CLYMER®
MANUALS

SUZUKI
DL650 V-STROM • 2004-2011

WHAT'S IN YOUR TOOLBOX?

More information available at Clymer.com
Phone: 805-498-6703

Haynes Publishing Group
Sparkford Nr Yeovil
Somerset BA22 7JJ England

Haynes North America, Inc
861 Lawrence Drive
Newbury Park
California 91320 USA

ISBN 10: 1-62092-152-9
ISBN-13: 978-1-62092-152-4
Library of Congress: 2015935183

Common spark plug conditions

NORMAL
Symptoms: Brown to grayish-tan color and slight electrode wear. Correct heat range for engine and operating conditions.
Recommendation: When new spark plugs are installed, replace with plugs of the same heat range.

WORN
Symptoms: Rounded electrodes with a small amount of deposits on the firing end. Normal color. Causes hard starting in damp or cold weather and poor fuel economy.
Recommendation: Plugs have been left in the engine too long. Replace with new plugs of the same heat range. Follow the recommended maintenance schedule.

CARBON DEPOSITS
Symptoms: Dry sooty deposits indicate a rich mixture or weak ignition. Causes misfiring, hard starting and hesitation.
Recommendation: Make sure the plug has the correct heat range. Check for a clogged air filter or problem in the fuel system or engine management system. Also check for ignition system problems.

ASH DEPOSITS
Symptoms: Light brown deposits encrusted on the side or center electrodes or both. Derived from oil and/or fuel additives. Excessive amounts may mask the spark, causing misfiring and hesitation during acceleration.
Recommendation: If excessive deposits accumulate over a short time or low mileage, install new valve guide seals to prevent seepage of oil into the combustion chambers. Also try changing gasoline brands.

OIL DEPOSITS
Symptoms: Oily coating caused by poor oil control. Oil is leaking past worn valve guides or piston rings into the combustion chamber. Causes hard starting, misfiring and hesitation.
Recommendation: Correct the mechanical condition with necessary repairs and install new plugs.

GAP BRIDGING
Symptoms: Combustion deposits lodge between the electrodes. Heavy deposits accumulate and bridge the electrode gap. The plug ceases to fire, resulting in a dead cylinder.
Recommendation: Locate the faulty plug and remove the deposits from between the electrodes.

TOO HOT
Symptoms: Blistered, white insulator, eroded electrode and absence of deposits. Results in shortened plug life.
Recommendation: Check for the correct plug heat range, over-advanced ignition timing, lean fuel mixture, intake manifold vacuum leaks, sticking valves and insufficient engine cooling.

PREIGNITION
Symptoms: Melted electrodes. Insulators are white, but may be dirty due to misfiring or flying debris in the combustion chamber. Can lead to engine damage.
Recommendation: Check for the correct plug heat range, over-advanced ignition timing, lean fuel mixture, insufficient engine cooling and lack of lubrication.

HIGH SPEED GLAZING
Symptoms: Insulator has yellowish, glazed appearance. Indicates that combustion chamber temperatures have risen suddenly during hard acceleration. Normal deposits melt to form a conductive coating. Causes misfiring at high speeds.
Recommendation: Install new plugs. Consider using a colder plug if driving habits warrant.

DETONATION
Symptoms: Insulators may be cracked or chipped. Improper gap setting techniques can also result in a fractured insulator tip. Can lead to piston damage.
Recommendation: Make sure the fuel anti-knock values meet engine requirements. Use care when setting the gaps on new plugs. Avoid lugging the engine.

MECHANICAL DAMAGE
Symptoms: May be caused by a foreign object in the combustion chamber or the piston striking an incorrect reach (too long) plug. Causes a dead cylinder and could result in piston damage.
Recommendation: Repair the mechanical damage. Remove the foreign object from the engine and/or install the correct reach plug.

CONTENTS

QUICK REFERENCE DATA

ENGINE INFORMATION

MODEL:_____ YEAR:_____
VIN NUMBER:_____
ENGINE SERIAL NUMBER:_____
THROTTLE BODY SERIAL NUMBER OR 1.D. MARK: _____

RECOMMENDED LUBRICANTS AND FLUIDS

Brake fluid	DOT 4
Engine coolant	
Type	Antifreeze coolant that is compatible with an aluminum radiator.
Ratio	50:50 with distilled water
Capacity	1900 ml (2.0 U.S. qt.)
Engine oil	
Grade	API SF or SG
Viscosity	SAE 10W40
Capacity	
Oil change only	2.3 L (2.4 US qt.)
Oil and filter change	2.7 L (2.9 US qt.)
When engine completely dry	3.1 L (3.3 US qt.)
Fork oil	
Viscosity	SS8 fork oil
Capacity per leg	524 ml (17.7 U.S. oz.)
Fuel	
Type	Unleaded
Octane	
U.S.A., California, and Canada models	87 [(R + M)/2 method] or research octane of 91or higher
Non- U.S.A., California, and Canada models91	
Fuel tank capacity, including reserve	22.0 L (5.8 U.S. gal.)

MAINTENANCE AND TUNE-UP SPECIFICATIONS

Battery	
Type	YTX12-BS Maintenance free (sealed)
Capacity	12 volt 10 amp hour
Brake pedal height	20-30 mm (0.79-1.18 in.)
Clutch lever free play	10-15 mm (0.4-0.6 in.)
Compression pressure (at sea level)	
Standard	1,300-1,700 kPa (185-242 psi)
Service limit	1,100 kPa (156 psi)
Maximum difference between cylinders	200 kPa (28 psi)
Drive chain 21-pin length	319.4 mm (12.6 in.)
Drive chain free play	20-30 mm (0.8-1.2 in.)
Engine oil pressure (hot)	100-400 kPa (14-57 psi) at 3,000 rpm
Fork spring preload adjuster*	3rd groove from top
Idle speed	1,200-1,400 rpm
Ignition timing	4 B.T.D.C. at 1,300 rpm
Radiator cap release pressure	95-125 kPa (13.5-17.8 psi)
Rear shock absorber preload adjuster*	2 nd groove from bottom
Rear shock absorber rebound damping adjuster*	
U.S.A., California and Canada models	1 turns out
Non- U.S.A., California and Canada models	1 turn out

(continued)

MAINTENANCE AND TUNE-UP SPECIFICATIONS (continued)

Rim runout (front and rear)
  Axial   2.0 mm (0.08 in.)
  Radial   2.0 mm (0.08 in.)
Spark plug   NGK CR8E, ND U24ESR-N
Spark plug gap   0.7-0.8 mm (0.028-0.031 in.)
Throttle cable free play   2.0-4.0 mm (0.08-0.16 in.)
Tire pressure
  Single rider
    Front   225 kPa (33 psi)
    Rear   250 kPa (36 psi)
  Dual riders
    Front   225 kPa (33 psi)
    Rear   280 kPa (41 psi)
Tire tread depth (minimum)
  Front   1.6 mm (0.06 in.)
  Rear   2.0 mm (0.08 in.)
Valve clearance (cold)
  Intake   0.10-0.20 mm (0.004-0.008 in.)
  Exhaust   0.20-0.30 mm (0.008-0.012 in.)
*Standard setting.

MAINTENANCE AND TUNE-UP TORQUE SPECIFICATIONS

Item	N•m	in.-lb.	ft.-lb.
Oil drain plug	21	186	–
Rear axle nut	100	–	74
Rear brake master cylinder locknut	17	150	–
Spark plug	11	98	–

CLYMER® MANUALS

SUZUKI
DL650 V-STROM • 2004-2011

Models covered:
DL650K4 through DL650K9 (2004-2009)
DL650AK7 through DL650AL1 (2007-2011)

CHAPTER ONE

GENERAL INFORMATION

This detailed and comprehensive manual covers the Suzuki DL650 and DL650A models 2004-2011.

The text provides complete information on maintenance, tune-up, repair and overhaul. Hundreds of photos and drawings guide the reader through every job. All procedures are in step-by-step format and designed for the reader who may be working on the motorcycle for the first time.

MANUAL ORGANIZATION

A shop manual is a reference tool and, as in all Clymer manuals, the chapters are thumb-tabbed for easy reference. Important items are indexed at the end of the manual. Frequently used specifications and capacities from individual chapters are summarized in the *Quick Reference Data* at the front of the manual.

During some of the procedures there will be references to headings in other chapters or sections of the manual. When a specific heading is called out in a step it is italicized as it appears in the manual. If a sub-heading is indicated as being "in this section" it is located within the same main heading. For example, the sub-heading *Handling Gasoline Safely* is located within the main headingSafety.

This chapter provides general information on shop safety, tool use, service fundamentals and shop supplies. **Tables 1-6** at the end of the chapter provide general motorcycle, mechanical and shop information.

Chapter Two provides methods for quick and accurate diagnoses of problems. Troubleshooting procedures present typical symptoms and logical methods to pinpoint and repair a problem.

Chapter Three explains all routine maintenance.

Subsequent chapters describe specific systems, such as engine, clutch, transmission, fuel system, electrical system, wheels, tires, drive chain, suspension, brakes and body components.

Specification tables, when applicable, are located at the end of each chapter.

WARNINGS, CAUTIONS AND NOTES

The terms WARNING, CAUTION and NOTE have specific meanings in this manual.

A WARNING emphasizes areas where injury or even death could result from negligence. Mechanical damage may also occur. WARNINGS (bf ital)are to be taken seriously.

A CAUTION emphasizes areas where equipment damage could result. Disregarding a CAUTION could cause permanent mechanical damage, though injury is unlikely.

A NOTE provides additional information to make a step or procedure easier or clearer. Disregarding a NOTE could cause inconvenience, but would not cause equipment damage or injury.

SAFETY

Professional mechanics can work for years and never sustain a serious injury or mishap. Follow these guidelines and practice common sense to safely service the motorcycle:

1. Do not operate the motorcycle in an enclosed area. The exhaust gasses contain carbon monoxide, an odorless, colorless and tasteless poisonous gas. Carbon monoxide levels build quickly in small enclosed areas and can cause unconsciousness and death in a short time. Make sure the work area is properly ventilated, or operate the motorcycle outside.

2. *Never* use gasoline or any flammable liquid to clean parts. Refer to Handling Gasoline Safely and *Cleaning Parts* in this section.

3. Never smoke or use a torch in the vicinity of flammable liquids, such as gasoline or cleaning solvent.

4. Do not remove the radiator cap or cooling system hose while the engine is hot. The cooling system is pressurized and the high temperature coolant may cause injury.

5. Dispose of and store coolant in a safe manner. Do not allow children or pets access to open containers of coolant. Animals are attracted to antifreeze.

6. Avoid contact with engine oil and other chemicals. Most are known carcinogens. Wash your hands thoroughly after coming in contact with engine oil. If possible, wear a pair of disposable gloves.

7. If welding or brazing on the motorcycle, remove the fuel tank and shocks to a safe distance at least 50 ft. (15 m) away.

8. Use the correct types and sizes of tools to avoid damaging fasteners.

9. Keep tools clean and in good condition. Replace or repair worn or damaged equipment.

10. When loosening a tight fastener, be guided by what would happen if the tool slips.

11. When replacing fasteners, make sure the new fasteners are the same size and strength as the originals.

12. Keep the work area clean and organized.

13. Wear eye protection any time the safety of your eyes is in question. This includes procedures involving drilling, grinding, hammering, compressed air and chemicals.

14. Wear the correct clothing for the job. Tie up or cover long hair so it can not catch in moving equipment.

15. Do not carry sharp tools in clothing pockets.

16. Always have an approved fire extinguisher available. Make sure it is rated for gasoline (Class B) and electrical (Class C) fires.

17. Do not use compressed air to clean clothes, the motorcycle or the work area. Debris may be blown into the eyes or skin. *Never* direct compressed air at anyone. Do not allow children to use or play with any compressed air equipment.

18. When using compressed air to dry rotating parts, hold the part so it cannot rotate. Do not allow the force of the air to spin the part. The air jet is capable of rotating parts at extreme speeds. The part may be damaged or disintegrate, causing serious injury.

19. Do not inhale the dust created by brake pad and clutch wear. These particles may contain asbestos. In addition, some types of insulating materials and gaskets may contain asbestos. Inhaling asbestos particles is hazardous to health.

20. Never work on the motorcycle while someone is working under it.

21. When placing the motorcycle on a stand or overhead lift, make sure it is secure before walking away.

Handling Gasoline Safely

Gasoline is a volatile flammable liquid and is one of the most dangerous items in the shop. Because gasoline is used so often, many people forget that it is hazardous. Only use gasoline as fuel for gasoline internal combustion engines. Keep in mind when working on a motorcycle, gasoline is always present in the fuel tank, fuel line and fuel body. To avoid an accident when working around the fuel system, carefully observe the following precautions:

1. Never use gasoline to clean parts. Refer to *Cleaning Parts* in this section.

2. When working on the fuel system, work outside or in a well-ventilated area.

3. Do not add fuel to the fuel tank or service the fuel system while the motorcycle is near open flames, sparks or where someone is smoking. Gasoline vapor is heavier than air, collects in low areas and is more easily ignited than liquid gasoline.

4. Allow the engine to cool completely before working on any fuel system component.

5. Do not store gasoline in glass containers. If the glass breaks, an explosion or fire may occur.

6. Immediately wipe up spilled gasoline with rags. Store the rags in a metal container with a lid until they can be properly disposed, or place them outside in a safe place for the fuel to evaporate.

7. Do not pour water onto a gasoline fire. Water spreads the fire and makes it more difficult to put out. Use a class B, BC or ABC fire extinguisher to extinguish the fire.

8. Always turn off the engine before refueling. Do not spill fuel onto the engine or exhaust system. Do not overfill the fuel tank. Leave an air space at the top of the tank to allow room for the fuel to expand due to temperature fluctuations.

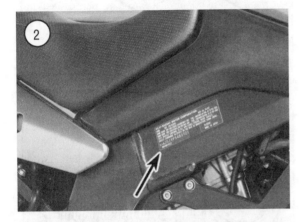

Cleaning Parts

Cleaning parts is one of the more tedious and difficult service jobs performed in the home garage. Many types of chemical cleaners and solvents are available for shop use. Most are poisonous and extremely flammable. To prevent chemical exposure, vapor buildup, fire and injury, observe each product's warning label and note the following:

1. Read and observe the entire product label before using any chemical. Always know what type of chemical is being used and whether it is poisonous and/or flammable.

2. Do not use more than one type of cleaning solvent at a time. If mixing chemicals is required, measure the proper amounts according to the manufacturer.

3. Work in a well-ventilated area.

4. Wear chemical-resistant gloves.

5. Wear safety glasses.

6. Wear a vapor respirator if the instructions call for it.

7. Wash hands and arms thoroughly after cleaning parts.

8. Keep chemicals away from children and pets, especially coolant. Animals are attracted to antifreeze.

9. Thoroughly clean all oil, grease and cleaner residue from any part that must be heated.

10. Use a nylon brush when cleaning parts. Metal brushes may cause a spark.

11. When using a parts washer, only use the solvent recommended by the manufacturer. Make sure the parts washer is equipped with a metal lid that will lower in case of fire.

Warning Labels

Most manufacturers attach information and warning labels to the motorcycle. These labels contain instructions that are important to safety when operating, servicing, transporting and storing the motorcycle Refer to the owner's manual for the description and location of labels. Order replacement labels from the manufacturer if they are missing or damaged.

SERIAL NUMBERS

Serial numbers are stamped on various locations on the frame, engine and carburetor. Record these numbers in the Quick Reference Data *section in the front of this manual. Have these numbers available when ordering parts.*

The frame serial number is stamped on the right side of the steering head (**Figure 1**).

The VIN number label (**Figure 2**) is located on the right side of the frame.

The engine serial number is stamped on the left, lower surface of the crankcase (**Figure 3**).

FASTENERS

WARNING
Do not install fasteners with a strength classification lower than what was originally installed by the manufacturer. Doing so may cause equipment failure and/or damage.

Proper fastener selection and installation is important to ensure the motorcycle operates as designed and can be serviced efficiently. The choice of original equipment fasteners is not arrived at by chance. Make sure replacement fasteners meet the requirements.

Threaded Fasteners

Threaded fasteners secure most of the components on the motorcycle. Most are tightened by turning them clockwise (right-hand threads). If the normal rotation of the component being tightened would loosen the fastener, it may have left-hand threads. If a left-hand threaded fastener is used, it is noted in the text.

Two dimensions are required to match the thread size of the fastener: the number of threads in a given distance and the outside diameter of the threads.

Two systems are currently used to specify threaded fastener dimensions: the U.S. Standard system and the metric system (**Figure 4**). Pay particular attention when working with unidentified fasteners; mismatching thread types can damage threads.

To ensure the fastener threads are not mismatched or cross-threaded, start all fasteners by hand. If a fastener is difficult to start or turn, determine the cause before tightening with a wrench.

Match fasteners by their length (L, **Figure 5**), diameter (D) and distance between thread crests (pitch, T). A typical metric bolt may be identified by the numbers, 8—1.25 × 130. This indicates the bolt has a diameter of 8 mm, the distance between thread crests is 1.25 mm and the length is 130 mm. Always measure bolt length as shown in L, **Figure 5** to avoid installing replacements of the wrong lengths.

If a number is located on the top of a metric fastener (**Figure 5**), this indicates the strength. The higher the number, the stronger the fastener. Typically, unnumbered fasteners are the weakest.

Many screws, bolts and studs are combined with nuts to secure particular components. To indicate the size of a nut, manufacturers specify the internal diameter and thread pitch.

The measurement across two flats on a nut or bolt indicates the wrench size.

Torque Specifications

The materials used in the manufacture of the motorcycle may be subjected to uneven stresses if fasteners are not installed and tightened correctly. Improperly installed fasteners or ones that worked loose can cause extensive damage. It is essential to use an accurate torque wrench, as described in this

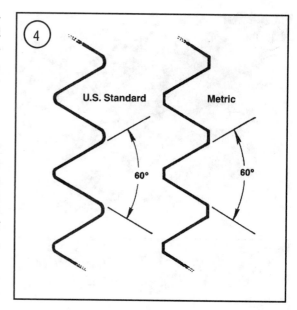

U.S. Standard   Metric

60°   60°

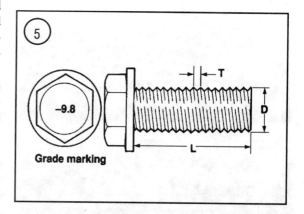

−9.8

Grade marking

chapter, with the torque specifications in this manual.

Specifications for torque are provided in Newton-meters (N•m), foot-pounds (ft.-lb.) and inch-pounds (in.-lb.). Refer to **Table 4** for general torque specifications. To use **Table 4**, first determine the size of the fastener as described in Threaded Fasteners in this section. Torque specifications for specific components are at the end of the appropriate chapters. Torque wrenches are covered in the *Tools* section.

Self-Locking Fasteners

Several types of bolts, screws and nuts incorporate a system that creates interference between the two fasteners. Interference is achieved in various ways. The most common type used is the nylon insert nut and a dry adhesive coating on the threads of a bolt.

Self-locking fasteners offer greater holding strength than standard fasteners, which improves their resistance to vibration. Self-locking fasteners cannot be reused. The materials used to form the lock become

distorted after the initial installation and removal. Do not replace self-locking fasteners with standard fasteners.

Some fasteners are equipped with a threadlock preapplied to the fastener threads (**Figure 6**). When replacing these fasteners, do not apply a separate threadlock. When it is necessary to reuse one of these fasteners, remove the threadlock residue from the threads. Then apply the threadlock specified in the text.

Washers

The two basic types of washers are flat washers and lockwashers. Flat washers are simple discs with a hole to fit a screw or bolt. Lockwashers are used to prevent a fastener from working loose. Washers can be used as spacers and seals or to help distribute fastener load and prevent the fastener from damaging the component.

As with fasteners, when replacing washers make sure the replacements meet the original specifications.

Cotter Pins

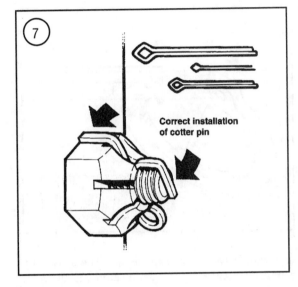

Correct installation of cotter pin

A cotter pin is a split metal pin inserted into a hole or slot to prevent a fastener from loosening. In certain applications, such as the rear axle, the fastener must be secured in this way. For these applications, a cotter pin and castellated (slotted) nut is used.

To use a cotter pin, first make sure the diameter is correct for the hole in the fastener. After correctly tightening the fastener and aligning the holes, insert the cotter pin through the hole and bend the ends over the fastener (**Figure 7**). Unless instructed to do so, never loosen a tightened fastener to align the holes. If the holes do not align, tighten the fastener just enough to achieve alignment.

Cotter pins are available in various diameters and lengths. Measure the length from the bottom of the head to the tip of the shortest pin.

Snap Rings and E-clips

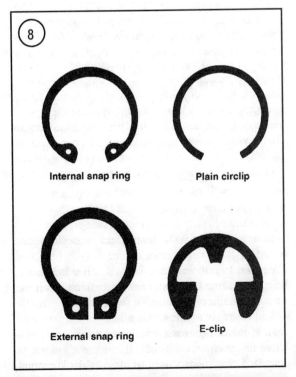

Internal snap ring   Plain circlip

External snap ring   E-clip

Snap rings (**Figure 8**) are circular-shaped metal retaining clips. They are required to secure parts and gears in place on parts such as shafts, pins or rods. External type snap rings are used to retain items on shafts. Internal type snap rings secure parts within housing bores. In some applications, in addition to securing the component(s), snap rings of varying thicknesses also determine endplay. These are usually called selective snap rings.

The two basic types of snap rings are machined and stamped snap rings. Machined snap rings (**Figure 9**) can be installed in either direction because both faces have sharp edges. Stamped snap rings (**Figure 10**) are manufactured with a sharp edge and round edge. When installing a stamped snap ring in a thrust application, install the sharp edge facing away from the part producing the thrust.

E-clips are used when it is not practical to use a snap ring. Remove E-clips with a flat blade screwdriver by prying between the shaft and E-clip. To install an E-clip, center it over the shaft groove and push or tap it into place.

Observe the following when installing snap rings:

1. Remove and install snap rings with snap ring pliers. Refer to Tools in this chapter.

2. In some applications, it may be necessary to replace snap rings after removing them.

3. Compress or expand snap rings only enough to install them. If overly expanded, they lose their retaining ability.

4. After installing a snap ring, make sure it seats completely.

5. Wear eye protection when removing and installing snap rings.

SHOP SUPPLIES

Lubricants and Fluids

Periodic lubrication helps ensure a long service life for any type of equipment. Using the correct type of lubricant is as important as performing the lubrication service, although in an emergency the wrong type is better than not using one. The following section describes the types of lubricants most often required. Make sure to follow the manufacturer's recommendations.

Engine oils

Engine oil for a four-stroke motorcycle engine use is classified by three standards: the American Petroleum Institute (API) service classification, the Society of Automotive Engineers (SAE) viscosity rating and the Japanese Automobile Standards Organization (JASO) T 903 certification standard.

The JASO certification specifies the oil has passed requirements specified by Japanese motorcycle manufacturers.

The API and SAE information is on all oil container labels. The JASO information is found on oil containers sold by the oil manufacturer specifically for motorcycle use. Two letters indicate the API service classification. The number or sequence of numbers

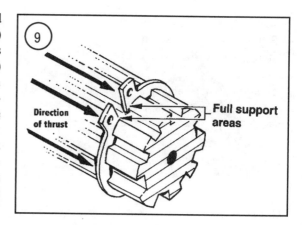

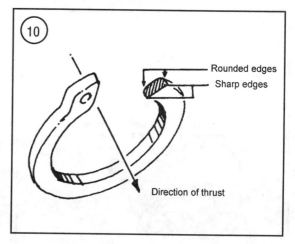

and letter (10W-40 for example) is the oil's viscosity rating. The API service classification and the SAE viscosity index are not indications of oil quality. The JASO certification label identifies two separate oil classifications and a registration number to ensure the oil has passed all JASO certification standards for use in four-stroke motorcycle engines.

The API service classification indicates that the oil meets specific lubrication standards and is not an indication of oil quality. The first letter in the classification S indicates that the oil is for gasoline engines. The second letter indicates the standard the oil satisfies.

The JASO certification label identifies two separate oil classifications and a registration number to ensure the oil has passed all JASO certification standards for use in four-stroke motorcycle engines. The classifications are: MA (high friction applications) and MB (low friction applications).

Viscosity is an indication of the oil's thickness. Thin oils have a lower number while thick oils have a higher number. Engine oils fall into the 5- to 50-weight range for single-grade oils.

Most manufacturers recommend multi-grade oil. These oils perform efficiently across a wide range of operating conditions. Multi-grade oils are identified by a W after the first number, which indicates the low-temperature viscosity.

Engine oils are most commonly mineral (petroleum) based; however, synthetic and semi-synthetic types are used more frequently. Always use oil with a classification recommended by the manufacturer (Chapter Three). Using oil with a different classification can cause engine damage.

Greases

Grease is lubricating oil with thickening agents added to it. The National Lubricating Grease Institute (NLGI) grades grease. Grades range from No. 000 to No. 6, with No. 6 being the thickest. Typical multipurpose grease is NLGI No. 2. For specific applications, manufacturers may recommend a water-resistant type grease or one with an additive, such as molybdenum disulfide (MoS_2).

Brake fluid

WARNING
Never put a mineral-based (petroleum) oil into the brake system. Mineral oil causes rubber parts in the system to swell and break apart, causing complete brake failure.

Brake fluid is the hydraulic fluid used to transmit hydraulic pressure (force) to the wheel brakes. Brake fluid is classified by the Department of Transportation (DOT). Current designations for brake fluid are DOT 3, DOT 4 and DOT 5. This classification appears on the fluid container. The models covered in this manual require DOT 4 brake fluid.

Each type of brake fluid has its own definite characteristics. Do not intermix different types of brake fluid; this may cause brake system failure. DOT 5 brake fluid is silicone based. DOT 5 is not compatible with other brake fluids or in systems for which it was not designed. Mixing DOT 5 fluid with other fluids may cause brake system failure. When adding brake fluid, only use DOT 4 brake fluid.

Brake fluid damages any plastic, painted or plated surface it contacts. Use extreme care when working with brake fluid, and remove any spills immediately with soap and water.

Hydraulic brake systems require clean and moisture free brake fluid. Never reuse brake fluid. Keep containers and reservoirs properly sealed.

Cleaners, Degreasers and Solvents

Many chemicals are available to remove oil, grease and other residue from the motorcycle. Before using cleaning solvents, consider their uses and disposal methods, particularly if they are not water-soluble. Local ordinances may require special procedures for the disposal of many types of cleaning chemicals. Refer to Safety and *Cleaning Parts* in this chapter for more information on their uses.

Use brake parts cleaner to clean brake system components when contact with petroleum-based products will damage seals. Brake parts cleaner leaves no residue. Use electrical contact cleaner to clean electrical connections and components without leaving any residue. Carburetor cleaner is a powerful solvent used to remove fuel deposits and varnish from fuel system components. Use this cleaner carefully; it may damage finishes.

Generally, degreasers are strong cleaners used to remove heavy accumulations of grease from engine and frame components.

Most solvents are designed to be used with a parts washing cabinet for individual component cleaning. For safety, use only nonflammable or high flash point solvents.

Gasket Sealant

Sealants are used in combination with a gasket or seal or occasionally alone. Use extreme care when choosing a sealant different from the type originally recommended. Choose sealants based on their resistance to heat, various fluids and their sealing capabilities.

One of the most common sealants is RTV, or room temperature vulcanizing, sealant. This sealant cures at room temperature over a specific time period. This allows the repositioning of components without damaging gaskets.

Moisture in the air causes the RTV sealant to cure. Always install the tube cap as soon as possible after applying RTV sealant. RTV sealant has a limited shelf life and will not cure properly if the shelf life has expired. Keep partial tubes sealed and discard them if they have surpassed the expiration date. If there is no expiration date on a sealant tube, use a permanent marker and write the date on the tube when it is first opened. Manufacturers usually specify a shelf life of one year after a container is opened, though it is recommended to contact the sealant manufacturer to confirm shelf life.

Removing RTV sealant

Silicone sealant is used on many engine gasket surfaces. When cleaning parts after disassembly, a razor blade or gasket scraper is required to remove the silicone residue that cannot be pulled off by hand from the gasket surfaces. To avoid damaging gasket surfaces, use Permatex Silicone Stripper (part No. 80647) to help soften the residue before scraping.

Applying RTV sealant

Clean all old sealer residue from the mating surfaces. Then inspect the mating surfaces for damage. Remove all sealer material from blind threaded holes; it can cause inaccurate bolt torque. Spray the mating surfaces with aerosol parts cleaner, and then wipe with a lint-free cloth. Because gasket surfaces must be dry and oil-free for the sealant to adhere, be thorough when cleaning and drying the parts.

Apply RTV sealant in a continuous bead 2-3 mm (0.08-0.12 in.) thick. Circle all the fastener holes unless otherwise specified. Do not allow any sealant to enter these holes. Drawings in specific chapters show how to apply the sealer to specific gasket surfaces. Assemble and tighten the fasteners to the specified torque within the time frame recommended by the RTV sealant manufacturer.

Gasket Remover

Aerosol gasket remover can help remove stubborn gaskets. This product can speed up the removal process and prevent damage to the mating surface that may be caused by using a scraping tool. Most of these types of products are very caustic. Follow the gasket remover manufacturer's instructions for use.

Threadlocking Compound

> *CAUTION*
> *Threadlocking compounds are anaerobic and damage most plastic parts and surfaces. Use caution when using these products in areas where plastic components are located.*

A threadlocking compound is a fluid applied to the threads of fasteners. After tightening the fastener, the fluid dries and becomes a solid filler between the threads. This makes it difficult for the fastener to work loose from vibration or heat expansion and contraction. Some threadlocking compounds also provide a seal against fluid leaks.

Before applying threadlocking compound, remove any old compound from both thread areas and clean them with aerosol parts cleaner. Use the compound sparingly. Excess fluid can run into adjoining parts.

Threadlocking compounds are available in various strengths, temperatures and repair applications.

TOOLS

Most of the procedures in this manual can be carried out with hand tools and test equipment familiar to the home mechanic. Always use the correct tools for the job. Keep tools organized and clean and store them in a tool chest with related tools organized together.

Quality tools are essential. The best are constructed of high-strength alloy steel. These tools are light, easy-to-use and resistant to wear. Their working surfaces are devoid of sharp edges and the tools are carefully polished. They have an easy-to-clean finish and are comfortable to use. Quality tools are a good investment.

Consider the tool's potential frequency of use when purchasing tools to perform the procedures covered in this manual. If a tool kit is just now being started, consider purchasing a tool set from a quality tool supplier. These sets are available in many tool combinations and offer substantial savings when compared to individually purchased tools. As work experience grows and tasks become more complicated, specialized tools can be added.

Some of the procedures in this manual specify special tools. In most cases, the tool is illustrated in use. In some case it may be possible to substitute similar tools or fabricate a suitable replacement. However, at times, the specialized equipment or expertise may make it impractical for the home mechanic to perform the procedure. When necessary, such operations are identified in the text with the recommendation to have a dealership or specialist perform the task.

Screwdrivers

The two basic types of screwdrivers are the slotted tip (flat blade) and the Phillips tip. These are available in sets that often include an assortment of tip sizes and shaft lengths.

As with all tools, use the correct screwdriver. Make sure the size of the tip conforms to the size and shape of the fastener. Use them only for driving screws. Never use a screwdriver for prying or chiseling. Repair or replace worn or damaged screwdrivers. A worn tip may damage the fastener, making it difficult to remove.

Phillips-head screws are often damaged by incorrectly fitting screwdrivers. Quality Phillips screwdrivers are manufactured with their crosshead tip

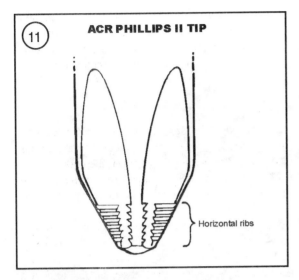

ACR PHILLIPS II TIP

Horizontal ribs

by the Phillips Screw Company. ACR stands for the horizontal anti-camout ribs found on the driving faces or flutes of the screwdrivers tip (**Figure 11**). ACR Phillips II screwdrivers were designed as part of a manufacturing drive system to be used with ACR Phillips II screws, but they work well on all common Phillips screws. A number of tool companies offer ACR Phillips II screwdrivers in different tip sizes and interchangeable bits to fit screwdriver bit holders.

Another way to prevent camout and increase the grip of a Phillips screwdriver is to apply valve grinding compound or Permatex Screw & Socket Gripper onto the screwdriver tip. After loosening/tightening the screw, clean the screw recess to prevent possible contamination.

Wrenches

Open-end, box-end and combination wrenches (**Figure 12**) are available in a variety of types and sizes.

The number stamped on the wrench refers to the distance between the work areas. This size must match the size of the fastener head.

The box-end wrench is an excellent tool because it grips the fastener on all sides. This reduces the chance of the tool slipping. The box-end wrench is designed with either a 6- or 12-point opening. For stubborn or damaged fasteners, the 6-point provides superior holding ability by contacting the fastener across a wider area at all six edges. For general use, the 12-point works well. It allows the wrench to be removed and reinstalled without moving the handle over such a wide arc.

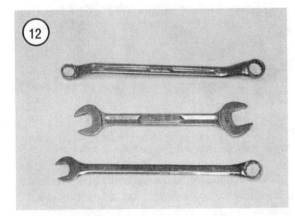

An open-end wrench is fast and works best in areas with limited overhead access. It contacts the fastener at only two points, and is subject to slipping under heavy force or if the tool or fastener is worn. A box-end wrench is preferred in most instances, especially when breaking loose and applying the final tightness to a fastener.

The combination wrench has a box-end on one end, and an open-end on the other. This combination makes it a convenient tool.

Adjustable Wrenches

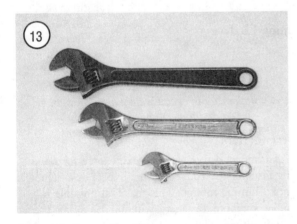

An adjustable wrench (**Figure 13**) can fit nearly any nut or bolt head that has clear access around its entire perimeter.

However, adjustable wrenches contact the fastener at only two points, which makes them more subject to slipping off the fastener. One jaw is adjustable and may loosen, which increases this possibility.

machined to Phillips Screw Company specifications. Poor quality or damaged Phillips screwdrivers can back out and round over the screw head (camout). Compounding the problem of using poor quality screwdrivers are Phillips-head screws made from weak or soft materials and screws initially installed with air tools.

The best type of screwdriver to use on Phillips screws is the ACR Phillips II screwdriver, patented

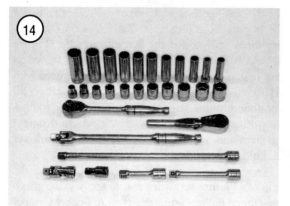

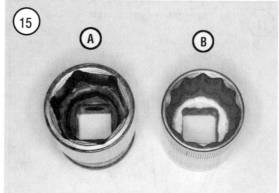

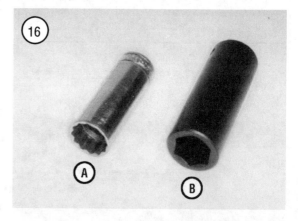

Make certain the solid jaw is the one transmitting the force.

However, adjustable wrenches are typically used to prevent a large nut or bolt from turning while the other end is being loosened or tightened with a box-end or socket wrench.

Socket Wrenches, Ratchets and Handles

> *WARNING*
> *Do not use hand sockets with air or impact tools; they may shatter and cause injury. Always wear eye protection when using impact or air tools.*

Sockets that attach to a ratchet handle (**Figure 14**) are available with 6-point (A, **Figure 15**) or 12-point (B) openings and different drive sizes. The drive size indicates the size of the square hole that accepts the ratchet handle. The number stamped on the socket is the size of the work area and must match the fastener head.

As with wrenches, a 6-point socket provides superior-holding ability, while a 12-point socket needs to be moved only half as far to reposition it on the fastener.

Sockets are designated for either hand or impact use. Impact sockets are made of a thicker material for more durability. Compare the size and wall thickness of a 19-mm hand socket (A, **Figure 16**) and the 19-mm impact socket (B). Use impact sockets when using an impact driver or air tool. Use hand sockets with hand-driven attachments.

Various handles are available for sockets. The speed handle is used for fast operation. Flexible ratchet heads in varying lengths allow the socket to be turned with varying force and at odd angles. Extension bars allow the socket setup to reach difficult areas. The ratchet is the most versatile. It allows the user to install or remove the nut without removing the socket.

Sockets combined with any number of drivers make them undoubtedly the fastest, safest and most convenient tool for fastener removal and installation.

Impact Driver

> *WARNING*
> *Do not use hand sockets with air or impact tools because they may shatter and cause injury. Always wear eye protection when using impact or air tools.*

An impact driver provides extra force for removing fasteners by converting the impact of a hammer into a turning motion. This makes it possible to remove stubborn fasteners without damaging them. Impact drivers and interchangeable bits (**Figure 17**) are available from most tool suppliers. When using a socket with an impact driver make sure the socket is designed for impact use. Refer to Socket Wrenches, Ratchets and Handles in this section.

Allen Wrenches

Allen, or setscrew wrenches (**Figure 18**), are used on fasteners with hexagonal recesses in the fastener

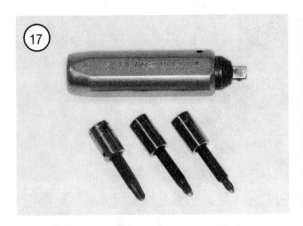

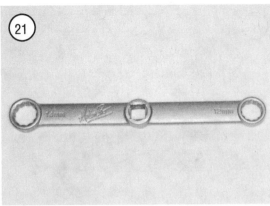

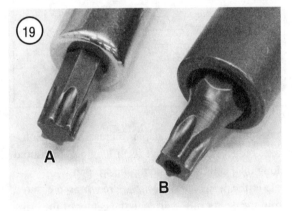

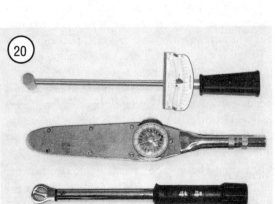

head. These wrenches are available in a L-shaped bar, socket and T-handle types. Allen bolts are sometimes called socket bolts.

Torx Fasteners

A Torx fastener head is a 6-point star-shaped pattern (A, **Figure 19**). Torx fasteners are identified with a T and a number indicating their drive size. For example, T25. Torx drivers are available in L-shaped bars, sockets and T-handles. Tamper-resistant Torx fasteners are also used and have a round shaft in the center of the fastener head. Tamper-resistance Torx fasteners require a Torx bit with a hole in the center of the bit (B, **Figure 19**).

Torque Wrenches

A torque wrench (**Figure 20**) is used with a socket, torque adapter or similar extension to tighten a fastener to a measured torque. Torque wrenches come in several drive sizes (1/4, 3/8, 1/2 and 3/4) and have various methods of reading the torque value. The drive size indicates the size of the square drive that accepts the socket, adapter or extension. Common methods of reading the torque value are the reflecting beam, the dial indicator and the audible click. When choosing a torque wrench, consider the torque range, drive size and accuracy. The torque specifications in this manual provide an indication of the range required. A torque wrench is a precision tool that must be properly cared for to remain accurate. Store torque wrenches in cases or separate padded drawers within a toolbox. Follow the manufacturer's instructions for their care and calibration.

Torque Adapters

Torque adapters (**Figure 21**), or extensions, extend or reduce the reach of a torque wrench. Specific adapters are required to perform some of the proce-

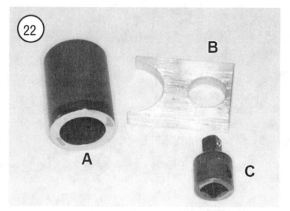

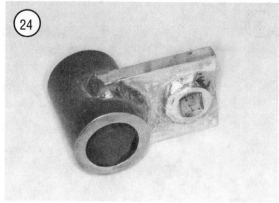

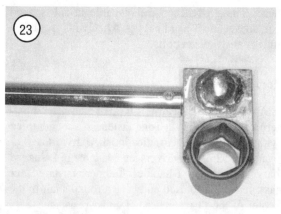

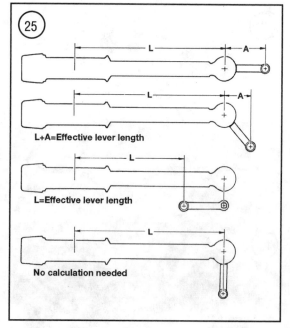

dures in this manual. These are available from the motorcycle manufacturer or can be fabricated by welding a socket (A, **Figure 22**) that matches the fastener onto a metal plate (B). Use another socket or extension (C, **Figure 22**) welded to the plate to attach to the torque wrench drive (**Figure 23**). The adapter shown (**Figure 24**) is used to tighten a fastener while preventing another fastener on the same shaft from turning.

If a torque adapter changes the effective lever length, the torque reading on the wrench will not equal the actual torque applied to the fastener. It is necessary to recalibrate the torque setting on the wrench to compensate for the change of lever length. When a torque adapter is used at a right angle to the drive head, calibration is not required because the lever length has not changed.

To recalculate a torque reading when using a torque adapter, use the following formula, and refer to **Figure 25**.

$$TW = \frac{TA \times L}{L + A}$$

TW is the torque setting or dial reading on the wrench.

TA is the torque specification and the actual amount of torque that will be applied to the fastener.

A is the amount the adapter increases (or in some cases reduces) the effective lever length as measured along the centerline of the torque wrench.

L is the lever length of the wrench as measured from the center of the drive to the center of the grip.

The effective lever length is the sum of L and A.

Example:

TA = 20 ft.-lb.

A = 3 in.

L = 14 in.

$$TW = \frac{20 \times 14}{14 + 3} = \frac{280}{17} = 16.5 \text{ ft.-lb.}$$

In this example, the torque wrench would be set to the recalculated torque value (TW = 16.5 ft.-lb.). When using a beam-type wrench, tighten the fastener until the pointer aligns with 16.5 ft.-lb. In this example, although the torque wrench is pre set to 16.5 ft.-lb., the actual torque is 20 ft.-lb.

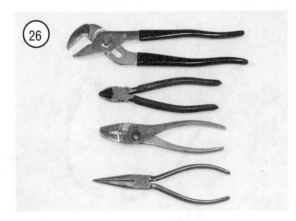

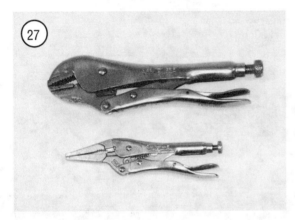

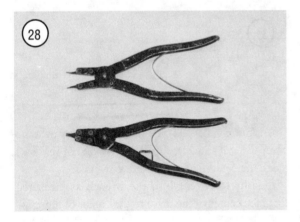

Pliers

Pliers come in a wide range of types and sizes. Pliers are useful for holding, cutting, bending, and crimping. Do not use them to turn fasteners unless they are designed to do so. **Figure 26** and **Figure 27** show several types of pliers. Each design has a specialized function. Slip-joint pliers are general-purpose pliers used for gripping and bending. Diagonal cutting pliers are needed to cut wire and can be used to remove cotter pins. Needlenose pliers are used to hold or bend small objects. Locking pliers (**Figure 27**), sometimes called Vise Grips, hold objects tight-

ly. They have many uses ranging from holding two parts together, to gripping the end of a broken stud. Use caution when using locking pliers; the sharp jaws will damage the objects they hold.

Snap Ring Pliers

> *WARNING*
> *Snap rings can slip and fly off when removing and installing them. In addition, the snap ring pliers tips may break. Always wear eye protection when using snap ring pliers.*

Snap ring pliers are specialized pliers with tips that fit into the ends of snap rings to remove and install them.

Snap ring pliers (**Figure 28**) are available with a fixed action (either internal or external) or are convertible (one tool works on both internal and external snap rings). They may have fixed tips or interchangeable ones of various sizes and angles. For general use, select convertible type pliers with interchangeable tips.

Hammers

> *WARNING*
> *Always wear eye protection when using hammers. Make sure the hammer face is in good condition and the handle is not cracked. Select the correct hammer for the job and make sure to strike the object squarely. Do not use the handle or the side of the hammer to strike an object.*

Various types of hammers are available to fit a number of applications. A ball-peen hammer is used to strike another tool, such as a punch or chisel. Soft-faced hammers are required when a metal object must be struck without damaging it. Never use a metal-faced hammer on engine and suspension components; damage will occur in most cases.

Ignition Grounding Tool

Some test procedures in this manual require turning the engine over without starting it. Do not remove the spark plug cap(s) and crank the engine without grounding the plug cap(s). Doing so will damage the ignition system.

An effective way to ground the system is to fabricate the tool shown in **Figure 29** from a No. 6 screw, two washers and a length of wire with an alligator clip soldered on one end. To use the tool, insert it into the spark plug cap and attach the alligator clip to a known engine ground. A separate grounding tool is required for each spark plug cap.

This tool is safer than a spark plug or spark tester because there is no spark firing across the end of the plug/tester to potentially ignite fuel vapor spraying from an open spark plug hole or leaking fuel component.

MEASURING TOOLS

The ability to accurately measure components is essential to successfully service many components. Equipment is manufactured to close tolerances, and obtaining consistently accurate measurements is essential.

Each type of measuring instrument is designed to measure a dimension with a certain degree of accuracy and within a certain range. When selecting the measuring tool, make sure it is applicable to the task.

As with all tools, measuring tools provide the best results if cared for properly. Improper use can damage the tool and cause inaccurate results. If any measurement is questionable, verify the measurement using another tool. A standard gauge is usually provided with measuring tools to check accuracy and calibrate the tool if necessary.

Accurate measurements are only possible if the mechanic possesses a feel for using the tool. Heavy-handed use of measuring tools produces less accurate results. Hold the tool gently by the fingertips so the point at which the tool contacts the object is easily felt. This feel for the equipment will produce more accurate measurements and reduce the risk of damaging the tool or component. Refer to the following sections for specific measuring tools.

Feeler Gauge

The feeler, or thickness gauge (**Figure 30**), is used for measuring the distance between two surfaces.

A feeler gauge set consists of an assortment of steel strips of graduated thicknesses. Each blade is marked with its thickness. Blades can be of various lengths and angles for different procedures.

A common use for a feeler gauge is to measure valve clearance. Wire (round) type gauges are used to measure spark plug gap.

Calipers

Calipers (**Figure 31**) are excellent tools for obtaining inside, outside and depth measurements.

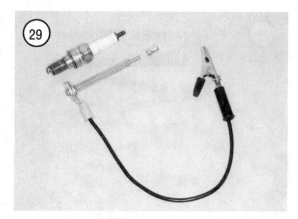

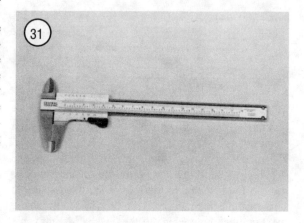

Although not as precise as a micrometer, they allow reasonable precision, typically to within 0.05 mm (0.001 in.). Most calipers have a range up to 150 mm (6 in.).

Calipers are available in dial, vernier or digital versions. Dial calipers have a dial readout that provides convenient reading. Vernier calipers have marked scales that must be compared to determine the measurement. The digital caliper uses a LCD to show the measurement.

Properly maintain the measuring surfaces of the caliper. There must not be any dirt or burrs between the tool and the object being measured. Never force

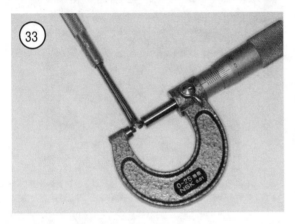

The outside micrometer is used to measure the outside diameter of cylindrical forms and the thicknesses of materials.

A micrometer's size indicates the minimum and maximum size of a part that it can measure. The usual sizes are 0-25 mm (0-1 in.), 25-50 mm (1-2 in.), 50-75 mm (2-3 in.) and 75-100 mm (3-4 in.).

Micrometers that cover a wider range of measurements are available. These use a large frame with interchangeable anvils of various lengths. This type of micrometer offers a cost savings; however, its overall size may make it less convenient.

Adjustment

Before using a micrometer, check its adjustment as follows.
1. Clean the anvil and spindle faces.
2A. To check a 0-1 in. or 0-25 mm micrometer:
    a. Turn the thimble until the spindle contacts the anvil. If the micrometer has a ratchet stop, use it to ensure the proper amount of pressure is applied.
    b. If the adjustment is correct, the 0 mark on the thimble will align exactly with the 0 mark on the sleeve line. If the marks do not align, the micrometer is out of adjustment.
    c. Follow the manufacturer's instructions to adjust the micrometer.
2B. To check a micrometer larger than 1 in. or 25 mm, use the standard gauge supplied by the manufacturer. A standard gauge is a steel block, disc or rod that is machined to an exact size.
    a. Place the standard gauge between the spindle and anvil and measure its outside diameter or length. If the micrometer has a ratchet stop, use it to ensure the proper amount of pressure is applied.
    b. If the adjustment is correct, the 0 mark on the thimble will align exactly with the 0 mark on the sleeve line. If the marks do not align, the micrometer is out of adjustment.
    c. Follow the manufacturer's instructions to adjust the micrometer.

Care

Micrometers are precision instruments. They must be used and maintained with great care. Note the following:
1. Store micrometers in protective cases or separate padded drawers in a toolbox.
2. When in storage, make sure the spindle and anvil faces do not contact each other or another object.

the caliper closed around an object; close the caliper around the highest point so it can be removed with a slight drag. Some calipers require calibration. Always refer to the manufacturer's instructions when using a new or unfamiliar caliper.

To read a vernier caliper refer to **Figure 32**. The fixed scale is marked in 1 mm increments. Ten individual lines on the fixed scale equal 1 cm. The moveable scale is marked in 0.05 mm (hundredth) increments. To obtain a reading, establish the first number by the location of the 0 line on the moveable scale in relation to the first line to the left on the fixed scale. In this example, the number is 10 mm. To determine the next number, note which of the lines on the movable scale align with a mark on the fixed scale. A number of lines will seem close, but only one will align exactly. In this case, 0.50 mm is the reading to add to the first number. The result of adding 10 mm and 0.50 mm is a measurement of 10.50 mm.

Micrometers

A micrometer (**Figure 33**) is an instrument designed for linear measurement using the decimal divisions of the inch or meter. While there are many types and styles of micrometers, most of the procedures in this manual call for an outside micrometer.

If they do, temperature changes and corrosion may damage the contact faces.

3. Do not clean a micrometer with compressed air. Dirt forced into the tool causes wear.

4. Lubricate micrometers to prevent corrosion.

Reading

When reading a micrometer, numbers are taken from different scales and added together.

For accurate results, properly maintain the measuring surfaces of the micrometer. There cannot be any dirt or burrs between the tool and the measured object. Never force the micrometer closed around an object. Close the micrometer around the highest point so it can be removed with a slight drag.

The standard metric micrometer is accurate to one one-hundredth of a millimeter (0.01 mm). The sleeve line is graduated in millimeter and half millimeter increments. The marks on the upper half of the sleeve line equal 1.00 mm. Each fifth mark above the sleeve line is identified with a number. The number sequence depends on the size of the micrometer. A 0-25 mm micrometer, for example, will have sleeve marks numbered 0 through 25 in 5 mm increments. This numbering sequence continues with larger micrometers. On all metric micrometers, each mark on the lower half of the sleeve equals 0.50 mm.

The tapered end of the thimble has 50 lines marked around it. Each mark equals 0.01 mm. One complete turn of the thimble aligns its 0 mark with the first line on the lower half of the sleeve line, or 0.50 mm.

When reading a metric micrometer, add the number of millimeters and half-millimeters on the sleeve line to the number of one one-hundredth millimeters on the thimble. Perform the following steps while referring to **Figure 34**.

1. Read the upper half of the sleeve line and count the number of lines visible. Each upper line equals 1 mm.

2. See if the half-millimeter line is visible on the lower sleeve line. If so, add 0.50 mm to the reading in Step 1.

3. Read the thimble mark that aligns with the sleeve line. Each thimble mark equals 0.01 mm.

4. If a thimble mark does not align exactly with the sleeve line, estimate the amount between the lines. For accurate readings in two-thousandths of a millimeter (0.002 mm), use a metric vernier micrometer.

5. Add the readings from Steps 1-4.

Telescoping and Small Hole Gauges

Use telescoping gauges (**Figure 35**) and small hole gauges (**Figure 36**) to measure bores. Neither gauge

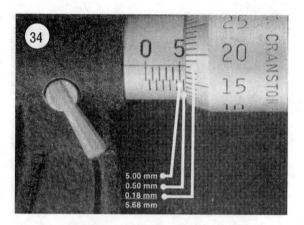

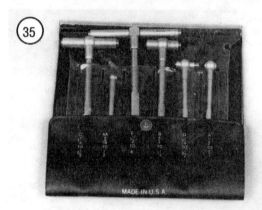

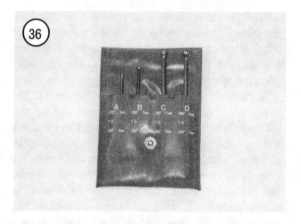

has a scale for direct readings. An outside micrometer must be used to determine the reading.

To use a telescoping gauge, select the correct size gauge for the bore. Compress the moveable post and carefully insert the gauge into the bore. Carefully move the gauge in the bore to make sure it is centered. Tighten the knurled end of the gauge to hold the moveable post in position. Remove the gauge and measure the length of the posts. Telescoping gauges are typically used to measure cylinder bores.

To use a small hole gauge, select the correct size gauge for the bore. Carefully insert the gauge into the bore. Tighten the knurled end of the gauge to care-

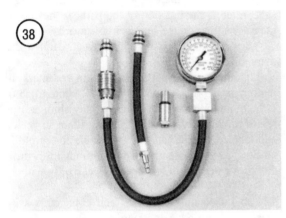

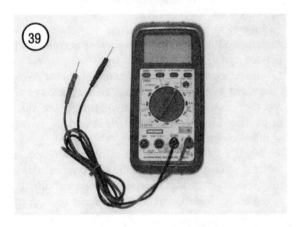

sions and movements. Measuring brake rotor runout is a typical use for a dial indicator.

Dial indicators are available in various ranges and graduations and with three types of mounting bases: magnetic, clamp or screw-in stud.

Cylinder Bore Gauge

A cylinder bore gauge is similar to a dial indicator. These typically consist of a dial indicator, handle and different length adapters (anvils) to fit the gauge to various bore sizes. The bore gauge is used to measure bore size, taper and out-of-round. When using a bore gauge, follow the manufacturer's instructions.

Compression Gauge

A compression gauge (**Figure 38**) measures combustion chamber (cylinder) pressure, usually in psi or kg/cm^2. The gauge adapter is either inserted and held in place or screwed into the spark plug hole to obtain the reading. Disable the engine so it will not start and hold the throttle in the wide-open position when performing a compression test. An engine that does not have adequate compression cannot be properly tuned. Refer to Chapter Three.

Multimeter

A multimeter (**Figure 39**) is an essential tool for electrical system diagnosis. The voltage function indicates the voltage applied or available to various electrical components. The ohmmeter function tests circuits for continuity, or lack of continuity, and measures the resistance of a circuit.

Some manufacturers' specifications for electrical components are based on results using a specific test meter. Results may vary if using a meter not recommend by the manufacturer. Such requirements are noted when applicable.

Ohmmeter (Analog) Calibration

Each time an analog ohmmeter is used or the scale is changed, the ohmmeter must be calibrated.

Digital ohmmeters do not require calibration.
1. Make sure the meter battery is in good condition.
2. Make sure the meter probes are in good condition.
3. Touch the two probes together and observe the needle location on the ohms scale. The needle must align with the 0 mark to obtain accurate measurements.
4. If necessary, rotate the meter ohms adjust knob until the needle and 0 mark align.

fully expand the gauge fingers to the limit within the bore. Do not overtighten the gauge; there is no built-in release. Excessive tightening can damage the bore surface and tool. Remove the gauge and measure the outside dimension with a micrometer (**Figure 33**). Small hole gauges are typically used to measure valve guides.

Dial Indicator

A dial indicator (**Figure 37**) is a gauge with a dial face and needle used to measure variations in dimen-

ELECTRICAL SYSTEM FUNDAMENTALS

A thorough study of the many types of electrical systems used in today's motorcycles is beyond the scope of this manual. However, a basic understanding of voltage, resistance and amperage is necessary to perform diagnostic tests.

Refer to Chapter Two for troubleshooting.

Voltage

Voltage is the electrical potential or pressure in an electrical circuit and is expressed in volts. The more pressure (voltage) in a circuit, the more work can be performed.

Direct current (DC) voltage means the electricity flows in one direction. All circuits powered by a battery are DC circuits.

Alternating current (AC) means the electricity flows in one direction momentarily and then switches to the opposite direction. Alternator output is an example of AC voltage. This voltage must be changed or rectified to direct current to operate in a battery powered system.

Resistance

Resistance is the opposition to the flow of electricity within a circuit or component and is measured in ohms. Resistance causes a reduction in available current and voltage.

Resistance is measured in an inactive circuit with an ohmmeter. The ohmmeter sends a small amount of current into the circuit and measures how difficult it is to push the current through the circuit.

An ohmmeter, although useful, is not always a good indicator of a circuit's actual ability under operating conditions. This is due to the low voltage (6-9 volts) that the meter uses to test the circuit. The voltage in an ignition coil secondary winding can be several thousand volts. Such high voltage can cause the coil to malfunction, even though it tests acceptable during a resistance test.

Resistance generally increases with temperature. Perform all testing with the component or circuit at room temperature. Resistance tests performed at high temperatures may indicate false resistance readings and cause the unnecessary replacement of a component.

Amperage

Amperage is the unit of measure for the amount of current within a circuit. Current is the actual flow of electricity. The higher the current, the more work

can be performed up to a given point. If the current flow exceeds the circuit or component capacity, the system will be damaged.

SERVICE METHODS

Many of the procedures in this manual are straightforward and can be performed by anyone reasonably competent with tools. However, consider previous experience carefully before performing any operation involving complicated procedures.

1. Front, in this manual, refers to the front of the motorcycle. The front of any component is the end closest to the front of the motorcycle. The left and right sides refer to the position of the parts as viewed by the rider sitting on the seat facing forward.

2. When servicing the motorcycle, secure it in a safe manner.

3. Label all similar parts for location and mark all mating parts for position. If possible, photograph or draw the number and thickness of any shim as it is removed. Identify parts by placing them in sealed and labeled plastic bags. It is possible for carefully laid out parts to become disturbed, making it difficult to reassemble the components correctly without a diagram.

4. Label disconnected wires and connectors with masking tape and a marking pen. Do not rely on memory alone.

5. Protect finished surfaces from physical damage or corrosion. Keep gasoline and other chemicals off painted surfaces.

6. Use penetrating oil on frozen or tight bolts. Avoid using heat where possible. Heat can warp, melt or affect the temper of parts. Heat also damages the finish of paint and plastics. Refer to *Heating Components* in this section.

7. When a part is a press fit or requires a special tool for removal, the information or type of tool is identified in the text. Otherwise, if a part is difficult to remove or install, determine the cause before proceeding.

8. To prevent objects or debris from falling into the engine, cover all openings.

9. Read each procedure thoroughly and compare the Figures to the actual components before starting the procedure. Perform the procedure in sequence.

10. Recommendations are occasionally made to refer service to a dealership or specialist. In these cases, the work can be performed more economically by the specialist than by the home mechanic.

11. The term replace means to discard a defective part and replace it with a new part. Overhaul means to remove, disassemble, inspect, measure, repair and/or replace parts as required to recondition an assembly.

12. Some operations require the use of a hydraulic press. If a press is not available, have these operations performed by a shop equipped with the necessary equipment. Do not use makeshift equipment that may damage the motorcycle. Do not direct high-pressure water at steering bearings, fuel body hoses, wheel bearings, suspension and electrical components. The water forces the grease out of the bearings and could damage the seals.

13. Repairs are much faster and easier if the motorcycle is clean before starting work. Degrease the motorcycle with a commercial degreaser; follow the directions on the container for the best results. Clean all parts with cleaning solvent.

14. If special tools are required, have them available before starting the procedure. When special tools are required, they will be described at the beginning of the procedure.

15. Make sure all shims and washers are reinstalled in the same location and position.

16. Whenever rotating parts contact a stationary part, look for a shim or washer.

17. Use new gaskets if there is any doubt about the condition of old ones.

18. If self-locking fasteners are used, replace them. Do not install standard fasteners in place of self-locking ones.

19. Use grease to hold small parts in place if they tend to fall out during assembly. Do not apply grease to electrical or brake components.

Heating Components

> *WARNING*
> *Wear protective gloves to prevent burns*
> *and injury when heating parts.*

> *CAUTION*
> *Do not use a welding torch when heating parts. A welding torch applies **excessive heat** to a small area very quickly, which can damage parts.*

A heat gun or propane torch is required to disassemble, assemble, remove and install many parts and components in this manual. Read the safety and operating information supplied by the manufacturer of the heat gun or propane torch while also noting the following:

1. The work area should be clean and dry. Remove all combustible components and materials from the work area. Wipe up all grease, oil and other fluids from parts. Check for leaking or damaged fuel system components. Repair or remove these parts before beginning work.

2. Never use a flame near the battery, fuel tank, fuel lines or other flammable materials.

3. When using a heat gun, remember that the temperature can be in excess of 540° C (1000° F).

4. Have a fire extinguisher near the job.

5. Always wear protective goggles and gloves when heating parts.

6. Before heating a part installed on the motorcycle, check areas around the part and those hidden that could be damaged or possibly ignite. Do not heat surfaces than can be damaged by heat. Shield materials near the part or area to be heated. For example, cables and wiring harnesses.

7. Before heating a part, read the entire procedure to make sure the required tools are available. This allows quick work while the part is at its optimum temperature.

8. The amount of heat recommended to remove or install a part is typically listed in the procedure. However, before heating parts without a specific recommendation, consider the possible effects. To avoid damaging a part, monitor the temperature with heat sticks or an infrared thermometer, if possible. Another way, though not as accurate, is to place tiny drops of water on the part. When the water starts to sizzle, the part is hot enough. Keep the heat in motion to prevent overheating.

Removing Frozen Fasteners

If a fastener cannot be removed, several methods may be used to loosen it. First, liberally apply penetrating oil, and let it penetrate for 10-15 minutes. Rap the fastener several times with a small hammer. Do not hit it hard enough to cause damage. Reapply the penetrating oil if necessary.

For frozen screws, apply penetrating oil as described, and then insert a screwdriver in the slot and rap the top of the screwdriver with a hammer. This loosens the rust so the screw can be removed in the normal way. If the screw head is too damaged to use this method, grip the head with locking pliers and twist it out.

If heat is required, refer to *Heating Components* in this section.

Removing Broken Fasteners

If the head breaks off a screw or bolt, several methods are available for removing the remaining portion. If a large portion of the remainder projects out, try gripping it with locking pliers. If the projecting portion is too small, file it to fit a wrench or cut a slot in it to fit a screwdriver (**Figure 40**).

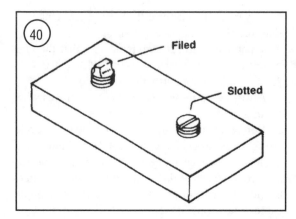

If the head breaks off flush, use a screw extractor. To do this, center punch the exact center of the screw or bolt (1, **Figure 41**), and then drill a small hole in the screw (2) and tap the extractor into the hole (3). Back the screw out with a wrench on the extractor (4, **Figure 41**).

Repairing Damaged Threads

Occasionally, threads are stripped through carelessness or impact damage. Often the threads can be repaired by running a tap (for internal threads on nuts) or die (for external threads on bolts) through the threads (**Figure 42**). To clean or repair spark plug threads, use a spark plug tap.

If an internal thread is damaged, it may be necessary to install a Helicoil or some other type of thread insert. Follow the manufacturer's instructions when installing its insert.

If it is necessary to drill and tap a hole, refer to **Table 6** for metric tap and drill sizes.

Stud Removal/Installation

A stud removal tool (**Figure 43**) is available from most tool suppliers. This tool makes the removal and installation of studs easier. If one is not available and the threads on the stud are not damaged, thread two nuts onto the stud and tighten them against each other. Remove the stud by turning the lower nut.

1. Measure the height of the stud above the surface.
2. Thread the stud removal tool onto the stud and tighten it, or thread two nuts onto the stud.
3. Remove the stud by turning the stud remover or the lower nut.
4. Remove any threadlocking compound from the threaded hole. Clean the threads with an aerosol parts cleaner.
5. Install the stud removal tool onto the new stud, or thread two nuts onto the stud.

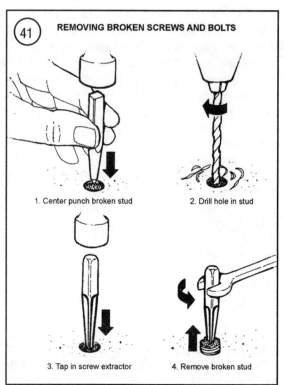

REMOVING BROKEN SCREWS AND BOLTS

1. Center punch broken stud

2. Drill hole in stud

3. Tap in screw extractor

4. Remove broken stud

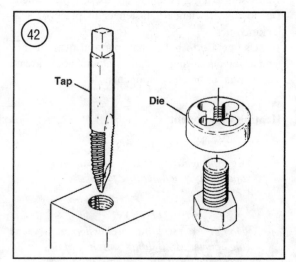

Tap

Die

6. Apply threadlocking compound to the threads of the stud.
7. Install the stud and tighten with the stud removal tool or the top nut.
8. Install the stud to the height noted in Step 1 or its torque specification.
9. Remove the stud removal tool or the two nuts.

Removing Hoses

When removing stubborn a hose, do not exert excessive force on the hose or fitting. Remove the hose

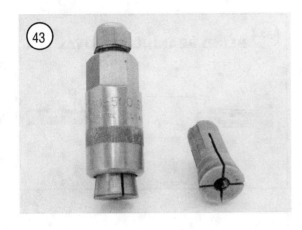

clamp and carefully insert a small screwdriver or similar blunt nose tool between the fitting and hose. Apply a spray lubricant under the hose and carefully twist the hose off the fitting. Clean the fitting of any corrosion or rubber hose material with a wire brush. Clean the inside of the hose thoroughly. Do not use any lubricant when installing the hose (new or old). The lubricant may allow the hose to come off the fitting, even with the clamp secure.

Bearings

Bearings are precision parts, they must be maintained with proper lubrication and maintenance. If a bearing is damaged, replace it immediately. When installing a new bearing, make sure to prevent damaging it. Bearing replacement procedures are included in the individual chapters where applicable; however, use the following sections as a guideline.

Unless otherwise specified, install bearings with the manufacturer's mark or number facing outward.

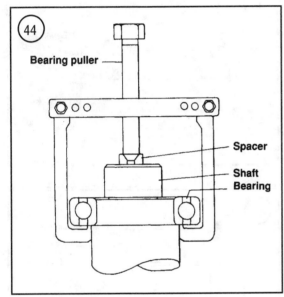

Removal

While bearings are normally removed only when damaged, there may be times when it is necessary to remove a bearing that is in good condition. However, improper bearing removal will damage the bearing and maybe the shaft or case half. Note the following when removing bearings:

1. Before removing the bearings, note the following:
   a. Refer to the bearing replacement procedure in the appropriate chapter for any special instructions.
   b. Remove any seals that interfere with bearing removal. Refer to Seal Replacement in this section.
   c. When removing more than one bearing, identify the bearings before removing them. Refer to the bearing manufacturer's numbers on the bearing.
   d. Note and record the direction in which the bearing numbers face for proper installation.
   e. Remove any set plates or bearing retainers before removing the bearings.

2. When using a puller to remove a bearing from a shaft, make sure the shaft is not damaged. Always place a piece of metal between the end of the shaft and the puller screw. In addition, place the puller arms next to the inner bearing race. Refer to **Figure 44**.

3. When using a hammer to remove a bearing from a shaft, do not strike the hammer directly against the shaft. Instead, use a brass or aluminum rod between the hammer and shaft (**Figure 45**) and make sure to

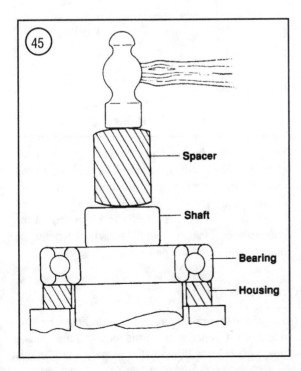

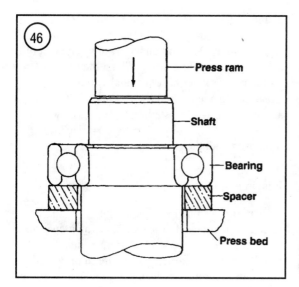

46
Press ram
Shaft
Bearing
Spacer
Press bed

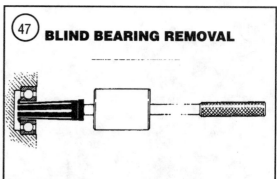

47 **BLIND BEARING REMOVAL**

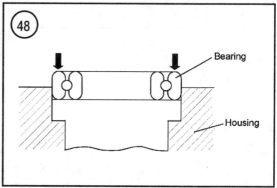

48
Bearing
Housing

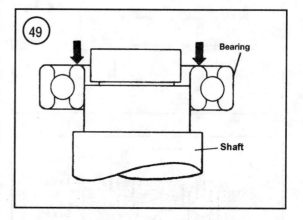

49
Bearing
Shaft

support both bearing races with wooden blocks as shown.

4. The ideal method of bearing removal is with a hydraulic press. Note the following when using a press:

a. Always support the inner and outer bearing races with a suitable size wooden or aluminum ring (**Figure 46**). If only the outer race is supported, pressure applied against the balls and/or the inner race will damage them.

b. Always make sure the press arm (**Figure 46**) aligns with the center of the shaft. If the arm is not centered, it may damage the bearing and/or shaft.

c. The moment the shaft is free of the bearing, it will drop to the floor. Secure or hold the shaft to prevent it from falling.

d. When removing bearings from a housing, support the housing with 4 × 4 in. wooden blocks to prevent damage to gasket surfaces.

5. Use a blind bearing puller to remove bearings installed in blind holes (**Figure 47**).

Installation

1. When installing a bearing in a housing, apply pressure to the outer bearing race (**Figure 48**). When installing a bearing on a shaft, apply pressure to the inner bearing race (**Figure 49**).

2. When installing a bearing as described in Step 1, a driver is required. Never strike the bearing directly with a hammer or the bearing will be damaged. When installing a bearing, use a piece of pipe or a driver with a diameter that matches the bearing race. **Figure 50** shows the correct way to use a driver and hammer to install a bearing on a shaft.

3. Step 1 describes how to install a bearing in a housing or over a shaft. However, when installing a bearing over a shaft and into the housing at the same time, a tight fit will be required for both outer and inner bearing races. In this situation, install a spacer underneath the driver tool so pressure is applied evenly across both races. Refer to **Figure 51**. If the outer race is not supported, the balls push against the outer bearing race and damage it.

Interference fit

1. Follow this procedure when installing a bearing over a shaft. When a tight fit is required, the bearing inside diameter will be smaller than the shaft. In this

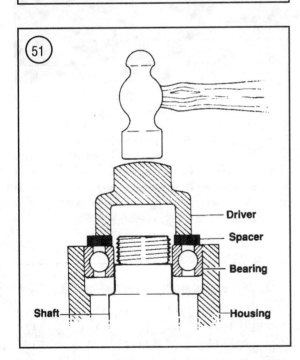

so it does not rest on the bottom or side of the pot.

d. Remove the bearing from its wrapper and secure it with a piece of heavy wire bent to hold it in the pot. Hang the bearing in the pot so it does not touch the bottom or sides of the pot.

e. Turn the heat on and monitor the thermometer. When the oil temperature rises to approximately 120° C (248° F), remove the bearing from the pot and quickly install it. If necessary, place a socket on the inner bearing race and tap the bearing into place. As the bearing chills, it tightens on the shaft, so installation must be done quickly. Make sure the bearing is installed completely.

2. Follow this step when installing a bearing in a housing. Bearings are generally installed in a housing with a slight interference fit. Driving the bearing into the housing using normal methods may damage the housing or cause bearing damage. Instead, heat the housing before the bearing is installed. Note the following:

a. Before heating the housing in this procedure, wash the housing thoroughly with detergent and water. Rinse and rewash the housing as required to remove all oil and chemicals.

b. Heat the housing to approximately 100° C (212° F) with a heat gun or on a hot plate. Monitor temperature with an infrared thermometer, heat sticks or place tiny drops of water on the housing; if they sizzle and evaporate immediately, the temperature is correct. Heat only one housing at a time.

c. If a hot plate is used, remove the housing and place it on wooden blocks.

d. Hold the housing with the bearing side down and tap the bearing out with a suitable size socket and extension. Repeat for all bearings in the housing.

e. Before heating the bearing housing, place the new bearing in a freezer, if possible. Chilling a bearing slightly reduces its outside diameter while the heated bearing housing assembly is slightly larger due to heat expansion. This makes bearing installation easier.

f. While the housing is still hot, install the new bearing(s) into the housing. Install the bearings by hand, if possible. If necessary, lightly tap the bearing(s) into the housing with a socket placed on the outer bearing race (**Figure 48**). Do not install bearings by driving on the inner-bearing race. Install the bearing(s) until it seats completely.

case, driving the bearing on the shaft using normal methods may cause bearing damage. Instead, heat the bearing before installation. Note the following:

a. Secure the shaft so it is ready for bearing installation.

b. Clean all residues from the bearing surface of the shaft. Remove burrs with a file.

c. Fill a suitable pot or beaker with clean mineral oil. Place a thermometer rated above 120° C (248° F) in the oil. Support the thermometer

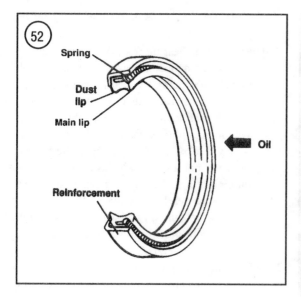

Spring
Dust lip
Main lip
Reinforcement
Oil

Seal Replacement

Seals are used to contain oil, water, grease or combustion gasses in a housing or shaft. Improper removal of a seal can damage the housing or shaft. Improper installation of the seal can damage the seal.

Before replacing a seal, identify it as a rubber or Teflon seal. Both types are used on the models covered in this manual. On a rubber seal (**Figure 52**), the body and sealing element will be made of the same material. The seal lip (element) will also be equipped with a garter spring. On a Teflon seal, the body and seal lip will be noticeably different. The outer part is normally made of rubber and the sealing lip, placed in the middle of the seal, is Teflon. A garter spring is not used.

Rubber seals

1. Prying is generally the easiest and most effective method of removing a seal from the housing. However, always place a rag under the pry tool (**Figure 53**) to prevent damage to the housing.
2. Before installing a typical rubber seal, pack waterproof grease in the seal lips.
3. In most cases, install seals with the manufacturer's numbers or marks face out.
4. Install seals either by hand or with tools. Center the seal in its bore and attempt to install it by hand. If necessary, install the seal with a socket or bearing driver placed on the outside of the seal as shown in **Figure 54**. Drive the seal squarely into the housing until it is flush with its mounting bore. Never install a seal by hitting against the top of the seal with a hammer.

STORAGE

Several months of non-use can cause a general deterioration of the motorcycle. This is especially true in areas of extreme temperature variations. This deterioration can be minimized with careful preparation for storage. A properly stored motorcycle is much easier to return to service.

Storage Area Selection

When selecting a storage area, consider the following:
1. The storage area must be dry. A heated area is best, but not necessary. It should be insulated to minimize extreme temperature variations.
2. If the building has large window areas, mask them to keep sunlight off the motorcycle.
3. Avoid storage areas close to saltwater.
4. Consider the area's risk of fire, theft or vandalism. Check with your insurer regarding motorcycle coverage while in storage.

Preparing the Motorcycle for Storage

The amount of preparation a motorcycle should undergo before storage depends on the expected length of non-use, storage area conditions and personal preference. Consider the following list the minimum requirement:

1. Wash the motorcycle thoroughly. Make sure all dirt, mud and road debris are removed.

2. Start the engine and allow it to reach operating temperature. Drain the engine oil regardless of the riding time since the last service. Fill the engine with the recommended type and quantity of oil.

3. Fill the fuel tank completely.

4. Remove the spark plug from the cylinder head. Ground the spark plug cap to the engine. Refer to *Ignition Ground Tool* in this chapter. Pour a teaspoon (15-20 ml) of engine oil into the cylinders. Place a rag over the openings and slowly turn the engine over to distribute the oil. Reinstall the spark plug.

5. Remove the battery. Store it in a cool, dry location. Charge the battery once a month. Refer to Battery in Chapter Nine for service.

6. Cover the exhaust and intake openings.

7. Apply a protective substance to the plastic and rubber components, including the tires. Make sure to follow the manufacturer's instructions for each type of product being used.

8. Rotate the front tire periodically to prevent a flat spot from developing and damaging the tire.

9. Cover the motorcycle with old bed sheets or something similar. Do not cover it with any plastic material that will trap moisture.

Returning the Motorcycle to Service

The amount of service required when returning a motorcycle to service after storage depends on the length of non-use and storage conditions. In addition to performing the reverse of the above procedure, make sure the brakes, clutch, throttle and engine stop switch work properly before operating the motorcycle. Refer to Chapter Three and evaluate the service intervals to determine which areas require service.

Table 1 GENERAL DIMENSIONS AND WEIGHT

Ground clearance	165 mm (6.5 in.)
Overall height*	1420 mm (55.9 in.)
Overall length	2290 mm (90.2 in.)
Overall width	840 mm (33.1 in.)
Seat height	820 mm (32.3 in.)
Wheelbase	1540 mm (60.6 in.)
Dry weight	190 kg (418 lb.)
* Middle windshield position	

TABLE 2 DECIMAL AND METRIC EQUIVALENTS

Fractions	Decimal in.	Metric mm	Fractions	Decimal in.	Metric mm
1/64	0.015625	0.39688	33/64	0.515625	13.09687
1/32	0.03125	0.79375	17/32	0.53125	13.49375
3/64	0.046875	1.19062	35/64	0.546875	13.89062
1/16	0.0625	1.58750	9/16	0.5625	14.28750
5/64	0.078125	1.98437	37/64	0.578125	14.68437
3/32	0.09375	2.38125	19/32	0.59375	15.08125
7/64	0.109375	2.77812	39/64	0.609375	15.47812
1/8	0.125	3.1750	5/8	0.625	15.87500
9/64	0.140625	3.57187	41/64	0.640625	16.27187
5/32	0.15625	3.96875	21/32	0.65625	16.66875
11/64	0.171875	4.36562	43/64	0.671875	17.06562
3/16	0.1875	4.76250	11/16	0.6875	17.46250
13/64	0.203125	5.15937	45/64	0.703125	17.85937
7/32	0.21875	5.55625	23/32	0.71875	18.25625
15/64	0.234375	5.95312	47/64	0.734375	18.65312
1/4	0.250	6.35000	3/4	0.750	19.05000
17/64	0.265625	6.74687	49/64	0.765625	19.44687

(continued)

TABLE 2 DECIMAL AND METRIC EQUIVALENTS (continued)

Fractions	Decimal in.	Metric mm	Fractions	Decimal in.	Metric mm
9/32	0.28125	7.14375	25/32	0.78125	19.84375
19/64	0.296875	7.54062	51/64	0.796875	20.24062
5/16	0.3125	7.93750	13/16	0.8125	20.63750
21/64	0.328125	8.33437	53/64	0.828125	21.03437
11/32	0.34375	8.73125	27/32	0.84375	21.43125
23/64	0.359375	9.12812	55/64	0.859375	22.82812
3/8	0.375	9.52500	7/8	0.875	22.22500
25/64	0.390625	9.92187	57/64	0.890625	22.62187
13/32	0.40625	10.31875	29/32	0.90625	23.01875
27/64	0.421875	10.71562	59/64	0.921875	23.41562
7/16	0.4375	11.11250	15/16	0.9375	23.81250
29/64	0.453125	11.50937	61/64	0.953125	24.20937
15/32	0.46875	11.90625	31/32	0.96875	24.60625
31/64	0.484375	12.30312	63/64	0.984375	25.00312
1/2	0.500	12.70000	1	1.00	25.40000

TABLE 3 CONVERSION FORMULAS

Multiply:	By:	To get the equivalent of:
Length		
Inches	25.4	Millimeter
Inches	2.54	Centimeter
Miles	1.609	Kilometer
Feet	0.3048	Meter
Millimeter	0.03937	Inches
Centimeter	0.3937	Inches
Kilometer	0.6214	Mile
Meter	3.281	Mile
Fluid volume		
U.S. quarts	0.9463	Liters
U.S. gallons	3.785	Liters
U.S. ounces	29.573529	Milliliters
Imperial gallons	4.54609	Liters
Imperial quarts	1.1365	Liters
Liters	0.2641721	U.S. gallons
Liters	1.0566882	U.S. quarts
Liters	33.814023	U.S. ounces
Liters	0.22	Imperial gallons
Liters	0.8799	Imperial quarts
Milliliters	0.033814	U.S. ounces
Milliliters	1.0	Cubic centimeters
Milliliters	0.001	Liters
Torque		
Foot-pounds	1.3558	Newton-meters
Foot-pounds	0.138255	Meters-kilograms
Inch-pounsd	0.11299	Newton-meters
Newton-meters	0.7375622	Foot-pounds
Newton-meters	8.8507	Inch-pounds
Meters-kilograms	7.2330139	Foot-pounds
Volume		
Cubic inches	16.387064	Cubic centimeters
Cubic centimeters	0.0610237	Cubic inches
Temperature		
Fahrenheit	(F-32°) 0.556	Centigrade
Centigrade	(C 1.8) + 32	Fahrenheit
Weight		
Ounces	28.3495	Grams
Pounds	0.4535924	Kilograms
Grams	0.035274	Ounces
Kilograms	2.2046224	Pounds

(continued)

TABLE 3 CONVERSION FORMULAS (continued)

Multiply:	By:	To get the equivalent of:
Pressure		
Pounds per square inch	0.070307	Kilograms per square centimeter
Kilograms per square centimeter	14.223343	Pounds per square inch
Kilopascals	0.1450	Pounds per square inch
Pounds per square inch	6.895	Kilopascals
Speed		
Miles per hour	1.609344	Kilometers per hour
Kilometers per hour	0.6213712	Miles per hour

Table 4 GENERAL TORQUE SPECIFICATIONS

Bolt diameter (mm)	Bolts with no hardness mark or marked 4			Bolts marked 7		
	N•m	in.-lb.	ft.-lb.	N•m	in.-lb.	ft.-lb.
4	1.5	13	-	2.3	20	-
5	3	27	-	4.5	40	-
6	5.5	49	-	10	89	-
8	13	115	-	23	-	17
10	29	-	21	50	-	36
12	45	-	33	85	-	63
14	65	-	48	135	-	100
16	105	-	77	210	-	155
18	160	-	118	240	-	177

Table 5 TECHNICAL ABBREVIATIONS

ABDC	After bottom dead center
ABS	Anti-lock brake system
ATDC	After top dead center
BBDC	Before bottom dead center
BDC	Bottom dead center
BTDC	Before top dead center
C	Celsius (centigrade)
cc	Cubic centimeters
cid	Cubic inch displacement
CKP sensor	Crankshaft position sensor
cu. in.	Cubic inches
ECM	Electronic control module
ECT	Engine coolant temperature sensor
ECU	Electronic control unit
EVAP	Evaporative emission system
F	Fahrenheit
ft.	Feet
ft.-lb.	Foot-pounds
gal.	Gallons
HO2 sensor	Heated oxygen sensor
IAP sensor	Intake air pressure sensor
IAT sensor	Intake air temperature sensor
hp	Horsepower
in.	Inches
in.-lb.	Inch-pounds
I.D.	Inside diameter
kg	Kilograms
kgm	Kilogram meters

(continued)

Table 5 TECHNICAL ABBREVIATIONS (continued)

km	Kilometer
kPa	Kilopascals
L	Liter
m	Meter
MAG	Magneto
MAP sensor	Manifold absolute pressure sensor
ml	Milliliter
mm	Millimeter
N•m	Newton-meter
O.D.	Outside diameter
oz.	Ounces
PAIR	Pulsed secondary air injection
psi	Pounds per square inch
pt.	Pint
qt.	Quart
rpm	Revolutions per minute
STP sensor	Secondary throttle position sensor
STVA	Secondary throttle valve actuator
TO sensor	Tip over sensor
TP sensor	Throttle position sensor
V	Volt
W	Watt

Table 6 METRIC TAP AND DRILL SIZES

Metric size	Drill equivalent	Decimal fraction	Nearest fraction
3 x 0.50	No. 39	0.0995	3/32
3 x 0.60	3/32	0.0937	3/32
4 x 0.70	No. 30	0.1285	1/8
4 x 0.75	1/8	0.125	1/8
5 x 0.80	No. 19	0.166	11/64
5 x 0.90	No. 20	0.161	5/32
6 x 1.00	No. 9	0.196	13/64
7 x 1.00	16/64	0.234	15-64
8 x 1.00	J	0.277	9/32
8 x 1.25	17/64	0.265	17/64
9 x 1.00	5/16	0.3125	5/16
9 x 1.25	5/16	0.3125	5/16
10 x 1.25	R	0.339	11/32
11 x 1.50	3/8	0.375	3/8
12 x 1.50	13/32	0.406	13/32
12 x 1.75	13/32	0.406	13/32

TROUBLESHOOTING

The troubleshooting procedures described in this chapter provide typical symptoms and logical methods for isolating the cause(s). There may be several ways to solve a problem, but only a systematic approach will be successful in avoiding wasted time and possibly unnecessary parts replacement. Gather as much information as possible to aid in diagnosis. Never assume anything and do not overlook the obvious. Make sure the engine stop switch is in the run position and there is fuel in the tank.

An engine needs three basics to run properly: correct air/ fuel mixture, compression and a spark at the correct time. If one of these is missing, the engine will not run.

Learning to recognize symptoms makes troubleshooting easier. In most cases, expensive and complicated test equipment is not needed to determine whether repairs can be performed at home. On the other hand, be realistic and do not start procedures that are beyond your experience and equipment available. If the motorcycle requires the attention of a professional, describe symptoms and conditions accurately and fully. The more information a technician has available, the easier it is to diagnose the problem.

STARTING THE ENGINE

The following sections described recommended starting procedures at various ambient temperatures and engine conditions.

CAUTION
Do not operate the starter for more than five seconds at a time. Wait for approximately ten seconds between starting attempts.

Starting System Operation

1. The position of the sidestand will affect engine starting. Note the following:
   a. The engine cannot start when the sidestand is down and the clutch lever released, or the transmission is not in neutral.
   b. The engine can start when the sidestand is down if the clutch lever is pulled in and the transmission is in neutral. The engine will remain running if the clutch lever is released with the transmission in neutral, but stop if the transmission is put in gear with the sidestand down.
   c. The engine can be started when the sidestand is up and the transmission is in neutral or in gear with the clutch lever pulled in.
2. Before starting the engine, shift the transmission into neutral and place the engine stop switch (A, **Figure 1**) in the run position.
3. The engine is now ready to start. Refer to the appropriate starting procedure.

Starting Procedures

All engine temperatures

1. Review Starting System Operation in this chapter.
2. Verify throttle is in closed position.
3. Turn the ignition switch on.
4. Place the engine stop switch (A, **Figure 1**) in the run position.

> *CAUTION*
> *The warning lights should go off after a few seconds or after the engine starts. If a light stays on, turn the engine off and check the relevant item.*

5. The following indicator lights should turn on when the ignition switch is on.
   a. The neutral indicator light (when the transmission is in neutral).
   b. Low oil pressure indicator light.
   c. Coolant temperature indicator light.
   d. Fuel level meter.
   e. On DL650A models, ABS indicator light.
   f. The speedometer and tachometer needles swing to their maximum settings and then return to zero.
6. Depress the starter button (B, **Figure 1**) and start the engine. Do not open the throttle when pressing the starter button.

Engine Flooded

If the engine will not start and a strong gasoline smell is present, the engine is probably flooded. To start a flooded engine:

1. Turn the engine stop switch off.
2. Turn the ignition switch on.

> *CAUTION*
> *The warning lights should go off after a few seconds or after the engine starts. If a light stays on, turn the engine off and check the relevant item.*

3. The following indicator lights should turn on when the ignition switch is on.
   a. The neutral indicator light (when the transmission is in neutral).
   b. Low oil pressure indicator light.
   c. Coolant temperature indicator light.
   d. Fuel level meter.
   e. On DL650A models, ABS indicator light.
   f. The speedometer and tachometer needles swing to their maximum settings and then return to zero.
4. Open the throttle one-eighth turn.

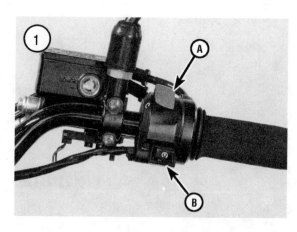

5. Operate the starter button for five seconds.
6. Follow the procedure under *All Engine Temperatures*. Note the following:
   a. If the engine starts but idles roughly, vary the throttle position slightly until the engine idles and responds smoothly.
   b. If the engine does not start, turn the ignition switch off and wait approximately ten seconds.

Then repeat Steps 1-5. If the engine still will not start, refer to *Engine Will Not Start* in this chapter.

ENGINE WILL NOT START

Identifying the Problem

If the engine does not start, perform the following procedure in sequence. If the engine fails to start after performing these checks, refer to the troubleshooting procedures indicated in the steps.

All models are equipped with an engine management system capable of self-diagnosis. Refer to *Electronic Diagnostic System)* in this chapter.

1. Refer to *Starting the Engine* in this chapter to make sure all switches and starting procedures are correct.
2. If the starter does not operate, refer to Starting System in this chapter.
3. If the starter operates, and the engine seems flooded, refer to *Starting the Engine* in this chapter. If the engine is not flooded, continue with Step 4.
4. Turn the ignition switch on and check the fuel meter. If the fuel level low-level light flickers the fuel level in the tank is low. The amount of fuel remaining in the tank when the fuel level light flickers is approximately 3.0 liter (0.8 gallon).
5. If there is sufficient fuel in the fuel tank, remove one of the spark plugs immediately after attempting to start the engine. The spark plug insulator should be wet, indicating that fuel is reaching the engine. If the plug tip is dry, fuel is not reaching the engine.

Confirm this condition by checking the other spark plug. A faulty fuel pump or a clogged fuel filter can cause this condition. Refer to *Fuel System* in this chapter. If there is fuel on the spark plug and the engine will not start, the engine may not have adequate spark. Continue with Step 6.

6. Make sure each spark plug cap is securely attached to the spark plug. If the engine does not start, continue with Step 7.

7. Perform the Spark Test described in this section. If there is a strong spark, perform Step 8. If there is no spark or if the spark is very weak, refer to Ignition System in this chapter.

8. If the fuel and ignition systems are working correctly, perform a leakdown test (this chapter) and compression test (Chapter Three). If the compression is low, refer to *Engine Performance* in this chapter. Check cylinder compression as described in Chapter Three.

Spark Test

Perform a spark test to determine if the ignition system is producing adequate spark. This test can be performed with a spark plug or a spark tester (Motion Pro part No. 08-0122). A spark tester is used as a substitute for the spark plug and allows the spark to be more easily observed between the adjustable air gap. If a spark tester is not available, use a new spark plug.

WARNING
Do not hold the spark plugs, tester, wire or connector, or a serious electrical shock may result.

1. Remove the spark plugs as described in Chapter Three.

2. Connect each spark plug wire and connector to a new spark plug or tester, and touch each spark plug base or tester to a good engine ground (**Figure 2**).

Position the spark plugs or tester away from the spark plug holes and so the electrodes are visible.

3. Shift the transmission to neutral, turn the ignition system on and place the engine stop switch in the run position.

4. Operate the starter button to turn the engine over. A fat blue spark must be evident across the spark plug electrodes or between the tester terminals. Repeat for each cylinder

5. If the spark is good at each spark plug, the ignition system is functioning properly. Check for one or more of the following possible malfunctions:

    a. Faulty fuel system component. Refer to *Fuel System* in this chapter.

    b. Engine damage (low compression).

    c. Engine flooded.

6. If the spark was weak or if there was no spark at one or both plugs, note the following:

    a. If there is no spark on both of the plugs, check for a problem on the input side of the ignition system or the ECM as described in *Ignition System* in this chapter

    b. If there is no spark at one spark plug only, the spark plug is probably faulty or there is a problem with the spark plug wire or plug cap. Retest with a spark tester, or use a new spark plug. If there is still no spark at that one plug, make sure the spark plug cap is installed correctly.

    c. If there is no spark, the ignition coil is faulty.

    d. Troubleshoot the ignition system as described in this chapter.

7. Install the spark plugs as described in Chapter Three.

Engine is Difficult to Start

1. After attempting to start the engine, remove one of the spark plugs as described in Chapter Three and check for the presence of fuel on the plug tip. Note the following:

    a. If there is no fuel visible on the plug, remove another spark plug. If there is no fuel on this plug, perform Step 2.

    b. If there is fuel on the plug tip, go to Step 4.

    c. If there is an excessive amount of fuel on the plug, check for a clogged or plugged air filter.

2. Test the fuel pump as described in Chapter Eight. Note the following:

    a. If the fuel pump operation is correct, go to Step 3.

    b. If there is fuel flow but the volume is minimal, check for a clogged fuel system.

    c. If the fuel pump operation is faulty, replace the fuel pump and retest the fuel system.

3. Perform the *Spark Test* in this section. Note the following:

    a. If the spark is weak or if there is no spark, go to Step 4.

    b. If the spark is good, go to Step 5.

4. If the spark is weak or if there is no spark, check the following:

    a. Fouled spark plug(s).

    b. Damaged spark plug(s).

    c. Loose or damaged spark plug wire(s).

    d. Loose or damaged spark plug cap(s).

    e. Faulty ECM.

    f. Faulty crankshaft position sensor.

    g. Faulty ignition coil(s).

    h. Faulty engine stop switch.

    i. Faulty ignition switch.

    j. Dirty or loose-fitting terminals.

5. If the engine turns over but does not start, the engine compression may be low. Check for the following possible malfunctions:

    a. Leaking cylinder head gasket.

    b. Valve clearance too tight.

    c. Bent or stuck valve(s).

    d. Incorrect valve timing. Worn cylinders and/or piston rings.

6. If the spark is good, try starting the engine by following normal starting procedures. If the engine starts but then stops, check for the following conditions:

    a. Leaking or damaged intake duct.

    b. Contaminated fuel.

    c. Incorrect ignition timing.

Engine Will Not Crank

If the engine will not turn over, check for one or more of the following possible malfunctions:

1. Blown main fuse.
2. Discharged battery.
3. Defective starter or starter relay switch.
4. Seized piston(s).
5. Seized crankshaft bearings.
6. Broken connecting rod(s).
7. Locked-up transmission or clutch assembly.
8. Defective starter clutch.

ENGINE PERFORMANCE

If the engine runs, but performance is unsatisfactory, refer to the following procedure(s) that best describes the symptom(s).

All models are equipped with an engine management system capable of self-diagnosis. Refer to *Electronic Diagnostic System* in this chapter for identification of malfunctioning components that may cause a performance problem.

The ignition timing is not adjustable. If incorrect ignition timing is suspected as being the cause of a malfunction, check the timing as described in Chapter Three. If the timing is incorrect, a defective ignition system component is indicated. Refer to Ignition System in this chapter.

Engine Will Not Idle

1. Clogged air filter element.
2. Poor fuel flow.
3. Incorrect throttle body synchronization.
4. Fouled or improperly gapped spark plug(s).
5. Leaking head gasket or vacuum leak.
6. Leaking or damaged intake duct.
7. Low engine compression.
8. Obstructed throttle body or defective fuel injector .
9. Incorrect ignition timing caused by a faulty ECM or crankshaft position sensor.

Poor Overall Performance

1. Position the motorcycle so the rear wheel is elevated, then spin the rear wheel by hand. If the wheel spins freely, perform Step 2. If the wheel does not spin freely, check for the following conditions:

    a. Dragging rear brake.

    b. Damaged rear axle assembly.

2. Check the clutch adjustment and operation. If the clutch slips, refer to Clutch in this chapter.

3. If Step 1 and Step 2 did not locate the problem, test ride the motorcycle and accelerate lightly. If the engine speed increases according to throttle position, perform Step 4. If the engine speed did not increase, check for one or more of the following problems:

    a. Clogged air filter.

    b. Restricted fuel flow.

    c. Clogged or damaged muffler.

4. Check for one or more of the following problems:

    a. Low engine compression.

    b. Worn spark plugs.

    c. Fouled spark plug(s).

    d. Incorrect spark plug heat range.

    e. Incorrect oil level (too high or too low).

    f. Contaminated oil.

    g. Worn or damaged valve train assembly.

    h. Engine overheating. Refer to *Engine Overheating* in this section.

    i. Incorrect ignition timing caused by a faulty ECM or crankshaft position sensor.

5. If the engine knocks during acceleration or when running at high speed, check for one or more of the following possible malfunctions:
   a. Incorrect type of fuel.
   b. Lean fuel mixture.
   c. Excessive carbon buildup in combustion chamber.
   d. Worn pistons and/or cylinder bores.
   e. Advanced ignition timing caused by a faulty ECM or crankshaft position sensor.

Poor Idle or Low Speed Performance

1. Check for damaged intake duct and air filter housing hose clamps.
2. Check the fuel system (Chapter Eight).
3. Perform the spark test in this section. Note the following:
   a. If the spark is good, go to Step 4.
   b. If the spark is weak, test the ignition system as described in this chapter.
4. Check the ignition timing as described in Chapter Three. Note the following:
   a. If the ignition timing is incorrect, check the ignition system (Chapter Nine).
   b. If the ignition timing is correct, recheck the fuel system.

Poor High Speed Performance

1. Check the fuel system (Chapter Eight).
2. Check ignition timing as described in Chapter Three. If ignition timing is incorrect, perform Step 3.
3. If the timing is incorrect, test the following ignition system components as described in Chapter Ten:
   a. Ignition coils.
   b. Crankshaft position sensor.
   c. ECM.
4. Check the valve clearance as described in Chapter Three. Note the following:
   a. If the valve clearance is correct, perform Step 5.
   b. If the clearance is incorrect, readjust the valves.
5. Incorrect valve timing and worn or damaged valve springs can cause poor high-speed performance. If the camshafts were timed just prior to the motorcycle experiencing this type of problem, the cam timing may be incorrect. If the cam timing was not set or changed, and all of the other inspection procedures in this section failed to locate the problem, inspect the camshafts and valve assembly.

Engine Overheating

Cooling system malfunction

1. Low coolant level.
2. Air in cooling system.
3. Clogged radiator, hose or engine coolant passages.
4. Thermostat stuck closed.
5. Worn or damaged radiator cap.
6. Damaged water pump.
7. Damaged fan motor switch.
8. Damaged fan motor.
9. Damaged coolant temperature sensor.

Other causes

1. Improper spark plug heat range.
2. Low oil level.
3. Oil not circulating properly.
4. Valves leaking.
5. Heavy engine carbon deposits in combustion chamber.
6. Dragging brake(s).
7. Clutch slip.

Engine Not Reaching Operating Temperature

1. Thermostat stuck open.
2. Defective fan motor switch.
3. Inaccurate temperature gauge.
4. Defective coolant temperature sensor.

Engine Backfires

1. Incorrect ignition timing due to loose or defective ignition system component.
2. Faulty ECM.

Engine Misfires During Acceleration

1. Incorrect ignition timing due to loose or defective ignition system component.
2. Faulty ECM.

ENGINE NOISES

Unusual noises are often the first indication of a developing problem. Investigate any new noises as soon as possible. Something that may be a minor problem, if corrected, could prevent the possibility of more extensive damage. Use a mechanic's stethoscope or a small section of hose held near the ear (not directly on the ear) with the other end close to the source of the noise to isolate the location. Determining the exact cause of a noise can be difficult. If this is the case, consult with a professional mechanic to determine the cause. Do not disassemble major components until all other possibilities have been eliminated.

Consider the following when troubleshooting engine noises:

1. Knocking or pinging during acceleration is usually caused by using a lower octane fuel than recommended. It may also be caused by poor fuel. Pinging can also be caused by an incorrect spark plug heat range or carbon build-up in the combustion chamber. Refer to *Spark Plugs and Compression Test* in Chapter Three.

2. A slapping or rattling noise at low speed or during acceleration is typically caused by excessive piston- to-cylinder wall clearance (piston slap). Piston slap is easier to detect when the engine is cold and before the pistons have expanded. Once the engine has warmed up, piston expansion reduces piston-to-cylinder clearance.

3. A knocking or rapping during deceleration is usually caused by excessive rod bearing clearance.

4. Persistent knocking and vibration at every crankshaft rotation are usually caused by worn rod or main bearing(s). It can also be caused by broken piston rings or damaged piston pins.

5. A rapid on-off squeal is due to a compression leak around the cylinder head gasket or spark plug(s).

6. In case of valve train noise, check for the following:
   a. Excessive valve clearance.
   b. Worn or damaged camshaft.
   c. Damaged camshaft, camshaft drive chain and guides.
   d. Worn or damaged valve lifter(s).
   e. Damaged valve lifter bore(s).
   f. Valve sticking in guide(s).
   g. Broken valve spring(s).
   h. Low oil pressure.
   i. Clogged cylinder oil hole or oil passage.

Engine Smoke

The color of engine smoke can help diagnose engine problems or operating conditions.

Black Smoke

Black smoke is an indication of a rich air/fuel mixture where an excessive amount of fuel is being burned in the combustion chamber. Check for a leaking fuel injector(s) or a damaged pressure regulator as described in Chapter Eight.

Blue Smoke

Blue smoke indicates that the engine is burning oil in the combustion chamber as it leaks past worn valve stem seals and piston rings. Excessive oil consumption is another indicator of an engine that is burning oil. Perform a compression test (Chapter Three) to isolate the problem.

White Smoke or Steam

It is normal to see white smoke or steam from the exhaust after first starting the engine in cold weather. This is actually condensed steam formed by the engine during combustion. If the motorcycle is ridden far enough, the water cannot buildup in the crankcase and should not be a problem. Once the engine heats up to normal operating temperature, the water evaporates and exits the engine through the crankcase vent system. However, if the motorcycle is ridden for short trips or repeatedly started and stopped and allowed to cool off without the engine getting warm enough, water will start to collect in the crankcase. With each short run of the engine, more water collects. As this water mixes with the oil in the crankcase, sludge is produced. Water sludge can eventually cause engine damage as it circulates through the lubrication system and blocks off oil passages. Water draining from drain holes in exhaust pipes indicates water buildup.

Large amounts of steam can also be caused by a cracked cylinder head or cylinder block surface that allows antifreeze to leak into the combustion chamber. Perform a coolant pressure test as described in Chapter Ten.

Low Engine Compression

Problems with the engine top end will affect engine performance and driveability. When the engine is suspect, perform the leakdown test in this chapter and do a compression test as described in Chapter Three. Interpret the results as described in each procedure to troubleshoot the suspect area.

An engine can lose compression through the following areas.

1. Valves:
   a. Incorrect valve adjustment.
   b. Incorrect valve timing.
   c. Worn or damaged valve seats (valve and/or cylinder head).
   d. Bent valves.
   e. Weak or broken valve springs.
2. Cylinder head:
   a. Loose spark plug or damaged spark plug hole.
   b. Damaged cylinder head gasket.

c. Warped or cracked cylinder head.

MOTORCYCLE NOISE

The following possible causes of noise will likely occur only when the bike is in motion.
1. Excessively loose drive chain.
2. Worn chain sliders.
3. Loose exhaust system.
4. Loose/missing body fasteners.
5. Loose shock absorber.
6. Loose engine mounting bolts.
7. Brake pads dragging on brake disc.
8. Worn/seized wheel bearings.

ENGINE LUBRICATION

An improperly operating engine lubrication system will quickly lead to engine seizure. Check the engine oil level before each ride, and top off as described in Chapter Three. Oil pump service is in Chapter Five.

High Oil Consumption or Excessive Exhaust Smoke

1. Worn valve guides.
2. Worn or damaged piston rings.

Oil Leaks

1. Clogged air filter housing breather hose.
2. Loose engine parts.
3. Damaged gasket sealing surfaces.

High Oil Pressure

1. Clogged oil filter.
2. Clogged oil passageways.
3. Incorrect type of engine oil.

Low Oil Pressure

1. Low oil level.
2. Defective oil pump.
3. Clogged oil strainer screen.
4. Clogged oil filter.
5. Internal oil leaks.
6. Incorrect type of engine oil.

No Oil Pressure

1. Low oil level.
2. Damaged oil pump drive shaft.
3. Damaged oil pump drive sprocket.
4. Incorrect oil pump installation.
5. Defective oil pump.

Oil Contamination

1. Blown head gasket allowing coolant to leak into the engine.
2. Water contamination.
3. Oil and filter not changed at specified intervals or when operating conditions demand more frequent changes.

OIL PRESSURE TEST

Check the oil pressure after installing a new oil pump, reassembling the engine or when troubleshooting the lubrication system.

To check the oil pressure, an oil pressure gauge hose (Suzuki part No. 09915-74521), gauge attachment (09915-74532) and high pressure meter (09915-77331) are required.
1. Make sure the engine oil level is correct as described in Chapter Three. Add oil if necessary.
2. Start the engine and allow it to reach normal operating temperature. Turn off the engine.
3. Place a drain pan under the main oil gallery plug (**Figure 3**) to catch the oil that drains out during the test.
4. Unscrew and remove the main oil gallery plug from the crankcase.

CAUTION
Keep the gauge hose away from the exhaust pipe during this test. If the hose contacts the exhaust pipes, it may melt and spray hot oil onto the hot exhaust pipe, resulting in a fire.

5. Install the adapter, then install the gauge into the main oil gallery. Make sure the fitting is tight to avoid oil loss.

6. Start the engine and let it idle. Increase engine speed to 3000 rpm. The oil pressure should be 100-400 kPa (14-57 psi) when the oil temperature is 60° C (140° F).

7. If the oil pressure is lower than specified, check the following:

    a. Low oil level.

    b. Incorrect type of engine oil.

    c. Clogged oil strainer screen.

    d. Clogged oil filter.

    e. Oil leak from oil passageway.

    f. Damaged oil seal(s).

    g. Defective oil pump.

    h. Combination of the above.

8. If the oil pressure is higher than specified check the following:

    a. Incorrect type of engine oil.

    b. Clogged oil passageways.

    c. Clogged oil filter.

    d. Combination of the above.

9. Shut off the engine and remove the test equipment.

10. Install the plug (**Figure 3**) and gasket onto the crankcase. Tighten the plug securely.

11. Check oil level and adjust if necessary (Chapter Three).

LEAKDOWN TEST

A leakdown test can locate engine problems from leaking valves, blown head gaskets or broken, worn or stuck piston rings. This test is performed by applying compressed air to the cylinder and then measuring the loss percentage. Use a cylinder leakdown tester (**Figure 4**) and an air compressor to perform this test.

Follow the manufacturer's directions along with the following information when performing a cylinder leak down test.

1. Start and run the engine until it reaches normal operating temperature, then turn off the engine.

2. Open and secure the throttle so it remains in the wide open position.

3. Remove the spark plugs as described in Chapter Three. This makes it easier to turn the engine by hand.

4. Remove the timing inspection plug (A, **Figure 5**).

5. Remove the flywheel bolt access plug (B, **Figure 5**).

6. Insert a suitably sized socket through the cover to engage the flywheel bolt (**Figure 6**).

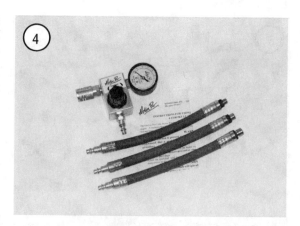

NOTE
The flywheel has lines marked F or R to indicate lop dead center for the front cylinder (F) or rear cylinder (R).

7. Rotate the engine counterclockwise, as viewed from the left side of the motorcycle. Rotate the flywheel until the F or R line, depending on the cylinder being tested, aligns with the mark on the timing inspection hole as shown in **Figure 7**. To determine if the piston is on the compression stroke, hold your finger on the spark plug hole of the cylinder being tested to feel for compression.

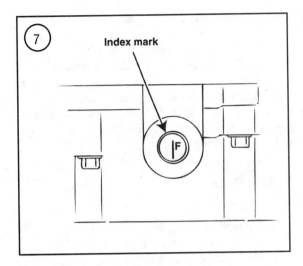

8. Install the leakdown tester into the spark plug hole. Connect an air compressor to the tester fitting.

NOTE
The engine may turn over when air pressure is applied to the cylinder To prevent this from happening, shift the transmission into sixth gear.

9. Apply compressed air to the leakdown tester. Read the leak rate on the gauge and record the measurement.

10. Listen for air escaping from the engine at the following points.

    a. Air leaking through the exhaust pipe indicates a leaking exhaust valve.

    b. Air leaking through the throttle body indicates a leaking intake valve.

    c. Air leaking through the crankcase breather tube indicates worn piston rings.

    d. Air leaking into the cooling system causes the coolant to bubble in the radiator. If this occurs, check for a damaged cylinder head gasket and/or a warped or cracked cylinder head or cylinder block surface.

11. Repeat Steps 7-10 for the remaining cylinder.

    a. For a new or rebuilt engine, a pressure loss of 0 to 5 percent per cylinder is desirable. A pressure loss of 6 to 14 percent is acceptable and means the engine is in good condition.

    b. If testing a used engine, the critical parameter is not each cylinder's leak rate, but the difference between the cylinders. On a used engine, a difference of 10 percent or less between the cylinders is acceptable,

    c. If the pressure loss between cylinders differs by more than 10 percent, the engine is in poor condition and further testing is required.

12. When finished, reinstall the spark plugs as described in Chapter Three and tightly install the tim-

ing inspection plug (A, **Figure 5**) and the flywheel bolt access plug (B).

CLUTCH

The two main clutch problems are clutch slip (clutch does not fully engage) and clutch drag (clutch does not fully disengage). These problems are often caused by incorrect clutch adjustment or a damaged/unlubricated cable. Perform the following checks before removing the right crankcase cover to troubleshoot the clutch:

1. Check the clutch cable routing from the handlebar to the engine. Check that the cable is free when the handlebar is turned lock to lock, and that the cable ends are installed correctly.

2. With the engine off, pull and release the clutch lever. If the lever is hard to pull, or the action is rough, check for the following:

    a. Damaged/kinked cable.

    b. Incorrect cable routing.

    c. Cable not lubricated.

    d. Worn/unlubricated lever at the handlebar.

    e. Damaged release lever at the engine.

3. If no damage was detected in the previous steps, and the lever moves without excessive roughness or binding, check the clutch adjustment as described in Chapter Three. Note the following:

    a. If the clutch cannot be adjusted to the specifications in Chapter Three, the clutch cable is stretched or damaged.

    b. If the clutch cable is in good condition and adjustment is correct, the clutch plates may be worn or warped.

Clutch Slipping

When the clutch slips, the engine accelerates faster than what the actual forward speed indicates. When continuous slipping occurs between the clutch plates, excessive heat quickly builds up in the assembly. This causes plate wear, warp and spring fatigue. One or more of the following can cause the clutch to slip:

1. Clutch wear or damage:

    a. Incorrect clutch adjustment.

    b. Weak or damaged clutch springs.

    c. Loose clutch springs.

    d. Worn friction plates.

    e. Warped clutch (steel) plates.

    f. Worn/damaged release lever assembly.

    g. Damaged pressure plate.

    h. Clutch housing and hub unevenly worn.

2. Clutch/engine oil:

    a. Excessive oil in crankcase.

b. Incorrect oil viscosity.

c. Oil additives.

Clutch Dragging

When the clutch drags, the plates are not completely separating. This causes the motorcycle to creep or lurch forward when the transmission is put into gear. Once underway, shifting is difficult. If this condition is not corrected, it can cause transmission gear and shift fork damage, due to the abnormal grinding and impacts on the parts. One or more of the following can cause the clutch to drag:

1. Clutch wear or damage:
   a. Worn/damaged release lever assembly.
   b. Warped clutch (steel) plates.
   c. Swollen friction plates.
   d. Warped pressure plate.
   e. Incorrect clutch spring tension.
   f. Galled clutch housing bushing.
   g. Uneven wear on clutch housing grooves or clutch hub splines.
   h. Incorrectly assembled clutch.
2. Clutch/engine oil:
   a. Low oil level.
   b. Incorrect viscosity oil.
   c. Oil additives.

Clutch Noise

Clutch noise is usually caused by worn or damaged parts, and is more noticeable at idle or low engine speeds. Clutch noise can be caused by the following conditions:

1. Wear in the clutch lifter bearing and/or lifter.
2. Excessive axial play in the clutch housing.
3. Excessive friction plate to clutch housing clearance.
4. Excessive wear between the clutch housing and primary drive gear.
5. Worn or damaged clutch housing and primary drive gear teeth.

GEAR SHIFT LINKAGE AND TRANSMISSION

Transmission problems are often difficult to distinguish from problems with the clutch and gear shift linkage. Often, the problem is symptomatic of one area, while the actual problem is in another area. For example, if the gears grind during shifting, the problem may be caused by a dragging clutch or a component of the shift linkage, not a damaged transmission. Of course, if the damaged part is not repaired, the transmission eventually becomes damaged, too.

Therefore, evaluate all the variables that exist when the problem occurs, and always start with the easiest checks before disassembling the engine.

When the transmission exhibits abnormal noise or operation, drain the engine oil and check it for contamination or metal particles. Examine a small quantity of oil under bright light. If a metallic cast or pieces of metal are seen, excessive wear and/or part failure is occurring.

Difficult Shifting

1. Clutch:
   a. Improper clutch operation.
   b. Incorrect clutch adjustment.
   c. Incorrect oil viscosity.
2. Shift shaft:
   a. Loose/stripped shift lever.
   b. Bent/damaged shift shaft.
   c. Worn pawl plate engagement points.
   d. Damaged pawl plate or pawl spring.
   e. Damaged return spring or loose spring post.
3. Lever:
   a. Damaged lever.
   b. Broken lever spring.
   c. Loose lever bolt.
4. Shift drum and shift forks:
   a. Worn/loose shift cam.
   b. Worn shift drum grooves.
   c. Worn shift forks/guide pins.
   d. Worn shift drum bearings.

Gears Do Not Stay Engaged

1. Lever:
   a. Damaged lever.
   b. Broken lever spring.
2. Shift drum and shift forks:
   a. Worn/loose shift cam.
   b. Worn shift drum grooves.
   c. Worn shift forks/guide pins.
3. Transmission:
   a. Worn gear dogs and mating recesses.
   b. Worn gear grooves for shift forks.
   c. Worn/damaged shaft snap rings or thrust washers.

ELECTRICAL TESTING

This section describes electrical troubleshooting and the use of test equipment. Never assume anything and do not overlook the obvious, such as a blown fuse or an electrical connector that has separated. Test the simplest and most obvious items first and try to make tests at easily accessible points on the motorcycle. Make sure to troubleshoot systematically.

Refer to the color wiring diagrams at the end of the manual for component and connector identification. Use the wiring diagrams to determine how the circuit should work by tracing the current paths from the power source through the circuit components to ground. Also check any circuits that share the same fuse, ground or switch. If the other circuits work properly and the shared wiring is good, the cause must be in the wiring used only by the suspect circuit. If all related circuits are faulty at the same time, the probable cause is a poor ground connection or a blown fuse(s).

Preliminary Checks and Precautions

Before starting any electrical troubleshooting, perform the following:

1. Inspect the battery. Make sure it is fully charged and the battery leads are clean and securely attached to the battery terminals.

2. Electrical connectors are often the cause of electrical system problems. Inspect the connectors as follows:

   a. Disconnect each electrical connector in the suspect circuit and make sure there are no bent terminals in the electrical connector. A bent terminal will not connect to its mate, causing an open circuit.

   b. Make sure the terminals are pushed all the way into the connector. If not, carefully push them in with a narrow blade screwdriver.

   c. Check the wires where they attach to the terminals for damage.

   d. Make sure each terminal is clean and free of corrosion. Clean them, if necessary, and pack the connectors with dielectric grease.

   e. Push the connector halves together. Make sure the connectors are fully engaged and locked together.

   f. Never pull the wires when disconnecting a connector. Pull only on the connector housing.

3. Never use a self-powered test light on circuits that contain solid-state devices. The solid-state devices may be damaged.

Intermittent Problems

Problems that do not occur all the time can be difficult to isolate during testing, such as when a problem only occurs when the motorcycle is ridden over rough roads (vibration) or in wet conditions (water penetration). Note the following:

1. Vibration. This is a common problem with loose or damaged electrical connectors.

   a. Perform a continuity test as described in the appropriate service procedure or under Continuity Test in this section.

   b. Lightly pull or wiggle the connectors while repeating the test. Do the same when checking the wiring harness and individual components, especially where the wires enter a housing or connector.

   c. A change in meter readings indicates a poor connection. Find and repair the problem or replace the part. Check for wires with cracked or broken insulation.

NOTE
An analog ohmmeter is useful when making this type of test. Slight needle movements are visibly apparent, which indicate a loose connection.

2. Heat. This is a common problem with connectors or joints that have loose or poor connections. As these connections heat up, the connection or joint expands and separates, causing an open circuit. Other heat related problems occur when a component starts to fail as it heats up.

   a. Troubleshoot the problem to isolate the circuit.

CAUTION
A heat gun will quickly raise the temperature of the component being tested. Do not apply heat directly to the Motronic unit or use heat in excess of 60° C (140° F) on any electrical component.

   b. To check a connector, perform a continuity test as described in the appropriate service procedure or under Continuity Test in this section. Then repeat the test while heating the connector with a heat gun. If the meter reading was normal (continuity) when the connector was cold, and then fluctuated or read infinity when heat was applied, the connection is bad.

   c. To check a component, allow the engine to cool, and then start and run the engine. Note operational differences when the engine is cold and hot.

   d. If the engine will not start, isolate and remove the suspect component. Test it at room temperature and again after heating it with a heat gun. A change in meter readings indicates a temperature problem.

3. Water. When the problem occurs when riding in wet conditions or in areas with high humidity, start

and run the engine in a dry area. Then, with the engine running, spray water onto the suspected component/circuit. Water-related problems often stop after the component heats up and dries.

Test Light or Voltmeter

Use a test light to check for voltage in a circuit. Attach one lead to ground and the other lead to various points along the circuit. It does not make a difference which test lead is attached to ground. The bulb lights when voltage is present.

Use a voltmeter in the same manner as the test light to find out if voltage is present in any given circuit. The voltmeter, unlike the test light, also indicates how much voltage is present at each test point.

Voltage test

Unless otherwise specified, make all voltage tests with the electrical connectors still connected. Insert the test leads into the backside of the connector and make sure the test lead touches the electrical terminal within the connector housing. If the test lead only touches the wire insulation, it will cause a false reading.

Always check both sides of the connector because one side may be loose or corroded, thus preventing electrical flow through the connector. This type of test can be performed with a test light or a voltmeter.
1. Attach the voltmeter negative test lead to a confirmed ground location. If possible, use the battery ground connection. Make sure the ground is not insulated.
2. Attach the voltmeter positive test lead to the point to be tested (**Figure 8**).
3. Turn the ignition switch on. If using a test light, the test light will come on if voltage is present. If using a voltmeter, note the voltage reading. The reading should be within 1 volt of battery voltage. If the voltage is less there is a problem in the circuit.

Voltage drop test

The wires, cables, connectors and switches in the electrical circuit are designed to carry current with low resistance. This ensures current can flow through the circuit with a minimum loss of voltage. Voltage drop indicates where there is resistance in a circuit. A higher-than-normal amount of resistance in a circuit decreases the flow of current and causes the voltage to drop between the source and destination in the circuit.

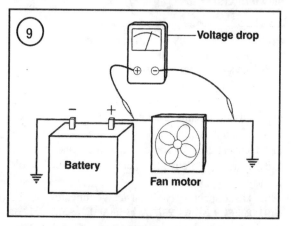

Because resistance causes voltage to drop, a voltmeter is used to measure voltage drop when current is running through the circuit. If the circuit has no resistance, there is no voltage drop so the voltmeter indicates 0 volts. The greater the resistance in a circuit, the greater the voltage drop reading.

To perform a voltage drop:
1. Connect the positive meter test lead to the electrical source (where electricity is coming from).
2. Connect the voltmeter negative test lead to the electrical load (where the electricity is going). Refer to **Figure 9**.
3. If necessary, activate the component(s) in the circuit.
4. Read the voltage drop (difference in voltage between the source and destination) on the voltmeter. Note the following:
   a. The voltmeter should indicate 0 volts. If there is a drop of 1 volt or more, there is a problem within the circuit. A voltage drop reading of 12 volts indicates an open in the circuit.
   b. A voltage drop of 1 or more volts indicates that a circuit has excessive resistance.
   c. For example, consider a starting problem where the battery is fully charged but the starter turns over slowly. Voltage drop would be the difference in the voltage at the battery (source)

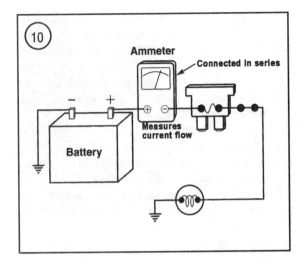

and the voltage at the starter (destination) as the engine is being started (current is flowing through the battery cables). A corroded battery cable would cause a high voltage drop (high resistance) and slow engine cranking.

d. Common sources of voltage drop are loose or contaminated connectors and poor ground connections.

Testing For a Short with a Voltmeter

A test light may also be used.
1. Remove the blown fuse from the fuse panel.
2. Connect the voltmeter across the fuse terminals in the fuse panel. Turn the ignition switch on and check for battery voltage.
3. With the voltmeter attached to the fuse terminals, wiggle the wiring harness relating to the suspect circuit at approximately 15.2 cm (6 in.) intervals. Start next to the fuse panel and work systematically away from the panel. Note the voltmeter reading while progressing along the harness.
4. If the voltmeter reading changes (test light blinks), there is a short-to-ground at that point in the harness.

Ammeter

Use an ammeter to measure the flow of current (amps) in a circuit (**Figure 10**). When connected in series in a circuit, the ammeter determines if current is flowing through the circuit and if that current flow is excessive because of a short in the circuit. Current flow is often referred to as current draw. Comparing actual current draw in the circuit or component to current draw specification (if specified by the manufacturer) provides useful diagnostic information.

Self-powered Test Light

A self-powered test light can be constructed from a 12-volt light bulb, a pair of test leads and a 12-volt battery. When the test leads are touched together the light bulb should go on.

Use a self-powered test light as follows:
1. Touch the test leads together to make sure the light bulb goes on. If not, correct the problem.
2. Disconnect the motorcycle's battery or remove the fuse(s) that protects the circuit to be tested. Do not connect a self-powered test light to a circuit that has power applied to it.
3. Select two points within the circuit where there should be continuity.
4. Attach one lead of the test light to each point.
5. If there is continuity, the test light bulb will come on.
6. If there is no continuity, the test light bulb will not come on, indicating an open circuit.

Ohmmeter

CAUTION
To prevent damage to the ohmmeter, never connect it to a circuit that has power applied to it. Always disconnect the battery negative lead before using an ohmmeter.

Use an ohmmeter to measure the resistance (in ohms) to current flow in a circuit or component.

Ohmmeters may be analog type (needle scale) or digital type (LCD or LED readout). Both types of ohmmeters have a switch that allows the user to select different ranges of resistance for accurate readings. The analog ohmmeter also has a set-adjust control which is used to zero or calibrate the meter (digital ohmmeters do not require calibration). Refer to the ohmmeter's instructions to determine the correct scale setting.

Use an ohmmeter by connecting its test leads to the circuit or component to be tested. If an analog meter is used, it must be calibrated by touching the test leads together and turning the set-adjust knob until the meter needle reads zero. When the leads are uncrossed, the needle should move to the other end of the scale, indicating infinite resistance.

During a continuity test, a reading of infinite resistance indicates there is an open in the circuit or component. A reading of zero indicates continuity, that is, there is no measurable resistance in the circuit or component. A measured reading indicates the actual resistance to current flow that is present in that circuit. Even though resistance is present, the circuit has continuity.

Continuity test

Perform a continuity test to determine the integrity of a circuit, wire or component. A circuit has continuity if it forms a complete circuit; that is if there are no opens in either the electrical wires or components within the circuit. A circuit with an open, on the other hand, has no continuity.

This type of test can be performed with a self-powered test light or an ohmmeter. An ohmmeter gives the best results.

1. Disconnect the negative battery cable or disconnect the test circuit/component from its power source.
2. Attach one test lead (test light or ohmmeter) to one end of the part of the circuit to be tested.
3. Attach the other test lead to the other end of the part or the circuit to be tested.
4. The self-powered test light comes on if there is continuity. An ohmmeter reads 0 or low resistance if there is continuity. A reading of infinite resistance indicates no continuity; the circuit is open.
5. If testing a component, note the resistance and compare this to the specification if available.

Testing for short with an ohmmeter

An analog ohmmeter or one with an audible continuity indicator works best for short testing. A self-powered test light may also be used.

1. Disconnect the negative battery cable.
2. If necessary, remove the blown fuse from the fuse panel.
3. Connect one test lead of the ohmmeter to the load side (battery side) of the fuse terminal in the fuse panel.
4. Connect the other test lead to a confirmed ground location. Make sure the ground is not insulated. If possible, use the battery ground connection.
5. Wiggle the wiring harness relating to the suspect circuit at approximately 15.2 cm (6 in.) intervals. Watch the ohmmeter while progressing along the harness.
6. If the ohmmeter needle moves or the ohmmeter beeps, there is a short-to-ground at that point in the harness.

Jumper Wire

Use a jumper wire to bypass a potential problem and isolate it to a particular point in a circuit. If a faulty circuit works properly with a jumper wire installed, an open exists between the two jumped points in the circuit.

To troubleshoot with a jumper wire, first use the wire to determine if the problem is on the ground side or the load side of a device. Test the ground by connecting the wire between the lamp and a good ground. If the lamp comes on, the problem is the connection between the lamp and ground. If the lamp does not come on with the wire installed, the lamp's connection to ground is good, so the problem is between the lamp and the power source.

To isolate the problem, connect the wire between the battery and the lamp. If it comes on, the problem is between these two points. Next, connect the wire between the battery and the fuse side of the switch. If the lamp comes on, the switch is good. By successively moving the wire from one point to another, the problem can be isolated to a particular place in the circuit.

Note the following when using a jumper wire:

1. Make sure the wire gauge (thickness) is the same as that used in the circuit being tested. Smaller gauge wire rapidly overheats and could melt.
2. Make sure the jumper wire has insulated alligator clips. This prevents accidental grounding (sparks) or possible shock. Install an inline fuse/fuse holder in the jumper wire.
3. A jumper wire is a temporary test measure. Do not leave a jumper wire installed as a permanent solution. This creates a fire hazard.
4. Never use a jumper wire across any load (a component that is connected and turned on). This would cause a direct short and blow the fuse(s).

STARTING SYSTEM

Starter Turns Slowly

1. Weak battery.
2. Poorly connected/corroded battery terminals and cables.
3. Loose starter motor cable.
4. Worn or damaged starter.

Starter Turns, But Does Not Crank Engine

1. Worn or damaged starter clutch.
2. Damaged teeth on starter motor shaft or starter gears.

Starter Does Not Operate

When the starter does not operate, refer to Starting System in Chapter Nine for the system diagram and component testing procedures. Begin testing at the starter relay.

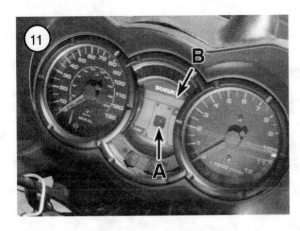

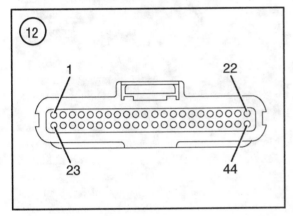

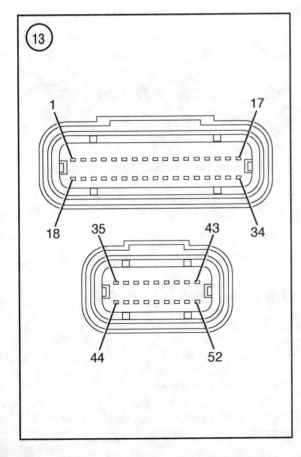

ELECTRONIC DIAGNOSTIC SYSTEM

The electronic control module (ECM) includes a self-diagnostic function that monitors electrical components of the ignition and fuel injection systems. Whenever an error is detected, the ECM stores the malfunction and sets a malfunction code. It also turns on the indicator LED (A, **Figure 11**) in the meter assembly and FI appears in the odometer panel (B) of the meter display.

Electrical Component Replacement

Most motorcycle dealerships and parts suppliers will not accept the return of any electrical part. Consider any test results carefully before replacing a component that tests only slightly out of specification, especially resistance.

ECM Testing

Fuel injection troubleshooting frequently includes testing the ECM wiring. Some wiring colors are used more than once in the ECM connector(s). To ensure the correct wire is tested, the test procedures include the wire color and pin location to describe a test point. The number in parentheses after a wiring color refers to the pin location number. Refer to **Figure 12** or **Figure 13** to determine where that terminal is located in the relevant ECM connector.

If testing indicates that the ECM is faulty, take the motorcycle to a dealership for further testing before purchasing a replacement ECM. If possible, install a known good ECM and confirm that the ECM is the problem.

Malfunction Code Retrieval

When the system is in dealer mode, the meter assembly LCD (odometer panel) displays any stored malfunction codes. A mode select switch (Suzuki part No. 09930-82720) is needed to enter the dealer mode (**Figure 14**).

> *CAUTION*
> *Do not attempt this procedure without the mode select switch. Shorting the terminals in the dealer mode connector could damage the ECM.*

1A. On non-ABS models, connect the mode select switch to the dealer mode connector (**Figure 15**) adjacent to the battery box.

1B. On ABS models, connect the mode select switch to the dealer mode connector (**Figure 16**) below the right side of the fuel tank.

2. Run the engine for four seconds. If the engine will not start, crank the engine for four seconds.

3. After four seconds, turn the mode select switch on. The system enters the dealer mode and displays a stored malfunction code in the LCD portion of the meter assembly. If more than one code is stored, codes are displayed in numeric order starting with the lowest numbered code.

4. Record any malfunction codes before disconnecting the ECM connector(s) from the ECM, the ECM ground wire from the harness or engine, or the battery cables or before pulling the main fuse. Any of these actions erases the malfunction code(s) from memory. The malfunction code table (**Figure 17**) lists the malfunction codes and the likely causes.

Fail-Safe Operation

For some malfunction codes, the ECM sets the affected component to a preset value so the motorcycle can still operate. This fail-safe operation allows the motorcycle to still run. Refer to **Figure 18** for the fail-safe actions taken when a particular malfunction code is set. This chart also describes whether the motorcycle can continue to operate once a code has been set or if it can be restarted after the engine has been turned off.

Even if the motorcycle continues to run with a malfunction code stored, troubleshoot the system and eliminate the problem immediately. If the problem cannot be solved, take the motorcycle to a dealership as soon as possible.

Malfunction Code Troubleshooting

Perform the following to troubleshoot a problem with the fuel injection system.

1. Enter the dealer mode as described in *Malfunction Code Retrieval* in this section.

2. Record any displayed malfunction code(s).

3. Refer to the troubleshooting chart (**Figure 19**), and identify the relevant diagnostic flow chart for the malfunction code.

> *NOTE*
> *The diagnostic flow charts refer to various test procedures for the affected components. The removal, adjustment and test procedures for most of the mentioned components are in this chapter. Any exceptions are noted in the flow charts.*

4. Turn to the indicated diagnostic flow chart (**Figures 20-35**). Perform the test procedures in order until the problem is resolved.

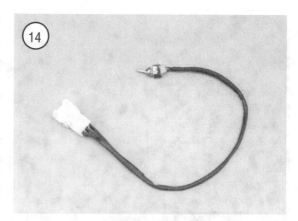

5. Once a fault has been corrected, reset the self-diagnostic system as described in this section.

Resetting the Self-diagnostic System

Perform the following to reset the system once a fuel injection system malfunction has been corrected.

1. While in the dealer mode, turn the ignition switch off and then turn it back on.

2. The LCD should display the no fault code: c00.

3. Turn the dealer mode switch to off and disconnect the switch from the dealer mode connector.

(17)

MALFUNCTION CODE TABLE*

Malfunction Code	Related Item	Detected Failure	Probable Cause
c00	No error	-	-
c12	Crankshaft position (CKP) sensor	The ECM has not received a signal from the crankshaft position sensor 3 seconds after it received the start signal.	Faulty crankshaft position sensor, its wiring or connector.
c13 (front cyl.) c17 (rear cyl.)	Intake air pressure (IAP) sensor	The sensor's voltage is outside the range 0.1-4.8 volts.	Faulty intake air pressure sensor, its wiring or connector.
c14	Throttle position (TP) sensor	The sensor's voltage is outside the range 0.1-4.8 volts.	Faulty throttle position sensor, its wiring or connector.
c15	Engine coolant temperature (ECT) sensor	The sensor's voltage is outside the range: 0.1-4.6 volts.	Faulty engine coolant temperature sensor, its wiring or connector.
c21	Intake air temperature (IAT) sensor	The sensor's voltage is outside the range 0.1-4.6 volts.	Faulty intake air temperature sensor, its wiring or connector.
c23	Tip-over (TO) sensor	The sensor's voltage is not within the range of 0.2 – 4.6 volts 2 seconds after the ignition switch has been turned on.	Faulty tip over sensor, its wiring or connector.
c24 (rear cyl.) c25 (front cyl.)	Ignition system malfunction	The ECM does not receive a proper signal from an ignition coil.	Faulty ignition coil, its wiring or connector. Faulty power supply from the battery.
c28	Secondary throttle valve actuator (STVA)	Signal voltage from the ECM is not reaching the actuator, the ECM is not receiving a signal from the actuator, or load voltage is not reaching the actuator motor.	Faulty secondary throttle valve actuator, its wiring or connector.
c29	Secondary throttle position (STP) sensor	The sensor's voltage is outside the range 0.1-4.8 volts.	Faulty secondary throttle position sensor, its wiring or connector.
c31	Gear position (GP) signal	The gear position sensor's voltage is less than 0.2 volts for 3 or more seconds.	Faulty gear position sensor, its wiring, connector or faulty shift cam.
c32 (rear cyl.) c33 (front cyl.)	Fuel injector	The ECM does not receive a proper signal from the fuel injector.	Faulty fuel injector, its wiring or connector. Faulty power supply to the injector.
c41	Fuel pump, fuel pump relay	The ECM does not receive a signal from the fuel pump relay.	Faulty fuel pump relay, wiring or connector. Faulty power source to the fuel pump relay or injectors.

(continued)

(17) **MALFUNCTION CODE TABLE* (continued)**

Malfunction Code	Related Item	Detected Failure	Probable Cause
c42	Ignition switch signal	The ECM does not receive a signal from ignition switch.	Faulty ignition switch, its wiring or connector.
c44	HO₂	No oxygen sensor voltage to ECM. No heater voltage to sensor.	Faulty wiring or connector. No battery voltage to sensor.
c49	PAIR control solenoid valve	The ECM does not receive voltage from PAIR control solenoid valve.	Faulty PAIR solenoid, wiring or connector.

*On 2004-2006 models, code c17 not used. Code c13 applies to the single IAP that serves both cylinders.

 (18) **FAIL SAFE ACTION**

Failed Item	Fail-safe Action	Operation Status
Crankshaft position sensor.	The motorcycle stops.	Engine stops operating; cannot restart.
Intake air pressure sensor.	Intake air pressure is set to 760 mmHg (29.92 in. Hg).	Engine continues operating; can restart.
Throttle position sensor.	Throttle valve is set to its fully open position. Ignition timing is set to a preset value	Engine continues operating; cannot restart.
Engine coolant temperature sensor.	Engine coolant temperature is set to 80° C (176° F).	Engine continues operating; can restart.
Intake air temperature sensor.	Intake air temperature set to 40° C (104° F).	Engine continues operating; can restart.
Ignition signal.	No spark at affected cylinder.	Opposite cylinder can operate.
Fuel injector.	Fuel cut-off to affected injector.	Opposite cylinder can operate.
Secondary throttle valve actuator.	Secondary throttle valve is set to the fully closed position.	Engine continues operating; can restart.
Secondary throttle position sensor.	Secondary throttle valve is set to a fixed position.	Engine continues operating; can restart.
Gear position signal.	Gear position signal set to fourth gear.	Engine continues operating; can restart.
Heated oxygen sensor.	Air/fuel ratio fixed to normal condition.	Engine continues operating; can restart.
PAIR control solenoid valve.	ECM ceases control of PAIR control solenoid valve.	Engine continues operating; can restart.

TROUBLESHOOTING CHART

Malfunction Code	Diagnostic Flow Chart
c00	No fault detected
c12	Figure 20
c13	Figure 21
c14	Figure 22
c15	Figure 23
c17	Figure 24
c21	Figure 25
c23	Figure 26
c24 or c25	Figure 27
c28	Figure 28
c29	Figure 29
c31	Figure 30
c32 or c33	Figure 31
c41	Figure 32
c42	Figure 33
c44	Figure 34
c49	Figure 35

2

BRAKES

The disc brakes are critical to riding performance and safety. Inspect the brakes frequently and replace worn or damaged parts immediately. The brake system used on this motorcycle uses DOT 4 brake fluid in both brake systems. Always use new fluid from a sealed container. The troubleshooting checks in **Figure 36** assist in isolating the majority of disc brake problems. On models equipped with an anti-lock brake system (ABS), also refer to the ABS Brakes section to troubleshoot problems related to ABS brake components.

When checking brake pad wear, check that the pads in each caliper squarely contact the disc. Uneven pad wear on one side of the disc can indicate a warped or bent disc, damaged caliper or pad pins.

ABS BRAKES

When the engine is started, the ECU performs self-diagnosis and checks the operating conditions of the ABS components. Self-diagnosis starts when the ig-nition switch is turned on and ends when the motor-cycle speed reaches 5 km/h (3 mph). If the system is operational, the ABS indicator (**Figure 37**) turns off. This check must be observed each time the motor-cycle is ridden.

If a problem is detected, the ABS stores a diagnos-tic trouble code (DTC) and the ABS indicator light will flash or stay on. A DTC is also set in the ECU memory. When the ABS indicator is flashing or stays on, the ABS function is disabled. However, even when the ABS is disabled, the primary brake system (both front and rear brakes) still operates normally. DTC(s) can be retrieved by performing the DTC re-trieval procedure described in this section.

Self-Diagnosis Check

Perform the following to initiate self-diagnosis.
1. Turn the ignition switch on.
2. Check that the ABS indicator (**Figure 37**) turns on

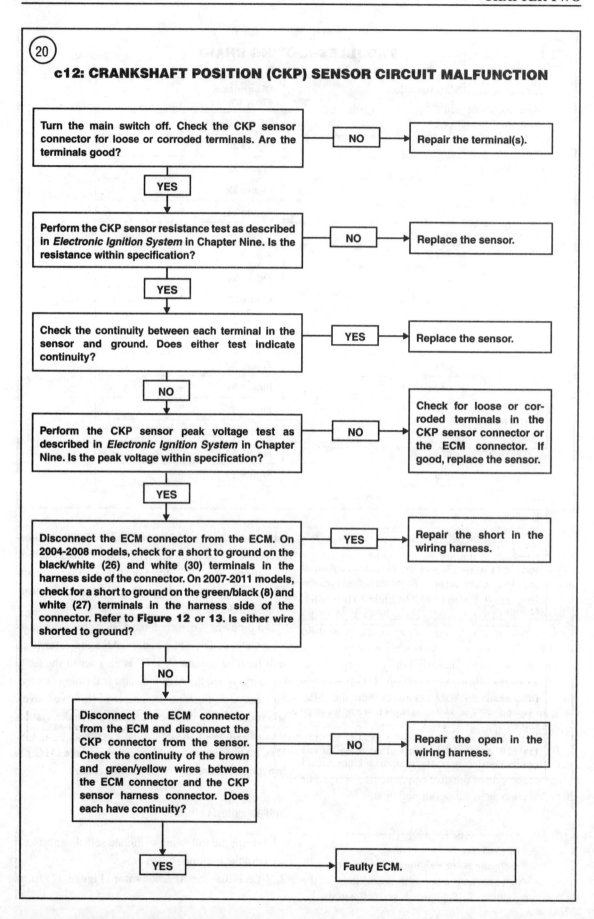

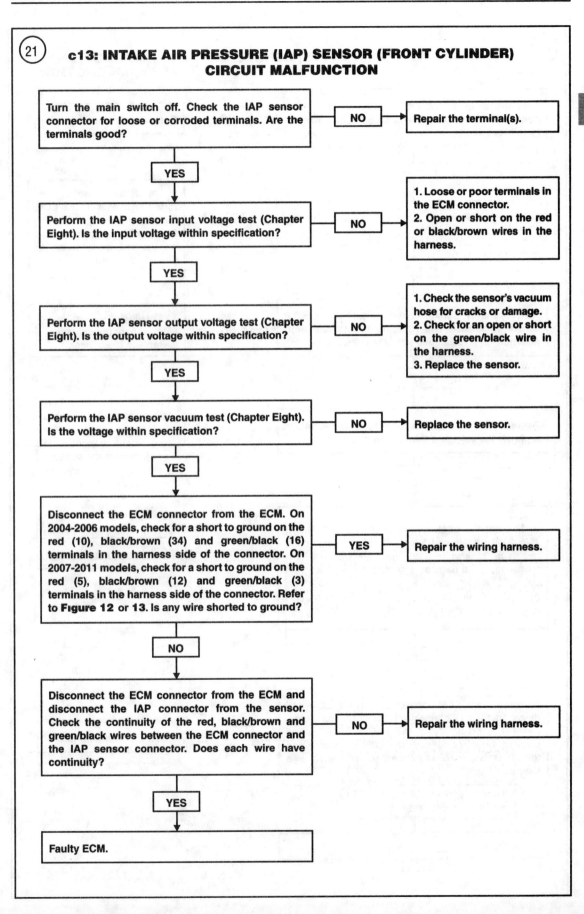

(21) **c13: INTAKE AIR PRESSURE (IAP) SENSOR (FRONT CYLINDER) CIRCUIT MALFUNCTION**

Turn the main switch off. Check the IAP sensor connector for loose or corroded terminals. Are the terminals good? — **NO** → Repair the terminal(s).

YES

Perform the IAP sensor input voltage test (Chapter Eight). Is the input voltage within specification? — **NO** →
1. Loose or poor terminals in the ECM connector.
2. Open or short on the red or black/brown wires in the harness.

YES

Perform the IAP sensor output voltage test (Chapter Eight). Is the output voltage within specification? — **NO** →
1. Check the sensor's vacuum hose for cracks or damage.
2. Check for an open or short on the green/black wire in the harness.
3. Replace the sensor.

YES

Perform the IAP sensor vacuum test (Chapter Eight). Is the voltage within specification? — **NO** → Replace the sensor.

YES

Disconnect the ECM connector from the ECM. On 2004-2006 models, check for a short to ground on the red (10), black/brown (34) and green/black (16) terminals in the harness side of the connector. On 2007-2011 models, check for a short to ground on the red (5), black/brown (12) and green/black (3) terminals in the harness side of the connector. Refer to **Figure 12** or **13**. Is any wire shorted to ground? — **YES** → Repair the wiring harness.

NO

Disconnect the ECM connector from the ECM and disconnect the IAP connector from the sensor. Check the continuity of the red, black/brown and green/black wires between the ECM connector and the IAP sensor connector. Does each wire have continuity? — **NO** → Repair the wiring harness.

YES

Faulty ECM.

2

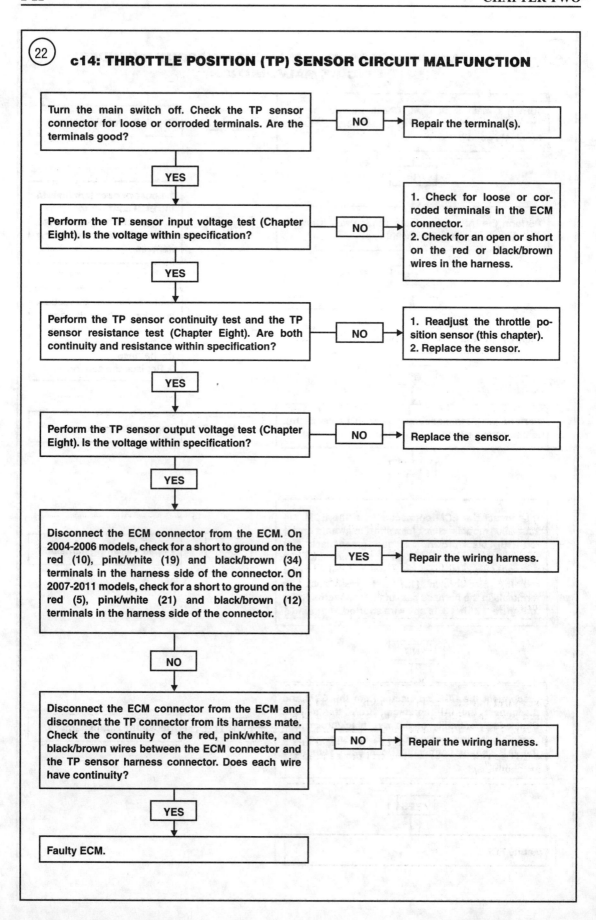

㉒ c14: THROTTLE POSITION (TP) SENSOR CIRCUIT MALFUNCTION

Turn the main switch off. Check the TP sensor connector for loose or corroded terminals. Are the terminals good?

→ **NO** → Repair the terminal(s).

↓ **YES**

Perform the TP sensor input voltage test (Chapter Eight). Is the voltage within specification?

→ **NO** →
1. Check for loose or corroded terminals in the ECM connector.
2. Check for an open or short on the red or black/brown wires in the harness.

↓ **YES**

Perform the TP sensor continuity test and the TP sensor resistance test (Chapter Eight). Are both continuity and resistance within specification?

→ **NO** →
1. Readjust the throttle position sensor (this chapter).
2. Replace the sensor.

↓ **YES**

Perform the TP sensor output voltage test (Chapter Eight). Is the voltage within specification?

→ **NO** → Replace the sensor.

↓ **YES**

Disconnect the ECM connector from the ECM. On 2004-2006 models, check for a short to ground on the red (10), pink/white (19) and black/brown (34) terminals in the harness side of the connector. On 2007-2011 models, check for a short to ground on the red (5), pink/white (21) and black/brown (12) terminals in the harness side of the connector.

→ **YES** → Repair the wiring harness.

↓ **NO**

Disconnect the ECM connector from the ECM and disconnect the TP connector from its harness mate. Check the continuity of the red, pink/white, and black/brown wires between the ECM connector and the TP sensor harness connector. Does each wire have continuity?

→ **NO** → Repair the wiring harness.

↓ **YES**

Faulty ECM.

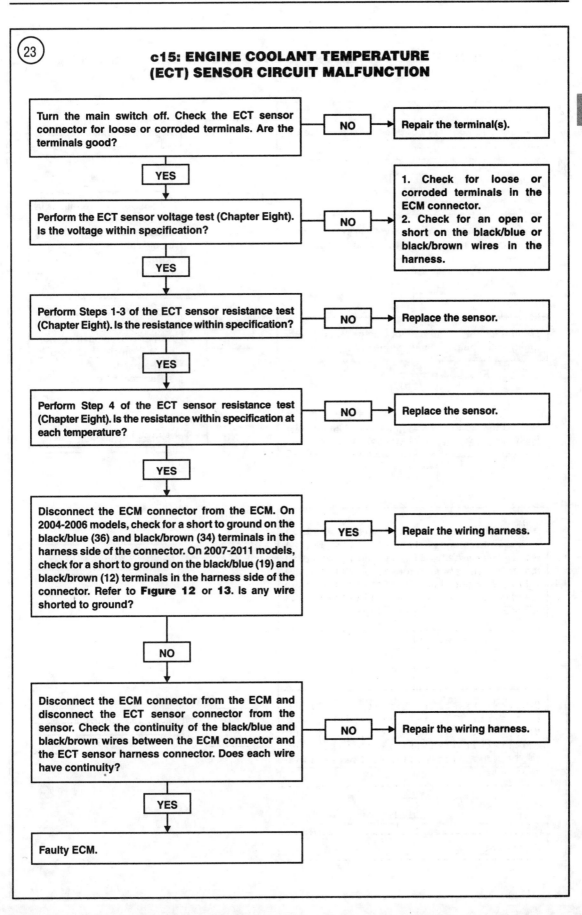

(23)

c15: ENGINE COOLANT TEMPERATURE (ECT) SENSOR CIRCUIT MALFUNCTION

Turn the main switch off. Check the ECT sensor connector for loose or corroded terminals. Are the terminals good? — **NO** → Repair the terminal(s).

YES

Perform the ECT sensor voltage test (Chapter Eight). Is the voltage within specification? — **NO** → 1. Check for loose or corroded terminals in the ECM connector. 2. Check for an open or short on the black/blue or black/brown wires in the harness.

YES

Perform Steps 1-3 of the ECT sensor resistance test (Chapter Eight). Is the resistance within specification? — **NO** → Replace the sensor.

YES

Perform Step 4 of the ECT sensor resistance test (Chapter Eight). Is the resistance within specification at each temperature? — **NO** → Replace the sensor.

YES

Disconnect the ECM connector from the ECM. On 2004-2006 models, check for a short to ground on the black/blue (36) and black/brown (34) terminals in the harness side of the connector. On 2007-2011 models, check for a short to ground on the black/blue (19) and black/brown (12) terminals in the harness side of the connector. Refer to **Figure 12** or **13**. Is any wire shorted to ground? — **YES** → Repair the wiring harness.

NO

Disconnect the ECM connector from the ECM and disconnect the ECT sensor connector from the sensor. Check the continuity of the black/blue and black/brown wires between the ECM connector and the ECT sensor harness connector. Does each wire have continuity? — **NO** → Repair the wiring harness.

YES

Faulty ECM.

2

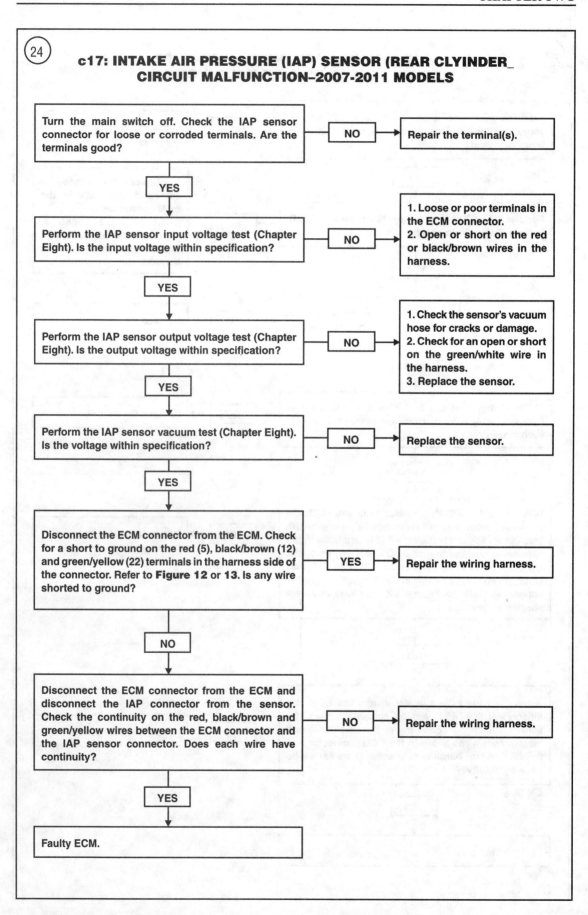

(24)

c17: INTAKE AIR PRESSURE (IAP) SENSOR (REAR CLYINDER_ CIRCUIT MALFUNCTION–2007-2011 MODELS

Turn the main switch off. Check the IAP sensor connector for loose or corroded terminals. Are the terminals good? → **NO** → Repair the terminal(s).

YES ↓

Perform the IAP sensor input voltage test (Chapter Eight). Is the input voltage within specification? → **NO** →
1. Loose or poor terminals in the ECM connector.
2. Open or short on the red or black/brown wires in the harness.

YES ↓

Perform the IAP sensor output voltage test (Chapter Eight). Is the output voltage within specification? → **NO** →
1. Check the sensor's vacuum hose for cracks or damage.
2. Check for an open or short on the green/white wire in the harness.
3. Replace the sensor.

YES ↓

Perform the IAP sensor vacuum test (Chapter Eight). Is the voltage within specification? → **NO** → Replace the sensor.

YES ↓

Disconnect the ECM connector from the ECM. Check for a short to ground on the red (5), black/brown (12) and green/yellow (22) terminals in the harness side of the connector. Refer to **Figure 12** or **13**. Is any wire shorted to ground? → **YES** → Repair the wiring harness.

NO ↓

Disconnect the ECM connector from the ECM and disconnect the IAP connector from the sensor. Check the continuity on the red, black/brown and green/yellow wires between the ECM connector and the IAP sensor connector. Does each wire have continuity? → **NO** → Repair the wiring harness.

YES ↓

Faulty ECM.

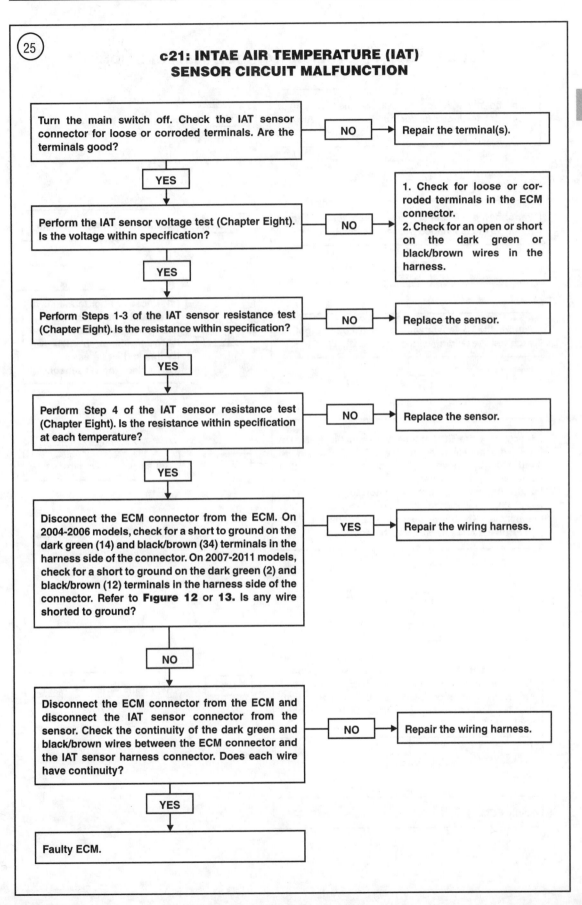

25

c21: INTAE AIR TEMPERATURE (IAT) SENSOR CIRCUIT MALFUNCTION

Turn the main switch off. Check the IAT sensor connector for loose or corroded terminals. Are the terminals good? → NO → Repair the terminal(s).

YES ↓

Perform the IAT sensor voltage test (Chapter Eight). Is the voltage within specification? → NO →
1. Check for loose or corroded terminals in the ECM connector.
2. Check for an open or short on the dark green or black/brown wires in the harness.

YES ↓

Perform Steps 1-3 of the IAT sensor resistance test (Chapter Eight). Is the resistance within specification? → NO → Replace the sensor.

YES ↓

Perform Step 4 of the IAT sensor resistance test (Chapter Eight). Is the resistance within specification at each temperature? → NO → Replace the sensor.

YES ↓

Disconnect the ECM connector from the ECM. On 2004-2006 models, check for a short to ground on the dark green (14) and black/brown (34) terminals in the harness side of the connector. On 2007-2011 models, check for a short to ground on the dark green (2) and black/brown (12) terminals in the harness side of the connector. Refer to **Figure 12** or **13.** Is any wire shorted to ground? → YES → Repair the wiring harness.

NO ↓

Disconnect the ECM connector from the ECM and disconnect the IAT sensor connector from the sensor. Check the continuity of the dark green and black/brown wires between the ECM connector and the IAT sensor harness connector. Does each wire have continuity? → NO → Repair the wiring harness.

YES ↓

Faulty ECM.

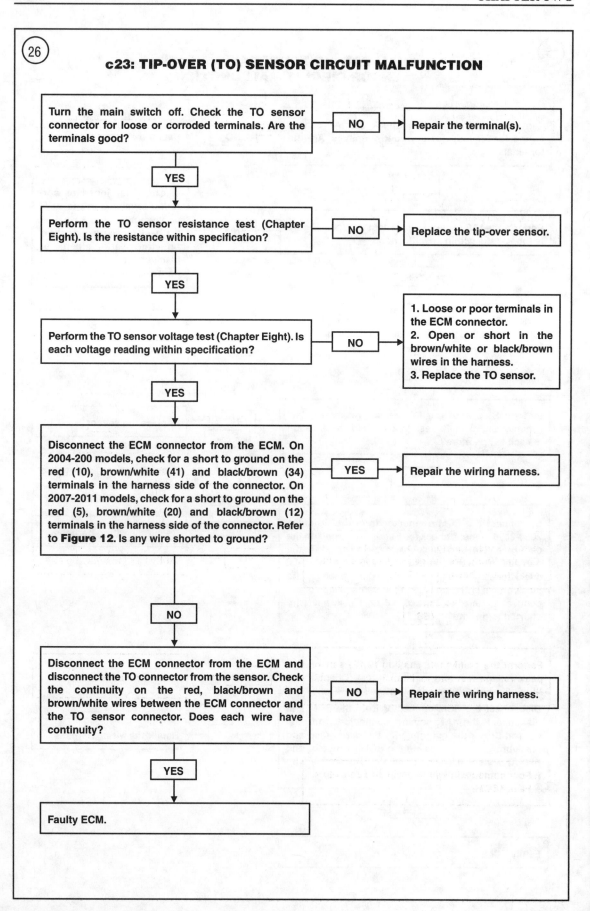

c23: TIP-OVER (TO) SENSOR CIRCUIT MALFUNCTION

Turn the main switch off. Check the TO sensor connector for loose or corroded terminals. Are the terminals good?

→ **NO** → Repair the terminal(s).

↓ **YES**

Perform the TO sensor resistance test (Chapter Eight). Is the resistance within specification?

→ **NO** → Replace the tip-over sensor.

↓ **YES**

Perform the TO sensor voltage test (Chapter Eight). Is each voltage reading within specification?

→ **NO** →
1. Loose or poor terminals in the ECM connector.
2. Open or short in the brown/white or black/brown wires in the harness.
3. Replace the TO sensor.

↓ **YES**

Disconnect the ECM connector from the ECM. On 2004-200 models, check for a short to ground on the red (10), brown/white (41) and black/brown (34) terminals in the harness side of the connector. On 2007-2011 models, check for a short to ground on the red (5), brown/white (20) and black/brown (12) terminals in the harness side of the connector. Refer to **Figure 12**. Is any wire shorted to ground?

→ **YES** → Repair the wiring harness.

↓ **NO**

Disconnect the ECM connector from the ECM and disconnect the TO connector from the sensor. Check the continuity on the red, black/brown and brown/white wires between the ECM connector and the TO sensor connector. Does each wire have continuity?

→ **NO** → Repair the wiring harness.

↓ **YES**

Faulty ECM.

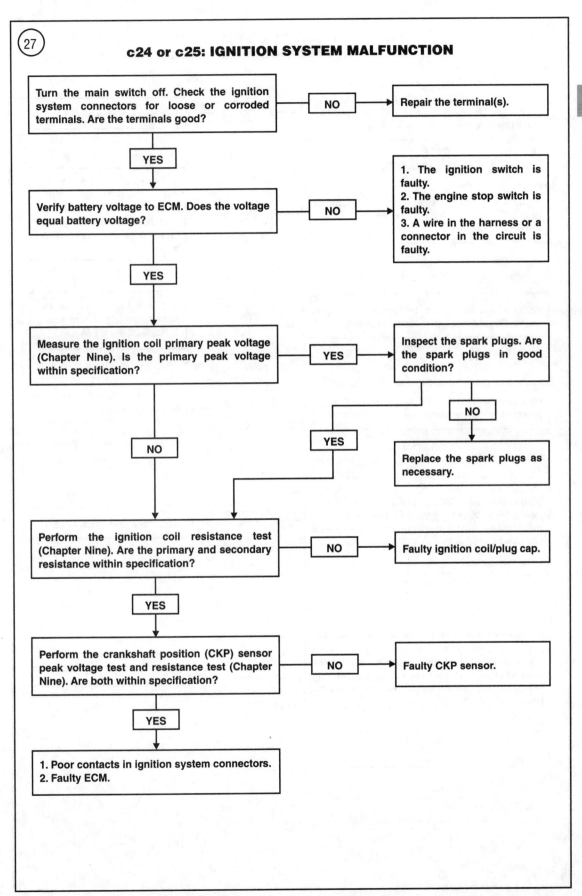

(27)

c24 or c25: IGNITION SYSTEM MALFUNCTION

Turn the main switch off. Check the ignition system connectors for loose or corroded terminals. Are the terminals good?

NO → Repair the terminal(s).

YES

Verify battery voltage to ECM. Does the voltage equal battery voltage?

NO →
1. The ignition switch is faulty.
2. The engine stop switch is faulty.
3. A wire in the harness or a connector in the circuit is faulty.

YES

Measure the ignition coil primary peak voltage (Chapter Nine). Is the primary peak voltage within specification?

YES → Inspect the spark plugs. Are the spark plugs in good condition?

NO → Replace the spark plugs as necessary.

YES

NO

Perform the ignition coil resistance test (Chapter Nine). Are the primary and secondary resistance within specification?

NO → Faulty ignition coil/plug cap.

YES

Perform the crankshaft position (CKP) sensor peak voltage test and resistance test (Chapter Nine). Are both within specification?

NO → Faulty CKP sensor.

YES

1. Poor contacts in ignition system connectors.
2. Faulty ECM.

2

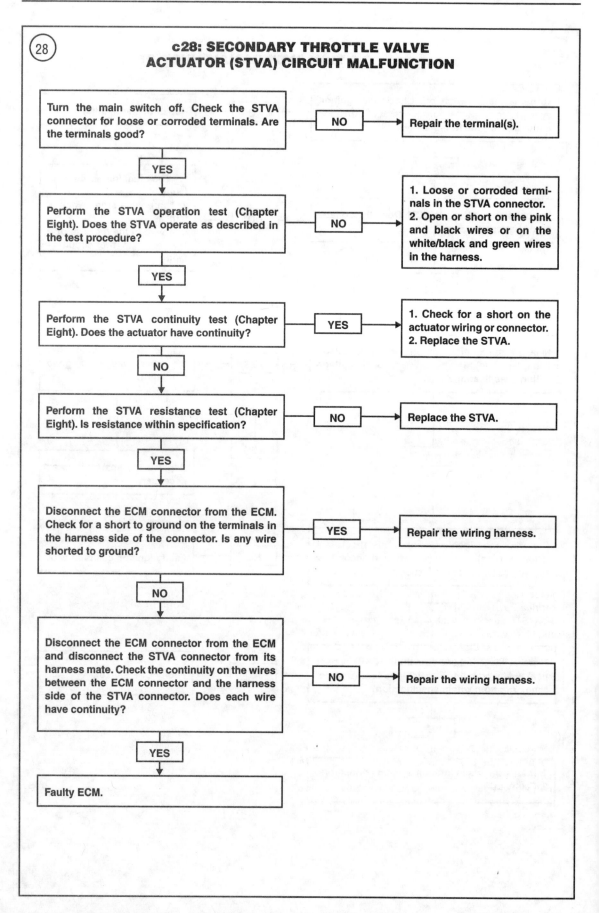

(28) **c28: SECONDARY THROTTLE VALVE ACTUATOR (STVA) CIRCUIT MALFUNCTION**

Turn the main switch off. Check the STVA connector for loose or corroded terminals. Are the terminals good? — **NO** → Repair the terminal(s).

YES ↓

Perform the STVA operation test (Chapter Eight). Does the STVA operate as described in the test procedure? — **NO** → 1. Loose or corroded terminals in the STVA connector. 2. Open or short on the pink and black wires or on the white/black and green wires in the harness.

YES ↓

Perform the STVA continuity test (Chapter Eight). Does the actuator have continuity? — **YES** → 1. Check for a short on the actuator wiring or connector. 2. Replace the STVA.

NO ↓

Perform the STVA resistance test (Chapter Eight). Is resistance within specification? — **NO** → Replace the STVA.

YES ↓

Disconnect the ECM connector from the ECM. Check for a short to ground on the terminals in the harness side of the connector. Is any wire shorted to ground? — **YES** → Repair the wiring harness.

NO ↓

Disconnect the ECM connector from the ECM and disconnect the STVA connector from its harness mate. Check the continuity on the wires between the ECM connector and the harness side of the STVA connector. Does each wire have continuity? — **NO** → Repair the wiring harness.

YES ↓

Faulty ECM.

(29)

c29: SECONDARY THROTTLE POSITION (STP) SENSOR CIRCUIT MALFUNCTION

Turn the main switch off. Check the STP sensor connector for loose or corroded terminals. Are the terminals good? → **NO** → Repair the terminal(s).

↓ **YES**

Perform the STP sensor input voltage test (Chapter Eight). Is the input voltage within specification? → **NO** → 1. Loose or corroded terminals in the ECM connector.
2. Open or short on the red and black/brown wires in the harness.

↓ **YES**

Perform the STP sensor continuity test (Chapter Eight). Does the sensor have continuity? → **YES** → 1. Repair the sensor wiring.
2. Replace the STP sensor.

↓ **NO**

Perform the STP sensor resistance test (Chapter Eight). Is resistance within specification? → **NO** → 1. Adjust the STP sensor.
2. Replace the secondary throttle position sensor.

↓ **YES**

Perform the STP sensor output voltage test (Chapter Eight). Is the voltage within specification? → **NO** → Replace the STP sensor

↓ **YES**

Refer to the wiring diagram for the model being serviced. Identify the wires in the harness end of the 3-pin STP connector that connect to the blue, yellow and black wires from the sensor. These are the circuit harness wires. Disconnect the ECM connector and check for a short to ground on these circuit harness wires. Is any wire shorted to ground? → **YES** → Repair the wiring harness.

↓ **NO**

Disconnect the ECM connector from the ECM and disconnect the STP sensor connector from the its harness mate. Check the continuity on each circuit harness wire between the ECM connector and the harness side of the STP sensor connector. Does each wire have continuity? → **NO** → Repair the wiring harness.

→ **YES** → Faulty ECM.

2

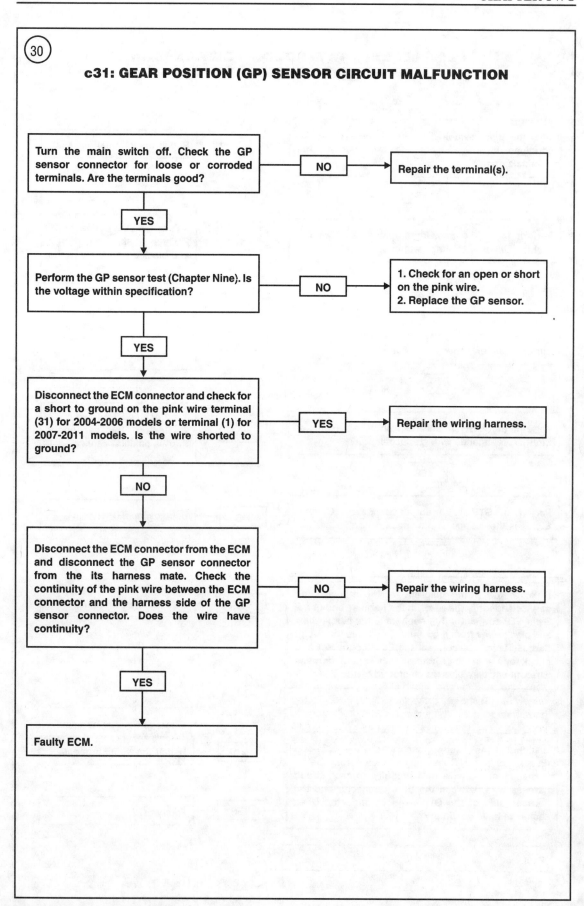

(30)

c31: GEAR POSITION (GP) SENSOR CIRCUIT MALFUNCTION

Turn the main switch off. Check the GP sensor connector for loose or corroded terminals. Are the terminals good? → **NO** → Repair the terminal(s).

YES ↓

Perform the GP sensor test (Chapter Nine). Is the voltage within specification? → **NO** → 1. Check for an open or short on the pink wire.
2. Replace the GP sensor.

YES ↓

Disconnect the ECM connector and check for a short to ground on the pink wire terminal (31) for 2004-2006 models or terminal (1) for 2007-2011 models. Is the wire shorted to ground? → **YES** → Repair the wiring harness.

NO ↓

Disconnect the ECM connector from the ECM and disconnect the GP sensor connector from the its harness mate. Check the continuity of the pink wire between the ECM connector and the harness side of the GP sensor connector. Does the wire have continuity? → **NO** → Repair the wiring harness.

YES ↓

Faulty ECM.

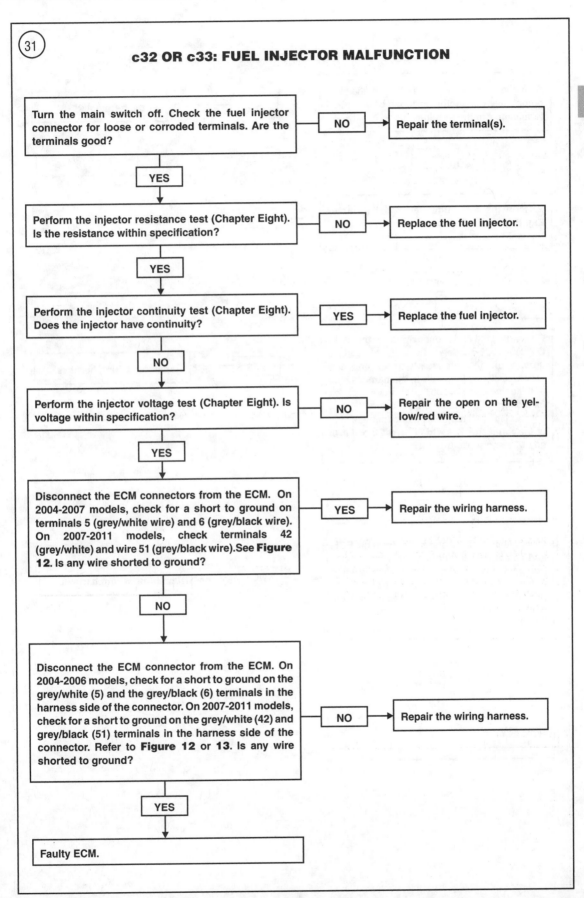

c32 OR c33: FUEL INJECTOR MALFUNCTION

Turn the main switch off. Check the fuel injector connector for loose or corroded terminals. Are the terminals good? — **NO** → Repair the terminal(s).

YES

Perform the injector resistance test (Chapter Eight). Is the resistance within specification? — **NO** → Replace the fuel injector.

YES

Perform the injector continuity test (Chapter Eight). Does the injector have continuity? — **YES** → Replace the fuel injector.

NO

Perform the injector voltage test (Chapter Eight). Is voltage within specification? — **NO** → Repair the open on the yellow/red wire.

YES

Disconnect the ECM connectors from the ECM. On 2004-2007 models, check for a short to ground on terminals 5 (grey/white wire) and 6 (grey/black wire). On 2007-2011 models, check terminals 42 (grey/white) and wire 51 (grey/black wire). See **Figure 12**. Is any wire shorted to ground? — **YES** → Repair the wiring harness.

NO

Disconnect the ECM connector from the ECM. On 2004-2006 models, check for a short to ground on the grey/white (5) and the grey/black (6) terminals in the harness side of the connector. On 2007-2011 models, check for a short to ground on the grey/white (42) and grey/black (51) terminals in the harness side of the connector. Refer to **Figure 12** or **13**. Is any wire shorted to ground? — **NO** → Repair the wiring harness.

YES

Faulty ECM.

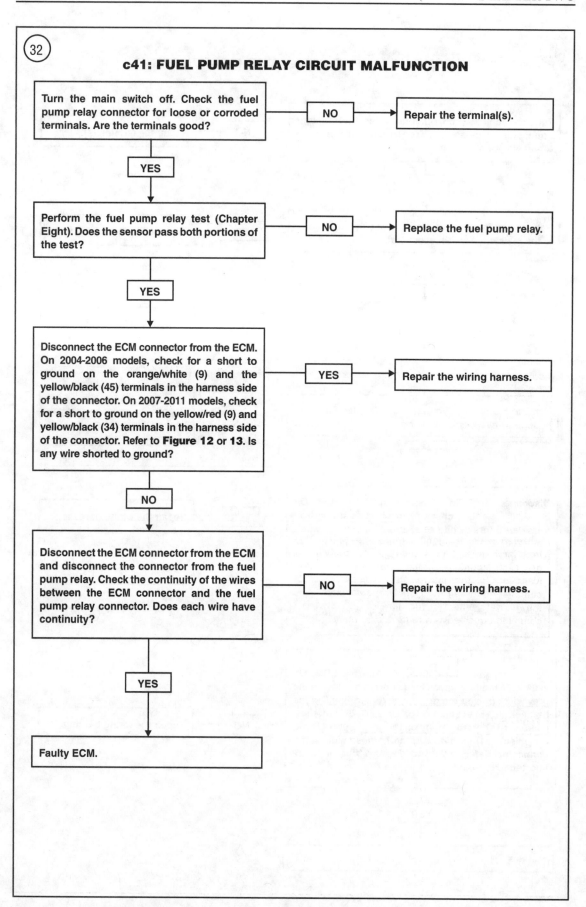

32

c41: FUEL PUMP RELAY CIRCUIT MALFUNCTION

Turn the main switch off. Check the fuel pump relay connector for loose or corroded terminals. Are the terminals good? → **NO** → Repair the terminal(s).

YES

Perform the fuel pump relay test (Chapter Eight). Does the sensor pass both portions of the test? → **NO** → Replace the fuel pump relay.

YES

Disconnect the ECM connector from the ECM. On 2004-2006 models, check for a short to ground on the orange/white (9) and the yellow/black (45) terminals in the harness side of the connector. On 2007-2011 models, check for a short to ground on the yellow/red (9) and yellow/black (34) terminals in the harness side of the connector. Refer to **Figure 12** or **13**. Is any wire shorted to ground? → **YES** → Repair the wiring harness.

NO

Disconnect the ECM connector from the ECM and disconnect the connector from the fuel pump relay. Check the continuity of the wires between the ECM connector and the fuel pump relay connector. Does each wire have continuity? → **NO** → Repair the wiring harness.

YES

Faulty ECM.

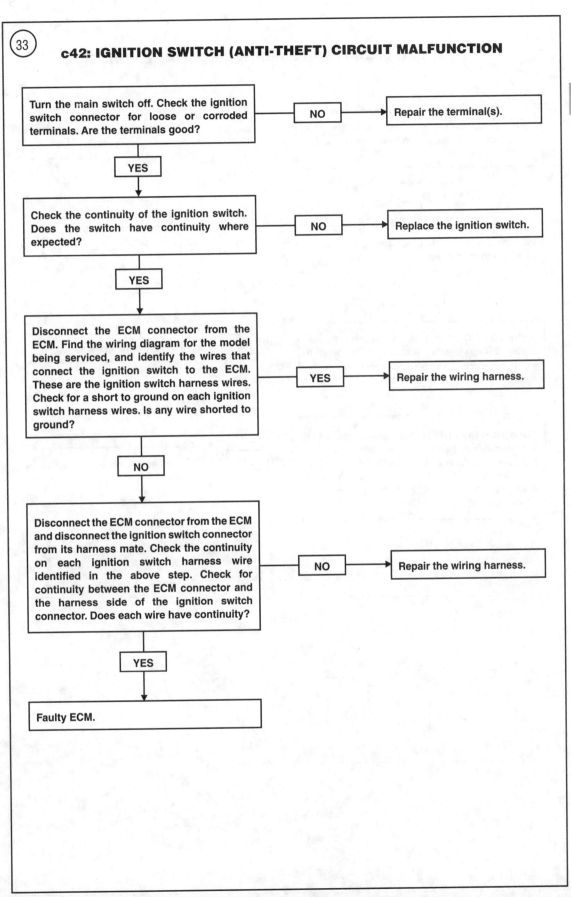

(33) c42: IGNITION SWITCH (ANTI-THEFT) CIRCUIT MALFUNCTION

Turn the main switch off. Check the ignition switch connector for loose or corroded terminals. Are the terminals good? — **NO** → Repair the terminal(s).

YES

Check the continuity of the ignition switch. Does the switch have continuity where expected? — **NO** → Replace the ignition switch.

YES

Disconnect the ECM connector from the ECM. Find the wiring diagram for the model being serviced, and identify the wires that connect the ignition switch to the ECM. These are the ignition switch harness wires. Check for a short to ground on each ignition switch harness wires. Is any wire shorted to ground? — **YES** → Repair the wiring harness.

NO

Disconnect the ECM connector from the ECM and disconnect the ignition switch connector from its harness mate. Check the continuity on each ignition switch harness wire identified in the above step. Check for continuity between the ECM connector and the harness side of the ignition switch connector. Does each wire have continuity? — **NO** → Repair the wiring harness.

YES

Faulty ECM.

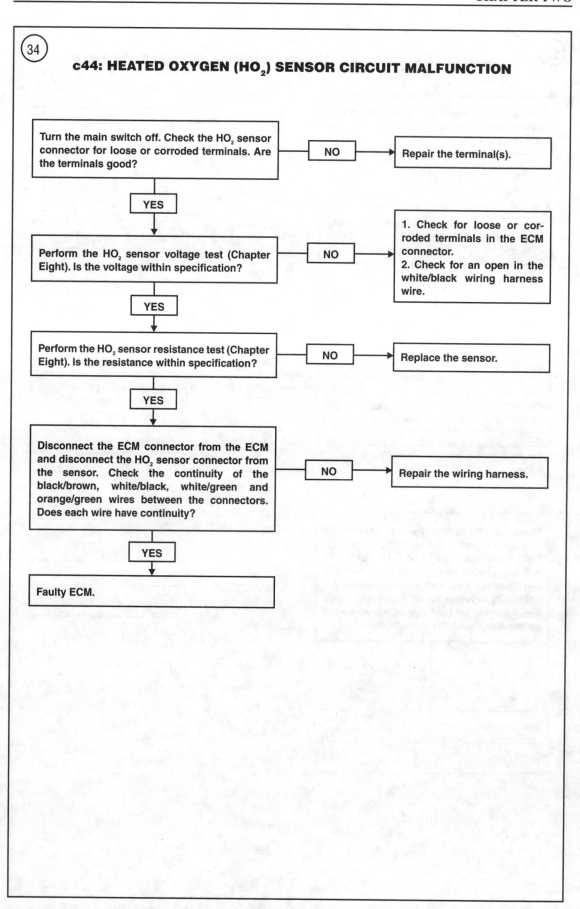

(34)

c44: HEATED OXYGEN (HO$_2$) SENSOR CIRCUIT MALFUNCTION

Turn the main switch off. Check the HO$_2$ sensor connector for loose or corroded terminals. Are the terminals good?

→ NO → Repair the terminal(s).

YES

Perform the HO$_2$ sensor voltage test (Chapter Eight). Is the voltage within specification?

→ NO →
1. Check for loose or corroded terminals in the ECM connector.
2. Check for an open in the white/black wiring harness wire.

YES

Perform the HO$_2$ sensor resistance test (Chapter Eight). Is the resistance within specification?

→ NO → Replace the sensor.

YES

Disconnect the ECM connector from the ECM and disconnect the HO$_2$ sensor connector from the sensor. Check the continuity of the black/brown, white/black, white/green and orange/green wires between the connectors. Does each wire have continuity?

→ NO → Repair the wiring harness.

YES

Faulty ECM.

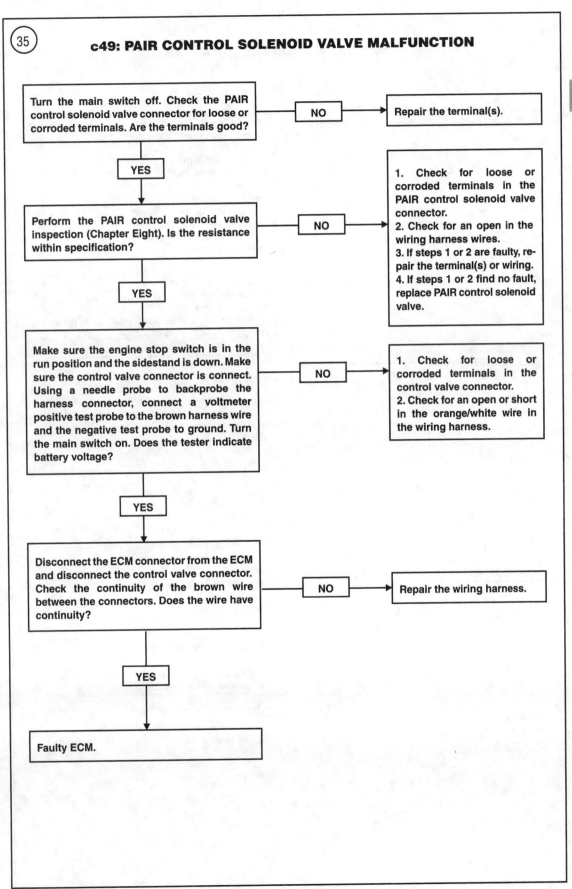

(35) **c49: PAIR CONTROL SOLENOID VALVE MALFUNCTION**

Turn the main switch off. Check the PAIR control solenoid valve connector for loose or corroded terminals. Are the terminals good? — **NO** → Repair the terminal(s).

YES

Perform the PAIR control solenoid valve inspection (Chapter Eight). Is the resistance within specification? — **NO** →
1. Check for loose or corroded terminals in the PAIR control solenoid valve connector.
2. Check for an open in the wiring harness wires.
3. If steps 1 or 2 are faulty, repair the terminal(s) or wiring.
4. If steps 1 or 2 find no fault, replace PAIR control solenoid valve.

YES

Make sure the engine stop switch is in the run position and the sidestand is down. Make sure the control valve connector is connect. Using a needle probe to backprobe the harness connector, connect a voltmeter positive test probe to the brown harness wire and the negative test probe to ground. Turn the main switch on. Does the tester indicate battery voltage? — **NO** →
1. Check for loose or corroded terminals in the control valve connector.
2. Check for an open or short in the orange/white wire in the wiring harness.

YES

Disconnect the ECM connector from the ECM and disconnect the control valve connector. Check the continuity of the brown wire between the connectors. Does the wire have continuity? — **NO** → Repair the wiring harness.

YES

Faulty ECM.

2

(36)

DISC BRAKE TROUBLESHOOTING

Disc brake fluid leakage

Check:
- Loose or damaged line fittings
- Worn caliper piston seals
- Scored caliper piston or bore
- Loose banjo bolts
- Damaged oil line washers
- Leaking master clyinder diaphragm
- Leaking master cylinder secondary seal
- Cracked master cylinder housing
- Too high brake fluid level
- Loose or damaged master cylinder

Brake overheating

Check:
- Warped brake disc
- Incorrect brake fluid
- Caliper piston and/or brake pads hanging up
- Riding brakes during riding

Brake chatter

Check:
- Warped brake disc
- Incorrect caliper alignment
- Loose caliper mounting bolts
- Loose front axle nut and/or clamps
- Worn wheel bearings
- Damaged hub
- Restricted brake hydraulic line
- Contaminated brake pads

Brake locking

Check:
- Incorrect brake fluid
- Plugged passages in master cylinder
- Caliper piston and/or brake pads hanging up
- Warped brake disc

Insufficient brakes

Check:
- Air in brake lines
- Worn brake pads
- Low brake fluid
- Incorrect brake fluid
- Worn brake disc
- Worn caliper piston seals
- Glazed brake pads
- Leaking primary cup seal in master cylinder
- Contaminated brake pads and/or disc

Brake squeal

Check:
- Contaminated brake pads and/or disc
- Dust or dirt collected behind brake pads
- Loose parts

NOTE
If the ABS indicator does not turn on when the ignition switch is turned on, verify that battery voltage is present at the ECU and the combination meter operates properly.

3. Start the engine.

4. Ride the motorcycle until the speed reaches approximately 5 km/h (3 mph).

5. Observe the ABS indicator (**Figure 37**):

   a. ABS is normal if the ABS indicator turns off.

   b. If the ABS indicator remains on or flashes, a malfunction has been detected by the ECU and the ABS system is turned off. Perform the *Pre-Inspection* described in this section.

Pre-Inspection

When the ABS indicator flashes or stays on, make the following general checks before testing the ABS:

1. Verify that the correct tires are installed and properly inflated. Inspect the wheels for damage. Abnormal motorcycle operation, such as wheelies, may trigger a DTC.

2. The electrical components in the ABS require a fully charged battery. When troubleshooting the ABS, make sure the battery is fully charged. When in doubt, test the battery. Refer to Battery in Chapter Nine. If the charging system is suspect, test the charging system output. Refer to *Charging System* in Chapter Nine.

3. Check the overall condition of the primary braking system. This includes brake pad wear, tightness of the component fasteners, and brake fluid levels in both master cylinder reservoirs. Check all union bolts and metal brake lines for tightness. Check for any brake fluid leaks.

4. Inspect the entire ABS wire harness, starting at the ECU (**Figure 38**). Check for chaffing and other apparent damage. Particularly check the front and rear wheel speed sensors, wiring harness and connectors.

5. Because electrical components in the ABS operate on low voltage, they are sensitive to any increase in resistance in the circuit. Visually inspect the ABS circuit for any loose or damaged connectors. Then check the voltage drop across the suspect connectors. Refer to this chapter for typical voltage drop testing. A voltage drop exceeding 0.5 volt indicates excessive resistance and a problem in the circuit.

6. If the ABS indicator flashed or stayed on after reinstalling a wheel, check the wheel speed sensor and sensor rotor for damage. Check the wheel sensor clearance as described in Chapter Fourteen. Check the sensor rotor for debris or chipped or damaged teeth.

7. After performing these general checks, retrieve the DTC(s), and then clear them. Refer to *Diagnostic Trouble Codes* in this section. If the ABS indicator flashes or remains on, retrieve the DTC and troubleshoot the system.

Diagnostic Trouble Codes

Diagnostic trouble codes (DTCs) are retrieved from the ECU by triggering a series of timed flashes from the ABS indicator (**Figure 37**). The number of flashes displayed by the ABS indicator indicates the stored DTC. See **Figure 39** for a description of each DTC.

Note the following before retrieving DTCs:

1. The DTC set in the ECU memory remains in memory until the problem is repaired and the DTC is erased. Turning the ignition switch off during or after retrieving the DTC does not erase it. However, to view the DTC again after turning the ignition switch off and then on, the retrieval procedure must be repeated. See DTC Retrieval.

2. The ECU can store six DTCs. The most current problem is displayed first.

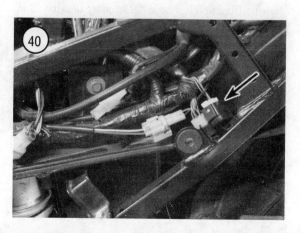

Fault code/flashes	Faulty component or symptoms	Possible causes
ABS light does not come on with ignition	No voltage at instrument cluster No voltage at ABS control unit	Damaged signal fuse Faulty wiring or wiring connector Faulty LED
ABS light stays on continuously	No voltage at ABS control unit ABS control unit Service check connector	Faulty wiring or wiring connector Internal fault
25	Front wheel speed sensor circuit Front wheel speed sensor Front wheel sensor rotor	Wrong tyre size or pressure Deformed wheel Faulty wiring or wiring connector Faulty sensor Damaged sensor rotor
35	ABS motor fuse No voltage at ABS control unit ABS control unit	Fuse blown Faulty wiring or wiring connector Internal fault
41	Front wheel speed sensor	Incorrect sensor installation Faulty wiring or wiring connector Damaged sensor rotor Faulty ABS control unit
42	Front wheel speed sensor open circuit	Faulty wiring or wiring connector Dirty or damaged sensor Faulty ABS control unit
44	Rear wheel speed sensor	Incorrect sensor installation Faulty wiring or wiring connector Damaged sensor rotor Faulty ABS control unit
45	Rear wheel speed sensor open circuit	Faulty wiring or wiring connector Dirty or damaged sensor Faulty ABS control unit
47	Supply voltage increased*	Faulty battery Faulty regulator/rectifier Faulty wiring
48	Supply voltage decreased*	Discharged or faulty battery Faulty alternator or regulator/rectifier Faulty wiring
55	ABS control unit	Internal fault
61	ABS valve fuse ABS solenoid	Fuse blown Faulty ABS control unit

*ABS light goes out when voltage returns to normal

3. Record each DTC in the order displayed.

4. After troubleshooting and repairing the ABS erase the DTC and perform the self-diagnosis. If the ABS indicator does not flash or stay on after completing the self-diagnosis, the problem has been repaired.

DTC Retrieval

A mode select switch (Suzuki part No. 09930-82710) is needed to enter the dealer mode (**Figure 14**).

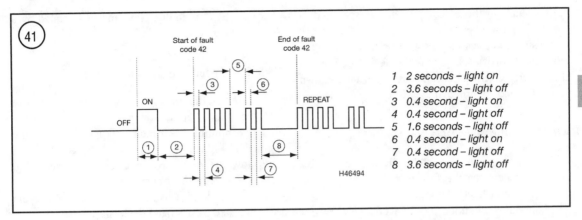

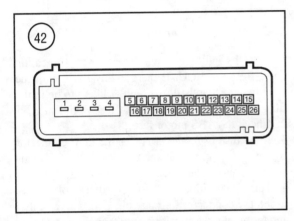

CAUTION
Do not attempt this procedure without the mode select switch. Shorting the terminals in the dealer mode connector could damage the ECU.

NOTE
Do not start the engine during this procedure.

1. Turn the ignition switch off.

NOTE
The dealer mode connector is adjacent to the positive terminal side of the battery box. In some instances the connector may be accessible after removing the seat. Otherwise, remove the left side cover.

2. Remove the seat, and if necessary, the left side cover as described in Chapter Fifteen.

3. Connect the mode select switch to the dealer mode connector (**Figure 40**) adjacent to the battery box.

4. Turn the mode select switch on.

5. Turn the ignition switch on and watch the ABS indicator (**Figure 37**).

6. The ABS indicator (**Figure 37**) will light and remain on for 2 seconds, blink off for 3.6 seconds, and then flash the DTC or begin flashing repeatedly.

7. If there is no DTC stored, the ABS indicator will flash repeatedly every 3.6 seconds and extinguish.

8. If there is a DTC stored, the ABS indicator will flash in a cyclic pattern that reflects the DTC. Refer to **Figure 41**.

9. The ECU can store up to six codes. When there are two codes, they are separated by a 3.6-second pause.

10. After retrieving and writing down any codes, refer to the ABS diagnostic trouble code chart in **Figure 39**. The chart lists the DTC number, the problem area and possible causes. Refer to the troubleshooting procedure related to the DTC.

11. After repairing the problem, erase the trouble code(s) and reset the self-diagnosis to confirm the problem has been repaired.

Erase DTC and Reset Self-diagnostic System

Perform the following to erase the DTC(s) and reset the system once an ABS malfunction has been corrected.

1. Perform steps 1-5 in DTC retrieval procedure.

2. While the ABS indicator flashes, move the dealer mode switch to off. Leave the switch in the off position for 13 seconds.

3. Move the dealer mode switch from off to on three times. Allow the switch to remain in the on position for more than one second each time.

4. Turn the ignition switch off.

5. Perform DTC retrieval procedure to verify that DTC has been erased.

ECU Testing

Troubleshooting the ABS frequently includes testing the ECU wiring. Refer to **Figure 42** to identify pin terminals in the ECU connector as specified in the test procedure.

If testing indicates that the ECU is faulty, take the motorcycle to a dealership for further testing before purchasing a replacement ECU. If possible, install a known good ECU and confirm that the ECU is the problem.

ABS Indicator Light Does Not Come On

1. Check the signal fuse, then check the orange/green wire between the fuse box and combination meter (refer to Chapter Nine).
2. Make sure the ignition is off. Disconnect the ECU wiring connector.
3. Turn the ignition on. Using a multimeter set to the dc volts function, measure the voltage between pin 12 (positive probe) and pin 4 (negative probe) in the connector.

Desired voltage is between 7.5 and 9.5 V. If no voltage is shown check the wiring to the combination meter and the terminals of the combination meter connector. If the wiring is good, the ABS indicator light may be faulty.

NOTE
If the indicator light LED has failed a new combination meter will have to be installed (refer to Chapter Nine).

4. Turn the ignition off.
5. If there is voltage in Step 3, using a continuity tester or multimeter, test for continuity between terminal pin 4 on the wire harness side (positive probe) of the connector and ground (negative probe). Continuity should exist if the ground circuit is good, indication that the ABS control unit is faulty. Have the ECU tested by a Suzuki dealership.

ABS Light Stays On Continuously

1. Check the ignition fuse.
2. Make sure the ignition is off. Disconnect the ECU wiring connector.
3. Turn the ignition on. Using a multimeter set to the dc volts function, measure the voltage between pin 18 (positive probe) and pin 4 (negative probe) in the connector . Desired voltage is between 7.5 and 9.5 V. If no voltage is shown check the wiring to the combination meter and the terminals of the combination meter connector. If the wiring is good, the ABS indicator light may be faulty.
4. If there is voltage check the orange and black/white wires between the ECU connector and the mode select switch connector for continuity. Make sure there is no short to ground. Otherwise, it is

likely the ECU is faulty. Have the ECU tested by a Suzuki dealership.

Code 25 – Speed Sensor Malfunction

1. Ensure that the tire size and pressure are correct.
2. Check the speed sensor rotor condition, particularly that nothing has become trapped between the segments.
3. Follow the procedure in Chapter Fourteen and check the speed sensor clearance.
4. If the checks fail to identify the fault, have the ECU checked by a Suzuki dealership.

Code 35 – ABS Motor Fuse

1. Turn the ignition on and listen for any operating noise from the ECU. If there is any noise with the machine at a standstill the fault is likely to be in the ECU. Have the ECU checked by a Suzuki dealer.
2. Check the ABS motor fuse.
3. If the fuse is good, verify that the ECU connector is secure. Disconnect it and check that the terminals are clean and undamaged.
4. Turn the ignition on. Test for battery voltage between the connector terminal pin 1 (negative probe) and terminal pin 2 (positive probe) on the wiring harness side of the connector. If there is no voltage, inspect the wiring for damage. If there is voltage, have the ECU tested by a Suzuki dealership.

Code 41 – Front Wheel Speed Sensor Signal Malfunction

1. Check that the sensor is mounted securely and the rotor is clean and in good condition without anything trapped between its segments.
2. Refer to Chapter Fourteen and measure the sensor rotor clearance. If necessary, adjust the sensor rotor clearance. If the clearance is correct and there is no damage, refer to Code 42.

Code 42 – Front Wheel Speed Sensor Open Circuit

1. Remove the air box (Chapter Eight) to access the front wheel speed sensor wiring connector. Check the wiring for damage and make sure that the connector is secure, then disconnect it and check that the terminals are clean and undamaged. Reconnect the connector.
2. Verify that the ECU connector is secure. Disconnect it and check that the terminals are clean and undamaged.

3. Test for continuity between the connector terminal pin 5 and terminal pin 16 on the wiring harness side of the ECU connector.

4. If no continuity is indicated, test between pin 16 and ground. No continuity should be shown. If it is, disconnect the wheel speed sensor connector and test for continuity between the white/red wire terminal and ground on the sensor side of the connector. No continuity should be shown. If continuity is shown, the speed sensor is faulty.

5. Test for continuity between terminal pin 5 and ground in the wiring harness side of the ECU connector. No continuity should be shown. If it is, disconnect the wheel speed sensor connector and test for continuity between the black/red wire terminal and ground on the sensor side of the connector. No continuity should be shown. If continuity is shown, the speed sensor is faulty.

6. Check the white/red wire between the ECU connector harness side and the wheel speed sensor connector. There should be continuity. Similarly check the black/red wire.

Code 44 – Rear Wheel Speed Sensor Signal Malfunction

1. Check that the sensor is mounted securely and the rotor is clean and in good condition without anything trapped between its segments.

2. Refer to Chapter Fourteen and measure the sensor rotor clearance. If necessary, adjust the sensor rotor clearance. If the clearance is correct and there is no damage, refer to Code 45.

Code 45 – Rear Wheel Speed Sensor Open Circuit

1. Remove the seat to access the rear wheel speed sensor wiring connector. Check the wiring for damage and make sure that the connector is secure, then disconnect it and check that the terminals are clean and undamaged. Reconnect the connector.

2. Verify that the ECU connector is secure. Disconnect it and check that the terminals are clean and undamaged.

3. Test for continuity between the connector terminal pin 7 and terminal pin 19 on the wiring harness side of the ECU connector.

4. If no continuity is indicated, test between pin 7 and ground. No continuity should be shown. If it is, disconnect the wheel speed sensor connector and test for continuity between the white/yellow wire terminal and ground on the sensor side of the connector. No continuity should be shown. If continuity is shown, the speed sensor is faulty.

5. Test for continuity between terminal pin 19 and ground in the wiring harness side of the ECU connector. No continuity should be shown. If it is, disconnect the wheel speed sensor connector and test for continuity between the black/yellow wire terminal and ground on the sensor side of the connector. No continuity should be shown. If continuity is shown, the speed sensor is faulty.

6. Check the white/yellow wire between the ECU connector harness side and the wheel speed sensor connector. There should be continuity. Similarly check the black/yellow wire.

Code 47, 48 – Supply Voltage

1. Check the battery voltage (refer to Chapter Nine). If the voltage is good, check the output of the charging system (refer to Chapter Nine).

2. Verify that the ECU connector is secure. Disconnect it and check that the terminals are clean and undamaged.

3. Connect a multimeter to connector pin 18 (positive probe) and pin 4 (negative probe). Start the engine and warm it up to normal operating temperature. Switch the headlight switch to HI beam and briefly increase the engine speed to 5000 rpm. Measure the voltage. Desired voltage is same as charging voltage measured in Step 1. If not, check the wiring. If the wiring is good, have the ECU tested by a Suzuki dealership.

Code 55 – Control Unit Malfunction

1. Check that the front and rear wheel speed sensors are mounted securely and each rotor is clean and in good condition without anything trapped between its segments.

2. Refer to Chapter Fourteen and measure the clearance of each sensor rotor. If necessary, adjust the sensor rotor clearance. If the clearance is correct and there is no damage, go to Step 3.

3. Erase the DTC, then check to see if the DTC has been reactivated. If the DTC reappears it is likely the ECU is faulty. Have the ECU tested by a Suzuki dealership.

Code 61 – ABS Solenoid Malfunction

1. Check the ABS valve relay fuse (25 amp). If the fuse is good, verify that the ECU connector is secure. Disconnect it and check that the terminals are clean and undamaged.

2. Turn the ignition on. Using a multimeter set to the dc volts function, measure the voltage between pin 3 (positive probe) and pin 4 (negative probe) in the

connector. If battery voltage is not present, inspect the wiring for damage. If the wiring is good, have the ECU tested by a Suzuki dealership.

STEERING AND HANDLING

Correct poor steering and handling immediately after it is detected, since loss of control is possible. Check the following areas:

1. Excessive handlebar vibration:
   a. Incorrect tire pressure.
   b. Unbalanced tire and rim.
   c. Damaged rim.
   d. Loose or damaged handlebar clamps.
   e. Loose steering stem nut.
   f. Worn or damaged front wheel bearings.
   g. Bent or loose axle.
   h. Cracked frame or steering head.
2. Handlebar is hard to turn:
   a. Tire pressure too low.
   b. Incorrect cable routing.
   c. Steering stem adjustment too tight.
   d. Bent steering stem.
   e. Improperly lubricated or damaged steering bearings.
3. Handlebar pulls to one side:
   a. Bent fork leg.
   b. Fork oil levels uneven.
   c. Bent steering stem.
   d. Bent frame or swing arm.
4. Shock absorption too soft:
   a. Low fork oil level.
   b. Fork oil viscosity too low.
   c. Shock absorber rebound damping too low.
   d. Shock absorber spring preload too low.
   e. Shock absorber spring weak.
5. Shock absorption too hard:
   a. High tire pressure.
   b. High fork oil level.
   c. Fork oil viscosity too high.
   d. Bent fork.
   e. Shock absorber rebound damping too high.
   f. Shock absorber spring preload too high.

CHAPTER THREE

LUBRICATION, MAINTENANCE AND TUNE-UP

This chapter describes lubrication, maintenance and tune-up procedures. Specifications are listed in **Tables 1-4** located at the end of this chapter.

To maximize the service life of the motorcycle and gain the utmost in safety and performance, it is necessary to perform periodic inspections and maintenance. Minor problems found during routine service can be corrected before they develop into major ones. A neglected motorcycle will be unreliable and may be dangerous to ride.

Table 1 lists the recommended lubrication, maintenance and tune-up intervals. If the motorcycle is operated in extreme conditions, it may be appropriate to reduce the interval between some maintenance items.

PRE-RIDE INSPECTION

Perform the following inspections before riding the motorcycle. When riding the motorcycle on extended travel and over rough terrain, perform the inspection at least once daily. Perform the inspection when the engine is cold.

1. Inspect fuel lines and fittings for leaks.
2. Inspect fuel level.
3. Inspect engine oil level.
4. Inspect brake operation and lever/pedal free play.
5. Inspect throttle operation and free play.
6. Inspect clutch operation and free play.

7. Inspect steering for smooth operation and no cable binding.
8. Inspect tire condition and air pressure.
9. Inspect wheel condition.
10. Inspect axle nut tightness.
11. Inspect for loose fasteners.
12. Inspect exhaust system.
13. Inspect drive chain condition and adjustment.
14. Inspect the rear sprocket for tightness.
15. Inspect the air filter for dirt/debris buildup.
16. Inspect the suspension for proper settings for riding conditions.
17. Inspect the engine stop switch for proper operation.
18. Inspect the lights for proper operation.

TUNE-UP

Perform the tune-up procedures at the intervals specified in **Table 1**. More frequent tune-ups may be required if the motorcycle is operated primarily in stop-and-go traffic or in areas where there is excessive dirt and dust.

Refer to **Table 3** for tune-up specifications. If the motorcycle is equipped with a label that provides tune-up specifications that differ from those in the table, use those in the label.

During a tune-up, inspect the battery as described in Chapter Nine. Also service the following items as described in this chapter:

1. Air filter.
2. Engine oil and filter.
3. Idle speed.
4. Spark plugs.
5. Battery.
6. Engine compression.
7. Brake system.
8. Clutch system.
9. Fuel system.
10. Tires.
11. Suspension components.
12. Steering.
13. Drive chain.
14. Fasteners.

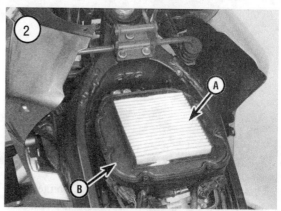

AIR FILTER

Remove and clean the air filter at the interval indicated in **Table 1**. Replace the element at the interval indicated in **Table 1** or whenever it is damaged or starting to deteriorate.

The air filter removes dust and abrasive particles before the air enters the carburetors and the engine. Without the air filter, very fine particles will enter the engine and cause rapid wear of the piston rings, cylinder bores and bearings. Never run the motorcycle without the air filter element installed.

Removal/Cleaning/Installation

1. Remove the fuel tank as described in Chapter Eight.
2. Thoroughly clean any debris from the area surrounding the air box cover (**Figure 1**).
3. Remove the air box cover (**Figure 1**).
4. Remove the air filter (A, **Figure 2**) from the air box.
5. Place a clean shop cloth into the opening in the air box to prevent the entry of debris.

> *NOTE*
> *If the air filter is extremely dirty or if there are any holes in the filter, wipe out the interior of the air box with a shop rag dampened in cleaning solvent. Remove any debris that may have passed through a broken element.*

6. Gently tap the air filter to loosen the trapped dirt and dust.

> *CAUTION*
> *In the next step, do not apply compressed air toward the outside surface of the filter. Air directed at the outside surface forces the dirt and dust into the*

pores of the element thus restricting air flow.

7. Apply compressed air to the *inside surface* (**Figure 3**) of the air filter and remove all loosened dirt and dust.
8. Thoroughly and carefully inspect the filter. If it is torn or broken in any area, replace the air filter. Do not run the motorcycle with a damaged air filter. It may allow dirt to enter the engine. If the filter is good, use it until the indicated time for replacement listed in **Table 1**.

9. Install the air filter (A, **Figure 2**). Make sure the filter is properly seated so there is no air leak.
10. Install the O-ring gasket (B, **Figure 2**) into the groove in the air box.
11. Install the air box cover and tighten the screws securely.

> *NOTE*
> *The air box is shown removed for clarity.*

12. Remove the drain plug in the bottom of the air box (**Figure 4**). Drain out water and other debris col-

lected in the air box. Reinstall the drain cap. Make sure it is clamped in place.
13. Install the fuel tank as described in Chapter Eight.

ENGINE OIL AND FILTER

Refer to **Table 2** for lubricant and fluid information.

3

Engine Oil Level Check

Engine oil level is checked with the oil level gauge located on the right crankcase cover.
1. If the motorcycle has not been run, start the engine and let it warm for several minutes.
2. Shut off the engine and let the oil settle for 2-3 minutes.

> *CAUTION*
> *Do not check the oil level reading with the motorcycle on the sidestand as the oil will flow away from the gauge giving a false reading.*

3. Have an assistant sit on the motorcycle to hold it vertically on level ground.
4. Check the engine oil level in the oil inspection window (**Figure 5**) on the right crankcase cover. The oil level must be between the upper and lower lines.
5. If the oil level is low, unscrew the oil filler cap (**Figure 6**) from the right crankcase cover. Add the recommended grade and viscosity oil (**Table 2**) to correct the level.

> *NOTE*
> *Refer to **Engine Oil and Filter Change** in this section for additional information on oil selection.*

6. Inspect the O-ring seal on the oil filler cap. Replace the O-ring if it is starting to deteriorate or harden.
7. Install the oil filler cap and tighten it securely.
8. If the oil level is too high, remove the oil filler cap and draw out the excess oil with a syringe or suitable pump.
9. Recheck the oil level and adjust if necessary.
10. Install the oil filler cap and tighten it securely.

Engine Oil and Filter Change

Change the oil and filter at the intervals recommended in **Table 1**. If the motorcycle is used in extreme conditions (hot, cold, wet or dusty) change the oil more often.

Always change the oil when the engine is warm. Contaminants will remain suspended in the oil and it will drain more completely and quickly.

> *WARNING*
> *Prolonged contact with used engine oil may cause skin cancer. Minimize contact with the engine oil.*

1. Start the engine and let it warm for approximately 2-3 minutes. Shut off the engine.

> *NOTE*
> *Warming the engine heats the oil so it flows freely and carries out contamination and sludge.*

2. Place the motorcycle on the sidestand on level ground.
3. Place a drain pan under the engine.
4. Remove the oil drain plug (**Figure 7**) and gasket from the bottom of the oil pan.
5. Loosen the oil filler cap (**Figure 6**). This speeds up the flow of oil.
6. Allow the oil to completely drain.
7. Inspect the condition of the drained oil for contamination. After it has cooled, check for any metal particles or clutch friction disc particles.

> *WARNING*
> *The exhaust system must be completely cool before removing the oil filter.*

8. To replace the oil filter, perform the following:
   a. Move the drain pan under the oil filter (**Figure 8**).
   b. Install an oil filter wrench onto the oil filter, and turn the filter counterclockwise *until oil begins to run out. Wait until the oil stops then loosen the filter until it is easy to turn.*
   c. Remove the oil filter wrench from the end of the filter then completely unscrew and remove the filter. Hold it with the open end facing up.
   d. Hold the filter over the drain pan and pour out any remaining oil. Place the old filter in a heavy-duty, freezer-grade recloseable plastic bag and close the bag. Discard the old filter properly.
   e. Thoroughly clean the filter-to-crankcase surface. This surface must be clean to prevent leakage.
   f. Apply a light coat of clean engine oil to the rubber seal on the new filter.
   g. Install a new oil filter onto the threaded fitting on the engine.
   h. Tighten the filter by hand until the rubber gasket contacts the crankcase surface, and then tighten it an additional two full turns.

9. Inspect the drain plug gasket for damage. Replace the gasket if necessary.
10. Install the drain plug (**Figure 7**) and its gasket. Tighten the oil drain plug to 21 N•m (186 in.-lb.).
11. Pour in the quantity of oil specified in **Table 2**.
12. Install the oil filler cap and tighten it securely.
13. Start the engine and let it idle.
14. Check the oil filter and drain plug for leaks.
15. Turn off the engine and check the engine oil level as described in this chapter. Adjust the oil level if necessary.

COOLING SYSTEM

> *WARNING*
> *Do not dispose of antifreeze by flushing it down a drain or pouring it onto the ground. Place old antifreeze into a suitable container and dispose of it properly. Do not store coolant where it is accessible to children or pets.*

> *WARNING*
> *Do not remove the radiator cap when the engine is hot. The coolant is very hot and under pressure. Severe scald-*

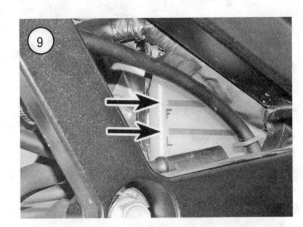

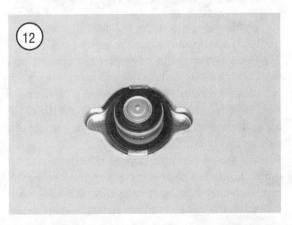

*ing could result if the coolant comes in
contact with your skin.*

Coolant

Use only a high-quality ethylene glycol-based
coolant formulated for aluminum radiators and engines. Mix the coolant with distilled water at a 50:50
ratio. Coolant capacity is listed in **Table 2**. When
mixing antifreeze and water, be sure to use only a
soft or distilled water. *Never* use tap water as this
damages engine parts.

Coolant Level

It is important to keep the coolant level at the upper mark on the coolant reserve tank. On 2004-2006
models, the coolant reserve tank is located on the left
side (**Figure 9**). On 2007-2011 models, the coolant
reserve tank is located under the seat (**Figure 10**).
1. Check the level with the engine at normal operating temperature and the motorcycle upright.
2. If the level is low, add coolant to the reserve
tank.
3. Raise the fuel tank as described in Chapter Eight
for access to the reserve tank cap.

Cooling System Inspection

Once a year, or whenever the cooling system requires repeated refilling, check the following items.
If the test equipment is not available, the tests can
be done by a dealership, radiator shop or competent
service station.
1. With the engine *cold,* remove the radiator cap (A,
Figure 11).
2. Check the rubber sealing washers on the radiator
cap (**Figure 12**). Replace the cap if the washers show
signs of deterioration, cracking or other damage. If
the radiator cap is acceptable, perform Step 3.

*NOTE
Apply water to the rubber washer in
the radiator cap before installing the
cap onto the pressure gauge.*

3. Test the radiator cap pressure (**Figure 13**). The radiator cap must be able to hold a pressure of 95-125
kPa (13.5-17.8 psi) for at least 10 seconds. Replace
the cap if it does not hold pressure or if the relief
pressure is too high or too low.
4. Have the radiator and cooling system pressure
tested. If the cooling system will not hold pressure,
determine the source of leakage and make the appropriate repairs.

5. With the engine cold, remove the radiator cap and test the specific gravity of the coolant. Use an antifreeze tester following the manufacturer's instructions. This ensures adequate temperature and corrosion protection. Never let the mixture become less than 50 percent antifreeze or corrosion protection will be impaired. Never use a mixture of 60 percent or greater or the cooling efficiency will be reduced.

6. Check all cooling system hoses and the radiator for damage or deterioration as described in Chapter Ten.

7. Install the radiator cap. Turn the radiator cap clockwise to the first stop. Then push down and turn it clockwise until it stops.

Coolant Change

Completely drain and refill the cooling system at the interval listed in **Table 1**.

It is sometimes necessary to drain the coolant from the system to perform a service procedure on some part of the engine. If the coolant is in good condition (and not due for replacement), it can be reused if it remains clean. Drain the coolant into a *clean* drain pan and then pour the coolant into a clean sealable container and screw on the cap. This coolant can then be reused.

> *CAUTION*
> *Be careful not to spill coolant on painted, plated or plastic surfaces. It may damage the finish and/or surface. Wash any applicable area with soapy water and rinse thoroughly with clean water.*

Perform the following procedure when the engine is cold.

1. Place the motorcycle on level ground on the sidestand.

2. With the engine *cold,* remove the radiator cap (A, **Figure 11**).

3. On the left side, place a drain pan under the water pump housing.

4. Remove the drain screw on the water pump (**Figure 14**) and drain the coolant into the pan.

5. Tip the motorcycle from side to side to drain residual coolant from the cooling system.

> *NOTE*
> *If the coolant is dirty, place another drain pan under a disconnected lower radiator hose and flush the system with clean water. Drain out all water from the system.*

6. Install the water pump drain screw.

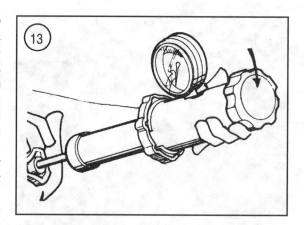

7. Detach the reservoir hose from the radiator (B, **Figure 11**) and drain the coolant from the coolant reservoir.

8. If necessary, clean the inside of the reservoir with a liquid detergent. Thoroughly rinse it with clean water.

9. Attach the reservoir hose to the radiator.

> *CAUTION*
> *Do not use a coolant-to-water ratio higher than 50:50. A higher concentration of coolant (60% or greater) actually **decreases** the performance of the cooling system.*

10. Place a funnel into the radiator filler neck and refill the radiator and engine.

11. Use a 50:50 mixture of coolant and distilled water. Slowly add the coolant through the radiator filler neck. Add it slowly so it expels as much air as possible from the engine and radiator. Top off the coolant to the bottom of the filler neck. Do not install the radiator cap at this time.

12. Tip the motorcycle from side to side several times. This helps bleed off some of the air trapped in the cooling system. If necessary, add additional coolant to the system until the coolant level is to the

bottom of the filler neck. Do not install the radiator cap at this time.

13. Start the engine and let it run at idle until the engine reaches normal operating temperature. Make sure there are no air bubbles in the coolant and that the coolant level stabilizes at the bottom of the radiator filler neck. Add coolant as needed.

14. Install the radiator cap.

15. Add coolant to the reservoir tank so the coolant level is between the two lines on the tank.

16. Test ride the motorcycle and readjust the coolant level in the reservoir tank if necessary.

BRAKE SYSTEM

WARNING
Use DOT 4 brake fluid. Others may cause brake failure. Do not intermix different brands or types of brake fluid, as they may not be compatible. Do not use silicone-based (DOT 5) brake fluid, as it can cause brake component damage and brake system failure.

CAUTION
Brake fluid will damage painted and plastic surfaces; handle it carefully. Wash spilled brake fluid immediately with soap and water and thoroughly rinse the area.

Check the brake fluid in each brake master cylinder at the intervals in **Table 1**. At the same time, inspect the brake pads for wear. Refer to Chapter Fourteen for brake bleeding, brake component servicing and brake pad replacement procedures.

Brake Hose Inspection

Check the brake calipers hoses and the front and rear master cylinders for leaks. If leaks are found,

tighten the union bolt or hose and then bleed the brake system as described in Chapter Fourteen. If this does not stop the leak or if a brake line is damaged, replace the brake hose and bleed the system.

Brake Fluid Type

The brake system requires DOT 4 brake fluid.

Brake Fluid Change

Every time the reservoir cap is removed, a small amount of dirt and moisture enters the brake fluid. The same thing happens if a leak occurs or when a brake hose is loosened. Dirt can clog the system and cause unnecessary wear. Water in the brake fluid will vaporize at high brake system temperatures, impairing the hydraulic action and reducing brake performance. To maintain peak performance, change the brake fluid at the interval in **Table 1** or whenever the caliper or master cylinder is overhauled. To change brake fluid, follow the brake bleeding procedure in Chapter Fourteen.

Brake Fluid Level Inspection

WARNING
If the reservoir is empty, air has probably entered the brake system. Bleed the brake system as described in Chapter Fourteen.

WARNING
A low brake fluid level usually indicates brake pad wear. As the pads wear, the brake caliper pistons automatically extend farther out of the bore and the brake fluid level drops in the reservoir. However, if the brake fluid level is low and the brake pads are not worn excessively, check all of the brake hoses for leaks.

1. Support the motorcycle so the brake fluid reservoir being checked (front or back) is level.

2. Inspect the front reservoir as follows:

   a. The fluid level should be between the lower mark and top of the sight glass (**Figure 15**).

   b. If the fluid level is below the low mark, remove the cover and diaphragm, then add DOT 4 brake fluid. Replace the diaphragm and cap.

   c. Check for master cylinder leaks and worn brake pads.

3. Inspect the rear reservoir as follows:

a. The fluid level should be between the upper and lower level marks on the reservoir (**Figure 16**).

b. If the fluid level is below the low mark, remove the right frame cover as described in Chapter Fifteen.

c. Remove the cap and diaphragm, then add DOT 4 brake fluid. Replace the diaphragm and cap.

d. Check for master cylinder leaks and worn brake pads.

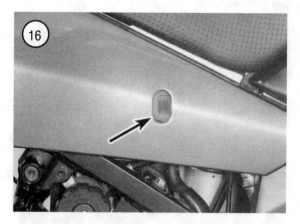

Brake Pad Wear Inspection

Inspect the brake pads for wear at the interval indicated in **Table 1**.

On the brake caliper, look at the brake pads where they contact the brake disc and inspect the brake pads for excessive or uneven wear.

> *NOTE*
> *A small inspection mirror may be helpful. The wear indicator grooves are visible on the installed pads. The pads shown in **Figure 17** were removed for clarity.*

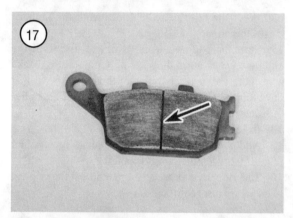

Each brake pad has one or more wear grooves (**Figure 17**) that serve as wear indicators. If any pad is worn so that any groove is no longer visible, replace both pads. Follow the pad replacement procedure in Chapter Fourteen.

> *NOTE*
> *Always replace both pads in each caliper at the same time to maintain even pressure on the brake disc.*

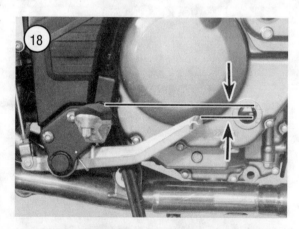

Rear Brake Pedal Height Adjustment

The pedal height will change as the brake pads wear. The top of the brake pedal should be positioned below the top surface of the footpeg. The distance between the top of the brake pedal and the top of the footpeg (**Figure 18**) should be 20-30 mm (0.8-1.2 in.). If the dimension is incorrect, adjust the brake pedal height by performing the following.

1. Place the motorcycle on level ground on the sidestand.

2. Make sure the brake pedal is in the at-rest position.

3. At the rear brake master cylinder, loosen the locknut (A, **Figure 19**) and turn the pushrod (B) in either direction until the brake pedal height equals the specified dimension.

4. Tighten the rear brake master cylinder locknut to 17 N•m (150 in.-lb.).

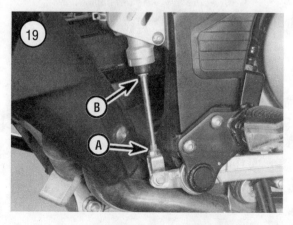

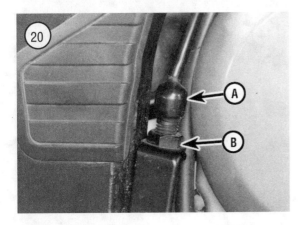

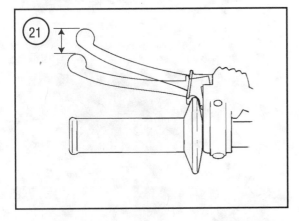

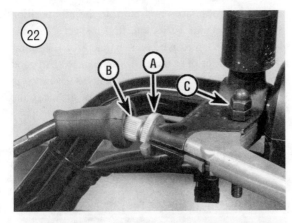

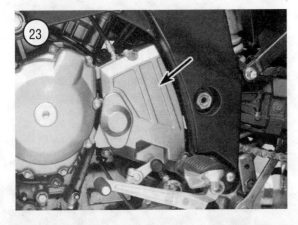

Rear Brake Light Switch Adjustment

1. Turn the ignition switch on.

2. Depress the brake pedal and watch the brake light. The brake light should come on just before feeling pressure at the brake pedal. If necessary, adjust the rear brake light switch by performing the following.

3. To adjust the brake light switch, hold the switch body (A, **Figure 20**) and turn the adjusting nut (B). To make the light come on earlier, turn the adjusting nut and move the switch body up. Move the switch body down to delay the light coming on.

4. Check that the brake light comes on when the pedal is depressed and goes off when the pedal is released. Readjust if necessary.

5. Turn the ignition switch off.

CLUTCH

Clutch Lever Adjustment

The clutch lever free play is continually changing due to the clutch cable wearing and stretching over time, as well as clutch plate wear. Maintain the clutch lever free play within the specification listed in this procedure. Insufficient free play causes clutch slippage and premature clutch plate wear. Excessive free play causes clutch drag and rough shift pedal operation.

NOTE
Clutch cable adjustment is possible at the handlebar clutch lever or at the release lever on the engine. Make minor adjustments at the clutch lever. Make major adjustments at the release lever.

1. Determine the clutch lever free play at the end of the clutch lever **Figure 21**. If the free play is more or less than 10-15 mm (0.4-0.6 in.), adjust the cable as described in the following steps.

2. Pull back the boot. Loosen the locknut (A, **Figure 22**) then turn the clutch lever cable end adjuster (B) as required to obtain the specified amount of free play.

3. If the proper amount of free play cannot be achieved by turning the clutch lever adjuster, perform the following.

4. Loosen the locknut (A, **Figure 22**) and turn the adjuster (B) all the way into the clutch lever.

5. Remove the engine sprocket cover (**Figure 23**).

6. Loosen the locknut (A, **Figure 24**) on the clutch release mechanism and turn the adjusting screw (B) two or three turns out.

7. Rotate the locknuts (C, **Figure 24**) so the angle of the clutch release arm is 80° from vertical.

8. Slowly turn in the clutch release adjusting screw (B, **Figure 24**) until resistance is felt.

9. Turn out the clutch release adjusting screw (B, **Figure 24**) 1/4 turn. Hold the position of the screw with a screwdriver and tighten the locknut (A).

10. Install the engine sprocket cover (**Figure 23**).

11. Turn the adjuster (B, **Figure 22**) to obtain the specified clutch lever free play of 10-15 mm (0.4-0.6 in.). Tighten the locknut (A).

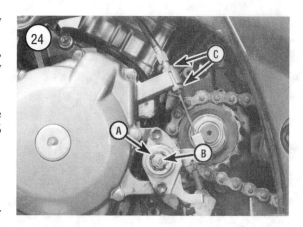

Clutch Cable Lubrication

1. Refer to Clutch Cable Replacement in Chapter Six and detach the upper and lower ends of the clutch cable.

2. Attach a cable lubricator, then lubricate the cable with an aerosol cable lubricant (**Figure 25**). Keep the cable in a vertical position so the lubricant can pass to the opposite end. Move the cable in the housing to help distribute the oil. Stop lubrication when oil is seen at the opposite end of the cable.

3. Remove the clutch lever pivot bolt (C, **Figure 22**), then remove the clutch lever.

4. Clean the lever pivot hole and the pivot bolt. Lubricate the lever and pivot bolt with lithium grease.

5. Install the clutch lever and reattach the clutch cable. Tighten the pivot bolt securely.

6. Adjust the clutch lever free play as described in this chapter.

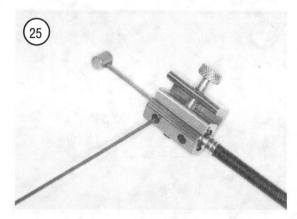

FUEL HOSE INSPECTION

1. Remove the fuel tank as described in Chapter Eight.

2. Inspect the fuel hoses for leaks, deterioration or other damage. Replace damaged fuel hoses.

3. Make sure all connections are leak free. Repair as needed.

4. Install the fuel tank.

THROTTLE CABLES

The throttle uses two cables. One cable pulls the throttle open during acceleration, while the other pulls the throttle closed during deceleration. In operation, the cables always move in opposite directions to one another.

Throttle Operation

1. Check for smooth throttle operation from the fully closed to the fully open positions. Rotate the throttle to the wide-open position and release it. The throttle must automatically return to the idle position without hesitation.

2. If the throttle does not return to the idle position smoothly without hesitation, first inspect the cable housings for excessive wear, damage or deterioration. If the exterior of the cables appears to be in good condition, lubricate the throttle cables as described in this chapter. Also, apply a light coat of grease to the throttle cable pulley.

3. If cable operation is still sluggish after lubrication, replace the throttle cables as described in Chapter Eight.

Throttle Cable Adjustment

WARNING
*With the engine idling, move the handlebar from side to side. If the idle speed increases during this movement, the throttle cables may need adjusting or may be incorrectly routed through the frame. Correct this problem immediately. Do **not** ride the motorcycle in this unsafe condition.*

Specified throttle cable free play is 2.0-4.0 mm (0.08-0.16 in.) as measured on the hand-contact area of the throttle grip.

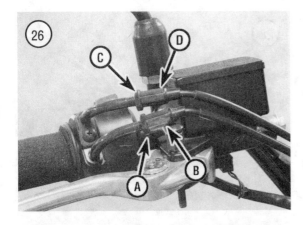

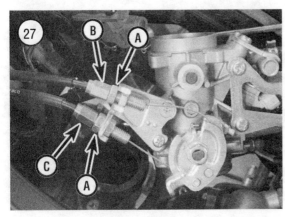

In time, the throttle cable free play becomes excessive from cable stretch. This delays throttle response and affects low speed operation. On the other hand, insufficient throttle cable free play can lead to an excessively high idle.

Minor adjustments can be made at the throttle grip end of the throttle cables. If proper adjustment cannot be achieved at this location, the cables must be adjusted at the throttle pulley on the throttle body assembly.

1. Shift the transmission into neutral.

2. Start the engine and allow it to idle.

3. With the engine at idle speed, slowly twist the throttle to raise engine speed. Note the amount of rotational movement of the throttle grip required to increase engine idle speed. This is the throttle cable free play.

4. If throttle cable free play is outside the specified range of 2.0-4.0 mm (0.08-0.16 in.), adjust it by performing the following procedure:

   a. Shut off the engine.

   b. Loosen the locknut on the return cable (A, **Figure 26**) and turn the adjuster (B) all the way in.

   c. Loosen the locknut on the pull cable (C, **Figure 26**) and turn the adjuster (D) in either direction until the correct amount of free play

is achieved. Hold the pull cable adjuster, then tighten the locknut securely.

   d. Hold the throttle grip in the fully closed position.

   e. Slowly turn the adjuster on the return cable (B, **Figure 26**) until there is resistance, then stop. Hold the return cable adjuster (B) and tighten the locknut (A).

5. Restart the engine and repeat Steps 2-4 to make sure the adjustment is correct.

6. If throttle cable free play cannot be properly adjusted with the adjusters at the throttle grip end of the cables, loosen the locknuts on both cables and turn the adjuster on each cable all the way in toward the throttle housing. Hold the adjuster and tighten the locknut.

7. Remove the air box as described in Chapter Eight.

8. At the throttle cables on the throttle body assembly, perform the following:

   a. Loosen both throttle cable adjuster locknuts (A, **Figure 27**) on each side of the cable bracket.

   b. Rotate each adjuster (B and C, **Figure 27**) so the locknut and adjuster are against the bracket.

   c. Rotate the pull adjuster (C, **Figure 27**) in either direction until the correct amount of free play is achieved. Hold the pull cable adjuster, then tighten the locknuts securely.

   d. Hold the throttle grip in the fully closed position.

   e. Slowly turn the adjuster on the return cable (B, **Figure 27**) until there is 1.0 mm (0.04 in) slack, then stop. Hold the return cable adjuster (B, **Figure 26**) and tighten the locknuts (A).

9. Recheck the throttle cable free play. If necessary, readjust free play using the adjusters at the throttle grip.

10. If the throttle cable free play cannot be adjusted to specification, the cable(s) is stretched beyond the wear limit and must be replaced. Refer to Chapter Eight for this service procedure.

11. Check the throttle cables from grip to throttle body. Make sure they are not kinked or chafed. Replace as necessary.

12. Install the air box as described in Chapter Eight.

13. Test ride the motorcycle, slowly at first, and make sure the throttle cables are operating correctly. Readjust if necessary.

Throttle Cable Lubrication

1. Remove the throttle cables from the throttle body and throttle as described in Chapter Eight.

2. Clean the throttle assembly and cable ends.

3. Attach a cable lubricator, then lubricate each cable with an aerosol cable lubricant (**Figure 25**). Keep the cable in a vertical position so the lubricant can pass to the opposite end. Move the cable in the housing to help distribute the oil. Stop lubrication when oil appears at the opposite end of the cable.

4. Lubricate the throttle drum, cable ends and housing with lithium grease.

5. Install the cables as described in Chapter Eight.

6. Adjust throttle free play as described in this chapter.

IDLE SPEED ADJUSTMENT

WARNING
With the engine running at idle speed, move the handlebars from side to side. If the idle speed increases during this movement, either the throttle cables require adjusting or they are incorrectly routed through the frame. Correct this problem immediately. Do not ride the motorcycle in this unsafe condition.

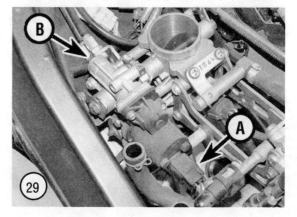

2004-2006 Models

Before adjusting the idle speed, make sure the air filter element is clean.

1. Make sure the throttle cable free play is adjusted correctly. Check and adjust if necessary as described in this chapter.

2. Connect a tachometer following the manufacturer's instructions.

3. Start the engine and let it warm approximately 2-3 minutes.

4. The idle speed knob (**Figure 28**) is located on the left side of the frame. Turn the idle speed knob in or out to adjust the idle speed to 1200-1400 rpm.

5. Open and close the throttle a couple of times. Check for variations in idle speed, and readjust if necessary.

6. Turn off the engine.

7. Disconnect the tachometer.

2007-2011 Models

The idle speed is controlled by the ECM and not adjustable. Refer to Chapter Eight.

FAST IDLE SPEED ADJUSTMENT

2004-2006 Models

The ECM increases the idle speed (fast idle speed) for a specific duration depending on the ambient temperature.

1. Remove the air box as described in Chapter Eight.

2. Check and, if necessary, adjust the throttle position (TP) sensor as described in Chapter Eight.

3. Disconnect the STVA electrical connector (A, **Figure 29**).

4. Connect a voltmeter positive lead to the red TP sensor wire by piercing the wire with a needle probe. Connect the voltmeter negative lead to the black/brown TP sensor wire by piercing the wire with a needle probe.

5. Turn the ignition switch on.

6. Rotate the secondary throttle valve (STV) shaft (B, **Figure 29**) so the valve is in the full open position.

7. Read the voltmeter. If the voltmeter does not indicate 1.21 volts, turn the fast idle speed adjuster on the front edge of the throttle cable pulley below the STV servo until the voltage is within specification.

8. If the specified fast idle cannot be obtained, note the following possible causes:

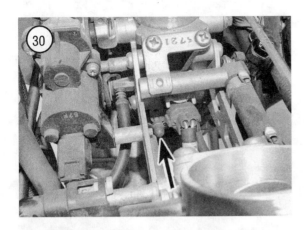

a. Faulty engine coolant (ECT) sensor.
b. Faulty secondary throttle valve actuator (STVA).
c. Faulty wiring or connectors.

2007-2011 Models

The fast idle speed is controlled by the ECM and not adjustable. Refer to Chapter Eight.

THROTTLE BODY SYNCHRONIZATION

To ensure maximum engine performance, the throttle bodies must be synchronized so that each throttle body is opening the same amount throughout the throttle range. Make sure the idle speed and valve clearances are properly adjusted before performing synchronization.

Synchronization tools are available in a number of different styles; some measure engine vacuum with a traditional vacuum gauge or by the movement of mercury within a glass tube, while some perform this function electronically. If this equipment is not available, have a Suzuki dealership or motorcycle specialist perform the operation. Do not attempt to synchronize the throttle bodies without the proper equipment. Doing so will result in misadjustment and poor engine performance.

2004-2006 Models

1. Start the engine and let it run until it reaches normal operating temperature, then shut it off.
2. Remove the fuel tank and air box as described in Chapter Eight.
3. Remove the intake air temperature and intake air pressure sensors from the air box and reconnect them to the wiring harness. Connect the vacuum hose to the IAP sensor. Remove the PAIR control valve from the air filter housing and reconnect the wiring connector and hose.
4. Remove the caps from the vacuum fitting (**Figure 30**).
5. Connect the gauge hoses to the vacuum fittings. Make sure the No. 1 gauge is attached to the No. 1 (front cylinder) throttle body.
6. Start the engine and let it idle, making sure the speed is still correct. If the gauges are fitted with damping adjustment, set this so that the needle flutter is just eliminated but so that they can still respond to small changes in pressure.
7. The vacuum readings for both cylinders should be the same, or at least within 10 mmHg of each other.
8. Turn the synchronizing screw (A, **Figure 31**) on the No. 2 (rear) throttle body to balance the throttle valves. During adjustment of the synchronizing screw, there should be slight clearance between the throttle lever and stopper screw (B, **Figure 31**).

NOTE
Do not press hard on the screw while adjusting it. Otherwise, a false reading will result.

9. After each adjustment, open and close the throttle quickly two or three times to settle the linkage, and recheck the gauge readings, readjusting if necessary. When the adjustment is complete, check and adjust the idle speed.
10. Remove the gauges and install the caps on the vacuum fittings. Reinstall the sensors and PAIR valve to the air box.
11. Install the air box and fuel tank as described in Chapter Eight.

2007-2011 Models

Throttle valve synchronization requires use of the Suzuki Diagnosis System tool (SDS). Contact a dealership for this procedure.

SPARK PLUGS

Inspect and replace the spark plugs at the service intervals in **Table 1**. A single spark plug in the top of the cylinder (A, **Figure 32**) is used on 2004-2006 models. On 2007-2011 models, a second spark plug is located in the side of the cylinder head (B) on each cylinder.

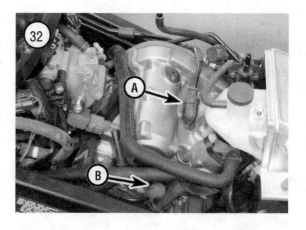

Removal

> *CAUTION*
> *Dirt around the spark plug hole, if allowed to enter the engine, can cause serious engine damage. Clean the area thoroughly. Use compressed air if available.*

> *NOTE*
> *When properly read, a spark plug can indicate the operating condition of its cylinder. As each spark plug is removed, label it according to cylinder and position.*

1. Grasp the spark plug cap, not the wire, and pull the cap off the plug.
2. Install the plug socket onto the spark plug. Make sure it seats correctly, then loosen and remove the spark plug.
3. Repeat for the remaining spark plug(s).
4. Inspect the spark plugs carefully. Look for plugs with broken center porcelain, excessively eroded electrodes and excessive carbon or oil fouling. Replace defective plugs. Refer to *Inspection* in this section.
5. Inspect the spark plug cap and wire. Replace the spark plug wire if the cap or wire is damaged.

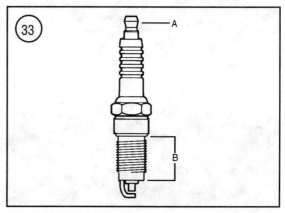

Gap

Carefully adjust the gap of new plugs to ensure a reliable, consistent spark.
1. Remove the new plugs from the box. If installed, unscrew the terminal nut (A, **Figure 33**) from the end of the spark plug. It is not used with this ignition system.
2. Insert a round feeler gauge between the center and the side electrode of the plug (**Figure 34**). When the gap is correct (**Table 3**), a slight drag will be felt as the gauge is pulled through. If there is no drag, or if the gauge will not pass through, bend the side electrode with the gapping tool (**Figure 35**) to set the gap.
3. Repeat for all spark plugs.

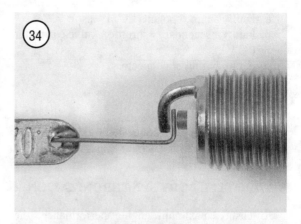

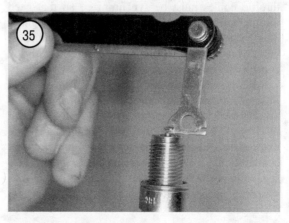

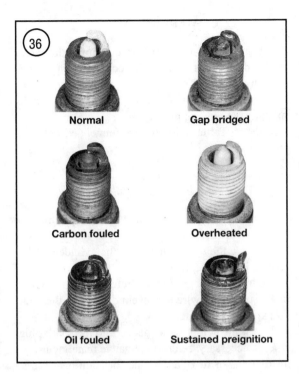

Normal   Gap bridged

Carbon fouled   Overheated

Oil fouled   Sustained preignition

Installation

1. Apply a light coat of antiseize compound onto the threads (B, **Figure 33**) of the spark plug before installing it. Remove any compound that contacts the plug electrodes. Do not use engine oil on the plug threads.

2. Carefully screw the spark plug in by hand until it seats. Very little effort is required. If force is necessary, the plug may be cross-threaded. Unscrew it and try again.

> *CAUTION*
> *Do not overtighten the spark plug. This will damage the gasket and may damage the spark plug threads in the cylinder head.*

3. Tighten the spark plugs to 11 N•m (98 in.-lb.).
4. Connect all spark plug leads and push them down until they are completely seated.

Heat Range

Spark plugs are available in various heat ranges, hotter or colder than the plugs originally installed by the manufacturer. Refer to **Table 3** for recommended spark plugs. Do not change the spark plug heat range to compensate for adverse engine or air/fuel mixture conditions. A plug with an incorrect heat range can foul or overheat and cause engine damage.

To determine if plug heat range is correct, remove each spark plug and examine the insulator. Compare the insulator to those in **Figure 36**. If necessary, select a plug with a heat range designed for the loads and conditions being encountered. In general, use a hot plug for low speeds and low temperatures. Use a cold plug for high speeds, high engine loads and high temperatures. The plug should operate hot enough to bum off unwanted deposits, but not so hot that it causes preignition. When replacing plugs, make sure the reach (B, **Figure 33**) is correct. A longer than standard plug could interfere with the piston, causing engine damage.

Inspection

Inspecting or reading the spark plugs can provide a significant amount of information regarding engine performance. Reading plugs that have been in use will give an indication of spark plug operation, air/fuel mixture composition and engine conditions. Before checking new spark plugs, operate the motorcycle under a medium load for approximately 6 miles (10 km). Avoid prolonged idling before shutting off the engine. Remove the spark plugs as described in this section. Examine each plug and compare it to those in **Figure 36**.

Normal condition

If the plug has a light tan- or gray-colored deposit and no abnormal gap wear or erosion, good engine, fuel system and ignition conditions are indicated. The plug in use is of the proper heat range and may be serviced and returned to use.

Carbon fouled

Soft, dry, sooty deposits covering the entire firing end of the plug are evidence of incomplete combustion. Even though the firing end of the plug is dry, the plug's insulation decreases when in this condition. The carbon forms an electrical path that bypasses the spark plug electrodes, resulting in a misfire condition. One or more of the following can cause carbon fouling:

1. Rich fuel mixture.
2. Cold spark plug heat range.
3. Clogged air filter.
4. Improperly operating ignition component.
5. Ignition component failure.
6. Low engine compression,
7. Prolonged idling.

Oil fouled

The tip of an oil fouled plug has a black insulator tip, a damp oily film over the firing end and a carbon layer over the entire nose. The electrodes are not worn. Oil fouled spark plugs may be cleaned in an emergency, but it is better to replace them. It is important to correct the cause of the fouling before the engine is returned to service. Common causes for this condition are:

1. Engine still being broken in.
2. Valve guides worn.
3. Piston rings worn or broken.

Gap bridging

Plugs with this condition exhibit gaps shorted out by combustion deposits between the electrodes. If this condition is encountered, check for excessive carbon or oil in the combustion chamber. Be sure to locate and correct the cause of this condition.

Overheating

Badly worn electrodes and premature gap wear are signs of overheating, along with a gray or white blistered porcelain insulator surface. The most common cause for this condition is using a spark plug of the wrong heat range (too hot). If the spark plug is the correct heat range and is overheating, consider the following causes:

1. Lean air/fuel mixture.
2. Improperly operating ignition component.
3. Engine lubrication system malfunction.
4. Engine air leak.
5. Improper spark plug installation.
6. No spark plug gasket.

Worn out

Corrosive gasses formed by combustion and high voltage sparks have eroded the electrodes. A spark plug in this condition requires more voltage to fire under hard acceleration. Replace with a new spark plug.

Preignition

If the electrodes are melted, preignition is almost certainly the cause. Check for intake air leaks at the manifolds and carburetors, or throttle bodies, and advanced ignition timing. It is also possible the plug is the wrong heat range (too hot). Find the cause of the preignition before returning the engine into service.

COMPRESSION TEST

A compression test can help determine the internal condition of the engine. Check the compression of each cylinder at each tune up, record the readings and compare them with subsequent reading to help spot any developing problems.

Refer to **Table 3** for the recommended cylinder compression.

NOTE
Make sure the battery is fully charged.

1. Warm the engine to normal operating temperature. Turn off the engine.
2. Remove the spark plug from the cylinder as described in this chapter.
3. Connect a grounding tool (refer to Chapter One) to the spark plug wire to prevent damage to the ignition system components.
4. Install the compression gauge into the spark plug hole. If necessary, refer to the gauge manufacturer's instructions or to Chapter One for additional information.

CAUTION
Do not operate the starter more than necessary.

5. Open the throttle completely and turn the engine over until there is no further rise in pressure. The cylinder should develop maximum pressure within 4-7 seconds. Record the reading. The recommended cylinder compression and the maximum allowable difference between cylinders is listed in **Table 4**.
6. Remove the compression gauge from the cylinder.
7. Repeat Steps 2-6 for the remaining cylinder and record the readings.
8. If a lower than specified reading is obtained, consider the following:
   a. Worn or damaged piston rings.
   b. Worn or damaged cylinder.
   c. Cylinder head gasket leak.
   d. Incorrect head gasket.
   e. Loose cylinder head bolts.
   f. Worn or damaged valve or valve seat.
   g. Worn valve guide.
8. A higher than specified reading may be caused by:
   a. Carbon buildup on piston and cylinder head.
   b. Incorrect head gasket.
9. To determine whether piston rings or valves are causing low compression, pour about a teaspoon of engine oil into the spark plug hole and repeat the procedure.

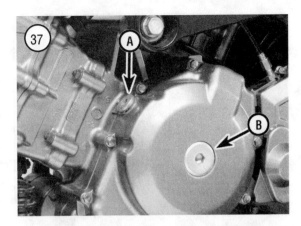

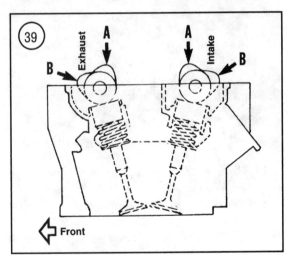

a. If the compression increases significantly, check for worn piston rings.

b. If the compression does not increase, the valves or head gasket is leaking.

10. Install the spark plug.

IGNITION TIMING INSPECTION

No procedure is available for checking the ignition timing.

VALVE CLEARANCE

The exhaust valves are located at the front of the cylinder head on the front cylinder and at the rear of the cylinder head on the rear cylinder. The intake valves are located on the opposite side of the cylinder head from the exhaust valves.

The cylinders are numbered from front to rear. The front cylinder is No. 1; the rear cylinder is No. 2. The left and right sides refer to the position of the parts as viewed by the rider sitting on the seat facing forward.

Measurement

The engine must be cold (below 35° C/95° F) to obtain accurate results.

1. Remove the cylinder head covers as described in Chapter Four.

2. Remove both spark plugs as described in this chapter. This makes it easier to turn the engine by hand.

3. Remove the timing plug (A, **Figure 37**).

4. Remove the flywheel bolt access cover (B, **Figure 37**).

5. Insert a suitably sized socket through the side cover to engage the flywheel bolt (**Figure 38**).

> *NOTE*
> *The flywheel has lines marked F or R to indicate top dead center for the front cylinder (F) or rear cylinder (R).*

> *NOTE*
> *The camshaft lobes must point away from the tappet as shown in either position A or B, **Figure 39**. Clearance dimensions taken with the camshaft in any other position give a false reading leading to incorrect valve clearance adjustment and possible engine damage.*

6A. On the front cylinder, rotate the engine counterclockwise, as viewed from the left side of the motorcycle. Rotate the flywheel until the F line aligns with the mark on the timing inspection hole as shown in **Figure 40**. The camshaft lobes must be in the position A shown in **Figure 39**. If the camshaft lobes are not as shown, rotate the crankshaft one complete turn, being sure to realign the F mark.

6B. On the rear cylinder, rotate the engine counterclockwise, as viewed from the left side of the motorcycle. Rotate the flywheel until the R line aligns with the mark on the timing inspection hole. The camshaft lobes must be in the position B shown in **Figure 39**.

If the camshaft lobes are not as shown, rotate the crankshaft one complete turn, being sure to realign the R mark.

7. With the engine in this position, check the valve clearance on the valves.

NOTE
When checking the clearance, start with a feeler gauge of the specified clearance thickness. If this thickness is too large or small, change the gauge thickness until there is a drag on the feeler gauge when it is inserted and withdrawn.

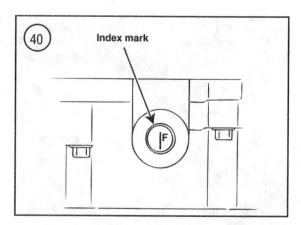

8. Check the clearance by inserting the feeler gauge between the tappet and the camshaft lobe (**Figure 41**). When the clearance is correct, there will be a slight resistance on the feeler gauge when it is inserted and withdrawn. Record the clearance dimension. Identify the clearance by cylinder number and by intake or exhaust valve. The clearance dimension is needed if adjustment is necessary.

9. Measure the clearance of all the valves on the cylinder head before beginning the valve adjustment procedure. Refer to **Table 3** for valve clearance specifications.

10. If the valves require adjustment, follow the adjustment procedure described below.

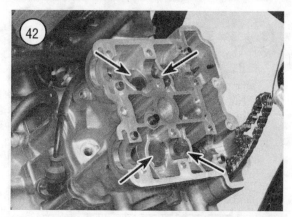

Valve Clearance Adjustment

To adjust the valve clearance, replace the shim located under the tappet with a shim of a different thickness. The camshaft(s) must be removed to gain access to the shims. The shims are available from Suzuki dealerships in thickness increments of 0.05 mm that range from 1.20 to 2.20 mm in thickness.

NOTE
Measure the thickness of the shims that are removed from the engine to confirm their dimensions. If the shim is worn to less than its indicated size, the valve clearance calculations will be inaccurate. Also measure replacement shims to make sure they are correctly marked.

1. Remove the camshaft(s) as described in Chapter Four.

2. To avoid confusion adjust one valve at a time.

3. Remove the tappet(s) (**Figure 42**) for the valve requiring adjustment.

4. Use needlenose pliers or tweezers to remove the shim(s) (**Figure 43**) from the top of the valve spring retainer.

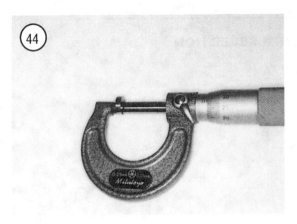

5. Check the number on the bottom of the shim. If the number is no longer legible, measure the shim with a micrometer (**Figure 44**).

6. Use the number on the installed shim and the measured valve clearance to select the new shim by performing the following:

   a. Refer to the appropriate chart (**Figure 45** or **Figure 46**) for the valve being serviced.

   b. The correct number for a new shim is listed at the intersection of the *Installed Shim No.* column and the *Measured Valve Clearance* row in each chart.

   c. For example, if the measured clearance for an intake valve is 0.23 mm and the installed shim number is 170 (1.70 mm), locate the 170 column and the 0.21-0.25 mm row on the intake valve chart (**Figure 45**). The new shim number is indicated where there row and column intersect. In this example, install a new No. 180 shim (1.80 mm).

   d. Replacing a 170 shim with a 180 shim increases shim thickness by 0.10 mm. This decreases the clearance from 0.23 mm to 0.13 mm, which is within specification.

7. Apply clean engine oil to both sides of the new shim and to the receptacle on top of the valve spring retainer. Position the shim so the side with the printed number faces down, and install the shim(s) (**Figure 43**) into the recess in the valve spring retainer.

8. Install the tappet(s) (**Figure 42**) into the cylinder head receptacle.

9. Repeat this procedure for all valve assemblies that are out of specification.

10. Install the camshaft(s) as described in Chapter Four.

11. Rotate the engine several complete revolutions counterclockwise, as viewed from the left side of the motorcycle (**Figure 38**). This seats the new shims and squeezes any excess oil from between the shim, the spring retainer and the tappet.

12. Recheck all valve clearances as described in the preceding procedure. If there is any clearance outside the specified range, repeat this procedure until all clearances are correct.

13. Install the cylinder head cover as described in Chapter Four.

CRANKCASE BREATHER

1. Raise and support the fuel tank as described in Chapter Eight.

2. Inspect the breather hoses (**Figure 47**). If either hose is cracked or deteriorated, replace it. Make sure the hose clamps are in place and are tight.

3. Lower the fuel tank.

EVAPORATIVE EMISSION CONTROL SYSTEM (CALIFORNIA MODELS)

The evaporative emissions control system captures fuel vapors and stores them so they will not be released into the atmosphere. The fuel vapors are routed to the charcoal canister (**Figure 48**), located on the right side of the rear sub-frame. When the engine is started, these stored vapors are drawn from the canister, through the purge control valves and into the throttle bodies. Make sure all evaporative emission control hoses are correctly routed and properly attached. Inspect the hoses and

replace any if necessary as described in Chapter Eight.

PAIR (AIR SUPPLY) SYSTEM EMISSION CONTROL SYSTEM

The PAIR system introduces fresh air into the exhaust ports to reduce the exhaust emission level.

Refer to *PAIR (Air Supply) System Emission Control System* in Chapter Eight for complete inspection and service procedures.

EXHAUST SYSTEM

1. Inspect the exhaust system for cracks or dents which could alter performance.

2. Check all exhaust system fasteners and mounting points for loose or damaged parts.

3. Make sure all mounting bolts and nuts are tight. If loose, refer to Chapter Four for torque specifications.

(45)

INTAKE VALVE SHIM SELECTION

VALVE CLEARANCE SPECIFICATION*

*Valve clearance specification (cold): 0.10-0.20 mm (0.004-0.008 in.)

Measured valve clearance (mm) \ Installed shim No.	120	125	130	135	140	145	150	155	160	165	170	175	180	185	190	195	200	205	210	215	220
Shim size (mm)	1.20	1.25	1.30	1.35	1.40	1.45	1.50	1.55	1.60	1.65	1.70	1.75	1.80	1.85	1.90	1.95	2.00	2.05	2.10	2.15	2.20
0.00-0.04			1.20	1.25	1.30	1.35	1.40	1.45	1.50	1.55	1.60	1.65	1.70	1.75	1.80	1.85	1.90	1.95	2.00	2.05	2.10
0.05-0.09		1.20	1.25	1.30	1.35	1.40	1.45	1.50	1.55	1.60	1.65	1.70	1.75	1.80	1.85	1.90	1.95	2.00	2.05	2.10	2.15
0.10-0.20																					
0.21-0.25	1.30	1.35	1.40	1.45	1.50	1.55	1.60	1.65	1.70	1.75	1.80	1.85	1.90	1.95	2.00	2.05	2.10	2.15	2.20		
0.26-0.30	1.35	1.40	1.45	1.50	1.55	1.60	1.65	1.70	1.75	1.80	1.85	1.90	1.95	2.00	2.05	2.10	2.15	2.20			
0.31-0.35	1.40	1.45	1.50	1.55	1.60	1.65	1.70	1.75	1.80	1.85	1.90	1.95	2.00	2.05	2.10	2.15	2.20				
0.36-0.40	1.45	1.50	1.55	1.60	1.65	1.70	1.75	1.80	1.85	1.90	1.95	2.00	2.05	2.10	2.15	2.20					
0.41-0.45	1.50	1.55	1.60	1.65	1.70	1.75	1.80	1.85	1.90	1.95	2.00	2.05	2.10	2.15	2.20						
0.46-0.50	1.55	1.60	1.65	1.70	1.75	1.80	1.85	1.90	1.95	2.00	2.05	2.10	2.15	2.20							
0.51-0.55	1.60	1.65	1.70	1.75	1.80	1.85	1.90	1.95	2.00	2.05	2.10	2.15	2.20								
0.56-0.60	1.65	1.70	1.75	1.80	1.85	1.90	1.95	2.00	2.05	2.10	2.15	2.20									
0.61-0.65	1.70	1.75	1.80	1.85	1.90	1.95	2.00	2.05	2.10	2.15	2.20										
0.66-0.70	1.75	1.80	1.85	1.90	1.95	2.00	2.05	2.10	2.15	2.20											
0.71-0.75	1.80	1.85	1.90	1.95	2.00	2.05	2.10	2.15	2.20												
0.76-0.80	1.85	1.90	1.95	2.00	2.05	2.10	2.15	2.20													
0.81-0.85	1.90	1.95	2.00	2.05	2.10	2.15	2.20														
0.86-0.90	1.95	2.00	2.05	2.10	2.15	2.20															
0.91-0.95	2.00	2.05	2.10	2.15	2.20																
0.96-1.00	2.05	2.10	2.15	2.20																	
1.01-1.05	2.10	2.15	2.20																		
1.06-1.10	2.15	2.20																			
1.11-1.15	2.20																				

46

EXHAUST VALVE SHIM SELECTION

VALVE CLEARANCE SPECIFICATION*

*Valve clearance specification (cold): 0.20-0.30 mm (0.008-0.012 in.)

Measured valve clearance (mm) \ Installed shim No. (Shim size mm)	120	125	130	135	140	145	150	155	160	165	170	175	180	185	190	195	200	205	210	215	220
0.05-0.09	1.20	1.25	1.30	1.35	1.40	1.45	1.50	1.55	1.60	1.65	1.70	1.75	1.80	1.85	1.90	1.95	2.00	2.05	2.10	2.15	2.20
0.10-0.14		1.20	1.25	1.30	1.35	1.40	1.45	1.50	1.55	1.60	1.65	1.70	1.75	1.80	1.85	1.90	1.95	2.00	2.05	2.10	2.15
0.15-0.19			1.20	1.25	1.30	1.35	1.40	1.45	1.50	1.55	1.60	1.65	1.70	1.75	1.80	1.85	1.90	1.95	2.00	2.05	2.10
0.20-0.30																					
0.31-0.35	1.30	1.35	1.40	1.45	1.50	1.55	1.60	1.65	1.70	1.75	1.80	1.85	1.90	1.95	2.00	2.05	2.10	2.15	2.20		
0.36-0.40	1.35	1.40	1.45	1.50	1.55	1.60	1.65	1.70	1.75	1.80	1.85	1.90	1.95	2.00	2.05	2.10	2.15	2.20			
0.41-0.45	1.40	1.45	1.50	1.55	1.60	1.65	1.70	1.75	1.80	1.85	1.90	1.95	2.00	2.05	2.10	2.15	2.20				
0.46-0.50	1.45	1.50	1.55	1.60	1.65	1.70	1.75	1.80	1.85	1.90	1.95	2.00	2.05	2.10	2.15	2.20					
0.51-0.55	1.50	1.55	1.60	1.65	1.70	1.75	1.80	1.85	1.90	1.95	2.00	2.05	2.10	2.15	2.20						
0.56-0.60	1.55	1.60	1.65	1.70	1.75	1.80	1.85	1.90	1.95	2.00	2.05	2.10	2.15	2.20							
0.61-0.65	1.60	1.65	1.70	1.75	1.80	1.85	1.90	1.95	2.00	2.05	2.10	2.15	2.20								
0.66-0.70	1.65	1.70	1.75	1.80	1.85	1.90	1.95	2.00	2.05	2.10	2.15	2.20									
0.71-0.75	1.70	1.75	1.80	1.85	1.90	1.95	2.00	2.05	2.10	2.15	2.20										
0.76-0.80	1.75	1.80	1.85	1.90	1.95	2.00	2.05	2.10	2.15	2.20											
0.81-0.85	1.80	1.85	1.90	1.95	2.00	2.05	2.10	2.15	2.20												
0.86-0.90	1.85	1.90	1.95	2.00	2.05	2.10	2.15	2.20													
0.91-0.95	1.90	1.95	2.00	2.05	2.10	2.15	2.20														
0.96-1.00	1.95	2.00	2.05	2.10	2.15	2.20															
1.01-1.05	2.00	2.05	2.10	2.15	2.20																
1.06-1.10	2.05	2.10	2.15	2.20																	
1.11-1.15	2.10	2.15	2.20																		
1.16-1.20	2.15	2.20																			
1.21-1.25	2.20																					

DRIVE CHAIN

The motorcycle is equipped with an O-ring chain that requires routine cleaning and lubrication. If the chain has been replaced with a standard chain, it too requires regular cleaning, lubrication and adjustment for long life. Although O-ring chains are internally lubricated and sealed, the O-rings must be kept clean and lubricated to prevent them from drying out and disintegrating.

Never clean chains with high-pressure water sprays or strong solvents. This is particularly true for O-ring chains. If water is forced past the O-rings, water will be trapped inside the links. Strong solvents can soften the O-rings so they tear or damage easily.

Although chains are often lubricated while they are installed on the motorcycle, the chain should periodically be removed from the motorcycle and thoroughly cleaned. The following procedure describes the preferred method for cleaning and lubricating the chain.

1. Refer to *Drive Chain Removal and Installation* in Chapter Eleven to remove the chain.
2. Immerse the chain in kerosene and work the links so dirt is loosened.

> **CAUTION**
> *Brushes with coarse or wire bristles can damage O-rings.*

3. Lightly scrub the chain with a soft-bristle brush.
4. Rinse the chain with clean kerosene and wipe dry.

> **CAUTION**
> *Because the links of an O-ring chain are permanently lubricated and sealed, O-ring chain lubricant is formulated to prevent exterior corrosion of the chain and to condition the O-rings. It is not tacky and resists the adhesion of dirt. Avoid lubricants that are tacky or designed for conventional chains. These lubricants attract dirt and subject the O-rings to unnecessary abrasion.*

5. Lubricate the chain with chain lubricant. Lubricate an O-ring chain with lubricant specifically for O-ring chains.

> **NOTE**
> *While the chain is removed, check that it is still within the wear limit as described in **Drive Chain and Sprockets Inspection** in this section.*

6. Install the chain as described in Chapter Eleven.
7. Adjust the chain as described in this section

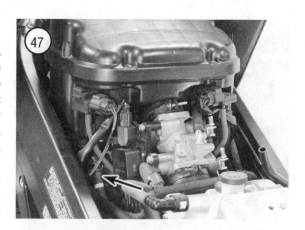

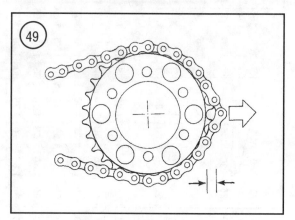

Drive Chain and Sprockets Inspection

A worn drive chain and sprockets is both unreliable and potentially dangerous. Inspect the chain and rear sprocket for wear and replace if necessary. If there is wear, replace both sprockets and the chain. Mixing old and new parts will prematurely wear the new parts.

Determine if the chain should be measured for wear by pulling one chain link away from the rear sprocket. Generally, if more than half the height of the sprocket tooth is visible (**Figure 49**), accurately measure the chain for wear. Refer to the following

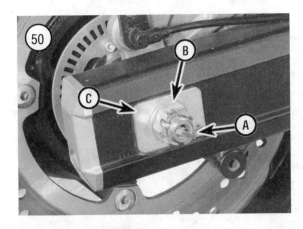

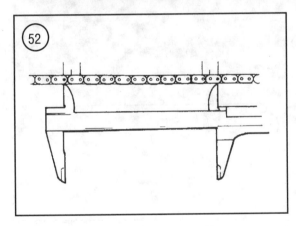

procedure to measure chain wear and inspect the sprockets.

1. Remove the cotter pin (A, **Figure 50**).

2. Loosen the rear axle nut (B, **Figure 50**).

3. On each side, tighten the chain adjuster (**Figure 51**) to move the wheel rearward until the chain is tight with no slack.

4. Place a vernier caliper along the chain run and measure the distance between 21 pins (20 links) in the chain as shown in **Figure 52**. If the 21-pin length exceeds 319.4 mm (12.6 in.), install a new drive chain as described in Chapter Eleven.

5. Inspect the inner plate chain faces (**Figure 53**). They should be lightly polished on both sides. If they show considerable uneven wear on one side, the engine and rear sprockets are not aligned properly. Excessive wear requires replacement of not only the drive chain but also the engine and rear sprockets.

NOTE
The engine sprocket cover must be partially removed to visually inspect the drive sprocket.

6. To inspect the engine sprocket, remove the engine sprocket cover (**Figure 54**).

7. If the drive chain is excessively worn, inspect both the engine and rear sprockets for the following defects:

　　a. Undercutting or sharp teeth (**Figure 55**).

　　b. Broken teeth.

8. If wear is evident, replace the drive chain, the engine sprocket and the rear sprocket as a complete set. If only the drive chain is replaced, the worn sprockets will quickly wear out the new chain.

9. Adjust the drive chain as described in this chapter.

10. Install the engine sprocket cover.

Drive Chain Free play Adjustment

The drive chain must have adequate play so the chain is not strung tight when the swing arm is horizontal. On the other hand, too much slack may cause the chain to jump off the sprockets with potentially dangerous results.

Check and adjust the drive chain at the interval listed in **Table 1**. A properly lubricated and adjusted drive chain provides maximum service life and reliability.

When adjusting the chain, check the free play at several places along its length by rotating the rear wheel. The chain rarely wears uniformly and as a result will be tighter at some places than at others. Measure the chain free play when the chain's tightest point is halfway between the sprockets.

1. Roll the motorcycle back and forth and check the chain for tightness at several points on the chain. Identify the tightest point, and mark this spot with a piece of chalk.

2. Turn the wheel until this mark is on the lower chain run, midway between the engine and drive sprockets.

3. Place the motorcycle on the sidestand on level ground.

4. Grasp the chain at the center of the chain run, and move the chain up and down. Measure the distance the chain moves vertically (**Figure 56**). Drive chain

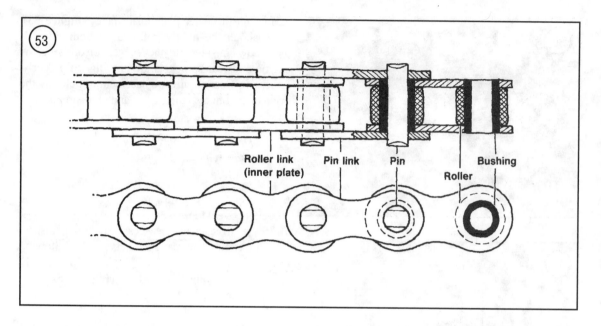

free play should be 20-30 mm (0.8-1.2 in.). If necessary, adjust the free play by performing the following.

NOTE
When adjusting the drive chain free
play, make sure to maintain rear wheel
alignment. A misaligned rear wheel
can cause poor handling. All models
are equipped with alignment marks on
the swing arm.

5. On U.S.A., California and Canada models, remove the rear axle nut cotter pin (A, **Figure 50**).
6. Loosen the rear axle nut (B, **Figure 50**).
7. On each side, loosen the chain adjuster (**Figure
51**).
8. Tighten or loosen the adjuster on each side an
equal amount until the chain free play is within the
specified range. Make sure the edge of each adjuster
plate (C, **Figure 50**) aligns with the same mark on
each side of the swing arm.
9. When drive chain free play is correct, check the
wheel alignment by sighting along the top of the
drive chain from the rear sprocket. The chain should
form a straight line as it leaves the rear sprocket and
travels to the front sprocket (A, **Figure 57**). If the
chain veers to one side or the other (B and C, **Figure
57**), perform the following:
   a. Check that the adjuster plates are set to the
      same positions on the swing arm.
   b. If not, readjust the drive chain so the adjuster
      plates are at the same position on both sides
      and the free play is within specification.
10. Tighten the rear axle nut to 100 N•m (74 ft.-lb.).
11. On U.S.A., California and Canada models, install the rear axle nut cotter pin (A, **Figure 50**).

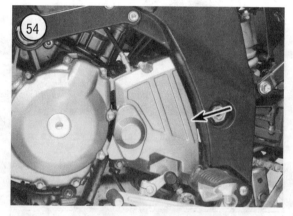

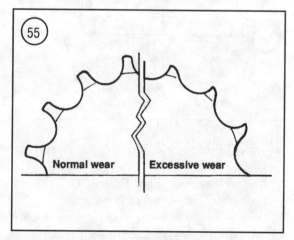

12. If the drive chain cannot be adjusted to the correct measurement, the drive chain is excessively
worn and must be replaced as described in Chapter
Eleven. Replace both the engine and rear sprockets
when replacing the drive chain. Never install a new
drive chain over worn sprockets.

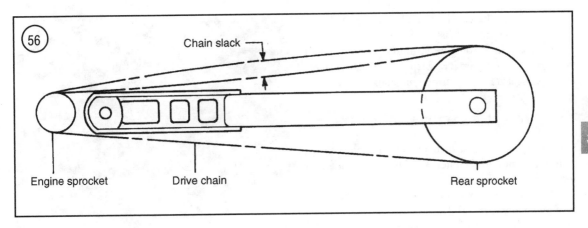

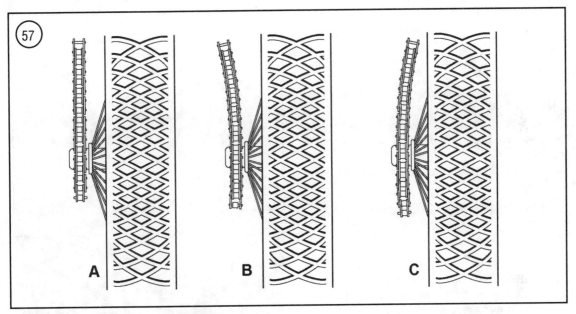

3

Drive Chain Slider Inspection

Inspect the drive chain slider (**Figure 58**) on the left side of the swing arm for wear. Replace the slider if it is excessively worn.

Routine inspection and replacement of the drive chain slider prevents the drive chain from damaging the swing arm. A chain that is too loose causes rapid wear to the slider. To replace the drive chain slider, remove the swing arm as described in Chapter Thirteen and remove the slider. Whenever the swing arm is removed for slider replacement, inspect and lubricate the swing arm bearings.

STEERING HEAD BEARING INSPECTION

Inspect the steering head bearing adjustment at the intervals specified in **Table 1**.

1. Support the motorcycle on a stand with the front wheel off the ground.

2. Hold onto the handlebars and move them from side to side. Note any binding or roughness.

3. Support the motorcycle so that both wheels are on the ground.

4. Sit on the motorcycle and hold onto the handlebars. Apply the front brake lever and try to push the front fork forward. Try to detect any movement in

the steering head area. If so, the bearing adjustment is loose and requires adjustment.

5. If there is any roughness, binding or looseness when performing Step 2 or Step 4, service the steering head bearings as described in Chapter Twelve.

FRONT SUSPENSION INSPECTION

Inspect the front suspension at the intervals in **Table 1**. Refer to Chapter Twelve for service and torque specifications.

1. Use a soft, wet cloth to wipe the front fork tubes to remove any dirt and debris. As this debris passes against the fork seals, it will eventually damage the seals and cause an oil leak.

2. Check the front fork for any oil seal leaks or damage.

3. Make sure the upper and lower fork tube pinch bolts are tight.

4. Check that the handlebar mounting bolts are tight.

5. Apply the front brake and pump the fork up and down as vigorously as possible. Check for smooth operation.

6. Make sure the front axle is tight (**Table 4**).

FORK SPRING PRELOAD ADJUSTMENT

WARNING
Each fork leg must be set to the same setting. If the fork legs are set differently, it will adversely affect the handling. Make sure the settings are identical on both fork leg assemblies.

Adjust the spring preload by turning the spring adjuster (**Figure 59**) on the top of each fork tube. Turn the spring adjuster clockwise to increase preload. Turn the adjuster counterclockwise to decrease preload.

The adjuster is marked with four equally spaced grooves as shown in **Figure 60**. Use the grooves to ensure that the spring preload is set to the same level on each fork leg. At position 0 the top of the adjuster is flush with the top of the fork cap. Position 0 provides the maximum spring preload; position 5 provides the minimum. The standard setting is position 3.

FRONT FORK OIL CHANGE

Suzuki does not specify an interval for changing the oil in the front fork. Changing the fork oil may be advisable if motorcycle operation is severe. Refer to Chapter Twelve for the oil changing procedure.

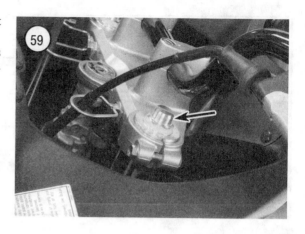

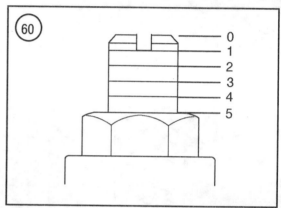

REAR SUSPENSION INSPECTION

1. Support the motorcycle' so the rear wheel is off the ground.

2. Push hard on the rear wheel (sideways) to check for side play in the rear swing arm bearings.

3. Refer to Chapter Thirteen and make sure the swing arm pivot bolt is tight. A special tool is required to tighten the locknut.

4. Remove the side covers as described in Chapter Fifteen.

5. Make sure the shock absorber upper (**Figure 61**) and lower (A, **Figure 62**) fasteners are tight.

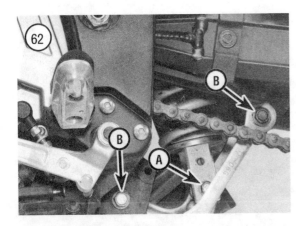

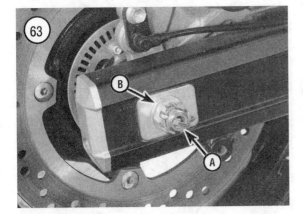

6. Make sure the shock absorber lever assembly fasteners are tight (B, **Figure 62**).

7B. Make sure the rear axle nut is tight (**Table 4**).

7A. On U.S.A., California and Canada models, make sure the rear axle nut cotter pin (A, **Figure 63**) is in place and that the nut (B) is tight (**Table 4**).

> *CAUTION*
> *If any of the previously mentioned bolts and nuts are loose, refer to Chapter Thirteen for correct procedures and torque specifications.*

REAR SUSPENSION ADJUSTMENT

Rear Shock Absorber Spring Preload Adjustment

Adjust the spring preload by turning the spring adjuster knob (**Figure 64**). Turn the spring adjuster clockwise to increase preload. Turn the adjuster counterclockwise to decrease preload.

The shock absorber spring retainer is marked with five equally spaced grooves as shown in **Figure 65**. At position 0 the top of the spring cover contacts the spring retainer flange. Position 0 provides the minimum spring preload: position 5 provides the maximum. The standard setting is position 2.

Rear Shock Absorber Rebound Damping Adjustment

Rebound damping affects the rate at which the shock absorber returns to its extended position after compression. Rebound damping does not affect the action of the shock on compression.

1. To adjust the rebound damping to the standard setting, perform the following:
   a. Turn the rebound adjuster (**Figure 66**) clockwise until it stops. This is the hardest setting.

b. Turn the adjuster counterclockwise the number of clicks indicated in **Table 3**. The rebound damper is set to the standard setting for an average size rider.

2. To fine tune the rebound damping, set the damping to the standard setting and then perform the following:

NOTE
When fine tuning the suspension, do so gradually. Turn the rebound damping adjuster in 1/8 turn increments and then test ride the motorcycle.

a. To reduce the rebound damping, turn the adjuster counterclockwise toward the S (soft) marked on the shock housing.

b. To increase the rebound damping, turn the adjuster clockwise toward the H (hard) marked on the shock housing.

TIRES AND WHEELS

Tire Pressure

Check and adjust tire pressure (**Table 3**) to maintain good traction and handling and to prevent rim damage.

NOTE
*After checking and adjusting the tire pressure, be sure to install the air valve cap (A, **Figure 67**). The cap prevents debris from collecting in the valve stem. This could allow air leakage or result in incorrect tire pressure readings.*

Tire Inspection

Inspect the tires for excessive wear, cuts, abrasions, etc. If an object has punctured the tire, mark its location with a light crayon before removing it. This will help locate the hole for repairs. Refer to the tire changing procedure in Chapter Eleven.

Measure the tread depth at the center of the tire (**Figure 68**) using a tread depth gauge or small ruler. Replace the original equipment tires when the tread has worn to the dimensions specified in **Table 2**.

Wheel Inspection

Frequently inspect the wheel rims (B, **Figure 67**) for cracks, warp or dents. A damaged rim may leak or affect wheel balance. If the rim portion of an alloy wheel is damaged, replace the wheel.

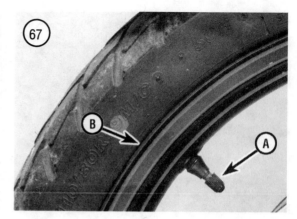

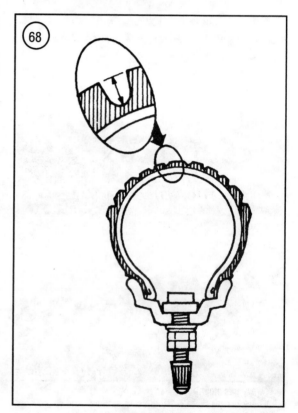

If the wheel appears to wobble, check wheel runout as described in Chapter Eleven.

LIGHTS AND HORN INSPECTION

Periodically check the headlight aim, the brake and turn signal lights, and horn operation. Refer to Chapter Nine for adjustment and repair procedures.

With the engine running, check as follows:

1. Pull the front brake lever and make sure the brake light comes on.

2. Push the rear brake pedal and make sure the brake light comes on.

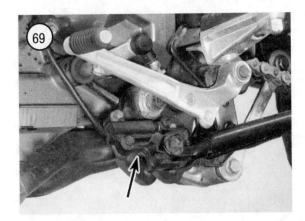

3. Move the dimmer switch up and down between the high and low positions, and make sure both headlights are working.

4. Move the turn signal switch to the left position and then to the right position and make sure the turn signal lights are working.

5. Operate the horn button and make sure the horn sounds.

SIDESTAND SWITCH AND IGNITION CUT-OFF SYSTEM

Periodically check the sidestand switch (**Figure 69**) and the ignition cut-off system operation.

1. Sit on the motorcycle so it is vertical and the sidestand is unloaded.

2. Operate the sidestand and check its movement and spring tension. Replace the spring if it is weak or damaged.

3. Lubricate the sidestand pivot bolt if necessary.

4. Check the sidestand ignition cut-off system as follows:

   a. Park the motorcycle so both wheels are on the ground.

   b. Sit on the motorcycle and raise the sidestand.

   c. Shift the transmission into neutral.

   d. Start the engine, then squeeze the clutch lever and shift the transmission into gear.

   e. Move the sidestand down. When doing so, the engine should stop.

   f. If the engine did not stop as the sidestand was lowered, test the sidestand switch as described in Chapter Nine.

FASTENERS

1. Vibration can loosen many fasteners on a motorcycle. Check the tightness of all exposed fasteners. Refer to the appropriate chapter for torque specifications.

2. Make sure all hose clamps, cable stays and safety clips are properly installed. Replace missing or damaged items.

Table 1 MAINTENANCE SCHEDULE

Weekly/gas stop
  Check tire pressure cold; adjust to suit load and speed
  Check condition of tires
  Check brake operation
  Check throttle grip for smooth operation and return
  Check for smooth but not loose steering
  Check axle, suspension, controls and linkage fasteners; tighten if necessary
  Check engine oil level; add oil if necessary
  Check lights and horn operation, especially brake light
  Check for any abnormal engine noise and leaks
  Check coolant level
  Check stop switch operation
Initial 600 miles (1000 km) or 1 month
  Change engine oil and replace oil filter
  Check idle speed; adjust if necessary
  Check throttle cable free play; adjust if necessary
  Clean and lubricate drive chain
  Check brake pads for wear and rear pedal height
  Check brake discs thickness; replace if necessary
  Check brake discs for rust and corrosion; clean if necessary

(continued)

Table 1 MAINTENANCE SCHEDULE (continued)

Initial 600 miles (1000 km) or 1 month (continued)
  Check steering play; adjust if necessary
  Check and tighten exhaust system fasteners
  Check tightness of all chassis fasteners; tighten if necessary
  On California models, synchronize the carburetors
Every 4000 miles (6000 km) or 6 months
  Check air filter element for contamination; clean or replace if necessary
  Check spark plugs; replace if necessary
  Check all fuel system hoses for leakage; repair or replace if necessary
  Change engine oil
  Check idle speed; adjust if necessary
  Check throttle cable free play; adjust if necessary
  Check clutch lever free play; adjust if necessary
  Check radiator and all coolant hoses for leakage
  Check battery charge and condition
  Clean and lubricate drive chain
  Check drive chain and sprockets for wear or damage
  Check drive chain free play; adjust if necessary
  Check brake pads for wear
  Check brake discs thickness; replace if necessary
  Check brake discs for rust and corrosion; clean if necessary
  Check brake system for leakage; repair if necessary
  Check brake fluid level in both reservoirs; add fluid if necessary
  Check tire and wheel rim condition
  Lubricate all pivot points
  Check tightness of all chassis fasteners; tighten if necessary
Every 7500 miles (12,000 km) or 12 months
  All items listed in 4000 miles (6000 km) or 6 months and the following:
  Replace the spark plugs
Every 7500 miles (12,000 km) or 12 months (continued)
  Check front fork operation and for leakage
  Check EVAP hoses (California models)
  Check PAIR (air supply) hoses (California models)
  Lubricate control cables
Every 11,000 miles (18,000 km) or 18 months
  All items listed in 7500 miles (12,000 km) or 12 months and the following:
  Replace air filter element
  Replace oil filter
Every 15,000 miles (24,000 km) or 24 months
  All items listed in 7500 miles (12,000 km) or 12 months and the following:
  Check valve clearance; adjust if necessary
Every 2 years
  Replace coolant
  Replace brake fluid
Every 4 years
  Replace all brake hoses
  Replace EVAP hoses (California models)

Table 2 RECOMMENDED LUBRICANTS AND FLUIDS

Brake fluid	DOT 4
Engine coolant	
Type	Antifreeze coolant that is compatible with an aluminum radiator.
Ratio	50:50 with distilled water
Capacity	1900 ml (2.0 U.S. qt.)
Engine oil	
Grade	API SF or SG
Viscosity	SAE 10W40
Capacity	
Oil change only	2.3 L (2.4 US qt.)
Oil and filter change	2.7 L (2.9 US qt.)
When engine completely dry	3.1 L (3.3 US qt.)

(continued)

Table 2 RECOMMENDED LUBRICANTS AND FLUIDS

Fork oil	
Viscosity	SS8 fork oil
Capacity per leg	524 ml (17.7 U.S. oz.)
Fuel	
Type	Unleaded
Octane	
U.S.A., California, and Canada models	87 [(R + M)/2 method] or research octane of 91 or higher
Non- U.S.A., California, and Canada models	91
Fuel tank capacity, including reserve	22.0 L (5.8 U.S. gal.)

Table 3 MAINTENANCE AND TUNE-UP SPECIFICATIONS

Battery	
Type	YTX12-BS Maintenance free (sealed)
Capacity	12 volt 10 amp hour
Brake pedal height	20-30 mm (0.79-1.18 in.)
Clutch lever free play	10-15 mm (0.4-0.6 in.)
Compression pressure (at sea level)	
Standard	1,300-1,700 kPa (185-242 psi)
Service limit	1,100 kPa (156 psi)
Maximum difference between cylinders	200 kPa (28 psi)
Drive chain 21-pin length	319.4 mm (12.6 in.)
Drive chain free play	20-30 mm (0.8-1.2 in.)
Engine oil pressure (hot)	100-400 kPa (14-57 psi) at 3,000 rpm
Fork spring preload adjuster*	3rd groove from top
Idle speed	1,200-1,400 rpm
Ignition timing	4 B.T.D.C. at 1,300 rpm
Radiator cap release pressure	95-125 kPa (13.5-17.8 psi)
Rear shock absorber preload adjuster*	2 nd groove from bottom
Rear shock absorber rebound damping adjuster*	
U.S.A., California and Canada models	1 1/2 turns out
Non- U.S.A., California and Canada models	1 turn out
Rim runout (front and rear)	
Axial	2.0 mm (0.08 in.)
Radial	2.0 mm (0.08 in.)
Spark plug	NGK CR8E, ND U24ESR-N59933
Spark plug gap	0.7-0.8 mm (0.028-0.031 in.)
Throttle cable free play	2.0-4.0 mm (0.08-0.16 in.)
Tire pressure	
Single rider	
Front	225 kPa (33 psi)
Rear	250 kPa (36 psi)
Dual riders	
Front	225 kPa (33 psi)
Rear	280 kPa (41 psi)
Tire tread depth (minimum)	
Front	1.6 mm (0.06 in.)
Rear	2.0 mm (0.08 in.)
Valve clearance (cold)	
Intake	0.10-0.20 mm (0.004-0.008 in.)
Exhaust	0.20-0.30 mm (0.008-0.012 in.)

*Standard setting.

Table 4 MAINTENANCE AND TUNE-UP TORQUE SPECIFICATIONS

Item	N•m	in.-lb.	ft.-lb.
Oil drain plug	21	186	–
Rear axle nut	100	–	74
Rear brake master cylinder			
pushrod locknut	17	150	–
Spark plug	11	98	–

MAINTENANCE LOG

Date	Miles	Type of Service

MAINTENANCE LOG

Date	Miles	Type of Service

3

MAINTENANCE LOG

Date	Miles	Type of Service

MAINTENANCE LOG

Date	Miles	Type of Service

3

Notes

ENGINE TOP END

4

All models covered in this book are equipped with a liquid-cooled, four-stroke, V-twin engine with dual overhead camshafts in each cylinder head. The crankshaft is supported by two main bearings, which are replaceable sleeve type bearings mounted in the vertically split crankcase.

The camshafts are chain-driven from the sprocket on the riitght end of the crankshaft. The camshaft lobes operate the valves directly.

An oil pump on the right side of the engine next to the clutch delivers oil under pressure throughout the engine. A gear on the clutch drives the oil pump gear. A filter screen on the oil pickup and a disposable oil filter remove contaminants from the oil.

This chapter contains information for removal, inspection, service and reassembly of the top end of the engine. The removal and installation of the engine assembly are covered in Chapter Five.

Tables 1-3 are located at the end of this chapter.

ENGINE COOLING

The vehicle is equipped with a liquid cooling system to remove engine heat. A water pump located on the right crankcase cover circulates a mixture of water and antifreeze through the engine and cooling system. Refer to Chapter Three for cooling system maintenance procedures. Refer to Chapter Ten for cooling system repair procedures.

SERVICING ENGINE IN FRAME

The following components can be serviced while the engine is mounted in the frame (the vehicle frame is a great holding fixture for breaking loose stubborn bolts and nuts):
1. Camshaft.
2. Cylinder head.
3. Cylinder.
4. Fuel injection system.
5. Starter.
6. Alternator.
7. Clutch.
8. Water pump.
9. Oil pump.
10 Exhaust system.

EXHAUST SYSTEM

WARNING
Do not service the exhaust system while hot.

Removal/Installation

1. Loosen but do not remove the muffler mounting bolts (**Figure 1**).
2. Loosen the exhaust pipe clamp bolt (A, **Figure 2**).

3. Remove the exhaust pipe mounting bolt below the right footpeg (**Figure 3**).

4. Remove the bolts (B, **Figure 2**) securing the exhaust pipe to the front cylinder head and remove the exhaust pipe.

5. Loosen the exhaust pipe clamp bolt on the rear cylinder exhaust pipe (**Figure 4**).

6. Remove the muffler mounting bolts (**Figure 1**) and remove the muffler/exhaust pipe.

7. Check the rubber mounting grommets. Replace the rubber grommet if it is starting to harden or deteriorate.

8. Remove the exhaust gasket from each cylinder head.

9. Installation is the reverse of removal.
   a. Install a new gasket into each cylinder head.
   b. Install a new gasket at each exhaust pipe joint.
   c. Apply exhaust system sealer such as Permatex 1372 to the exhaust joints.
   d. Tighten all fasteners to 23 N•m (17 ft.-lb.).
   e. After installation is complete, start the engine and make sure there are no exhaust leaks.

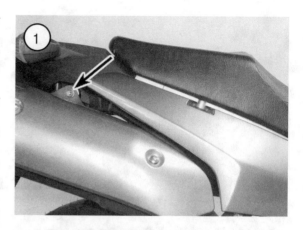

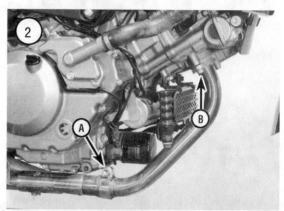

CYLINDER HEAD COVERS

The cylinder head covers can be removed with the engine mounted in the frame. However, for clarity, some of the illustrations depict the engine removed.

Removal

> *NOTE*
> *If removing only one cylinder head cover (front or rear), note the steps that provide specific information for that cylinder head cover.*

1. Disconnect the negative battery cable as described in Chapter Three.

2A. Rear cylinder head cover, proceed as follows:
   a. Remove the fuel tank as described in Chapter Eight.
   b. On 2007-2011 models, remove the coolant reservoir.
   c. Detach the PAIR hose (**Figure 5**) from the cylinder head cover.

2B. Front cylinder head cover, proceed as follows:
   a. Remove the radiator as described in Chapter Ten.
   b. Detach the PAIR hose (**Figure 6**) from the cylinder head cover.

3. Detach the spark plug leads and move out of the way.

4. Remove the cylinder head cover retaining bolts (A, **Figure 7**).

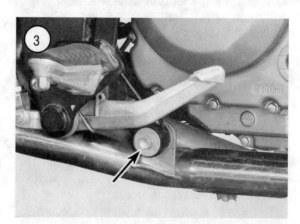

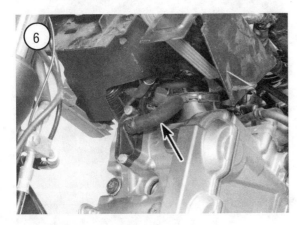

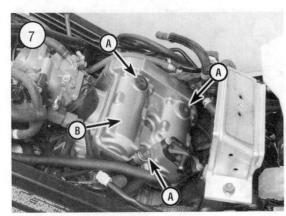

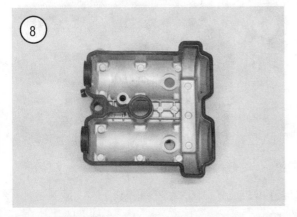

5. Remove the cylinder head cover (B, **Figure 7**) and gasket.

Inspection and Gasket Replacement

1. Make sure the gasket sealing surface in the cover groove is clean and free of any oil. This surface must be clean and smooth to provide a tight seal.

2. Inspect the cylinder head cover gasket around its perimeter for wear or damage. Replace the gasket if it is not in excellent condition.

3. Remove all old gasket sealer residue from the gasket sealing surface around the perimeter of the cylinder head. Make sure to clean off all old sealer from the crescent-shaped machined surfaces at the end of the cylinder head.

4. Check the cylinder head cover (**Figure 8**) for warpage, cracks or damage, and replace if necessary.

5. Inspect the cover bolts for thread damage and rubber/metal sealing rings for damage or hardness. Replace as necessary.

6. Inspect dowel pin and O-ring (**Figure 9**). Replace the O-ring if damaged or deteriorated.

7. Install the new gasket onto the cylinder head cover. Make sure it is completely seated around the perimeter.

8. Apply a light coat of Suzuki Bond No. 1207B, or equivalent, to the half-round shaped portions (A, **Figure 10**) of the gasket. This ensures a tight seal between the cylinder head cover and the cylinder head.

Installation

1. If removed, install the dowel pin and O-ring (**Figure 9**) into the cylinder head.

2. Make sure the gasket is installed correctly in the cylinder head cover.

3. Before installation, make sure to identify the cylinder head covers. The front cylinder head cover is equipped

with a threaded radiator mounting hole (B, **Figure 10**). The covers are also embossed with F or R.

4. Install the cylinder head cover onto the cylinder head. Make sure the half-round portions of the cover gasket properly engage the crescent shaped areas of the cylinder head.

5. Refer to **Figure 11** and install the correct gasket washer on the cylinder head bolts. If so equipped, position the metal side of the washer next to the bolt head.

6. Install the cover bolts making sure the gaskets are installed under each bolt. Tighten the bolts in a crossing pattern to 14 N•m (124 in.-lb.).

7. Connect the spark plug leads.

8A. Rear cylinder head cover, proceed as follows:

    a. Attach the PAIR hose (**Figure 5**) to the cylinder head cover.

    b. On 2007-2011 models, install the coolant reservoir as described in Chapter Ten.

    c. Install the fuel tank as described in Chapter Eight.

8B. Front cylinder head cover, proceed as follows:

    a. Install the radiator as described in Chapter Ten.

    b. Attach the PAIR hose (**Figure 6**) to the cylinder head cover.

9. Connect the negative battery cable as described in Chapter Three.

CAMSHAFT

The procedures for servicing the camshafts on the front and rear cylinders are similar. However, due to the restricted space available around the rear cylinder, follow the additional steps described in the following procedures when servicing the camshafts on the rear cylinder.

Removal

1. Remove the cylinder head cover as described in this chapter.

2. Remove the spark plugs as described in Chapter Three. This makes it easier to turn the engine by hand.

3. Remove the flywheel inspection plug (A, **Figure 12**) in the left crankcase cover.

4. Remove the left crankcase cover access plug (**Figure 12**).

5. Remove the cam chain guide (**Figure 13**).

6A. Front cylinder—Correctly position the camshafts as follows:

    a. Insert a suitably sized socket through the side cover to engage the flywheel bolt (**Figure 14**). Rotate the engine *counterclockwise*, as viewed

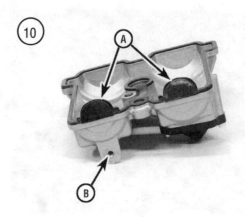

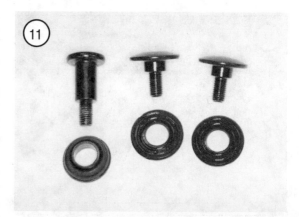

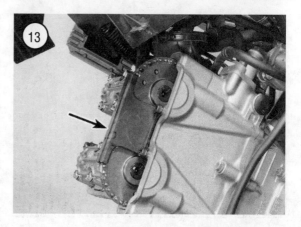

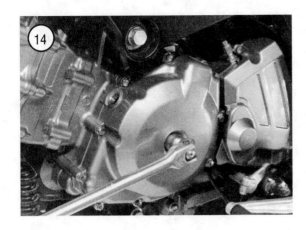

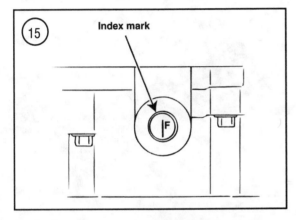

Index mark

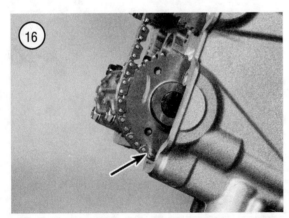

from the left side of the motorcycle, until the F line on the flywheel aligns with the mark on the timing inspection hole as shown in **Figure 15**.

b. Make sure the exhaust camshaft sprocket is positioned so the 1F mark on the sprocket is aligned with the top surface of the cylinder head as shown in **Figure 16**. If the sprocket is not positioned correctly, rotate the crankshaft one full revolution (360°).

c. If it was necessary to rotate the crankshaft an additional revolution, recheck that the F line on the flywheel is once again aligned with the mark on the timing inspection hole (**Figure 15**). Realign if necessary.

6B. Rear cylinder—Correctly position the camshafts as follows:

a. Insert a suitably sized socket through the side cover to engage the flywheel bolt (**Figure 14**). Rotate the engine *counterclockwise*, as viewed from the left side of the motorcycle, until the F line on the alternator rotor aligns with the mark on the timing inspection hole as shown in **Figure 15**.

b. Make sure the intake camshaft sprocket is positioned so the 1R mark on the sprocket is aligned with the top surface of the cylinder head as shown in **Figure 17**. If the sprocket is not positioned correctly, rotate the crankshaft one full revolution (360°).

c. If it was necessary to rotate the crankshaft an additional revolution, recheck that the F line on the flywheel is once again aligned with the mark on the timing inspection hole (**Figure 15**). Realign if necessary.

7. Remove the cam chain tensioner as described in this chapter.

NOTE
Mark the camshaft holder so it can be installed in the original location.

8. Using a crossing pattern, loosen then remove the bolts securing the camshaft holders (**Figure 18**). Pull the holders straight up and off the cylinder head.

9. Disengage the cam chain from the camshaft sprockets. Attach a piece of wire to the cam chain and tie it to the engine or frame. This will prevent the chain from falling into the crankcase.

10. Remove the intake and the exhaust camshafts (**Figure 19**) from the cylinder head one at a time.

CAUTION
If the crankshaft must be rotated while the camshafts are removed, pull up on the cam chain so it properly engages the crankshaft timing sprocket. Hold

the chain taut on the timing sprocket while rotating the crankshaft. If this is not done, the cam chain could become kinked, which could cause damage to the chain, timing sprocket and surrounding crankcase area.

Inspection

When measuring the camshafts in this section, compare the actual measurements to the new and wear limit specifications listed in **Table 2**. Replace parts that are out of specification or show damage as described in this section.

1. Check the camshaft lobes (A, **Figure 20**) for wear. The lobes should not be scored and the edges should be square.
2. Measure the height of each lobe (**Figure 21**) with a micrometer. Replace the camshaft if any lobe is out of specification.
3. Check each camshaft bearing journal (B, **Figure 20**) for wear and scoring.
4. Measure the diameter of each camshaft bearing journal (**Figure 22**) with a micrometer. Record each measurement. It is necessary to have them when measuring camshaft bearing clearance. Replace the camshaft if any journal diameter is out of specification.
5. If the camshaft bearing journals are excessively worn or damaged, check the bearing surfaces in the cylinder head (**Figure 23**) and in the camshaft holders (**Figure 24**). They should not be scored or excessively worn. If any of the bearing surfaces are worn or scored, replace the cylinder head assembly and camshaft holders as a set.
6. Place the camshaft on a set of V-blocks (**Figure 25**) and check the runout with a dial indicator. Replace the camshaft if its runout is out of specification.
7. Inspect the camshaft sprocket (**Figure 26**) for broken or chipped teeth. Also check the teeth for cracking or rounding. If the camshaft sprocket(s) is

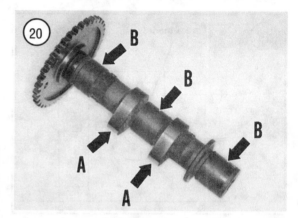

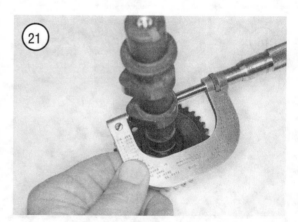

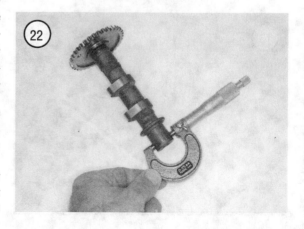

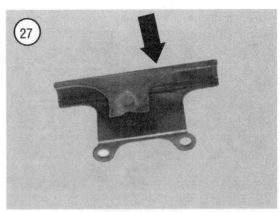

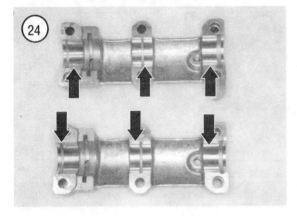

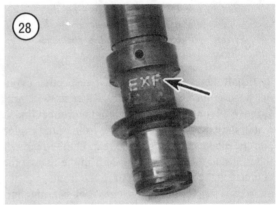

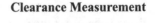

damaged or excessively worn, replace the camshaft. Also, inspect the camshaft timing sprocket mounted on the crankshaft as described in Chapter Five.

NOTE
If the camshaft sprockets are worn, check the cam chain, chain guides and chain tensioner for damage.

8. Inspect the sliding surface of the top cam chain guide (**Figure 27**) for wear or damage. Also check both ends of the guide. Replace the top guide as necessary.

Clearance Measurement

This procedure requires the use of Plastigage. The camshafts must be installed into the cylinder head. Before installing the camshafts, wipe all oil residue from each camshaft bearing journal and from the bearing surface of the cylinder head and camshaft holders.

1. Do not install the drive chain onto the camshafts for this procedure.

NOTE
*The camshafts are identified according to location by embossed letters on each camshaft (**Figure 28**). The identifying*

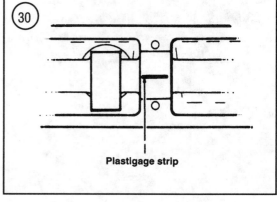

Plastigage strip

letters are IN for the intake camshaft, EX for the exhaust camshaft, F for the front cylinder, and R for the rear cylinder.

2. Install the camshafts into their respective cylinder head in the correct location. Refer to the marks (**Figure 29**) on each camshaft. On the front cylinder, install the exhaust camshaft in the front of the engine and the intake camshaft in the rear. On the rear cylinder, install the exhaust camshaft in the rear of the engine and the intake camshaft in the front.

3. Place a strip of Plastigage onto each bearing journal (**Figure 30**). The Plastigage must be parallel to the camshaft.

4. Install each camshaft holder in its correct location. Refer to the **IN** *and* **EX** marks (**Figure 31**) on each holder, as well as the marks made during disassembly to indicate original cylinder location. The groove at the end of each camshaft holder (**Figure 32**) must fit over the flange on the camshaft.

5. Install the camshaft holder bolts fingertight at this time.

> *CAUTION*
> *Failure to tighten the bolts in a crossing pattern will result in damage to the bearing surfaces in the cylinder head and camshaft holders.*

6. Install the bolts and tighten them evenly in a crossing pattern to 10 N•m (88 in.-lb.).

> *CAUTION*
> *Do not rotate the camshafts with the Plastigage in place.*

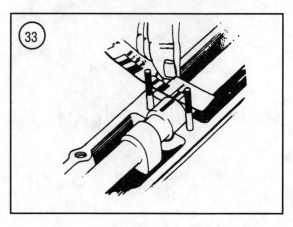

7. Loosen the bolts in a crossing pattern.

8. Pull straight up and carefully remove the camshaft holders.

9. Measure the flattened Plastigage (**Figure 33**) at the widest point, according to the manufacturer's instructions.

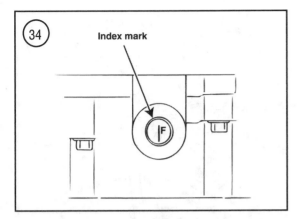

Index mark

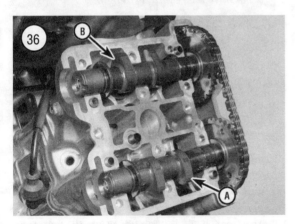

CAUTION
Make sure to remove all traces of Plastigage from the camshaft holders and from the camshaft bearing journal. If any of the material is left in the engine, it can plug an oil control orifice and cause severe engine damage.

10. Remove *all* Plastigage from the camshafts and camshaft holders.

11. If the camshaft bearing oil clearance is greater than specified in **Table 2**, refer to the camshaft bearing outer diameter dimension recorded in *Inspection* Step 4. If the bearing surface is worn to the service limit; replace the camshaft. If the camshaft is within specification; replace the cylinder head assembly.

Camshaft Installation
Front Cylinder

NOTE
The camshafts are identified according to location by embossed letters on each camshaft (Figure 28). The identifying letters are IN for the intake camshaft, EX for the exhaust camshaft, F for the front cylinder, and R for the rear cylinder.

1. Pull up on the cam chain and make sure it is properly meshed with the crankshaft timing sprocket.

NOTE
If the crankshaft has not been disturbed since the camshafts were removed, the engine may still be at the correct position for camshaft installation. If the F line on the alternator rotor is still aligned with the mark on the timing inspection hole (Figure 34) then the engine is in the correct position for camshaft installation. If alignment is incorrect, perform Step 2.

2. Use a suitable wrench on the alternator retaining bolt (**Figure 35**). Rotate the engine *counterclockwise*, as viewed from the left side of the bike, until the F line on the alternator rotor is aligned with the mark on the timing inspection hole (**Figure 34**).

3. Apply a light coat of molybdenum disulfide grease to each camshaft journal (B, **Figure 20**). Coat all bearing surfaces in the cylinder head (**Figure 23**) and camshaft holders (**Figure 24**) with clean engine oil.

4. Set the exhaust camshaft into the cam chain and install the camshaft onto the cylinder head bearing surface (A, **Figure 36**).

5. Lift up on the chain and rotate the exhaust camshaft until the 1F arrow mark (A, **Figure 37**) is level with

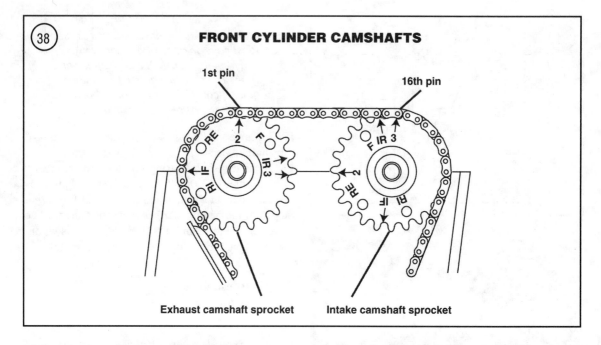

FRONT CYLINDER CAMSHAFTS

1st pin

16th pin

Exhaust camshaft sprocket   Intake camshaft sprocket

the top surface of the cylinder head. The No. 2 arrow mark (B) is now pointing straight up. Properly mesh the cam chain with the sprocket and install a short cable tie to secure the cam chain to the cam sprocket.

6. Fit the intake camshaft (B, **Figure 36**) through the cam chain and install the camshaft onto the cylinder head bearing surface.

7. Note that the No. 2 arrow on the exhaust cam sprocket points to a pin on the cam chain. This is the first pin (**Figure 38**). Starting at this pin, count back to the 16th pin. Properly mesh the cam chain with the intake cam sprocket so the 16th pin is opposite the No. 3 arrow on the intake cam sprocket (**Figure 38**). Install a short cable tie to secure the cam chain to the sprocket.

> *CAUTION*
> *Engine damage is likely if the cam chain-to-camshaft installation and alignment is incorrect. Recheck the work several times to make sure alignment is correct.*

> *NOTE*
> *The cam chain is now riding on the crankshaft timing sprocket, the exhaust cam sprocket and the intake cam sprocket. Do not disturb this alignment until the camshaft holders and cam chain tensioner are properly installed.*

8. Install the camshaft holders onto the correct camshaft. Refer to the **IN** *and* **EX** marks (**Figure 31**) and install the camshaft holder onto the respective camshaft. The groove at the end of each camshaft holder (**Figure 32**) must fit over the flange on the camshaft.

> *CAUTION*
> *Do not substitute any other type of bolt for the original camshaft holder bolts. These special bolts are marked with a 9 on the head and are of a superior strength grade. Substitute bolts may not have the required strength.*

9. Install the camshaft holder bolts fingertight at this time.

> *CAUTION*
> *Failure to tighten the bolts in a crossing pattern will result in damage to the bearing surfaces in the cylinder head and camshaft holders.*

10. Install the bolts and tighten them evenly in a crossing pattern to 10 N•m (88 in.-lb.).

11. Remove the cable ties securing the cam chain to the sprockets.

12. As a final check, insert a finger into the tensioner receptacle in the cylinder, push on the chain and take out the chain slack. Recheck all the timing marks to make sure all marks are still aligned properly as shown in **Figure 38**. If incorrect, reposition the cam chain on the sprockets.

13. Install the top cam chain guide (**Figure 13**) and tighten the mounting bolts to 10 N•m (88 in.-lb.).

14. Install the cam chain tensioner as described in this chapter.

15. Fill the pockets in the cylinder head with clean engine oil.

16. After the tensioner is installed correctly, recheck the alignment as shown in **Figure 38**. If any of the

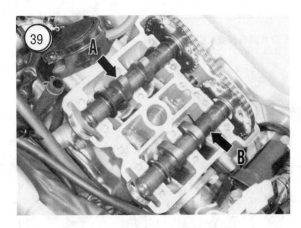

alignment points are incorrect, repeat this procedure until *all* are correct.

> *CAUTION*
> *If there is any binding while rotating the crankshaft, **stop**. Determine the cause before proceeding.*

17. Insert a suitably sized socket through the side cover to engage the alternator bolt (**Figure 35**). Rotate the crankshaft *counterclockwise* as viewed from the left side of the motorcycle. Rotate the crankshaft several complete revolutions and check the operation of the valve train.

18. Adjust the valves as described in Chapter Three.

19. Install the spark plug as described in Chapter Three.

20. Install the cylinder head cover as described in this chapter.

Camshaft Installation
Rear Cylinder

> *NOTE*
> *The camshafts are identified according to location by embossed letters on each camshaft (**Figure 28**). The identifying*

letters are IN for the intake camshaft, EX for the exhaust camshaft, F for the front cylinder, and R for the rear cylinder.

1. Pull up on the cam chain and make sure it is properly meshed with the crankshaft timing sprocket.

2. If the crankshaft has not been disturbed since the front cylinder camshafts were installed, use a suitable wrench on the flywheel retaining bolt (**Figure 35**). Rotate the crankshaft 360° *counterclockwise*, as viewed from the left side of the motorcycle, until the F line on the flywheel is aligned with the mark on the timing inspection hole (**Figure 34**). Proceed to Step 4.

3. If the crankshaft position is not known, proceed as follows:

  a. If the cylinder head cover on the front cylinder is installed, remove it as described in this chapter.

> *CAUTION*
> *Pull up on the rear cylinder cam chain when rotating the crankshaft to prevent internal damage due to chain binding.*

  b. Insert a suitably sized socket through the side cover to engage the alternator bolt (**Figure 35**). Rotate the crankshaft *counterclockwise*, as viewed from the left side of the motorcycle, until the F line on the alternator rotor aligns with the mark on the timing inspection hole as shown in **Figure 34**.

  c. Make sure the holes marked F on the front cylinder camshaft sprockets are positioned as shown in **Figure 16**. If the sprocket holes are not positioned as shown, rotate the crankshaft one full revolution (360°) until the sprocket holes are positioned correctly.

  d. With the crankshaft now positioned properly for the front cylinder, rotate the crankshaft one full revolution (360°) *counterclockwise*, as viewed from the left side of the motorcycle, until the F line on the flywheel aligns with the mark on the timing inspection hole as shown in **Figure 34**. The rear cylinder will now be on the compression stroke and in position for installation of the camshafts.

4. Apply a light coat of molybdenum disulfide grease to each camshaft journal (B, **Figure 20**). Coat all bearing surfaces in the cylinder head (**Figure 23**) and camshaft holders (**Figure 24**) with clean engine oil.

5. Set the intake camshaft into the cam chain and install the camshaft onto the cylinder head bearing surface (A, **Figure 39**).

6. Lift up on the chain and rotate the intake camshaft until the 1R arrow mark is level with the top surface of the cylinder head (**Figure 40**). The No. 2 arrow

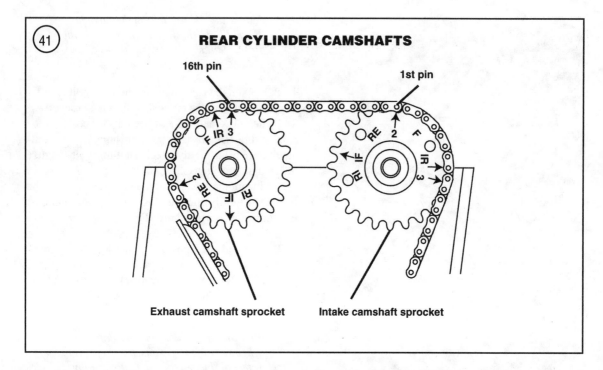

REAR CYLINDER CAMSHAFTS

16th pin

1st pin

Exhaust camshaft sprocket

Intake camshaft sprocket

mark is now pointing straight up. Properly mesh the cam chain with the sprocket and install a short cable tie to secure the cam chain to the cam sprocket.

7. Fit the exhaust camshaft (B, **Figure 39**) through the cam chain and install the camshaft onto the cylinder head bearing surface.

8. Note that the No. 2 arrow on the intake cam sprocket points to a pin on the cam chain. This is the first pin (**Figure 41**). Starting at this pin, count back to the 16th pin.

Properly mesh the cam chain with the exhaust cam sprocket so the 16th pin is opposite the No. 3 arrow on the intake cam sprocket (**Figure 41**). Install a short cable tie to secure the cam chain to the sprocket.

CAUTION
Engine damage is likely if the cam chain-to-camshaft installation and alignment is incorrect. Recheck the work several times to make sure alignment is correct.

NOTE
The cam chain is now riding on the crankshaft timing sprocket, the exhaust cam sprocket and the intake cam sprocket. Do not disturb this alignment until the camshaft holders and cam chain tensioner are properly installed.

9. Install the camshaft holders onto the correct camshaft. Refer to the **IN** *and* **EX** marks (**Figure 31**) and install the camshaft holder onto the respective

camshaft. The groove at the end of each camshaft holder (**Figure 32**) must fit over the flange on the camshaft.

CAUTION
Do not substitute any other type of bolt for the original camshaft holder bolts. These special bolts are marked with a 9 on the head and are of a superior strength grade. Substitute bolts may not have the required strength.

10. Install the camshaft holder bolts fingertight at this time.

CAUTION
Failure to tighten the bolts in a crossing pattern will result in damage to the bearing surfaces in the cylinder head and camshaft holders.

11. Install the bolts and tighten them evenly in a crossing pattern to 10 N•m (88 in.-lb.).

12. Remove the cable ties securing the cam chain to the sprockets.

13. As a final check, insert a finger into the tensioner receptacle in the cylinder, push on the chain and take out the chain slack. Recheck all the timing marks to make sure all marks are still aligned properly as shown in **Figure 41**. If incorrect, reposition the cam chain on the sprockets.

14. Install the top cam chain guide (**Figure 13**) and tighten the mounting bolts to 10 N•m (88 in.-lb.).

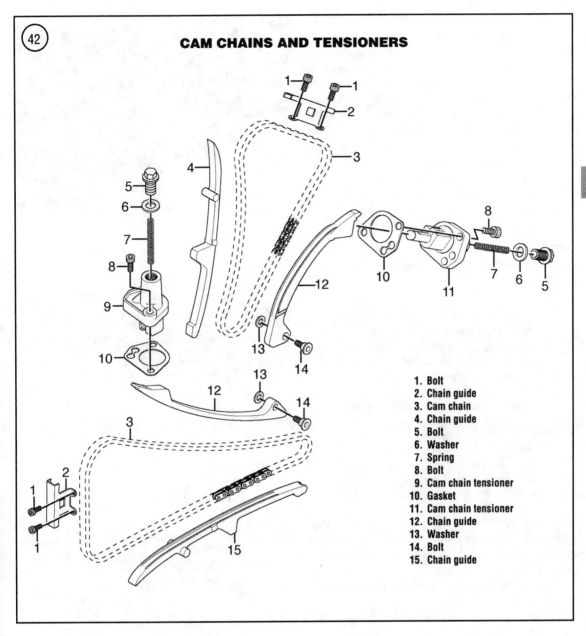

CAM CHAINS AND TENSIONERS

1. Bolt
2. Chain guide
3. Cam chain
4. Chain guide
5. Bolt
6. Washer
7. Spring
8. Bolt
9. Cam chain tensioner
10. Gasket
11. Cam chain tensioner
12. Chain guide
13. Washer
14. Bolt
15. Chain guide

15. Install the cam chain tensioner as described in this chapter.

16. Fill the pockets in the cylinder head with clean engine oil.

17. After the tensioner is installed correctly, recheck the alignment as shown in **Figure 41**. If any of the alignment points are incorrect, repeat this procedure until *all* are correct.

CAUTION
If there is any binding while rotating the crankshaft, stop. Determine the cause before proceeding.

18. Insert a suitably sized socket through the side cover to engage the alternator bolt (**Figure 35**).

Rotate the crankshaft *counterclockwise* as viewed from the left side of the motorcycle. Rotate the crankshaft several complete revolutions and check the operation of the valve train.

19. Adjust the valves as described in Chapter Three.

20. Install the spark plugs as described in Chapter Three.

21. Install the cylinder head cover as described in this chapter.

CAM CHAIN TENSIONER AND GUIDES

The engine is equipped with a cam chain tensioner and guides for each cylinder (**Figure 42**). The cam chain tensioner on the front cylinder is located on the left, rear of the cylinder and is relatively accessible. The cam chain tensioner on the rear cylinder is located on the right, rear of the cylinder. While the rear cylinder cam tensioner is accessible, it is difficult to service with the engine in the frame. Before servicing the rear cylinder cam tensioner, particularly if other major work will be performed, read the following procedure as well as the procedure for engine removal and installation. Servicing the cam tensioner with the engine on the workbench may be the better procedure.

The cam chain tensioner is lubricated by an oil jet located in the cylinder head.

Cam Chain Tensioner
Removal/Inspection/Installation

CAUTION
*The cam chain tensioner is a non-return type. The internal push rod will not return to its original position once it has moved out, even the slightest amount. After the tensioner mounting bolts are loosened, the tensioner assembly must be **completely removed** and the pushrod reset. If the mounting bolts are loosened, do not simply retighten the mounting bolts. The pushrod has already moved out to an extended position, and it will exert excessive pressure on the chain leading to costly engine damage.*

Refer to **Figure 42**.
1. If removing the cam chain tensioner on the front cylinder, remove the throttle bodies as described in Chapter Eight.
2. If removing the cam chain tensioner on the rear cylinder, note the following:
   a. Accessibility is dependent on the tools available.
   b. On ABS models, swing arm removal may be necessary to gain access to the cam tensioner:
3. Unscrew and remove the cap bolt (**Figure 43**) and washer from the end of the tensioner.
4. Remove the spring.
5. Remove the socket-head bolts securing the cam chain tensioner. On 2007-2011 models, note the spark plug wire holder under the mounting bolt.
6. Remove the cam chain tensioner (A, **Figure 44**) and gasket.
7. Inspect the tensioner push rod, spring and body (**Figure 45**) for damage.
8. Check tensioner operation as follows. Attempt to push in the push rod; it should not move inward. Push in the ratchet stopper (B, **Figure 44**), then push in the push rod (C). The push rod should move freely

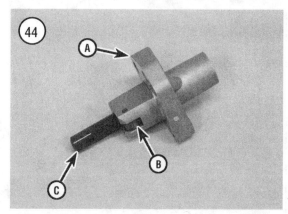

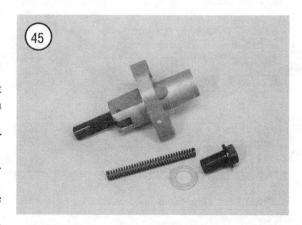

in and out of the tensioner body. With the ratchet stopper released, the push rod should extend fully.
9. Remove and inspect the oil jet (**Figure 46**). Clean the jet and install a new O-ring. Reinstall the jet slotted end out.
10. Prior to installation, push in the ratchet stopper and push in the push rod so it is in the fully retracted position.
11. The front and rear chain tensioners are different. The tensioner is identified by F-UP or R-UP cast on the tensioner adjacent to UP on the body (**Figure 47**).
12. Install a new gasket onto the tensioner.

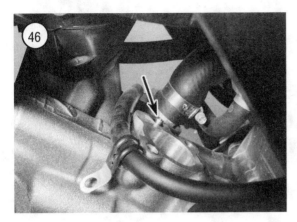

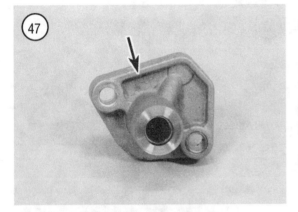

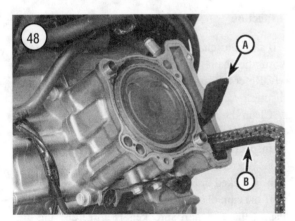

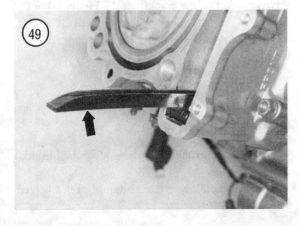

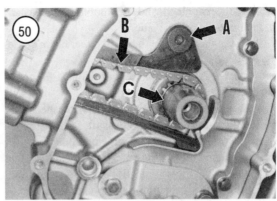

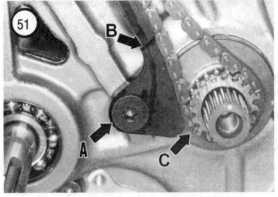

13. Install the tensioner so the UP mark (**Figure 47**) is properly positioned. Install the mounting bolts and tighten to 10 N•m (88 in.-lb.).

14. Install the spring, washer and cap bolt. Tighten the cap bolt to 23 N•m (17 ft.-lb.).

Cam Chain Guides
Removal/Inspection/Installation

Refer to **Figure 42**. The rear cam chain guide (A, **Figure 48**) on each cylinder is secured at its lower end by a bolt on the side of the crankcase. The front cam chain guide (B) on each cylinder rests in pockets in the crankcase and cylinder.

1. Remove the cylinder head as described in this chapter.

2. Front cylinder cam chain guides—Remove the starter clutch assembly as described in Chapter Five.

3. Rear cylinder cam chain guides—Remove the primary drive gear as described in Chapter Six.

4. Pull straight up and withdraw the front cam chain guide (**Figure 49**).

5A. Front cylinder—To remove the rear cam chain guide, remove the bolt and washer (A, **Figure 50**) securing the rear chain guide. Do not lose the washer on the backside of the guide.

5B. Rear cylinder—To remove the rear cam chain guide, remove the bolt and washer (A, **Figure 51**) securing the rear chain guide. Do not lose the washer on the backside of the guide.

6. Pull straight up and withdraw the rear chain guide (B, **Figure 51**).

7. Inspect both guides for wear or damage. Replace as necessary.

8. Make sure the cam chain is properly meshed with the timing sprocket on the crankshaft.

9. Install the rear cam chain guide into position.

10. Install the bolt (A, **Figure 52**) part way through the guide. Install the washer (B) behind the guide and push the bolt the rest of the way through the guide.

11. Tighten the bolt to 10 N•m (88 in.-lb.).

12. Install the front cam chain guide (**Figure 49**) and push it down until it seats in the pockets in the crankcase and cylinder.

13. Front cylinder cam chain guides—Install the starter clutch assembly as described in Chapter Five.

14. Rear cylinder cam chain guides—Install the primary drive gear as described in Chapter Six.

15. Install the cylinder head as described in this chapter.

CAM CHAINS

The engine is equipped with two cam chains, one for each cylinder. The cam chain in the front cylinder is driven by a sprocket on the crankshaft behind the starter driven gear. The cam chain in the rear cylinder is driven by a sprocket on the crankshaft behind the primary drive gear.

A continuous cam chain is used on all models. Do not cut the chain; replacement link components are not available.

> *CAUTION*
> *Do not install a new chain onto worn or damaged sprockets. Doing so will quickly wear the new chain.*

Removal/Installation

1. Remove the cylinder head as described in this chapter.

2. Remove the cam chain guides as described in this chapter.

3. Remove the cam chain from the sprocket (C, **Figure 50** or C, **Figure 51**) on the crankshaft.

4. Pull the cam chain up through the chain tunnel in the cylinder and remove the chain.

5. If cam chain sprocket service is required, refer to Chapter Five.

6. Install the cam chain by reversing the preceding removal steps.

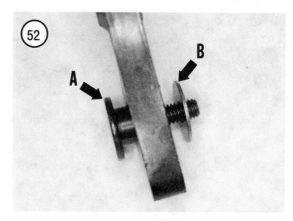

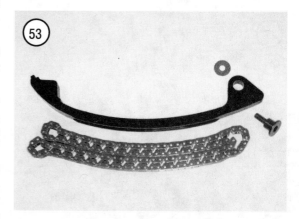

Inspection

If the cam chain or chain guides are excessively worn, the chain tensioner may not be working properly. Refer to *Cam Chain Tensioner Inspection* in this chapter.

1. Clean the cam chain in solvent. Blow it dry with compressed air.

2. Inspect the cam chain (**Figure 53**) for:
   a. Worn or damaged pins and rollers.
   b. Cracked or damaged side plates.

3. If the cam chain is excessively worn or damaged, inspect the camshaft sprockets (**Figure 26**) and the drive sprocket on the crankshaft (C, **Figure 50** or C, **Figure 51**) for the same wear conditions. If any of the sprockets show signs of wear or damage, replace them.

CYLINDER HEAD

Removal

1. Remove the exhaust system as described in this chapter.

2. Drain the cooling system as described in Chapter Three.

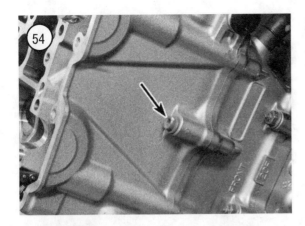

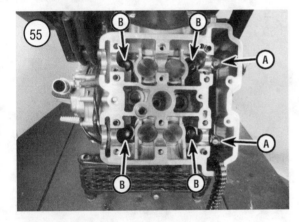

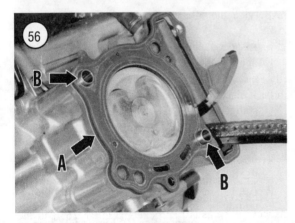

3. Remove the throttle bodies as described in Chapter Eight.

4. Remove the camshafts as described in this chapter.

> *CAUTION*
> *The valve lifters and shims can remain in the cylinder head if it is not going to be serviced. Do not allow the lifters and shims to fall out by turning the cylinder head over or on its side. If these parts fall out, they may be damaged and it will be impossible to return them to their original locations, making it necessary to adjust the valve clearances.*

5. If the cylinder head is going to be inspected and/or serviced, remove the valve lifters and shims before removing the head. Refer to *Valve Lifter and Shim Removal and Installation* in this chapter.

6. Tie a piece of wire to the cam chain and secure it so the cam chain cannot fall into the engine.

7. Remove the cylinder head-to-cylinder socket-head bolt (**Figure 54**) on the side of the cylinder head.

8. Remove the bolts in the cam chain compartment (A, **Figure 55**).

9. In a crossing pattern, remove the cylinder head bolts (B, **Figure 55**) securing the cylinder head.

10. Loosen the cylinder head by tapping around the perimeter with a rubber or soft-faced mallet. Do not use a metal hammer.

11. Lift off cylinder head. Guide the camshaft chain through the opening in the cylinder head and retie the wire to the exterior of the engine. This will prevent the drive chain from falling down into the crankcase.

12. Remove the cylinder head gasket (A, **Figure 56**) and discard it. Don't lose the locating dowels (B).

13. Place a clean shop cloth into the cam chain opening in the cylinder to prevent the entry of foreign matter.

Inspection

> *NOTE*
> *The cylinder heads are not identical. A cavity on each cylinder head contains either an F or R (**Figure 57**) to designate the location of the cylinder head.*

1. If not already removed, remove the valve lifters and shims. Make sure to keep them in order so they can be reinstalled in their original locations. Refer to Step 6 in the cylinder head removal procedure.

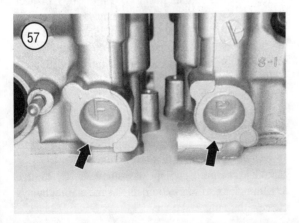

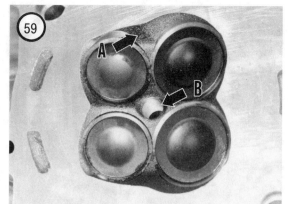

2. Remove all traces of gasket residue from the cylinder head (**Figure 58**) and cylinder mating surfaces. Do not scratch the gasket surfaces.

3. *Without removing the valves*, remove all carbon deposits from the combustion chamber (A, **Figure 59**). Take care not to damage the head, valves or spark plug threads.

> *CAUTION*
> *Cleaning the combustion chamber with the valves removed can damage the valve seat surfaces. A damaged or even slightly scratched valve seat causes poor valve seating.*

4. Inspect the threads in the spark plug hole(s) (B, **Figure 59**). If the threads are dirty or mildly damaged, use a spark plug thread tap as instructed by the manufacturer to clean and straighten the threads. If thread damage is excessive, the threads can be restored by installing a steel thread insert. Thread insert kits can be purchased at automotive supply stores or the inserts can be installed by a dealership or machine shop.

5. After all carbon is removed from combustion chambers and valve ports, and the spark plug thread hole is repaired, clean the entire head in solvent. Blow it dry with compressed air.

6. Examine the crown on both pistons. A crown should show no signs of wear or damage. If a crown appears pecked or spongy-looking, also check the spark plug, valves and combustion chamber for aluminum deposits. If these deposits are found, the cylinder is suffering from excessive heat caused by a lean fuel mixture or preignition.

> *NOTE*
> *The intake tubes (A, **Figure 60**) are marked according to location. The intake tube for the front cylinder head is marked F on the lip of the tube, while the intake tube for the rear cylinder head is marked R.*

7. Service the intake tube (A, **Figure 60**) as follows:

   a. Inspect the intake tube for cracks or other damage that would allow unfiltered air to enter the engine.

   b. If necessary, remove the intake tube and install a new O-ring between the intake tube and the cylinder head. Lubricate the O-ring using Suzuki Super Grease A or equivalent.

   c. Install the intake tube so the UP on the lip of the tube is toward the top of the cylinder head.

   d. Apply Threadlock 1342 to the intake tube retaining bolts and tighten them securely.

8. Remove the coolant fitting (B, **Figure 60**). Inspect the fitting for cracks or other damage and replace if necessary. Install a new O-ring onto the fitting. Coat the O-ring with coolant before installing the fitting.

9. Check for cracks in the combustion chamber, intake port and exhaust. Replace a cracked head if it cannot be repaired by welding.

10. On the rear cylinder head, remove the exhaust pipe (**Figure 61**). On both cylinder heads, inspect the threads on the exhaust pipe mounting studs for damage. Clean with a metric die if damaged.

11. Make sure all coolant passageways (C, **Figure 59**) are clear. If necessary, blow the passageways clear with compressed air.

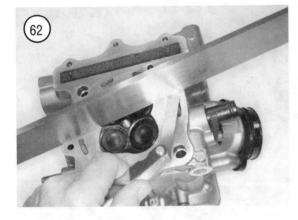

12. Run a tap through each threaded hole to remove any debris accumulation. Make sure the engine mounting bolt holes are in good condition.

13. Thoroughly clean the cylinder head in solvent and then hot soap water.

NOTE
If the cylinder head was bead blasted, grit in small crevices can be hard to remove. Any residual grit left in the engine will contaminate the oil and cause premature wear. Repeatedly wash the cylinder head in a solution of hot soap and water to remove this debris.

14. After the head has been thoroughly cleaned, place a straightedge across the gasket surface at several points. Measure warp (**Figure 62**) by attempting to insert a feeler gauge between the straightedge and cylinder head at each location. The maximum warp limit is 0.05 mm (0.002 in.). A warped or nicked cylinder head surface could cause an air leak and result in overheating. If the warp limit exceeds the specification, the cylinder head must be resurfaced or replaced. Consult a dealership or machine shop experienced in this type of work.

Installation

1. Make sure the cylinder head and cylinder mating surfaces are clean of all gasket residue.

2. If removed, install the two locating dowels (B, **Figure 56**) into the cylinder.

3. Install a new cylinder head gasket (A, **Figure 56**). Make sure all the gasket holes align with those in the cylinder.

4. Position the cylinder head over the cylinder and run the cam chain and its safety wire through the cam chain tunnel. Tie the safety wire to the exterior of the engine.

5. Carefully slide the cylinder head onto the engine and seat the cylinder head onto the cylinder. Make sure the locating dowels engage the cylinder head.

6. Pull up on the cam chain and make sure it is properly engaged with the crankshaft timing sprocket before continuing.

7. Make sure the cylinder head bolt, threads and washers are free of debris.

NOTE
Apply clean engine oil to the washers and threads on the cylinder head bolts before installation.

8. Install the cylinder head 10 mm bolts and washers (B, **Figure 55**). Tighten the bolts in a crossing pattern. Initially, tighten all the bolts to 25 N•m (18 ft.-lb.), then tighten them to a final torque of 42 N•m (31 ft.-lb.).

9. Install the 8 mm bolts in the cam chain compartment (A, **Figure 55**) and tighten to 10 N•m (88 in.-lb.).

10. Install the cylinder head-to-cylinder socket-head bolt (**Figure 54**) on the side of the cylinder head. Tighten the bolt to 10 N•m (88 in.-lb.).

11. If the valve lifters and shims were removed, install them at this time as described in *Valve Lifter and Shim Removal and Installation* later in this chapter.

12. Install the camshafts as described in this chapter.

13. Install the throttle bodies as described in Chapter Eight.

14. Fill the cooling system as described in Chapter Three.

15. Install the exhaust system as described in this chapter.

VALVE LIFTERS AND SHIMS

Removal and Installation

Refer to **Figure 63**.

If the cylinder head is going to be inspected and/or serviced, remove the valve lifters and shims before

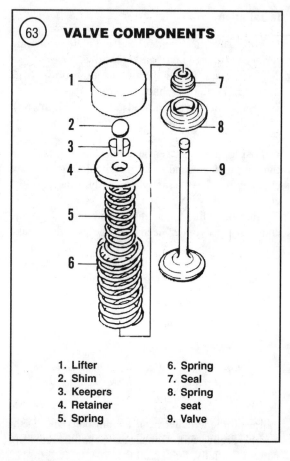

VALVE COMPONENTS

1. Lifter
2. Shim
3. Keepers
4. Retainer
5. Spring
6. Spring
7. Seal
8. Spring seat
9. Valve

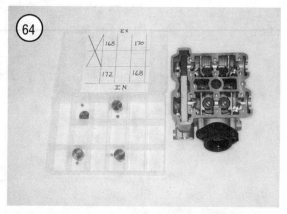

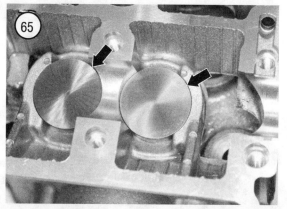

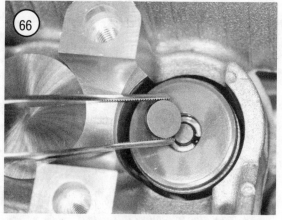

removing the head. To avoid mixing the parts, do this procedure very systematically.

1. Make or use a holder for the valve lifters and shims (**Figure 64**). Mark it with the cylinder name (front or rear), valve type (intake or exhaust) and valve location (right or left).

2. Remove the valve lifters (**Figure 65**) and their respective shims (**Figure 66**) and place both of them in the correct location in the holder. Repeat this step for all of the valve lifters and shims.

3. Inspect the valve lifters and shims for wear or heat damage. Service specifications for the outer diameter of the lifter and the inner diameter of the lifter receptacle in the cylinder head are not available. The lifter (with clean oil applied to its sides) should move up and down in the cylinder head with no binding or chatter. If the side of the lifter is scuffed or scratched, replace it.

NOTE
*To avoid mixing the parts, perform Steps 4-7 carefully and work on one cylinder at a time. Position the holder containing the valve lifters and shims (**Figure 64**) with the same orientation as the cylinder head.*

4. Install the shim onto the top of the valve keepers and make sure it is seated correctly.

5. Apply clean engine oil to the side of the valve lifter and install it.

6. Rotate the lifter to make sure it is seated correctly and rotates freely.

7. Install all the shims and lifters.

VALVES AND VALVE COMPONENTS

Due to the number of special tools required for valve service, it is general practice to remove the

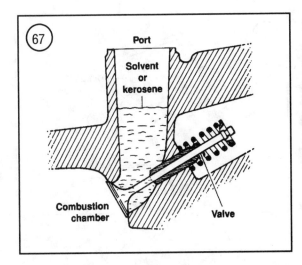

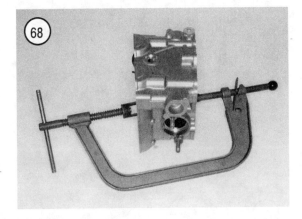

a. A worn or damaged valve face.

b. A worn or damaged valve seat (in the cylinder head).

c. A bent valve stem.

d. A crack in the combustion chamber.

Valve Removal

1. Remove the cylinder head, valve lifters and shims as described in this chapter.

2. Install a valve spring compressor (**Figure 68**) squarely onto the valve spring retainer (A, **Figure 69**) and place the other end of tool against the valve head.

CAUTION
To avoid loss of spring tension, do not compress the spring any more than necessary to remove the valve keepers.

3. Tighten the valve spring compressor until the valve keepers (B, **Figure 69**) separate from the valve stem. Lift the valve keepers out through the valve spring compressor with a magnet or needlenose pliers.

4. Gradually loosen the valve spring compressor and remove it from the cylinder head.

5. Remove the spring retainer and the two valve springs.

CAUTION
Remove any burrs from the valve stem groove before removing the valve (Figure 70); otherwise the valve guide will be damaged as the valve stem passes through it.

6. Remove the valve from the cylinder while rotating it slightly.

7. Remove the spring seat.

8. Pull the oil seal off the valve guide. Discard the oil seal.

cylinder head and refer valve service to a dealership or machine shop.

The following procedures describe how to check for valve component wear and to determine what type of service is required.

Refer to **Figure 63**.

Solvent Test

Perform the solvent test with the valve assembly in the cylinder head. The test can reveal if valves are fully seating, as well as expose undetected cracks in the cylinder head.

1. Remove the cylinder head as described in this chapter.

2. Check that the combustion chamber is dry and the valves are seated.

3. Support the cylinder head so the port faces up (**Figure 67**).

4. Pour solvent or kerosene into the port.

5. Inspect the combustion chamber for leakage around the valve.

6. Repeat Steps 3-5 for the other valves.

7. If there is leakage, it can be caused by:

CAUTION
*All component parts of each valve as-sembly must be kept together (**Figure 71**). Place each set into a divided car-ton, into separate small boxes or into small reclosable plastic bags. Label each valve set. Identify a valve set by its cylinder name (front or rear), type of valve (intake or exhaust) and loca-tion in the cylinder head (right or left). This will prevent parts mixing and will make installation simpler. Do not in-termix components from the valves or excessive wear may result.*

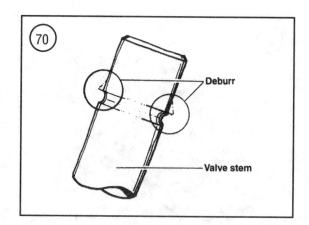

9. Repeat Steps 2-8 and remove the remaining valves. keep all valve sets separate.

Valve Inspection

When measuring the valves and valve components in this section, compare the measurements to the new and wear limit specifications listed in **Table 2**. Replace parts that are out of specification or show damage as described in this section.

1. Clean valves in solvent. Do not gouge or damage the valve seating surface.
2. Inspect the valve face (**Figure 72**). Minor rough-ness and pitting can be removed by lapping the valve as described in this chapter. Excessive unevenness to the contact surface is an indication that the valve is not serviceable.
3. Inspect the valve stem for wear and roughness. Then measure the valve stem outside diameter with a micrometer (**Figure 73**).
4. Remove all carbon and varnish from the valve guides with a stiff spiral wire brush before measur-ing wear.

NOTE
If the required measuring tools are not available, proceed to Step 6.

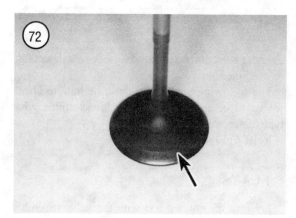

5. Measure the valve guide inside diameter with a small hole gauge. Measure at the top, center and bot-tom positions. Then measure the small hole gauge and check against the dimension in **Table 2**.
6. If a small hole gauge is not available, insert each valve into its guide. Position a dial indicator against the valve head (**Figure 74**) and check the valve stem deflection. Hold the valve 10 mm (0.4 in.) off its seat and rock it sideways in two directions 90° to each other. If the valve stem deflection in either direc-tion exceeds the service limit in **Table 2**, the guide is probably worn. However, as a final check, take the cylinder head to a Suzuki dealership or machine shop and have the valve guides measured.

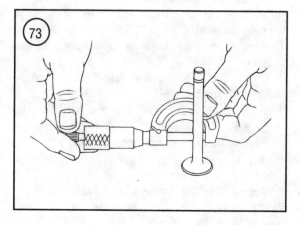

Dial indicator

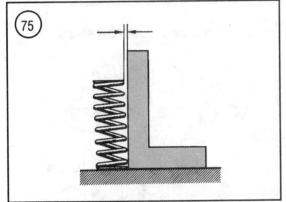

7. Check the inner and outer valve springs as follows:

    a. Check each of the valve springs for visual damage.

    b. Use a square and check the spring for distortion or tilt (**Figure 75**).

    c. Measure the valve spring free length with a vernier caliper (**Figure 76**) and compare with the dimension in **Table 2**.

    d. Repeat for each valve spring.

    e. Replace defective springs as a set (inner and outer).

8. Check the valve spring seats and valve keepers for cracks or other damage.

9. Inspect the valve seats (**Figure 77**, typical) in the cylinder head. If worn or burned, they may be reconditioned as described in this chapter. Seats and valves in near-perfect condition can be reconditioned by lapping with fine carborundum paste. Check as follows:

    a. Clean the valve seat and corresponding valve mating areas with contact cleaner.

    b. Coat the valve seat with layout fluid.

    c. Install the valve into its guide. Using the valve lapping tool, tap the valve against the valve seat with a light rotating motion in both directions. See *Valve Lapping* in this chapter.

    d. Lift the valve out of the guide and measure the seat width with a vernier caliper.

    e. The seat width of each valve should be within the specifications listed in **Table 2** all the way around the seat. If the seat width is outside the specified range (**Table 2**), regrind the seats as described in this chapter.

    f. Remove all layout fluid residue from the seats and valves.

10. Check the valve stem runout with a V-block and dial indicator as shown in **Figure 78**. Replace the valve if the valve stem runout exceeds the service limit listed in **Table 2**.

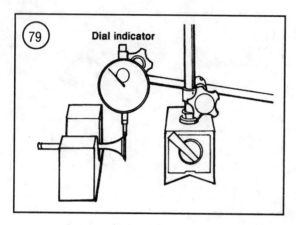

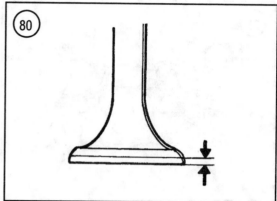

11. Measure valve head radial runout with a dial indicator as shown in **Figure 79**. Replace the valve if the valve head radial runout exceeds the wear limit in **Table 2**.

12. Measure the valve head margin with a vernier caliper (**Figure 80**). Replace the valve if valve head margin is less than the service limit in **Table 2**.

Valve Installation

Refer to **Figure 81**.

1. Clean the end of the valve guide.

2. Install the spring seat around the valve guide.

3. Lubricate the inside of the new oil seal and install it over the end of the valve guide. Push the seal down until it is completely seated on the valve guide.

4. Coat the valve stem with molybdenum disulfide paste. Install the valve part way into the guide. Then, slowly turn the valve as it enters the oil seal and continue turning it until the valve is completely installed.

5. Position the valve springs with their *closer* wound coils (**Figure 82**) toward the cylinder head.

6. Install the outer valve spring and make sure it is properly seated on the spring seat.

7. Install the inner valve spring and make sure it is properly seated on the lower spring seat.

8. Install the spring retainer on top of the valve springs.

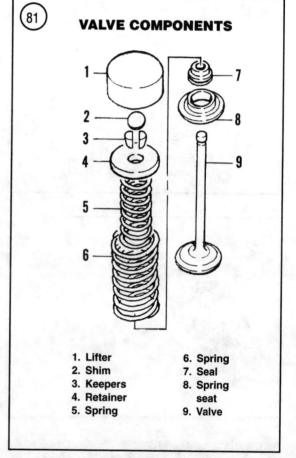

VALVE COMPONENTS

1. Lifter	6. Spring
2. Shim	7. Seal
3. Keepers	8. Spring
4. Retainer	seat
5. Spring	9. Valve

CAUTION
To avoid loss of spring tension, do not compress the spring any more than necessary to remove the valve keepers.

9. Compress the valve springs with a valve spring compressor (**Figure 68**) and install the valve keepers (B, **Figure 69**).

10. Make sure both keepers are seated around the valve stem before releasing the compressor.

11. Slowly release tension from the compressor and remove it. After removing the compressor, inspect the valve keepers to make sure they are properly seated. Tap the end of the valve stem with a drift and hammer. This ensures that the keepers are properly seated.

12. Repeat Steps 1-11 for the remaining valves.

13. Install the shims and valve lifters as described in this chapter.

14. Install the cylinder head as described in this chapter.

15. Adjust the valve clearance as described in Chapter Three.

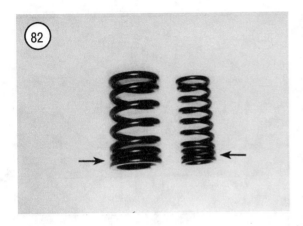

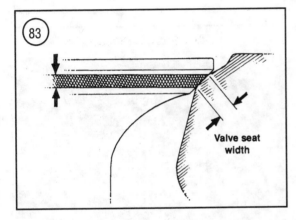

Valve seat width

Valve Guide Replacement

If the valve guide-to-valve stem clearance is excessive, replace the valve guides and valves. Special tools and experience are required to replace the valve guides. If these tools are not available, it is more economical to have this procedure performed by a machine shop.

Valve Seat Inspection

The most accurate method for checking the valve seat is to use a layout fluid, available from auto parts

and tool stores. Layout fluids are used for locating high or irregular spots when checking or making close fits and when scraping bearing surfaces. Follow the manufacturer's directions.

NOTE
Because of the close operating tolerances within the valve assembly, the valve stem and guide must be within tolerance; otherwise the inspection results will be inaccurate.

1. Remove the valves as described in this chapter.
2. Clean the valve seat in the cylinder head and valve mating areas with contact cleaner.
3. Thoroughly clean off all carbon deposits from the valve face with solvent or detergent and dry the valve thoroughly.
4. Spread a thin layer of layout fluid evenly on the valve face. Allow the fluid to air dry.
5. Moisten the end of a suction cup valve tool and attach it to the valve. Insert the valve into the guide.
6. Using the valve lapping tool, tap the valve against the valve seat with a light rotating motion in both directions.
7. Remove the valve and examine the impression left by the layout fluid. If the impression (on the valve or in the cylinder head) is not even and continuous and if the valve seat width (**Figure 83**) is not within the specified tolerance listed in **Table 2**, the valve seat must be reconditioned.
8. Closely examine the valve seat in the cylinder head (**Figure 77**). It should be smooth and even with a polished seating surface.
9. If the valve seat is good, install the valve as described in this chapter.
10. If the valve seat is not correct, recondition the valve seat(s).
11. Repeat for the other valves.

Valve Seat Reconditioning

Considerable expertise and specialized equipment are required to recondition valve seats. If these are not available, have the procedure performed by a machine shop that specializes in valve service.

Valve Lapping

Valve lapping is a simple operation which can restore the valve seal without machining if the amount of wear or distortion is not too great.

Perform this procedure only after determining that the valve seat width and outside diameter are within specifications. A lapping stick (**Figure 84**) is required.

1. Smear a light coat of fine grade valve lapping compound onto the seating surface of the valve.

2. Insert the valve into the cylinder head.

3. Wet the suction cup of the lapping stick and stick in onto the head of the valve. Spin the stick in both directions, while pressing it against the valve seat and lap the valve to the seat. See **Figure 85**. Every 5 to 10 seconds, rotate the valve 180° in the valve seat. Continue with this action until the mating surfaces on the valve and seat are smooth and equal in size.

4. Closely examine the valve seat in the cylinder head (**Figure 77**). It should be smooth and even with a polished seating ring.

5. Repeat Steps 1-4 for the remaining valves.

6. Thoroughly clean the valves and cylinder head in solvent or detergent and hot water to remove all valve grinding compound. Dry the components thoroughly.

CAUTION
Any compound left on the valves or the cylinder head will contaminate the oil and cause premature engine wear.

7. Install the valve assemblies as described in this chapter.

8. After the valves are installed in the head, perform a *Solvent Test* as described in this section. If there is leakage, remove that valve and repeat the lapping process.

9. Apply a light coat of engine oil to all bare metal surfaces to prevent rust.

CYLINDER

Removal

NOTE
If it is necessary to rotate the crankshaft, pull up the cam chains so they cannot bind internally.

1. Remove the cylinder head cover and cylinder head as described in this chapter.

2. On the rear cylinder, detach the wires from the wire clamp (A, **Figure 86**).

3. Remove the nuts (B, **Figure 86**) securing the cylinder to the crankcase.

4. Loosen the cylinder by tapping around the perimeter with a rubber or plastic mallet. If necessary, *gently* pry the cylinder loose with a broad-tipped screwdriver.

5. Pull the cylinder straight off the crankcase dowel pins and piston. Work the cam chain wire through the opening in the cylinder.

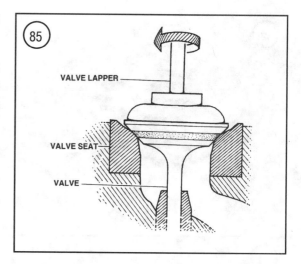

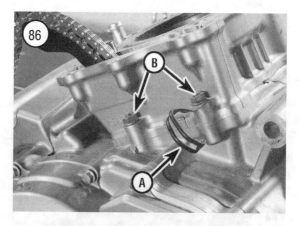

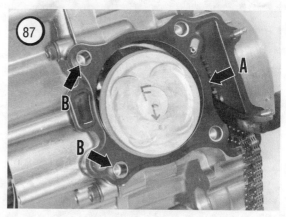

6. Remove the cylinder base gasket (A, **Figure 87**) and discard it. Remove the dowel pins (B) from the crankcase.

7. Install a piston holding fixture under the piston (**Figure 88**) to protect the piston skirt from damage. This fixture may be purchased or constructed of wood. See **Figure 89** for basic dimensions.

8. Place a clean shop cloth into the openings in the crankcase to prevent the entry of foreign material.

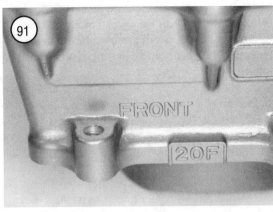

4

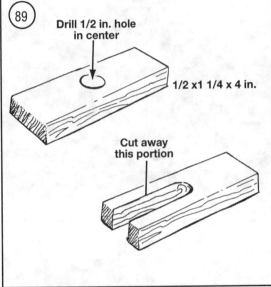

NOTE
*An oil passage jet is located on the top side of the crankcase (**Figure 90**). Refer to **Crankcase Inspection** in Chapter Five if service is necessary.*

9. Inspect the cylinder as described in this chapter.

Installation

NOTE
*The front and rear cylinders are not identical. Each cylinder is identified with FRONT or REAR embossed on the cylinder (**Figure 91**).*

NOTE
If it is necessary to rotate the crankshaft, pull up the cam chains so they cannot bind internally.

1. If used, remove the piston holding fixtures.

NOTE
When rotating the crankshaft, pull up the cam chains so they cannot bind internally. Protect the pistons so they will not be damaged when retracting into the crankcase.

2. Rotate the crankshaft so the piston being serviced is below the crankcase opening.

NOTE
Protect the piston and rings when applying sealer in Step 4.

3. Check that the top surface of the crankcase and the bottom surface of the cylinder are clean.
4. Apply a light coat of Suzuki Bond No. 1207B, or equivalent, to the crankcase mating surface joint on the crankcase-to-cylinder mating surface (A, **Figure 92**).
5. If removed, install the locating dowels (A, **Figure 93**).
6. Install a new cylinder base gasket (B, **Figure 93**).

NOTE
Be careful when installing the piston holding fixture so the cylinder base gasket is not damaged.

7. Rotate the crankshaft so the piston is above the crankcase, then install the piston holding fixture.

8. Apply a liberal coat of clean engine oil to the cylinder wall, especially at the lower end where the piston will enter.

9. Apply clean engine oil to the piston and piston rings. This will make it easier to guide the piston into the cylinder bore.

10. Make sure the piston ring end gaps are not aligned—they must be staggered evenly around the piston circumference.

11. Start the cylinder down over the piston. Compress each piston ring with your fingers as it enters the cylinder.

12. Push the cylinder down past the piston rings.

13. Carefully feed the cam chain and wire up through the opening in the cylinder and tie it to the engine.

14. Slide the cylinder down until it bottoms on the piston holding fixture.

15. Remove the piston holding fixture and push the cylinder down into place onto the crankcase until it bottoms.

16. Install the lower nuts (B, **Figure 86**) securing the cylinder to the crankcase and tighten only fingertight at this time. On the rear cylinder, install the wiring clamp (A).

17. Install the cylinder head as described in this chapter.

18. Tighten the cylinder-to-crankcase lower nuts (B, **Figure 86**), installed in Step 16, to 10 N•m (88 in.lb.).

19. Install the cylinder head as described in this chapter.

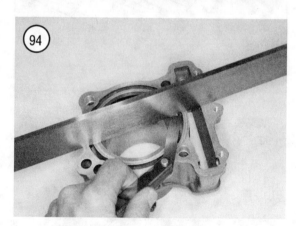

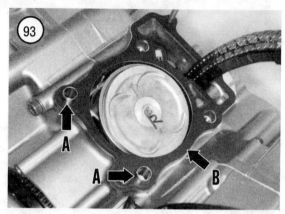

Inspection

1. Thoroughly clean the cylinder with solvent. Then, using a dull gasket scraper, carefully remove all gasket material from the top and bottom mating surfaces on the cylinder. Do not nick or gouge the gasket surfaces or leakage will result.

2. After the cylinder has been thoroughly cleaned, place a straightedge across the cylinder-to-cylinder head gasket surface at several points. Measure warp (**Figure 94**) by attempting to insert a feeler gauge between the straightedge and cylinder at each location. The maximum warp limit is 0.05 mm (0.002 in.). There should be no warpage. Replace the cylinder if the gasket surface is warped to or beyond the specified limit.

3. Thoroughly check the bore surface for scratches or gouges. If damaged in any way, the bore will require boring and reconditioning.

4. Determine piston-to-cylinder clearance as described in *Piston Clearance* in this chapter.

5. If the cylinder requires service, such as boring, remove all dowel pins from the cylinder prior to taking it to a dealer or machine shop for service.

6. After the cylinder has been serviced, perform the following:

CAUTION
A combination of soap and hot water is the only solution that will completely clean cylinder walls. Solvent and kerosene cannot wash fine grit out of cylinder crevices. Any grit left in the cylinder will act as a grinding com-

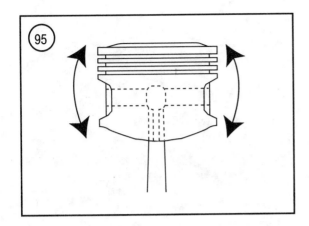

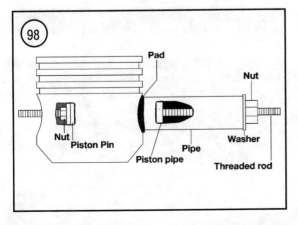

Pad

Nut

Nut
Piston Pin

Washer

Pipe

Piston pipe

Threaded rod

pound and cause premature wear to the new rings.

a. Wash the cylinder bore in hot soapy water. This is the only way to clean the cylinder of the fine grit material left from the honing procedure.

b. Also wash out any fine grit material from the cooling passages surrounding the cylinder.

c. After washing the cylinder wall, wipe the cylinder wall with a clean white cloth. It should not show any traces of grit or debris. If the rag is the slightest bit dirty, the wall is not thoroughly cleaned and must be washed again.

PISTON AND PISTON RINGS

The pistons are made of an aluminum alloy. The piston pin is made of steel and is a precision fit in the pistons. The piston pins are secured by a clip at each end.

Piston Removal

NOTE
If it is necessary to rotate the crankshaft, pull up the cam chains so they cannot bind internally. Protect the pistons so they will not be damaged when retracting into the crankcase.

1. Remove the cylinder head and cylinder as described in this chapter.

2. Mark the top of the piston with an identification letter (F or R).

3. Block off the crankcase below the piston with a clean shop cloth to prevent the piston pin circlips from falling into the crankcase.

4. Before removing the piston, hold the rod tightly and rock the piston (**Figure 95**). Any rocking motion (do not confuse with the normal sliding motion) indicates wear on the piston pin, rod bushing, pin bore, or more likely, a combination of all three.

5. Remove the circlip (**Figure 96**) from one side of the piston pin bore.

6. From the other side, push the piston pin (**Figure 97**) out of the piston by hand. If the pin is tight, use a homemade tool (**Figure 98**) and remove it. Do not drive the piston pin out. This action could damage the piston pin, connecting rod or piston.

7. Lift the piston off the connecting rod.

8. Inspect the piston as described in this chapter.

Piston Inspection

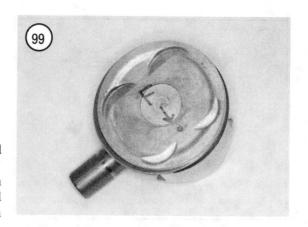

CAUTION
*If piston and/or piston ring replacement is necessary, verify that piston and piston rings are compatible. Refer to **Piston Ring Inspection** in this section.*

1. If necessary, remove the piston rings as described in this chapter.
2. Carefully clean the carbon from the piston crown (**Figure 99**) with a soft scraper or wire wheel mounted in a drill. Large carbon accumulations reduce piston cooling and result in detonation and piston damage. Renumber the piston as soon as it is cleaned.

CAUTION
Be careful not to gouge or damage the piston when removing carbon. Never use a wire brush to clean the piston skirt or ring grooves. Do not attempt to remove carbon from the sides of the piston above the top ring or from the cylinder bore near the top. Removal of carbon from these two areas may cause increased oil consumption.

3. After cleaning the piston, examine the crown. The crown should show no signs of wear or damage. If the crown appears pecked or spongy-looking, also check the spark plug, valves and combustion chamber for aluminum deposits. If these deposits are found, the engine is overheating.
4. Examine each ring groove (A, **Figure 100**) for burrs, dented edges or other damage. Pay particular attention to the top compression ring groove. It usually wears more than the others. Because the oil rings are constantly bathed in oil, these rings and grooves wear little compared to compression rings and their grooves. If there is evidence of oil ring groove wear or if the oil ring assembly is tight and difficult to remove, the piston skirt may have collapsed due to excessive heat. Replace the piston.

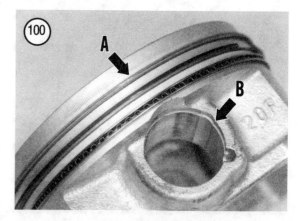

5. Check the oil control holes (**Figure 101**) in the piston for carbon or oil sludge buildup. Clean the holes with wire and blow them clear with compressed air.
6. Inspect the piston skirt (**Figure 102**) for cracks or other damage. If a piston shows signs of partial seizure (bits of aluminum buildup on the piston skirt), it should be replaced to reduce the possibility of engine noise and further engine damage.

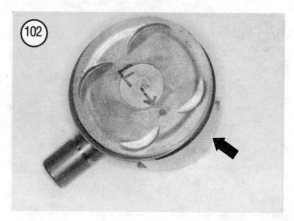

NOTE
If the piston skirt is worn or scuffed unevenly from side-to-side, the connecting rod may be bent or twisted.

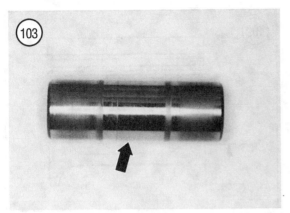

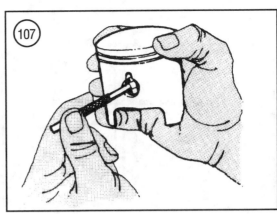

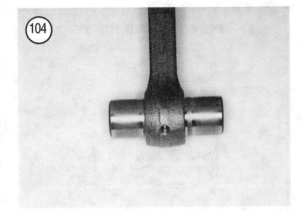

7. Check the circlip groove (B, **Figure 100**) on each side for wear, cracks or other damage. If the grooves are questionable, check the circlip fit by installing a new circlip into each groove and then attempt to move the circlip from side-to-side. If the circlip has any side play, the groove is worn and the piston must be replaced.

8. Measure piston-to-cylinder clearance as described in *Piston Clearance* in this chapter.

9. If damage or wear indicate piston replacement, select a new piston as described under *Piston Clearance* in this chapter. If the piston, rings and cylinder are not damaged and are dimensionally correct, they can be reused.

Piston Pin
Inspection

1. Clean the piston pin in solvent, and dry it thoroughly.

2. Inspect the piston pin (**Figure 103**) for chrome flaking or cracks. Replace if necessary.

3. Lubricate the piston pin with engine oil and install it into the connecting rod (**Figure 104**). Slowly rotate the piston pin and check for radial play.

4. Lubricate the piston pin and partially install it into the piston (**Figure 105**). Check the piston pin for excessive play (**Figure 106**).

5. Measure the piston pin outside diameter with a micrometer. If the piston pin outside diameter is less than 19.980 mm (0.7866 in.), replace the piston pin.

6. Measure the inside diameter of the piston pin bore (**Figure 107**) with a small hole gauge. Measure the small hole gauge with a micrometer. If the measurement exceeds 20.030 mm (0.7886 in.), replace the piston.

7. Replace the piston pin and/or piston or connecting rod if necessary.

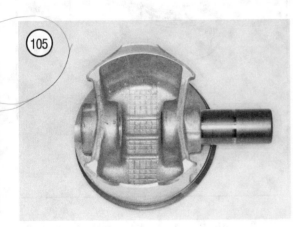

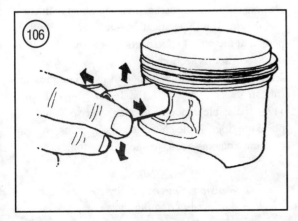

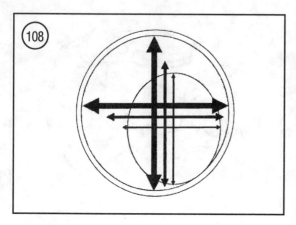

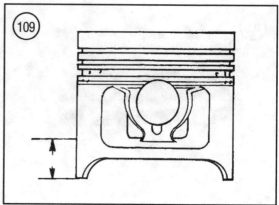

Piston Clearance

1. Make sure the piston skirt and cylinder wall are clean and dry.
2. Measure the cylinder bore with a bore gauge or inside micrometer. Measure the cylinder bore at the three positions shown in **Figure 108**. Measure in line with the piston pin and 90° to the pin. Record the bore inner diameter measurement.
3. Measure the piston outside diameter with a micrometer at a right angle to the piston pin bore. Measure up 20 mm (0.79 in.) from the bottom edge of the piston skirt (**Figure 109**).
4. Subtract the piston outside diameter from the largest bore diameter; the difference is piston-to-cylinder clearance. If the clearance exceeds 0.055-0.065 mm (0.0021-0.0026 in.), determine if the piston, cylinder or both are worn. If necessary, take the cylinder to a dealership that can rebore the cylinder to accept an oversize piston.

Piston Ring
Inspection and Removal

The piston and ring assembly is a 3-ring type (**Figure 110**). The top and second rings are compression rings. The lower ring is an oil control ring assembly (consisting of two ring rails and an expander spacer).

Note the configuration of the top ring used on 2004-2006 models and 2007-2011 models as shown in **Figure 111** as well as the piston groove shape. The piston and piston rings must match.

CAUTION
Make sure the piston and piston rings are compatible when ordering parts. Parts installed during a previous repair may have been selected from another model year.

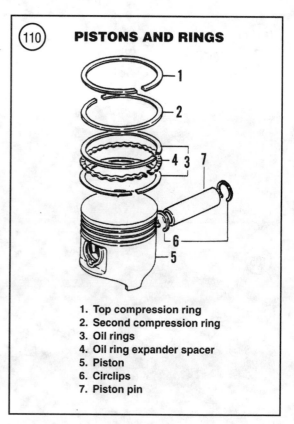

PISTONS AND RINGS

1. Top compression ring
2. Second compression ring
3. Oil rings
4. Oil ring expander spacer
5. Piston
6. Circlips
7. Piston pin

When measuring the piston rings and piston in this section, compare the actual measurements to the new and service limit specifications in **Table 2**. Replace parts that are out of specification or show damage as described in this section.

1. Measure the side clearance of each compression ring in its groove with a flat feeler gauge (**Figure 112**). If the clearance is greater than specified, replace the rings. If the clearance is still excessive with the new rings installed, replace the piston.

WARNING
The piston ring edges are sharp. Be careful when handling them.

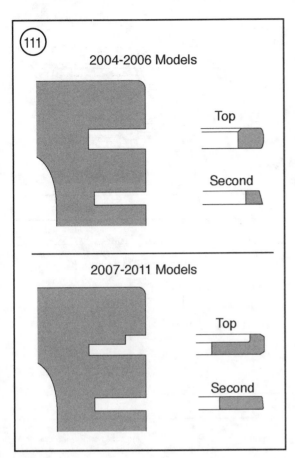

2004-2006 Models

Top

Second

2007-2011 Models

Top

Second

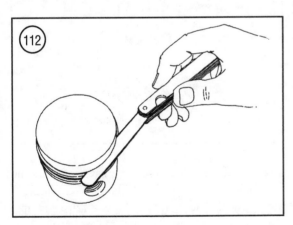

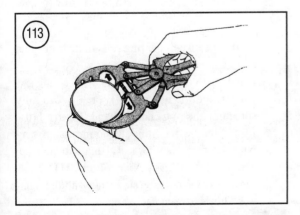

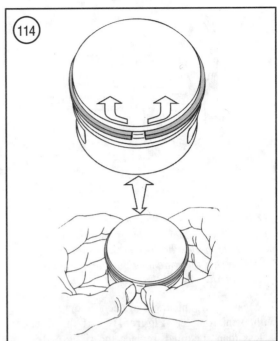

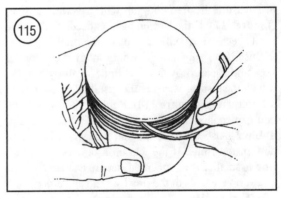

NOTE
Store the old rings in the order they were removed.

2. Remove the compression rings with a ring expander tool (**Figure 113**) or by spreading the ring ends by hand (**Figure 114**).

3. Remove the oil ring assembly by first removing the upper and then the lower ring rails. Then remove the expander spacer.

4. Using a broken piston ring, carefully remove carbon and oil residue from the piston ring grooves (**Figure 115**). Do not remove aluminum material from the ring grooves as this increases ring side clearance.

5. Measure each compression ring groove width with a vernier caliper. Measure each groove at several points around the piston. Replace the piston if any groove is outside the specified range.

6. Inspect grooves carefully for burrs, nicks or broken or cracked lands. Replace the piston if necessary.

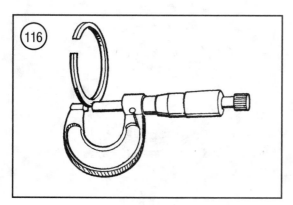

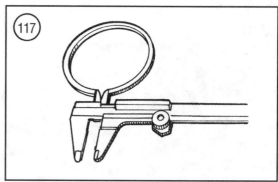

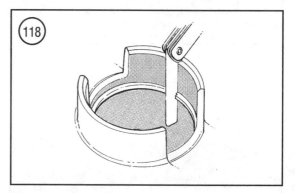

NOTE
The top compression ring on 2007-2011 models has two measurable thicknesses: the wide face thickness and the narrower inner thickness.

7. Measure the thickness of each compression ring with a micrometer (**Figure 116**). If the thickness is less than specified, replace the ring(s). Refer to **Table 2**.

8. Measure the free end gap with a vernier caliper (**Figure 117**). If the free end gap exceeds the service limit specified in **Table 2**, replace the ring(s).

9. Insert the ring into the bottom of the cylinder bore and square it with the cylinder wall by tapping it with the piston. Measure the installed end gap with a feeler gauge (**Figure 118**). Replace the rings if the end gap equals or exceeds service limit specified in **Table 2**. Also measure the end gap when installing new piston rings. If the gap on a new compression ring is smaller than specified, secure a small file in a vise, grip the ends of the ring by hand and enlarge the gap (**Figure 119**).

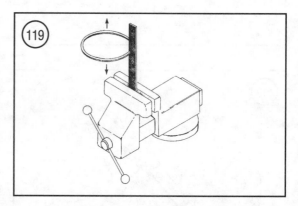

Piston Ring Installation

1. If new rings will be installed, deglaze or hone the cylinder. This helps seat the new rings. Refer honing service to a dealership or machine shop. After honing, measure the ring end gap for each compression ring.

2. Clean the piston and rings. Dry them with compressed air.

3. Install the piston rings as follows:

WARNING
The piston ring edges are sharp. Be careful when handling them.

NOTE
When installing aftermarket piston rings, follow the manufacturer's directions.

a. Install the oil control ring assembly into the bottom ring groove. Install the oil ring expander spacer first (A, **Figure 120**), and then install each ring rail (B). Make sure the ends of the expander spacer butt together (**Figure 121**). They should not overlap. If reassembling used parts, install the ring rails in their original positions.

b. Install the compression rings with a ring expander tool (**Figure 109**) or by carefully spreading the ring ends by hand (**Figure 110**).

c. Install the 2nd or middle compression ring with the manufacturer's RN mark facing up. This ring has a slight taper (**Figure 111**).

d. Install the top compression ring with the manufacturer's R mark facing up.

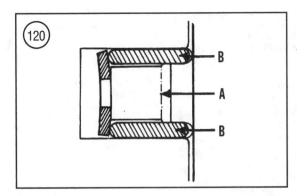

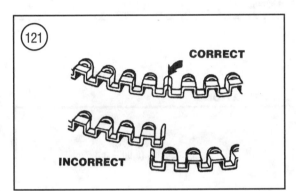

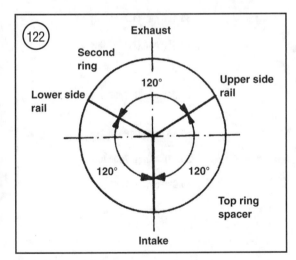

4. Make sure the rings are seated completely in their grooves all the way around the piston and that the end gaps are distributed around the piston as shown in **Figure 122**. To prevent the compressed air from escaping past them, the ring gaps must not align.

5. If new parts were installed, follow the *Engine Break-In* procedure in Chapter Five.

Piston Installation

NOTE
If it is necessary to rotate the crank-shaft, pull up the cam chains so they cannot bind internally.

1. Coat the connecting rod bushing, piston pin and piston with molybdenum grease.

2. Install a *new* circlip into one side of the piston. Make sure it is correctly seated in the piston groove. The circlip ends must not align with the notch adjacent to the piston pin bore (**Figure 123**).

3. Slide the piston pin into the piston until its end is flush with the piston pin boss.

4. Place the correct piston onto the connecting rod so the indexing dot on the piston crown is toward the exhaust side of the engine (**Figure 124**).

5. Align the piston pin with the hole in the connecting rod. Push the piston pin through the connecting rod and into the other side of the piston until it is centered in the piston.

6. Install a *new* piston pin circlip into the other side of the pin boss. Make sure the circlip is seated correctly in the piston groove.

7. If removed, install the piston rings as described in this chapter.

8. Install the cylinder and cylinder head as described in this chapter.

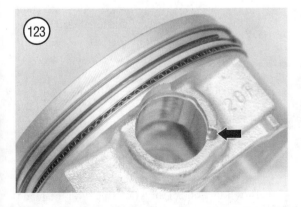

Table 1 GENERAL ENGINE SPECIFICATIONS

Item	Specification
Type	4 stroke, liquid cooled, DOHC
Number of cylinders	2
Firing order	front, then rear cylinder
Bore and stroke	81.0x 62.6 mm
	(3.189x2.465 in.)
Displacement	645 cc (39.4 cu. in.)
Compression ratio	11.5 to 1
Compression pressure (at sea level)	
Standard	1,300-1,700 kPa (185-242 psi)
Service limit	1,100 kPa (156 psi)
Maximum difference between cylinders	200 kPa (28 psi)
Ignition timing	4° BTDC @ 1300 rpm
Lubrication	Wet sump

Table 2 TOP END SPECIFICATIONS

Camshaft		
Cam journal holder		–
Inner diameter	22.012 22.025 mm	
	(0.8666 0.8671 in.)	
Cam journal oil clearance	0.032 0.066 mm	0.150 mm (0.0059 in.)
	(0.0013 0.0026 in.)	
Cam journal outer diameter	21.959 21.980 mm	–
	(0.8645 0.8654 in.)	
Cam lobe height		
Intake	35.480 35.530 mm	35.180 mm (1.3850 in.)
	(1.3968 1.3988 in.)	
Exhaust	33.480 33.530 mm	33.180 mm (1.3063 in.)
	(1.3181 1.3201 in.)	
Runout	–	0.10 mm (0.004 in.)
Connecting rod		
Small end inner diameter	20.010 20.018 mm	20.040 mm (0.7890 in.)
	(0.7878 0.7881 in.)	
Cylinder head warpage (max.)	0.05 mm (0.002 in.)	
Piston diameter	80.950 80.955 mm	80.88 mm (3.184 in.)
	(3.1870 3.1872 in.)	
Piston pin bore diameter	20.002 20.008 mm	20.030 mm (0.7886 in.)
	(0.7875 0.7877 in.)	
Piston pin diameter	19.992 20.000 mm	19.980 mm (0.7866 in.)
	(0.7871 0.7874 in.)	
Piston-to-cylinder clearance	0.055-0.065 mm	0.120 mm (0.0047 in.)
	(0.0022-0.0026 in.)	
Piston ring groove width*		
2004-2006 models		
Top ring	1.21-1.23	–
	(0.0476-0.0484	
Second ring	1.01-1.03	–
	(0.0398-0.0406)	
Oil control ring	2.01-2.03	–
	(0.0791-0.0799)	
2007-2011 models		
Top ring**		
At face	1.30-1.32	–
	(0.0512-0.0520	
Internal groove	0.83-0.85	–
	(0.0327-0.0335)	
Second ring	1.01-1.03	–
	(0.0398-0.0406)	
Oil control ring	2.01-2.03	–
	(0.0791-0.0799)	

(continued)

Table 2 TOP END SPECIFICATIONS (continued)

Piston rings		
Number of rings		
Compression	2	
Oil control	1	
Ring free end gap		
Top		
2004-2006 models	Approx. 9.5 mm (0.37 in.)	7.6 mm (0.30 in.)
2007-2011 models	Approx. 7.0 mm (0.28 in.)	5.6 mm (0.22 in.)
Second	Approx. 11.0 mm (0.43 in.)	8.8 mm (0.35 in.)
Ring end gap (in cylinder bore)		
Top & second	0.20 0.35 mm (0.008 0.014 in.)	0.70 mm (0.028 in.)
Ring side clearance		
Top	–	0.180 mm (0.0071 in.)
Second	–	0.150 mm (0.0059 in.)
Ring thickness*		
Top		
2004-2006 models	1.17 1.19 mm (0.046 0.047 in.)	–
2007-2011 models**		
At face	1.08 1.10 mm (0.042 0.043 in.)	–
Internal blade	0.76 0.81 mm (0.030 0.032 in.)	–
Second	0.97 0.99 mm (0.038 0.039 in.)	–
Valve stem outer diameter		
Intake	4.465 4.480 mm (0.1758 0.1764 in.)	–
Exhaust	4.455 4.470 mm (0.1754 0.1760 in.)	–
Valve guide inner diameter		
Intake and exhaust	4.500 4.512 mm (0.1772 0.1776 in.)	–
Valve stem to guide clearance		
Intake	0.020 0.047 mm (0.0008 0.0018 in.)	–
Exhaust	0.030 0.057 mm (0.0012 0.0022 in.)	–
Valve seat width		
Intake and exhaust	0.9 1.1 mm (0.035 0.043 in.)	–
Valve stem runout	–	0.05 mm (0.002 in.)
Valve head radial runout	–	0.03 mm (0.001 in.)
Valve spring free length		
(intake and exhaust)		
Inner spring	–	36.8 mm (1.45 in.)
Outer spring	–	39.8 mm (1.57 in.)
Valve spring pressure		
(intake and exhaust)		
Inner spring	4.2-4.8 kg @ 29.9 mm (9.3-10.6 lb. @ 1.18 in.)	–
Outer spring	17.0-19.6 kg @ 33.4 mm (37.5-43.2 lb. @ 1.31 in.)	–

*Refer to text to verify piston and piston ring design.
**L-shaped piston ring.

Table 3 TOP END TORQUE SPECIFICATIONS

Item	N•m	in. lb.	ft.-lb.
Cam chain guide mounting bolt	10	88	–
Cam chain tensioner cap bolt	23	–	17
Cam chain tensioner mounting bolt	10	88	–
Camshaft holder	10	88	–
Camshaft top chain guide	10	88	–
Cylinder head bolts			
6 mm	10	88	–
10 mm			
Initial	25	–	18
Final	42	–	31
Cylinder head cover bolt	14	124	–
Cylinder head side socket head bolt	10	88	–
Cylinder head to crankcase lower nuts	10	88	–
Exhaust system fasteners	23	–	17

Notes

4

Notes

CHAPTER FIVE

ENGINE LOWER END

This chapter provides service procedures for lower end components. These include the crankcases, crankshaft and connecting rods, and the oil pump/ lubrication system. Service procedures for the transmission and internal shift mechanism assemblies are described in Chapter Seven.

Refer to **Tables 1-4** at the end of this chapter for specifications and bearing selection information.

References to the left and right sides refer to the position of the parts as viewed by the rider siting on the seat facing forward, not how the engine sits on the workbench.

SERVICING ENGINE IN FRAME

Many components can be serviced with the engine mounted in the frame–(the frame is a great holding fixture, especially for breaking loose stubborn bolts and nuts):

1. External gearshift mechanism.
2. Clutch.
3. Oil pump.
4. Throttle bodies.
5. Alternator.
6. Starter motor and gears.

ENGINE

Removal

This procedure describes engine removal and installation. It may be easier in some cases to remove as many engine assemblies as possible before removing the lower end from the frame. Following this method reduces the weight of the engine and allows the frame to be used as a holding fixture. Disassembling the engine on the workbench without some type of holding fixture can be difficult and time consuming.

NOTE
A special tool, Suzuki Engine Mounting Thrust Adjuster Socket Wrench (part No. 09940-14990) or equivalent, is required to remove and install the engine in the frame. Failure to use the tool will damage the engine mounting fasteners. Read the following procedure before removing the engine.

1. Securely support the bike on level ground.
2. Drain the engine oil and remove the oil filter as described in Chapter Three.
3. Drain the engine coolant as described in Chapter Three.
4. Remove the seat as described in Chapter Fifteen.

5. Disconnect the negative battery cable as described in Chapter Three.

6. Remove the fuel tank as described in Chapter Eight.

7. Remove the exhaust system as described in Chapter Four.

8. Remove the air box and throttle body assembly as described in Chapter Four.

9. Disconnect the spark plug leads.

10. Remove the radiator assembly and hoses as described in Chapter Ten.

11. Remove the coolant reservoir.

12. Remove the oil cooler as described in Chapter Ten.

13. Detach the clutch cable from the engine as described in Chapter Six.

14. Remove the engine sprocket and drive chain from the engine as described in Chapter Eleven.

15. Remove both footpeg brackets as described in Chapter Fifteen.

16. Disconnect the following electrical connectors:
   a. Engine ground cable
   b. Starter motor lead
   c. Alternator connector
   d. ECT sensor lead
   e. Neutral switch connector
   f. Oil pressure switch connector
   g. CKP connector

17. If the engine requires disassembly, remove the following sub-assemblies:
   a. Alternator (Chapter Nine).
   b. Clutch (Chapter Six).
   c. Oil pump (this chapter).
   d. Starter motor (Chapter Nine).

18. Move all electrical wires, harnesses and hoses out of the way.

19. Place a floor jack underneath the engine. Raise the jack so the pad just rests against the bottom of the engine. Place a thick wooden block on the jack pad to protect the engine.

CAUTION
*Use Suzuki special tool, Engine Mounting Thrust Adjuster Socket Wrench (part No. 09940-14990), to loosen the engine mounting fasteners. A socket wrench tool may be created from a suitable impact socket (**Figure 1**). This tool is also required to tighten the fasteners to the correct torque specification during installation.*

NOTE
The locknuts are self-locking and must be discarded after removal. Do not re-

use a self-locking nut or substitute another type of locknut.

20. Remove the nut (**Figure 2**) from the upper mounting bolt, then remove the bolt.

21. Use the special tool and remove the thrust adjuster locknut (A, **Figure 3**).

22. Loosen the thrust adjuster (B, **Figure 3**).

23. Remove the bolts (A, **Figure 4**) securing the left side engine mounting bracket (B).

24. Detach the ignition coil wires and coolant hose clamp. Remove the left side mounting bracket with the ignition coil. Note routing of spark plug wire(s).

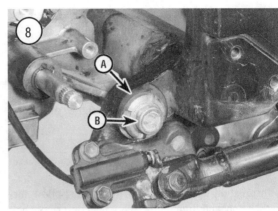

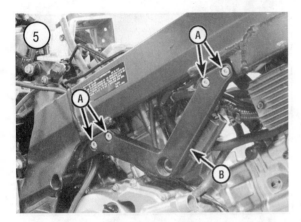

25. Remove the bolts (A, **Figure 5**) securing the right side engine mounting bracket (B).

26. Detach the ignition coil wires. Remove the right side mounting bracket and ignition coil. Note routing of spark plug wire(s).

27. Check to make sure the floor jack is still positioned correctly against the engine.

28. Detach the wires from the wire clamp (**Figure 6**).

29. Remove the nut (**Figure 7**) from the lower mounting bolt, then remove the bolt.

30. Use the special tool and remove the thrust adjuster locknut (A, **Figure 8**).

31. Loosen the thrust adjuster (B, **Figure 8**).

32. Loosen the clamp bolt (**Figure 9**).

33. Have an assistant steady the engine assembly, then remove the center mounting bolt (**Figure 10**) from the right side.

NOTE
While removing the engine, be sure the exhaust pipe on the rear cylinder head does not obstruct removal.

34. Carefully lower the engine from the frame.

35. Place the engine on a workbench.

36. While the engine is removed, check all the engine mounting points on the frame for cracks or other

damage. Also check the mounting bolts and holes for thread damage and repair them if necessary.

37. Remove corrosion from bolts and their threads with a wire wheel. Check the threads on all parts for wear or damage. Clean with the appropriate size metric tap or die and clean with solvent.

38. Before installation, spray the engine mounting bolts with a rust inhibitor.

Installation

Installation is the reverse of removal. Follow the installation and tightening sequence described below.

1. Verify that the center mounting sleeve (**Figure 11**) is properly positioned in the frame leg. A clamp bolt (**Figure 9**) secures the sleeve in the frame.

2. Make sure the engine mounting thrust adjuster (B, **Figure 8**) is installed in the frame.

3. Position the engine into the frame and align the mounting bolt holes with the frame.

4. Install the left and right mounting brackets (B, **Figure 4** and **Figure 5**). Apply ThreeBond 1342 to the bracket mounting bolts. Tighten the mounting bolts to 35 N•m (25 ft.-lb.).

5. Install the engine mounting bolts. Tighten until just snug.

6. Tighten the engine mounting thrust adjusters (B, **Figure 3** and **Figure 8**) to 12 N•m (106 in.-lb.).

7. Use the special tool and tighten the engine mounting thrust adjuster locknuts (A, **Figure 3** and **Figure 8**) to 45 N•m (33 ft.-lb.).

8. Tighten the center mounting bolt (**Figure 10**) to 55 N•m (40 ft.-lb.).

9. Tighten the clamp bolt (**Figure 9**) to 25 N•m (18 ft.-lb.).

10. Tighten the nut on the upper mounting bolt (**Figure 2**) to 93 N•m (68 ft.-lb.).

11. Tighten the nut on the lower mounting bolt (**Figure 7**) to 55 N•m (40 ft.-lb.).

12. Assemble the engine by reversing engine removal steps. Note the following:

   a. Fill the engine with the recommended type and quantity of engine oil and coolant as described in Chapter Three.

   b. Adjust the drive chain as described in Chapter Three.

LEFT CRANKCASE COVER

Removal/Installation

1. Remove the engine sprocket cover (**Figure 12**).

2. Detach the clutch release return spring (A, **Figure 13**).

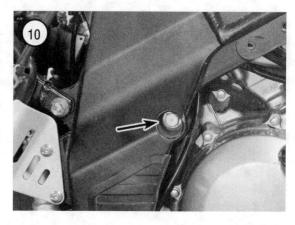

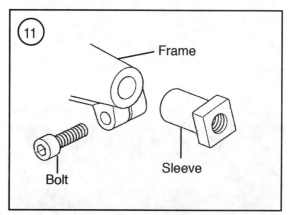

Frame

Sleeve

Bolt

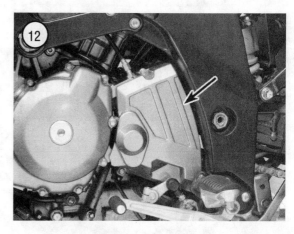

3. Loosen the clutch adjusting nut (B, **Figure 13**).

4. Remove the two retaining bolts, then remove the clutch release assembly (C, **Figure 13**).

5. Loosen the clutch cable mounting nuts (D, **Figure 13**) and separate the cable from the mounting arm on the left crankcase cover.

6. Remove the air box as described in Chapter Eight.

7. Disconnect the alternator three-wire electrical connector (A, **Figure 14**) and the CKP sensor two-wire connector (B).

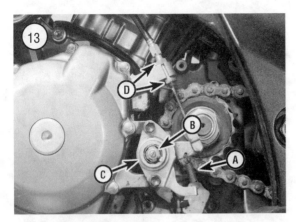

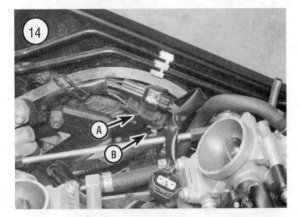

8. Remove the bolts securing the left crankcase cover (A, **Figure 15**) to the crankcase.

NOTE
Note the path of the wiring harness when withdrawing it in Step 8.

9. Extract the wiring harness from the engine.

10. Remove the left crankcase cover. Do not lose the two locating dowels which may reside in the side of the engine (**Figure 16**) or in the left crankcase cover.

11. If necessary, inspect the stator and CKP sensor as described in Chapter Nine.

12. Install by reversing the preceding removal steps while noting the following:

    a. If removed, install the two locating dowels (**Figure 16**).

    b. Install a new gasket.

    c. Note the location of the long bolts (B, **Figure 15**).

    d. Install a new gasket washer onto each of the bolts (C, **Figure 15**).

FLYWHEEL (ALTERNATOR ROTOR) AND STARTER CLUTCH

The alternator rotor mounted on the flywheel contains the magnets that energize the alternator stator coils. The alternator rotor and flywheel are available only as a unit assembly. The flywheel can be removed with the engine in the frame.

Flywheel Puller

A flywheel puller is required to remove the flywheel from the crankshaft. Use one of the following pullers or an equivalent:

    a. Suzuki flywheel puller (part No. 09930-30450).

    b. Motion Pro flywheel puller (part No. 08-0085).

CAUTION
Do not attempt to remove the flywheel without a puller. Doing so may damage the flywheel and crankshaft.

Removal/installation

1. Place a wrench on the flats of the flywheel (A, **Figure 17**), then remove the flywheel bolt (B) and washer.

2. Install the flywheel puller (A, **Figure 18**) into the threads of the flywheel.

3. Hold the flywheel with a suitable wrench (B, **Figure 18**). Turn the bolt or handle of the flywheel

puller until the flywheel disengages from the crankshaft taper. Remove the flywheel from the crankshaft.

> *CAUTION*
> *If the flywheel is difficult to remove, strike the end of the flywheel puller with a hammer. Do not strike the flywheel.*

> *CAUTION*
> *Do not apply excessive pressure to the puller. This could strip the threads in the flywheel. If the flywheel is difficult to remove, have a dealership perform the procedure.*

4. Remove the flywheel puller.

5. Inspect the inside of the flywheel for any metal debris that may have been picked up by the magnets. These small metal bits can damage the alternator stator assembly.

6. Install by reversing the preceding removal steps while noting the following:
   a. Use aerosol parts cleaner to clean all oil residue from the crankshaft taper and the matching tapered surface in the flywheel. This ensures a good tight fit between the flywheel and the crankshaft.
   b. Be sure the key is in place on the crankshaft (A, **Figure 19**).
   c. Apply a light coat engine oil to the mounting bolt threads before installation.
   d. Be sure the washer is mounted on the flywheel bolt, then tighten the flywheel bolt to 120 N•m (88 ft.-lb.).

STARTER CLUTCH AND IDLER GEAR

Removal

1. Remove the flywheel as described in this chapter.
2. Remove the drive key (A, **Figure 19**).
3. Remove the starter driven gear (B, **Figure 19**).
4. Extract the idler shaft (A, **Figure 20**), then remove the starter idler gear (B).
5. Inspect all components as described in the following section.
6. Install by reversing the removal steps.

Disassembly/Inspection/Assembly

Refer to **Figure 21** for this procedure.

1. Inspect the starter idler gear and shaft (**Figure 22**) for wear or damage. Replace if necessary.
2. Set the flywheel and starter driven gear on the workbench with the flywheel facing down.
3. Inspect the one-way clutch as follows:

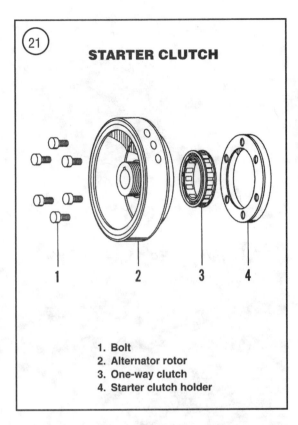

STARTER CLUTCH

1. Bolt
2. Alternator rotor
3. One-way clutch
4. Starter clutch holder

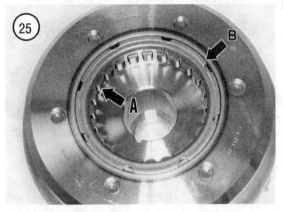

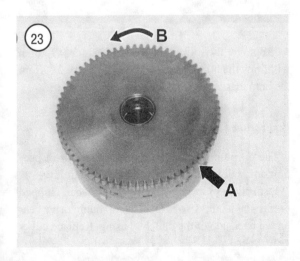

a. Rotate the starter driven gear (A, **Figure 23**) clockwise (B); it should not rotate.
b. Rotate the starter driven gear (A, **Figure 23**) counterclockwise (C); it should rotate.
c. If the one-way clutch fails either of these tests, replace the one-way clutch.

NOTE
The starter driven gear, starter clutch holder and one-way clutch are only available as an assembly.

4. Rotate the starter driven gear (A, **Figure 23**) counterclockwise (B) and pull it up at the same time. Remove the gear from the backside of the AC generator flywheel.

5. Inspect the starter driven gear for wear, chipped or missing teeth (A, **Figure 24**). Replace the gear if necessary.

6. Inspect the starter driven gear bushing (B, **Figure 24**) for wear or damage. The bushing is not available separately from the gear.

7. Inspect the starter driven gear outer surface (C, **Figure 24**) where it rides on the one-way clutch. If the surface is damaged, replace the gear.

8. Inspect the rollers (A, **Figure 25**) of the one-way clutch for burrs, wear or damage. If necessary, remove the one-way clutch as follows:

a. Use a wrench on the hex portion (A, **Figure 26**) of the flywheel or a strap-type wrench (B). Hold the flywheel stationary while loosening the Allen bolts in the next step.

> *CAUTION*
> *The Allen bolts have a locking agent applied to them during installation. Use the correct size wrench to loosen the screws, otherwise, the screw heads will be damaged.*

b. Loosen, then remove the Allen bolts (C, **Figure 26**) securing the starter clutch holder and one-way clutch to the backside of the AC generator flywheel.

c. Remove the starter clutch holder (B, **Figure 25**) and the one-way clutch from the backside of the flywheel.

d. If removed, install the one-way clutch so the flanged side fits into the notch on the starter clutch holder. Install the starter clutch holder (B, **Figure 25**) so the stepped side is toward the flywheel and align the bolt holes.

e. Apply Threadlock Super 1303 to the Allen bolt threads prior to installation, then install the bolts (C, **Figure 26**). Use the same tool set up used for loosening the bolts and tighten the bolts to 25 N•m (18 ft.-lb.).

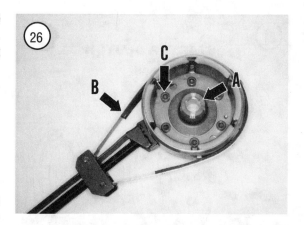

OIL PUMP

The oil pump is mounted behind the clutch on the right side of the engine. The oil pump can be removed with the engine mounted in the frame. Replacement parts are not available for the oil pump with the exception of the oil pump gear. If the oil pump is not operating properly, replace the entire oil pump assembly.

If abnormal oil pressure is suspected, perform the oil pressure test described in Chapter Two.

Removal

1. Remove the clutch as described in Chapter Six.
2. Remove the circlip (A, **Figure 27**) securing the gear, then remove the gear (B).
3. Remove the pin (A, **Figure 28**) and washer (B).

> *CAUTION*
> *Use an impact driver or air tool to loosen the screws. The screw heads may be damaged if removal is tried using a hand-held, regular Phillips head screwdriver.*

4. Remove the oil pump mounting screws, then withdraw the oil pump assembly (C, **Figure 28**) from the crankcase.

Inspection

The oil pump cannot be disassembled for inspection or service and must be replaced as a unit.

Inspect the oil pump driven gear for wear, chipped or missing teeth. Also inspect the oil pump drive gear on the backside of the clutch housing. Replace either gear if necessary.

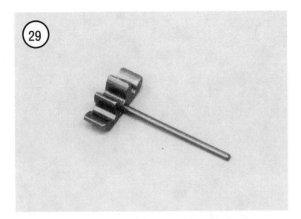

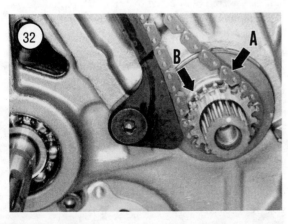

Installation

1. If a new oil pump is being installed or the existing oil pump was cleaned in solvent, the oil pump must be primed. Pour fresh engine oil into one of the openings in the backside of the oil pump until it runs out the other opening. Rotate the drive shaft several times by hand to make sure the internal flywheels within the oil pump are coated with oil.

2. Reverse the removal steps to install the oil pump. Apply suitable threadlock to the oil pump mounting screws. Tighten the oil pump mounting screws securely.

PRIMARY AND WATER PUMP DRIVE GEARS

The primary drive gear is located between the water pump drive gear and rear cylinder cam chain drive sprocket on the right end of the crankshaft. Removing the primary drive gear requires clutch removal.

Removal/Installation

1. Remove the clutch plates and clutch hub as described in the clutch removal section in Chapter Six.

2. To prevent gear rotation when loosening the retaining bolt, the following methods may be used.

   a. Place a gear holder tool (**Figure 29**) or small gear in mesh with the clutch and primary drive gears (A, **Figure 30**).

   b. Place a soft copper washer (copper penny) or shop cloth into mesh with the gears. This will prevent the primary drive gear from turning in the next step.

NOTE
The primary drive gear retaining bolt has left-hand threads. Loosen it by turning it clockwise.

3. Remove the primary drive gear retaining bolt (B, **Figure 30**) by turning the bolt clockwise (left-hand threads).

4. Remove the water pump drive gear (A, **Figure 31**).

5. Remove the clutch housing as described in Chapter Six.

6. Remove the primary drive gear (B, **Figure 31**). The rear cylinder cam chain (A, **Figure 32**) and sprocket (B) are now accessible.

7. Inspect the gears for excessive wear and damage. Replace if necessary.

8. Install the primary drive gear and water pump drive gear by reversing the removal procedure. Clean

the threads of any oil, then tighten the retaining bolt to 70 N•m (51 ft.-lb.).

> *NOTE*
> *The primary drive gear retaining bolt has left-hand threads. Tighten it by turning it counterclockwise.*

CAM CHAIN SPROCKETS

The cam chain in the front cylinder is driven by an integral sprocket on the crankshaft behind the starter driven gear. The cam chain in the rear cylinder is driven by a removable sprocket on the crankshaft behind the primary drive gear.

Proceed as follows to service the removable cam chain sprocket for the rear cylinder.

1. Remove the primary drive gear as previously described.

2. Remove the cam chain drive sprocket (A, **Figure 33**).

3. Inspect the sprocket for excessive wear and damage. Replace if necessary.

> *NOTE*
> *If replacing the drive sprocket, also install a new cam chain.*

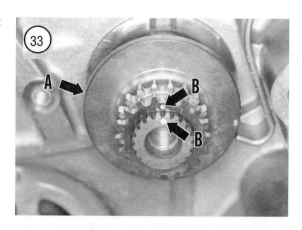

4. Install the cam chain drive sprocket by reversing the removal procedure. Be sure to align the timing marks (B, **Figure 33**) on the sprocket and crankshaft end when installing the sprocket on the crankshaft.

CRANKCASE

The following procedures detail the disassembly and reassembly of the crankcase. When the two halves of the crankcase are disassembled-or split-the crankshaft, balancer shaft and transmission assemblies can be removed for inspection and repair. Before proceeding with this procedure, remove the engine from the frame as described in this chapter. All assemblies located in the crankcase covers must be removed. It may be easier to remove these assemblies with the engine in the frame. The engine will remain steady during the disassembly process.

The crankcase halves are made of cast aluminum alloy. Do not hammer or pry on the cases. The cases will fracture or break. The cases are aligned at the joint by dowels and joined with liquid sealant.

Special Tools

Crankcase disassembly requires the use of a crankcase separation tool: Suzuki part No. 09920-13120. A

suitable equivalent tool is offered by K&L or Motion Pro and can be ordered at motorcycle dealerships.

Crankcase Disassembly

The procedure that follows is presented as a complete, step-by-step, major lower end rebuild that should be followed if an engine is to be completely reconditioned. However, if replacing a defective part, the disassembly should be carried out only until the failed part is accessible; there is no need to disassemble the engine beyond that point so long as you know the remaining components are in good condition and that they were not affected by the failed part.

Remember that the right and left side of the engine relates to the engine as it sits in the frame, not as it sits on the workbench.

1. Remove the engine as described in this chapter.

2. Place the engine on wood blocks or a wood fixture (**Figure 34**). Make certain the engine is supported at the crankcase and not the crankshaft.

3. Remove all exterior engine assemblies as described in this chapter and related chapters. Be sure to also remove the following components:

   a. External shift mechanism as described in Chapter Six.

   b. Oil seal retainer (A, **Figure 35**).

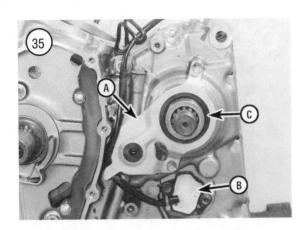

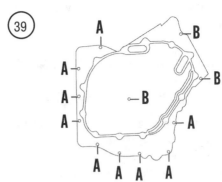

c. Neutral switch, contact pins and springs (B, **Figure 35**) as described in Chapter Nine.

d. Spacer (C, **Figure 35**).

e. Cam chains and rear cylinder sprocket as described in Chapter Four and this chapter.

f. Oil pipe retainer (**Figure 36**) and oil pipe (**Figure 37**).

4. Remove the four crankcase bolts on the left side as shown at A, **Figure 38**. Loosen the bolts in two steps in a crossing pattern. The upper, rear bolt also secures the wire clamp (B). Remove the oil plate (C, **Figure 38**).

5. Remove the crankcase bolts on the right side indicated in **Figure 39**. Note the location of the 6 mm bolts (A) and 8 mm bolts (B).

> *CAUTION*
> *Perform the next step directly over and close to the workbench as the crankcase halves may separate easily. Do not hammer on the crankcase halves.*

6. Place the crankcase assembly on the wooden box or wooden blocks on its left side with the right side facing up.

7. Install the crankcase separating tool (**Figure 40**). If the proper tools are not available, take the crankcase assembly to a dealer and have it separated. Do

not risk expensive crankcase damage with improper tools or techniques.

> *NOTE*
> *Never pry between case halves. Doing so may result in oil leaks, requiring replacement of the case halves as a set.*

8. Don't lose the locating dowels (**Figure 41**) if they are loose in the case. They do not have to be removed from the case if they are secure.

9. Remove the transmission, shift drum and shift fork shaft assemblies as described in Chapter Seven.

10. The crankshaft assembly (**Figure 42**) can be removed at this time, if desired.

11. Inspect the crankcase halves and crankshaft assembly as described in this chapter.

Crankcase Reassembly

Before assembling the crankcase, make sure the following components are properly installed, if removed:

    a. Connecting rods
    b. Main bearings
    c. Oil strainer and oil regulator
    d. Oil jets
    e. Oil seals
    f. Transmission assembly and bearings

> *NOTE*
> *Set the left crankcase half assembly on wooden blocks or the wooden holding fixture (shown in the disassembly procedure.*

> *NOTE*
> *Lubricate the lips of all oil seals with clean engine oil.*

1. Apply a light coat of molybdenum disulfide grease to the thrust surfaces at both ends on the crankshaft (A, **Figure 43**).

2. Apply a light coat of molybdenum disulfide grease to the main bearing surfaces at both ends on the crankshaft (B, **Figure 43**).

3. Carefully install the crankshaft into the left crankcase half (tapered crankshaft end toward left crankcase half) while positioning the connecting rods into their respective cylinder openings.

4. Make sure the dowel pins (**Figure 41**) are installed.

> *NOTE*
> *Apply a light coat of grease to the O-rings in Step 8 to hold them in*

place when assembling the crankcase halves.

5. Install the O-rings (**Figure 44**) into the recesses in the left crankcase half.

> *NOTE*
> *Make sure the crankcase mating surfaces are clean and free of all old sealant material.*

6. Apply a light coat of Suzuki Bond No. 1207B or 1215, or equivalent, to the mating surface of the left crankcase half as shown in **Figure 45**.

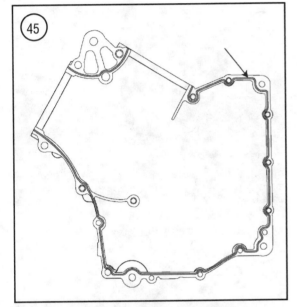

9. Be sure to install the wire clamp onto the upper crankcase bolt (B, **Figure 38**).

10. Tighten the crankcase 8 mm bolts (A, **Figure 38**) on the left crankcase half in a crossing pattern to 26 N•m (19 ft.-lb.).

11. Install the oil plate (C, **Figure 38**) onto the left crankcase half. Tighten the bolts to 10 N•m (88 in.-lb.).

12. Reassemble the remainder of the crankcase by reversing the removal procedure while noting the following:

   a. Install the oil pipe so the crimped end is out (**Figure 37**). Install the oil pipe retainer as shown in **Figure 36**.

   b. Install a new O-ring into the groove into the output shaft spacer (**Figure 46**). Lubricate the O-ring and oil seal, then install the spacer so the grooved end is in and the flat end (**Figure 47**) is out.

Crankcase Inspection

1. Clean the crankcase halves and clean all crankcase bearings with cleaning solvent. Thoroughly dry all components with compressed air. Make sure there is no solvent residue left in the cases as it will contaminate the new engine oil.

2. Using a scraper, *carefully* remove any remaining sealer residue from all crankcase sealing surfaces.

3. Carefully check the sealing surface of both crankcase halves. Check for gouges or nicks that may lead to an oil leak.

4. Service the piston cooling jets as follows:

   a. Remove the piston cooling oil jet retainer (**Figure 48**) and the cooling jet (**Figure 49**). Each crankcase half is equipped with a cooling jet.

   b. Clean the jet and the jet passage.

   c. Install a new O-ring onto the jet before installing it. Lubricate the O-ring with engine oil.

7. Install the right crankcase half onto the left crankcase half.

8. Install the crankcase bolts (**Figure 39**) and tighten in a crossing pattern. Tighten the 6 mm bolts to 11 N•m (97 in.-lb.). Tighten the 8 mm bolts to 26 N•m (19 ft.-lb.).

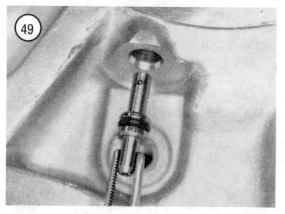

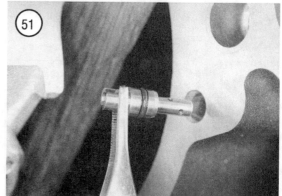

d. Install the jet so the hole in the tip points toward the cylinder opening in the crankcase. Be sure the jet is properly seated in the crankcase.

e. Apply Threadlock 1342 or equivalent to the threads of the Allen bolt. Tighten the bolt 10 N•m to (88 in.-lb.).

5. Service the oil passage jets as follows:

a. Remove the oil passage jet (**Figure 50**) from the cylinder mating surface. Each crankcase half is equipped with an oil passage jet.

b. Clean the jet and the jet passage.

c. Install a new O-ring onto the jet before installing it. Lubricate the O-ring with engine oil.

d. Install the jet so the slotted end points upward the cylinder (**Figure 51**).

6. Service the transmission oil jet as follows:

a. Remove the oil passage bolt (A, **Figure 52**) and the transmission oil jet (**Figure 53**) in the crankcase half.

NOTE
It may be necessary to dislodge the jet by directing a wire into the oil passage behind the jet. Insert the wire through the oil hole in the transmission shaft bore (A, Figure 54).

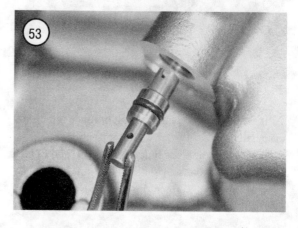

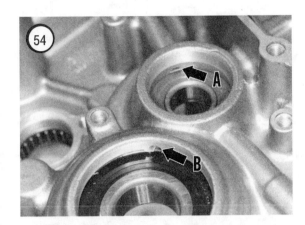

b. Clean the jet and the jet passage.

c. Install a new O-ring onto the jet before installing it. Lubricate the O-ring with engine oil.

d. Install the jet so the slotted end points inward (**Figure 53**). Insert the jet until it bottoms in the oil passage.

e. Tighten the oil passage bolt to 18 N•m (159 in.-lb.).

7. Remove the oil passage plugs and washers (B, **Figure 52**) from the left crankcase half.

8. Direct compressed air to the oil passages and blow out any accumulated residue. If necessary, rinse out the passages with solvent and once again apply compressed air to thoroughly clean out the gallery.

9. Install the oil gallery plugs with new sealing washers and tighten them securely.

10. Inspect the cases for cracks and fractures, especially in the lower areas where they are vulnerable to rock damage. Check the areas around the stiffening ribs, around bearing bosses and threaded holes for damage. If damage is found, have it repaired by a shop specializing in the repair of precision aluminum castings or replace the crankcases as a set.

11. Check the tightness of the shift lever stopper pin (**Figure 55**). If loose, remove the stopper pin. Apply Threadlock Super 1303 to the stopper pin threads and reinstall it. Tighten the stopper pin to 19 N•m (168 in.-lb.).

12. Inspect the main bearings (**Figure 56**). Replace the main bearings if damaged or excessively worn. Measure the main bearing clearance as described in this chapter.

NOTE
The crankcase is equipped with insert-type main bearings in each crankcase half. A Suzuki special tool is required to install the bearings. If the bearings are excessively worn or damaged, take the crankcase and crankshaft to a Suzuki dealership for bearing installation.

13. Check the shift drum bearing (**Figure 57**) for wear. Rotate the inner race of the bearing by hand. The bearing must rotate freely with no signs of binding. If necessary, replace the bearing as described in this chapter.

CAUTION
If oil seal removal is necessary, be careful not to damage the crankcase bore. When removing the transmission mainshaft or transmission output shaft seal, the crankcase may be damaged if the removal tool snags the adjacent oil passage in the crankcase bore (A or B, Figure 54).

14. Inspect the oil seals for the transmission main-shaft (A, **Figure 58**), transmission output shaft (B) and transmission shift shaft (C). Check for hardness, deterioration and wear. Replace if necessary. Install the mainshaft and output shaft seals so they are flush with the crankcase; if installed too deeply, the seals may block the oil passages. Install the shift shaft seal so it bottoms in the crankcase.

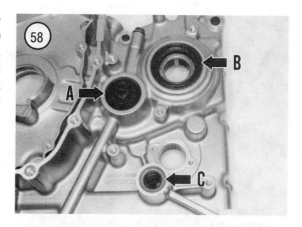

Oil Strainer

The oil strainer is contained in a compartment in the right crankcase half (**Figure 59**).

1. Remove the retainer plate (**Figure 59**).
2. Remove the oil strainer (A, **Figure 60**).
3. Thoroughly clean the strainer, retainer plate and crankcase in solvent and dry them with compressed air.
4. Inspect the strainer screen for broken areas or damage. Replace the strainer if damaged or if it cannot be cleaned adequately.

> *NOTE*
> *Perform service to the crankcase halves before installing the oil strainer.*

5. Install the oil strainer into the crankcase half so the projection (B, **Figure 60**) is toward the bottom of the crankcase.
6. Install the retainer plate. Tighten the retainer bolts to 10 N•m (88 in.-lb.).

Oil Pressure Regulator

The oil pressure regulator valve is located inside the left crankcase half (**Figure 61**).

> *NOTE*
> *There are no replacement parts for the valve. If damaged, the entire valve must be replaced.*

1. Unscrew the valve (**Figure 61**) from the crankcase.
2. To check the valve operation, use a piece of plastic rod or wood and push down on the piston within the valve. The piston must slide smoothly and return to the fully closed position when released. If piston operation is not smooth, clean the valve in solvent and thoroughly dry it with compressed air.
3. Repeat Step 3 to check valve operation. If cleaning does not solve the problem, replace the valve.
4. Install the valve (**Figure 61**) and tighten it to 27 N•m (20 ft.-lb.).

Bearing Replacement

Before removing a bearing, note and record which side of the bearing has markings on the races. Install the new bearing so the markings appear on the same side with relation to the crankcase.

1. On a bearing so equipped, remove the screws (**Figure 62**, typical) securing the bearing retainer plate(s) and remove the retainer plate(s). If the bearing is not going to be replaced, check the retaining screws for tightness.

> *CAUTION*
> *Before heating the crankcase halves in this procedure to remove the bearings, wash the cases thoroughly with hot water and detergent. Rinse and rewash the cases as required to remove all traces of oil and other chemical deposits.*

> *CAUTION*
> *Even after the cases have been thoroughly washed, there may be a slight residual oil or solvent odor left in the oven after heating the crankcase. This may be undesirable if using a household oven.*

2A. The bearings are installed with a slight interference fit. The crankcase must be heated in an oven or hot plate to a temperature of about 215° F (100° C). An easy way to check the proper temperature is to drop tiny drops of water on the case; if they sizzle and evaporate immediately, the temperature is correct. Heat only one crankcase at a time.

> *CAUTION*
> *Do not heat the cases with a torch (propane or acetylene); never bring a flame into contact with the bearing or case. The direct heat will destroy the case hardening of the bearing and will likely cause warpage of the case.*

2B. A hydraulic press may be used instead of heat to remove and install the bearings and oil seals.

3. Remove the case from the oven or hot plate using a kitchen pot holder, heavy gloves or heavy shop cloths—it is hot.

4. Hold the crankcase with the bearing side down and tap it squarely on a piece of soft wood. Continue to tap until the bearing(s) fall out. Repeat for the other case half.

> *CAUTION*
> *Be sure to tap the crankcase squarely on the piece of wood. Avoid damaging the sealing surface of the crankcase.*

5. If the bearings are difficult to remove, they can be gently tapped out with a suitable size socket or piece of pipe the same size as the bearing inner race.

> *NOTE*
> *If the bearings or seals are difficult to remove or install, don't take a chance on expensive damage. Have the work performed by a dealer or competent machine shop.*

6. While heating the crankcase halves, place the new bearings in a freezer if possible. Chilling them will slightly reduce their overall diameter while the hot crankcase is slightly larger due to heat expansion. This will make bearing installation much easier.

> *NOTE*
> *Prior to installing the new bearing(s) apply a light coat of lithium-based grease to the inside and outside to aid in installation.*

> *NOTE*
> *Install a new bearing so that the manufacturer's name and size code face in the same direction recorded during disassembly. If you did not note this information prior to removing the bearings, install the bearings so that their marks are visible after the bearing has been installed.*

7. While the crankcase is still hot, press each new bearing(s) into place in the crankcase by hand until it seats completely. Install the bearings by hand, if possible. If necessary, lightly tap the bearing(s) into the case with a socket placed on the outer race. Do not install new bearings by driving on the inner bearing race. Install the bearing(s) until it seats completely. If the bearing will not seat, remove it and cool it again. Reheat the crankcase and install the bearing again.

CRANKSHAFT

Removal/Installation

1. Remove the crankshaft/connecting rod assembly as previously described in *Crankcase Disassembly* in this chapter.

2. Inspect the crankshaft and main bearings as described in this chapter.

3. Install the crankshaft/connecting rod assembly as described in *Crankcase Assembly* in this chapter.

Crankshaft Inspection

1. Clean the crankshaft thoroughly with solvent. Clean the crankshaft oil passageways with compressed air. If necessary, clean them with rifle cleaning brushes, then flush the passageways with solvent. Dry the crankshaft with compressed air, then lubricate all bearing surfaces with a light coat of engine oil.

2. Inspect each crankshaft main journal and each connecting rod journal for scratches, ridges, scoring, nicks or heat discoloration. Very small nicks and scratches may be removed with crocus cloth. Anything more serious must be referred to a machine shop.

3. If the surface finish on each crankshaft main bearing journal is satisfactory, measure the main journals with a micrometer for runout, taper and wear (**Figure 63**). Compare the measurements with the specifications listed in **Table 1**.

4. If the surface finish on each connecting rod journal is satisfactory, measure the journals with a micrometer and check runout, taper and wear. Compare the measurements with the specifications listed in **Table 1**.

5. Inspect the crankshaft outer splines (A, **Figure 64**) and threads (B) on the right end of the crankshaft. If damaged, replace the crankshaft. If the crankshaft splines are damaged, also inspect the inner splines on the cam chain sprocket and primary drive gear.

6. On the left end, inspect the threads (A, **Figure 65**), cam chain sprocket (B) and keyway (C) for wear or damage. If damaged, replace the crankshaft.

Crankshaft Main Bearings

The crankcase is equipped with insert-type main bearings in each crankcase half. A Suzuki special tool is required to install the bearings. If the bearings are excessively worn or damaged, take the crankcase and crankshaft to a Suzuki dealership for bearing installation. Use the following procedure to determine the condition of the crankshaft and bearings.

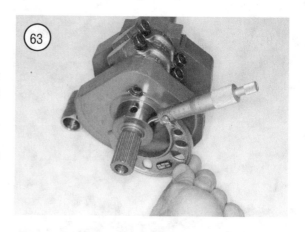

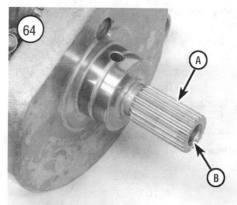

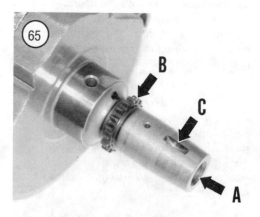

1. Check each crankshaft main bearing insert (**Figure 66**) for evidence of wear, abrasion and scoring. If the bearing inserts are good, they may be reused. If any insert is questionable, replace the entire set.

2. Clean the bearing surfaces of the crankshaft and the bearing inserts for the crankshaft.

3. Measure the main bearing inside diameter with an inside micrometer. Record the bearing inner diameter measurement.

4. Measure the crankshaft main journal outside diameter with a micrometer (**Figure 63**). Record the main journal diameter.

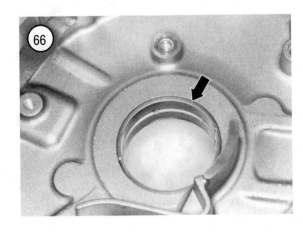

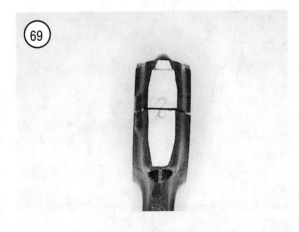

5. Subtract the crankshaft main journal diameter from the main bearing diameter; the difference is crankshaft main bearing oil clearance. If the clearance exceeds the service limit specified in **Table 1**, the crankshaft, main bearings, or both must be replaced. Take the crankshaft and crankcase to a Suzuki dealership for further service.

CONNECTING RODS

Removal/Installation

1. Remove the crankshaft/connecting rod assembly as described in *Crankcase Disassembly* in this chapter.

2. Insert a flat feeler gauge between the connecting rod and the crankshaft machined surface (**Figure 67**). Compare the measurement to the connecting rod big end side clearance service limit in **Table 1**. Measure each connecting rod. If the measurement is not within the service limit refer to Connecting Rod Inspection in this chapter to determine which component requires replacement.

3. Remove the connecting rod cap bolts (**Figure 68**), remove the cap and separate the rods from the crankshaft. Keep each cap with its original rod. The weight mark on the end of the cap should align with the mark on its connecting rod (**Figure 69**).

> *CAUTION*
> *If old bearing inserts are reused, they must be installed in their original locations. Keep each bearing insert in the connecting rod and cap. If they are removed, label the backside of each insert with a F or R that corresponds to the cylinder location and with rod (R) and cap (C) identification.*

4. Inspect the connecting rods and bearings as described in this chapter.

5. If new bearing inserts are being installed, check the bearing clearance as described in this chapter.

6. Apply a light even coat of clean engine oil and molybdenum disulfide grease to the crankpin journals.

7. Make sure the inserts are locked into place (**Figure 70**). Apply clean engine and molybdenum disulfide grease oil to the bearing surface of both bearing inserts.

8. Install each connecting rod onto the crankshaft in the correct location and with the weight mark (**Figure 71**) facing toward the *middle* of the engine. Be careful not to damage the bearing surface of the crankshaft with the sharp edge of the connecting rod and upper insert.

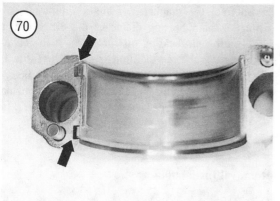

9. Align the weight mark on the end of the cap with the mark on the rod and install the cap onto the rod. Push it on until it contacts the connecting rod.

> NOTE
> *A torque angle gauge (available at auto parts stores) should be used to measure the wrench angle in Step 10.*

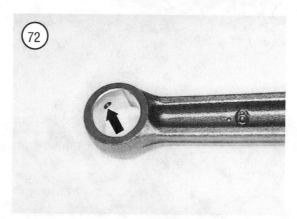

10. Install the connecting rod cap bolts (**Figure 68**). Initially, tighten the bolts to 21 N•m (186 in.-lb.). Tighten the bolts an additional 90°.

11. After installing the connecting rods and tightening the cap nuts tightened correctly, rotate each connecting rod on the crankshaft and make sure there is no binding.

Connecting Rod Inspection

1. Check each connecting rod assembly for obvious damage such as cracks or burns.

2. Make sure the small end oil hole (**Figure 72**) is open. Clean it if necessary.

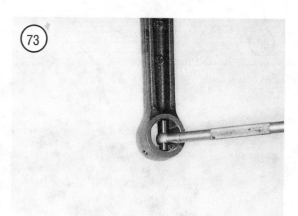

3. Measure the small end inside diameter with a small hole gauge (**Figure 73**) and measure the gauge with a micrometer. Replace the connecting rod if the small end inside diameter is worn to the wear limit specified in **Table 1**.

4. Check the piston pin (**Figure 74**) for chrome flaking or cracks. Replace the pin if necessary.

5. Check the piston pin where it contacts the surface of the small end (**Figure 74**) for wear or abrasion.

6. Lubricate the piston pin and install it in the connecting rod (**Figure 75**). Slowly rotate the piston pin and check for radial play.

7. Inspect the alignment of each connecting rod. If there is evidence of abnormal piston or cylinder wear, have the connecting rod inspected at a machine shop. Specialized equipment is required to accurately determine if a rod is bent or twisted.

8. Examine the bearing inserts (**Figure 76**) for wear, scoring or burned surfaces. They are reusable if in

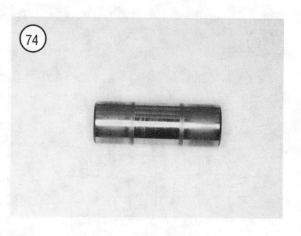

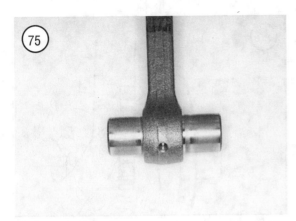

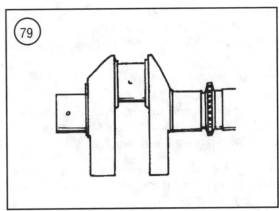

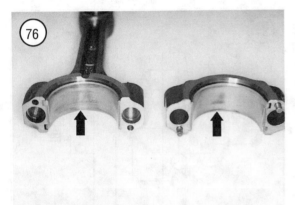

good condition. Make a note of the bearing color identification on the side of the insert if the bearing is to be discarded. A previous owner may have installed undersize bearings.

9. If the connecting rod big end side clearance (*Connecting Rod Removal/Installation*) is greater than specified, perform the following:

    a. Measure the width of the connecting rod big end with a micrometer (**Figure 77**). If the width is less than the value specified in **Table 1**, replace the connecting rod assembly.

    b. Measure the crankpin width with a dial caliper or vernier caliper (**Figure 78**) and compare the measurement to the dimension listed in **Table 1**. If the width is greater than specified, replace the crankshaft.

Connecting Rod Bearing Clearance Measurement

1. Inspect each connecting rod insert (**Figure 76**) for evidence of wear, abrasion and scoring. If the bearing inserts are good they may be reused. If any insert is questionable, replace all of the inserts as a set.

2. Clean the crankshaft crankpin (**Figure 79**) and check for damage.

3. If removed, install the existing bearing inserts into the connecting rod and cap. Make sure they are locked into place (**Figure 70**).

4. Install the connecting rods onto the crankshaft in the correct location with the weight mark (**Figure 71**) facing the *middle* of the engine. Be careful not to damage the bearing surface of the crankshaft.

5. Place a piece of Plastigage onto the rod journal. Make sure the Plastigage runs parallel to the crankshaft as shown in **Figure 80**. Do not place the Plastigage material over the oil hole in the crankshaft.

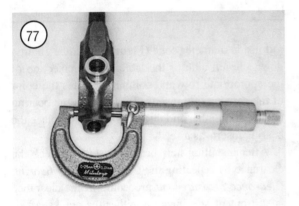

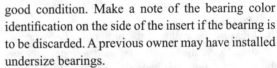

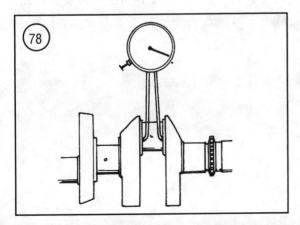

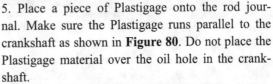

CAUTION
Do not rotate the crankshaft or the con-
necting rod while the Plastigage is in
place.

NOTE
A torque angle gauge (available at auto
parts stores) should be used to measure
the wrench angle in Step 6.

6. Align the weight mark on the end of the cap with
the mark on the rod (**Figure 71**) and install the cap.
Install the bolts. Initially, tighten the bolts to 21 N•m
(186 in.-lb.). Tighten the bolts an additional 90°.
7. Loosen the cap bolts. Carefully lift the cap straight
up and off the connecting rod.
8. Measure the width of the flattened Plastigage according to the manufacturer's instructions. Measure
both ends of the Plastigage strip (**Figure 80**).
   a. A difference of 0.025 mm (0.001 in.) or more
      indicates a tapered journal. Confirm the mea-
      surement using a micrometer.
   b. If the connecting rod bearing clearance is
      greater than the wear limit specified in **Table 1**,
      select new bearings as described in this chap-
      ter.
9. Remove all of the Plastigage from the crankshaft
rod journals.

Connecting Rod-to-Crankcase
Bearing Selection

1. The crankpin is identified by a code (1, 2 or 3)
stamped into the counterbalance web on the crankshaft. The codes coincide with the crankpin journal
outside diameter as shown in **Figure 81**.
2. The connecting rods are coded with a weight
number (1 or 2) marked on the side of the connecting
rod (**Figure 69**). The codes coincide with the inside
diameter of the connecting rod.
3. Select new bearings by cross-referencing the
crankpin outside diameter code (**Figure 81**) in the
row across the top of **Table 2** with the connecting

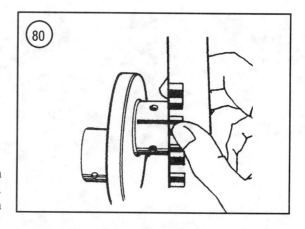

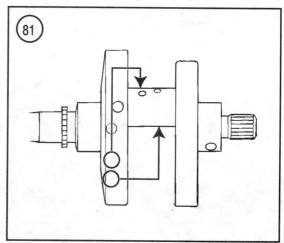

rod inside diameter code (**Figure 69**) in the column
down the left side of the table. The intersection of
the appropriate row and column indicates the color
of the new bearing inserts. **Table 3** lists the bearing
color, part number and thickness. Always replace the
bearing inserts as a set.
4. After installing new bearing inserts, recheck the
clearance by repeating the *Connecting Rod Bearing*
Clearance Measurement procedure. If the clearance
is still out of specification, either the crankshaft or
the connecting rod(s) is worn to the service limit and
requires replacement.

Table 1 LOWER END SPECIFICATIONS

Item	Specification	Wear limit
Connecting rod		
Big end diameter		
Code 1	41.000-41.008 mm	–
	(1.6142-1.6145 in.)	
Code 2	41.008-41.016 mm	–
	(1.6145-1.6148 in.)	
Big end side clearance	0.170 0.320 mm	0.5 mm
	(0.0067 0.0126 in.)	(0.02 in.)
Big end width	20.95-21.00 mm	–
	(0.825-0.827 in.)	
Big end oil clearance	0.032-0.056 mm	0.080 mm
	(0.0013-0.0022 in.)	(0.0031 in.)
Small end inner diameter	20.010-20.018 mm	20.040 mm
	(0.7878-0.7881 in.)	(0.7890 in.)
Crankpin standard diameter	37.976-38.000 mm	–
	(1.4951-1.4960 in.)	
Code 1	37.992-38.000 mm	–
	(1.4957-1.4960 in.)	
Code 2	37.984-37.992 mm	–
	(1.4954-1.4957 in.)	
Code 3	37.976-37.984 mm	–
	(1.4951-1.4954 in.)	
Crankpin width	42.17-42.22 mm	–
	(1.660-1.662 in.)	
Crankshaft end play	0.050-0.110 mm	–
	(0.0020-0.0043 in.)	
Crankshaft main bearing journal	41.985-42.000 mm	–
	(1.6529-1.6535 in.)	
Crankshaft main bearing oil clearance	0.002-0.029 mm	0.080 mm
	(0.0001-0.0011 in.)	(0.0031 in.)
Crankshaft runout	–	0.05 mm (0.002 in.)

Table 2 CONNECTING ROD BEARING SELECTION

Crankshaft outer diameter code	1	2	3
Connecting rod inside diameter code			
1	Green	Black	Brown
2	Black	Brown	Yellow

Table 3 CONNECTING ROD BEARING INSERT COLOR, PART NO., THICKNESS

Color and part No.	Specification	Wear limit
Green	1.480-1.484 mm	–
12164-46E01-0A0	(0.0583-0.0584 in.)	
Black	1.484-1.488 mm	–
12164-46E01-0B0	(0.0584-0.0586 in.)	
Brown	1.488-1.492 mm	–
12164-46E01-0C0	(0.0586-0.0587 in.)	
Yellow	1.492-1.496 mm	–
12164-46E01-0D0	(0.0587-0.0589 in.)	

Table 4 LOWER END TORQUE SPECIFICATIONS

Item	N•m	in. lb.	ft.-lb.
Connecting rod bolt			
Initial torque	21	186	–
Final torque*			

(continued)

Table 4 LOWER END TORQUE SPECIFICATIONS (cont.)

Item	N•m	in. lb.	ft.-lb.
Crankcase bolts			
6 mm	11	97	–
8 mm	26	–	19
Engine bracket mounting bolts	35	–	25
Engine center mounting bolt	55	–	40
Engine lower mounting bolt nut	55	–	40
Engine mounting spacer clamp bolt	25	–	18
Engine mounting thrust adjuster locknut	45	–	33
Engine mounting thrust adjuster	12	106	–
Engine upper mounting bolt	93	–	68
Flywheel bolt	120	–	88
Oil plate bolts	10	88	–
Oil passage bolt	18	159	–
Oil pressure regulator	27	–	20
Oil strainer bolt	10	88	–
Piston cooling jet retaining bolt	10	88	–
Primary gear retaining bolt	70	–	51
Shift lever stopper pin	19	168	–
Starter clutch bolts	25	–	18

*Refer to text.

CHAPTER SIX

CLUTCH AND PRIMARY DRIVE GEAR

This chapter provides service procedures for the clutch, clutch release mechanism and external shift mechanism. Clutch specifications are in **Tables 1** and **2** at the end of the chapter.

The DL650 clutch is a wet multi-plate design that operates in the engine oil. The clutch assembly is located on the right side of the engine. The clutch hub is mounted on the splines on the transmission input (main) shaft. The outer clutch housing is driven by the primary drive gear on the crankshaft. A gear on the inner side of the clutch housing drives the oil pump.

Clutch release is accomplished via a pushrod/push piece assembly operating on the pressure plate. The pushrods pass through the transmission input shaft and are actuated by the clutch cable pulling on the clutch lifter mechanism mounted in the drive sprocket cover on the left side of the engine. This system requires routine adjustment (Chapter Three) to compensate for cable stretch.

CLUTCH CABLE REPLACEMENT

1. Slide the rubber boot (**Figure 1**) off the clutch hand lever adjuster.
2. At the clutch hand lever, loosen the large jam nut (A, **Figure 2**) and turn the adjuster (B) all the way in toward the clutch lever holder to allow maximum cable slack. Disconnect the cable from the clutch lever.
3. Raise and support the fuel tank as described in Chapter Eight.
4. Remove the clamp bolt (A, **Figure 3**) and slide the shift arm (B) off the shift shaft.
5. Remove the engine sprocket cover (C, **Figure 3**).
6. Loosen the jam nuts (A, **Figure 4**) on the lower cable housing.
7. Rotate the adjuster (B, **Figure 4**) to increase cable slack.
8. Disconnect the clutch cable end from the clutch release arm (C, **Figure 4**).
9. Tie a piece of heavy string onto the lower end of the old cable. Cut the string to a length that is longer than the new clutch cable.
10. Tie the lower end of the string to the frame or engine component.

NOTE
It may be necessary to detach cable clamps to extract or install the cable.

11. Remove the old clutch cable by pulling it from the top (upper cable end). Continue until the cable is removed from the frame, leaving the attached piece of string in its mounting position.
12. Untie the string from the old cable and discard the old cable.

13. Lubricate the new clutch cable as described in Chapter Three.

14. Tie the string onto the bottom end of the new clutch cable.

15. Slowly pull the string and cable to install the cable along the path of the original clutch cable. Continue until the clutch cable is correctly routed through the engine and frame. Untie and remove the string.

16. Visually check the entire length of the clutch cable as it runs through the frame and engine. Make sure there are no kinks or sharp bends.

17. Connect the upper cable end to the clutch lever.

18. Reattach the lower end of the clutch cable as shown in **Figure 4**. Be sure to bend up the locking tab (**Figure 5**) so the cable end is secured in the swivel fitting.

19. Install the engine sprocket cover.

20. Install the shift arm onto the shift shaft. The shift arm position should be approximately 64° from vertical (**Figure 6**).

21. Return the fuel tank to the installed position.

22. Adjust the clutch cable as described in Chapter Three.

EXTERNAL GEARSHIFT MECHANISM

The external gearshift mechanism is located on the right (clutch) side of the engine. Access to the internal gearshift mechanism requires removing the engine and splitting the crankcase as described in Chapter Five. Internal gearshift mechanism service is described in Chapter Seven.

Removal

Refer to **Figure 7**.

1. Remove the clamp bolt (A, **Figure 3**) and slide the shift arm (B) off the shift shaft.

2. Remove the clutch assembly as described in this chapter.

3. Remove the circlip (A, **Figure 8**) and washer (B) from the left end of the shift shaft.

4. On the right side of the engine, withdraw the shift shaft (**Figure 9**) from the crankcase. Reinstall the washer and circlip removed in Step 3 onto the shift shaft to avoid misplacing them.

5. Remove the Allen bolt (A, **Figure 10**).

6. Push back the gearshift cam stopper (B, **Figure 10**) and remove the gearshift cam plate (C).

7. Remove the bolt (A, **Figure 11**), washer, spring (B) and gearshift cam stopper (C). Note the washer (**Figure 12**) located between the stopper and spring.

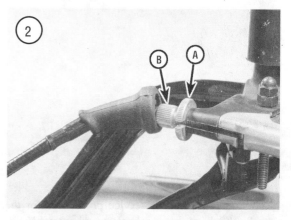

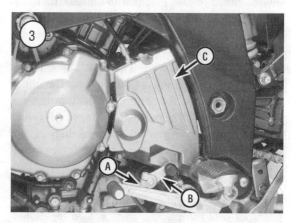

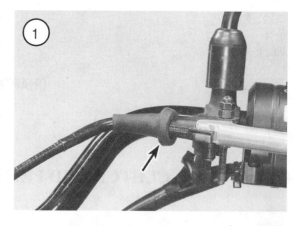

8. If the locating pins (D, **Figure 11**) in the end of the shift drum are loose, remove them. If not, leave them in place.

9. Inspect the components as described in this chapter.

Inspection

1. Inspect the gearshift shaft (A, **Figure 13**) for bending, wear or other damage; replace if necessary.

2. Inspect the return spring (B, **Figure 13**). If broken or weak, replace it.

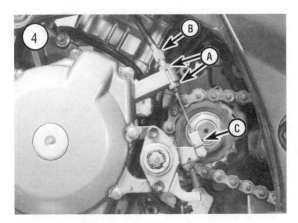

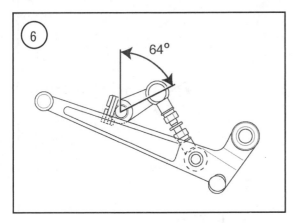

3. Inspect the shift cam (A, **Figure 14**) and pins (B) for wear or damage. Replace the shift cam if excessively worn or damaged.

Installation

1. Make sure the locating pins (D, **Figure 11**) are in place in the end of the shift drum.

NOTE
If the cam stopper was removed as an assembly and not disassembled, the components may be installed onto the

*crankcase as an assembly (**Figure 11**) instead of following Steps 2 and 3. Tighten the bolt 10 N•m to (88 in.-lb.).*

2. Assemble the cam stopper components (**Figure 12**) as shown in **Figure 15**. Install the washer between the spring and arm. Note that the spring end must fit into the notch (**Figure 15**) on the back of the cam stopper and force the stopper down.
3. Install the cam stopper assembly and tighten the bolt 10 N•m to (88 in.-lb.).
4. Push up the cam stopper (B, **Figure 10**), then install the shift cam (C) onto the shift drum end while aligning the holes in the shift cam with the locating pins.
5. Apply Threadlocker 1342 or equivalent to the threads of the Allen bolt, then secure the shift cam by installing the bolt (A, **Figure 10**). Tighten the Allen bolt to 13 N•m (115 in.-lb.).
6. Install the spring onto the shift shaft so the spring ends fit around the tab (A, **Figure 16**). Install the washer (B) onto the shift shaft next to the spring.
7. Install the shift plate (A, **Figure 17**), spring (B), washer (C) and circlip (D) onto the shift shaft as shown in **Figure 17**.
8. Install the shift lever assembly (**Figure 18**). While inserting the shaft, position the legs of the return spring around the shift arm stopper (**Figure 19**).
9. Install the washer (B, **Figure 20**) and circlip (A) onto the left end of the shift shaft.
10. Install the clutch assembly as described in this chapter.
11. Install the shift arm onto the shift shaft. The shift arm position should be approximately 64° from vertical (**Figure 6**).

CLUTCH

Removal/Disassembly

Refer to **Figure 21** when performing this procedure.
1. Drain the cooling system as described in Chapter Three.
2. Drain the engine oil as described in Chapter Three.
3. Remove the right footpeg and bracket as described in Chapter Fifteen.
4. Detach the bypass hose (A, **Figure 22**) from the water pump.
5. Loosen the hose clamp (B, **Figure 22**) and disconnect the inlet hose from the water pump.
6. Remove the bolts retaining the right crankcase cover (**Figure 23**). Note that three bolts also retain the water pump.
7. Remove the right crankcase cover.

⑦ **EXTERNAL SHIFT MECHANISM**

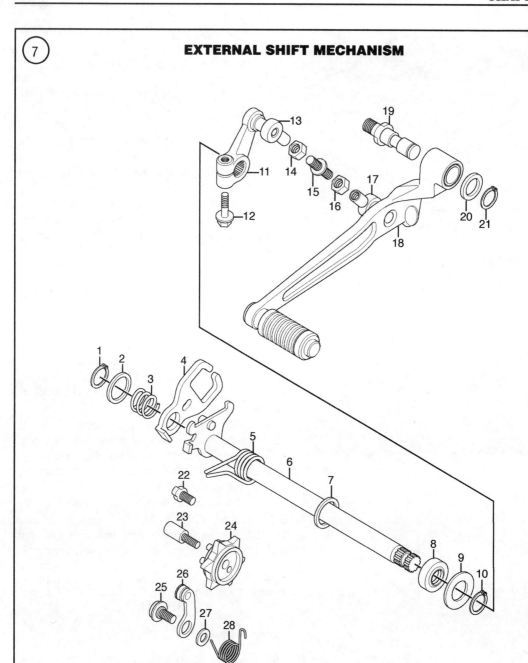

1. Snap ring
2. Washer
3. Spring
4. Shift plate
5. Return spring
6. Shift shaft
7. Washer
8. Seal
9. Washer
10. Snap ring
11. Shift arm
12. Bolt
13. Boot
14. Nut
15. Shift rod
16. Nut
17. Boot
18. Shift lever
19. Shaft
20. Washer
21. Snap ring
22. Spring stopper bolt
23. Allen bolt
24. Shift cam
25. Bolt
26. Cam stopper
27. Washer
28. Spring

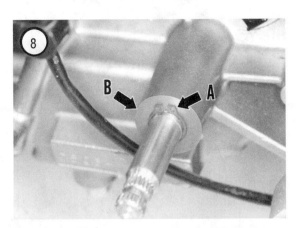

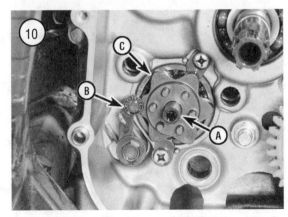

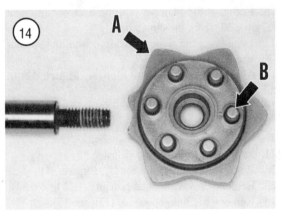

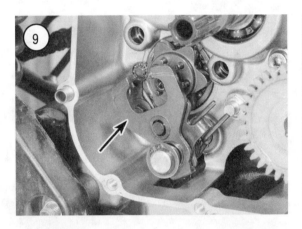

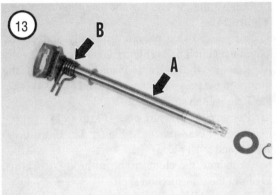

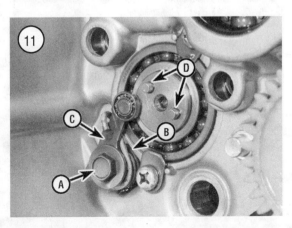

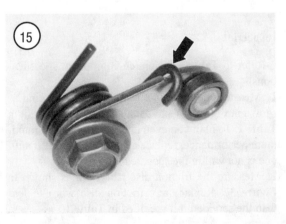

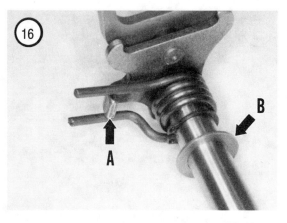

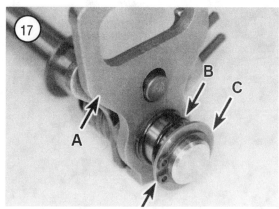

8. Remove the gasket. Do not lose the dowel pins (**Figure 24**).

9. Using a crossing pattern, gradually and evenly loosen the clutch bolts (**Figure 25**).

10. Remove the bolts and spacers securing the springs to the pressure plate (**Figure 26**).

11. Remove the springs.

12. Remove the pressure plate (**Figure 27**).

13. Remove the washer (A, **Figure 28**), thrust bearing (B) and push piece (C).

14. Withdraw the clutch right pushrod (A, **Figure 29**) from the transmission shaft.

15. Remove all the friction discs and clutch plates (B, **Figure 29**) and keep in their order.

16. Remove the damper spring and spring seat (**Figure 30**) from the clutch hub.

17. Bend back the folded portion of the lockwasher (**Figure 31**).

18. Attach a clutch holding tool (A, **Figure 32**) to the clutch hub.

19. While grasping the holding tool, loosen the nut (B, **Figure 32**).

20. Remove the nut and lockwasher.

21. Remove the clutch hub (**Figure 33**).

22. Remove the thrust washer (A, **Figure 34**).

23. Remove the clutch outer housing (B, **Figure 34**).

24. Remove the flanged sleeve (**Figure 35**).

25. Inspect all parts as described in this chapter.

Inspection

Refer to **Table 1** for clutch component specifications.

1. Measure the free length of each clutch spring as shown in **Figure 36** and compare to the wear limit in **Table 1**. To maintain even clutch pressure and maximum performance, replace all springs as a set if anyone is not within the specified tolerance.

2. Measure the friction disc tab width as shown in **Figure 37**. Replace any friction disc worn to less than the service limit specified in **Table 1**.

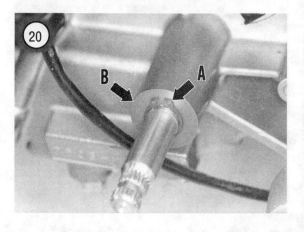

(21) **CLUTCH AND RELEASE MECHANISM**

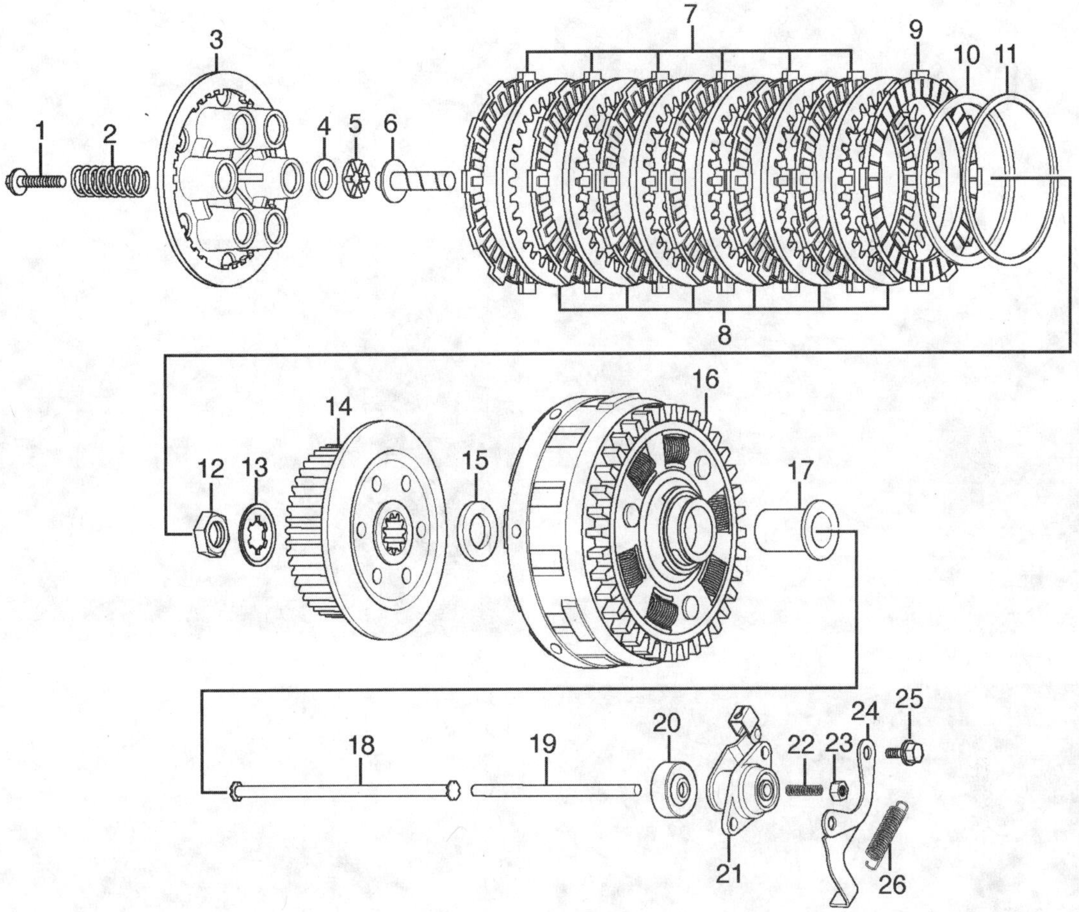

6

1. Screw
2. Spring
3. Pressure plate
4. Washer
5. Thrust bearing
6. Push piece
7. No. 1 friction plates
8. Steel plates
9. No. 2 friction plate
10. Damper spring
11. Spring seat
12. Nut
13. Splined washer
14. Clutch hub

15. Thrust washer
16. Outer housing
17. Flanged sleeve
18. Pushrod (right)
19. Pushrod (left)
20. Oil seal
21. Clutch release
    mechanism
22. Threaded stud
23. Nut
24. Spring bracket
25. Bolt
26. Spring

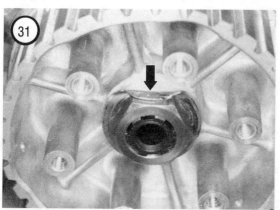

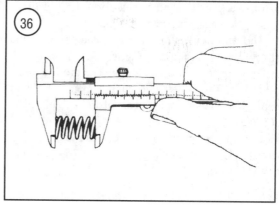

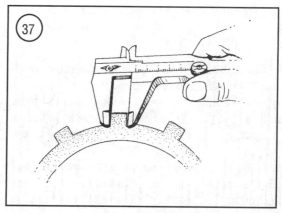

6

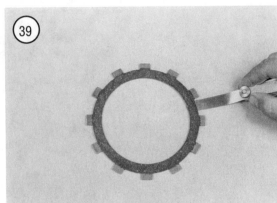

3. The friction material on the friction disc is bonded to an aluminum plate for warp resistance and durability. Measure the thickness of the friction disc at several places as shown in **Figure 38**. Replace all discs if any are worn to less than the service limit in **Table 1**.

4. Place each steel clutch plate on a flat surface like a piece of plate glass, and check for warpage with a feeler gauge (**Figure 39**). If any plate is warped more than specified in **Table 1**, replace the entire set of clutch plates. Do not replace only one or two plates as clutch operation will be unsatisfactory.

5. The steel clutch plate's inner teeth mesh with the clutch hub splines. They must be smooth for chatter-free clutch operation. If the sleeve hub splines are worn, check the steel plate teeth for wear or damage as they may also require replacement.

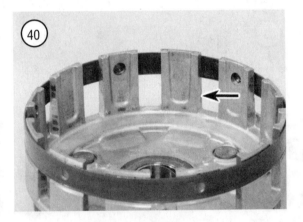

6. The tabs on the clutch friction plates slide in the clutch housing grooves (**Figure 40**). Inspect the groove tabs for cracks or galling. The grooves must be smooth for chatter-free clutch operation. Light damage can be repaired with an oilstone. Replace the clutch housing if required.

7. Inspect the clutch pressure plate splines (A, **Figure 41**) for wear or damage. Replace the pressure plate if required.

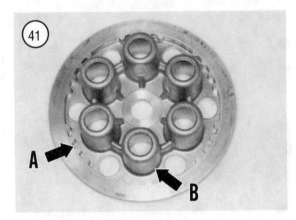

NOTE
If the clutch outer housing teeth are damaged, the primary drive gear may also be damaged. Inspect it and replace if necessary.

8. Check the gear teeth (A, **Figure 42**) on the clutch outer housing. Check for damaged, chipped or missing teeth. Remove any small nicks with an oilstone. If damaged, the outer housing must be replaced. Also, check the gear teeth on the primary drive gear as it may also be damaged. Refer to Chapter Five.

9. Inspect the clutch outer housing damper springs (B, **Figure 42**). If they are sagged or broken, replace the housing.

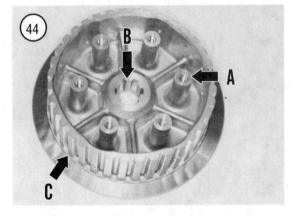

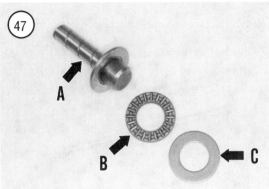

10. Check the inner bushing surface (A, **Figure 43**) of the clutch outer housing. Replace the outer housing if necessary.

11. Inspect the sleeve (B, **Figure 43**) on which the clutch rides. Replace the sleeve if it is galled, excessively worn or otherwise damaged.

12. Inspect the clutch spring bolt studs on the clutch hub (A, **Figure 44**) for thread damage or cracks at the base of the studs. Thread damage may be repaired with a correct size metric tap. Use kerosene on the tap threads. If the bolt stud is cracked or damaged, replace the clutch hub.

13. Inspect the inner splines (B, **Figure 44**) in the clutch hub for damage. Remove any small nicks with a file. Replace the clutch hub if damage is excessive.

14. Inspect the clutch spring towers on the pressure plate (B, **Figure 41**). If any are worn or damaged, replace the pressure plate.

15. Inspect the outer grooves on the clutch hub (C, **Figure 44**). If any are worn or damaged, replace the pressure plate.

16. If necessary, replace the oil pump drive gear as follows:

NOTE
The oil pump drive gear pin may be loose
and fall out when removing the gear.

a. Remove the circlip (A, **Figure 45**) securing the drive gear and remove the drive gear (B).

b. If removed, install the locating pin (A, **Figure 46**) into the clutch outer housing.

c. One side of the drive gear hub is raised. Install the drive gear onto the clutch outer housing so the raised side (B, **Figure 46**) is toward the clutch hub. The notch in the drive gear must align with the drive pin.

d. Push the gear down until it bottoms, then install the circlip with the flat side facing out.

e. Be sure the circlip is properly seated in the groove.

17. Examine the push piece (A, **Figure 47**) for wear or scoring. Install it into the end of the transmission

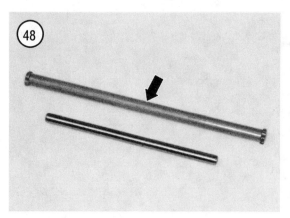

shaft and push it in and out. It should move freely with no hesitation. Replace if necessary.

18. Install the thrust bearing (B, **Figure 47**) and washer (C) onto the push piece and rotate slowly. The bearing must rotate freely with no sign of wear or chatter. Check the thrust bearing needles for wear or damage. Replace the thrust bearing and push piece as a set if necessary.

19. Inspect the right pushrod (**Figure 48**) for bending, wear or damage. Replace if necessary.

Assembly/Installation

1. Install the flanged sleeve (**Figure 49**) onto the transmission shaft.

2. Apply clean engine oil to the inner bushing area of the clutch housing.

3. Install the clutch housing assembly (A, **Figure 50**). Make sure it is meshed properly with the primary drive gear (B) and the oil pump driven gear (C), then push it onto the transmission shaft until it bottoms out. Double check all gear engagements.

4. Install the thrust washer (D, **Figure 50**).

5. Install the clutch hub (**Figure 51**).

NOTE
Install the clutch hub nut so the chamfered side is facing out.

6. Install a new lockwasher (A, **Figure 52**), then install the clutch hub nut (B).

7. Use the same tool arrangement used in Step 17 of Removal/Disassembly and tighten the clutch hub nut (**Figure 53**) to 50 N•m (37 ft.-lb.).

8. Fold over a portion of the lockwasher securely against the nut as shown in **Figure 54**.

9. Remove the holding tool from the clutch hub.

10. Install the damper spring seat (A, **Figure 55**) onto the clutch hub.

11. Install the damper spring (B, **Figure 55**) onto the clutch hub so the concave side faces out.

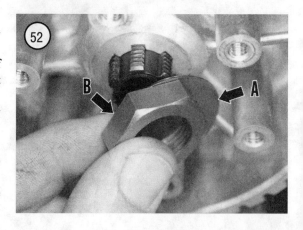

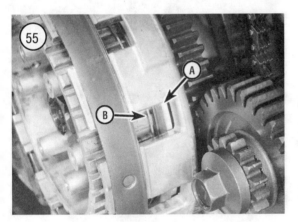

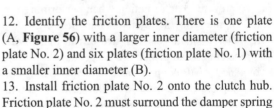

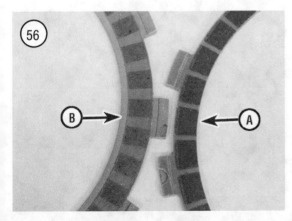

NOTE
Lubricate the contact surfaces of the friction plates and steel plates with clean engine oil prior to assembly.

12. Identify the friction plates. There is one plate (A, **Figure 56**) with a larger inner diameter (friction plate No. 2) and six plates (friction plate No. 1) with a smaller inner diameter (B).

13. Install friction plate No. 2 onto the clutch hub. Friction plate No. 2 must surround the damper spring and spring seat (**Figure 57**).

14. Install a steel plate next to friction plate No. 2.

15. Install a No. 1 friction plate, then continue to install a steel plate, a friction plate and alternate them until all are installed. The last item installed is a friction plate (A, **Figure 58**).

16. Install the right clutch pushrod (B, **Figure 58**) into the transmission shaft. Push it in until it bottoms against the left pushrod still located in the transmission shaft.

17. Install the push piece (A, **Figure 59**) into the transmission shaft.

18. Apply a light coat of clean engine oil to both sides of the washer and thrust bearing.

19. Install the thrust bearing (B, **Figure 59**) onto the push piece, then install the washer (C).

20. Install the clutch pressure plate (**Figure 60**) and push it on until it bottoms.

21. Install the springs (**Figure 61**), spacers and bolts. Start the bolts and tighten only fingertight.

22. To prevent clutch rotation when performing the next step, the following methods may be used.

    a. Place a small gear (**Figure 62**) in mesh with the clutch and primary drive gears.

    b. Place a soft copper washer (copper penny) or shop cloth into mesh with the gears. This will prevent the primary drive gear from turning in the next step.

23. Tighten the clutch bolts in a crossing pattern in 2-3 stages. Tighten the bolts to 10 N•m (88 in.-lb.).

24. Be sure the dowel pins (**Figure 24**) are in place and install a new right crankcase cover gasket (**Figure 63**).

25. Install the right crankcase cover while carefully engaging the water pump gears.

26. Tighten the right crankcase cover bolts securely.

27. Make sure to install the bypass hose (A, **Figure 64**).

28. The radiator hose is a shaped hose and must be installed properly. Push the hose onto the water pump until it bottoms against the stop on the pump inlet. The paint dot on the hose end must be just above

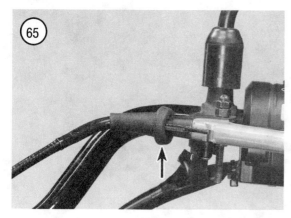

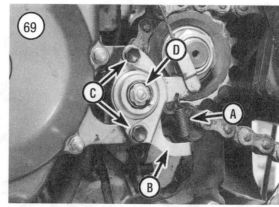

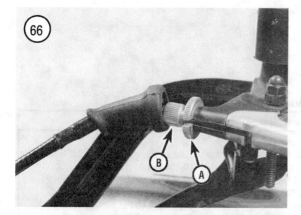

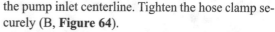

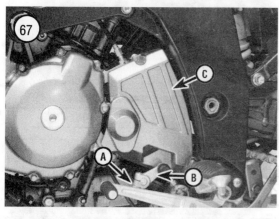

the pump inlet centerline. Tighten the hose clamp securely (B, **Figure 64**).

29. Refill the cooling system with the recommended type and quantity of coolant as described in Chapter Three.

30. Refill the engine with oil as described in Chapter Three.

CLUTCH RELEASE MECHANISM

Removal/Installation

1. Slide the rubber boot (**Figure 65**) off the clutch hand lever adjuster.

2. At the clutch hand lever, loosen the large jam nut (A, **Figure 66**) and turn the adjuster (B) all the way in toward the clutch lever holder to allow maximum cable slack. Disconnect the cable from the clutch lever.

3. Remove the clamp bolt (A, **Figure 67**) and slide the shift arm (B) off the shift shaft.

4. Remove the engine sprocket cover (C, **Figure 67**).

5. Loosen the jam nuts (A, **Figure 68**) on the lower cable housing.

6. Rotate the adjuster (B, **Figure 68**) to increase cable slack.

7. Disconnect the clutch cable end from the clutch release arm (C, **Figure 68**).

8. Detach the return spring (A, **Figure 69**) from the spring bracket (B).

9. Remove the mounting bolts (C, **Figure 69**), then remove the clutch release assembly (D).

10. Operate the release mechanism and check for binding or other signs of faulty operation. Inspect the mechanism for damage. Replace if necessary.

11. Install by reversing the removal procedure while noting the following:

    a. Apply molybdenum grease to the spiral splines before assembly.

b. Loosen the stud and nut (**Figure 70**) several turns before assembly.

c. Assemble the mechanism and spring bracket as shown in **Figure 69**.

d. When properly assembled the clutch release arm should be approximately 80° from vertical.

e. Tighten the mounting bolts securely.

f. Adjust the clutch as described in Chapter Three.

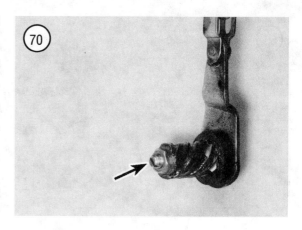

Table 1 CLUTCH SERVICE SPECIFICATIONS

Item	Standard	Wear limit
Friction disc thickness		
No. 1 and No. 2	2.92-3.08 mm	2.62 mm
	(0.115-0.121 in.)	(0.104 in.)
Friction disc tab width	13.7-13.8 mm	12.9 mm
	(0.539-0.543 in.)	(0.51 in.)
Clutch plate warpage	–	0.1 mm (0.004 in.)
Clutch spring free length	53.1 mm (2.09 in.)	50.5 mm (1.99 in.)
Number of clutch plates		
Friction plates No. 1	6	
Friction plate No. 2	1	
Steel plates	6	

Table 2 CLUTCH AND GEARSHIFT MECHANISM TORQUE SPECIFICATIONS

Item	N•m	in. lb.	ft.-lb.
Cam stopper bolt	10	88	–
Clutch hub nut	50	–	37
Clutch spring bolts	10	88	–
Shift cam Allen bolt	13	115	–

CHAPTER SEVEN

TRANSMISSION AND INTERNAL SHIFT MECHANISM

This chapter covers service to the transmission and internal gearshift assemblies. Specifications are listed in **Table 1** and **Table 2** at the end of this chapter.

When the clutch is engaged, the input (main) shaft is driven by the clutch hub, which is driven by the primary crankshaft drive gear/clutch outer housing. Power is transferred from the input shaft through the selected gear combination to the output (counter) shaft, which drives the engine drive sprocket.

To gain access to the transmission and internal shift mechanism, it is necessary to remove the engine and disassemble the crankcase as described in Chapter Five.

> *NOTE*
> *Suzuki terminology for the transmission shafts is different than most manufacturers. Suzuki refers to the input (main) shaft as the countershaft and the output shaft as the driveshaft. Most manufacturers, if they do not use the input/output shaft terms, refer to the input shaft as the mainshaft and the output shaft as the countershaft. In this manual, the input shaft is termed the mainshaft and the output shaft is called the countershaft. Make sure to identify the correct part when ordering parts.*

INTERNAL SHIFT MECHANISM

Removal

Refer to **Figure 1**.
1. Disassemble the crankcase as described in Chapter Five.
2. Remove the shift fork shafts (**Figure 2**).
3. Remove the shift drum (**Figure 3**).
4. Remove the shift forks (**Figure 4**).

Inspection

Refer to **Figure 1**.
1. Clean all parts in solvent and thoroughly dry them with compressed air.
2. Inspect each shift fork for signs of wear or cracking. Check for any burned marks on the fingers of the shift forks (A, **Figure 5**). This indicates that the shift fork has come in contact with the gear. Replace the fork if the fork fingers have become excessively worn.
3. Check the bore of each shift fork and the shift fork shaft for burrs, wear or pitting. Replace any worn parts.
4. Install each shift fork onto its shaft (**Figure 6**) and make sure it moves freely on the shaft with no binding.

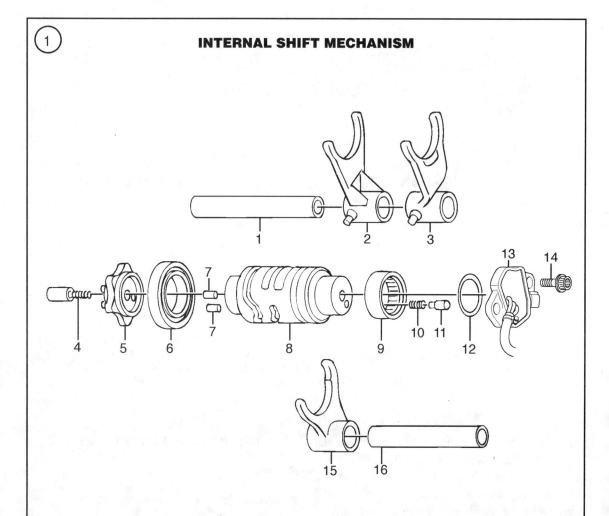

INTERNAL SHIFT MECHANISM

1. Shift shaft
2. Shift fork (right)
3. Shift fork (left)
4. Allen bolt
5. Cam stopper plate
6. Bearing
7. Locating pins
8. Shift drum
9. Bearing
10. Spring
11. Contact pin
12. O-ring
13. Neutral switch
14. Bolt
15. Shift fork (center)
16. Shift shaft

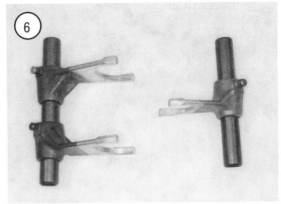

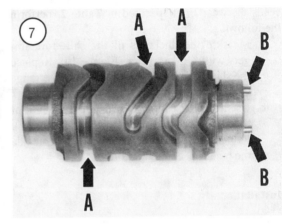

5. Check the guide pin (B, **Figure 5**) on each shift fork for wear or damage. Replace the shift fork(s) as necessary.

6. Roll each shift fork shaft on a surface plate or a piece of plate glass. If a shaft is bent, replace it.

7. Check the grooves in the shift drum (A, **Figure 7**) for wear or roughness. If any of the groove profiles have excessive wear or damage, replace the shift drum.

8. Inspect the cam gear locating pins (B, **Figure 7**) and threaded hole in the end of the shift drum for wear or damage. Replace the shift drum if necessary.

9. Check the neutral switch contact plungers and springs (**Figure 8**) for wear or damage. If the springs have sagged, replace them.

CAUTION
Replace marginally worn shift forks.
Worn forks can cause the transmission
to slip out of gear, leading to serious
damage.

10. Install each shift fork into the groove in its respective gear. Use a flat feeler gauge and measure the clearance between the fork and the groove as shown in **Figure 9**. If the shift fork-to-groove clearance ex-

ceeds the wear limit specified in **Table 2**, perform the following:

    a. Measure the thickness of the shift fork fingers with a micrometer (**Figure 10**). Replace the shift fork if the width is outside the range specified in **Table 2**.

    b. Use a vernier caliper to measure the width of the shift fork groove in the gear (**Figure 11**). Replace the gear if the groove width is outside the range specified in **Table 2**.

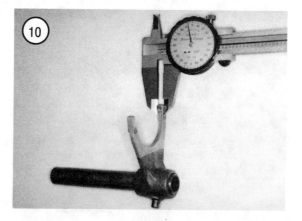

Installation

> *NOTE*
> *Lubricate all rotating and sliding surfaces with engine oil during assembly.*

1. Be sure the mainshaft and countershaft assemblies are properly installed.

2. Note the identifying number cast into each shift fork (C, **Figure 5**).

> *NOTE*
> *All shift forks have a pin that must engage the proper groove in the shift drum. Be sure to install the shift forks so the pin points toward the shift drum.*

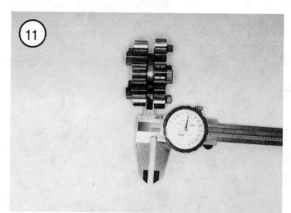

3. Install the shift forks as follows:

    a. Install the left shift fork–identifying number 42E1-2J–into the sixth driven gear groove (A, **Figure 12**).

    b. Install the right shift fork–identifying number 42E-1R–into the fifth driven gear groove (B, **Figure 12**).

    c. Install the center shift fork–identifying number 42E-3J–into the third/fourth drive gear groove (**Figure 13**).

4. Install the shift drum (A, **Figure 14**). Position the shift drum and shift forks so the pins on the shift forks properly engage the grooves in the shift drum.

5. Install the long shift shaft (B, **Figure 14**).

6. Install the short shift shaft (C, **Figure 14**).

7. Rotate the transmission shafts and shift through all gears using the shift drum. Make sure the mechanism will shift into all gears. This is the time to find that something may be installed incorrectly—not after the crankcase is completely assembled.

> *NOTE*
> *This procedure is easier with the aid of a helper as the assemblies are loose and won't spin very easily. Have the helper spin the transmission shaft while you turn the shift drum through all the gears.*

8. Reassemble the crankcase as described in Chapter Five.

TRANSMISSION

Removal/Installation

1. Remove the internal shift mechanism as described in this chapter.

2. Remove the washer (A, **Figure 15**) on the countershaft.

> *NOTE*
> *It may be necessary to tap the outer end (drive sprocket) of the countershaft to dislodge the countershaft from the bearing.*

3. Pull out both the countershaft assembly (B, **Figure 15**) and the mainshaft assembly (C) from the left crankcase half as shown in **Figure 16**.

4. If necessary, disassemble and inspect the transmission assemblies as described in this chapter.

5. To install the transmission, assemble the countershaft and mainshaft assemblies so all gears are meshed (**Figure 16**).

6. Install the transmission assemblies into the left crankshaft half (**Figure 15**). It may be necessary to gently tap the inner end of the countershaft so it will pass through the bearing in the crankcase half.

7. Install the washer (A, **Figure 15**) onto the countershaft.

8. Install the internal shift mechanism as described in this chapter.

Preliminary Inspection

1. Clean and inspect the assemblies before disassembling them. Place the assembled shaft into a large can or plastic bucket and thoroughly clean the assembly with a stiff brush and petroleum-based solvent. Dry

TRANSMISSION

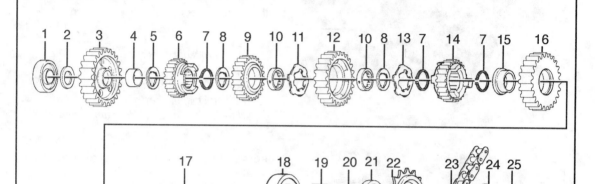

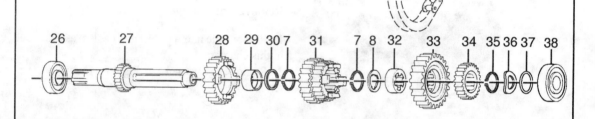

1. Bearing
2. Thrust washer
3. Countershaft first gear
4. Countershaft first gear bushing
5. Washer
6. Countershaft fifth gear
7. Snap ring
8. Splined washer
9. Countershaft fourth gear
10. Splined bushing
11. Lockwasher
12. Countershaft third gear
13. Lockwasher
14. Countershaft sixth gear
15. Flanged bushing
16. Countershaft second gear
17. Countershaft
18. Bearing
19. Spacer

20. O-ring
21. Oil seal
22. Drive sprocket
23. Drive chain
24. Washer
25. Nut
26. Bearing
27. Mainshaft/first gear
28. Mainshaft fifth gear
29. Mainshaft fifth gear bushing
30. Washer
31. Mainshaft third/fourth gear
32. Splined bushing
33. Mainshaft sixth gear
34. Mainshaft second gear
35. Circlip
36. Wave washer
37. O-ring
38. Bearing

the assembly with compressed air or let it sit on rags to drip dry. Do this for both shaft assemblies.

2. Visually inspect the components for excessive wear. Check the gear teeth for chips, burrs or pitting. Remove burrs with an oilstone. Replace any damaged components.

3. Carefully check the engagement dogs. If any is chipped, worn, rounded or missing, replace the affected gear.

4. Rotate the transmission bearings in the crankcase halves by hand. Check for roughness, noise and radial play. Replace any bearing that is suspect as described in Chapter Five.

5. Slide the clutch pushrods into the mainshaft and check for binding. If binding occurs, check the pushrods for damage. Inspect the mainshaft bore for debris. Clean out the bore if necessary.

6. If the transmission shafts are satisfactory and are not going to be disassembled, apply assembly oil or engine oil to all components and reinstall them into the crankcase as described in this chapter.

Transmission Service Notes

1. After removing a part from the shaft, set it in an egg crate in the exact order of removal and with the same orientation the part had when installed on the shaft. This is an easy way to remember the correct relationship of all parts.

2. The snap rings fit tightly on the transmission shafts. It is recommended that all snap rings be replaced during assembly.

3. Snap rings will turn and fold over making removal and installation difficult. To ease replacement, open a snap ring with a pair of snap ring pliers while at the same time holding the back of the snap ring with a pair of pliers and remove it. Repeat for installation.

Countershaft Disassembly

Refer to **Figure 17**.

1. If not cleaned during *Preliminary Inspection*, place the assembled shaft into a large can or plastic bucket. Thoroughly clean it with solvent and a stiff brush. Dry the shaft assembly with compressed air or let it sit on rags to dry.

2. Remove the thrust washer (A, **Figure 18**) and first gear (B).

3. Remove the first gear bushing (A, **Figure 19**), thrust washer (B) and fifth gear (C).

4. Remove the snap ring (A, **Figure 20**), splined washer (B) and fourth gear (C).

5. Remove the fourth gear bushing (A, **Figure 21**).

6. Slide off the tab lockwasher (A, **Figure 22**).

7. Rotate the notched lockwasher (B, **Figure 22**) in either direction to disengage its tangs from the grooves on the countershaft. Slide off the notched lockwasher.

8. Slide off the third gear (**Figure 23**).

9. Remove the third gear bushing (A, **Figure 24**) and splined washer (B).

10. Remove the snap ring (C, **Figure 24**) and sixth gear (D).

11. Remove the snap ring (A, **Figure 25**).

12. Slide off the second gear (B, **Figure 25**) with the flanged bushing (C).

13. Inspect the components as described in *Transmission Inspection*.

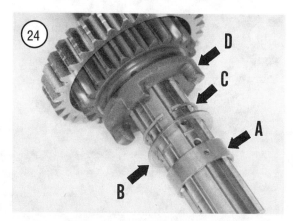

Countershaft Assembly

NOTE
Install new snap rings during assembly to ensure proper gear alignment. Do not expand a snap ring more than necessary to slide it over the shaft.

1. Apply a light coat of molybdenum oil to all sliding surfaces prior to installing any parts.

2. Slide the second gear (A, **Figure 26**) and flange bushing (B) onto the countershaft. The gear's engagement slots should face out, away from the threaded shaft end. The flanged end of the bushing must face the adjacent snap ring.

3. Install the snap ring (A, **Figure 25**) so the flat side is away from the bushing flange. Make sure the snap ring is correctly seated in the snap ring groove.

4. Install sixth gear (D, **Figure 24**) so its shift-fork groove faces out, away from second gear.

5. Install the snap ring (C, **Figure 24**) so it is properly seated in the snap ring groove.

6. Install the splined washer (B, **Figure 24**) and the third gear bushing (A). Make sure the oil hole in the bushing aligns with the oil hole in the countershaft. These holes must align to ensure proper gear lubrication.

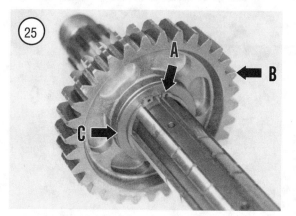

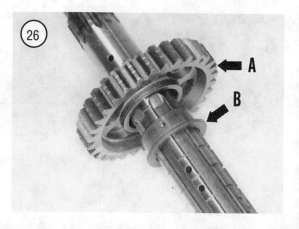

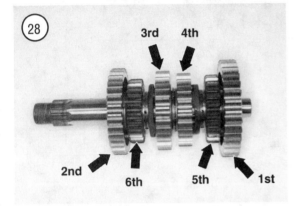

17. Refer to **Figure 28** for correct placement of all gears. Make sure all snap rings are correctly seated in the countershaft grooves.

18. Make sure each gear properly engages an adjoining gear where applicable.

Mainshaft Disassembly

Refer to **Figure 29**.

1. If not cleaned during *Preliminary Inspection*, place the assembled mainshaft into a large can or plastic bucket, and thoroughly clean the assembly with solvent and a stiff brush. Dry with compressed air or let it sit on rags to dry.

2. Remove the O-ring (A, **Figure 30**) and wave washer (B) from the end of the mainshaft.

NOTE
The snap ring is recessed inside the second gear. Steps 3-5 must be performed to expose this snap ring for removal.

3. Slide the third-fourth combination gear (A, **Figure 31**) away from the sixth gear (B) to expose the snap ring (**Figure 32**) and splined washer.

4. Using angled snap ring pliers, open the snap ring (**Figure 33**) and slide the snap ring and the splined washer away from the sixth and second gears.

5. Slide the sixth and second gears toward the third-fourth combination gear to expose the snap ring (A, **Figure 34**) under the second gear. If necessary, use the sixth and second gears to tap the sixth-gear snap ring and splined washer inward until the snap ring is exposed.

6. Remove the snap ring (A, **Figure 34**), then remove second gear (B) and sixth gear (C).

7. Remove the sixth gear bushing (A, **Figure 35**), splined washer (B) and snap ring (C).

8. Slide off the third-fourth combination gear (**Figure 36**).

9. Remove the snap ring (A, **Figure 37**), washer (B) and fifth gear (C).

10. Remove the fifth gear bushing (A, **Figure 38**).

11. Inspect the components as described in *Transmission Inspection*.

Mainshaft Assembly

NOTE
*The first gear (B, **Figure 38**) is part of the mainshaft. If the gear is defective, replace the mainshaft.*

1. Apply a light coat of molybdenum oil to all sliding surfaces prior to installing any parts.

7. Install third gear (**Figure 23**) so its engagement slots face in toward sixth gear.

8. Install lockwasher No.1 (A, **Figure 27**). Rotate the lockwasher in either direction so the tangs on the lockwasher engage the grooves in the countershaft.

9. Install lockwasher No.2 (B, **Figure 27**) and press it into place. The tangs on lockwasher No.2 should engage the cutouts in lockwasher No.1 (A).

10. Align the oil hole in the fourth gear bushing (A, **Figure 21**) with the oil hole (B) in the countershaft and slide the bushing into place. This alignment is necessary for proper gear lubrication.

11. Install the fourth gear (C, **Figure 20**) so its engagement slots face out.

12. Install the splined washer (B, **Figure 20**) and snap ring (A). Install the snap ring so the flat side is away from the washer. Make sure the snap ring is correctly seated in the snap ring groove.

13. Install fifth gear (C, **Figure 19**) so its shift fork groove faces in toward fourth gear.

14. Slide on the thrust washer (B, **Figure 19**) and the first gear bushing (A).

15. Slide on the first gear (B, **Figure 18**) so its flat side faces out, away from fifth gear.

16. Install the thrust washer (A, **Figure 18**).

TRANSMISSION

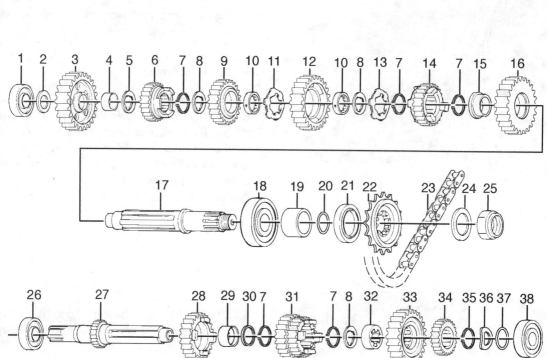

1. Bearing
2. Thrust washer
3. Countershaft first gear
4. Countershaft first gear bushing
5. Washer
6. Countershaft fifth gear
7. Snap ring
8. Splined washer
9. Countershaft fourth gear
10. Splined bushing
11. Lockwasher
12. Countershaft third gear
13. Lockwasher
14. Countershaft sixth gear
15. Flanged bushing
16. Countershaft second gear
17. Countershaft
18. Bearing
19. Spacer

20. O-ring
21. Oil seal
22. Drive sprocket
23. Drive chain
24. Washer
25. Nut
26. Bearing
27. Mainshaft/first gear
28. Mainshaft fifth gear
29. Mainshaft fifth gear bushing
30. Washer
31. Mainshaft third/fourth gear
32. Splined bushing
33. Mainshaft sixth gear
34. Mainshaft second gear
35. Circlip
36. Wave washer
37. O-ring
38. Bearing

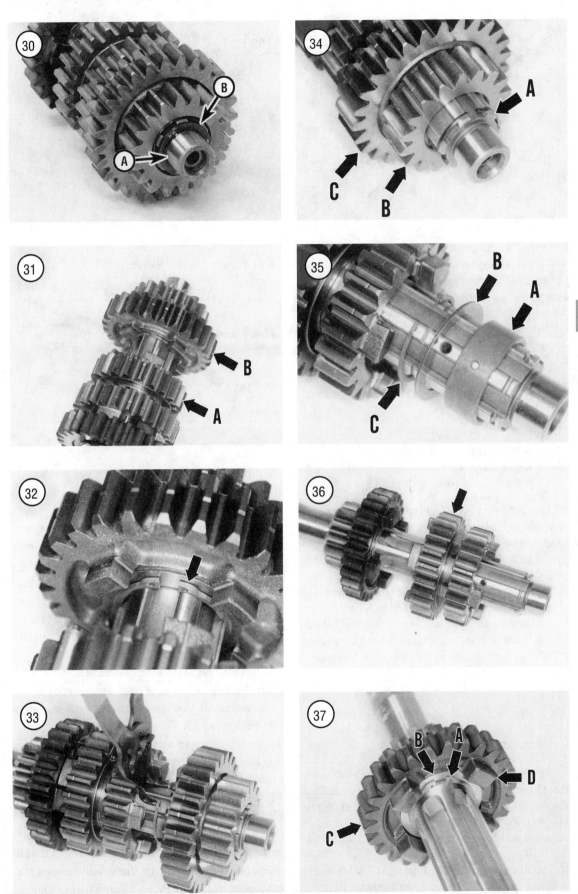

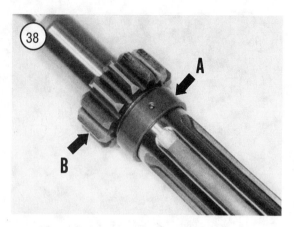

2. Install the fifth gear bushing (A, **Figure 38**) and fifth gear (C, **Figure 37**) onto the mainshaft. Install the gear so the engagement dogs face out, away from first gear (D, **Figure 37**).

3. Install the washer (B, **Figure 37**) and snap ring (A). Install the snap ring so its flat side faces out away from fifth gear. Make sure the snap ring is correctly seated in the snap ring groove.

4. Install third-fourth combination gear with the larger diameter fourth gear (**Figure 36**) going on first.

NOTE
In Step 5 do not seat the snap ring in its respective groove at this time. It will be positioned correctly in Step 10.

5. Install the snap ring (C, **Figure 35**) but do not seat it in its respective groove in the shaft. Position the snap ring so its faces in toward third-fourth combination gear. Move the snap ring past the snap ring groove toward the third-fourth combination gear.

6. Install the splined washer (B, **Figure 35**) and slide it up against the snap ring installed in Step 5.

7. Install the sixth gear bushing (A, Figure 35) then install the sixth gear (C, **Figure 34**) so its engagement dogs face in toward the third-fourth combination gear.

NOTE
After the second gear is installed on the shaft, the outermost snap ring groove in the shaft must be exposed.

8. Install the second gear so the relieved inner diameter (**Figure 39**) is toward the end of the shaft. Slide the second gear (B, **Figure 34**) toward the sixth gear (C) until the snap ring groove is exposed. If necessary, use the second and sixth gears to tap the splined washer farther down the shaft.

9. Install the snap ring (A, **Figure 34**). Make sure it is correctly seated in the mainshaft groove.

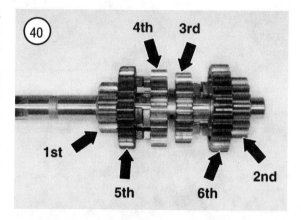

10. Slide the second and sixth gears against the snap ring at the end of the shaft to expose the snap ring and splined washer installed in Step 5.

11. Slide the splined washer toward the sixth gear.

12. Using angled snap ring pliers, move the snap ring into its respective groove (**Figure 33**). Make sure it is correctly seated in the mainshaft groove.

13. After the snap ring is installed, spin the sixth gear to make sure it rotates correctly and that the splined washer and snap ring are installed correctly. Reposition the snap ring if necessary.

14. Refer to **Figure 40** for correct placement of all gears. Make sure the snap rings are correctly seated in the mainshaft grooves. Check that each gear properly engages an adjoining gear where applicable.

15. Install the wave washer (B, **Figure 30**).

16. Install the O-ring (A, **Figure 30**) into the groove in the mainshaft.

17. After both transmission shafts have been assembled, mesh the two assemblies together in the correct position (**Figure 41**). Check that each gear properly engages its mate on the opposite shaft. This is the last check prior to installing the shaft assemblies into the crankcase; make sure they are correctly assembled.

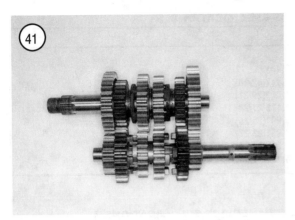

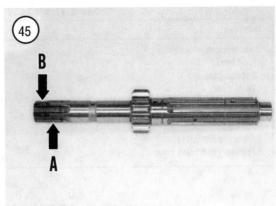

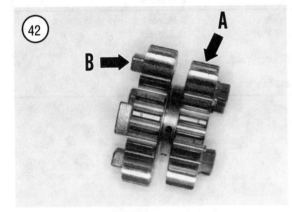

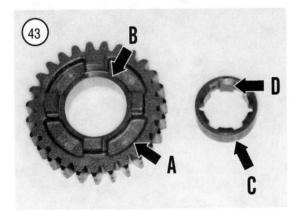

Transmission Inspection

> *NOTE*
> *Replace defective gears and their mating gears on the other shaft as well, even though they may not show as much wear or damage.*

1. Check each gear for excessive wear, burrs, pitting, chipped or missing teeth (A, **Figure 42**). Make sure the engagement dogs (B, **Figure 42**) on the gears are in good condition. Also inspect the engagement slots (A, **Figure 43**) for wear or damage.

2. On splined gears, check the inner splines for excessive wear or damage. Replace the gear if necessary.

3. On gears with bushings, inspect the inner surface of the gear (B, **Figure 43**) for wear, pitting or damage. Insert the bushing into the gear and check for smooth operation.

4. Check each bushing (C, **Figure 43**) for excessive wear, pitting or damage. Replace any bushing if necessary.

5. On splined bushings, check the inner splines (D, **Figure 43**) for excessive wear or damage. Replace if necessary.

6. Make sure that all gears and bushings slide smoothly on the shaft splines.

7. Inspect countershaft lockwashers (**Figure 44**) for wear, cracks, or damage. Replace if necessary.

8. Inspect the washers for bending wear or damage. Replace if necessary.

9. Inspect the splines and snap ring grooves in a shaft. If any are damaged, replace the shaft.

10. Inspect the clutch hub splines (A, **Figure 45**) and clutch nut threads (B) on the end of the mainshaft. If any of the splines are damaged, the shaft must be replaced.

11. Inspect the shift fork-to-gear clearance as described in the *Internal Gearshift Mechanism* section.

Table 1 TRANSMISSION SPECIFICATIONS

Item	
Transmission gear ratios	
First gear	2.461 (32/13)
Second gear	1.777(32/18)
Third gear	1.380(29/21)
Fourth gear	1.125(27/24)
Fifth gear	0.961(25/26)
Sixth gear	0.851(23/27)
Primary reduction ratio	2.088(71/34)
Secondary reduction ratio	3.133(47/15)

Table 2 INTERNAL SHIFT MECHANISM SERVICE SPECIFICATIONS

Item	Standard	Wear limit
Shift fork-to-groove clearance	0.1-0.3 mm (0.004-0.012 in.)	0.50 mm (0.020 in.)
Shift fork groove width	5.5-5.6 mm (0.217-0.220 in.)	–
Shift fork thickness	5.3-5.4 mm (0.209-0.213 in.)	–

CHAPTER EIGHT

FUEL AND EMISSION CONTROL SYSTEMS

This chapter covers the service procedures for the fuel and emission control systems. Air filter service is covered in Chapter Three. Specifications are listed in **Tables 1-4** at the end of this chapter.

The fuel system consists of the fuel tank, fuel pump, fuel pump relay, fuel injectors, throttle body, ECM and associated electrical components.

The emission system components vary depending on the model. A crankcase breather system and a PAIR (air supply) system is used on all models. California models are equipped with an evaporative emissions control system.

FUEL TANK

Raising/Supporting the Fuel Tank

1. Remove the front seat as described in Chapter Fifteen.
2. Remove the side covers around the fuel tank as described in Chapter Fifteen.
3. Remove the center cowling panel as described in Chapter Fifteen.
4. Remove the bolt (**Figure 1**) securing the cowling to the fuel tank on each side.
5. Disengage the mounting bosses and holes on the cowling and fuel tank.
6. Remove the fuel tank retaining bolt (A, **Figure 2**) and prop (B).

NOTE
Protect the fuel tank to prevent scratches during raising.

7. Raise the rear of the fuel tank and position the prop so it supports the fuel tank (**Figure 3**).
8. Reverse the procedure to lower the fuel tank. Tighten the fuel tank retaining bolt securely.

Removal/Installation

WARNING
Some fuel may spill from the fuel tank hose when performing this procedure. Because gasoline is extremely flammable and explosive, perform this procedure away from all open flames (including appliance pilot lights) and sparks. Do not smoke or allow someone who is smoking in the work area. Always work in a well-ventilated area. Wipe up any spills immediately.

1. Disconnect the negative battery cable as described in Chapter Nine.
2. Raise and support the fuel tank as previously described.
3. Disconnect the fuel pump electrical connector (A, **Figure 4**).
4. Disconnect the fuel hose connector (B, **Figure 4**).
5. Detach the fuel drain hose (A, **Figure 5**).

6. On California models, detach the fuel vapor hose (B, **Figure 5**).

7. Remove the bolt (**Figure 6**) securing the front of the tank.

8. Carefully remove the fuel tank.

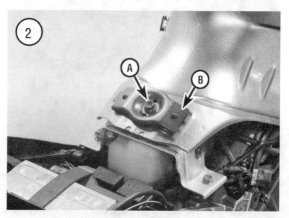

Inspection

1. Inspect the rubber cushions for damage or deterioration and replace if necessary.

2. Inspect the filler cap gaskets. If the cap gasket is damaged or deteriorating, replace the filler cap assembly. The gasket cannot be replaced separately. If the mounting flange gasket is damaged, replace it.

3. To remove the fuel filler cap, remove the screws and the filler cap assembly. Install the new filler cap and tighten the screws securely.

4. Inspect the entire fuel tank for leaks or damage. Repair or replace the fuel tank if any fuel leakage is found.

ELECTRONIC FUEL INJECTION (EFI)

This section describes the components and operation of the electronic fuel injection (EFI) system. The EFI system consists of a fuel delivery system and electronic control system.

Components in the fuel delivery system include the fuel tank, fuel pump, fuel pump relay, throttle body and fuel injectors. The fuel pump resides in the fuel tank and directs fuel to the fuel injectors at a regulated pressure of 300 kPa (43 psi). The fuel injectors are mounted on the throttle body, which is attached to both cylinder heads.

The electronic control system consists of the electronic control module (ECM) and sensors. The electronic control system determines the output of the fuel injectors, the position of the secondary throttle valve, as well as controlling ignition timing. Refer also to the following section.

Refer to Chapter Two for troubleshooting procedures.

Electronic Control Module (ECM) and Sensors

The electronic control module (ECM) is mounted next to the battery. The ECM contains a program map that determines the optimum fuel injection and ignition timing based on input from sensors.

The sensors and their locations and functions are as follows:

1. The throttle position sensor (TP), located on the rear throttle body and attached directly to the throttle shaft, indicates throttle angle. The ECM determines the air volume entering the engine based on the throttle angle.

2. The crankshaft position sensor (CKP), located in the left crankcase cover, is an inductive type sensor. The ECM determines the engine speed by how fast the machined teeth on the flywheel pass by the sensor.

3. The engine coolant temperature sensor (ECT) is located on the thermostat housing. The ECM adjusts the injector opening time based on input from this sensor.

4. The intake air temperature sensor (IAT) is located on the right side of the air box. The ECM determines

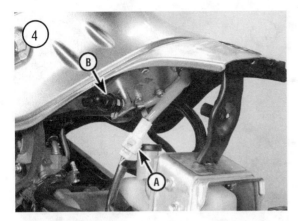

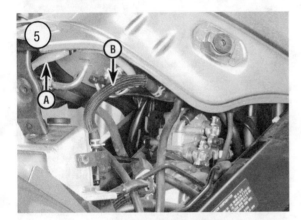

to the throttle shaft of the secondary throttle valves, indicates secondary throttle angle.

8. U.K., EU Models–The heated oxygen sensor (HOS) on the muffler provides the ECM with exhaust gas mixture information. The sensor decreases voltage output if it detects a large amount of oxygen in the exhaust gas, which indicates a lean air/fuel mixture. The heater element improves sensor performance.

Fuel Supply System

Fuel Pump and filters

The fuel pump and filter assembly is located inside the fuel tank. This assembly is attached to a mounting plate on the bottom of the fuel tank. A fuel regulator attached to the fuel pump mounting bracket maintains fuel pressure.

A mesh-type inlet screen on the fuel pump prevents solid material in the fuel tank from entering the fuel pump. A filter at the outlet of the fuel pump prevents contaminants from entering the fuel lines and fuel injectors.

Fuel line

The fuel line is attached to the fuel tank tubing with quick-disconnect fittings.

The fuel supply line pressure is 300 kPa (43 psi). A check valve is located on the fuel line where it attaches to the fuel tank.

Fuel injectors

The pintle-type fuel injector consists of a solenoid plunger, needle valve and housing. The injector has a fixed orifice size and operates at a constant pressure.

Throttle Body

A throttle body with primary and secondary throttle valves sits atop the intake tube on each cylinder head. The front (no. 1cylinder) throttle body contains the throttle-grip controlled primary throttle valve. A link transmits throttle valve motion to the primary valve on the rear (no. 2 cylinder) throttle body.

On 2004-2006 models, the secondary throttle valve actuator (SVTA) rotates the secondary throttle valve shaft as directed by the ECM. Using air/fuel maps, the ECM sets the secondary throttle valve position to optimize air flow through the throttle body bore. A link transmits throttle valve motion to the secondary valve on the rear (no. 2 cylinder) throttle body.

the air density and adjusts the injector opening time based on input from this sensor.

5. The intake air pressure sensor (IAP) is attached to the rear of the air box. The IAP monitors intake manifold pressure (vacuum) and sends this information to the ECM.

6. The tip-over sensor (TO), located under the seat, interrupts the ignition and shuts off the engine if the motorcycle's lean angle is greater than 65° from vertical.

7. The secondary throttle position sensor (STP), located on the rear throttle body and attached directly

On 2007-2011 models, the SVTA is mounted on the rear throttle body and a link transmits throttle valve motion to the secondary valve on the front throttle body.

A fuel injector is mounted on each throttle body. Mounted on the rear throttle body are the throttle position sensor and secondary throttle position sensor.

FUEL DELIVERY SYSTEM TESTS

WARNING
Before disconnecting the fuel fittings, turn the ignition switch off and allow the system to internally release fuel pressure.

WARNING
Some fuel may spill from the fuel hoses when performing this procedure. Because gasoline is extremely flammable and explosive, perform this procedure away from all open flames (including appliance pilot lights) and sparks. Do not smoke or allow someone who is smoking in the work area. Always work in a well-ventilated area. Wipe up any spills immediately.

The following tests evaluate the performance of the fuel delivery system components (fuel pump, pressure regulator and filters).

Fuel Pressure Test

Tools

The following Suzuki tools, or equivalents, are needed to perform this test:
1. Fuel pressure gauge adapter (part No. 09940-40211).
2. Fuel pressure gauge hose attachment (part No. 09940-40220).
3. Oil pressure gauge set (part No. 09915-74511).

Test procedure

1. Raise and support the fuel tank as described in this chapter.

NOTE
To disengage the hose end from the fuel pump pipe in Step 2, press in on the upper tabs of the coupler.

2. Disconnect the fuel hose (A, **Figure 7**) from the output pipe on the fuel pump. Be prepared to catch residual gasoline.

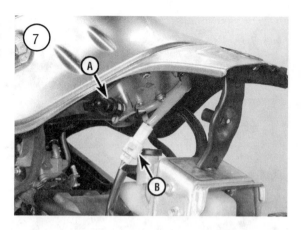

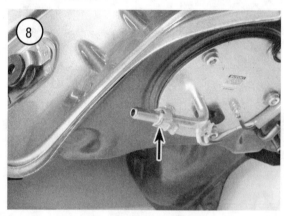

NOTE
*The plastic coupler (**Figure 8**) may remain on the tank pipe. Carefully remove the coupler and insert it into the fuel hose end.*

3. Use the adapters to install the gauge inline between the fuel pump and the throttle body. Follow the manufacturer's instructions. See **Figure 9**.
4. Turn the ignition switch on, and read the fuel pressure. It should equal approximately 300 kPa (43 psi).
5. If fuel pressure is less than specified, check for a leak in the fuel system, a clogged fuel filter, faulty pressure regulator or faulty fuel pump.
6. If fuel pressure exceeds specification, the fuel pump check valve or the pressure regulator is faulty. The check valve is an integral part of the fuel pump and cannot be replaced separately. If the pressure regulator is faulty, replace the fuel pump mounting plate assembly.

Fuel Pump Operation Test

1. Turn the ignition switch on and listen for operation of the fuel pump.

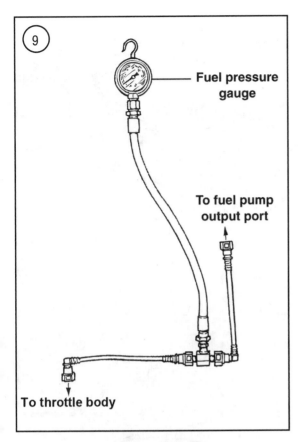

2. If no sound is heard, test the fuel pump relay and the tip over sensor as described in this chapter. If both of these components are within specification, replace the fuel pump.

Fuel Pump Discharge Test

A graduated cylinder or similar graduated container with a capacity of at least 1.0 liter (1.0 qt.) is needed for this test.

1. Raise and support the fuel tank as described in this chapter.
2. Disconnect the fuel pump connector (B, **Figure 7**).

NOTE
To disengage the hose end from the fuel pump pipe in Step 2, press in on the upper tabs of the coupler.

3. Disconnect the fuel hose (A, **Figure 7**) from the output pipe on the fuel pump. Be prepared to catch residual gasoline.

NOTE
*The plastic coupler (**Figure 8**) may remain on the tank pipe. Carefully remove the coupler and insert it into the fuel hose end.*

4. Connect a suitable hose to the fuel pump output pipe and feed the opposite end of the hose into a graduated cylinder.
5. Apply battery voltage directly to the fuel pump for 10 seconds as follows:
   a. Use a jumper to connect the battery positive terminal to the yellow/red wire in the pump end of the fuel pump connector. Connect the negative battery terminal to the black/white terminal in the pump end of the connector.
   b. Keep the jumpers connected to the terminals for 10 seconds, and then disconnect them from the connector and from the battery terminal.
6. Measure the amount of fuel in the graduated cylinder. It should equal the fuel pump output volume specified in **Table 1**. The fuel pump is faulty or the fuel filters are obstructed if the volume is significantly less than specified.

FUEL PUMP (2004-2006 MODELS)

The fuel pump is located inside the fuel tank and operates whenever the ignition switch is on. The pressure regulator, which is an integral part of the fuel pump plate assembly, maintains fuel line pressure at 300 kPa (43 psi). The pressure regulator bypasses fuel back into the fuel tank internally, so there is no fuel return line. The fuel meter sending unit is attached to the fuel pump.

Removal/Installation

1. Remove the fuel tank as described in this chapter. Drain the fuel into a suitable container.
2. Set the fuel tank on towels or a blanket on the workbench.
3. Evenly loosen the fuel pump mounting plate bolts (**Figure 10**) in a crossing pattern and remove the bolts.

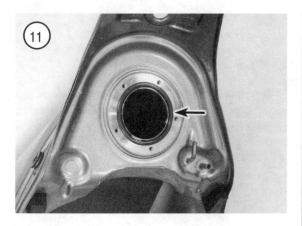

4. Remove the fuel pump from the tank. Remove and discard the O-ring (**Figure 11**) which may remain on the fuel tank or fuel pump.

5. If necessary, test the fuel meter sending unit as described in Chapter Nine.

6. Install the fuel pump by reversing the preceding removal steps and noting the following:

    a. Apply Suzuki Super Grease A to a new O-ring, and fit the O-ring into the channel in the tank (**Figure 11**).

    b. Apply Suzuki Thread Lock 1342, or equivalent, to the threads of the fuel pump bolts and install the bolts (**Figure 10**).

    c. Evenly tighten the bolts in a crossing pattern to 10 N•m (88 in.-lb.).

Disassembly

NOTE
Verify parts availability before disassembling the fuel pump assembly.

Refer to **Figure 12**.

1. Remove the fuel pump as described in this section.

2. Remove the fuel meter sending unit as follows:

    a. Note the location of the sending unit wires.

    b. Disconnect the sending unit wires.

    c. Remove the wire clamp.

    d. Remove the sending unit mounting screws.

    e. Remove the sending unit.

3. Disconnect the electrical lead from each terminal as follows:

    a. Label each wire and its terminal. Each wire must be reconnected to the correct terminal during assembly.

    b. Remove the terminal nut, lockwasher, wire ring terminal and washer from each terminal.

4. Remove the screw from the mounting arms of the pump base (A, **Figure 13**). Watch for the special nut installed on the mounting arm.

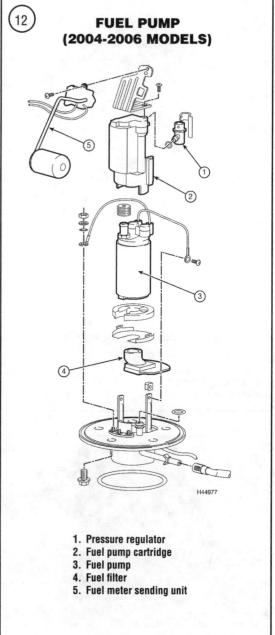

**FUEL PUMP
(2004-2006 MODELS)**

1. Pressure regulator
2. Fuel pump cartridge
3. Fuel pump
4. Fuel filter
5. Fuel meter sending unit

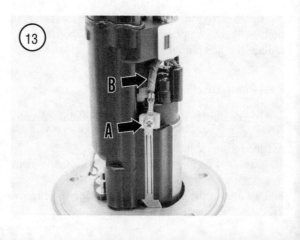

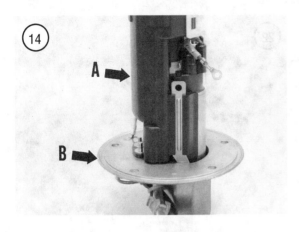

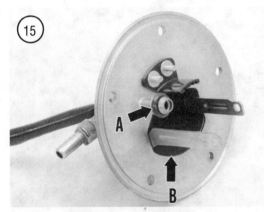

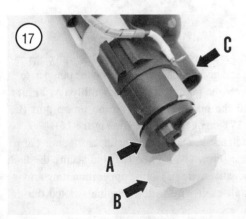

5. Slide the fuel pump/cartridge assembly (A, **Figure 14**) from the pump base (B). Discard the O-ring (A, **Figure 15**) from the fitting on the pump base.

6. Release the pump holder (**Figure 16**) from the tabs on the pump and remove the holder.

7. Remove the damper (A, **Figure 17**), and pull the fuel filter (B) from the pump.

8. Release the safety clip (**Figure 18**) from the tab on the pump and pull the clip from the pressure regulator.

9. Pull the pressure regulator (**Figure 19**) from the cartridge. Discard the O-ring (**Figure 20**) from the

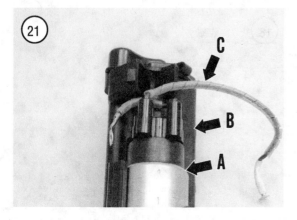

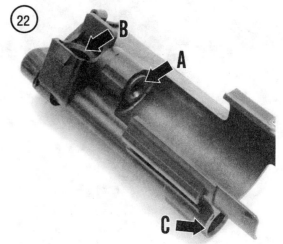

regulator fitting. Note that the fuel pump wires sit behind the pressure regulator.

10. Slide the fuel pump (A, **Figure 21**) from the cartridge (B). Note that the fuel pump wires (C) sit above the top of the pump. The wire must be rerouted the same way during assembly.

11. Slide the bushing (A, **Figure 22**) from the cartridge or remove the bushing on the fuel pump. Discard the bushing.

Inspection

1. Clean any sediment from the fuel pump base (B, **Figure 15**).
2. Blow the filter element clear with compressed air. Replace the element if it remains clogged.
3. Clear the ports (A, B and C, **Figure 22**) in the cartridge assembly.

Assembly

1. Press a new bushing (A, **Figure 22**) into the fuel pump port.
2. Slide the fuel pump into the cartridge (**Figure 23**) so the pump fitting (**Figure 24**) engages the bushing (A, **Figure 22**) in the fuel pump port. Make sure the pump wires (C, **Figure 21**) cross above the top of the pump as noted during disassembly.
3. Lubricate a new O-ring (**Figure 20**) with clean engine oil, and install it onto the pressure regulator.
4. Seat the pressure regulator (**Figure 19**) in the regulator port on the cartridge. Make sure the pump wires cross behind the pressure regulator.
5. Press the safety clip (**Figure 18**) onto the pump until the clip snaps into place.
6. Install the fuel filter (A, **Figure 25**) so it engages the indexing post in the pump.
7. Install the damper (B, **Figure 25**), and seat it (A, **Figure 17**) onto the pump.
8. Install the pump holder (**Figure 18**) so it locks onto the pump tabs.

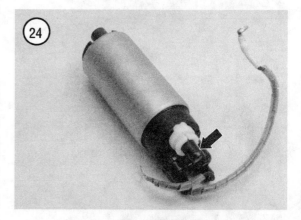

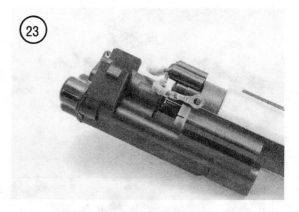

9. Lubricate a new O-ring (A, **Figure 15**) with clean engine oil, and install it onto the fitting on the pump base.
10. Lower the pump/cartridge assembly (A, **Figure 14**) onto the pump base (B) so the pump port (C, **Figure 17**) engages the base (B, **Figure 15**).
11. Install a special nut onto the upper mounting arm. Install the screw (A, **Figure 13**), and secure the fuel pump negative wire (B) to the upper mounting arm.
12. Install each wire to the terminals noted during removal.

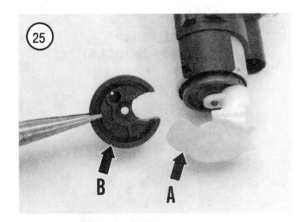

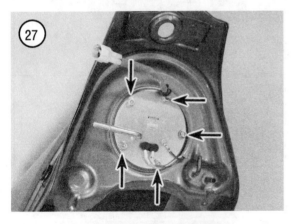

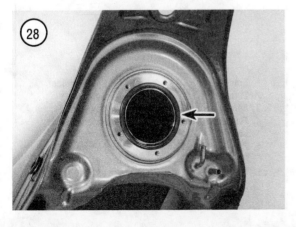

13. Assemble each terminal in the following order: install a washer, the wire ring terminal lockwasher and then the nut. Note the terminal connections:

    a. Positive fuel pump wire (A, **Figure 26**).

    b. Positive fuel meter sending unit wire (B, **Figure 26**).

FUEL PUMP (2007-2011 MODELS)

The fuel pump is located inside the fuel tank and operates whenever the ignition switch is on. The pressure regulator, which is an integral part of the fuel pump plate assembly, maintains fuel line pressure at 300 kPa (43 psi). The pressure regulator bypasses fuel back into the fuel tank internally, so there is no fuel return line.

Removal/Installation

1. Remove the fuel tank as described in this chapter. Drain the fuel into a suitable container.

2. Set the fuel tank on towels or a blanket on the workbench.

3. Evenly loosen the fuel pump mounting plate bolts (**Figure 27**) in a crossing pattern and remove the bolts.

4. Remove the fuel pump assembly from the tank. Remove and discard the fuel pump O-ring (**Figure 28**).

5. Install the fuel pump by reversing the preceding removal steps and noting the following:

    a. Apply Suzuki Super Grease A to a new O-ring, and fit the O-ring into the channel in the tank (**Figure 28**).

    b. Apply Suzuki Thread Lock 1342, or equivalent, to the threads of the fuel pump bolts and install the bolts (**Figure 27**).

    c. Evenly tighten the bolts in a crossing pattern to 10 N•m (88 in.-lb.).

Disassembly/Reassembly

Refer to **Figure 29**.

1. Remove the fuel pump as described in this section.

2. Remove the fuel meter sending unit as follows:

    a. Note the location of the sending unit wires.

    b. Disconnect the sending unit wires.

    c. Remove the sending unit mounting screws (A, **Figure 30**).

    d. Remove the sending unit (B, **Figure 30**).

3. Remove the fuel pressure regulator holder (**Figure 31**).

4. Remove the fuel pressure regulator retainer (**Figure 32**).

8

5. Remove the O-ring (A, **Figure 33**).

6. Remove the fuel pressure regulator (B, **Figure 33**).

7. Remove the O-ring (A, **Figure 34**).

8. Remove the fuel pump holder (B, **Figure 34**).

9. Remove the fuel filter (**Figure 35**).

10. Remove the fuel pump (**Figure 36**).

11. Remove the fuel joint pipe (**Figure 37**) from the fuel pump.

12. Reverse disassembly steps for reassembly while noting the following:

    a. Install new O-rings.

    b. Apply engine oil to O-rings before installation.

    c. Connect the positive fuel pump wire to terminal (A, **Figure 38**).

    d. Connect fuel gauge wire to terminal (B, **Figure 38**).

Inspection

1. If not previously cleaned, clean the fuel pump and plate assembly, but do not allow foreign matter to enter pump or line openings.

2. Clean the filter element. Replace the element if it remains obstructed.

FUEL PUMP RELAY

Removal/Installation

1. Disconnect the negative battery terminal cable.

2. Pull the relay (**Figure 39**) out of the connector.

3. Installation is the reverse of removal.

Test

1. Remove the relay from the motorcycle as described in this section.

2. Check the continuity between the A and B terminals on the relay (**Figure 40**). The relay should not have continuity.

3. Use jumpers to connect the positive terminal of a 12-volt battery to the C terminal on the relay (**Figure 40**); connect the negative battery terminal to the D relay terminal.

4. Check the continuity between the A and B relay terminals. The relay should have continuity while voltage is applied.

5. Replace the relay if it fails either portion of this test.

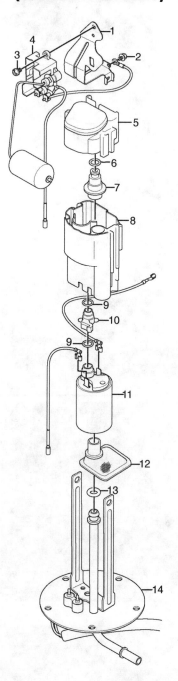

(29) **FUEL PUMP (2007-2011 MODELS)**

1. Bracket
2. Screw
3. Screw
4. Fuel meter sending unit
5. Pressure regulator holder
6. O-ring
7. Pressure regulator
8. Fuel pump holder
9. O-ring
10. Pressure regulator retainer
11. Fuel pump
12. Fuel filter
13. O-ring
14. Base

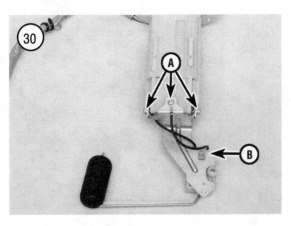

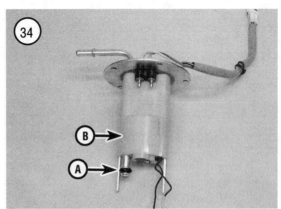

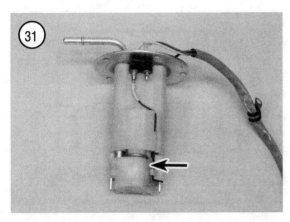

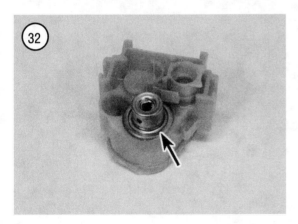

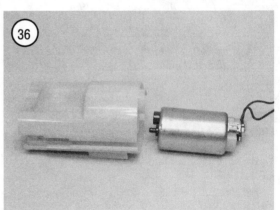

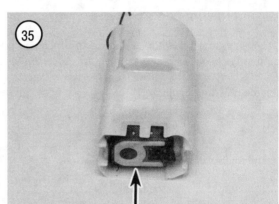

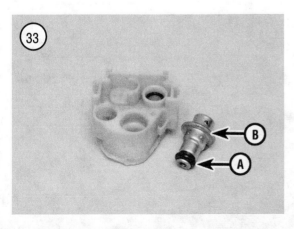

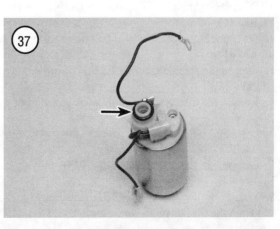

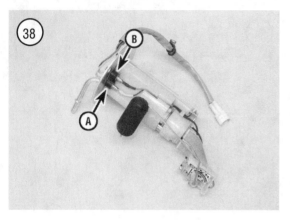

FUEL PRESSURE REGULATOR

The pressure regulator is part of the fuel pump mounting plate assembly. Refer to *Fuel Pump Disassembly/Assembly* in this chapter when servicing the pressure regulator.

AIR BOX

The air box is located under the fuel tank.

> *NOTE*
> *Label each hose and its air box fitting so the hose can be easily identified and reinstalled onto the correct fitting during assembly. Color-coded plugs are available at motorcycle and auto parts stores. Also plug the hoses and fittings so debris cannot enter.*

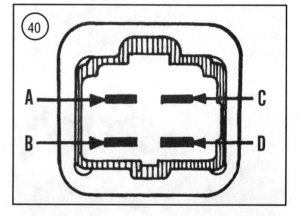

Removal/Installation (2004-2006 Models)

1. Remove the fuel tank as described in this chapter.

2. Disconnect the connector on the IAT sensor (A, **Figure 41**).

3. Disconnect the connector on the IAP sensor (B, **Figure 41**).

4. Disconnect the IAP sensor vacuum hose (C, **Figure 41**).

5. Loosen the clamp screw on the front throttle body (**Figure 42**).

6. Loosen the clamp screw on the rear throttle body (**Figure 43**).

7. Disconnect the PAIR hose (A, **Figure 44**) from the PAIR valve.

8. Disconnect the connector on the PAIR valve (B, **Figure 44**).

9. Detach the crankcase ventilation hoses (**Figure 45**) from the fittings on the breather box.

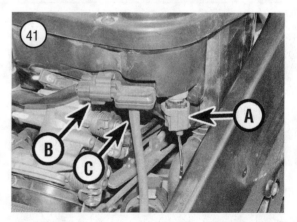

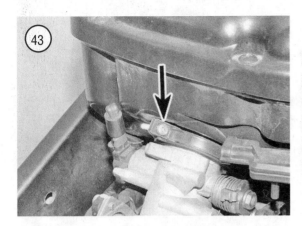

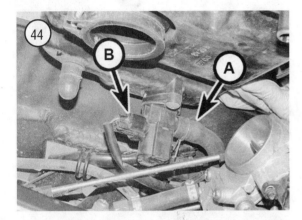

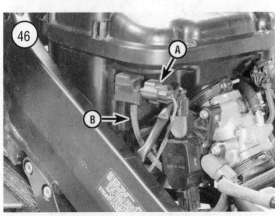

10. Pull the air box up and off the throttle bodies.

11. Remove the air box from the engine and frame.

12. Plug the throttle body inlets to prevent debris from entering.

13. Inspect the air box and the air inlet ducts for cracks, wear or damage. If any damage is noted, replace the air box to avoid the possibility of unfiltered air entering the engine.

14. Inspect the air box-to-throttle body tubes for hardness, deterioration or damage. Replace them if necessary.

15. Remove the drain plug and clean out all residue from the plug and air box. Reinstall the drain plug.

16. Install by reversing the preceding removal steps. Be sure all hoses are securely connected to prevent air leaks.

Removal/Installation
(2007-2011 Models)

1. Raise and support the fuel tank as described in this chapter.

2. Disconnect the connectors on the IAP sensors (A, **Figure 46**).

3. Disconnect the IAP sensor vacuum hoses (B, **Figure 46**).

4. Loosen the clamp screw on the front throttle body (**Figure 47**).

5. Loosen the clamp screw on the rear throttle body (**Figure 48**).

6. Disconnect the ISC valve hose (A, **Figure 49**).

7. Disconnect the PAIR hose (B, **Figure 49**) from the PAIR valve.

8. Disconnect the connector on the PAIR valve (**Figure 50**).

9. Detach the crankcase ventilation hoses (A, **Figure 51**) from the fittings on the breather box.

10. Disconnect the connector on the IAT sensor (B, **Figure 51**).

11. Pull the air box up and off the throttle bodies.

12. Remove the air box from the engine and frame.

13. Plug the throttle body inlets to prevent debris from entering.

14. Inspect the air box and the air inlet ducts for cracks, wear or damage. If any damage is noted, replace the air box to avoid the possibility of unfiltered air entering the engine.

15. Inspect the air box-to-throttle body tubes for hardness, deterioration or damage. Replace them if necessary.

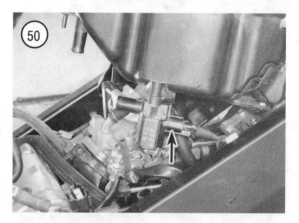

16. Remove the drain plug and clean out all residue from the plug and air box. Reinstall the drain plug.

17. Install by reversing the preceding removal steps. Note the following:

    a. Install the air box-to-throttle body tubes so the ▲ or ■ mark on the tube and air box are aligned (**Figure 52**).

    b. Be sure all hoses are securely connected to prevent air leaks.

THROTTLE BODIES

Each cylinder is equipped with a throttle body that houses a fuel injector. The throttle bodies are secured together by parallel brackets. Except for attached sensors and the fuel injectors, individual components are not available. Both throttle bodies and the connecting brackets must be serviced as a unit assembly.

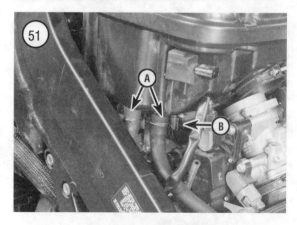

Each throttle body is equipped with two throttle valves—a primary throttle valve and a secondary throttle valve. The primary throttle valve is at the lower end of the throttle body.

Removal/Installation
(2004-2006 Models)

1. Remove the fuel tank as described in this chapter.

2. Remove the air box as described in this chapter.

3. Disconnect the TP sensor connector (A, **Figure 53**).

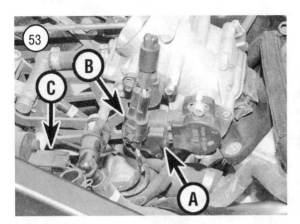

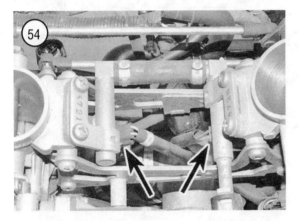

4. Disconnect the STP sensor connector (B, **Figure 53**).

5. Disconnect the connector from the secondary throttle valve actuator (C, **Figure 53**).

6. Disconnect the connector from each fuel injector (**Figure 54**).

7. Dislodge the idle speed screw cable from the mounting bracket (**Figure 55**).

8. Loosen the clamp screw on the front throttle body intake tube (**Figure 56**).

9. Loosen the clamp screw on the rear throttle body intake tube (**Figure 57**, typical).

CAUTION
Do not allow the throttle valve in the throttle body to snap shut. Doing so may damage the throttle valve or throttle body.

NOTE
It is helpful to label or tag each throttle cable so it can be installed in its original location.

10. Lift the throttle body assembly off the intake tubes. Refer to *Throttle Cables* in this chapter and disconnect the throttle cables from the throttle body.

11. Remove the throttle body.

12. Install the throttle body by reversing the removal steps while noting the following:

    a. After installing the throttle cables, operate the throttle lever and make sure the throttle body throttle linkage is operating correctly with no binding. If operation is incorrect or there is binding, carefully check that the cables are attached correctly and there are no tight bends in either cable.

    b. Adjust the throttle cables as described in Chapter Three.

    c. Check secondary throttle synchronization as described in this chapter.

    d. If disturbed, adjust the STP sensor as described in this chapter.

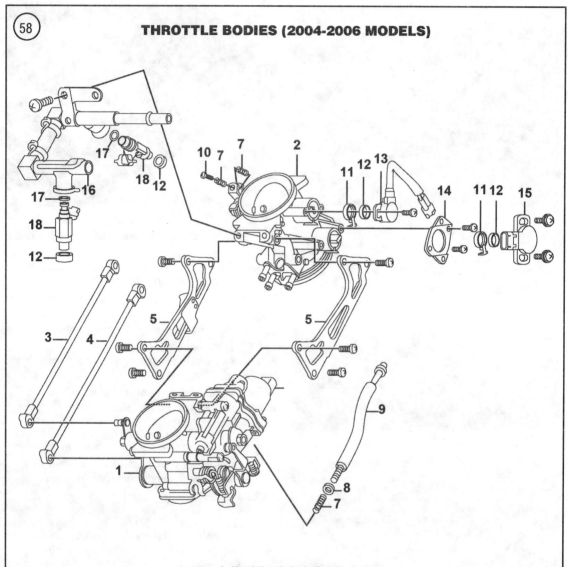

THROTTLE BODIES (2004-2006 MODELS)

1. No. 1 throttle body (front)
2. No. 2 throttle body (rear)
3. Secondary throttle link rod
4. Throttle link rod
5. Link plate
6. Secondary throttle valve actuator
7. Spring
8. Washer
9. Throttle stop screw
10. Secondary throttle valve screw
11. Bushing
12. Seal
13. Secondary throttle position sensor
14. Gasket
15. Throttle position sensor
16. Fuel delivery pipe
17. O-ring
18. Fuel injector

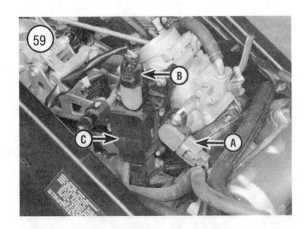

e. If disturbed, adjust the TP sensor as described in this chapter.

f. Adjust the fast idle as described in Chapter Three.

g. Adjust throttle valve synchronization as described in Chapter Three.

Disassembly/Assembly (2004-2006 Models)

WARNING
Some fuel may spill from the throttle body when performing this procedure. Because gasoline is extremely flammable and explosive, perform this procedure away from all open flames (including appliance pilot lights) and sparks. Do not smoke or allow someone who is smoking in the work area. Always work in a well-ventilated area. Wipe up any spills immediately.

Refer to **Figure 58**.

NOTE
Do not turn screws that affect throttle position. Doing so will require adjust-

ment to obtain desired engine operation.

NOTE
To disengage the hose end from the fuel manifold pipe in Step 1, press in on the tabs of the coupler.

1. Detach the fuel supply hose from the fuel manifold.

2. Detach the IAP vacuum hose and vacuum damper from the throttle body.

3. Remove the fuel injectors as described in the *Fuel Injectors* section in this chapter.

4. Remove the TP and STP sensors as described in this chapter.

CAUTION
Do not remove the secondary throttle valve actuator from the throttle body.

5. Further disassembly is neither necessary nor recommended. Note the following:

a. Do not remove the primary or secondary throttle shaft and throttle valve assemblies. If these parts are damaged, replace the throttle body as these items are not available separately.

b. If removed, note that the primary throttle link is longer than the secondary throttle link.

6. Reverse the disassembly procedure for assembly.

NOTE
Install the IAP sensor vacuum damper so the stamped end is toward the throttle body.

Removal/Installation (2007-2011 Models)

1. Remove the fuel tank as described in this chapter.

2. Remove the air box as described in this chapter.

3. Disconnect the TP sensor connector (A, **Figure 59**).

4. Disconnect the STP sensor connector (B, **Figure 59**).

5. Disconnect the connector from the secondary throttle valve actuator (C, **Figure 59**).

6. Disconnect the connector from each fuel injector (**Figure 60**).

7. Detach the hoses from the idle speed control valves (**Figure 61**).

8. Loosen the clamp screw on the front throttle body intake tube (**Figure 56**).

9. Loosen the clamp screw on the rear throttle body intake tube (**Figure 57**).

10. Refer to *Throttle Cables* in this chapter and disconnect the throttle cables from the throttle body.

11. Remove the throttle body.

12. Install the throttle body by reversing the removal steps while noting the following:

   a. After installing the throttle cables, operate the throttle lever and make sure the throttle body throttle linkage is operating correctly with no binding. If operation is incorrect or there is binding, carefully check that the cables are attached correctly and there are no tight bends in either cable.

   b. Adjust the throttle cables as described in Chapter Three.

   c. If disturbed, adjust the STP sensor as described in this chapter.

   d. If disturbed, adjust the TP sensor as described in this chapter.

   e. Adjust throttle valve synchronization as described in Chapter Three.

**Disassembly/Assembly
(2007-2011 Models)**

Refer to **Figure 62**.

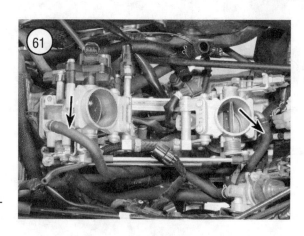

1. Mark for reference, then detach the vacuum hoses (**Figure 63**).

2. Detach the fuel supply hose (A, **Figure 64**) from the fuel manifold.

3. Remove the fuel injectors as described in the *Fuel Injectors* section in this chapter.

4. Remove the TP and STP sensors as described in this chapter.

5. Further disassembly is neither necessary nor recommended. Note the following:

   a. Do not remove the primary or secondary throttle shaft and throttle valve assemblies. If these parts are damaged, replace the throttle body as these items are not available separately.

   b. If removed, note that the primary throttle link is longer than the secondary throttle link.

6. Reverse the disassembly procedure for assembly.

**SECONDARY THROTTLE VALVE
SYNCHRONIZATION (2004-2006 MODELS)**

The secondary throttle valve (STV) synchronization procedure can be performed with the throttle bodies removed or installed on the motorcycle. The purpose of the procedure is to identically set both secondary throttle valves so the valves are parallel to the top surface of their respective throttle body.

1. If the throttle body assembly is installed on the motorcycle, do the following:

   a. Remove the air box as described in this section

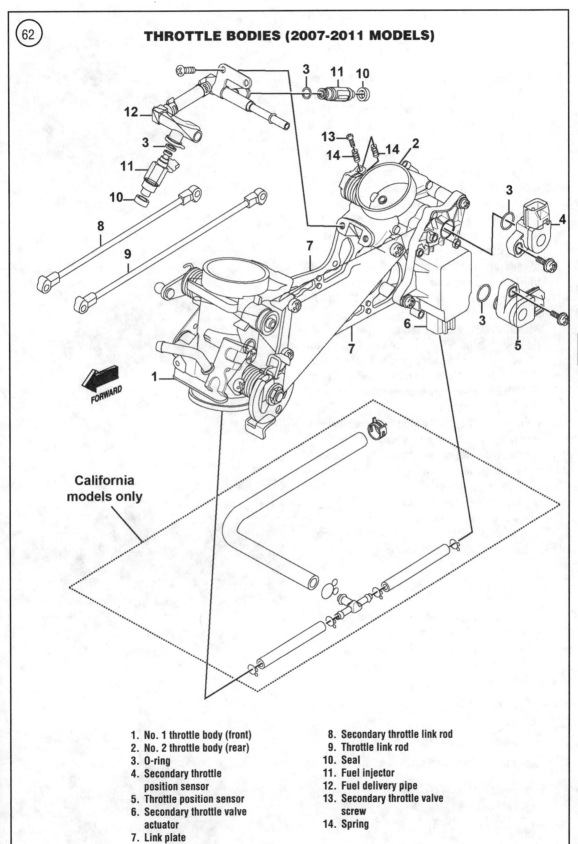

(62)

THROTTLE BODIES (2007-2011 MODELS)

FORWARD

California models only

8

1. No. 1 throttle body (front)
2. No. 2 throttle body (rear)
3. O-ring
4. Secondary throttle position sensor
5. Throttle position sensor
6. Secondary throttle valve actuator
7. Link plate
8. Secondary throttle link rod
9. Throttle link rod
10. Seal
11. Fuel injector
12. Fuel delivery pipe
13. Secondary throttle valve screw
14. Spring

b. Do not turn on the ignition switch during the adjustment procedure.

2. Begin adjustment at the No. 1 (front) throttle body as follows:

   a. Measure the distance from the top of the throttle body to the STV surface (A, **Figure 65**). Make the measurement at a point 90° to the axis of the STV shaft and centered with the STV. Record the measurement.

   b. Repeat the measurement at the point directly opposite (B, **Figure 65**) the first measurement point. Record the measurement.

   c. Compare the two measurements. If the measurements are not identical, turn the shaft on the secondary throttle valve actuator (STVA) (C, **Figure 65**) to open/close the STV. Continue to measure and adjust the position of the STV until the two measurements are identical.

3. Adjust the No. 2 (rear) throttle body. Do the following:

   a. Measure the distance from the top of the throttle body to the STV surface (A, **Figure 66**). Make the measurement at a point 90° to the axis of the STV shaft and centered with the STV. Record the measurement.

   b. Repeat the measurement at the point directly opposite (B, **Figure 66**) the first measurement point. Record the measurement.

   c. Compare the two measurements. If the measurements are not identical, turn the adjustment screw (C, **Figure 66**) to open/close the STV. Continue to measure and adjust the position of the STV until the two measurements are identical.

4. Check secondary throttle position (STP) sensor adjustment as described in this section.

FUEL INJECTORS

A multi-hole type fuel injector is mounted on the throttle body for each cylinder. The ECM controls the opening time of the injector. The fuel injector is not serviceable, but must be replaced as a unit assembly.

Removal/Installation

1. Remove the fuel tank as described in this chapter.

2. Remove the air box as described in this chapter.

> *NOTE*
> *To disengage the hose end from the fuel manifold pipe in Step 3, press in on the tabs of the coupler.*

3. Detach the fuel supply hose (A, **Figure 67**) from the fuel manifold.

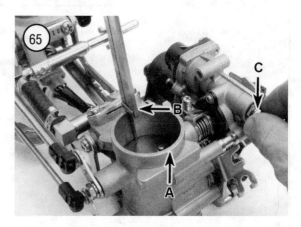

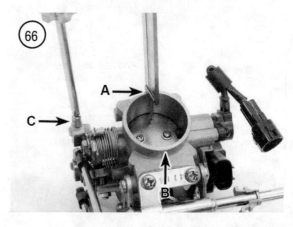

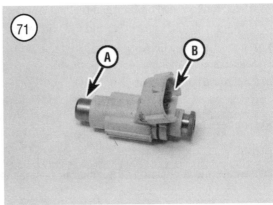

4. Disconnect the connector from each fuel injector (B, **Figure 67**).

5. Remove the fuel manifold mounting screws (C, **Figure 67**).

6. Remove the fuel manifold and attached fuel injectors (**Figure 68**).

7. Separate each fuel injector from the fuel manifold.

8. Inspect the fuel injectors as described in this section.

9. Install the upper and lower O-rings onto the fuel injectors. The upper O-ring (A, **Figure 69**) has a round cross-section. The lower O-ring (B) has a square cross-section.

10. Make sure the mounting bore for the fuel injector in the throttle body is clean.

NOTE
Lubricate all O-rings with engine oil prior to installation.

NOTE
Do not turn the fuel injector during installation in Step 11.

11. Install each fuel injector into the fuel manifold so the electrical connector on the injector (A, **Figure 70**) fits between the flange tips (B) on the fuel manifold.

12. Install the fuel manifold and injectors.

13. Tighten the fuel manifold retaining screws to 5.0 N•m (44 in.-lb.).

14. Connect the fuel supply hose to the fuel manifold.

15. Install the air box as described in this chapter.

16. Install the fuel tank as described in this chapter.

Inspection

1. Visually inspect the fuel injectors for damage. Inspect the injector nozzle (A, **Figure 71**) for carbon buildup or damage.

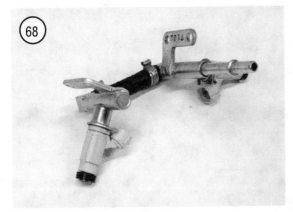

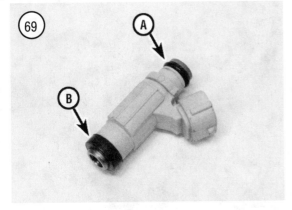

2. Check for corroded or damaged fuel injector connector terminals (B, **Figure 71**) and the wiring connector.

3. Make sure the mounting bore for the fuel injector in the throttle body is clean.

Resistance Test

1. Turn the ignition switch off.

2. Remove the fuel tank as described in this chapter.

3. Remove the air box as described in this chapter.

4. Disconnect the connector (B, **Figure 67**) from the fuel injector.

5. Use an ohmmeter to measure the resistance between the two terminals in the fuel injector. The resistance should be within the range specified in **Table 2** or **Table 3**.

6. Repeat this test for the remaining fuel injector.

Continuity Test

1. Perform Steps 1-4 of the injector resistance test.

2. Check the continuity between each injector terminal and ground. No continuity (infinity) should be indicated.

3. Repeat this test for the remaining fuel injector.

Voltage Test

1. Perform Steps 1-4 of the injector resistance test.

2. Connect a voltmeter positive test probe to the yellow/red wire in the injector connector; connect the negative test probe to a good ground.

> *NOTE*
> *Injector voltage will be present for only three seconds after the ignition switch is turned on. If necessary, turn the switch off and then back on.*

3. Turn the ignition switch on and measure the voltage. It should equal battery voltage.

4. Repeat this test for the remaining fuel injector.

CRANKSHAFT POSITION (CKP) SENSOR

Refer to Chapter Nine for information concerning service and testing of the crankshaft position sensor.

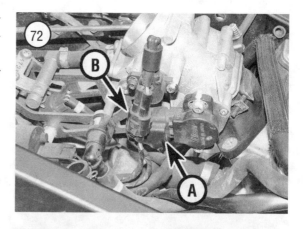

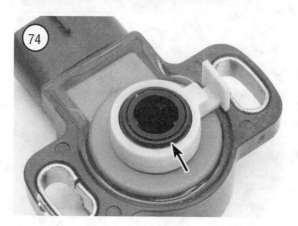

THROTTLE POSITION (TP) SENSOR

Removal/Installation

1. Disconnect the negative battery cable (Chapter Nine).

2. Remove the fuel tank as described in this chapter.

3A. On 2004-2006 models, disconnect the throttle position sensor connector (A, **Figure 72**).

3B. On 2007-2011 models, disconnect the throttle position sensor connector (A, **Figure 73**).

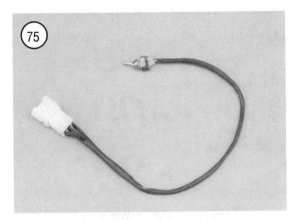

4. Make an index line across the sensor and throttle body so the sensor can be reinstalled in the same position during assembly.

5. Use a Torx security wrench to remove the mounting screws. Pull the sensor (B, **Figure 72** or **Figure 73**) from the throttle shaft, and remove the sensor. Note how the sensor engages the throttle shaft.

6A. On 2004-2006 models, inspect the seal and bushing (**Figure 74**). If necessary, replace the seal and/or bushing.

6B. On 2007-2011 models, inspect the O-ring on the sensor. Replace if damaged.

7. Installation is the reverse of removal. Note the following:
   a. Apply Suzuki Super Grease A to the end of the throttle shaft.
   b. On 2004-2006 models, install the bushing so it fits into the notch on the throttle body.
   c. Align the end of the throttle shaft with the slot in the sensor and slide the sensor onto the shaft.
   d. Position the sensor so the index mark on the sensor aligns with the mark on the throttle body.
   e. Install the mounting screw(s) and tighten to 3.5 N•m (31 in.-lb.).

Adjustment

The Suzuki mode select switch (part No. 09930-82720) shown in **Figure 75** is needed to perform this adjustment.

CAUTION
Do not attempt this procedure without the mode select switch. Shorting the terminals in the dealer mode connector could damage the ECM.

1. Run the engine until it reaches normal operating temperature. Check the idle speed. If necessary, adjust the idle to specification as described in Chapter Three.
2. Stop the engine.
3. Lift and support the fuel tank as described in this chapter.
4A. On non-ABS models, connect the mode select switch to the dealer mode connector (**Figure 76**) adjacent to the battery box.
4B. On ABS models, connect the mode select switch to the dealer mode connector (**Figure 77**) below the right side of the fuel tank.
5. Turn the mode select switch to on.
6. The malfunction code cOO should appear in the meter display. The dash before the code indicates the state of the TP sensor adjustment. The dash should be in the middle position as shown in **Figure 78**. If the dash is in the upper or lower position, adjust the sensor as follows:
   a. Loosen the screw(s) securing the sensor.
   b. Rotate the sensor until the dash moves to the center position.
   c. Tighten the screw(s) to 3.5 N•m (31 in.-lb.).

Continuity Test

1. Lift and support the fuel tank as described in this chapter.

2A. On 2004-2006 models, disconnect the throttle position sensor connector (A, **Figure 72**).

2B. On 2007-2011 models, disconnect the throttle position sensor connector (A, **Figure 73**).

3. Check the continuity between the center wire terminal in the sensor end of the connector and a good ground.

4. Reverse the test probes, and check the continuity in the opposite direction.

5. Both readings should indicate no continuity (infinity).

Resistance Test

1. Perform Steps 1-2 of the *Continuity Test*.

2. Connect an ohmmeter to the center wire terminal in the sensor end of the connector and the black/brown wire terminal in the sensor end of the connector.

3. Read the resistance when the throttle is fully closed and fully open. Record each reading.

4. The fully open and fully closed resistance should be within the range specified in **Table 2** or **Table 3**.

Input Voltage Test

1. Perform Steps 1-2 of the *Continuity Test*.

2. Connect a voltmeter positive test probe to the red terminal in the harness end of the sensor connector; connect the voltmeter negative probe to ground.

3. Turn the ignition switch on, and measure the input voltage. It should be within the range specified in **Table 2** or **Table 3**.

4. Connect the voltmeter positive test probe to the red terminal in the harness end of the sensor connector; connect the negative test probe to the black/brown terminal in the harness end of the connector.

5. The input voltage should be within the range specified in **Table 2** or **Table 3**.

Output Voltage Test

1. Lift and support the fuel tank as described in this chapter.

2. Make sure the sensor connector is securely connected to the sensor.

3. Using a needle probe to back probe the harness connector, connect a voltmeter positive test probe to the pink/white harness wire and the negative test probe to the black/brown harness wire.

4. Turn the ignition switch on.

5. Measure the output voltage when the throttle is fully closed and fully opened. Each measurement should be within the range specified in **Table 2** or **Table 3**.

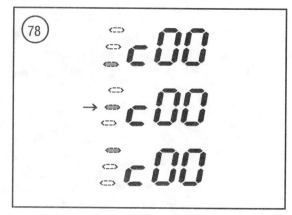

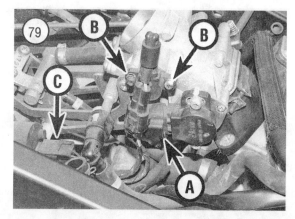

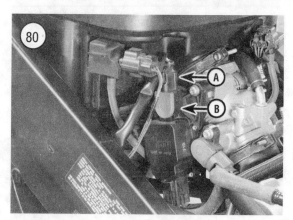

SECONDARY THROTTLE POSITION (STP) SENSOR

Removal/Installation

1. Disconnect the negative battery cable (Chapter Nine).

2. Remove the fuel tank as described in this chapter.

3. Remove the air box as described in this chapter.

4A. On 2004-2006 models, disconnect the STP sensor connector (A, **Figure 79**).

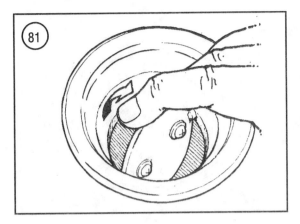

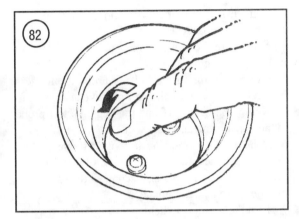

4B. On 2007-2011 models, disconnect the STP sensor connector (A, **Figure 80**).

5. Make an index line across the sensor and throttle body so the sensor can be reinstalled in the same position during assembly.

6. Use a Torx security wrench to remove the mounting screw(s), pull the sensor (B, **Figure 79** or B, **Figure 80**) from the throttle shaft, and remove the sensor. Note how the sensor engages the throttle shaft.

7A. On 2004-2006 models, inspect the seal and bushing (**Figure 74**). If necessary, replace the seal and/or bushing.

7B. On 2007-2011 models, inspect the O-ring on the sensor. Replace if damaged.

8. Installation is the reverse of removal. Note the following:

    a. Apply Suzuki Super Grease A to the end of the throttle shaft.

    b. On 2004-2006 models, install the bushing so it fits into the notch on the throttle body.

    c. Align the end of the throttle shaft with the slot in the sensor and slide the sensor onto the shaft.

    d. Position the sensor so the index mark on the sensor aligns with the mark on the throttle body.

    e. Install the mounting screw(s) and tighten to 3.5 N•m (31 in.-lb.).

Adjustment (2004-2006 Models)

1. Remove the fuel tank as described in this chapter.

2. Remove the air box as described in this chapter.

3. Make sure the STP sensor connector (A, **Figure 79**) is properly connected.

4. Using a needle probe to back probe the harness connector, connect a voltmeter positive test probe to the yellow harness wire and the negative test probe to the black harness wire.

5. Disconnect the secondary throttle valve actuator connector (C, **Figure 79**).

6. Turn the ignition switch on.

7. Manually move the secondary throttle valve (**Figure 81**) to the fully open position. Measure the output voltage. The voltage should be approximately 4.38 volts.

8. If the measured voltage is out of specification, loosen the sensor mounting screws and rotate the sensor (B, **Figure 79**) until the voltage is within specification.

9. Tighten the mounting screw to torque specified in **Table 4**.

Adjustment (2007-2011 Models)

1. Remove the fuel tank as described in this chapter.

2. Remove the air box as described in this chapter.

3. Make sure the STP sensor connector (A, **Figure 80**) is securely connected to the sensor.

4. Using a needle probe to back probe the harness connector, connect a voltmeter positive test probe to the yellow harness wire and the negative test probe to the black/brown harness wire.

5. Disconnect the secondary throttle valve actuator connector.

6. Turn the ignition switch on.

7. Manually move the secondary throttle valve (**Figure 82**) to the fully closed position. Measure the output voltage. The voltage should be approximately 0.6 volts.

8. If the measured voltage is out of specification, loosen the sensor mounting screw and rotate the sensor (B, **Figure 80**) until the voltage is within specification.

9. Tighten the mounting screw to torque specified in **Table 4**.

Continuity Test (2004-2006 Models)

1. Remove the fuel tank as described in this chapter.
2. Remove the air box as described in this chapter.
3. Disconnect the STP sensor connector (A, **Figure 79**).
4. Check the continuity between the yellow wire terminal in the sensor end of the connector and a good ground.
5. Reverse the test probes, and check the continuity in the opposite direction.
6. Both readings should indicate no continuity (infinity).

Resistance Test (2004-2006 Models)

1. Perform Steps 1-3 of the *Continuity Test*.
2. Connect an ohmmeter to the yellow wire terminal in the sensor end of the connector and the black wire terminal in the sensor end of the connector.
3. Manually move the secondary throttle valve (**Figure 83**). Read the resistance when the throttle is fully closed and fully open. Record each reading.
4. The fully open and fully closed resistance should be within the range specified in **Table 2** or **Table 3**.

Input Voltage Test

1. Remove the fuel tank as described in this chapter.
2A. On 2004-2006 models, disconnect the STP sensor connector (A, **Figure 79**).
2B. On 2007-2011 models, disconnect the STP sensor connector (A, **Figure 80**).
3. Connect a voltmeter positive test probe to the red terminal in the harness end of the sensor connector; connect the voltmeter negative probe to ground.
4. Turn the ignition switch on, and measure the input voltage. It should be within the range specified in **Table 2** or **Table 3**.
5. Connect the voltmeter positive test probe to the red terminal in the harness end of the sensor connector; connect the negative test probe to the black/brown terminal in the harness end of the connector.
6. The input voltage should be within the range specified in **Table 2** or **Table 3**.

Output Voltage Test

1. Remove the fuel tank as described in this chapter.
2. Remove the air box as described in this chapter.
3A. On 2004-2006 models, disconnect the STP sensor connector (A, **Figure 79**).

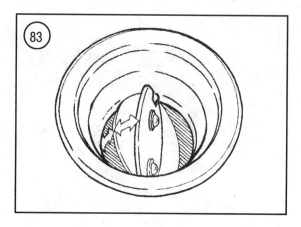

3B. On 2007-2011 models, disconnect the black STP sensor connector (A, **Figure 80**).
4. Make sure the sensor connector is connected to its harness mate.
5. Using a needle probe to back probe the harness connector, connect a voltmeter positive test probe to the yellow harness wire and the negative test probe to the black/brown harness wire.
6A. On 2004-2006 models, disconnect the secondary throttle valve actuator connector (C, **Figure 79**).
6B. On 2007-2011 models, disconnect the secondary throttle valve actuator connector.
7. Turn the ignition switch on.
8. Manually move the secondary throttle valve (**Figure 83**). Measure the output voltage when the throttle is fully closed and fully opened. Each measurement should be within the range specified in **Table 2** or **Table 3**.

SECONDARY THROTTLE VALVE ACTUATOR (STVA)

STVA Operation Test

1. Remove the fuel tank as described in this chapter.
2. Remove the air box as described in this chapter.
3. Turn the ignition switch on, and watch the movement of the secondary throttle valves. Each should move to the fully open position, and then to its operating position within approximately one second. See **Figure 83**.

Continuity Test

1. Remove the fuel tank as described in this chapter.
2. Remove the air box as described in this chapter.
3A. On 2004-2006 models, disconnect the secondary throttle valve actuator connector (C, **Figure 79**).

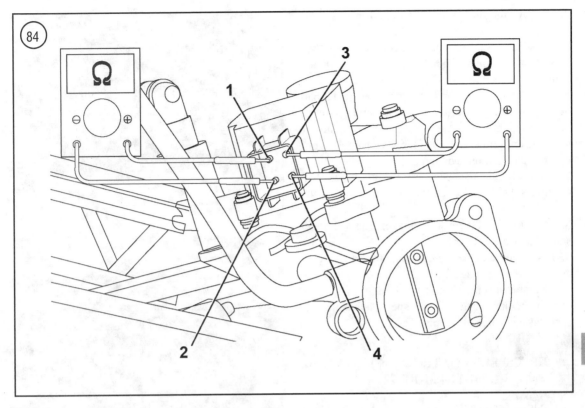

3B. On 2007-2011 models, disconnect the secondary throttle valve actuator connector (C, **Figure 80**).

4. Check the continuity between the wire terminals in the sensor end of the connector and a good ground.

5. The tester should indicate no continuity (infinity).

Resistance Test

1. Perform Steps 1-3 of the *Continuity Test*.

2A. On 2004-2006 models, connect an ohmmeter to the terminals in the sensor. The resistance should equal the value in **Table 2**.

2B. On 2007-2011 models, refer to **Figure 84** and proceed as follows:

   a. Connect an ohmmeter positive test probe to terminal 1; connect the negative test probe to terrminal 2. The resistance should equal the value in **Table 3**.

   b. Connect an ohmmeter negative test probe to terminal 3; connect the positive test probe to terminal 4. The resistance should equal the value in **Table 3**.

FAST IDLE SPEED (2004-2006 MODELS)

The fuel system includes a fast idle system that adjusts throttle valve position during engine warm-up. When operated, a fast idle cam (A, **Figure 85**) pushes the fast idle lever (B) that opens and closes the throttle valves. The fast idle cam is controlled by the secondary throttle valve actuator. During operation, the ECM monitors engine coolant temperature and ambient air temperature, then signals the secondary throttle valve actuator to set throttle valve position at fast idle so the engine idles at 1500-2000 rpm. When engine temperature reaches 40-50°C (104-122° F) the fast idle function is deactivated.

Adjustment

1. Make sure the engine is cold.

2. Remove the fuel tank as described in this chapter.

3. Remove the air box as described in this chapter.

4. Disconnect the secondary throttle valve actuator connector (C, **Figure 79**).

5. Using a needle probe to back probe the TP harness connector (A, **Figure 79**), connect a voltmeter positive test probe to the red harness wire and the negative test probe to the black/brown harness wire.

6. Turn the ignition switch on.

7. Manually turn the secondary throttle valve shaft (**Figure 86**) so the secondary throttle valves are fully open.

8. Measure the TP sensor voltage. The voltmeter should indicate 1.21 volts.

9. If the voltmeter does not indicate the correct voltage, turn the fast idle adjuster screw (C, **Figure 85**) to obtain the specified voltage reading.

10. After adjusting the fast idle speed, adjust the idle speed as described in Chapter Three.

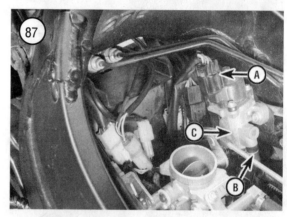

IDLE SPEED CONTROL (ISC) VALVE
(2007-2011 MODELS)

The idle speed control (ISC) valve determines engine speed at idle by adjusting the amount air bypassing the primary throttle valve in both throttle bodies. The ECM controls the ISC. A sensor within the ISC informs the ECM of the valve position.

CAUTION
Do not disconnect the ISC or ECM electrical connectors until at least 5 seconds have passed after the ignition key was turned off. If insufficient time is allowed, ISC or ECM operation may be affected.

Removal/Installation

NOTE
If the ISC valve is removed, preset the valve using Suzuki mode select switch (part No. 09930-82720) shown in Figure 75.

1. Remove the air box as described in this chapter.

2. Disconnect the connector (A, **Figure 87**).

3. Label the vacuum hoses, then detach the hoses (B, **Figure 87**) from the valve (C).

4. Remove the two mounting bolts and remove the valve.

5. Reverse the removal steps for installation. Perform the following preset procedure:

   a. Turn the ignition switch off.

b. Connect Suzuki mode select switch (part No. 09930-82720) shown in **Figure 75** to the dealer mode coupler (**Figure 77**).

c. Turn the Suzuki mode select switch on.

d. Turn the ignition switch on.

e. Turn the ignition switch off.

f. Allow at least 5 seconds to pass.

g. Turn the Suzuki mode select switch off and remove it.

Inspection

NOTE
Parts for the ISC valve are not available, including the internal O-ring.

1. Remove the screws securing the control unit to the housing.

2. Carefully separate the control unit from the housing to prevent damage to the O-ring.

3. Replace the ISC valve if worn, damaged or clogged by deposits.

Resistance Test

1. Remove the air box as described in this chapter.

2. Disconnect the connector (A, **Figure 87**).

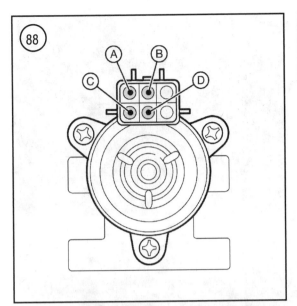

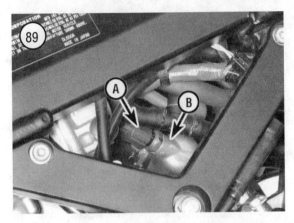

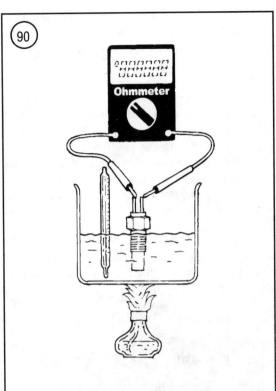

3. Connect an ohmmeter to terminals A and C shown in **Figure 88**. The ohmmeter should indicate no continuity.

4. Connect an ohmmeter to terminals B and D. The ohmmeter should indicate no continuity.

5. Connect an ohmmeter to terminals A and B. The ohmmeter should read 28.8-31.2 ohms.

6. Connect an ohmmeter to terminals C and D. The ohmmeter should read 28.8-31.2 ohms.

ENGINE COOLANT TEMPERATURE (ECT) SENSOR

Resistance Test

1. Disconnect the connector (A, **Figure 89**) from the coolant sensor (B).

NOTE
The motorcycle must be at room temperature (approximately 68° F) when performing this test.

2. Connect the ohmmeter positive test probe to the black/blue terminal in the sensor; connect the negative test probe to the black/brown terminal.

3. Measure the resistance. It should be within the range specified in **Table 2** or **Table 3**.

4. If necessary, remove the sensor and test at various temperatures as follows:

  a. Fill a beaker or pan with water, and place it on a stove or hot plate.

NOTE
The thermometer and the sensor must not touch the container sides or bottom. If either does, test readings will be inaccurate.

  b. Place a thermometer in the pan of water. Use a cooking or candy thermometer that is rated higher than the test temperature.

  c. Mount the sensor so that the temperature sensing tip and the threaded portion of the body are submerged as shown in **Figure 90**.

  d. Attach an ohmmeter to the sensor terminals as shown in **Figure 90**.

  e. Gradually heat the water to the temperatures specified in **Table 2** or **Table 3**. Note the resistance of the sensor when the water temperature reaches the specified values.

f. Replace the sensor if any reading equals infinity or is considerably different than the specified resistance at a given temperature.

Voltage Test

1. Disconnect the connector (A, **Figure 89**) from the coolant sensor (B).
2. Connect the voltmeter positive test probe to the black/blue terminal in the connector; connect the negative test probe to a good ground.
3. Turn on the ignition switch and measure the voltage. It should be within the range specified in **Table 2** or **Table 3**.
4. Connect the voltmeter positive test probe to the black/blue terminal in the connector; connect the negative test probe to the black/brown terminal in the connector.
5. Turn on the ignition switch. The voltage should be within the specified range.

Removal/Installation

Refer to Chapter Ten for removal/installation procedure.

INTAKE AIR TEMPERATURE (IAT) SENSOR

Removal/Installation

1A. On 2004-2006 models, proceed as follows:
   a. Raise and support the fuel tank as described in this chapter.
   b. Disconnect the connector (A, **Figure 91**) from the sensor.
   c. Unscrew the sensor and remove it and the sealing washer from the thermostat housing.
1B. On 2007-2011 models, proceed as follows:
   a. Remove the air box as described in Chapter Eight.
   b. Remove the sensor mounting screw (A, **Figure 92**), then remove the sensor (B). Discard the O-ring on the sensor.
2. Installation is the reverse of removal. On 2004-2006 models, install a new sealing washer onto the sensor. On 2007-2011 models, install a new O-ring onto the sensor.

Resistance Test

1. Lift and support the fuel tank as described in Chapter Eight.
2A. On 2004-2006 models, disconnect the connector (A, **Figure 91**) from the sensor.

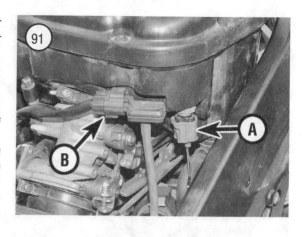

NOTE
The air box was raised for clarity in Step 2B.

2B. On 2007-2011 models, disconnect the connector (**Figure 93**) from the sensor.
3. Connect the positive test probe of an ohmmeter to the dark green wire terminal in the sensor; connect the negative test probe to the black/brown wire terminal.
4. Measure the resistance. It should be within specification in **Table 2** or **Table 3**.
5. If further testing is necessary, remove the IAT sensor as described in this section, and proceed as follows:
   a. Fill a beaker or pan with water, and place it on a stove or hot plate.

NOTE
The thermometer and the sensor must not touch the container sides or bottom. If either does, it will result in a false reading.

   b. Place a thermometer in the pan of water. Use a cooking or candy thermometer that is rated higher than the test temperature.
   c. Mount the IAT sensor so the temperature sensing tip and the mounting portion of the body are submerged as shown in **Figure 90**.

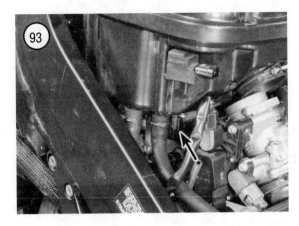

d. Attach an ohmmeter to the sensor terminals as shown in **Figure 90**.

e. Gradually heat the water to the temperatures specified in **Table 2** or **Table 3**. Note the resistance of the sensor when the water temperature reaches the specified values.

f. Replace the IAT sensor if any reading is considerably different than the specified resistance at a given temperature.

Voltage Test

1. Lift and support the fuel tank as described in Chapter Eight.

2A. On 2004-2006 models, disconnect the connector (A, **Figure 91**) from the sensor.

NOTE
The air box was raised for clarity in Step 2B.

2B. On 2007-2011 models, disconnect the connector (**Figure 93**) from the sensor.

3. Connect the positive test probe of a voltmeter to the dark green wire terminal in the connector; connect the negative test probe to a good ground.

4. Turn on the ignition switch and measure the voltage. It should be within the range specified in **Table 2** or **Table 3**.

5. Connect the voltmeter positive test probe to the dark green wire terminal in the connector; connect the negative test probe to the black/brown wire terminal.

6. Turn on the ignition switch. The voltage should be within the specified range.

INTAKE AIR PRESSURE (IAP) SENSOR (2004-2006 MODELS)

A single intake air pressure (IAP) sensor is used on 2004-2006 models. The sensor is mounted on the air box.

Removal/Installation

1. Disconnect the negative battery cable.
2. Lift and support the fuel tank as described in this chapter.
3. Disconnect the connector (B, **Figure 91**) from the IAP sensor.
4. Remove the screw securing the sensor to the air box, then remove the sensor.
5. Installation is the reverse of removal.

Input Voltage Test

1. Lift and support the fuel tank as described in this chapter.
2. Disconnect the connector (B, **Figure 91**) from the IAP sensor.
3. Connect a voltmeter positive test probe to the red terminal in the harness connector; connect the negative test probe to ground.
4. Turn the ignition switch on, and measure the voltage. It should be within the input voltage range specified in **Table 2** or **Table 3**.
5. Turn the ignition switch off.
6. Connect the voltmeter's positive test probe to the red terminal in the harness connector; connect the negative test probe to the black/brown terminal in the harness connector.
7. Turn the ignition switch on, and measure the voltage. It should be within the input voltage range specified in **Table 2** or **Table 3**.

Output Voltage Test

NOTE
*Test results may vary due to changes in altitude and atmospheric pressure. Refer also to the **Vacuum Test**.*

1. Run the engine until it reaches normal operating temperature, then shut off the engine.
2. Lift and support the fuel tank as described in this chapter.
3. Make sure the connector is securely mated to the pressure sensor.
4. Using a needle probe to back probe the harness connector, connect a voltmeter positive test probe to the green/black wire terminal in the IAP sensor connector.
5. Connect the negative test probe to the black/brown terminal.
6. Start the engine and let run at idle speed.
7. Measure the voltage. It should equal the output voltage value specified in **Table 2** or **Table 3**.

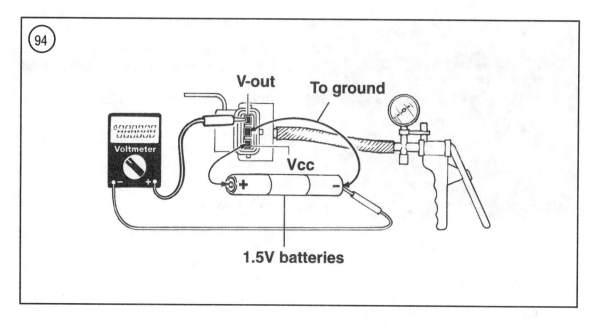

V-out   **To ground**

Voltmeter

Vcc

1.5V batteries

Vacuum Test

1. Remove the IAP sensor as described in this section.

2. Make sure the sensor air passage is clear, and connect a vacuum pump and gauge to the air tube (**Figure 94**).

3. Connect three new 1.5 volt batteries in series as shown in **Figure 94**. Measure the total voltage of the batteries. The voltage must be 4.5-5.0 volts.

4. Connect the battery positive terminal to the Vcc terminal in the sensor; connect the battery negative terminal to the ground terminal in the sensor.

5. Connect the voltmeter positive test probe to the V-out terminal in the sensor; connect the negative test probe to the battery negative terminal.

6. Use the vacuum pump to apply vacuum to the sensor. The voltage reading should be within the V-out voltage range specified in **Table 2** or **Table 3**.

INTAKE AIR PRESSURE (IAP) SENSORS (2007-2011 MODELS)

Two intake air pressure (IAP) sensors are used on 2006-2011 models to monitor air pressure for each cylinder. The sensors are mounted on the air box.

The IAP sensor for the front cylinder is the same as used for 2004-2006 models. Refer to the preceding section for service on the front cylinder IAP sensor.

The following service procedure applies to the IAP sensor for the rear cylinder.

Removal/Installation

1. Disconnect the negative battery cable.

2. Lift and support the fuel tank as described in this chapter.

3. Disconnect the connector (A, **Figure 95**) from the IAP sensor (B) for the rear cylinder.

4. Disengage the sensor from the mount, then remove the sensor.

5. Installation is the reverse of removal.

Input Voltage Test

1. Lift and support the fuel tank as described in this chapter.

2. Disconnect the connector (A, **Figure 95**) from the IAP sensor (B).

3. Connect a voltmeter positive test probe to the red terminal in the harness connector; connect the negative test probe to ground.

4. Turn the ignition switch on, and measure the voltage. It should be within the input voltage range specified in **Table 2** or **Table 3**.

5. Turn the ignition switch off.

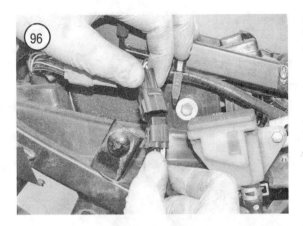

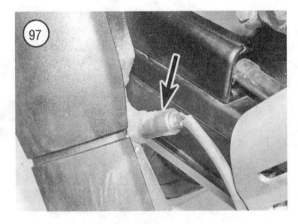

6. Connect the voltmeter's positive test probe to the red terminal in the harness connector; connect the negative test probe to the black/brown terminal in the harness connector.

7. Turn the ignition switch on, and measure the voltage. It should be within the input voltage range specified in **Table 2** or **Table 3**.

Output Voltage Test

NOTE
Test results may vary due to changes in altitude and atmospheric pressure. Refer also to the Vacuum Test.

1. Run the engine until it reaches normal operating temperature, then shut off the engine.
2. Lift and support the fuel tank as described in this chapter.
3. Make sure the connector is securely mated to the pressure sensor.
4. Using a needle probe to back probe the harness connector, connect a voltmeter positive test probe to the green/yellow wire terminal in the IAP sensor connector.
5. Connect the negative test probe to the black/brown terminal.

6. Start the engine and let run at idle speed.
7. Measure the voltage. It should equal the output voltage value specified in **Table 2** or **Table 3**.

Vacuum Test

Refer to test procedure described in section for 2004-2006 models.

OXYGEN (HO$_2$) SENSOR

A heated oxygen sensor is used on U.K., EU and Australian models. The sensor is mounted on the exhaust pipe.

Removal/Installation

1. Lift and support the fuel tank as described in this chapter.
2. Disconnect the sensor connector (**Figure 96**).
3. Unscrew the sensor from the exhaust pipe (**Figure 97**).
4. Reverse the removal steps to install the sensor. Tighten the sensor to 47.5 N•m (34 ft.-lb.).

Voltage Test

1. Lift and support the fuel tank as described in this chapter.
2. Using a needle probe to back probe the harness connector (**Figure 96**), connect a voltmeter positive test probe to the orange/white wire terminal in the oxygen sensor connector.
3. Connect the negative test probe to ground.

NOTE
A voltage will only be detected for a few seconds in Step 4 after the ignition switch is turned on.

4. Turn the ignition switch to on. The voltage reading should indicate battery voltage.
5. Run the engine until it reaches normal operating temperature.
6. Using a needle probe to back probe the harness connector, connect a voltmeter positive test probe to the white/green wire terminal in the oxygen sensor connector.
7. Using a needle probe to back probe the harness connector, connect a voltmeter negative test probe to the black/brown wire terminal in the oxygen sensor connector.
8. Run the engine at idle and observe the voltage reading.

9. Run the engine at 5000 rpm and observe the voltage reading.

10. The voltage readings should be within the ranges specified in **Table 2** or **Table 3**.

Resistance Test

1. Lift and support the fuel tank as described in this chapter.
2. Disconnect the sensor connector (**Figure 96**).
3. Using an ohmmeter measure the resistance between the white wire terminals in the sensor connector.
4. The resistance reading should equal the value in **Table 2** or **Table 3**. If the resistance reading is incorrect, replace the sensor.

TIP-OVER (TO) SENSOR

Whenever the TO sensor is activated, the ECM cuts off power to the fuel pump, ignition system and fuel injection circuits.

Removal/Installation

1. Remove the seat as described in Chapter Fifteen.
2. Disconnect the tip-over sensor connector (A, **Figure 98**).
3. Remove the sensor (B, **Figure 98**) from the mounting bracket on the frame.
4. Installation is the reverse of removal. Make sure the arrow on the sensor points upward and the UP mark is properly positioned.

Resistance Test

1. Remove the right side cover as described in Chapter Fifteen.
2. Disconnect the tip-over sensor connector (A, **Figure 98**).
3. Connect the ohmmeter test probes to the red terminal and to the black/brown terminal in the sensor. Read the resistance.
4. The resistance should be within the range specified in **Table 2** or **Table 3**.

Voltage Test

1. Remove the tip-over sensor as described in this section.
2. Reconnect the harness connector to the sensor. If disconnected, reconnect the electrical cable to the negative battery terminal.

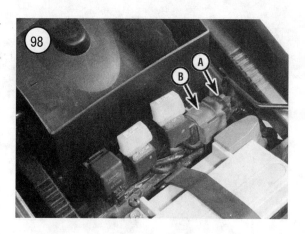

3. Using a needle probe to back probe the harness connector, connect a voltmeter positive test probe to the brown/white terminal in the harness end of the connector; connect the negative test probe to the black/brown terminal (harness end).
4. Turn the ignition switch on.
5. Hold the sensor so the side marked with an arrow faces up, and read the voltage.
6. Tilt the sensor more than 65° and read the voltage.
7. Each reading should be within the range specified in **Table 2** or **Table 3**.

PAIR (AIR SUPPLY) SYSTEM

All models are equipped with the PAIR system that lowers emissions output by introducing secondary air into the exhaust ports (**Figure 99**). The introduction of air raises the exhaust temperature, which consumes some of the unburned fuel in the exhaust.

The PAIR system consists of a control valve, reed valves, inlet and outlet hoses, and ECM (**Figure 99**). The ECM operates a solenoid valve that opens and closes the inlet air passage in the control valve. The reed valves use the momentary pressure variations created by the exhaust gas pulses to introduce additional air into the exhaust ports.

PAIR Reed Valve
Removal/Inspection/Installation

1. Lift and support the fuel tank as described in this chapter.
2. On 2007-2011 models, remove the coolant reservoir tank.
3. Detach the hose (A, **Figure 100**).
4. Remove the bolts securing the PAIR reed valve cover (B, **Figure 100**).
5. Remove the reed valve (**Figure 101**) from the cylinder head cover.

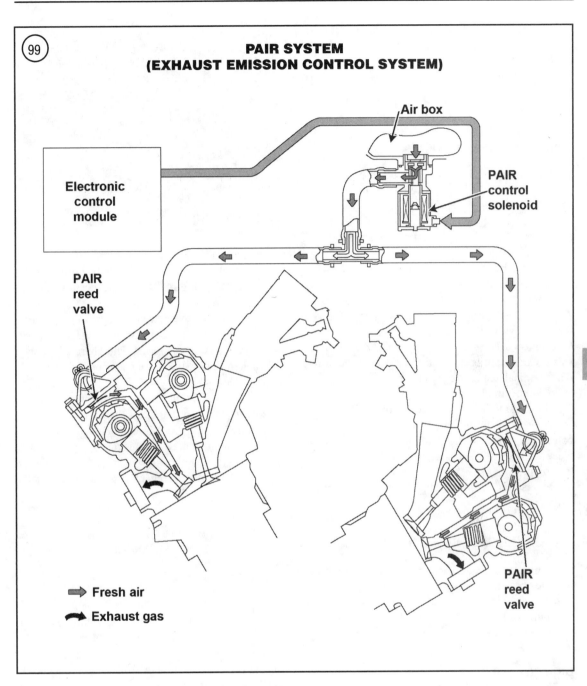

PAIR SYSTEM
(EXHAUST EMISSION CONTROL SYSTEM)

Air box

Electronic control module

PAIR control solenoid

PAIR reed valve

PAIR reed valve

⇒ Fresh air

⇒ Exhaust gas

8

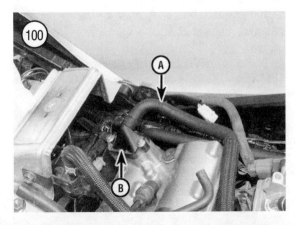

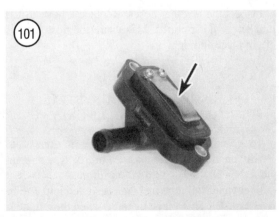

6. Inspect the reed valve for carbon deposits. Replace the reed valve if there are deposits or the reeds are damaged.

7. Reverse the removal steps to install the reed valve

PAIR Control Valve
Removal/Inspection/Installation

1. Remove the air box as described in this chapter. The PAIR control valve is located on the underside of the air box (**Figure 102**).

2. Connect an ohmmeter to the solenoid connector terminals. The resistance should equal the value in **Table 2** or **Table 3**.

3. Remove the control valve mounting bolts.

4. Pull out the control valve from the air box.

5. Blow air into the inlet port of the control valve. Air should flow from the two outlet ports. Replace the control valve if it does not.

6. Connect a 12-volt battery to the terminals on the valve. Connect the positive battery wire to the brown wire terminal and the negative battery wire to the orange/white wire terminal.

7. Blow into the control valve inlet port. Air should not flow from the outlet ports when the battery is connected to the solenoid connector. If it does, replace the control valve. Disconnect the battery from the solenoid.

8. Reverse the removal steps to install the control valve.

CRANKCASE BREATHER SYSTEM

All models are equipped with a closed crankcase breather system. This system routes crankcase vapors into the air box, then they are drawn into the engine and burned. Breather hoses are connected between the air box, crankcase and front cylinder.

Inspection and Cleaning

Inspect the breather hoses. Replace a hose if it is cracked or deteriorated. Make sure the hose clamps are in place and tight.

EVAPORATIVE
EMISSION CONTROL SYSTEM
(CALIFORNIA MODELS ONLY)

To comply with the California Air Resources Board, an evaporative emission control system is installed on all models sold in California.

Fuel vapor from the fuel tank is routed into a charcoal canister. This vapor is stored when the engine is

not running. When the engine is running these vapors are drawn into the throttle bodies to be burned. Refer to **Figure 103** or **Figure 104** for the location of hoses and system components.

Make sure the hoses are correctly routed and attached to the various components. Inspect the hoses and replace any if necessary. The charcoal canister and fuel shutoff valve are located on the right side of the frame.

On most models, the hoses and fittings are color coded with labels or bands. If these labels or bands are deteriorated or are missing, mark the hose and the fitting with a piece of masking tape to identify the hose. There are many hoses on these models. Without clear identifying marks, reconnecting the hoses correctly can be difficult.

THROTTLE CABLES
(2004-2006 MODELS)

Removal/Installation

The throttle uses two cables. One cable pulls the throttle open during acceleration, while the other pulls the throttle closed during deceleration. In operation, the cables always move in opposite directions to one another. Use the following procedure to replace the throttle cables.

1. Remove the air box.

2. At the handlebar, slide back the sleeves on each cable.

3. On each cable, loosen the locknut (A, **Figure 105**). Turn the adjuster on the cable (B) to obtain maximum cable slack.

4. Identify the accelerator and decelerator cables so the new cables can be matched and installed in the correct position.

5. At the throttle body, loosen the locknut (A, **Figure 106**) on each cable. Turn the adjuster on each cable (B). Detach each cable from the holder and the throttle pulley.

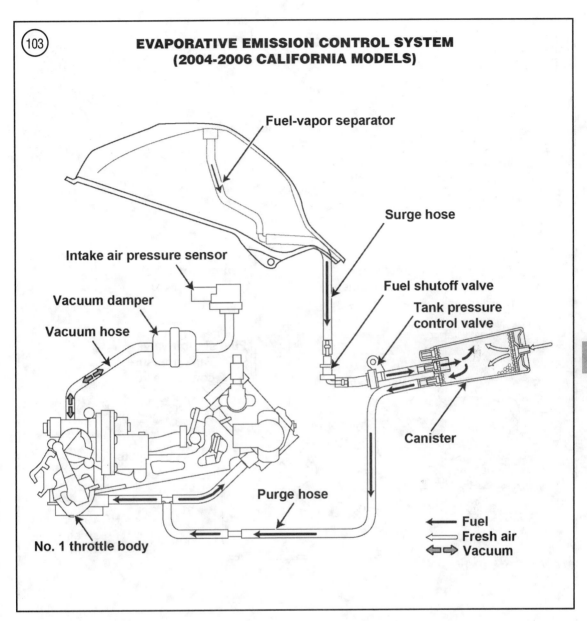

(103)

**EVAPORATIVE EMISSION CONTROL SYSTEM
(2004-2006 CALIFORNIA MODELS)**

Fuel-vapor separator

Surge hose

Intake air pressure sensor

Fuel shutoff valve

Tank pressure
control valve

Vacuum damper

Vacuum hose

Canister

Purge hose

No. 1 throttle body

⟵ Fuel
⟸ Fresh air
⟺ Vacuum

6. Note how the cables are routed, then remove the cables from the frame.

7. Slide the rubber cable cover (**Figure 107**) off the throttle housing and cables.

8. Remove the screws from the housing and separate the housing halves.

NOTE
The throttle cables are only available as a set.

9. Separate each cable guide from its housing half. Note that each cable guide will only fit into its corresponding housing half.

10. Detach the cable ends from the throttle pulley (**Figure 108**).

11. Clean the throttle assembly.

12. Lubricate the new cables as described in Chapter Three. Lubricate the throttle pulley and cable ends with lithium grease.

13. Install the new cables by reversing the removal procedure while noting the following:

a. Pull all slack out of the cables, then check that they move in the correct direction when the throttle is operated.

b. Connect the cables to the throttle body pulley, then adjust the cables as described in Chapter Three.

WARNING
An improperly adjusted or incorrectly routed throttle cable can cause the throttle to hang open. This could cause

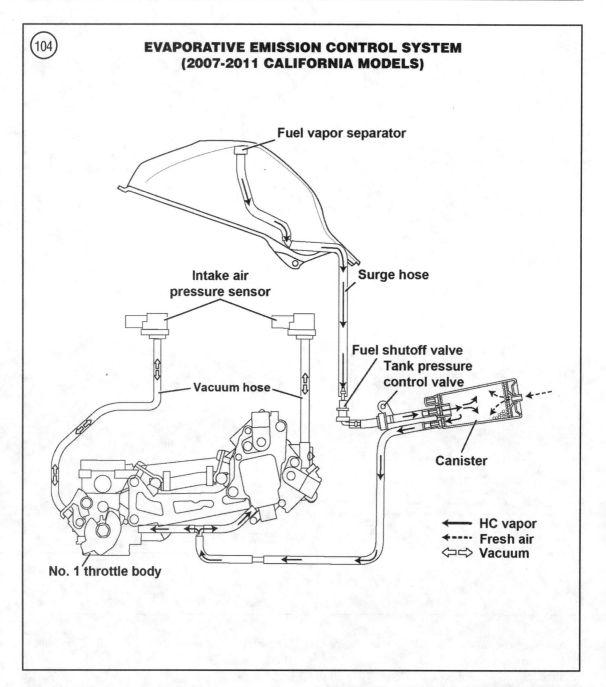

(104)

EVAPORATIVE EMISSION CONTROL SYSTEM
(2007-2011 CALIFORNIA MODELS)

Fuel vapor separator

Intake air
pressure sensor

Surge hose

Fuel shutoff valve
Tank pressure
control valve

Vacuum hose

Canister

⟵ HC vapor
⟵---- Fresh air
⟸⟹ Vacuum

No. 1 throttle body

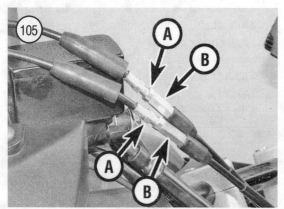

(105)

A
B
A
B

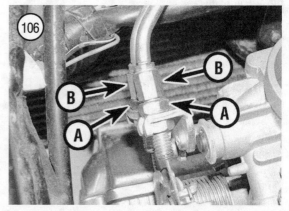

(106)

B
B
A
A

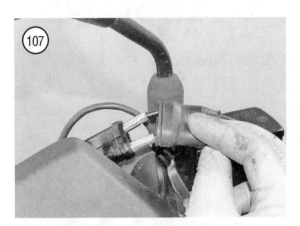

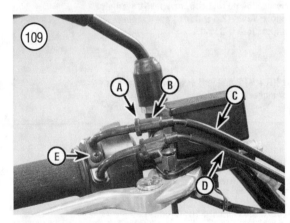

a crash. Do not ride the vehicle until throttle cable operation is correct.

c. Start the engine and let it idle. Turn the handlebar from side to side and listen to the engine speed. Make sure the idle speed does not increase. If it does, the throttle cables are adjusted incorrectly or the throttle cable(s) is improperly routed. Find and correct the source of the problem before riding.

THROTTLE CABLE (2007-2011 MODELS)

Removal/Installation

The throttle uses two cables. One cable pulls the throttle open during acceleration, while the other pulls the throttle closed during deceleration. In operation, the cables always move in opposite directions to one another. Use the following procedure to replace the throttle cables.

1. Remove the air box as described in this chapter.
2. At the throttle grip, loosen the throttle cable locknut (A, **Figure 109**) and turn the adjuster (B) all the way into the switch assembly to allow maximum slack in the accelerator cable (C). Repeat this procedure for the decelerator cable (D).
3. Remove the screws (E, **Figure 109**) securing the right switch assembly together and separate the assembly halves (**Figure 110**).
4. Disconnect the throttle pull cable and the return cable from the throttle grip. Note that a retaining plate (A, **Figure 109**) secures the cables in the throttle housing.
5. Identify the accelerator and decelerator cables so the new cables can be matched and installed in the correct position.
6. At the throttle body, loosen the locknut (A, **Figure 106**) on each cable. Turn the adjuster on each cable (B). Detach each cable from the holder and the throttle pulley.
7. Note how the cables are routed, then remove the cables from the frame.
8. Lubricate the new cables as described in Chapter Three. Lubricate the throttle pulley and cable ends with lithium grease.
9. Install the new cables by reversing the removal procedure while noting the following:
   a. Pull all slack out of the cables, then check that they move in the correct direction when the throttle is operated.
   b. Install the mounting pad so the pin fits into the hole in the handlebar (**Figure 110**).
   c. Operate the throttle and make sure the linkage operates correctly without binding. If opera-

tion is incorrect or if there is binding, carefully check that the cables are attached correctly and there are no tight bends in the cable.

d. Adjust the throttle cables as described in Chapter Three.

WARNING
An improperly adjusted or incorrectly routed throttle cable can cause the throttle to hang open. This could cause a crash. Do not ride the vehicle until throttle cable operation is correct.

e. Start the engine and let it idle. Turn the handlebar from side to side and listen to the engine speed. Make sure the idle speed does not increase. If it does, the throttle cables are adjusted incorrectly or the throttle cable(s) is improperly routed. Locate and correct the source of the problem before riding.

Table 1 FUEL SYSTEM SPECIFICATIONS

Item	Specification
Throttle body bore size	39 mm
Throttle body No.	
2004-2006 models	
All models except California	27G0
California models	27G1
2007-2011 models	
All models except California	27G2
California models	27G3
Idle speed	1200-1400 rpm
Fast idle speed	
2004-2006 models	1800-2400 rpm
2007-2011 models	1800-2200 rpm
Throttle cable free play	2.0-4.0 mm (0.08-0.16 in.)
Fuel pump output pressure	Approx. 300 kPa (43 psi)
Fuel pump output volume	
2004-2006	Approx. 168 ml (5.7 U.S. oz.) per 10 seconds
2007-2011 models	Approx. 75 ml (2.5 U.S. oz.) per 6 seconds
Fuel tank capacity (total)	22 liters (5.8 U.S. gal.)
Fuel	
Type	Unleaded
Octane	
U.S.A., California, and Canada models	87 [(R + M)/2 method] or research octane of 91 or higher
Non- U.S.A., California, and Canada models	91

Table 2 FUEL SYSTEM TEST SPECIFICATIONS (2004-2006 Models)

Item	Specification
Engine coolant temperature sensor	
Resistance	Approx. 2.45 ohms @ 20° C (68° F)
Voltage	4.5-5.5 volts
Resistance at temperature	
20° C (68° F)	Approx. 2.45 ohms
40° C (104° F)	Approx. 1.148 ohms
60° C (140° F)	Approx. 0.587 ohms
80° C (176° F)	Approx. 0.322 ohms
Fuel injector resistance	11-13 ohms @ 20° C (68° F)
Intake air pressure sensor	
Input voltage	4.5-5.5 volts
Output voltage	Approx. 2.7 volts @ idle speed
V-out voltage	
94-100 kPa (707-760 mmHg)	3.3-3.6 volts
85-94 kPa (634-707 mmHg)	3.0-3.3 volts
76-85 kPa (567-634 mmHg)	2.7-3.0 volts
70-76 kPa (526-567 mmHg)	2.5-2.7 volts

(continued)

Table 2 FUEL SYSTEM TEST SPECIFICATIONS (2004-2006 Models) (cont.)

Item	Specification
Intake air temperature sensor	
Resistance	Approx. 2.45 ohms @ 20° C (68° F)
Voltage	4.5-5.5 volts
Resistance at temperature	
20° C (68° F)	Approx. 2.45 ohms
40° C (122° F)	Approx. 1.148 ohms
60° C (176° F)	Approx. 0.587 ohms
80° C (230° F)	Approx. 0.322 ohms
Heated oxygen sensor	
Heater voltage	Battery voltage
Voltage at idle speed	0.4 volts or less
Voltage at 5000 rpm	0.6 volts or more
Resistance	
2004-2006 models	4-5 ohms at 23° C (73.4° F)
2007-2011 models	11-15 ohms at 23° C (73.4° F)
PAIR solenoid resistance	20-24 ohms at 20° C (68° F)
Secondary throttle position sensor	
Resistance	
Fully closed	Approx. 0.58 ohms
Fully open	Approx. 4.38 ohms
Input voltage	4.5-5.5 volts
Output voltage	
Fully closed	Approx. 0.58 volts
Fully open	Approx. 4.40 volts
Secondary throttle valve actuator resistance	Approx. 7-14 ohms
Throttle position sensor	
Resistance	
Fully closed	Approx. 1.22 k ohms
Fully open	Approx. 4.26 k ohms
Input voltage	4.5-5.5 volts
Output voltage	
Fully closed	Approx. 0.58 volts
Fully open	Approx. 0.40 volts
Tip-over sensor	
Resistance	19.1-19.7 ohms
Voltage	Upright: 0.4-1.4 volts
	Leaning 65°: 3.7-4.4 volts

Table 3 FUEL SYSTEM TEST SPECIFICATIONS (2007-2011 MODELS)

Item	Specification
Engine coolant temperature sensor	
Resistance	Approx. 2.45 ohms @ 20° C (68° F)
Voltage	4.5-5.5 volts
Resistance at temperature	
20° C (68° F)	Approx. 2.45 ohms
40° C (104° F)	Approx. 1.148 ohms
60° C (140° F)	Approx. 0.587 ohms
80° C (176° F)	Approx. 0.322 ohms
Fuel injector resistance	11-13 ohms @ 20° C (68° F)
Intake air pressure sensor	
Input voltage	4.5-5.5 volts
Output voltage	Approx. 1.6 volts @ idle speed
V-out voltage	
94-100 kPa (707-760 mmHg)	3.4-4.0 volts
85-94 kPa (634-707 mmHg)	3.0-3.7 volts
76-85 kPa (567-634 mmHg)	2.6-3.4 volts
70-76 kPa (526-567 mmHg)	2.4-3.1 volts
Intake air temperature sensor	
Resistance	Approx. 2.6K ohms @ 20° C (68° F)
Voltage	4.5-5.5 volts

(continued)

Table 3 FUEL SYSTEM TEST SPECIFICATIONS (2007-2011 MODELS) (cont.)

Item	Specification
Intake air temperature sensor (cont.)	
Resistance at temperature	
20° C (68° F)	Approx. 2.56 ohms
40° C (122° F)	Approx. 1.20 ohms
60° C (176° F)	Approx. 0.61 ohms
80° C (230° F)	Approx. 0.33 ohms
Heated oxygen sensor	
Heater voltage	Battery voltage
Voltage at idle speed	0.4 volts or less
Voltage at 5000 rpm	0.6 volts or more
Resistance	11-15 ohms at 23° C (73.4° F)
ISC valve resistance	28.8-31.2 ohms at 20° C (68° F)
PAIR solenoid resistance	20-24 ohms at 20° C (68° F)
Secondary throttle position sensor	
Input voltage	4.5-5.5 volts
Output voltage	
Fully closed	Approx. 0.6 volts
Fully open	Approx. 4.5 volts
Secondary throttle valve actuator resistance	Approx. 7 ohms
Throttle position sensor	
Input voltage	4.5-5.5 volts
Output voltage	
Fully closed	Approx. 1.1 volts
Fully open	Approx. 4.3 volts
Tip-over sensor	
Resistance	19.1-19.7 ohms
Voltage	Upright: 0.4-1.4 volts
	Leaning 65°: 3.7-4.4 volts

Table 4 FUEL SYSTEM TORQUE SPECIFICATIONS

Item	N•m	in. lb.	ft.-lb.
Engine coolant sensor	19	168	–
Fuel delivery pipe screws	5	44	–
Fuel pump mounting bolts	10	88	–
Oxygen sensor	47.5	–	34
Secondary throttle position sensor screw			
2004-2006 models	2	18	–
2007-20011 models	3.5	31	–
Throttle position sensor screw	3.5	31	–

ELECTRICAL SYSTEM

9

This chapter contains service and test procedures for the following systems/components:

1. Electrical components.
2. Charging system.
3. Ignition system.
4. Starting system.
5. Lighting system.
6. Switches.
7. Fuses.

Refer to **Tables 1-3** at the end of this chapter for specifications.

ELECTRICAL COMPONENT REPLACEMENT

Most vehicle dealerships and parts suppliers will not accept the return of any electrical part. If the exact cause of an electrical system malfunction cannot be determined, have a dealership retest that specific system to verify the test results. This may help avert the possibility of purchasing an expensive, un-returnable part that does not fix the problem.

Consider any test results carefully before replacing a component that tests only slightly out of specification, especially resistance. A number of variables can affect test results dramatically. These include the testing meter's internal circuitry, ambient tempera-

ture and conditions under which the machine has been operated. All instructions and specifications have been checked for accuracy; however, successful test results depend to a great extent upon individual accuracy.

CONTINUITY TESTING GUIDELINES

Circuits, switches, light bulbs and fuses can be checked for continuity (a completed circuit) using an ohmmeter connected to the appropriate color-coded wires in the circuit. Tests can be made at the connector or at the part. Use the following procedure as a guide to performing general continuity tests.

CAUTION
Do not turn on the ignition switch when performing continuity checks. Damage to parts and test equipment could occur. Also, verify that power from the battery is not routed directly into the test circuit, regardless of ignition switch position.

1. Refer to the wiring diagram at the back of this manual and find the part to be checked.
2. Identify the wire colors leading to the part and determine which pairs of wires should be checked. For

any check, the circuit should begin at the connector, pass through the part, then return to the connector.

3. Determine when continuity should exist.

  a. Typically, whenever a switch or button is turned on, it closes the circuit, and the meter should indicate continuity.

  b. When the switch or button is turned off, it opens the circuit, and the meter should not indicate continuity.

4. Trace the wires from the part to the nearest connector. Separate the connector.

5. Connect an ohmmeter to the connector half that leads to the part being checked. If the test is being made at the terminals on the part, remove all other wires connected to the terminals so they do not influence the meter reading.

6. Operate the switch/button and check for continuity.

ELECTRICAL CONNECTORS

All models are equipped with numerous electrical components, connectors and wires. Corrosion-causing moisture can enter these electrical connectors and cause poor electrical connections, leading to component failure. Troubleshooting an electrical circuit with one or more corroded electrical connectors can be time-consuming and frustrating. Pack the electrical connectors with a dielectric grease compound when reconnecting them. Dielectric grease is specially formulated for sealing and waterproofing electrical connections without affecting current flow. Use only this compound or an equivalent designed for this specific purpose. Do not use a substitute that may interfere with the current flow within the electrical connector. Do not use silicone sealant.

After cleaning both the male and female connectors, make sure they are thoroughly dry. Apply dielectric grease to the interior of one of the connectors prior to connecting the connector halves. For best results, the compound should fill the entire inner area of the connector. On multi-pin connectors, also pack the backside of both the male and female end with the compound to prevent moisture from entering the connector. After the connector is fully packed, wipe all excessive compound from the exterior.

BATTERY NEGATIVE TERMINAL

Some of the component replacement procedures and some of the test procedures in this chapter require disconnecting the negative (—) battery cable as a safety precaution.

1. Turn the ignition switch off.

2. Remove the seat as described in Chapter Fifteen.

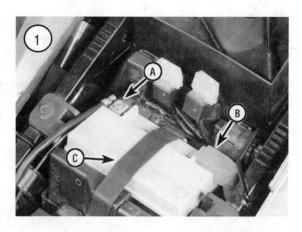

3. Remove the bolt and disconnect the negative battery cable (A, **Figure 1**) from the battery terminal.

4. Move the cable out of the way so it does not accidentally make contact with the battery terminal.

5. Once the procedure is completed, connect the negative battery cable to the terminal and tighten the bolt securely.

6. Install the seat as described in Chapter Fifteen.

BATTERY

A sealed, maintenance-free battery is installed on all models. The battery electrolyte level cannot be serviced. When replacing the battery, use a sealed type; do not install a non-sealed battery. Never attempt to remove the sealing caps from the top of the battery. The battery does not require periodic electrolyte inspection or refilling. Refer to **Table 1** for battery specifications.

To prevent accidental shorts that could blow a fuse when working on the electrical system, always disconnect the negative battery cable from the battery.

> *WARNING*
> *Even though the battery is a sealed type, protect eyes, skin and clothing; electrolyte is corrosive and can cause severe burns and permanent injury. The battery case may be cracked and leaking electrolyte. If electrolyte gets into the eyes, flush both eyes thoroughly with clean, running water and get immediate medical attention. Always wear safety goggles when servicing the battery.*

> *WARNING*
> *While batteries are being charged, highly explosive hydrogen gas forms in each cell. Some of this gas escapes through filler cap openings and may form an explosive atmosphere in and around the battery. This condition can*

persist for several hours. Sparks, an open flame or a lighted cigarette can ignite the gas, causing an internal battery explosion and possible serious personal injury.

NOTE
Recycle the old battery. When replacing the old battery, be sure to turn in the old battery at that time. The lead plates and the plastic case can be recycled. Most vehicle dealerships accept old batteries in trade when purchasing a new one. Never place an old battery in household trash; it is illegal, in most states, to place any acid or lead (heavy metal) contents in landfills.

Safety Precautions

Heed the following precautions to prevent an explosion.
1. Do not smoke or permit any open flame near any battery being charged or which has been recently charged.
2. Do not disconnect live circuits at the battery. A spark usually occurs when a live circuit is broken.
3. Take care when connecting or disconnecting a battery charger. Turn the ignition switch OFF before making or breaking connections. Poor connections are a common cause of electrical arcs, which cause explosions.
4. Keep children and pets away from the charging equipment and the battery.

Removal/Installation

1. Make sure the ignition switch is off.
2. Disconnect the negative battery terminal (A, **Figure 1**) as described in this chapter.
3. Remove the insulator cover from the positive cable (B, **Figure 1**), then detach the cable from the battery terminal
4. Detach the retaining strap (C, **Figure 1**).
5. Detach the vent tube and remove the battery.
6. Clean and check the components for damage.
7. Reverse the preceding procedure to install the battery while noting the following:
   a. To prevent corrosion, apply a thin coating of dielectric grease to the battery terminals and cable ends.
   b. Tighten the terminal bolts firmly. Do not apply excessive force.

Cleaning/Inspection

The battery electrolyte level cannot be serviced. Never attempt to remove the sealing bar cap from the top of the battery. The battery does not require periodic electrolyte inspection or refilling.
1. Read *Safety Precautions* in this section.
2. Remove the battery from the vehicle as described in the previous section. Do not clean the battery while it is mounted in the vehicle.
3. Clean the battery exterior with a solution of warm water and baking soda. Rinse thoroughly with clean water.
4. Inspect the physical condition of the battery. Look for bulges or cracks in the case, leaking electrolyte or corrosion buildup.
5. Check the battery terminal bolts and nuts for corrosion and damage. Clean parts with a solution of baking soda and water, and rinse thoroughly. Replace if damaged.
6. Check the battery cable clamps for corrosion and damage. If corrosion is minor, clean the battery cable clamps with a stiff brush. Replace excessively worn or damaged cables.

Testing

The maintenance-free battery can be tested while mounted in the vehicle. A digital voltmeter is required for this procedure. See **Table 1** for battery voltage readings for the maintenance free battery.
1. Read *Safety Precautions* in this section.

NOTE
To prevent false test readings, do not test the battery if the battery terminals are corroded. Remove and clean the battery and terminals as described in this chapter, then reinstall it.

2. Connect a digital voltmeter between the battery negative and positive leads. Note the following:
   a. If the battery voltage is 13.0-13.2 volts (at 20° C [68° F]), the battery is fully charged.
   b. If the battery voltage is below 12.8 volts (at 20° C [68° F]), the battery is undercharged and requires charging.
3. If the battery is undercharged, recharge it as described in this chapter. Then test the charging system as described in this chapter.

Battery Current Draw Test

If the battery is in good condition, but it discharges at a rapid rate when the motorcycle is not used, check the electrical system for a current draw. Machines that have a clock or some other type of aftermarket accessory (such as an alarm) will have a continuous parasitic current loss to operate these types of devices. This will show up as a current draw on the battery. However, any current draw present when all electrical devices are shut off indicates a problem.

A short in a wire or component can allow the battery to discharge to ground. Dirt and moisture can also create a path to ground. To isolate the problem, an ammeter is connected to the battery and various circuits/components disconnected while observing the current reading.

1. Make sure the ignition switch is off.
2. Disconnect the negative battery terminal as described in this chapter.
3. Make sure the battery is fully charged.

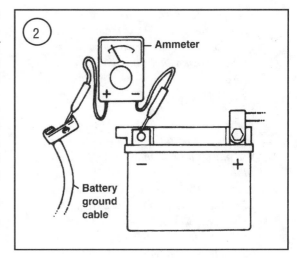

> *CAUTION*
> *Before connecting the ammeter in the next step, set the amperage range to the highest setting. If there is an excessive amount of current flow, the meter may be damaged.*

4. Connect the ammeter to the negative battery cable and terminal as shown in **Figure 2**.
   a. The meter should indicate a current draw of 3 mA or less.
   b. If excessive current draw is indicated, continue the test.
5. Remove the fuses from the fuse box. Observe the meter.
   a. If the current draw lessens, there is a problem indicated in one of the fused circuits. Install the fuse(s) and continue to isolate the problem by separating the connectors in the circuit.
   b. If the current draw remains the same, there is a problem indicated in the main circuit.
6. Check the connector as follows:
   a. Refer to the system diagrams in this chapter, and if necessary, the wiring diagram at the back of the manual for additional circuits and part identifications.
   b. Separate the individual connectors of the appropriate parts. Work with one connector at a time, disconnecting and connecting the connectors until the meter indicates no current draw. When this occurs, the shorted circuit has been isolated.

Charging

Refer to *Battery Initialization* in this chapter if the battery is new.

To recharge a maintenance-free battery, a digital voltmeter and a charger with an adjustable or automat-

ically variable amperage output are required. If this equipment is not available, have the battery charged by a shop with the proper equipment. Excessive voltage and amperage from an unregulated charger can damage the battery and shorten service life.

The battery should only self-discharge approximately one percent of its given capacity each day. If a battery not in use, without any loads connected, loses its charge within a week after charging, the battery is defective.

If the vehicle is not used for long periods of time, an automatic battery charger (**Figure 3**) with variable voltage and amperage outputs is recommended for optimum battery service life.

> *WARNING*
> *During the charging process, highly explosive hydrogen gas is released from the battery. Charge the battery only in a well-ventilated area away from any open flames (including pilot lights on home gas appliances). Do not allow any smoking in the area. Never check the charge of the battery by connecting screwdriver blades or other metal objects between the terminals; the resulting spark can ignite the hydrogen gas.*

> *CAUTION*
> *Always remove the battery from the vehicle before connecting the battery charger. Never recharge a battery in the frame; corrosive gasses emitted during the charging process will damage surfaces.*

1. Remove the battery as described in this chapter.
2. Connect the positive charger lead to the positive battery terminal and the negative charger lead to the negative battery terminal.

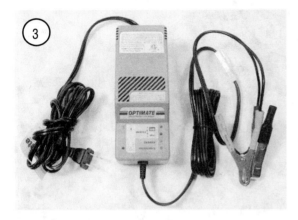

3. Set the charger at 12 volts and switch it on. Normally, a battery should be charged at a slow charge rate of 1/10 its given capacity. **Table 1** lists the battery capacity and charge rate for all models.

4. After the battery has been charged, turn the charger OFF, disconnect the leads and check the battery with a digital voltmeter. It should be within the limits specified in **Table 1**. If it is, and remains stable for one hour, the battery is charged.

Battery Initialization

A *new* battery must be fully charged before installation. Failure to do so reduces the life of the battery. Using a new battery without an initial charge causes permanent battery damage. That is, the battery will never be able to hold more than an 80% charge. Charging a *new* battery after it has been used will not bring its charge to 100%. When purchasing a new battery from a dealership or parts store, verify its charge status. If necessary, have them perform the initial or booster charge before accepting the battery.

CHARGING SYSTEM

The charging system consists of the battery, alternator and a voltage regulator/rectifier. Alternating current generated by the alternator is rectified to direct current. The voltage regulator maintains the voltage to the battery and additional electrical loads at a constant voltage regardless of variations in engine speed.

A malfunction in the charging system generally causes the battery to remain undercharged. To prevent damage to the alternator and the regulator/rectifier when testing and repairing the charging system, note the following precautions:

1. Always disconnect the negative battery cable, as described in this chapter, before removing a component from the charging system.

2. When it is necessary to charge the battery, remove the battery from the motorcycle and recharge it as described in this chapter.

3. Inspect the physical condition of the battery. Look for bulges or cracks in the case, leaking electrolyte or corrosion buildup.

4. Check the wiring in the charging system for signs of chafing, deterioration or other damage.

5. Check the wiring for corroded or loose connections. Clean, tighten or reconnect as required.

Charging System Output Test

Whenever a charging system trouble is suspected, make sure the battery is fully charged and in good condition before going any further. Clean and test the battery as described in Chapter Three. Make sure all electrical connectors are tight and free of corrosion.

1. Start the engine and let it reach normal operating temperature. Shut off the engine.

2. Remove the front seat as described in Chapter Fifteen.

3. Remove the red plastic cover from the positive battery terminal (B, **Figure 1**).

4. Turn the headlight dimmer switch to the HI position.

5. Connect the positive test lead of a 0-25 DC voltmeter to the positive battery terminal. Connect the negative test lead to the negative battery terminal.

6. Restart the engine and let it idle.

7. Increase engine speed to 5,000 rpm. The voltage reading should be 14.0-15.5 volts. If the voltage is outside the specified range, inspect the alternator and the voltage regulator as described in this chapter. The voltage regulator/rectifier is a separate unit from the alternator and can be replaced individually.

8. If the charging voltage is too high; the voltage regulator/rectifier is probably faulty.

9. After completing the test, shut off the engine and disconnect the voltmeter.

10. Install the front seat.

Charging System No-Load Test

1. Remove the air box as described in Chapter Eight.

2. Disconnect the alternator three-wire (black wires) electrical connector (A, **Figure 4**).

3. Start the engine and let it idle.

NOTE
In Step 4 connect the voltmeter test leads to the alternator end of the electrical connector disconnected in Step 2.

4. Connect a 0-250 V (AC) voltmeter between each of the three terminals to the alternator end of the connector as shown in **Figure 5**.

5. Increase engine speed to 5000 rpm and check the voltage on the meter. The voltage should be greater than 60 volts.

6. Repeat this test for the remaining terminals. Take a total of three readings.

7. If the voltage in any test is less than the specified no-load voltage, shut off the engine and check the charging system wiring harness and connectors for dirt or loose-fitting terminals. Clean and repair as required. If the wiring and connectors are good, the alternator is defective and must be replaced.

8. Disconnect and remove the voltmeter.

9. Reconnect the alternator connector (A, **Figure 4**). Make sure the connector is corrosion free and secure.

10. Install the air box.

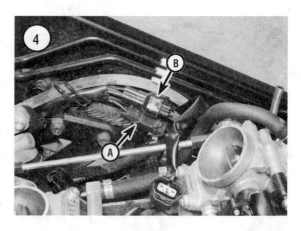

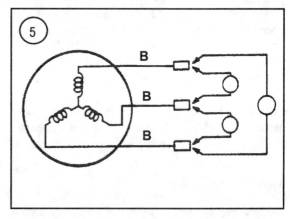

VOLTAGE REGULATOR/RECTIFIER

Testing

Suzuki specifies the use of the Suzuki Multi Circuit Tester (part No. 09900-25008) for testing the regulator/rectifier unit. If this tester is not available, have a Suzuki dealership test the unit.

> *NOTE*
> *Before making this test, check the condition of the tester battery. To ensure an accurate reading, install a new battery.*

1. Remove the regulator/rectifier as described in this section.

2. Connect the Suzuki Multi Circuit Tester regulator/rectifier to the terminals indicated in **Figure 6** and check the voltage across each pair of terminals.

3. If any voltage reading differs from the stated value, replace the regulator/rectifier unit.

Voltage Regulator/Rectifier Removal/Installation

1. Remove the air box as described in Chapter Eight.

2. Disconnect the negative battery lead as described in this chapter.

3. Disconnect the regulator/rectifier electrical connector (B, **Figure 4**).

4. Remove the two mounting bolts (A, **Figure 7**) and remove the regulator/rectifier (B).

5. Install by reversing the removal steps. Make sure the electrical connectors are tight and free of corrosion. Tighten the bolts securely.

ALTERNATOR

The alternator consists of the flywheel rotor and stator coil assembly. The rotor is a part of the flywheel. The stator coil assembly is located inside the left crankcase cover. The stator coil consists of separate coils that generate voltage for the charging system and lighting system.

Refer to Chapter Five for removal and installation of the flywheel and left crankcase cover.

Rotor Testing

The rotor is permanently magnetized and cannot be tested except by replacing it with a known good one. The rotor can lose magnetism over time or from a sharp impact. If defective, replace the rotor.

Stator Coil Resistance Test

1. Remove the air box as described in Chapter Eight.

⑥ REGULATOR/RECTIFIER TEST

		+ Probe of tester to:				
		B/R	B1	B2	B3	B/W
- Probe of tester to:	B/R		0.4~0.7	0.4~0.7	0.4~0.7	0.5~1.2
	B1	Approx. 1.5		Approx. 1.5	Approx. 1.5	0.4~0.7
	B2	Approx. 1.5	Approx. 1.5		Approx. 1.5	0.4~0.7
	B3	Approx. 1.5	Approx. 1.5	Approx. 1.5		0.4~0.7
	B/W	Approx. 1.5	Approx. 1.5	Approx. 1.5	Approx. 1.5	

R: Red, B: Black

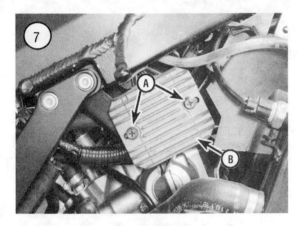

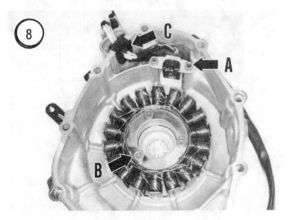

5. Check continuity from each black stator wire to ground.

6. Replace the stator coil if any black terminal has continuity to ground. Continuity indicates a short within the stator coil winding.

NOTE
Before replacing the stator assembly, check the electrical wires to and within the electrical connector, including the three-wire stator connector, for any opens or poor connections.

7. If the stator coil fails either of these tests, replace it as described in this section.

8. Make sure the electrical connector is secure and corrosion-free.

9. Reconnect the alternator electrical connector. Make sure the connector is corrosion free and tight.

10. Install the air box as described in Chapter Eight.

Stator Assembly Removal/Installation

The stator assembly is located within the left crankcase cover.

NOTE
The stator coil and crankshaft position sensor are wired together and must be serviced as a unit assembly.

1. Remove the left crankcase cover as described in Chapter Five.

2. Remove the bolts securing the crankshaft position sensor (A, **Figure 8**).

2. Disconnect the alternator three-wire (black wires) electrical connector (A, **Figure 4**).

3. Measure resistance between each black wire terminal in the alternator end of the connector. **Table 2** lists the specified stator coil resistance.

4. Replace the stator if the resistance is not as specified.

3. Remove the stator coil mounting bolts (B, **Figure 8**).

4. Pull the wire harness grommet (C, **Figure 8**) out of the crankcase cover notch.

5. Remove the stator coil and crankshaft position sensor assembly (**Figure 9**).

6. Do not clean the stator coils with solvent. Wipe off with a clean rag.

7. Install the stator coil and crankshaft position sensor assembly by reversing the preceding steps while noting the following:

   a. Tighten the stator coil bolts to 11 N•m (97 in.-lb.).

   b. Tighten the crankshaft position sensor bolts to 6.5 N•m (58 in.-lb.).

   c. Make sure the wire grommet is securely seated in the left crankcase cover.

ELECTRONIC IGNITION SYSTEM

The engine is equipped with an electronic ignition system. The system consists of an engine control module (ECM), crankshaft position (CKP) sensor, throttle position sensor (TPS), engine coolant temperature (ECT) sensor, gear position sensor, two ignition coils and spark plugs. On 2004-2006 models, the engine is equipped with two spark plugs. On 2007-2011 models, the engine is equipped with four spark plugs.

The crankshaft position portion of the system consists of external projections on the alternator rotor and the CKP sensor. The TPS is mounted on the throttle body assembly. The ECT sensor is located on the thermostat housing. The gear position sensor is mounted on the left crankcase half.

As the crankshaft rotates, the projections on the alternator rotor pass the CKP sensor, which sends a signal to the ECM. The ECM uses this signal, input from the throttle position sensor and a stored digital data map to determine the optimum ignition timing for the operating conditions.

Ignition System Precautions

Certain measures must be taken to protect the ignition system. Damage to the semiconductors in the system may occur if any of the electrical connections are disconnected while the engine is running.

Troubleshooting

Refer to *Ignition System* in Chapter Two.

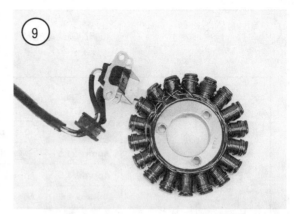

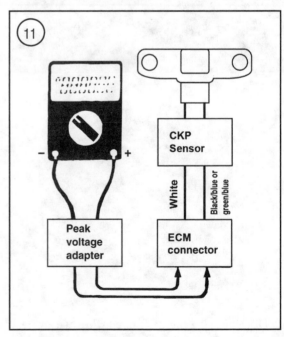

Crankshaft Position Sensor

Peak voltage test

Refer to *Preliminary Information* at the beginning of this chapter.

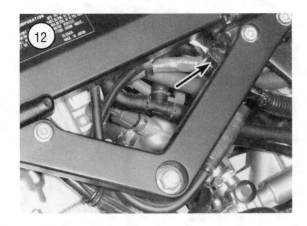

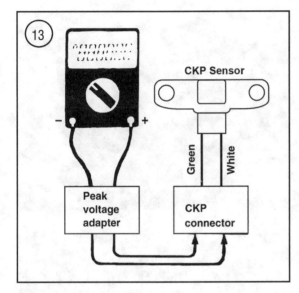

WARNING
High voltage is present during ignition system operation. Do not touch ignition components, wires or test leads while the engine is running or cranking.

NOTE
All peak voltage specifications are minimum values. If the measured voltage meets or exceeds the specifications, the test results are acceptable.

1. Remove the seat as described in Chapter Fifteen.
2. Disconnect the ECM connector (**Figure 10**) from the ECM.
3. Turn the tester's knob to voltage.
4A. On 2004-2006 models, connect the negative test probe to the black/white terminal on the connector, and connect the positive test probe to the white terminal (**Figure 11**).
4B. On 2007-2011 models, connect the negative test probe to the green/blue terminal on the connector,

and connect the positive test probe to the white terminal (**Figure 11**).
5. Shift the transmission into neutral and turn the ignition switch ON.
6. Press the starter button and crank the engine for a few seconds and record the highest reading.
7. If the CKP sensor peak voltage is less than 3.7 volts, check the peak voltage at the CKP sensor coupler (**Figure 12**) by performing the following:
   a. Remove the right cowling as described in Chapter Fifteen.
   b. Disconnect the two-wire CKP sensor connector (**Figure 12**).
   c. Connect the positive test probe to the green wire terminal in the CKP sensor connector and connect the negative test probe to the white wire terminal (**Figure 13**).
   d. Shift the transmission into neutral and turn the ignition switch ON.
   e. Press the starter button and crank the engine for a few seconds and record the highest reading.
8. If the peak voltage measured at the CKP sensor connector is normal but the peak voltage at the igniter connector is less than 3.7 volts, replace the wiring.
9. If the peak voltage at both the CKP sensor connector and the igniter connector are less than 3.7 volts, replace the CKP sensor.
10. If all tests are acceptable, reconnect the electrical connector. Make sure the electrical connector is free of corrosion and is tight.
11. Install the right cowling and seat.

Resistance test

1. Remove the right cowling as described in Chapter Fifteen.
2. Disconnect the two-wire CKP sensor connector (**Figure 12**).
3. Set the ohmmeter to the R × 100 scale, and check the resistance between the white and green terminals in the CKP sensor end of the connector (**Figure 14**). If the CKP sensor coil resistance is outside the range of 130-240 ohms, replace the CKP sensor.
4. Check the continuity between the green terminal in the CKP sensor connector and ground (**Figure 14**). There should be no continuity (infinite resistance). If there is continuity, replace the CKP sensor.
5. If all tests are acceptable, reconnect the electrical connector. Make sure the electrical connector is free of corrosion and is secure.
6. Install the right cowling.

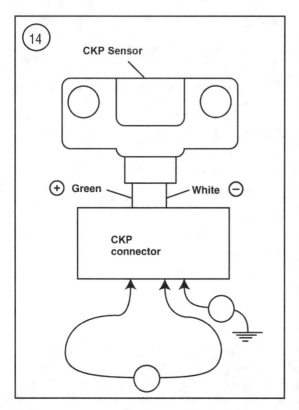

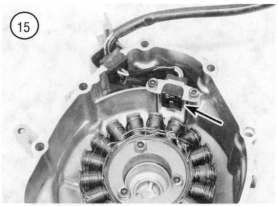

Crankshaft Position Sensor Replacement

The CKP sensor (**Figure 15**) is located inside the alternator cover. The CKP sensor and stator are only available as a unit assembly. If the CKP sensor is faulty, replace it by following the stator replacement procedure found in this chapter.

Ignition Coil

The ignition coil for the No. 1 (front) cylinder is located on the left side (**Figure 16**). The ignition coil for the No. 2 (rear) cylinder is located on the right side (**Figure 17**).

Primary peak voltage test

The Suzuki Multi-Circuit Tester (part No. 09900-25008) with the peak voltage adapter, the Motion Pro IgnitionMate (part No.08-0193), or an equivalent peak voltage tester is required for this test.
1. Lift and support the fuel tank as described in Chapter Eight.
2. Remove the spark plugs as described in Chapter Three.
3. Connect a new spark plug to each plug cap.
4. Ground the spark plugs to the crankcase.

WARNING
High voltage is present during ignition system operation. Do not touch ignition components, wires or test leads while cranking or running the engine.

NOTE
All peak voltage specifications are minimum values. If the measured voltage meets or exceeds the specification, the test results are satisfactory. On some components, the voltage may greatly exceed the minimum specification.

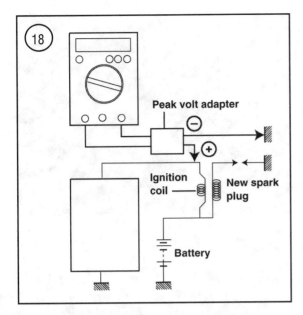

Peak volt adapter

Ignition coil

New spark plug

Battery

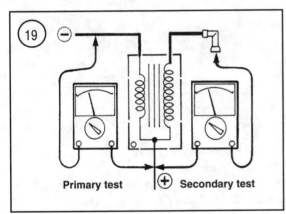

Primary test

Secondary test

5. Check the peak voltage for the No.1 cylinder by performing the following:

   a. Turn the tester knob to voltage.

> *NOTE*
> *Do not disconnect the wires from the ignition coil when performing the following test. If it is not possible to contact the coil terminal with the tester probe, pierce the wire using a needle probe.*

   b. Connect the positive test probe to the white/blue wire or terminal on the ignition coil and connect the negative test probe to ground (**Figure 18**).

   c. Shift the transmission into neutral and turn the ignition switch ON.

   d. Press the starter button and crank the engine for a few seconds while reading the meter. Record the highest meter reading. The minimum peak voltage is 150 volts.

6. Check the peak voltage for the No.2 cylinder by performing Step 5, except connect the positive test probe to the black wire or terminal on the ignition coil.

7. If the peak voltage reading on either ignition coil is less than specified, measure the resistance on that ignition coil.

Resistance test

The Suzuki Multi-Circuit Tester (part No. 09900-25008) is required for accurate resistance testing of the ignition coil/plug cap. Refer to Preliminary Information section at the beginning of this chapter.

1. Disconnect all ignition coil wires (including the spark plug leads from the spark plugs) before testing.

2. Set an ohmmeter to the R × 1 scale and measure the primary coil resistance between the positive (orange/white or black/orange wire) and the negative terminals (white/blue or black wire) on the ignition coil (**Figure 19**). Specified primary coil resistance is 2.0-5.0 ohms.

3. Set the ohmmeter to the R × 1,000 scale and measure the secondary coil resistance between the spark plug lead (with the spark plug cap attached) and the positive coil terminal. Refer to **Table 3** for specified primary coil resistance.

4. If either measurement does not meet specification, replace the coil. If the coil exhibits visible damage, replace it.

5. Reconnect all ignition coil wires to the ignition coil.

6. Repeat this procedure for the other ignition coil.

Removal/installation

1. Remove the air box as described in Chapter Eight.

2. Disconnect the negative battery cable.

3. Disconnect all ignition coil wires (including the spark plug leads from the spark plugs).

4. Remove the screws securing the ignition coil to the frame.

5. Install by reversing the preceding removal steps. Make sure all electrical connections are corrosion-free and secure.

ENGINE CONTROL MODULE (ECM)

The engine control module (ECM) controls the ignition and fuel injection systems.

No test specifications are available for the PCM. The PCM should be replaced only after all other components, including wiring and connections, have been eliminated through troubleshooting as the possible cause of the malfunction. Refer to Chapter Two.

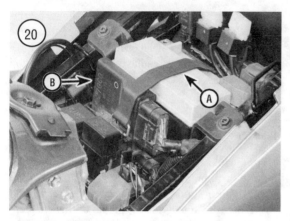

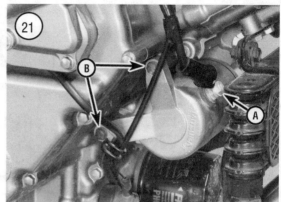

Replacement

1. Remove the seat as described in Chapter Fifteen.
2. Disconnect the negative battery cable as described in this chapter.
3. Detach the retaining strap (A, **Figure 20**).
4. Lift up the ECM (B, **Figure 20**) and detach the connector(s) from the unit.
5. Remove the ECM.
6. Reinstall the ECM by reversing the preceding removal steps.

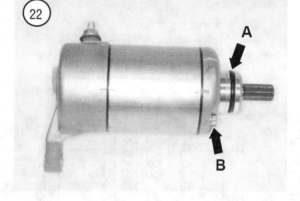

STARTING SYSTEM

The starting system consists of the starter motor, starter relay, clutch switch, sidestand switch, turn signal/sidestand relay, neutral switch, engine stop switch, starter button and ignition switch. When the starter button is pressed, it engages the starter relay and completes the circuit allowing electricity to flow from the battery to the starter motor.

The starter motor rotates the engine crankshaft through the starter idler gear and the starter clutch. Refer to Chapter Five for service information related to those components.

> *CAUTION*
> *Do not operate the starter for more than 5 seconds at a time. Let it cool approximately 10 seconds before operating it again.*

Troubleshooting

Refer to Chapter Two.

STARTER MOTOR (2004-2009 MODELS)

Removal/Installation

1. Disconnect the negative battery cable as described in this chapter.

2. Pull back the rubber boot from the starter motor electrical connector.
3. Remove the starter motor cable retaining nut (A, **Figure 21**) and disconnect the starter motor cable from the starter.
4. Remove the two bolts (B, **Figure 21**) securing the starter to the crankcase.
5. Remove the starter.
6. Thoroughly clean the starter mounting pads on the crankcase and the mounting lugs on the starter motor.
7. Inspect the O-ring (A, **Figure 22**) on the drive end of the starter motor for hardness or deterioration. Replace the O-ring if necessary. Apply clean engine oil to the O-ring before installing the starter motor.
8. Install the starter motor by reversing the removal procedure while noting the following:
   a. Place the starter motor cable clamp on the lower starter motor bolt.
   b. Tighten the starter motor mounting bolts securely.
   c. Connect the starter motor cable so it points at a 45° angle toward the rear of the starter.

Disassembly

Refer to **Figure 23** when performing this procedure.

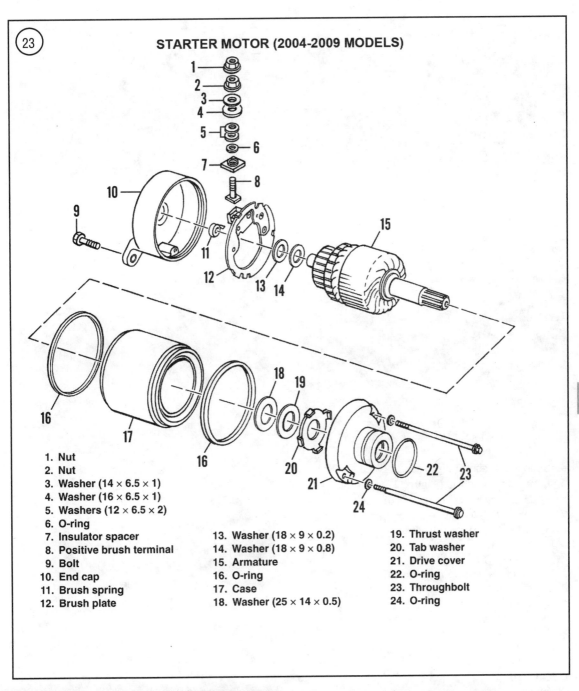

STARTER MOTOR (2004-2009 MODELS)

1. Nut
2. Nut
3. Washer (14 × 6.5 × 1)
4. Washer (16 × 6.5 × 1)
5. Washers (12 × 6.5 × 2)
6. O-ring
7. Insulator spacer
8. Positive brush terminal
9. Bolt
10. End cap
11. Brush spring
12. Brush plate
13. Washer (18 × 9 × 0.2)
14. Washer (18 × 9 × 0.8)
15. Armature
16. O-ring
17. Case
18. Washer (25 × 14 × 0.5)
19. Thrust washer
20. Tab washer
21. Drive cover
22. O-ring
23. Throughbolt
24. O-ring

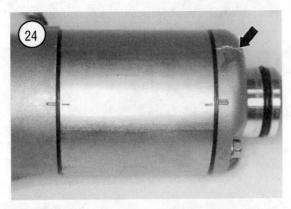

NOTE
While disassembling the starter motor, lay the parts out in the order of removal. While removing a part from the starter, set it next to the one previously removed. This is an easy way to remember the correct relationship of all parts.

1. Remove the throughbolts (B, **Figure 22**) and O-ring seals.
2. Remove the drive cover (**Figure 24**) from the case.
3. Remove the tab washer (**Figure 25**).

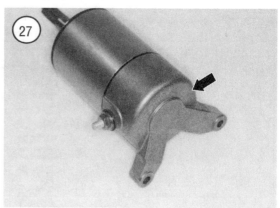

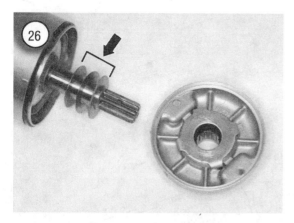

4. Slide the washers (**Figure 26**) off the shaft.
5. Remove the end cap (**Figure 27**) from the case.
6. Slide the washers (**Figure 28**) off the armature.
7. Remove the armature from the starter case (**Figure 29**).

> *NOTE*
> *Before removing the nuts and washers, record their descriptions and order. They must be reinstalled in the same order to insulate the positive (+) brush plate assembly from the case.*

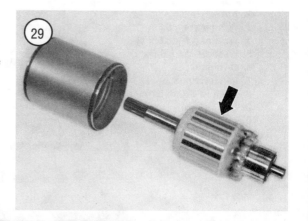

8. Remove the nut, washers, bushing and O-ring (**Figure 30**) securing the brush holder assembly to the end cap.
9. Pull the brush holder assembly (**Figure 31**) out of the end cap and remove it.

> *CAUTION*
> *Do not immerse the wire windings of the armature (**Figure 32**) in solvent as the insulation may be damaged. To clean the windings, wipe them with a cloth lightly moistened with solvent, then thoroughly dry.*

10. Clean all grease, dirt and carbon from all components.

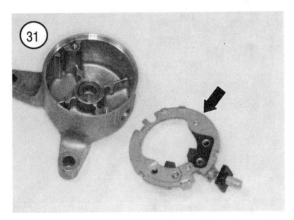

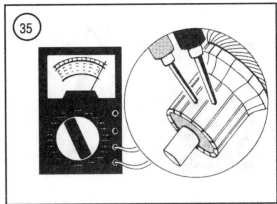

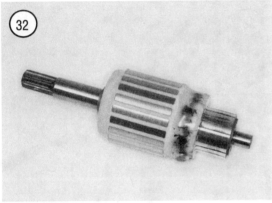

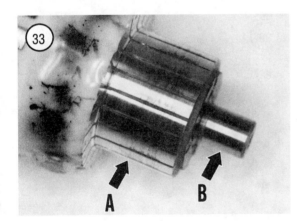

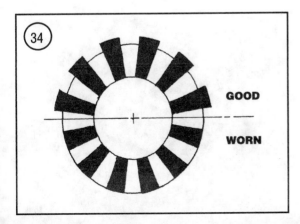

11. Inspect all starter components as described in this chapter.

Inspection

The only parts that are available separately are the brushes, the washer, the O-rings and the case bolts. If any other part of the starter motor is faulty, replace the starter motor as an assembly.

1. Inspect each brush for abnormal wear. Replace as necessary.

2. Inspect the commutator (A, **Figure 33**). The mica in a good commutator is below the surface of the copper bars. On a worn commutator, the mica and copper bars may be worn to the same level (**Figure 34**). If necessary, have the commutator serviced by a dealership or electrical repair shop.

3. Check the entire length of the armature coil for straightness or heat damage. Rotate the ball bearing and check for roughness or binding.

4. Inspect the armature shaft where it rides in the bushing (B, **Figure 33**). Check for wear, burrs or other damage. If worn or damaged, replace the starter assembly.

5. Inspect the commutator copper bars (A, **Figure 33**) for discoloration. If a pair of bars are discolored, grounded armature coils are indicated.

6. Use an ohmmeter and perform the following:
    a. Check for continuity between the commutator bars (**Figure 35**); there should be continuity between pairs of bars.
    b. Check for continuity between the commutator bars and the shaft (**Figure 36**); there should be no continuity (infinite resistance).
    c. If the unit fails either of these tests, replace the starter assembly. The armature cannot be replaced individually.

7. Use an ohmmeter and perform the following:
    a. Check for continuity between the starter cable terminal (**Figure 37**) and the end cap. There should be no continuity.

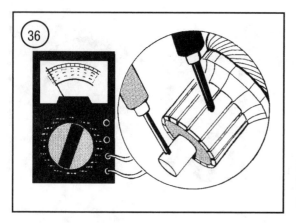

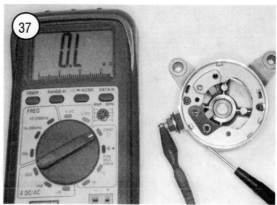

b. Check for continuity between the starter cable terminal and the positive brushes (**Figure 38**); there should be continuity (indicated resistance).

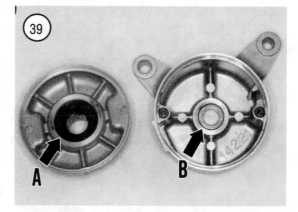

8. Inspect the seal and needle bearing (A, **Figure 39**) in the drive cover. Inspect the seal for wear, hardness or damage. The bearing must turn smoothly without excessive play or noise. Neither the seal or bearing is available separate from the drive cover.

9. Inspect the bushing (B, **Figure 39**) in the end cap for wear or damage. The bushing cannot be replaced if damaged. The starter must be replaced as this is not a separate part.

10. Inspect the magnets within the case. If they have picked up any small metal particles, remove the particles prior to reassembly. Then inspect for loose, chipped or damaged magnets.

11. Inspect the brush holder and springs for wear or damage. Replace if necessary.

12. Inspect the end cover and drive cover for wear or damage. If either is damaged, replace the starter.

13. Check the throughbolts for thread damage; clean up with the appropriate size metric die. Inspect the O-rings for hardness, deterioration or damage. Replace as necessary.

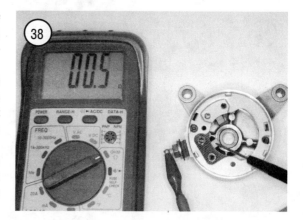

Assembly

NOTE
In the next step, reinstall all parts in the same order as noted during removal. This is essential to insulate the positive (+) brush plate assembly from the case.

1. Install the insulator spacer (7, **Figure 23**) onto the positive terminal stud and bottom the spacer on the stud.

2. Install the brush holder assembly into the end cap. Align the notches (**Figure 40**) on the brush holder plate with the projections on the end cap.

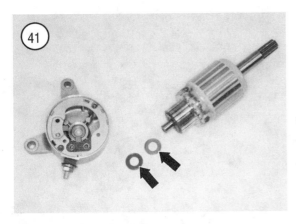

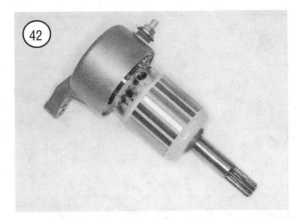

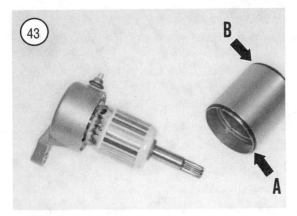

3. Install the nut, washers, bushing and O-ring (**Figure 30**) securing the brush holder assembly to the end cap. Refer to notes made during disassembly and **Figure 23** for proper sequence of parts.

4. Install the washers (**Figure 41**) onto the armature.

5. Hold the armature upright and insert the commutator end of the armature into the end cap (**Figure 42**). Do not damage the brushes during this step. Hold hack the brushes as the commutator passes by them, then ensure both brushes are in correct contact with the armature. Push the assembly down until it bottoms.

6. Keep the assembly in this position and slowly rotate the armature coil assembly to make sure it rotates freely with the brushes in place.

NOTE
Hold the armature and end cap together during the next step. The magnets in the case will try to pull the armature out of the end cap and disengage the brushes.

7. Install the O-ring (A, **Figure 43**) into the recess at the end of the case.

8. Install the case onto the armature and end cap. Align the marks on the case and end cap (**Figure 44**).

9. Install the washers (**Figure 26**) onto the armature shaft.

10. Install the tab washer (**Figure 45**) into the drive cover so the tabs on the washer fit into the recesses in the cover.

11. Install an O-ring (B, **Figure 43**) onto the case recess.

12. Install the drive cover onto the case. Align the marks on the case and cover (**Figure 46**).

13. Install the O-rings (**Figure 47**) onto the through-bolts and apply a light coat of clean engine oil to them.

14. Install the throughbolts and tighten securely. After the throughbolts are tightened, check the seams to ensure the end covers are pulled tight against the case.

STARTER MOTOR (2010-2011 MODELS)

Removal/Installation

1. Disconnect the negative battery cable as described in this chapter.

2. Pull back the rubber boot from the starter motor electrical connector.

3. Remove the starter motor cable retaining nut (A, **Figure 48**) and disconnect the starter motor cable from the starter.

4. Remove the two bolts (B, **Figure 48**) securing the starter to the crankcase.

5. Remove the starter.

6. Thoroughly clean the starter mounting pads on the crankcase and the mounting lugs on the starter motor.

7. Inspect the O-ring (A, **Figure 49**) on the drive end of the starter motor for hardness or deterioration. Replace the O-ring if necessary. Apply clean engine oil to the O-ring before installing the starter motor.

8. Install the starter motor by reversing the removal procedure while noting the following:

    a. Place the starter motor cable clamp on the lower starter motor bolt.

    b. Tighten the starter motor mounting bolts to 10 N•m (88 in.-lb.).

    c. Tighten the starter motor cable retaining nut to 6 N•m (53 in.-lb.).

Disassembly

Refer to **Figure 50** while performing this procedure.

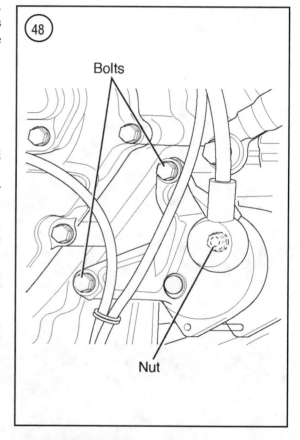

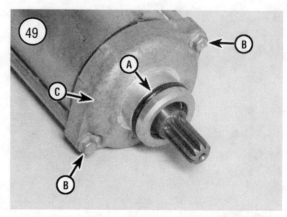

⑤⓪ **STARTER MOTOR (2010-2011 MODELS)**

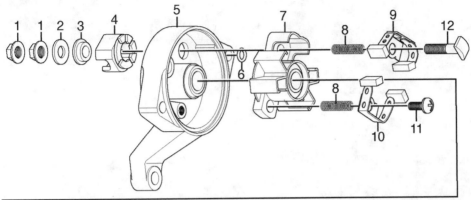

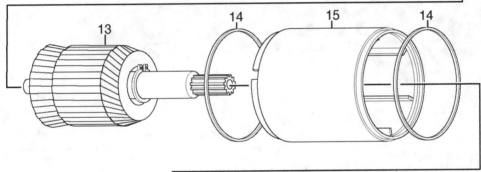

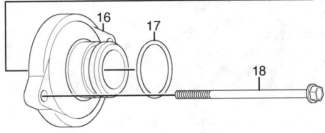

1. Nuts
2. Washer
3. Insulated washer
4. Terminal stopper
5. Rear cover
6. O-ring
7. Brush holder plate assembly
8. Springs
9. Positive brushes
10. Negative brushes
11. Screw
12. Terminal bolt
13. Armature
14. O-ring
15. Case
16. Front cover
17. O-ring
18. Throughbolt

9

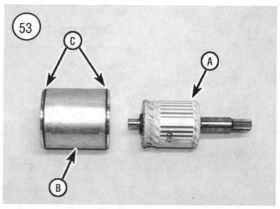

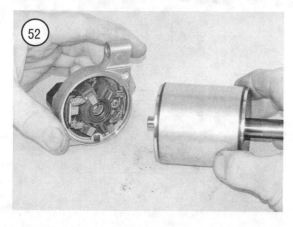

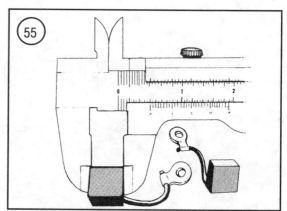

1. Locate the alignment marks on the case and front end cover (**Figure 51**). If necessary, highlight the existing marks or scribe new marks.

2. Remove the two case bolts (B, **Figure 49**).

3. Remove the front cover (C, **Figure 49**).

4. Remove the rear cover (**Figure 52**).

5. Separate the armature (A, **Figure 53**) from the case (B).

6. Remove the O-rings on the case (C, **Figure 53**).

7. Clean all grease, dirt and carbon from the armature, case and end covers.

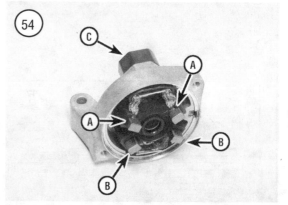

> *CAUTION*
> *Do not immerse the armature in solvent as the insulation may be damaged. Wipe the windings with a cloth lightly moistened with solvent.*

Inspection

1. Note the location of the positive brushes (A, **Figure 54**) and negative brushes (B).

2. Use an ohmmeter and perform the following:

   a. Check for continuity between the starter cable terminal (C, **Figure 54**) and the positive brushes (A); there should be continuity.

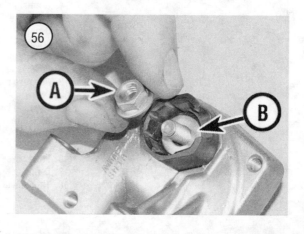

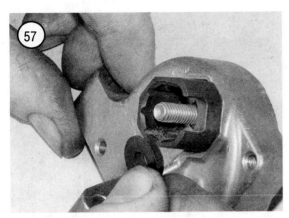

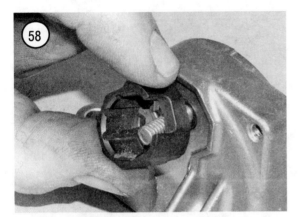

b. Check for continuity between the positive brushes (A, **Figure 54**) and the rear cover; there should be no continuity.

c. Check for continuity between the positive brushes (A, **Figure 54**) and the negative brushes (B); there should be no continuity.

d. Check for continuity between the starter cable terminal and the rear cover; there should be no continuity.

3. Measure the length of each brush with a vernier caliper (**Figure 55**). If the length is less than the service limit in **Table 1**, replace the brushes.

4. To replace the positive brush set, proceed as follows:

   a. Remove the nut (A, **Figure 56**) and washer (B).

   b. Remove the insulating washer (**Figure 57**).

   c. Remove the terminal stopper (**Figure 58**).

   d. Remove the O-ring (**Figure 59**).

   e. Remove the terminal bolt and brush set (**Figure 60**).

   f. Remove the springs from the brush holder (**Figure 61**).

   g. Reverse the removal steps for installation. Make sure the O-ring is installed on the terminal bolt (**Figure 59**). Install the insulating washer (**Figure 57**) so the small ID is toward the terminal stopper.

5. To replace the negative brush set, proceed as follows:

   a. Remove the screw and washer and the brush set (**Figure 62**).

   b. Remove the springs (**Figure 63**).

   c. Remove the brush holder (**Figure 64**).

6. Inspect the commutator (**Figure 65**). The mica in a good commutator is below the surface of the copper bars. On a worn commutator the mica and copper bars may be worn to the same level. Clean any foreign material from between the commutator bars. If necessary, have the commutator serviced by a dealer or electrical repair shop.

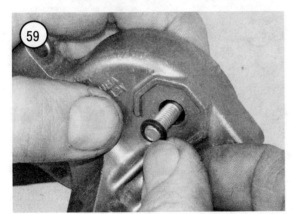

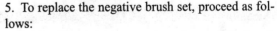

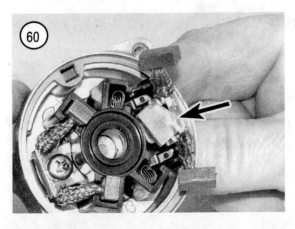

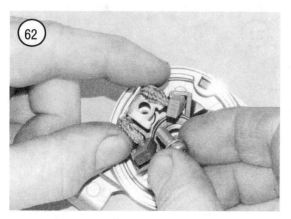

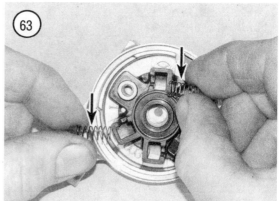

7. Inspect the commutator copper bars for discoloration. If a pair of bars are discolored, the armature coils are grounded.

8. Use an ohmmeter and perform the following:

    a. Check for continuity between the commutator bars (**Figure 66**); there should be continuity (indicated resistance) between pairs of bars.

    b. Check for continuity between the commutator bars and the shaft (**Figure 67**); there should be no continuity (infinite resistance).

    c. If the unit fails either of these tests, replace the starter. The armature cannot be replaced individually.

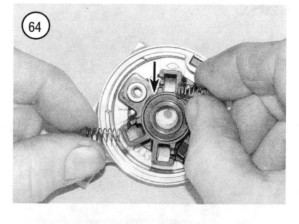

9. Inspect the oil seal and bearing in the front cover (**Figure 68**) for wear or damage. If either is damaged, replace the starter.

10. Inspect the bushing in the rear cover (**Figure 69**) for wear or damage. If it is damaged, replace the starter.

11. Inspect the case assembly for wear or damage. Make sure the field magnets are bonded securely in place. If there is damage, or if any field magnets are loose, replace the case.

12. Inspect the armature (**Figure 70**) for damage or wear. Inspect the gear splines on the armature shaft for wear or damage. If the armature is damaged, replace the starter motor.

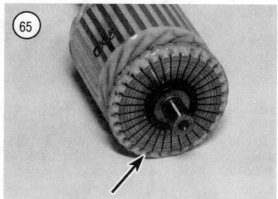

Assembly

1. Install the two O-rings onto the case.

2. Carefully insert the armature into the rear cover.

3. Install the case. Position the case so the notch in the case (A, **Figure 71**) engages the tab (B) in the rim of the rear cover.

4. Install the front cover onto the case. Align the mark on the case and front cover.

NOTE
If the correct alignment marks are unknown, position the front cover so the

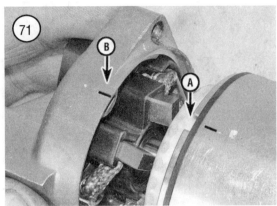

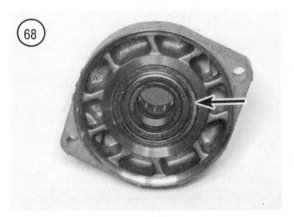

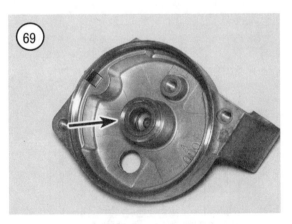

bolt holes align with the rear cover bolt holes.

5. Install the bolts and tighten securely.

6. Replace the front cover O-ring seal (A, **Figure 49**) if deteriorated or damaged.

STARTER RELAY

Removal/Installation

1. Remove the seat as described in Chapter Fifteen.

2. Disconnect the negative battery cable as described in this chapter.

3. Lift up the cover (**Figure 72**) from the starter relay.

4. Disconnect the starter relay primary connector (A, **Figure 73**).

5. Disconnect the starter motor lead (B, **Figure 73**) and the positive battery cable (C) from the starter relay.

6. Remove the starter relay.

7. Install by reversing the removal steps. Make sure the electrical connectors are tight.

Testing

1. Remove the starter relay as described in this chapter.

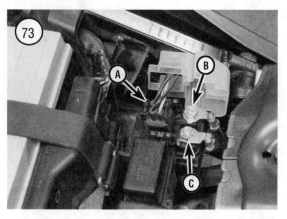

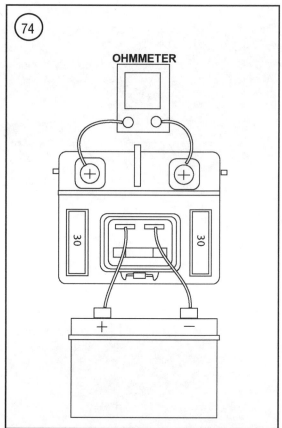

2. Connect a 12-volt battery and ohmmeter to the starter relay terminals (**Figure 74**). When the battery is connected, there should be continuity (low to zero ohms) across the two terminals. When the battery is disconnected, there should be no continuity (infinity).

3. Connect an ohmmeter to the starter relay terminals (**Figure 75**) and measure the resistance between the terminals. The resistance should be 3-6 ohms.

4. If the starter relay did not test correctly, replace the relay and retest.

SIDESTAND SWITCH

Testing

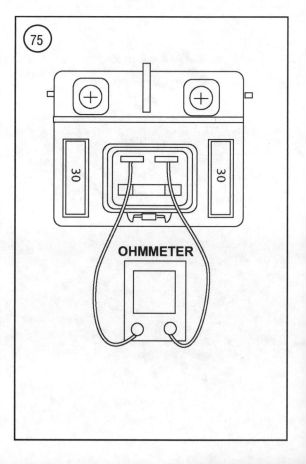

A multicircuit tester (Suzuki part No. 09900-25008 or equivalent) is needed to perform this test.

1. Support the motorcycle so the sidestand can move freely.

2. Remove the left frame cover as described in Chapter Fifteen.

3. Disconnect the 2-pin sidestand switch connector (**Figure 76**).

4. Turn the test knob on the tester to diode.

5. Connect the tester positive probe to the green terminal in the switch end of the connector; connect the negative test probe to the black/white terminal.

6. Raise the sidestand and read the voltage on the meter.

7. Lower the sidestand and read the voltage on the meter.

8. If either reading is outside the sidestand test voltage range specified in **Table 1**, replace the sidestand switch.

9. If the sidestand switch test cannot be performed, test the continuity of the sidestand switch by performing the following:

10. Connect an ohmmeter to the terminals in the switch end of the connector.

9. Make sure the electrical connectors are free of corrosion and are tight.
10. Install the left frame cover.
11. Reconnect the negative battery cable.

GEAR POSITION SWITCH

Continuity Test

1. Remove the left frame cover as described in Chapter Fifteen.
2. Disconnect the negative battery cable as described in this chapter.
3. Disconnect the three-wire gear position switch connector (**Figure 78**).
4. Shift the transmission into neutral.
5. Connect an ohmmeter to the blue wire and black/white wire terminals in the switch end of the electrical connector. Check that there is continuity.
6. Shift the transmission into any gear. There should be no continuity.
7. If the switch fails these tests, replace the switch.

11. Raise the sidestand. The meter should indicate continuity.
12. Lower the sidestand. The meter should indicate no continuity.
13. If the switch fails these tests, it is faulty and must be replaced.
14. Reconnect the sidestand switch connector.
15. Install the left frame cover.

Removal/Installation

1. Support the motorcycle so the sidestand can move freely.
2. Disconnect the negative battery cable as described in this chapter.
3. Remove the left frame cover as described in Chapter Fifteen.
4. Disconnect the 2-pin sidestand switch connector (**Figure 76**).
5. Lower the sidestand.
6. Remove the sidestand switch bolts and remove the switch (**Figure 77**). Note how the switch wiring is routed through the motorcycle.
7. Install a new switch. Tighten the mounting bolts securely.
8. Raise the sidestand and make sure the switch plunger moves in.

Voltage Test

1. Support the motorcycle so the sidestand can move freely.
2. Make sure the ignition switch is off.
3. Remove the left frame cover as described in Chapter Fifteen.
4. Locate the three-wire gear position switch connector (**Figure 78**). Do not disconnect the connector.
5. Use back-probe pins as follows. Connect a voltmeter positive test probe to the pink terminal in the harness end of the gear position switch connector. Connect the negative test probe to the black/white wire terminal.
6. Raise the sidestand and turn the ignition switch on.

7. Read the voltage with the transmission in neutral.

8. Shift the transmission into each gear, first through sixth, and read the voltage. It should equal or exceed the specified gear position switch voltage (**Table 1**) in every gear except neutral.

Removal/Installation

The gear position switch is mounted on the left crankcase below the drive sprocket.

1. Remove the drive sprocket cover as described in Chapter Eleven.

2. Remove the left frame cover as described in Chapter Fifteen.

3. Disconnect the negative battery cable as described in this chapter.

4. Disconnect the three-wire gear position switch connector (**Figure 78**).

5. Remove the mounting screws and the gear position switch (**Figure 79**) from the crankcase.

6. Remove the spring-loaded contact pins (A, **Figure 80**) and the O-ring (B).

7. Inspect the pins and springs for damage. Replace if necessary.

8. Installation is the reverse of the preceding removal steps while noting the following:

    a. Before installation, clean the switch contacts.

    b. Install a *new* O-ring. Lubricate the O-ring with Suzuki Super Grease A or equivalent.

    c. Install the switch and tighten the mounting screws securely.

    d. Check switch operation.

TURN SIGNAL/SIDESTAND RELAY

The turn signal relay/sidestand relay consists of the turn signal relay, sidestand relay and the diode as a unit assembly.

Removal/Installation

1. Remove the seat.

2. Remove the relay (**Figure 81**) from the mounting base.

3. Install the relay by reversing the removal steps. Make sure the relay is fully seated.

Sidestand Relay Testing

1. Remove the relay as described in this section.

2. Apply 12 volts to the relay by connecting the negative terminal of the battery to the C terminal in the relay assembly. Connect the positive battery terminal to the D terminal (**Figure 82**).

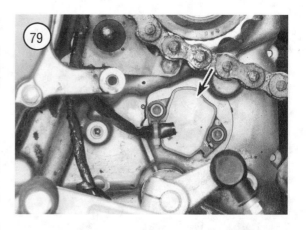

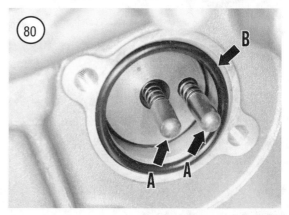

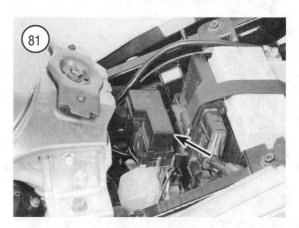

3. Use an ohmmeter to check the continuity between terminals D and E on the relay assembly. There should be continuity.

4. Replace the relay assembly if there is no continuity.

Turn Signal Relay Testing

If the turn signal light does not light, first look for a defective bulb. If the bulbs are good, check the turn signal switch as described in this chapter and all electrical connections within the turn signal circuit.

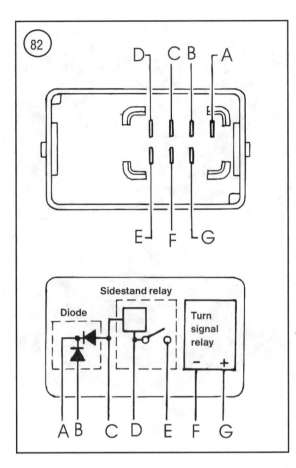

82

85

If all of these components test good, replace the relay unit.

Diode Testing

A multicircuit tester (Suzuki part No. 09900-25008 or equivalent) is needed to perform this test.
1. Remove the relay unit as described in this section.
2. Set the tester to diode test.
3. Connect the tester probes to the terminals indicated in **Figure 83**. Also see **Figure 82**.
4. Replace the relay assembly if any measurement is outside the specified range.

9

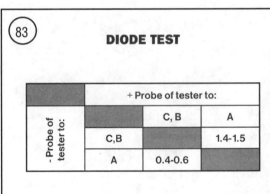

83

DIODE TEST

	+ Probe of tester to:		
		C, B	A
- Probe of tester to:	C,B		1.4-1.5
	A	0.4-0.6	

LIGHTING SYSTEM

Headlight Bulb Replacement

> *WARNING*
> *If the headlight has just burned out or has just been turned off, it will be **hot**! Do not touch the bulb. Wait for the bulb to cool before removing it.*

> *CAUTION*
> *All models are equipped with quartz-halogen bulbs. Do not touch the bulb glass (**Figure 84**) with bare fingers because traces of oil on the bulb will drastically reduce the life of the bulb. Clean any traces of oil or other chemicals from the bulb with a cloth moistened in alcohol or lacquer thinner.*

1. Disconnect the electrical connector (A, **Figure 85**) by pulling it *straight out* from the back of the headlight assembly.
2. Pull the tab and remove the rubber dust cover (B, **Figure 85**). Check the rubber cover for tears or deterioration; replace it if necessary.

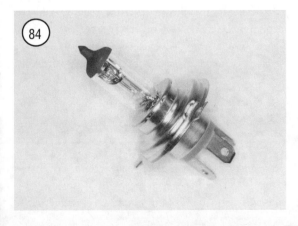

84

3. Unhook the light bulb retaining clip (**Figure 86**) and pivot it out of the way.

4. Remove the defective bulb.

5. Align the three tangs on the new bulb with the notches in the headlight housing and install the bulb.

6. Hook the retaining clip (**Figure 86**) over the bulb to hold it in place.

7. Install the rubber cover so the TOP mark is positioned at the top of the headlight assembly. Make sure the cover is correctly seated against the lens assembly and the bulb.

8. Correctly align the electrical connector terminals with the bulb and connect it to the bulb. Push it *straight* on until it bottoms on the bulb and the rubber cover.

9. Check headlight operation.

Headlight Lens/Housing Removal/Installation

1. Remove the cowling as described in Chapter Fifteen.

2. Remove the headlight housing retaining nuts (**Figure 87**) and separate the headlight housing assembly from the cowling.

3. Inspect the headlight lens/housing for damage and internal moisture. If damaged, replace the entire unit. No replacement parts available.

4. After installation, adjust the headlights as described below.

Headlight Adjustment

Adjust the headlight horizontally and vertically according to local Department of Motor Vehicle regulations.

> *NOTE*
> *There are four adjustment screws, two for each headlight.*

To adjust the headlight horizontally, turn the horizontal adjustment screw (A, **Figure 88**) in either direction until the aim is correct.

For vertical adjustment, turn the vertical adjustment screw (B, **Figure 88**) in either direction until the aim is correct.

Taillight/Brake Light Bulb Replacement

1. Remove the seat as described in Chapter Fifteen.

2. Push the defective bulb (**Figure 89**) into the socket, turn it counterclockwise and remove it.

3. Install a new bulb.

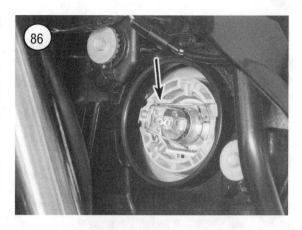

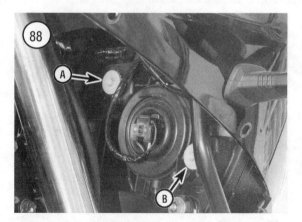

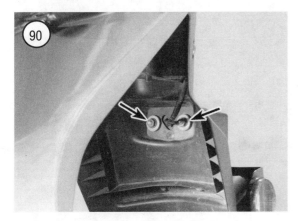

License Plate Light Bulb Replacement

1. Remove the nuts (**Figure 90**) securing the light housing. Remove the light housing from the fender.
2. Extract the defective bulb from the socket.
3. Install a new bulb.

Front and Rear Turn Signal Bulb Replacement

1. Remove the screw (**Figure 91**) securing the lens to the housing. Remove the lens.
2. Push the defective bulb into the socket, turn it counterclockwise and remove it.
3. Install a new bulb.
4. Check the turn signal light operation.
5. Install the lens into the housing.

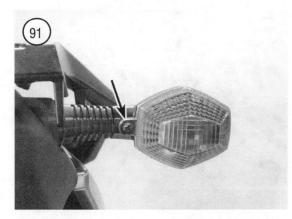

Combination Meter

All illumination on the combination meter is provided by non-replaceable electrical devices. Any malfunctions require replacement of the combination meter. Refer to combination meter replacement in this chapter.

SWITCHES

Left Handlebar Switch Assembly

The left handlebar switch assembly houses the headlight dimmer switch (A, **Figure 92**), turn signal switch (B), horn button (C), hazard warning switch (D) and passing switch (E). The switches can be checked for continuity using an ohmmeter connected to the appropriate color-coded wires in the connector plug. Refer to *Continuity Testing Guidelines* in this chapter for the test procedure.

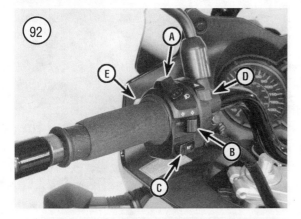

NOTE
The switches mounted in the left handlebar switch housing are not available separately. If one switch is damaged, the housing must be replaced as an assembly.

Replacement

1. Remove the air box as described in Chapter Eight.
2. Remove the left handlebar switch screws and separate the switch halves.
3. Disconnect the switch connectors (**Figure 93**).
4. Detach any wire clamps.
5. Remove the switch assembly. The mounting pad may remain on the handlebar (**Figure 94**).

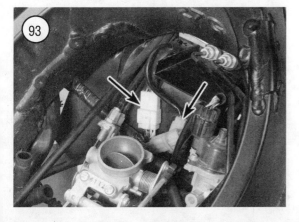

6. Reverse the removal procedure to install the switch housing. Install the mounting pad so the pin fits into the hole in the handlebar (**Figure 94**).

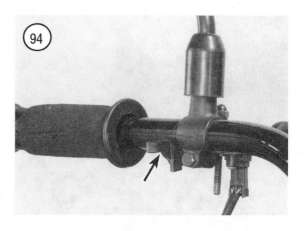

Right Handlebar Switch Assembly

The right handlebar switch assembly houses the engine stop switch (A, **Figure 95**) and starter button (B). The switches can be checked for continuity using an ohmmeter connected to the appropriate color-coded wires in the connector plug. Refer to *Continuity Testing Guidelines* in this chapter for the test procedure.

> *NOTE*
> *The switches mounted in the right handlebar switch housing are not available separately. If one switch is damaged, the housing must be replaced as an assembly.*

Replacement–2004-2006 Models

1. Remove the air box as described in Chapter Eight.
2. Disconnect the switch connector (**Figure 96**).
3. Remove the right handlebar switch screws and separate the switch halves.
4. Detach any wire clamps.
5. Reverse the removal procedure to install the switch housing. Note the following:
   a. Make sure the pin in the switch housing fits into the hole in the handlebar.
   b. Tighten the right handlebar switch housing screws securely.

Replacement–2007-2011 models

1. Remove the air box as described in Chapter Eight.
2. Disconnect the switch connector (**Figure 96**).
3. Disconnect the two-wire connector (C, **Figure 95**) from the front brake light switch.
4. Detach any wire clamps.
5. At the throttle grip, loosen the throttle cable locknut (A, **Figure 97**) and turn the adjust nut (B) all the way into the switch assembly to allow maximum slack in both cables. Perform this on both the throttle opening (C, **Figure 97**) and closing (D) cables.
6. Remove the right handlebar switch screws and separate the switch halves.
7. Disconnect the throttle opening cable, then the throttle closing cable from the throttle grip.
8. Remove the switch assembly. The mounting pad may remain on the handlebar (**Figure 98**).

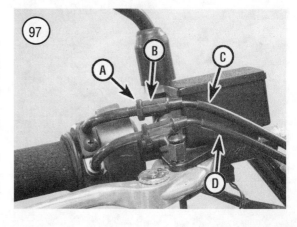

9. Install by reversing the preceding removal steps while noting the following:

   a. Connect the throttle cables to the throttle grip and switch housing.

   b. Install the mounting pad so the pin fits into the hole in the handlebar (**Figure 94**).

   c. Operate the throttle and make sure the linkage operates correctly without binding. If operation is incorrect or if there is binding, carefully check that the cables are attached correctly and there are no tight bends in the cable.

   d. Adjust the throttle cables as described in Chapter Three.

Ignition Switch
Replacement

> *NOTE*
> *A tamper-resistant T-40 Torx bit is required to remove and install the ignition switch retaining bolts.*

1. Remove the front side covers as described in Chapter Fifteen.

2. Disconnect the negative battery cable as described in this chapter.

3. Remove the air box as described in Chapter Eight.

4. Disconnect the ignition switch connector (**Figure 99**).

5. Remove the Torx bolt (**Figure 100**) on each side securing the ignition switch to the bottom of the upper steering stem bracket.

6. Install a new ignition switch and tighten the Torx bolts securely.

7. Make sure the electrical connectors are free of corrosion and secure.

Oil Pressure Switch

Testing

   When the ignition switch is turned on, the low oil pressure symbol in the combination meter should flicker and the indicator light should turn on. As soon as the engine starts, the symbol and the indicator light should go out. If there is a problem within the oil pressure system or if the oil pressure drops under the normal operating pressure range, the symbol flickers and indicator light turns on and stays on.

   If the warning light is not operating correctly or does not come on when the ignition switch is in the ON position (engine not running), perform the following test. The oil pressure switch (**Figure 101**) is

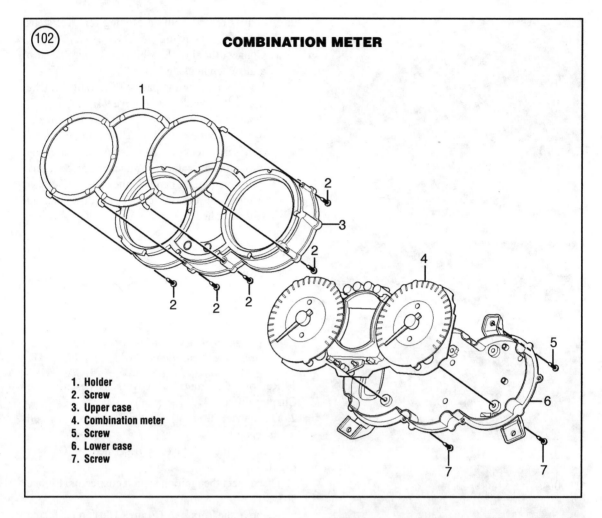

COMBINATION METER

1. Holder
2. Screw
3. Upper case
4. Combination meter
5. Screw
6. Lower case
7. Screw

mounted on the bottom of the engine adjacent to the oil filter.

1. Check the engine oil level as described in Chapter Three. Add oil if necessary.
2. Disconnect the electrical connector from the oil pressure switch (**Figure 101**).
3. Turn the ignition switch on.
4. Connect a jumper wire from the electrical connector to ground. The oil pressure warning light should come on.
5. If the light does not come on, check the wiring and connectors. If good, replace the combination meter.
6. If the combination meter and wiring are good, replace the switch as described below.

Replacement

The oil pressure switch (**Figure 101**) is mounted on the bottom of the engine adjacent to the oil filter.

1. Disconnect the electrical connector from the oil pressure switch.
2. Unscrew and remove the oil pressure switch from the crankcase.

3. Installation is the reverse of the preceding steps. Note the following:
   a. Apply a light coat of Suzuki Bond 1207B or equivalent sealant to the switch threads before installation.
   b. Install the switch and tighten to 14 N•m (124 in.-lb.).

METER ASSEMBLY

The meter assembly consists of the combination meter, cover and housing (**Figure 102**). The combination meter is a single integrated unit. The individual gauges and LEDs cannot be replaced. If any component fails, replace the complete combination meter unit.

Removal/Installation

1. Remove the instrument panel as described in Chapter Fifteen.
2. Remove the screws (**Figure 103**) securing the meter assembly to the instrument panel.

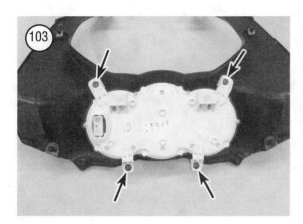

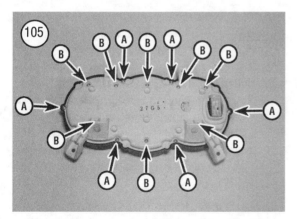

3. Separate the meter assembly (**Figure 104**) from the instrument panel.

4. To remove the upper case, remove the retaining screws (A, **Figure 105**).

5. The combination meter is now exposed (**Figure 106**).

6. To separate the combination meter from the lower case, remove the retaining screws (B, **Figure 105**).

7. Reverse the removal procedure to install the combination meter.

Resetting the Tachometer

Whenever the ignition switch is turned on, the tachometer needle swings to its maximum setting and then returns to zero. This is part of the self-check operation. If the needle does not return to zero, reset the tachometer by performing the following.

1. Press and hold the meter adjust button (**Figure 107**).

2. Turn the ignition switch on.

NOTE
The adjust button must be pressed twice within one second after it has been released.

3. Three to five seconds after turning on the ignition switch, release the adjust button, and quickly press it twice. The entire resetting process should be completed within 10 seconds after turning on the ignition switch.

4. The tachometer needle should return to zero. If the needle does not return to zero, replace the meter assembly.

Odometer/Tripmeter

If the odometer or tripmeter displays — the combination meter is faulty. The combination meter must be replaced to restore the odometer or tripmeter function.

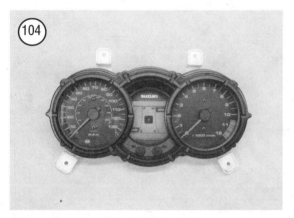

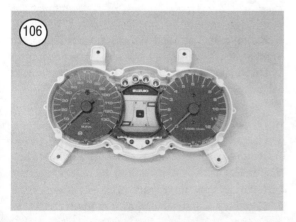

Coolant Temperature Meter Test

Before performing this test, check the engine coolant temperature sensor by performing the ECT sensor test described in Chapter Eight. Replace the sensor if it is out of specification. If the meter is still not working, perform the following test.

1. Remove the right frame cover as described in Chapter Fifteen.

> *CAUTION*
> *The ignition switch must be off whenever the 2-pin connector is disconnected from or connected to the engine coolant temperature sensor. Electronic parts can be damaged if the power is on when this connector is removed or installed.*

2. Disconnect the 2-pin connector (**Figure 108**) from the ECT sensor.
3. Connect a variable resistor between the two terminals in the harness end of the engine coolant temperature sensor connector (note the resistance values in Table 1.
4. Turn the ignition switch on.
5. Set the resistor to each resistance listed in Table 1 and check the meter. The coolant temperature display should appear as listed in **Table 1**.
6. Replace the combination meter if it fails this test.

Fuel Level Meter Testing

The fuel level meter changes according to the resistance of the fuel level sender in the fuel tank. To isolate a meter problem, perform the following tests.
1. Raise the fuel tank as described in Chapter Eight.
2. Disconnect the fuel pump connector (**Figure 109**).
3. Refer to **Table 1** and connect a resistor of the listed value to the yellow/black wire and black/white wire terminals in the harness end of the fuel pump connector.
4. Turn the ignition switch on. After approximately 40 seconds the fuel level meter should turn on and indicated fuel level should correspond to the resistor value specified in **Table 1**. Resistance values greater than 167 ohms will cause the lowest box to flicker, which indicates a low fuel condition.
5A. If the fuel level meter does not function as described above, replace the combination meter.
5B. If the fuel level meter functions properly, check the fuel level sending unit in the fuel tank as follows:
   a. Remove the fuel pump as described in Chapter Eight.

   b. Connect an ohmmeter to the yellow/black wire and black/white wire terminals in the fuel pump connector.
   c. Move the float to both the full and empty positions.
   d. Record the ohmmeter readings in both positions and compare to the specifications listed in **Table 1**.
   e. If the readings are not within specification, replace the fuel level meter sending unit.

SPEEDOMETER SENSOR

Testing

1. Remove the air box as described in Chapter Eight.
2. Disconnect the three-wire speedometer sensor connector (**Figure 110**).
3. Support the front of the motorcycle so the front wheel can be rotated.
4. Connect four 1.5 volt batteries in series to the center connector terminal as shown in **Figure 111**.
5. Connect a 1 K ohm resistor to the outer connector terminals as shown in **Figure 111**.
6. Connect a voltmeter as shown in **Figure 111**.

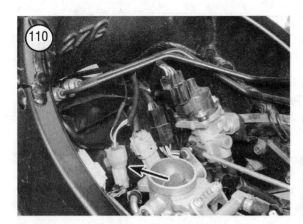

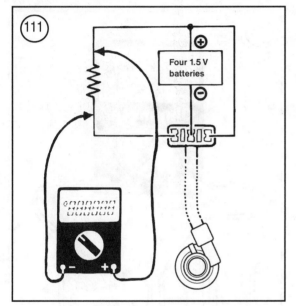

2. Disconnect the electrical connectors (A, **Figure 112**) from the horn.
3. Connect a 12 volt battery to the horn terminals. The horn should sound.
4. If it does not, replace the horn.

Removal/Installation

1. Disconnect the negative battery cable as described in this chapter.
2. Disconnect the electrical connectors (A, **Figure 112**) from the horn.
3. Remove the bolt (B, **Figure 112**) securing the horn bracket to the radiator.

> *NOTE*
> *Due to the confined space when accessing the mounting bolt, it may be necessary to remove the radiator as described in Chapter Ten.*

4. Remove the horn and bracket. The horn and bracket are available only as a unit.
5. Install by reversing the preceding removal steps while noting the following:
   a. Make sure the electrical connectors are free of corrosion and are tight.
   b. Test the horn to make sure it operates correctly.

7. Rotate the front wheel while observing the voltmeter. The voltage reading should be between 0 to 6 volts. If otherwise, replace the speed sensor.

Removal/Installation

1. Remove the air box as described in Chapter Eight.
2. Disconnect the three-wire speedometer sensor connector (**Figure 110**).
3. Remove the front wheel as described in Chapter Ten.
4. Reverse the removal procedure for installation.

HORN

Testing

1. Disconnect the negative battery cable as described in this chapter.

COOLING SYSTEM

Fan Motor Testing

Use an ammeter and a fully charged 12-volt battery for this test.
1. Remove the right cowling as described in Chapter Fifteen.
2. Disconnect the fan motor electrical connector (**Figure 113**) on the radiator shroud.

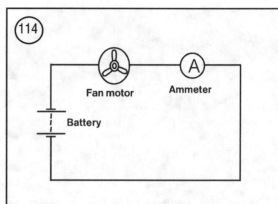

3. Use jumper wires to connect the test battery to the motor lead of the fan motor connector. Also connect an ammeter in line as shown in **Figure 114**.

4. The fan should operate when power is applied. Replace the fan assembly if the motor does not operate.

5. With the motor running at full speed, monitor the ammeter and note the load current. Replace the fan assembly if the load current exceeds 5 amps.

Cooling Fan Switch Testing

The cooling fan switch controls the radiator fan according to the engine coolant temperature using a thermostatic element in the switch. Refer also to Chapter Ten.

1. Remove the fan switch as described in Chapter Ten.

2. Fill a beaker or pan with water, and place it on a stove or hot plate.

3. Position the fan switch so that the temperature sensing tip and the threaded portion of the body are submerged as shown in **Figure 115**.

> *NOTE*
> *The thermometer and the fan switch must not touch the container sides or bottom. If either does, it will result in a false reading.*

4. Place a thermometer in the pan of water (use a cooking thermometer that is rated higher than the test temperature).

5. Attach ohmmeter leads to the fan switch terminals. Check the resistance as follows:

   a. Gradually heat the water.

   b. When the temperature reaches 208° F (98° C), the meter should read continuity (switch on).

   c. Gradually reduce the heat.

   d. When the temperature lowers to approximately 198° F (92° C), the meter should not read continuity (switch off).

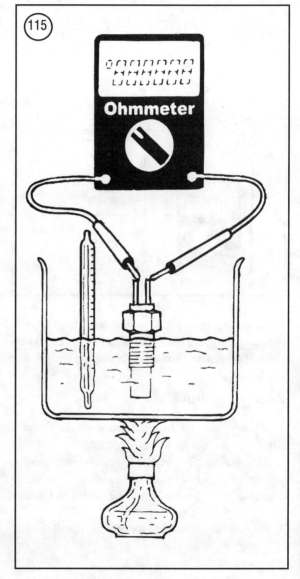

6. Replace the fan switch if it failed to operate as described in Step 5.

7. If the fan switch tests good, install the fan switch onto the radiator as described in Chapter Ten.

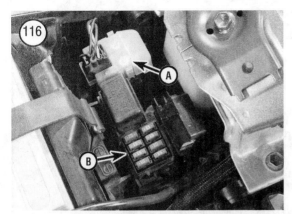

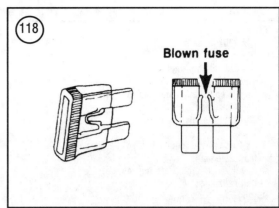

Blown fuse

FUSES

Fuse Replacement

All models are equipped with a single 30-amp main fuse that is located in the starter relay housing (A, **Figure 116**). The remaining fuses (except ABS fuses) are located in the auxiliary fuse box (B) located under the seat.

On ABS models, fuses for the ABS motor relay and valve relay are located under the seat (**Figure 117**).

If there is an electrical failure, first check for a blown fuse. A blown fuse will have a break in the element (**Figure 118**).

Whenever the fuse blows, determine the reason for the failure before replacing the fuse. Usually, the trouble is a short circuit in the wiring. This may be caused by worn-through insulation or a disconnected wire shorted to ground. Check by testing the circuit the fuse protects.

When installing a fuse, push it in all the way until it bottoms.

The fuse box, starter relay housing and ABS fuse holders have slots available to carry spare fuses.

WIRING DIAGRAMS

The wiring diagrams are located at the end of this manual

TABLES 1-3 CAN BE FOUND ON THE FOLLOWING PAGES

Table 1 ELECTRICAL SYSTEM SPECIFICATIONS

Alternator	
2004-2007 models	
Type	Three-phase AC
No-load voltage (engine cold)	60 volts (AC) @ 5000 rpm
Maximum output	375 watts @ 5000 rpm
Regulated voltage (charging voltage)	14.0-15.5 volts @ 5000 rpm
Coil resistance	0.2-0.7 ohms
2008-2011 models	
Type	Three-phase AC
No-load voltage (engine cold)	65 volts (AC) @ 5000 rpm
Maximum output	400 watts @ 5000 rpm
Regulated voltage (charging voltage)	14.0-15.5 volts @ 5000 rpm
Coil resistance	0.2-0.8 ohms
Battery	
Type	YT12X-BS Maintenance free (sealed)
Capacity	12 volt 10 amp-hour
Charging	6 amp for 1 hour or 1.4 amp for 5-10 hours
	(if test reading below 12.0 volts)
Cooling fan current (max.)	5 amps
Engine coolant temperature indicator	
Resistor	
0.111 k ohms or less	5 bars and coolant symbol
0.116 k ohms or less	5 bars
0.140-0.116 k ohms	4 bars
0.188-0.140 k ohms	3 bars
0.587-0.188 k ohms	2 bars
1.148-0.587 k ohms	1 bar
Greater than 1.148 k ohms	no bars
Fuel level meter	
2004-2006 models	
Resistor	
6.5 ohms or less	5 bars
6.5-26 ohms	4 bars
26-50 ohms	3 bars
50-87.5 ohms	2 bars
87.5-167 ohms	1 bar
Greater than 167 ohms	flicker
2007-2011 models	
Resistor	
9 ohms or less	5 bars
9-26 ohms	4 bars
26-50 ohms	3 bars
50-87.5 ohms	2 bars
87.5-167 ohms	1 bar
Greater than 167 ohms	flicker
Fuel level meter sending unit	
Empty	Approximately 182 ohms
Full	Approximately 4 ohms
Gear position switch voltage*	
1 st gear	1.36 V
2 nd gear	1.77 V
3 rd gear	2.49 V
4 th gear	3.23 V
5 th gear	4.10 V
6 th gear	4.55 V
Ignition coil	
2004-2006 models	
Primary peak voltage (min.)	150 volts
Primary resistance	2.0 5.0 ohms
Secondary resistance	24,000 37,000 ohms
2007-2011 models	
Primary peak voltage (min.)	150 volts
Primary resistance	
	1.0 5.0 ohms
Secondary resistance	25,000 40,000 ohms

(continued)

Table 1 ELECTRICAL SYSTEM SPECIFICATIONS (continued)

Ignition System	
Type	Electronic
Ignition timing	
2004-2008 models	4° BTDC @ 1300 rpm
2009-2011 models	8° BTDC @ 1300 rpm
Crankshaft position sensor	
Coil resistance	130-240 ohms
Peak voltage	3.7 V minimum
Sidestand switch	
Raised position	0.4-0.6 volt
Lowed position	1.4 volts or more
Speed sensor voltage	0-6 volts
Starter motor (2010-2011 models)	
brush service limit	6.5 mm (0.26 in.)

*Gear position switch voltages are approximate.

Table 2 REPLACEMENT BULBS

Item	Specification
Headlight	12 volt, 60/55W
License plate	12 volt, 5W
Taillight/brakelight	12 volt, 21/5W
Turn signal	12 volt, 21W

Table 3 ELECTRICAL SYSTEM TORQUE SPECIFICATIONS

Item	N•m	in. lb.	ft.-lb.
Alternator stator coil bolts	11	97	–
Crankshaft position sensor	6.5	58	–
Oil pressure switch	14	124	–
Starter motor bolts			
2004-2009 models	11	97	–
2010-2011	10	88	–
Starter motor cable retaining nut	6	53	–

9

Notes

CHAPTER TEN

COOLING SYSTEM

This chapter covers repair and replacement procedures for the radiator and cap, thermostat, electric fan, coolant reservoir and oil cooler. Routine maintenance operations are described in Chapter Three. Cooling system specifications are listed in **Table 1** and **Table 2** at the end of this chapter.

Refer to **Figure 1** for a diagram that depicts the coolant flow in the cooling system.

WARNING
Do not remove the radiator cap or any cooling system component that is under pressure when the engine is hot. The coolant is very hot and under pressure. Severe scalding could result if the coolant comes in contact with your skin. The cooling system must be cool before removing any system component.

WARNING
If the engine is warm or hot, the fan may come on (even with the ignition off). Never work around the fan until the engine is completely cool.

WARNING
Antifreeze is an environmental toxic waste. Do not dispose of it by flushing down a drain or pouring it onto the ground. Place old antifreeze into a suitable container and dispose of it properly. Do not store coolant where it is accessible to children or animals.

CAUTION
When adding coolant or refilling the system use a mixture of ethylene glycol antifreeze formulated for aluminum engines and distilled water. Do not use only distilled water (even if freezing temperatures are not expected); the antifreeze inhibits internal engine corrosion and provides lubrication for moving parts.

HOSES AND HOSE CLAMPS

After removing any cooling system component, inspect the adjoining hose(s) to determine if replacement is necessary. Hoses deteriorate with age and should be inspected carefully for conditions, which may cause them to fail. The possibility of a hose failing should be taken seriously. Loss of coolant will cause the engine to overheat and spray from a leaking hose can injure the rider. Observe the following when servicing hoses:

1. Make sure the cooling system is cool before removing any coolant hose or component.

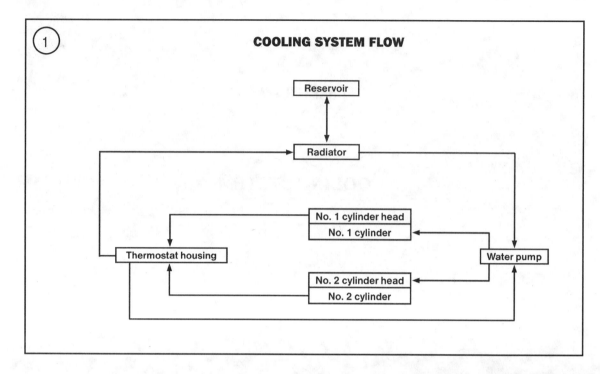

COOLING SYSTEM FLOW

2. Use original equipment replacement hoses; they are formed to a specific shape and dimension for correct fit.

3. Do not use excessive force when removing a hose from a fitting.

4. If the hose is difficult to install onto the fitting, soak the hose in hot water to make it more pliable. Do not use lubricant when installing hoses.

5. Inspect the hose clamps for damage. Position the clamp head so it is accessible for future removal and it does not contact other parts.

COOLING SYSTEM INSPECTION

1. If steam is observed at the muffler outlet, the head gasket might be damaged. If enough coolant leaks into a cylinder(s), the cylinder could hydrolock preventing the engine from being cranked. Coolant may also be present in the engine oil. If the oil visible in the oil level gauge (located on the right crankcase cover) appears foamy or milky, there is coolant in the oil. If so, correct the problem before returning the motorcycle to service.

> *CAUTION*
> *If the engine oil is contaminated with coolant, change the oil and filter after performing the coolant system repair. Refer to Chapter Three.*

2. Check the radiator for clogged or damaged fins. If excessive, take the radiator to a shop for repair.

3. Check all coolant hoses for cracks or damage. Replace all questionable parts. Make sure all hose clamps are tight, but not so tight that they cut the hoses.

4. Pressure test the cooling system as described in Chapter Three.

RADIATOR AND COOLING FAN

> *WARNING*
> *Whenever the engine is warm or hot, the fan may start even with the main (ignition) switch turned OFF. Never work around the fan or touch the fan until the engine and coolant are completely cool.*

Removal/Installation

1. Remove the cowling as described in Chapter Fifteen.

2. Drain the cooling system as described in Chapter Three.

3. Detach the upper radiator hose (**Figure 2**) and lower radiator hose (A, **Figure 3**) from the radiator.

4. Disconnect the reservoir hose (B, **Figure 3**) from the radiator, then drain the coolant in the reservoir out through the hose.

5. Disconnect the horn electrical connector (**Figure 4**).

6. Remove the lower radiator mounting bolt (**Figure 5**).

7. Detach the electrical connector for the cooling fan motor and the cooling fan switch (**Figure 6**) from the shroud, then disconnect the connector.

8. Remove the upper radiator mounting bolt (A, **Figure 7**).

9. Detach the speed sensor wire from the clamp (B, **Figure 7**).

10. Disengage the tabs (C, **Figure 7**) on each side securing the radiator to the shroud. Secure the shroud so it cannot fall down.

NOTE
The cooling fan, cooling fan switch and horn are mounted on the radiator. They are removed and installed as an assembly.

11. Disengage the radiator from the left side mounting stud and remove the radiator.

12. Note the following when removing or installing the cooling fan (A, **Figure 8**), cooling fan switch (B) and horn (C) on the radiator:

    a. Hold the horn mounting bolt and nut securely to prevent damage to the bracket. Tighten the bolt to 8 N•m (71 in.-lb.).

    b. Tighten the cooling fan mounting bolts to 8 N•m (71 in.-lb.).

10

c. Refer to Cooling Fan Switch in this chapter for service information.

13. Install the radiator by reversing the removal steps while noting the following:

a. Replace any hoses if they are deteriorating or are damaged in any way as described in this chapter.

b. Make sure the mounting cushion and sleeve (**Figure 9**) are in place on each radiator mount.

c. The radiator hoses are shaped hoses and must be installed properly. The paint dot on the hose end of the lower hose (A, **Figure 3**) must be on the outside of the hose when installed.

d. The bolt head on the radiator hose clamps should face downward.

e. Make sure the electrical connections are free of corrosion and secure.

f. Refill the cooling system with the recommended type and quantity of coolant as described in Chapter Three.

Radiator Inspection

1. Remove the cooling fan assembly (A, **Figure 8**) for inspection as described in this chapter.

2. Remove the horn assembly (C, **Figure 8**).

3. If compressed air is available, use short spurts of air directed to the *backside* of the radiator core to blow out debris.

4. Flush the exterior of the radiator with a garden hose on low pressure. Spray both the front and the back to remove all debris. Carefully use a whisk broom or stiff paint brush to remove any stubborn dirt from the cooling fins.

> *CAUTION*
> *Do not press hard on the cooling fins or tubes.*

5. Carefully straighten any bent cooling fins with a broad tipped screwdriver or putty knife.

6. Check for cracks or leakage (usually a moss-green colored residue) at all hose fittings (A, **Figure 10**) and both side tank seams (B).

7. To prevent oxidation of the radiator, touch up any areas where the paint is worn off. Use a quality spray paint and apply several *light* coats. Do not apply heavy coats as this reduces the cooling efficiency of the radiator.

8. Inspect the rubber dampers in the radiator mounts. Replace any that are damaged or deteriorating.

9. Check for leaks at the cooling fan switch (B, **Figure 8**).

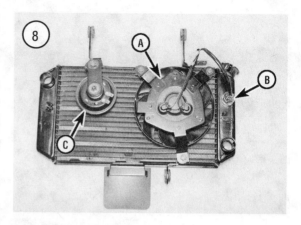

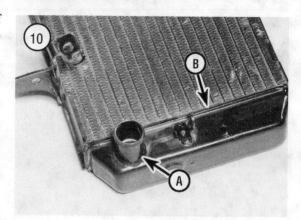

COOLING FAN

Removal/Installation

Replacement parts for the fan assembly are not available. If the fan motor is defective, replace the entire fan assembly.

1. Remove the radiator as described in this chapter.

2. Place a blanket or large towels on the workbench to protect the radiator.

3. Remove the screws securing the fan shroud (A, **Figure 8**) to the radiator and carefully detach the fan assembly from the radiator.

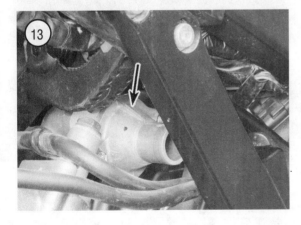

4. Test the cooling fan motor as described in Chapter Nine.

5. Install by reversing the preceding removal steps.

THERMOSTAT

Removal/Installation

1. Drain the cooling system as described in Chapter Three.

2. Remove both bolts securing the thermostat cover (A, **Figure 11**). Move the cover and attached hose out of the way.

3. Remove the thermostat (A, **Figure 12**) from the thermostat housing.

4. If necessary, test the thermostat as described in this chapter.

5. Inspect the thermostat for damage and make sure the spring has not sagged or broken. Replace the thermostat if necessary.

6. Clean the inside of the thermostat housing of any debris or old coolant residue.

7. Install by reversing the preceding removal steps while noting the following:

    a. Position the thermostat with the air bleed hole (B, **Figure 12**) toward the top of the cover.

    b. If loose, install the thermostat cover so the rib is up (**Figure 13**).

    c. If detached, install the radiator hose so the paint dot on the hose end aligns with the rib (B, **Figure 11**). Push the hose onto the thermostat cover until it contacts the rib.

    d. Refill the cooling system with the recommended type and quantity of coolant as described in Chapter Three.

Testing

Test the thermostat to ensure proper operation. Replace the thermostat if it remains open at normal room temperature or stays closed after the specified temperature has been reached during the test procedure.

> *NOTE*
> *The thermometer and the thermostat must not touch the container sides or bottom. If either does, it will result in a false reading.*

1. Suspend the thermostat and an accurate thermometer in a container of water (**Figure 14**). Do not allow the parts to touch the bottom or side of the container.

2. Slowly heat the water and observe the thermostat valve.

3. When the thermostat begins to open, observe the temperature on the thermometer. The thermostat should open at 88° C (190°F).

4. Continue to raise the temperature to 100° C (212° F). At this temperature, the thermostat valve should reach full lift, which is 8 mm (0.31 in.) or greater.

5. Replace the thermostat if it fails the tests.

THERMOSTAT HOUSING

The thermostat housing contains the thermostat as well as serving as a manifold. Hoses route the coolant from the cylinders to the manifold, while a bypass hose directs coolant to the water pump when the thermostat is closed. The coolant temperature sensor is mounted on the thermostat housing. Refer to **Figure 1** for a diagram of the cooling system.

Removal/Installation

1. Drain the cooling system as described in Chapter Three.

2. Remove the throttle bodies as described in Chapter Five.

3. Disconnect the wire connector from the coolant temperature sensor (A, **Figure 15**).

4. Detach the bypass hose (**Figure 16**) from the water pump.

5. Loosen the hose clamp and disconnect the hose from the thermostat cover (B, **Figure 15**).

6. Loosen the hose clamps and disconnect the hoses (C, **Figure 15**) from the fittings on the cylinder heads.

7. Remove the thermostat housing (D, **Figure 15**).

8. Reverse the removal procedure to install the thermostat housing while noting the following:

   a. The radiator hose is a shaped hose and must be installed properly.

   b. Refill the cooling system with the recommended type and quantity of coolant as described in Chapter Three.

WATER PUMP

The water pump is mounted on the clutch cover. The water pump cannot be removed from the clutch cover unless the clutch cover is removed from the engine.

Removal/Installation

1. Perform Steps 1-7 under *Clutch Removal/ Disassembly* in the Clutch section of Chapter Six.

2. Remove the snap ring (A, **Figure 17**), then remove the gear (B).

3. Remove the drive pin (A, **Figure 18**) and washer (B).

4. Remove the water pump from the clutch cover.

5. To install the water pump, reverse the removal procedure while noting the following:

   a. Install new O-rings around the coolant passages (A, **Figure 19**) and around the shaft housing (B).

   b. Lubricate the O-rings using Suzuki Super Grease A or equivalent.

   c. Be sure the drive slot in the gear engages the drive pin (A, **Figure 18**).

   d. Install a new snap ring (A, **Figure 17**).

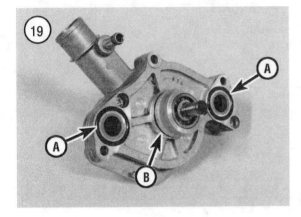

e. Perform Steps 24-29 under *Clutch Assembly/ Installation* in the Clutch section of Chapter Six.

Disassembly/Inspection/Assembly

Refer to **Figure 20**.

1. Remove the mounting screws (**Figure 21**) and separate the base assembly from the housing.
2. Detach the E-ring (**Figure 22**) from the impeller shaft.
3. Lift out the impeller and shaft (**Figure 23**).
4. Using a chisel, raise the outer lip of the mechanical seal (**Figure 24**).
5. Using a heat gun, heat the area around the mechanical seal.
6. Using a suitable tool, pry the mechanical seal out of the base (**Figure 25**).
7. Pry out the oil seal (**Figure 26**).
8. Rotate the bearing (**Figure 27**) and check for excessive noise or roughness. If bearing operation is rough, replace the bearing by using a suitable puller or driving out the bearing.
9. Remove the seal ring from the impeller (**Figure 28**).
10. Thoroughly clean the water pump base and housing to remove all old coolant residue.

11. Check the impeller blades for corrosion or damage. If corrosion is excessive or if the blades are cracked or broken, replace the impeller.
12. Install the bearing so the numbered side is out. Drive in the bearing until it bottoms in the base.
13. Install the oil seal (**Figure 29**) so the side marked A will be toward the mechanical seal. Lubricate the seal lip using Suzuki Super Grease A or equivalent.
14. Position the mechanical seal in the base (**Figure 30**). Use a socket that matches the outside diameter of the new mechanical seal and drive the new seal into the base until it bottoms (**Figure 31**).
15. Wrap tape around the gear end of the shaft to protect the seal lip.
16. Lubricate the shaft using Suzuki Super Grease A or equivalent, then install the shaft. Remove the tape.
17. Install the original snap ring (A, **Figure 32**) into the shaft groove.

NOTE
When installing the E-ring, push the E-ring into the groove using a wood or soft tool to avoid damaging the surrounding surfaces.

18. Pull up the shaft using the snap ring (A, **Figure 32**) to expose the E-ring groove in the shaft. Install the E-ring (B, **Figure 32**) with the flat side toward the shaft end.
19. Remove the original snap ring (A, **Figure 32**).
20. Install a new O-ring gasket onto the housing (**Figure 33**).
21. Install the housing onto the base assembly. Tighten the retaining screws (**Figure 21**) to 4.5 N•m (40 in.-lb.).

COOLING FAN SWITCH

Removal/Installation

1. Remove the cowling as described in Chapter Fifteen.
2. Drain the cooling system as described under *Coolant Change* in Chapter Three.
3. Detach the electrical connector from the fan switch (**Figure 34**).
4. Remove the switch.
5. If necessary, test the switch as described in Chapter Nine.
6. Install by reversing the preceding removal steps while noting the following:
   a. Install a new O-ring. Apply engine coolant to the O-ring.
   b. Install the switch and tighten it to 17 N•m (150 in.-lb.).

10

WATER PUMP

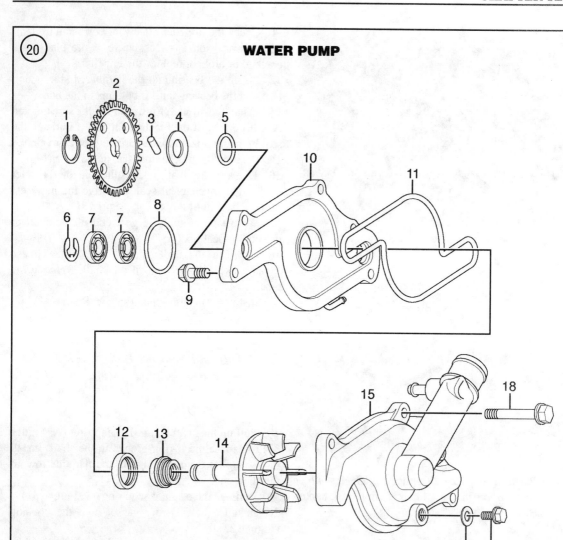

1. Snap ring
2. Gear
3. Pin
4. Washer
5. O-ring
6. E-ring
7. Bearings
8. O-ring
9. Screw
10. Base
11. O-ring
12. Oil seal
13. Mechanical seal
14. Impeller & shaft
15. Housing
16. Gasket
17. Drain bolt
18. Bolt

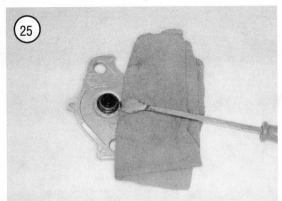

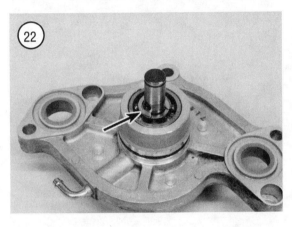

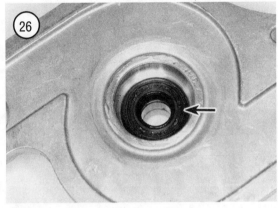

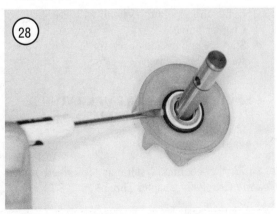

10

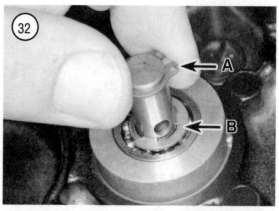

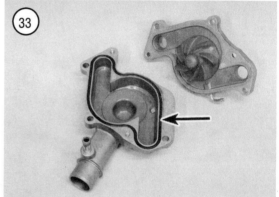

c. Refill the cooling system as described in Chapter Three.

d. Start the engine and check for leaks before installing the cowling.

ENGINE COOLANT TEMPERATURE (ECT) SENSOR

Removal/Installation

1. Drain the cooling system as described under *Coolant Change* in Chapter Three.

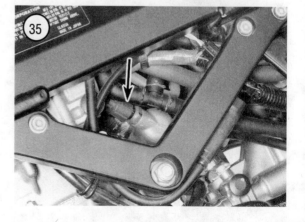

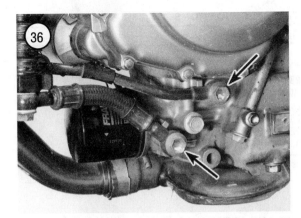

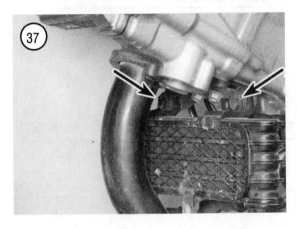

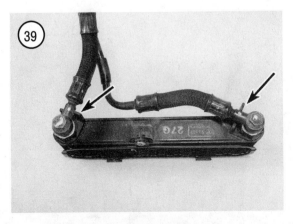

2. Disconnect the electrical connector from the ECT sensor (**Figure 35**).

3. Unscrew the ECT sensor from the thermostat housing and remove it.

4. Install by reversing the preceding removal steps while noting the following:

    a. Install a new sealing washer onto the ECT sensor.

    b. Tighten the switch to 19 N•m (168 in.-lb.).

    c. Refill the cooling system as described in Chapter Three.

    d. Start the engine and check for leaks.

Testing

Refer to Chapter Eight for testing procedure.

OIL COOLER

Removal/Installation

1. Drain the engine oil as described in Chapter Three.

2. Place an oil pan beneath the lower fittings on the oil cooler hoses to catch oil that drains from the fittings as the hoses are disconnected.

3. Remove the union bolts and sealing washers (**Figure 36**) securing each oil hose fitting to the engine. Place the oil hose ends in recloseable plastic bags to prevent the entry of debris.

4. Remove the bolts (**Figure 37**) securing the oil cooler to the mounting bracket and remove the oil cooler (**Figure 38**).

5. If necessary, remove the bolts securing the hoses to the base of the oil cooler.

6. Clean all dirt and road debris from the oil cooler core with a stiff paint brush. Do not press hard as the cooling fins may be damaged.

7. Install by reversing these removal steps while noting the following:

    a. Clean all road dirt and oil residue from the mating surfaces on the engine and the oil hose fittings.

    b. Install a new sealing washer on each side of the oil hose fittings when installing each union bolt.

    c. Position the oil fitting against the adjacent stop (**Figure 39**) before tightening the union bolt.

    d. Tighten each union bolt to 23 N•m (17 ft.-lb.).

    e. Tighten the mounting bolts to 10 N•m (88 in.-Lb.).

    f. Refill the engine with the recommended type and quantity oil as described in Chapter Three.

10

Table 1 COOLING SYSTEM SPECIFICATIONS

Item	Specification
Coolant capacity	
Engine cooling system	1.65 L (1.74 qt.)
Coolant reservoir	250 mL (0.26 qt.)
Coolant type	High-quality ethylene glycol antifreeze compounded for aluminum engines
Coolant mix ratio	50/50
Radiator cap opening pressure	95-125 kPa (13.5-17.8 psi)
Thermostat opening	88° C (190° F)

*Includes reserve tank.

Table 2 COOLING SYSTEM TORQUE SPECIFICATIONS

Item	N•m	in.-lb.	ft.-lb.
Cooling fan bolts	8	71	–
Cooling fan switch	17	150	–
ECT sensor	19	168	–
Horn mounting bracket	8	71	--
Oil cooler			
Union bolts	23	–	17
Mounting bolts	10	88	–
Water pump housing screws	4.5	40	–

CHAPTER ELEVEN

WHEELS, TIRES AND DRIVE CHAIN

This chapter describes repair and maintenance procedures for the front and rear wheels, tires and drive chain.

Specifications are located in **Tables 1-3** at the end of this chapter.

MOTORCYCLE STAND

Many procedures in this chapter require that the motorcycle be supported with a wheel off the ground. A motorcycle front end stand (**Figure 1**), swing arm stand or centerstand does this safely and effectively. Before purchasing or using a stand, check the manufacturer's instructions to make sure it is designed for the DL650. If the motorcycle or stand requires any adjustment or the installation of accessories (tie-downs), perform the required modification(s) before lifting the motorcycle. When using a motorcycle stand, have an assistant nearby.

CAUTION
Regardless of the method used to lift a motorcycle, make sure the motorcycle is properly supported before walking away from it.

FRONT WHEEL

Removal

CAUTION
Use care when removing, handling and installing a wheel with disc brake rotors, as well as a wheel equipped with an ABS speed sensor rotor. A disc brake rotor or speed sensor rotor can easily be damaged by side impacts. A disc brake rotor that is not true will cause brake pulsation. The rotors cannot be machined to repair excessive runout.

1. Place the motorcycle on the sidestand.
2. Shift the transmission into gear to prevent the motorcycle from rolling in either direction while the motorcycle is on a jack or wooden blocks.

NOTE
Insert a wood block between the brake pads after caliper removal. This prevents the caliper piston from extending if the lever is operated.

3. Remove both brake calipers as described in Chapter Fourteen.

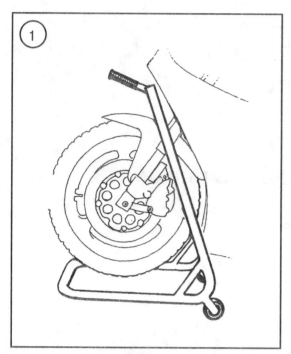

4. On DL650A models, remove the ABS speed sensor retaining bolt (A, **Figure 2**). Remove the sensor (B) and suspend out of the way.

5. On the right fork leg, loosen the axle pinch bolt (C, **Figure 2**), then loosen the front axle (D).

6. Place a suitable size jack, wooden blocks or other lifting device under the motorcycle to support the motorcycle securely with the front wheel off the ground.

7. Completely unscrew the axle from the left fork leg and remove the axle.

8. Pull the wheel down and forward and remove the wheel from the front fork.

> *CAUTION*
> *Do not set the wheel down on the disc surface. Set the tire sidewalls on two wooden blocks.*

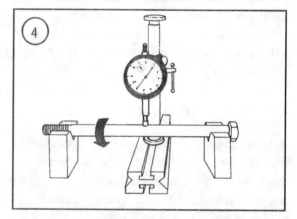

9. On DL650A models, remove the ABS speed sensor holder (A, **Figure 3**).

10. Inspect the wheel as described in this chapter.

Inspection

1. Remove any corrosion from the front axle with a piece of fine emery cloth. Clean the axle with solvent, and then wipe the axle clean with a lint-free cloth. Make sure all axle contact surfaces in both fork legs are clean.

2. Set the axle on V-blocks and place the tip of a dial indicator in the middle of the axle (**Figure 4**). Rotate the axle and measure axle runout. If axle runout ex-

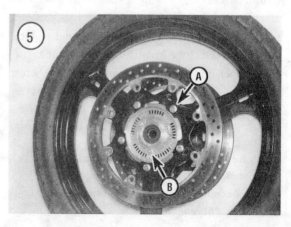

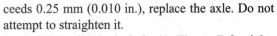

ceeds 0.25 mm (0.010 in.), replace the axle. Do not attempt to straighten it.

3. Check the disc brake bolts (A, **Figure 5**) for tightness on each side. Correct tightening torque is 23 N•m (17 ft.-lb.). Tighten if necessary.

4. On DL650A models, check the ABS speed sensor rotor bolts (B, **Figure 5**) for tightness. Tighten if necessary.

5. Inspect the seal on the right side of the wheel (**Figure 6**) for:

    a. Nicked, damaged or missing rubber.

    b. Grease or water seepage from the seal. If water or corrosion is evident in the bearing, the seal is leaking.

6. Inspect the front wheel bearings as described in *Front Wheel Hub* in this chapter.

7. Inspect the wheel rim for dents, bending or cracks. Check the rim and rim sealing surface for scratches or damage that may allow air leakage. If any of these conditions are present, replace the wheel.

8. Inspect the brake pads (Chapter Fourteen).

11

Installation

1. Make sure the contact surfaces of each fork leg and the axle are free from burrs and nicks.

2. Position the drive lugs on the speedometer sensor (A, **Figure 7**) so they align with the recesses in the wheel hub (B), then install the sensor into the wheel hub (figure 8).

3. On DL650A models, install the ABS sensor holder (A, **Figure 3**) into the wheel hub.

4. Correctly position the wheel so the directional arrow (**Figure 9**) on the tire points in the direction of normal wheel rotation.

5. Apply a light coat of grease to the front axle.

6. Position the wheel between the fork legs and lift the wheel into position between the fork legs.

7. Position the speed sensor so the boss on the sensor contacts the lug on the fork leg (**Figure 10**).

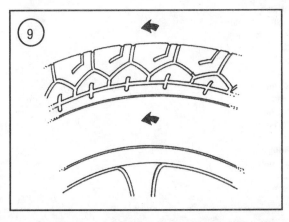

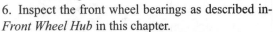

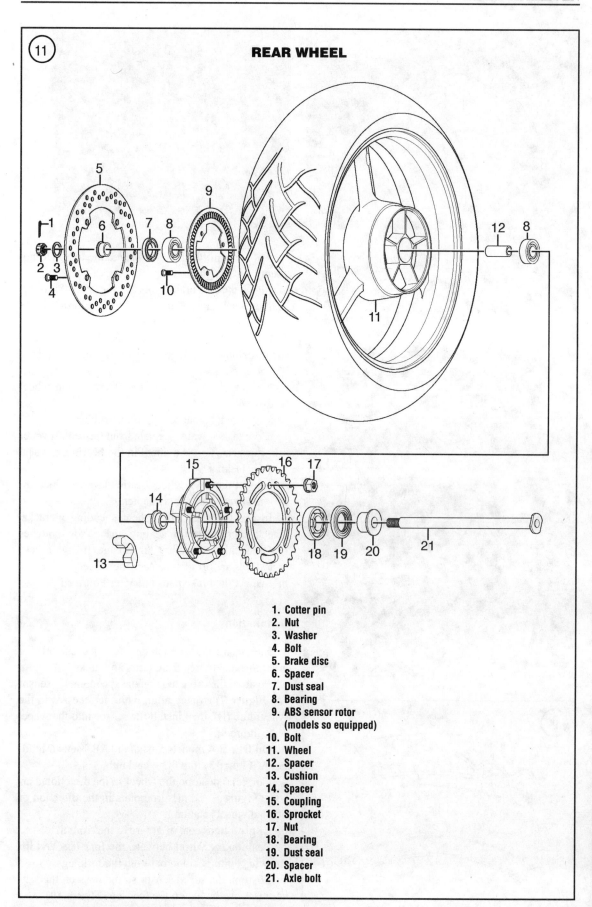

REAR WHEEL

1. Cotter pin
2. Nut
3. Washer
4. Bolt
5. Brake disc
6. Spacer
7. Dust seal
8. Bearing
9. ABS sensor rotor
   (models so equipped)
10. Bolt
11. Wheel
12. Spacer
13. Cushion
14. Spacer
15. Coupling
16. Sprocket
17. Nut
18. Bearing
19. Dust seal
20. Spacer
21. Axle bolt

REAR WHEEL

Removal

Refer to **Figure 11**.

1. On DL650A models, remove the ABS speed sensor retaining bolt (A, **Figure 12**). Remove the sensor (B) and suspend out of the way.

2. Remove the cotter pin (C, **Figure 12**) from the rear axle nut.

3. Have an assistant apply the rear brake, and then loosen the axle nut (D, **Figure 12**).

4. Block the front wheel to prevent the motorcycle from rolling in either direction while the motorcycle is on a jack or wooden blocks.

8. On DL650A models, position the ABS speed sensor holder so the slot (B, **Figure 3**) fits around the lug on the right fork leg.

9. Insert the front axle through the right fork leg, front wheel assembly and into the left fork leg.

10. Screw the axle (D, **Figure 2**) into the left fork leg and tighten the axle securely.

11. Install both brake calipers as described in Chapter Fourteen.

12. On DL650A models, install the ABS speed sensor (B, **Figure 2**). Tighten the retaining bolt securely.

13. Remove the jack, wooden block(s) or lifting device.

14. Have an assistant apply the front brake and tighten the axle (D, **Figure 2**) to 65 N•m (48 ft.-lb.).

15. Apply the front brake, push down hard on the handlebars and pump the fork four or five times to seat the front axle.

16. Tighten the front axle pinch bolt (C, **Figure 2**) to 23 N•m (17 ft.-lb.).

17. Shift the transmission into neutral.

18. Roll the motorcycle back and forth several times. Apply the front brake as many times as necessary to make sure the brake pads seat against the brake discs correctly.

5. Place a suitable size jack, wooden blocks or other lifting device under the motorcycle to support the motorcycle securely with the rear wheel off the ground.

6. Loosen the adjuster (E, **Figure 12**) on each side of the swing arm to allow maximum slack in the drive chain.

7. Remove the rear axle nut (D, **Figure 12**) and the washer.

8. Remove the rear axle from the left side of the motorcycle.

9. Push the wheel forward and remove the chain from the sprocket.

10. Remove the wheel and brake rotor assembly (**Figure 13**).

11. Insert a wood block between the brake pads until the wheel is installed. This prevents the caliper piston from extending if the pedal is operated. If dislodged, slide the brake caliper assembly back into the swing arm.

NOTE
Identify and mark all spacers when removing the rear wheel so they may be returned to their original locations.

12. Remove the spacer (A, **Figure 14** and A, **Figure 15**) from the hub and rear sprocket coupling.

11

13. Inspect and/or repair the wheel and axle assembly as described in this chapter.

Inspection

NOTE
The rear wheel hub is equipped with a single seal that is located in the rear sprocket assembly.

1. If still in place, remove the spacer (A, **Figure 14** and A, **Figure 15**) from the hub and rear sprocket coupling.

2. Clean the axle and spacers in solvent to remove all old grease and dirt. Make sure all axle contact surfaces are clean and free of dirt and old grease before installation. If these surfaces are not cleaned, the axle may be difficult to remove later.

3. Place the axle on V-blocks and place the tip of a dial indicator in the middle of the axle (**Figure 4**). Rotate the axle and check the runout. If axle runout exceeds 0.25 mm (0.010 in.), replace the axle. Do not attempt to straighten it.

4. Check the rear sprocket nuts (B, **Figure 15**) for tightness. Correct tightening torque is 60 N•m (44 ft.-lb.). Tighten if necessary.

5. Check the disc brake bolts (B, **Figure 14**) for tightness. Correct tightening torque is 23 N•m (17 ft.-lb.). Tighten if necessary.

6. On DL650A models, check the ABS speed sensor rotor bolts (C, **Figure 14**) for tightness. Tighten if necessary.

7. Inspect the seal on the right side of the wheel (**Figure 16**) and rear sprocket coupling (**Figure 17**) for:

 a. Nicked, damaged or missing rubber.
 b. Grease or water seepage from the seal. If water or corrosion is evident in the bearing, the seal is leaking.

8. Inspect the rear wheel bearings as described in *Rear Wheel Hub* in this chapter.

9. Inspect the wheel rim for dents, bending or cracks. Check the rim and rim sealing surface for scratches or damage that may allow air leakage. If any of these conditions are present, replace the wheel.

10. Inspect the rubber damper cushions in the wheel hub (**Figure 18**). The sprocket hub should fit firmly in the damper with little or no play. A damaged damper creates excessive lash in the driveline, which can be felt during acceleration and deceleration.

11. Inspect the brake pads (Chapter Fourteen).

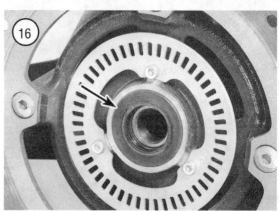

Installation

1. Make sure all axle contact surfaces on the swing arm and axle spacers are free of dirt and small burrs.

2. If the sprocket coupling was removed, apply grease to the spacer and install it into the sprocket coupling so the tapered side is out (**Figure 19**).

3. Install the sprocket coupling assembly into the rear wheel hub.

4. Apply a light coat of grease to the axle, bearings, spacers and grease seal.

5. Install the left (A, **Figure 14**) and right (A, **Figure 15**) axle spacers.

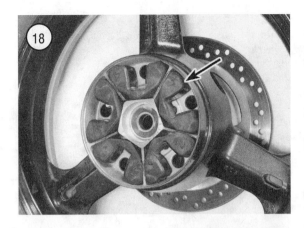

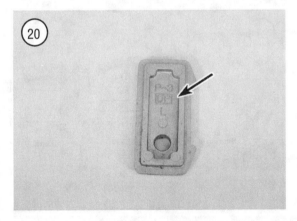

11. Install the rear axle nut (D, **Figure 12**). Hand-tighten the nut at this time.

12. Adjust the drive chain as described in Chapter Three.

13. Tighten the axle nut to 100 N•m (74 ft. lb.).

14. Install a new cotter pin onto the rear axle nut (C, **Figure 12**).

15. On DL650A models, install the ABS speed sensor (B, **Figure 12**). Tighten the retaining bolt securely.

16. Make sure the wheel spins freely and the brake operates properly.

FRONT WHEEL HUB

Preliminary Inspection

1. Support the motorcycle with the wheel to be inspected off the ground. The axle nut must be tight.

2. Grasp the wheel, placing the hands 180° apart. Lever the wheel up and down and side to side to check for radial and axial play. Have an assistant apply the brake while the test is repeated. Play will be detected in excessively worn bearings, even though the wheel is locked.

NOTE
If the disc brake drags and the bearings cannot be heard, remove the wheel. Place the axle in the wheel, and then support the axle so the wheel spins freely.

3. Spin the wheel and listen for bearing noise. A damaged bearing inconsistently sounds rough and smooth. An excessively worn bearing sounds consistently rough. In either case, replace the bearing.

4. If damage is evident, replace the bearings as a set.

Seal Replacement

Seals prevent the entry of moisture and dirt into the bearings and hub. Replace seals when they are obviously damaged or when water or corrosion is evident in the bearings and hub.

1. Pry out the old seal (**Figure 21**). Protect the hub from tool damage. Do not allow the end of the tool to touch the hub bore. Scratches in the bore cause leaks.

2. If installing a new bearing, replace it before installing the new seal.

3. Clean the seal bore.

4. Apply waterproof grease to the lip and sides of the new seal.

5. Install the seal as follows:

6. Remove the piece of wood from the brake caliper.

7. Position the wheel into place and roll it forward. Install the drive chain onto the rear sprocket.

8. Move the rear brake caliper and bracket assembly onto the disc. Make sure the right axle spacer is still in place.

9. If removed, install the drive chain adjusters onto the swing arm with the UP mark (**Figure 20**) on each adjuster correctly oriented.

10. From the left side of the motorcycle insert the rear axle. Push the axle all the way in until it bottoms in the swing arm.

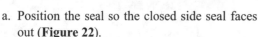

a. Position the seal so the closed side seal faces out (**Figure 22**).

b. Place the seal squarely over the bore.

c. Press the seal into place. If a driver is used, use a driver that contacts the perimeter of the seal.

Disassembly

1. Remove the front wheel as described in this chapter.

2. On DL650A models, remove the ABS front wheel speed sensor rotor as described in Chapter Fourteen.

> *CAUTION*
> *If the brake discs are not removed in the following procedure, do not allow the wheel to rest on the brake disc. Support the wheel to prevent pressure being applied to the disc.*

3. If necessary, remove the brake discs as described in Chapter Fourteen.

> *WARNING*
> *Wear safety glasses while removing the wheel bearings.*

4A. A special tool such as the Kowa Seiki wheel bearing remover set (**Figure 23**) is used in this procedure. The set uses a remover head that is wedged against the inner bearing race. The remover head and bearing are driven from the hub.

  a. Insert the remover head (**Figure 24**) into one of the wheel bearings from the outer surface of the wheel hub.

  b. Turn the wheel over and insert the remover shaft (**Figure 24**) into the backside of the adapter. Tap the wedge and force it into the slit in the remover head (**Figure 24**). This will force the remover head against the bearing inner race.

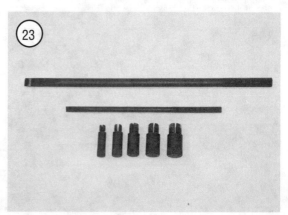

c. Tap on the end of the remover shaft with a hammer and drive the bearing out of the hub. Remove the bearing and the spacer.

d. Repeat for the bearing on the other side.

4B. If the special tools are not used, perform following:

  a. To remove the right and left bearings and spacer, insert a soft aluminum brass drift into one side of the hub.

  b. Push the inner spacer over to one side and place the drift on the inner race of the lower bearing (**Figure 25**).

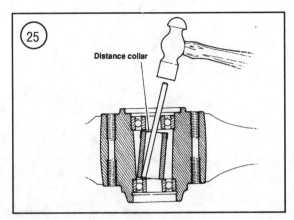

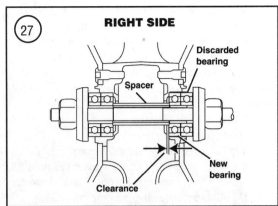

RIGHT SIDE

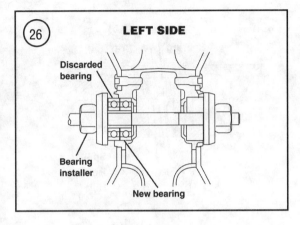

LEFT SIDE

c. Tap the bearing out of the hub with a hammer, working around the perimeter of the inner race. Remove the bearing and inner spacer.

d. Repeat for the other bearing.

5. Clean the inside and outside of the hub with solvent. Dry with compressed air.

Assembly

> *CAUTION*
> *Always reinstall **new** bearings. The bearings are damaged during removal and must not be reused.*

> *NOTE*
> *Replace bearings as a set. If either one bearing in a wheel is worn, replace both bearings.*

1. On non-sealed bearings, pack the bearings with a good quality waterproof bearing grease. To pack bearings, spread some grease in the palm of your hand and scrape the open side of the bearing across your palm until the bearing is packed completely full with grease. Spin the bearing a few times to deter-

mine if there are any open areas. Repack if necessary.

2. Blow any dirt or foreign matter out of the hub prior to installing the new bearings.

> *CAUTION*
> *Tap the bearings squarely into place. Tap on the outer race only; do no tap on the inner race or the bearing may be damaged. Be sure that the bearings are completely seated.*

3A. A special Suzuki tool (part No.09941-34513) can be used to install the wheel bearings as follows:

a. Install the left bearing into the hub first.

b. Position the bearing with the sealed side facing out.

> *NOTE*
> *When using a discarded bearing as a spacer, grind away a slight amount of the outside of the outer bearing race. This will prevent the old bearing from sticking in the hub bearing bore. Be sure to clean the old bearing before using it to prevent any debris from entering the hub or new bearing.*

c. Place a discarded bearing or suitably sized socket against the new bearing and install the bearing installer as shown in **Figure 26**.

d. Tighten the installer (**Figure 26**) and pull the left bearing into the hub until it is completely seated. Remove the bearing installer.

d. Turn the wheel over (right side up) on the workbench. Apply a light coat of grease to the spacer and install it in the hub.

e. Position the right bearing with the sealed side facing out.

f. Place a discarded bearing or suitably sized socket against the new bearing and install the bearing installer as shown in **Figure 27**.

11

g. Tighten the installer and pull the right bearing into the hub until there is a small amount of clearance between the inner race and the spacer. At this time the bearing is correctly seated. Remove the bearing installer.

3B. If the special tools are not used, perform the following:

a. Place the left bearing onto the hub with the sealed side facing out.

b. Tap the left bearing squarely into place. Tap on the outer race only. Use a socket (**Figure 28**, typical) that matches the outer race diameter. Do not tap on the inner race or the bearing will be damaged. Be sure the bearing is completely seated.

c. Turn the wheel over (right side up) on the workbench. Apply a light coat of grease to the spacer and install it in the hub.

d. Place the right bearing on the hub with the sealed side facing out.

> *NOTE*
> *Suzuki does not provide a specification for the slight clearance between the bearing and the spacer. The important thing is that these two parts are not pressed up against each other.*

e. Tap the right bearing squarely into place. Tap on the outer race only. Use a socket (**Figure 28**) that matches the outer race diameter. Do not tap on the inner race or the bearing will be damaged. Tap the right bearing into the hub until there is a small amount of clearance between the inner race and the spacer. At this time, the bearing is correctly seated.

4. Check that both bearings are installed squarely. Turn each bearing's inner race with your finger. The bearing must turn smoothly with no roughness or binding. If a bearing does not turn smoothly, it was damaged during installation. Remove and replace that bearing.

5. Install the dust seal.

6. If removed, install the brake discs as described in Chapter Fourteen.

7. On DL650A models, install the ABS front wheel speed sensor rotor as described in Chapter Fourteen.

REAR WHEEL HUB

Preliminary Inspection

1. Support the motorcycle with the wheel to be inspected off the ground. The axle nut must be tight. Remove the chain from the sprocket.

2. Grasp the wheel, placing the hands 180° apart. Lever the wheel up and down and side to side to

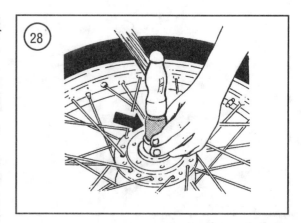

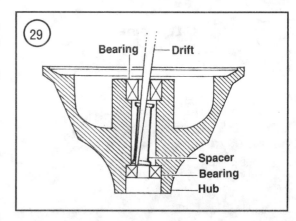

check for radial and axial play. Have an assistant apply the brake while the test is repeated. Play will be detected in excessively worn bearings, even though the wheel is locked.

> *NOTE*
> *If the disc brake drags and the bearings cannot be heard, remove the wheel. Place the axle in the wheel, and then support the axle so the wheel spins freely.*

3. Spin the wheel and listen for bearing noise. A damaged bearing inconsistently sounds rough and smooth. An excessively worn bearing sounds consistently rough. In either case, replace the bearing.

4. If damage is evident, replace the bearings as a set.

Seal Replacement

Refer to *Front Wheel Hub.*

Disassembly

Refer to **Figure 11**.

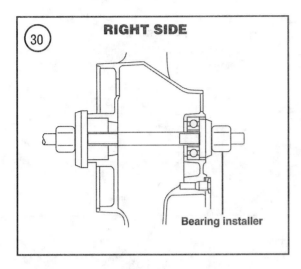

RIGHT SIDE

30

Bearing installer

1. Remove the rear wheel as described in this chapter.
2. If still in place, remove the right and left axle spacers.
3. If still installed, remove the rear sprocket and coupling assembly from the rear hub.
4. On DL650A models, remove the ABS rear wheel speed sensor rotor as described in Chapter Fourteen.

CAUTION
If the brake disc is not removed in the following procedure, do not allow the wheel to rest on the brake disc. Support the wheel to prevent pressure being applied to the disc.

5. If necessary, remove the brake disc as described in Chapter Fourteen.
6. Remove the rubber dampers (**Figure 18**) from the rear hub.

WARNING
Wear safety glasses while removing the wheel bearings.

7A. If special tools are not used, perform the following:
   a. To remove the right and left bearings and spacer, insert a soft aluminum or brass drift into one side of the hub.
   b. Push the spacer over to one side and place the drift on the inner race of the lower bearing.
   c. Tap the bearing out of the hub with a hammer, working around the perimeter of the inner race (**Figure 29**). Remove the bearing and spacer.
   d. Repeat for the bearing on the other side.
7B. A special tool such as the Kowa Seiki wheel bearing remover set (**Figure 23**) is used in this procedure. The set uses a remover head that is wedged against the inner bearing race. The remover head and bearing are driven from the hub.
   a. Select the correct size remover head tool and insert it into the bearing.
   b. Turn the wheel over and insert the remover shaft into the backside of the adapter. Tap the shaft and force it into the slit in the adapter (**Figure 24**). This will force the adapter against the bearing inner race.
   c. Tap on the end of the shaft with a hammer and drive the bearing out of the hub. Remove the bearing and the distance collar.
   d. Repeat for the bearing on the other side.
8. Clean the inside and the outside of the hub with solvent. Dry with compressed air.

Assembly

CAUTION
*Always reinstall **new** bearings. The bearings are damaged during removal and must not be reused.*

NOTE
Replace bearings as a set. If either bearing in a wheel is worn, replace all the bearings. Replace both wheel bearings as well as the rear coupling bearing.

1. On non-sealed bearings, pack the bearings with water-proof bearing grease. To pack the bearings, spread some grease in the palm of your hand and scrape the open side of the bearing across your palm until the bearing is completely packed full of grease. Spin the bearing a few times to determine if there are any open areas; repack if necessary.
2. Blow any dirt or foreign matter out of the hub before installing the new bearings.

CAUTION
Install non-sealed bearings with the single sealed side facing outward. Tap the bearings squarely into place and tap on the outer race only. Applying pressure to the inner race will damage the bearing. Be sure the bearings are completely seated.

3A. A special Suzuki tool set (part No. 09941-34513) can be used to install the wheel bearings as follows:
   a. Install the right bearing into the hub first.
   b. Place the right bearing with the sealed side facing out, and install the bearing installer as shown in **Figure 30**.

c. Tighten the bearing installer and pull the right bearing into the hub until it is completely seated. Remove the bearing installer.

d. Turn the wheel over (left side up) on the workbench and install the spacer.

e. Place the left bearing into the hub with the sealed side facing out, and install the bearing installer as shown in **Figure 31**.

> *NOTE*
> *Suzuki does not provide a specification for the slight clearance between the bearing and the spacer. The important thing is that these two parts are not pressed up against each other.*

f. Tighten the bearing installer and pull the left bearing into the hub until there is a *slight* clearance between the inner race and the spacer.

g. Remove the bearing installer.

3B. If special tools are not used, perform the following:

a. Install the right bearing first.

b. Using a socket that matches the outer race diameter, tap the right bearing squarely into place in the hub. Tap on the outer race only (**Figure 28**, typical). Do not tap on the inner race or the bearing might become damaged. Make sure the bearing is completely seated.

c. Turn the wheel over on the workbench and install the spacer.

d. Use the same tool set-up and drive the left bearing into the hub until there is a *slight* clearance between the inner race and the distance collar.

5. Install the dust seal.

6. If removed, install the brake discs as described in Chapter Fourteen.

7. On DL650A models, install the ABS front wheel speed sensor rotor as described in Chapter Fourteen.

8. Install the right and left axle spacers.

9. Install the rubber dampers (**Figure 18**) into the rear hub.

10. Install the rear sprocket and coupling assembly into the rear hub as described in this chapter.

WHEELS

Wheel Balance

An unbalanced wheel is unsafe. Depending upon the degree of imbalance and the speed of the motorcycle, the rider may experience anything from a mild vibration to a violent shimmy that could lead to a loss of control.

The balance weights attach to the rim on the DL650. Weight kits are available from motorcycle dealerships. These kits contain test weights and

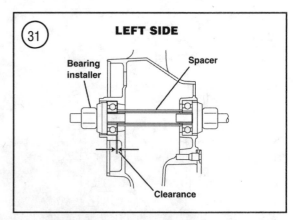

LEFT SIDE

Bearing installer · Spacer · Clearance

strips of adhesive backed weights that can be cut to the desired weight and attached to the rim.

Before attempting to balance the wheel, make sure the wheel bearings are in good condition and properly lubricated and that the brakes do not drag. The wheel must rotate freely.

> *NOTE*
> *When balancing the wheels, do so with the brake disc(s) and the rear coupling attached. These components rotate with the wheel and they affect the balance.*

1A. Remove the front wheel as described in this chapter.

1B. Remove the rear wheel as described in this chapter.

2. Mount the wheel on a fixture such as the one shown in **Figure 32** so the wheel can rotate freely.

3. Spin the wheel and let it coast to a stop. Mark the tire at the lowest point with chalk or light colored crayon.

4. Spin the wheel several more times. If the wheel keeps coming to rest at the same point, it is out of balance.

5. Attach a test weight to the upper (or light) side of the wheel.

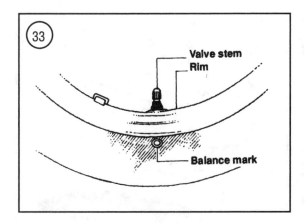

6. Experiment with different weights until the wheel, when spun, comes to rest at a different position each time.

7. Remove the test weight, thoroughly clean the rim surface, then install the correct size weight onto the rim. Make sure it is secured in place so it does not fly off when riding.

TIRES

Tire Safety

Tire wear and performance is greatly affected by tire pressure. Have a good tire gauge on hand and make a habit of frequent pressure checks. Maintain the tire inflation pressure recommended in **Table 1** for original equipment tires. If using another tire brand, follow their recommendation.

Follow a sensible break in period when running on new tires. New tires will exhibit significantly less adhesion ability. Do not subject a new tire to hard cornering, hard acceleration or hard braking for the first 100 miles (160 km).

TUBELESS TIRE CHANGING

The original equipment cast alloy wheels are designed for use with tubeless tires only. These wheels can easily be damaged during tire removal. Take special care to avoid scratching and gouging the outer rim surface, especially when using tire irons. Insert scraps of leather between the tire iron and the rim to protect the rim from damage.

When removing a tubeless tire, take care not to damage the tire beads, inner liner of the tire or the wheel rim flange. Use tire levers or flat-handle tire irons with rounded heads.

Tire Removal

CAUTION
Suzuki recommends that the tires be removed with a tire changer. Due to the large and rigid tires, tire removal with tire irons can be difficult and result in rim damage. On the other hand, a pneumatic tire changer can easily break the beads loose as well as remove and install the tire without damaging the cast wheel. The following procedure is provided if this alternative is not chosen.

CAUTION
To avoid damage when removing the tire, support the wheel on two blocks of wood so the brake discs or the rear sprocket does not contact the floor.

NOTE
To make tire removal easier, warming the tire will make it softer and more pliable. Place the wheel and tire assembly in the sun. If possible, place the wheel assembly in a completely closed vehicle. At the same time, place the new tire in the same location.

1A. Remove the front wheel as described in this chapter.
1B. Remove the rear wheel as described in this chapter.
2. If not already marked by the tire manufacturer, mark the valve stem location on the tire (**Figure 33**), in order to install the tire in the same location for easier balancing.
3. Remove the valve core from the valve stem and deflate the tire.

NOTE
*Removal of tubeless tires from their rims can be very difficult because of the exceptional tight tire bead-to-rim seal. Breaking the bead seal may require the use of a special tool (**Figure 34**). If the seal does not break loose, take the wheel to a motorcycle repair shop and have them break it loose on a tire changing machine.*

CAUTION
The inner rim and bead area are the sealing surfaces on the tubeless tire. Do not scratch the inside of the rim or damage the tire bead.

11

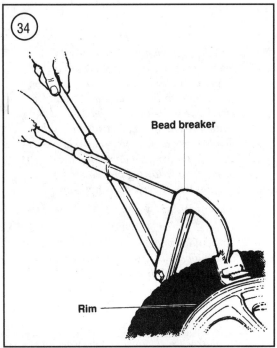

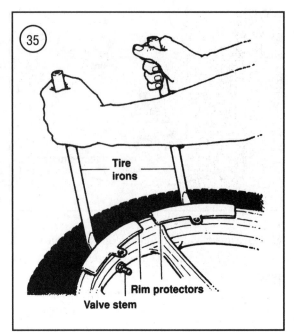

4. Press the entire bead on both sides of the tire away from the rim and into the center of the rim.

5. Lubricate both beads with soapy water.

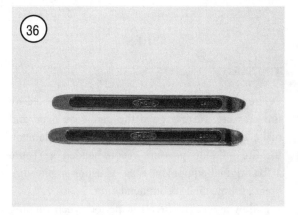

CAUTION
*Use rim protectors (**Figure 35**) or insert scraps of leather between the tire iron and the rim to protect the rim from damage.*

NOTE
*Use only quality tire irons without sharp edges (**Figure 36**). If necessary, file the ends of the tire irons to remove rough edges.*

6. Insert a tire iron under the top bead next to the valve stem (**Figure 37**). Force the bead on the opposite side of the tire into the center of the rim and pry the bead over the rim with the tire iron.

7. Insert a second tire iron next to the first iron to hold the bead over the rim. Then work around the tire with the first tire iron, prying the bead over the rim (**Figure 38**).

8. Stand the wheel upright. Insert a tire iron between the second bead and the side of the rim that the first bead was pried over (**Figure 39**). Force the bead on the opposite side from the tire iron into the center of the rim. Pry the back bead off the rim working around as with the first bead.

9. Inspect the valve stem seal. It is advisable to replace the valve stem when replacing the tire.

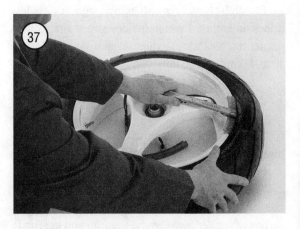

10. Remove the old valve stem and discard it. Inspect the valve stem hole (**Figure 40**) in the rim. Remove any dirt or corrosion from the hole and wipe it dry with a clean cloth. Install a new valve stem and make sure it properly seats in the rim.

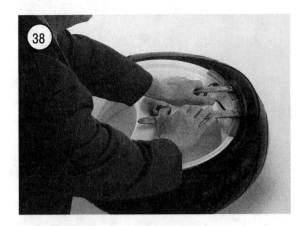

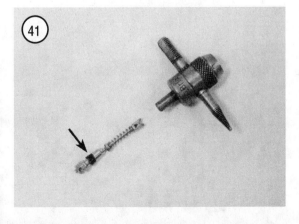

11. Carefully inspect the tire and wheel rim for any damage as described in the following.

Tire and Wheel Rim Inspection

1. Wipe off the inner surfaces of the wheel rim. Clean off any rubber residue or any oxidation.

> *WARNING*
> *Carefully consider whether a tire should be replaced. If there is any doubt about the quality of the existing tire, replace it with a new one. Do not take a chance on a tire failure at any speed.*

2. If any one of the following are observed; replace the tire with a new one:
   a. A puncture or split with a total length or diameter exceeding 6 mm (0.24 in.).
   b. A scratch or split on the side wall.
   c. Any type of ply separation.
   d. Tread separation or excessive abnormal wear pattern.
   e. Tread depth of less than the minimum value specified (**Table 1**) for original equipment tires. Aftermarket tire tread depth minimum may vary.
   f. Scratches on either sealing bead.
   g. The cord is cut in any place.
   h. Flat spots in the tread from skidding.
   i. Any abnormality in the inner liner.

3. Inspect the valve stem hole in the rim. Remove any dirt or corrosion from the hole, and wipe it dry with a clean cloth.

Tire Installation

1. Inspect the valve stem core rubber seal (**Figure 41**) for hardness or deterioration. Replace the valve core if necessary.

2. A new tire may have balancing rubbers inside. These are not patches and must be left in place. Most tires are marked with a colored spot near the bead (**Figure 33**) that indicates a lighter point on the tire. This should be placed next to the valve stem.

3. Lubricate both beads of the tire with soapy water.

4. When installing the tire on the rim, make sure the correct tire, either front or rear is installed on the correct wheel. Also, install the tire so the direction arrow on the tire (**Figure 42**) corresponds with the rotation arrow on the wheel (**Figure 43**).

5. If remounting the old tire, align the mark made in Step 2 of *Removal* with the valve stem. If installing a new tire, align the colored stop near the bead (in-

11

dicating the lightest point of the tire) with the valve stem. See **Figure 33**.

6. Place the backside of the tire onto the rim so the lower bead sits in the center of the rim while the upper bead remains outside the rim (**Figure 44**). Work around the tire in both directions and press the lower bead, by hand, into the center of the rim (**Figure 45**). Use a tire iron for the last few inches of bead (**Figure 46**).

7. Press the upper bead into the rim opposite the valve stem. Working on both sides of this initial point, pry the bead into the rim with a tire tool, and work around the rim to the valve stem. If the tire wants to pull up on one side, use either another tire iron or a knee to hold the tire in place. The last few inches are usually the toughest to install. If possible, continue to push the tire into the rim with by hand. Relubricate the bead if necessary. If the tire bead wants to pull out from under the rim use both knees to hold the tire in place. If necessary, use a tire iron for the last few inches.

8. Bounce the wheel several times, rotating it each time. This forces the tire bead against the rim flanges. After the tire beads are in contact with the rim, inflate the tire to seat the beads.

9. Place an inflatable band around the circumference of the tire. Slowly inflate the band until the tire beads are pressed against the rim. Inflate the tire enough to seat it. Deflate the band and remove it.

> *WARNING*
> *In the next step, never exceed 400 kPa (56 psi) inflation pressure as the tire could burst causing severe injury. Never stand directly over a tire while inflating it.*

10. After inflating the tire, check to see that the beads are fully seated and that the rim lines are the same distance from the rim all the way around the tire (**Figure 47**). If the beads are seated, deflate the tire and lubricate the rim and beads with soapy water.

11. Reinflate the tire to the required pressure as listed in **Table 1**. Install the valve stem cap.

12. Balance the wheel as described in this chapter.

13A. Install the front wheel as described in this chapter.

13B. Install the rear wheel as described in this chapter.

TIRE REPAIRS

> *WARNING*
> *Do not install an inner tube inside a tubeless tire. The tube will cause an abnormal heat buildup in the tire.*

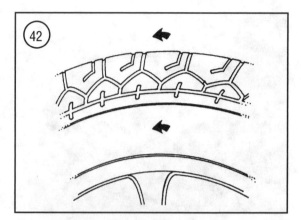

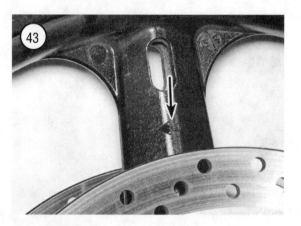

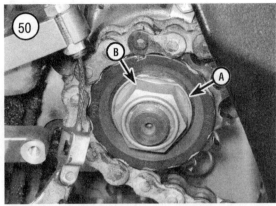

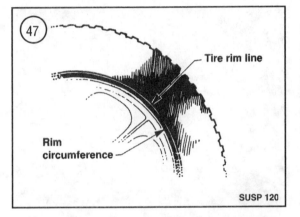

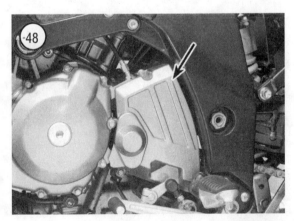

Only use tire plugs as an emergency repair. Follow the manufacturer's instructions and note the motorcycle weight and speed restrictions. A combination plug/patch applied from the inside is preferred to a plug applied from the outside. After performing an emergency tire repair with a plug, consider the repair temporary and replace the tire at the earliest opportunity.

SPROCKETS

Inspection

Refer to *Drive Chain and Sprocket Wear Inspection* in Chapter Three.

Drive Sprocket Removal

1. Place the motorcycle on the sidestand on level ground.
2. Shift the transmission into sixth gear.
3. Remove the sprocket cover bolts, then remove the sprocket cover (**Figure 48**).
4. Detach the clutch release spring (A, **Figure 49**).
5. Remove the clutch release mechanism bolts (B, **Figure 49**) and move the mechanism out of the way.
6. Using a suitable tool, bend back the washer (A, **Figure 50**) from the sprocket nut (B).
7. Remove the cotter pin (A, **Figure 51**) from the rear axle nut.
8. Loosen the axle nut (B, **Figure 51**) and the sprocket nut (B, **Figure 50**).
9. Loosen the chain adjusters (C, **Figure 51**) on both ends of the swing arm. Push the rear wheel forward until maximum chain slack is obtained.
10. Disengage the drive chain from the drive sprocket.
11. Remove the nut, washer and drive sprocket (**Figure 52**).

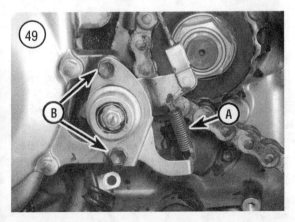

Drive Sprocket Installation

1. Install the drive sprocket (**Figure 52**), washer and nut onto the countershaft.

NOTE
The transmission must be in sixth gear when tightening the drive sprocket nut.

2. Tighten the drive sprocket nut to 145 N•m (105 ft.-lb.).
3. Bend the washer (A, **Figure 50**) and flatten it against one of the flats on the sprocket nut.
4. Install the drive chain onto the drive sprocket.
5. Install the clutch release mechanism and the clutch release spring (A, **Figure 49**).
6. Install the sprocket cover (**Figure 48**).
7. Adjust the drive chain tension as described in Chapter Three.

Driven Sprocket
Removal/Installation

1. Remove the rear wheel as described in this chapter.
2. Support the wheel so it does not rest directly on the brake disc, or remove the sprocket and rear coupling from the wheel. It may be easier to leave the rear coupling in the wheel until the sprocket nuts are loosened.
3. Remove the nuts securing the sprocket to the coupling (**Figure 53**).
4. Inspect the sprocket as described in Chapter Three.
5. Reverse this procedure to install the driven sprocket and rear wheel while noting the following:
   a. Mount the sprocket so the tooth identification number (**Figure 54**) faces out.
   b. Tighten the nuts in several passes, working in a crossing pattern. Tighten the nuts to 60 N•m (44 ft.-lb.).
   c. Adjust the drive chain tension as described in Chapter Three.

DRIVE CHAIN

Refer to Chapter Three for drive chain cleaning, lubrication, adjustment and measurement. Refer to **Table 2** in this chapter for chain specifications.

When checking the condition of the chain, also check the condition of the sprockets, as described in Chapter Three. If either the chain or sprockets are worn, replace all drive components. Using new sprockets with a worn chain, or a new chain on worn sprockets will shorten the life of the new part.

The motorcycle was originally equipped with an endless O-ring type chain. To remove the chain, the

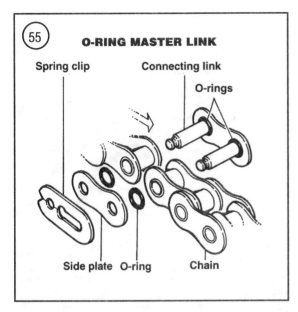

55 **O-RING MASTER LINK**

Spring clip — Connecting link — O-rings — Side plate — O-ring — Chain

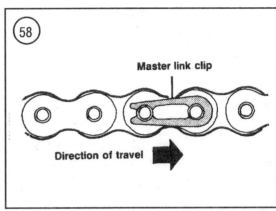

58 Master link clip — Direction of travel

chain may have been installed that uses a master link and spring clip (**Figure 55**), or a pressed-on master link (**Figure 56**). Refer to the appropriate following procedure for chain service.

Chain With No Master Link
Removal/Installation

1. Remove the swing arm as described in this chapter.
2. Remove the sprocket guard so the chain can be removed from the drive sprocket (**Figure 57**).
3. Disengage the chain from the sprocket, then remove the chain.
4. Reverse this procedure to install the chain. Note the following:
   a. Clean and inspect the swing arm before assembly. Apply waterproof grease to the parts before installing.
   b. Adjust the chain (Chapter Three).

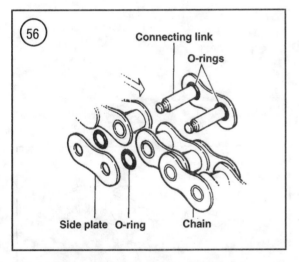

56 Connecting link — O-rings — Side plate — O-ring — Chain

Clip Type Master Link Drive Chain
Removal/Installation

1. Support the motorcycle on a workstand with its rear wheel off the ground and shift the transmission into neutral.
2. Find the master link on the chain. Remove the spring clip (**Figure 58**) with a pair of pliers, then remove the link from the chain (**Figure 55**).
3. Remove the drive chain.
4. Clean and inspect the chain as described in Chapter Three.
5. Clean the drive and driven sprockets.
6. Check the drive chain sliders for worn or damaged parts.
7. Reverse this procedure to install the chain. Note the following:
   a. Install the chain and reassemble a new master link (**Figure 55**).

57

swing arm must be removed so the chain can pass by the swing arm pivot.

The following procedure describes the removal and installation of the chain. The original chain is the endless type with no master link. A replacement

b. Install the spring clip on the master link with the closed end of the clip pointing toward the direction of travel (**Figure 58**).

c. Adjust the chain as described in Chapter Three.

Staked Type Master Link Drive Chain Removal/Installation

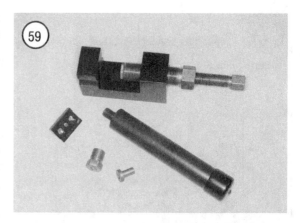

The drive chain uses a staked master link (**Figure 56**) and can be removed/replaced with the swing arm mounted on the motorcycle by breaking the chain at the master link. The following section describes chain removal and installation using the Motion Pro Jumbo Chain Tool (part no. 08-0135 [**Figure 59**]). The Jumbo Chain Tool can be used to break roller chains up to No. 630 and can be used to rivet chain sizes up to No. 530. Always follow the tool manufacturer's instructions provided with the tool. Use the following steps to supplement the instructions provided with the chain tool.

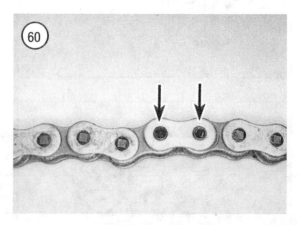

1. Support the motorcycle with the rear wheel off the ground.

2. Loosen the rear axle nut and the chain adjusters. Push the rear wheel forward until maximum chain slack is obtained.

3. Assemble the extractor bolt onto the body bolt. Then turn the extractor bolt until its pin is withdrawn into the pin guide chain tool, following the manufacturer's instructions.

4. Turn the chain to locate the crimped pin ends (**Figure 60**) on the master link. Break the chain at this point.

5. Install the chain tool across the master link, then operate the tool and push the connecting link out of the side plate to break the chain. Remove the side plate, connecting link and O-rings (**Figure 56**) and discard them.

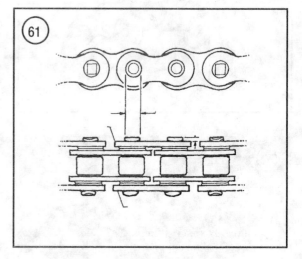

> *WARNING*
> *Discard the connecting link, side plate and O-rings after removing them. Never reuse these parts as they could break and cause the chain to separate. Reusing a staked master link may cause the chain to come apart and lock the rear wheel, causing a serious accident.*

6. If installing a new drive chain, count the links of the new chain, and if necessary, cut the chain to length as described under *Cutting A Drive Chain to Length* in this section. See **Table 2** for the original equipment chain sizes and lengths.

7. Install the chain around the drive sprocket, swing arm and driven sprocket.

> *NOTE*
> *Always install the drive chain around the swing arm before connecting and staking the master link.*

8. Assemble the new master link as follows:

a. Install an O-ring on each connecting link pin (**Figure 56**).

b. Insert the connecting link through the inside of the chain and connect both chain ends together.

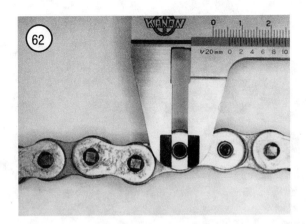

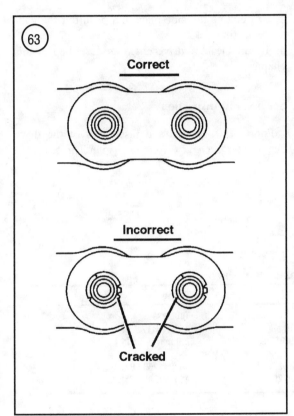

turer. If the height measurement is incorrect, confirm that the correct master link is being installed. If so, readjust the side plate height position on the connecting link.

b. Assemble the chain tool onto the master link and carefully stake each connecting link pin until its outside diameter (**Figure 61**) is as specified by the drive chain manufacturer. Work carefully and do not exceed the specified outside diameter measurement. Measure with a vernier caliper (**Figure 62**) in two places on each pin, 90° apart.

NOTE
If the diameter of one pin end is out of specification, remove and discard the master link. Then install a new master link assembly.

10. Remove the chain tool and inspect the master link for any cracks or other damage. Check the staked area for cracks (**Figure 63**). Then make sure the master link O-rings were not crushed. If there are cracks on the staked link surfaces or other damage, remove the master link and install a new one.

11. If there are no cracks, pivot the chain ends where they hook onto the master link. Each chain end must pivot freely. Compare by pivoting other links of the chain. If one or both drive chain ends cannot pivot on the master link, the chain is too tight. Remove and install a new master link assembly.

WARNING
An incorrectly installed master link may cause the chain to come apart and lock the rear wheel, causing a serious accident. If the tools to safely rivet the chain together are not available, take it to a Suzuki dealership. Do not ride the motorcycle unless absolutely certain the master link is installed correctly.

c. Install the remaining two O-rings (**Figure 56**) onto the connecting link pins.

d. Install the side plate (**Figure 56**) so the identification mark faces out (away from chain).

9. Stake each connecting link pin as follows:

NOTE
Refer to the drive chain manufacturer's specifications when pressing on the master link.

a. Measure the height of the connecting link from the outer side plate surface to the top of the connecting link (**Figure 61**). The height measurement is specified by the chain manufac-

12. Adjust the drive chain and tighten the rear axle nut as described in Chapter Three.

Cutting A Drive Chain To Length

Table 2 lists the correct number of chain links required for original equipment gearing. If the replacement drive chain is too long, cut it to length as follows.

1. Stretch the new chain on a workbench.

2. If installing a new chain over stock gearing, refer to **Table 2** for the correct number of links for the new chain. If sprocket sizes were changed, install the new chain over both sprockets, with the rear wheel moved forward, to determine the correct number of

links to remove (**Figure 64**). Make a chalk mark on the two chain pins to cut. Count the chain links one more time or check the chain length before cutting. Include the master link when counting the drive chain links.

WARNING
Using a hand or bench grinder as described in Step 3 will cause flying particles. Do not operate a grinding tool without proper eye protection.

3A. If using a chain breaker, use it to break the drive chain.

3B. To break the drive chain with a grinder, perform the following:

   a. Grind the head of two pins flush with the face of the side plate with a grinder or suitable grinding tool.

   b. Press the side plate out of the chain with a chain breaker; support the chain carefully while doing this. If the pins are still tight, grind more material from the end of the pins and then try again.

   c. Remove the side plate and push out the connecting link.

4. Install the new drive chain as described in this chapter.

Service and Inspection

For routine service and inspection of the drive chain, refer to *Drive Chain* in Chapter Three.

Table 1 TIRE SPECIFICATIONS

Item	Front	Rear
Tire type	Tubeless	Tubeless
Size	110/80 R19	150/70 R17
Minimum tread depth	1.6 mm (0.06 in.)	2.0 mm (0.08 in.)
Inflation pressure (cold)		
Single rider	33 psi (225 kPa)	36 psi (250 kPa)
Two riders	33 psi (225 kPa)	41 psi (280 kPa)

Table 2 WHEEL AND DRIVE CHAIN SPECIFICATIONS

Item	New	Service limit
Drive chain slack	20-30 mm (0.79-1.18 in.)	–
Drive chain	DID 525 V8 (116 links)	
Front axle runout (max.)	–	0.25 mm (0.010 in.)
Rear axle runout (max.)	–	0.25 mm (0.010 in.)
Sprocket sizes		
Drive (front)	15 teeth	
Driven (rear)	47 teeth	
Wheel rim size		
Front	19M/CxMT2.50	
Rear	17M/CxMT4.00	
Wheel rim axial runout (max.)	–	2.0 mm (0.08 in.)
Wheel rim radial runout (max.)	–	2.0 mm (0.08 in.)

Table 3 WHEELS, TIRES AND DRIVE CHAIN TORQUE SPECIFICATIONS

Item	N•m	in. lb.	ft.-lb.
Drive sprocket nut	143	–	105
Front axle	65	–	48
Front axle pinch bol	23	–	17
Front brake disc mounting bolt	23	–	17
Rear axle nut	100	–	74
Rear brake disc mounting bolt	23	–	17
Rear driven sprocket nut	60	–	44

11

Notes

CHAPTER TWELVE

FRONT SUSPENSION AND STEERING

This chapter provides service procedures for the front suspension and steering components. This includes the handlebar, fork and steering head. Refer to the **Table 1** and **Table 2** at the end of this chapter.

HANDLEBAR

Removal

CAUTION
Cover the front fender and front wheel with a heavy cloth or plastic tarp to protect them from accidental brake fluid spills. Brake fluid can mar or discolor painted or plastic surfaces. Immediately wash the surface using soapy water and rinse completely.

1. Remove the rear view mirrors.
2. Detach any cable or wiring clamps.
3. Disconnect the clutch switch electrical connector (**Figure 1**).
4. Refer to Chapter Nine and remove the left and right handlebar switch assemblies. Lay the assemblies out of the way.

NOTE
It is not necessary to disconnect the brake line from the master cylinder when performing Step 4.

5. Refer to Chapter Fourteen and remove the front brake master cylinder from the handlebar. Position the master cylinder after removal so the reservoir is in the upright position to minimize the loss of brake fluid and to keep air from entering the brake system.
6. Disconnect the clutch cable from the clutch control lever.
7. Remove the trim caps from the top of the handlebar upper holder Allen bolts.
8. Remove the handlebar upper holder bolts (A, **Figure 2**) and the handlebar upper holders (B, **Figure 2**).
9. Remove the handlebar.
10. If necessary, remove the handlebar balancer weight assemblies and left hand grip as described in this chapter.
11. If necessary, loosen the clamp bolt and remove the clutch lever assembly.

Installation

1. Install the handlebar onto the lower holders, then install the upper holders, washers and bolts. Install the upper holder so the punch mark (C, **Figure 2**) is toward the front. Do not tighten the bolts at this time.
2. Position the handlebar so the punch mark on the handlebar aligns with the gap between the holders as shown in **Figure 3**.

12

3. Tighten the holder bolts to 23 N•m (17 ft.-lb.). Tighten the front holder bolts first, then tighten the rear holder bolts.

4. If removed, install the clutch lever assembly onto the left handlebar. Align the lever body gap with the punch mark on the underside of the handlebar. Tighten the clamping bolt to 10 N•m (88 in.-lb.).

5. Install the front brake master cylinder as described in Chapter Fourteen.

6. Install the left and right handlebar switch assemblies as described in Chapter Nine.

7. Install the throttle housing and right hand throttle grip as described in Chapter Eight.

8. If removed, install the left hand grip as described in this chapter.

9. Connect the clutch switch connector (**Figure 1**).

10. Install the rear view mirrors.

11. Adjust the clutch lever free play as described in Chapter Three.

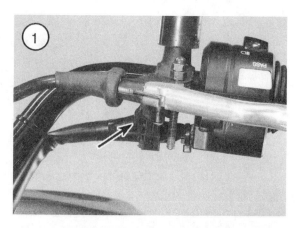

Inspection

> *WARNING*
> *Never straighten, weld or heat a damaged handlebar. The metal can weaken and possibly break when subjected to the shocks and stresses that occur when riding the motorcycle.*

1. Inspect the handlebar for cracks, bending or other damage.

2. Inspect the threads on the mounting bolts and the holders. Clean all residue from the threads. Replace damaged bolts.

3. Clean the handlebar, holders and caps with solvent or electrical contact cleaner. Use a stiff brush to clean the residue from the knurled areas on the handlebar. Use a soft brush on aluminum handlebars.

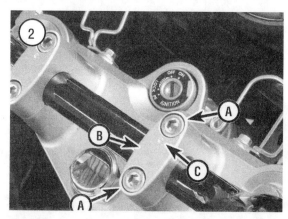

HANDLEBAR LEFT HAND GRIP REPLACEMENT

> *NOTE*
> *The factory equipped right hand grip is part of the throttle grip assembly and cannot be replaced separately.*

1. Remove the balancer assembly from the end of the left handlebar as described in this chapter.

2. Slide a thin screwdriver between the left hand grip and handlebar. Spray electrical contact cleaner into the opening under the grip.

3. Pull the screwdriver out and quickly twist the grip to break its bond with the handlebar, then slide the grip off.

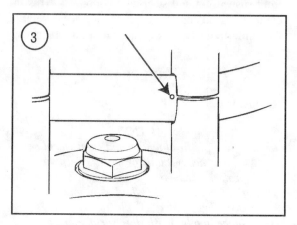

4. Clean the handlebar of all rubber or sealer residue.

5. Install the new grip following the manufacturer's directions. Apply an adhesive, such as ThreeBond Griplock, between the grip and handlebar. When applying an adhesive, follow the manufacturer's directions regarding drying time before operating the motorcycle.

6. Install the balancer assembly onto the left end of the handlebar.

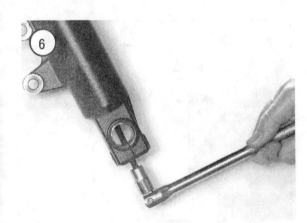

HANDLEBAR BALANCER WEIGHTS

A balancer weight (anti-vibration) assembly is located in each handlebar end. The weight assembly must be removed for access to the handlebar grips.

Removal/Installation

NOTE
If the bolt is removed, the retaining nut will fall into the handlebar.

1. Loosen the balancer weight mounting bolt (**Figure 4**) and remove the weight assembly.
2. If necessary, remove the nut (**Figure 5**), then separate the inner rubber center from the end weight.
3. Inspect the rubber center. Replace if deteriorated or otherwise damaged.
4. Assemble and install the weight assembly by reversing the removal procedure. Note the following:
   a. If removed, assemble the inner rubber center and end weight. Install the nut and tighten securely.
   b. Install the balancer weight mounting bolt and tighten securely after installation in the handlebar.

FRONT FORK

To simplify fork service and to prevent mixing parts, service the fork assemblies individually.

If a problem with the fork is suspected, first drain the fork oil and refill with the proper type and quantity. If a problem still exists, such as poor damping, a tendency to bottom out or top out or leakage around the slider seal, follow the service procedures in this section.

Removal/Installation

1. Remove the brake caliper and brake hose from each fork leg as described in Chapter Fourteen.
2. Remove the front wheel as described in Chapter Eleven.
3. Remove the front fender as described in Chapter Fifteen.

CAUTION
Press very hard on the wrench in the next step to ensure the wrench is completely seated within the Allen bolt head. If the Allen wrench starts to rotate with the socket it will damage the Allen bolt head. Apply coarse grit valve lapping compound to the wrench end to improve grip.

4. If the fork leg(s) will be disassembled, proceed as follows:
   a. On the right fork leg, remove the axle clamp bolt.
   b. Loosen the Allen bolt (**Figure 6**) in the bottom of the fork leg.
   c. Loosen the fork cap bolt (A, **Figure 7**).
5. Loosen the upper (B, **Figure 7**) fork tube clamp bolt.
6. Loosen the lower fork tube clamp bolts (**Figure 8**).

12

7. Carefully pull the fork leg down and out of the upper and lower steering brackets. It may be necessary to rotate the fork tube slightly while pulling it down and out.

8. Clean the fork legs and steering brackets.

9. Install by reversing the removal steps while noting the following:

    a. Insert the fork leg upward until the upper end of the fork tube is flush with the top surface of the upper steering bracket (**Figure 9**).

    b. Tighten the lower fork clamp bolts (**Figure 8**) to 23 N•m (17 ft.-lb.).

    c. If loosened or removed, tighten the fork cap (A, **Figure 7**) to 23 N•m (17 ft.-lb.).

    d. Tighten the upper fork clamp bolt (B, **Figure 7**) to 23 N•m (17 ft.-lb.).

Disassembly

Refer to **Figure 10**.

Service one fork leg before servicing the remaining leg. Do not intermix parts. If performing a routine fork oil change, perform Steps 1-7, and then go to *Fork Oil Refilling and Final Assembly* in this section.

The fork tubes are easily scratched and damaged. Handle them carefully. Work stands (**Figure 11**, www.parktool.com) appropriate for holding the fork are available.

1. Remove the front forks as described in this chapter.

2. Install the fork in a work stand or vise with soft jaws.

> *WARNING*
> *Be careful when removing the fork cap bolt as the spring is under pressure. Protect eyes accordingly.*

3. Slowly unscrew and remove the fork cap bolt (**Figure 12**).

4. Remove the spacer, washer and spring.

5. Turn the fork assembly upside down over a drain pan and completely drain the fork oil. Stroke the fork several times to pump out any oil that remains. Stand the fork tube upside-down in the drain pan and allow the oil to drain for several minutes.

6. Remove the Allen bolt and washer from the end of the slider. If the Allen bolt was not loosened during fork removal, proceed as follows:

    a. Install the attachment A tool (Suzuki part No. 09940-34531) onto the T handle (part No. 09940-34520).

    b. Insert this tool setup (A, **Figure 13**) into the fork tube and index it into the hex receptacle in the top of the damper rod to hold the damper rod in place.

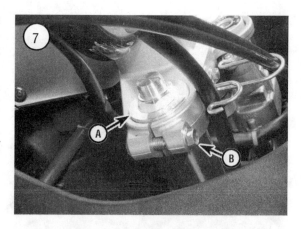

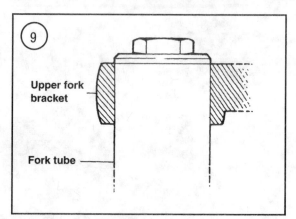

    c. Using an Allen wrench, loosen then remove the Allen bolt and washer (B, **Figure 13**) from the base of the slider.

> *NOTE*
> *The oil lock piece is often stuck to the bottom of the slider and may not come out with the damper rod. Do not lose the oil lock piece.*

7. Turn the fork assembly upside down and slide out the damper rod assembly complete with the rebound spring and oil lock piece.

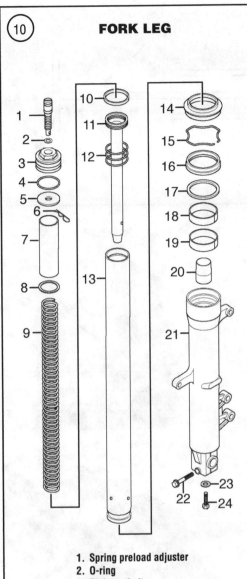

FORK LEG

1. Spring preload adjuster
2. O-ring
3. Fork cap bolt
4. O-ring
5. Plate
6. Pin
7. Spacer
8. Washer
9. Spring
10. Piston ring
11. Damper rod
12. Spring
13. Inner tube
14. Dust seal
15. Stopper ring
16. Oil seal
17. Retainer
18. Inner tube bushing
19. Outer tube bushing
20. Oil lock piece
21. Slider
22. Pinch bolt
23. Washer
24. Allen bolt

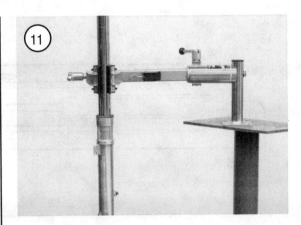

8. Remove the dust seal (**Figure 14**) from the slider.

9. Remove the stopper ring (**Figure 15**).

10. There is an interference fit between the bushing in the fork slider and bushing in the fork tube. To remove the fork tube from the slider, pull hard on the fork tube using quick in-and-out strokes (**Figure 16**). Doing so will withdraw the slider bushing, oil seal retainer and oil seal from the slider.

11. Withdraw the fork tube from the slider.

NOTE
Do not remove the fork tube bushing unless it is going to be replaced. Inspect it as described in this section.

12. Remove the oil lock piece from the slider if it did not come out in Step 9.

13. Slide off the oil seal (A, **Figure 17**), oil seal retainer (B) and slider bushing (C) from the fork tube.

14. Remove the oil seal lock piece (D, **Figure 17**).

15. Inspect all parts as described in this chapter.

Inspection

1. Thoroughly clean all parts in solvent and dry them completely.

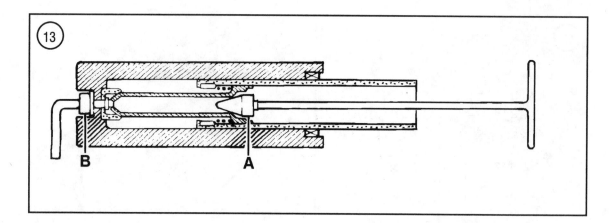

2. Inspect the damper rod for straightness (**Figure 18**), damage or roughness. Check for galling, deep scores or excessive wear. Replace the damper rod if necessary.

3. Make sure the oil holes (**Figure 19**) in the damper rod are clear. Clean out if necessary.

4. Inspect the piston ring (**Figure 20**) on the end of the damper rod for wear or damage. Replace if necessary.

5. Inspect the fork cap bolt threads (A, **Figure 21**) for wear or damage. If damage is minimal, clean with the appropriate size metric die.

6. Check the fork cap bolt O-ring (B, **Figure 21**) for hardness or deterioration. Replace if necessary to avoid an oil leak.

7. Inspect the spring adjuster components in the top cap. If necessary, remove the clip (**Figure 22**) and disassemble the components (**Figure 23**). Replace the O-ring on the adjuster if damaged.

8. Check the fork tube for straightness. If bent or scratched, replace the fork tube.

9. Inspect the fork tube fork cap bolt threads (**Figure 24**) for wear or damage. If damage is minimal, clean with the appropriate size metric tap.

10. Check the slider for dents or exterior damage that may cause the fork tube to bind during riding. Replace if necessary.

11. Check the front brake caliper mounting bosses on the fork legs. Check the front axle clamp bolt area (**Figure 25**) on the right slider for cracks or damage. Replace if necessary.

12. Check the slider stopper ring groove (A, **Figure 26**) for cracks or damage. Inspect the oil seal area (B) and the slider bushing area (C) for dents or other damage and replace the slider if necessary.

13. Measure the free length of the fork spring (not the rebound spring). If the spring length is less than 435 mm (11.1 in.), replace the spring.

14. Inspect the slider (A, **Figure 27**) and fork tube (B) bushings. Replace them if either is scratched or scored. If the Teflon coating is worn off so the copper

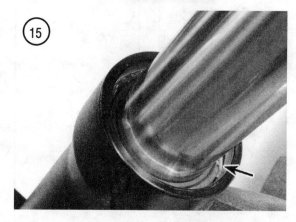

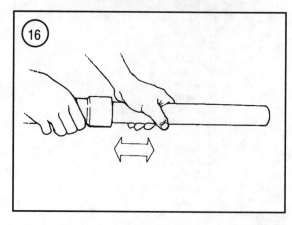

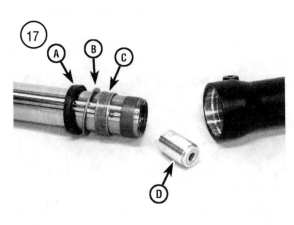

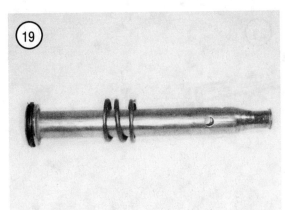

12

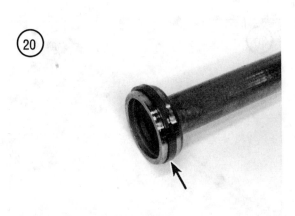

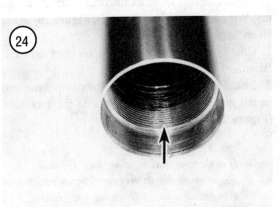

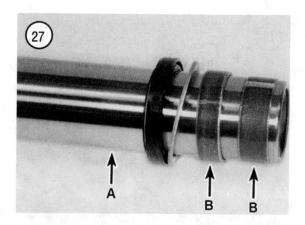

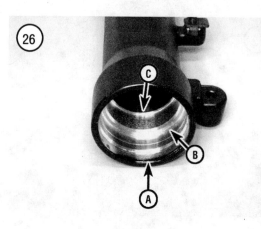

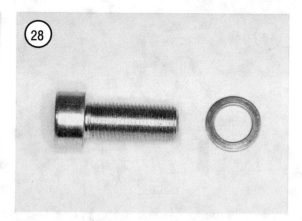

base material is showing on 3/4 of the total surface area, replace both bushings.

15. Inspect the gasket washer (**Figure 28**) on the Allen bolt and replace if necessary.

16. Replace any parts that are worn or damaged. Simply cleaning and reinstalling unserviceable components will not improve performance of the front suspension.

Assembly

Refer to **Figure 10**.

1. Make sure that all fork components are clean and dry. Wipe out the seal bore area (B, **Figure 26**) in the slider with a lint-free cloth.

2. Coat all parts with SAE 10 fork oil prior to installation.

3. Install the rebound spring on the damper rod and install the damper rod assembly into the fork tube (**Figure 29**).

NOTE
If a damper rod holding tool (Figure 30) is available to prevent damper rod movement when tightening the Allen bolt, proceed to Step 5.

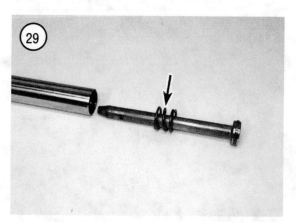

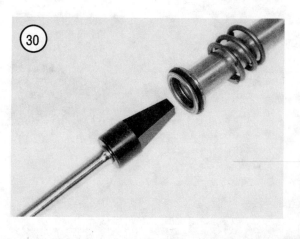

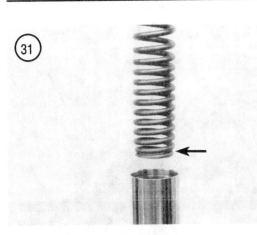

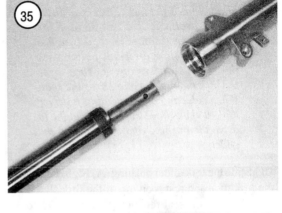

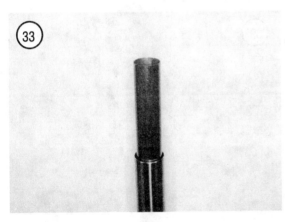

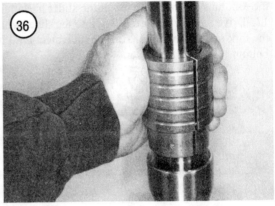

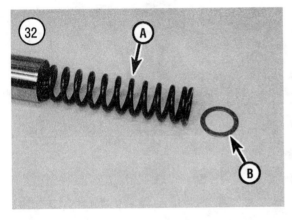

NOTE
*Install the fork spring so the end with closely wound coils enters first (**Figure 31**).*

4. Temporarily install the fork spring (A, **Figure 32**), washer (B), spacer (**Figure 33**) and fork cap bolt (**Figure 12**) to hold the damper rod in place. Only hand-tighten the fork cap bolt at this time. The tension of the fork spring will keep the damper rod in place in the fork tube and ease the assembly process.

5. Install the oil lock piece onto the damper rod (**Figure 34**).

6. Carefully install the fork tube and the damper rod assembly into the slider as shown in **Figure 35**.

7. Clean the threads of the Allen bolt thoroughly. Make sure that the gasket/washer is in place on the Allen bolt. Apply Threadlock 1342 to the bolt threads.

8. Install the Allen bolt and gasket washer. If available, hold the damper rod using the holder tool (**Figure 13**) described in the disassembly procedure. Tighten the Allen bolt to 20 N•m (177 in.-lb.).

9. Secure the fork vertically.

NOTE
*A fork seal driver (**Figure 36**) is required to install the fork slider bushing*

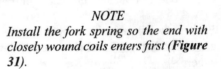

and fork seal into the slider. A number of different aftermarket fork seal drivers are available that can be used for this purpose. Another method is to use a piece of pipe or metal collar with the correct dimensions to slide over the fork tube and seat against the seal. When selecting or fabricating a driver tool, it must have sufficient weight to drive the bushing and oil seal into the slider.

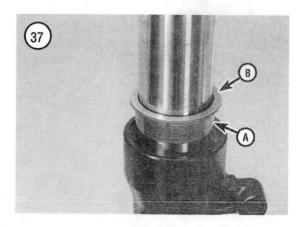

10. Slide the fork slider bushing (A, **Figure 37**) down the fork tube and rest it on top of the fork slider.

11. Slide the oil seal retainer (B, **Figure 37**) down the fork tube and rest it on top of the slider bushing.

12. Drive the new slider bushing into the slider with the fork seal driver (**Figure 36**) or equivalent until it bottoms. Remove the driver.

NOTE
*To avoid damage to the oil seal lips and dust seal when installing them over the top of the fork tube, place a plastic bag over the fork tube and coat it with fork oil. Then slide both seals over the fork tube and plastic bag (**Figure 38**) without damaging them.*

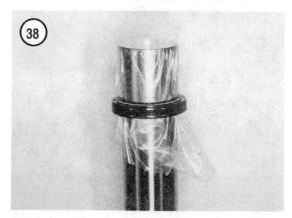

13. Coat the lips of the new oil seal with fresh fork oil.

14. Position the oil seal with its open groove facing upward and slide the oil seal (**Figure 39**) down the fork tube.

15. Slide the fork seal driver down the fork tube (**Figure 36**) and drive the seal into the slider until it bottoms. Make sure the groove in the slider can be seen above the top surface of the oil seal. If not, continue to drive the oil seal in until the groove is visible.

16. Slide the stopper ring (**Figure 40**) down the fork tube and rest it on top of the oil seal.

17. Carefully install the stopper ring into the slider groove (**Figure 41**). Make sure the stopper ring is locked into the groove in the fork tube.

18. Install the dust seal into the slider. Press it in until it is completely seated (**Figure 42**).

NOTE
Measure the fork oil level, if possible, to ensure a more accurate filling. This results in a better handling bike.

19. Remove the fork cap bolt, spacer, washer and fork spring.

20. Fill the fork with oil. Set the oil level and complete fork assembly as described in *Fork Oil Refilling and Final Assembly* (this section).

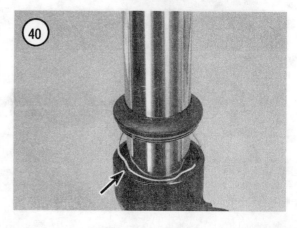

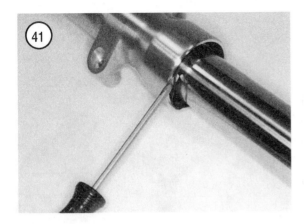

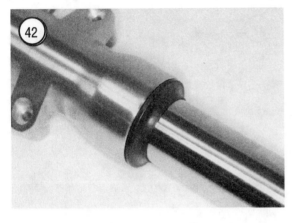

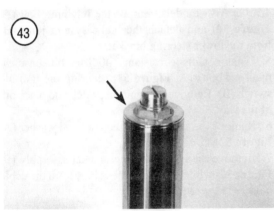

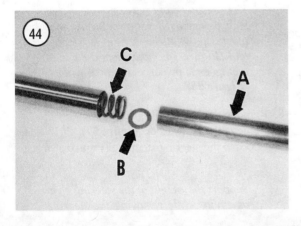

Fork Oil Refilling and Final Assembly

Use the following procedure to fill the fork legs with oil, either after rebuilding the fork legs, or during a routine fork oil change. This procedure also details the assembly of the fork legs after the oil level has been set. Refer to **Table 1** for the recommended fork oil and quantity.

> *NOTE*
> *To measure the correct amount of fluid, use a plastic baby bottle. These bottles have measurements in milliliters (ml).*

1. If refilling the forks with oil, perform the following:
   a. Remove the front forks as described in this chapter.
   b. Install the fork in a work stand or vise with soft jaws.

> *WARNING*
> *Be careful when removing the fork cap bolt as the spring is under pressure. Protect eyes accordingly.*

   c. Slowly unscrew and remove the fork cap bolt (**Figure 43**).
   d. Remove the spacer (A, **Figure 44**), washer (B) and spring (C).
2. Compress the fork completely.
3. Add the recommended amount of SS-08 fork oil to the fork assembly listed in **Table 1**.
4. Pump the fork leg several times to thoroughly distribute the oil. Bottom the fork tube in the fork slider and allow it to stand in the vertical position for several minutes.

> *NOTE*
> *Make sure the tube is bottomed by pushing down slowly on the last stroke. Otherwise, hydraulic force may produce the feeling that the tube is bottomed.*

5. Hold the fork assembly as close to perfectly vertical as possible.
6. Use an accurate ruler (**Figure 45**) or oil level gauge (Motion Pro part No. 08-121 [**Figure 46**]) to obtain the correct oil level listed in **Table 1**.
7. Allow the oil to settle completely and recheck the oil level measurement. Adjust the oil level if necessary.

> *NOTE*
> *The following photographs depict the fork on its side for clarity. Keep the fork assembly vertical or some of the fork oil will drain out.*

12

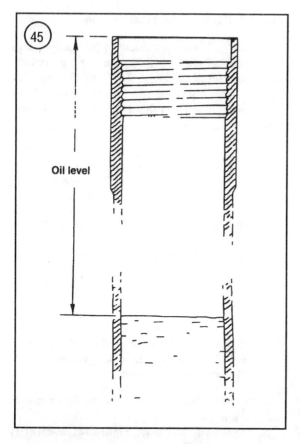

Oil level

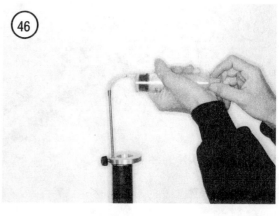

8. Install the fork spring (C, **Figure 44**), washer (B) and spacer (A). Install the fork spring so the end with closely wound coils enters first (**Figure 31**).

9. Inspect the O-ring (**Figure 47**) on the fork top cap for hardness or deterioration. Replace the O-ring if necessary.

10. Install the fork cap bolt (**Figure 43**) hand tight at this time. Tighten the cap bolt to 23 N•m (17 ft.-lb.) after the fork assembly has been installed. Keep the fork tube vertical until it is installed on the bike to prevent the loss of fork oil. Adjust spring preload adjustment after installation as described in Chapter Three.

STEERING STEM AND HEAD

Removal

Refer to **Figure 48**.

1. Remove the front fork as described in this chapter.

2. Remove the handlebar as described in this chapter.

3. Detach the wire guides (**Figure 49**) from the upper steering bracket.

4A. On non-ABS models, detach the front brake hose guide from the lower steering bracket.

4B, On ABS models, remove the retaining bolt (A, **Figure 50**) and detach the brake system joint (B) from the lower steering bracket.

5. Using a tamper-resistant T40 Torx bit, unscrew the Torx bolts (A, **Figure 51**) securing the ignition switch (B). Remove the ignition switch and place out of the way.

6. Remove the steering stem cap nut and washer (A, **Figure 52**).

7. Remove the upper steering bracket assembly (B, **Figure 52**) while detaching the cables from the cable holders (**Figure 53**).

NOTE
*The locknut and steering stem nut may be removed using a Suzuki tool (part No.09940-14911), a fabricated tool (**Figure 54**) made from a piece of tubing or pipe, or a spanner wrench (**Figure 55**).*

8. Remove the locknut (**Figure 56**).

9. Remove the tab washer (**Figure 57**).

10. Loosen the steering stem nut (**Figure 58**).

NOTE
Support the weight of the steering stem assembly while removing the steering

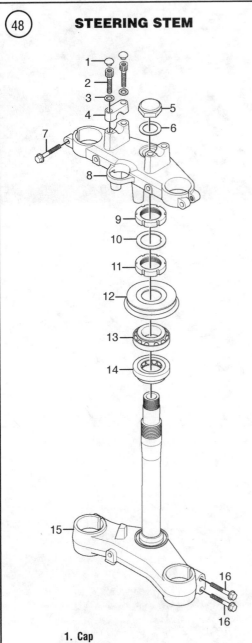

STEERING STEM

48

1. Cap
2. Allen bolt
3. Washer
4. Upper handlebar holder
5. Cap nut
6. Washer
7. Bolt
8. Upper steering bracket
9. Locknut
10. Tab washer
11. Steering stem nut
12. Dust seal
13. Bearing
14. Bearing
15. Steering stem
16. Bolt

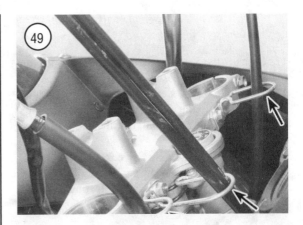

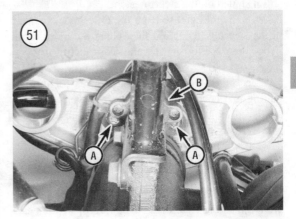

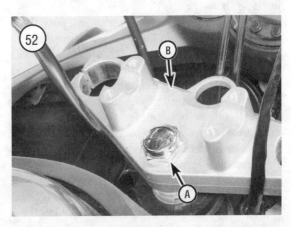

12

*stem nut or the assembly will drop out
of the steering head.*

11. Support the steering stem and remove the nut
(**Figure 58**).

12. Gently lower the steering stem out of the frame.
Do not worry about catching loose bearing balls.
Both bearings are caged ball bearings with no loose
parts.

13. Lift off the dust seal (**Figure 59**).

14. Carefully remove the upper bearing (**Figure 60**)
from the upper bearing race in the steering head.

CAUTION
*Do not attempt to remove the lower
bearing race from the steering stem
unless bearing replacement is necessary. The bearing race is pressed on
the steering stem and will be damaged
during removal.*

Inspection

1. Clean the upper and lower bearings in a bearing degreaser. Make certain the bearing degreaser is
compatible with the rubber covers on each bearing.
Hold onto the bearing so it does not spin and thoroughly dry both bearings with compressed air. Make
sure all solvent is removed from the lower bearing
still installed on the steering stem.

2. Wipe the old grease from the outer races located
in the steering head, and then clean the outer races
with a rag soaked in solvent. Thoroughly dry the
races with a lint-free cloth.

3. Check the steering stem outer races for pitting,
galling and corrosion. If any race is worn or damaged, replace the race(s) and bearing as an assembly
as described in this chapter.

4. Check the steering head for cracks and fractures.
If any damage is found, have the frame repaired at a
competent frame shop or welding service.

5. Check the balls for pitting, scratches or discoloration indicating wear or corrosion. Replace the bearing if any balls are less than perfect.

6. If the bearings are in good condition, pack them
thoroughly with Suzuki Super Grease A or an equivalent waterproof bearing grease. To pack the bearings, spread some grease in the palm of your hand
and scrape the open side of the bearing across your
palm until the bearing is packed completely full of
grease. Rotate the bearing a few times to determine if
there are any open areas; repack if necessary.

7. Thoroughly clean all mounting parts in solvent.
Dry them completely.

8. Inspect the nut and washers for wear or damage.
Inspect the threads. If necessary, clean them with an
appropriate size metric tap or replace the nut(s). If the

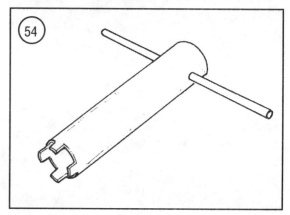

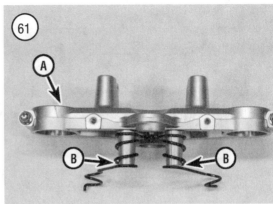

threads are damaged, inspect the appropriate steering stem thread(s) for damage. If necessary, clean the threads with an appropriate size metric die.

9. Inspect the steering stem nut washer for damage. Replace it if necessary. If damaged, check the underside of the steering stem nut for damage. Replace it as necessary.

10. Inspect the steering stem and the lower bracket for cracks or other damage. Make sure the lower bracket clamping areas are free of burrs and the bolt holes are in good condition.

11. Inspect the upper steering bracket (A, **Figure 61**). If necessary, replace the cable holders (B). Check both the upper and lower surface of the bracket. Make sure the bracket clamping areas are free of burrs and the bolt holes are in good condition.

Installation

Refer to **Figure 48**.

1. Make sure the steering head outer races are properly seated and clean.

2. Apply an even, complete coat of Suzuki Super Grease A or equivalent to the steering head outer races, to both bearings, and to the dust seal.

3. Install the upper bearing into the race in the top of the steering head.

4. Carefully slide the steering stem up into the frame. Take care not to dislodge the upper bearing.

5. Hold the steering stem in position and install the dust seal (**Figure 62**) on top of the upper bearing.

6. Install the steering stem nut (**Figure 58**). Use the same tool setup used during disassembly and tighten the steering stem nut to 45 N•m (33 ft.-lb.).

7. Move the steering stem back and forth from lock to lock five or six times to make sure the bearings are completely seated.

8. Loosen the steering stem nut 1/4 to 1/2 turn. Verify that the steering stem moves freely.

9. Install the tab washer (**Figure 57**) so the tab engages the groove in the steering stem.

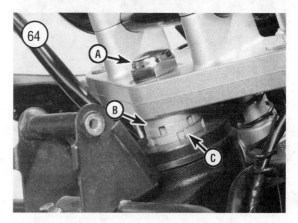

10. Install the locknut (**Figure 56**). Tighten the lock-nut to 80 N•m (58 ft.-lb.).

11. Insert the cables into the cable holders (**Figure 53**) on the upper steering bracket.

12. Install the upper steering bracket assembly (B, **Figure 52**), washer and cap nut (A). Tighten the cap nut only fingertight at this time. Do not tighten the cap nut until the front forks are installed. This will ensure proper alignment between the steering stem and the upper steering bracket.

13. Install the ignition switch. Apply Threadlock 1342 to the bolt threads. Tighten the bolts securely.

14A. On non-ABS models, attach the front brake hose guide to the lower steering bracket.

14B. On ABS models, attach the brake system joint (B, **Figure 50**) to the lower steering bracket with the retaining bolt (A).

15. Install the wire guides (**Figure 49**).

16. Install the front fork as described in this chapter. Tighten the lower fork clamp bolts to 23 N•m (17 ft.-lb.).

17. Check the movement of the front fork and steering stem assembly. The steering stem must turn freely from side to side, but without any free play when the fork legs are moved fore and aft.

18. Tighten the steering stem cap nut (A, **Figure 52**) to 90 N•m (65 ft.-lb.). Recheck the movement of the front end and readjust if necessary.

19. Complete installation of the front forks as described in this chapter.

20. Install the handlebar assembly as described in this chapter.

Adjustment

1. Raise the motorcycle with a jack and place wooden blocks under the frame to support the bike securely with the front wheel off the ground 20-30 mm (0.8-1.2 in.).

2. Grasp each fork leg at the lower end and attempt to move the forks back and forth. If any fore and aft

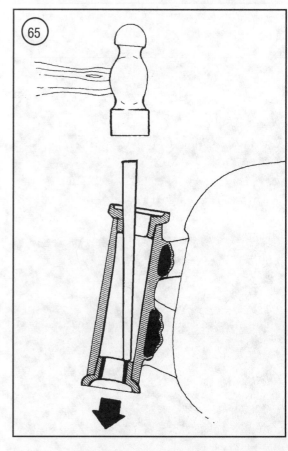

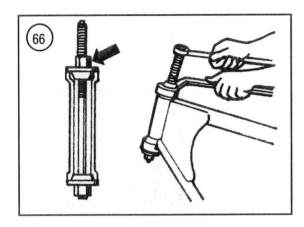

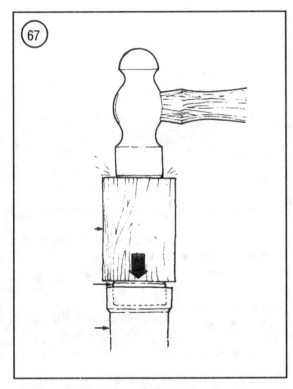

10. Loosen the steering stem cap nut (A, **Figure 64**).

11. Loosen the locknut (B, **Figure 64**).

12. Turn the steering stem nut (C, **Figure 64**) to adjust steering movement.

13. Tighten the locknut to 80 N•m (58 ft.-lb.).

14. Tighten the steering stem cap nut (A, **Figure 64**) to 90 N•m (65 ft.-lb.).

15. Tighten the upper fork clamp bolts to 23 N•m (17 ft.-lb.).

16. Recheck steering movement and, if necessary, repeat adjustment.

STEERING HEAD BEARING RACES

The headset and steering stem bearing races are pressed into the headset portion of the frame. Because the races are easily bent, do not remove them unless they require replacement.

**Headset Bearing Race
Removal/Installation**

1. Remove the steering stem as described in this chapter.

2. Insert a hardwood stick or soft punch into the head tube and carefully tap the outer race out from the inside (**Figure 65**).

3. After first movement of the bearing race, work around the outer race in a crossing pattern so that neither the race nor the head tube is damaged.

4A. Use the Suzuki bearing installer (part No. 09941-34513) to install the headset bearing race as follows:

  a. Position the outer races into the headset and just start them into position lightly with a soft-faced mallet. Just tap them in enough to hold them in place.

  b. Position the bearing installer (**Figure 66**) into both of the outer races.

  c. Tighten the nuts on the bearing installer and pull the outer races into place in the headset. Tighten the nuts until both bearing outer races are completely seated in the head set and is flush with the steering head surface.

  d. Remove the special tool.

4B. If the special tools are not used, perform the following:

  a. Position one of the outer races into the headset and just start it into position lightly with a soft-faced mallet. Just tap it in enough to hold it in place.

  b. Tap the outer race in slowly with a block of wood or a suitable size socket or pipe (**Figure 67**). Make sure that the race is squarely seated

movement of the front end is detected, the steering stem nut must be adjusted.

3. Attach a spring scale to the outer end of either hand grip.

4. Point the front wheel straight ahead.

5. Pull the spring scale while keeping the scale at right angle to the handlebar.

6. The spring scale should read 200-500 grams just as the handlebar starts to move. Make sure no cables, wires or other objects prevent the movement.

7. Repeat the procedure using the opposite throttle grip.

8. If the scale reading is incorrect, adjust the steering as follows.

9. Loosen the upper fork clamp bolts (**Figure 63**).

12

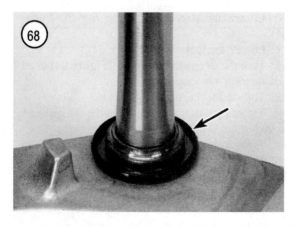

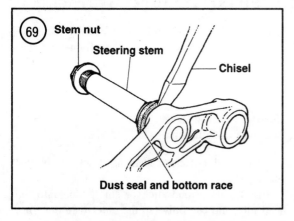

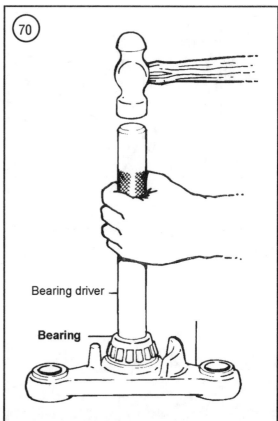

in the headset race bore before tapping it into place. Tap the race in until it is flush with the steering head surface.

c. Repeat for the other outer race.

Steering Stem Lower Bearing Race Removal/Installation

Do not remove the steering stem lower bearing race and seal (**Figure 68**) unless replacement is necessary. The lower bearing race can be difficult to remove. If you cannot remove it as described in this procedure, take the steering stem to a dealership service department and have them replace the bearing race.

Never reinstall a lower bearing race that has been removed as it is no longer true and will damage the rest of the bearing assembly if reused.

1. Install the steering stem bolt onto the top of the steering stem to protect the threads.

2. Loosen the lower bearing race from the shoulder at the base or the steering stem using a chisel as shown in **Figure 69**. Slide the lower bearing race and grease seal off the steering stem. Discard the lower bearing race and the grease seal.

3. Clean the steering stem with solvent and dry thoroughly.

4. Position the new grease seal so the seal outer lip faces up.

5. Slide the new grease seal and the lower bearing race onto the steering stem until they stop on the raised shoulder.

6. Using a piece of pipe with the same ID as the bearing race ID, or Suzuki steering stem bearing race installer (part No. 09925-18011), carefully tap on the bearing installer and drive the lower bearing race into place (**Figure 70**).

7. Remove the bearing race installer and verify that the race is seated squarely and is all the way down.

Table 1 FRONT SUSPENSION SPECIFICATIONS

Item	Specification	Service limit
Front fork oil		
Viscosity	SS-08 fork oil	
Capacity per leg	524 mL	
	(17.7 US oz., 18.5 lmp. oz.)	
Front fork oil level	143 mm (5.63 in.)	
Front fork spring free length	–	444 mm (17.5 in.)
Front wheel travel	150 mm (5.9 in.)	
Steering		
Caster angle	26°	
Trail	110 mm (4.33 in.)	

Table 2 FRONT SUSPENSION TORQUE SPECIFICATIONS

Item	N•m	in. lb.	ft.-lb.
Clutch lever clamping bolt	10	–	88
Front fork cap bolt	23	–	17
Front fork clamp bolts	23	–	17
Front fork damper rod Allen bolt	20	177	–
Handlebar holder bolt	23	–	17
Steering stem cap nut	90	–	65
Steering stem locknut	80	–	58
Steering stem nut*			
*Refer to text.			

12

Notes

CHAPTER THIRTEEN

REAR SUSPENSION

This chapter contains repair and replacement procedures for the rear suspension. Rear suspension specifications and torque specifications are listed in **Tables 1-2** at the end of this chapter.

NOTE
In the following procedures, whenever grease is referenced, a molydisulfide or waterproof grease should be used. Molydisulfide grease has excellent antiwear characteristics when subjected to extreme pressure. Waterproof grease, which is very durable, has a high tack and is very resistant to washout when subjected to wet conditions. Which grease to use is a preference of the rider and the conditions in which the motorcycle is operated. If the linkage is regularly maintained, either grease will perform well.

SHOCK ABSORBER

Removal/Installation

1. Support the motorcycle securely with the rear wheel off the ground. If a motorcycle stand or jack is not available, place wooden block(s) under the engine.

2. Remove the rear side covers as described in Chapter Fifteen.
3. Remove the bolts (**Figure 1**) securing the rear shock absorber adjuster.
4. Remove the lower tie rod bolt and nut (**Figure 2**) and allow the tie rods to hang down.
5. Remove the lower shock mounting bolt (**Figure 3**), and separate the lower shock mount from the shock lever.
6. Detach the shock absorber adjuster hose from the retaining clamp.
7. Remove the upper shock mounting bolt (**Figure 4**).
8. Remove the shock absorber by lowering it down through the swing arm.
9. Inspect the shock absorber as described in this chapter.
10. Reverse the removal procedure to install the shock absorber. Note the following:
    a. Install the shock absorber and tie rod bolts from the left side.
    b. Tighten the shock absorber mounting nuts to 50 N•m (37 ft.-lb.).
    c. Tighten the tie rod nut to 78 N•m (57 ft.-lb.).

Inspection

No replacement parts are available for the original equipment shock absorber. If any part of the shock

13

absorber is defective, replace the shock absorber assembly.

1. Inspect the shock absorber for oil leaks.

2. Check the spring (A, **Figure 5**) for cracks or other damage.

3. Inspect the upper (B, **Figure 5**) and lower (C) mounts for wear or damage.

4. Check operation of the spring preload control (D, **Figure 5**). If faulty, the shock absorber must be replaced.

SWING ARM

Swing Arm Bearing

Preliminary inspection

The condition of the swing arm bearings can greatly affect the handling of the motorcycle. Worn bearings causes wheel hop, pulling to one side under acceleration and pulling to the other side during braking. To check the condition of the swing arm bearings, perform the following steps.

1. Remove the rear wheel as described in Chapter Eleven.

2. Remove the rear tie rod mounting bolt and nut (**Figure 2**) and lower the tie rods away from the swing arm.

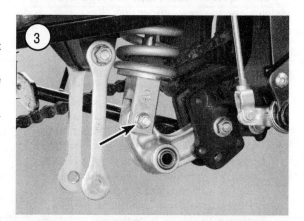

3. Remove the cover (**Figure 6**).

4. On the right side, make sure the swing arm pivot locknut nut (A, **Figure 7**) is tight.

5. On the left side, make sure the pivot nut (**Figure 8**) is tight.

6. The swing arm is now free to move under its own weight.

> *NOTE*
> *Have an assistant steady the motorcycle when performing Step 6 and Step 7.*

7. Grasp both ends of the swing arm and attempt to move it from side to side in a horizontal arc. If more than a slight amount of movement is felt, the bearings are worn and must be replaced.

8. Grasp both ends of the swing arm and move it up and down. The swing arm should move smoothly with no binding or abnormal noise from the bearings. If there is binding or noise, the bearings are worn and must be replaced.

9. Move the swing arm and the tie rods into position. Install the rear tie rod bolt from the left side. Install the tie rod nut and tighten to 78 N•m (57 ft.-lb.).

10. Install the rear wheel as described in this chapter.

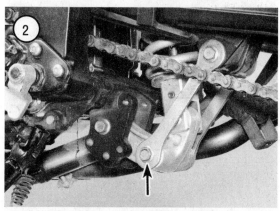

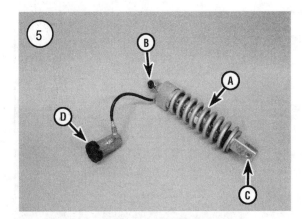

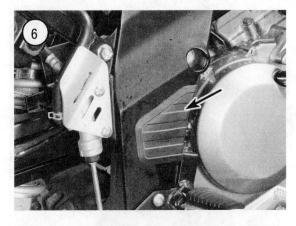

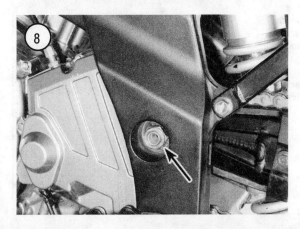

Removal

Refer to **Figure 9**.

1. Remove the exhaust system as described in Chapter Four.

2. Remove the rear wheel as described in Chapter Eleven.

3. Remove the chain guard from the swing arm.

4. Remove the bolts securing the rear brake hose clamp (**Figure 10**).

5. Remove the rear brake caliper as described in Chapter Fourteen. Suspend the caliper out of the way.

6. Remove the brake caliper bracket from the swing arm (**Figure 11**).

7. Remove the shock linkage as described in this chapter.

8. On the right side, use the Suzuki Swing Arm Pivot Thrust Adjuster Socket Wrench, (part No. 09940-14940) and remove the pivot locknut (A, **Figure 7**).

> *NOTE*
> *A socket wrench tool may be created from a suitable impact socket (**Figure 12**).*

9. Tie the end of the swing arm to the frame or place a box under the end of the swing arm and support it securely.

10. Hold the pivot shaft (B, **Figure 7**) with a suitable socket.

11. On the left side, remove the pivot nut (**Figure 8**) and washer.

12. From the left side, carefully tap the pivot shaft out of the frame and swing arm. Pull the pivot shaft (**Figure 13**) from the right side of the frame.

13. Lower the swing arm from the frame or from the box.

14. Rotate the swing arm and separate it from the drive chain.

15. If the swing arm bearings are not going to be serviced, place a strip of duct tape over each pivot. This protects the bearing assemblies and prevents the loss of any small parts.

16. If necessary, remove the mud guard flap from the swing arm.

17. Inspect the swing arm as described in this chapter. Lubricate all bearings as described in this chapter.

Installation

1. Lubricate the swing arm and shock linkage bearings, the pivot bolts and collars with waterproof grease before installation.

13

⑨

SWING ARM

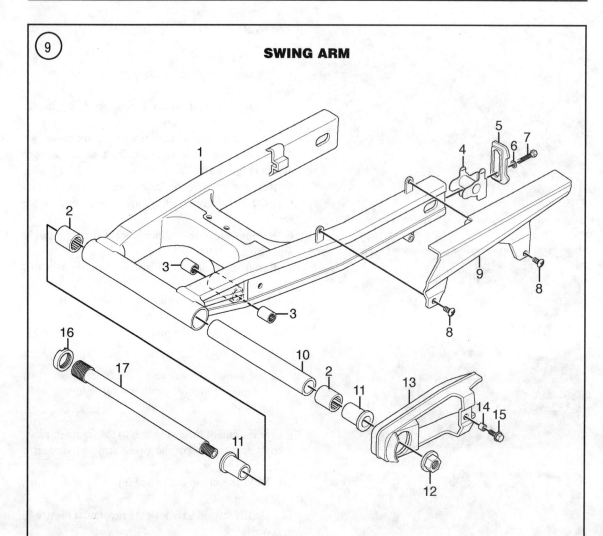

1. Swing arm
2. Bearing
3. Bearing
4. Chain adjuster
5. Chain adjuster guide
6. Washer
7. Chain adjuster bolt
8. Bolt
9. Chain guard
10. Spacer
11. Bushing
12. Locknut
13. Chain slider
14. Spacer
15. Bolt
16. Locknut
17 Pivot shaft

2. If removed, reattach the mud guard flap onto the swing arm.

3. Place the drive chain around the swing arm and set the swing arm in place beneath the frame.

4. Raise the swing arm and install it between the frame pivots. From the right side of the motorcycle, install the swing arm pivot shaft (**Figure 13**) through the frame and the swing arm pivots.

5. Loosely install the nut (**Figure 8**) onto the left end of the pivot shaft.

6. Set the thrust clearance by tightening the swing arm pivot fasteners in the order described below.

    a. Tighten the swing arm pivot shaft (B, **Figure 7**) to 15 N•m (133 in.-lb.).

    b. Hold the pivot shaft with a suitable hex tool and tighten the pivot nut (**Figure 8**) to 100 N•m (74 ft.-lb.).

    c. Install the pivot locknut (A, **Figure 7**). Tighten the pivot locknut to 90 N•m (66 ft.-lb.).

7. After tightening all of the fasteners in Step 6, move the swing arm up and down and check for smooth movement. If the swing arm is tight or loose, then the fasteners in Step 6 were either tightened in the wrong sequence or to the incorrect torque specification; repeat Step 6.

8. Install the shock linkage as described in this chapter.

9. Install the rear brake caliper bracket (**Figure 11**).

10. Install the rear brake caliper as described in Chapter Fourteen.

11. Attach the rear brake hose clamp (**Figure 10**) to the swing arm.

12. Install the chain guard onto the swing arm.

13. Install the rear wheel as described in Chapter Eleven.

14. Install the exhaust system as described in Chapter Four.

15. Adjust the drive chain as described in Chapter Three.

13

Disassembly

Refer to **Figure 9**.

1. Remove the swing arm assembly as described in this chapter.

2. Remove the bushing (**Figure 14**) from each needle bearing.

4. Remove the spacer (A, **Figure 15**) from the pivot boss (B, **Figure 15**) on the swing arm.

5. If necessary, remove the chain slider from the swing arm.

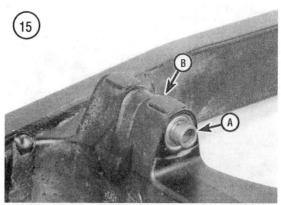

Inspection

1. Wash the bolts, collar and bushings in solvent, and thoroughly dry them.

2. Inspect the spacer and bushings for wear, scratches or score marks.

3. Inspect the swing arm pivot bearings as follows:

   a. Use a clean lint-free rag and wipe off surface grease from the pivot area needle bearings.

   b. Turn each bearing (**Figure 16**) by hand. The bearing should turn smoothly without excessive play or noise. Check the rollers for wear, pitting or rust.

   c. Inspect the bushings (**Figure 17**) for wear, scratches or score marks.

   d. Reinstall the bushing (**Figure 14**) into the bearings and slowly rotate each bushing. The bushings must turn smoothly without excessive play or noise.

   e. Remove the bushings.

4. Inspect the tie-rod pivot boss (B, **Figure 15**) on the swing arm as follows:

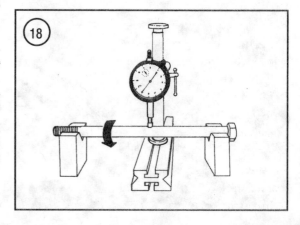

   a. Use a clean lint-free rag and wipe off surface grease from the needle bearings.

   b. Turn each bearing by hand. The bearing should turn smoothly without excessive play or noise. Check the rollers for wear, pitting or rust.

   c. Insert the spacer (A, **Figure 15**) into each bearing and slowly rotate the collar. It should turn smoothly without excessive play or noise.

   d. Remove the spacer.

5. Replace any worn or damaged bearing as described in *Swing Arm Needle Bearing Replacement* in this chapter.

6. Check the welded sections on the swing arm for cracks or fractures.

7. Check the pivot shaft for straightness with V-blocks and a dial indicator (**Figure 18**). Replace the pivot shaft if the runout exceeds 0.3 mm (0.012 in.).

8. Inspect the drive chain slider for wear or damage. Replace if necessary.

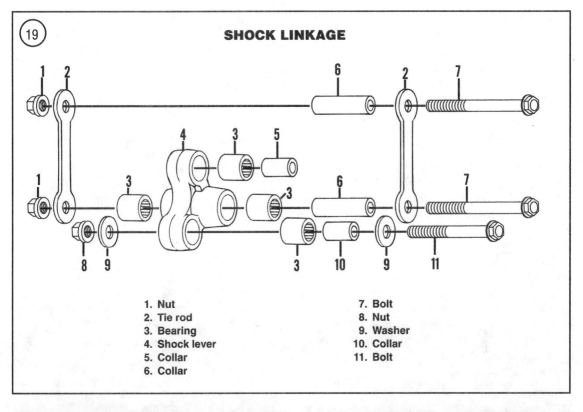

19

SHOCK LINKAGE

1. Nut
2. Tie rod
3. Bearing
4. Shock lever
5. Collar
6. Collar
7. Bolt
8. Nut
9. Washer
10. Collar
11. Bolt

20

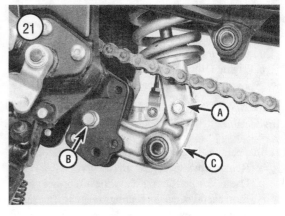

21

13

Assembly

1. If removed, install the chain slider onto the swing arm.

2. Lubricate the following parts with grease:
   a. Needle bearings.
   b. Spacers and bushings.

3. Install the spacer (A, **Figure 15**) into the tie-rod pivot boss (B) on the swing arm. Make sure the ends of the collar are flush with the end of each needle bearing.

4. Install the bushing (**Figure 14**) into the needle bearing on each side of the swing arm pivot.

5. Install the swing arm as described in this chapter.

SHOCK LINKAGE

Removal

Refer to **Figure 19**.

1. Support the motorcycle securely with the rear wheel off the ground. If a motorcycle stand or jack is not available, place wooden block(s) under the engine.

2. Remove the nuts and bolts securing the tie rods (**Figure 20**) to the shock lever and swing arm. Remove the tie rods.

3. Remove the bolt (A, **Figure 21**) securing the lower shock mount to the shock lever.

4. Remove the shock lever mounting bolt (B, **Figure 21**). Pull the shock lever pivot bolt from the left side

of the motorcycle and lower the shock lever (C, **Figure 21**) from the frame bracket.

Installation

NOTE
Install all bolts from the left side of the motorcycle.

1. Apply grease to the pivot points on the lower end of the shock absorber and to the frame mounting boss.
2. Install a washer (**Figure 22**) on each side of the shock lever. Then insert the shock lever into the frame bracket. Insert the shock lever pivot bolt from the left side. Install but do not tighten the nut at this time.
3. Move the shock lever up and align the lever rear pivot with the shock absorber lower mount. Loosely insert the shock mounting bolt (A, **Figure 21**) from the right side. Fingertighten the bolt at this time.
4. Rotate the tie rods forward and align their mounting holes with the center pivot on the shock lever.
5. Install the tie rod bolts and loosely install the tie-rod mounting nuts.
6. Tighten the mounting hardware in the following order:
   a. Tighten the shock lever mounting nut to 78 N•m (57 ft.-lb.).
   b. Tighten the tie-rod retaining nuts to 78 N•m (57 ft.-lb.).
   c. Tighten the lower shock mounting bolt (A, **Figure 21**) to 50 N•m (37 ft.-lb.).

Inspection

1. Inspect the shock lever pivot bearings as follows:
   a. Remove the spacers from the pivot.
   b. Use a clean lint-free rag and wipe off surface grease from the pivot needle bearings (**Figure 23**).
   c. Turn each bearing by hand. The bearing should turn smoothly without excessive play or noise. Check the rollers for wear, pitting or rust.
   d. Reinstall the spacers (**Figure 24**) into the bearings and slowly rotate each spacer. The collars must turn smoothly without excessive play or noise.
   e. Remove the spacers.
   f. If the needle bearings must be replaced, refer to *Shock Lever Needle Bearing Replacement* in this chapter.
2. Inspect the spacers for wear and damage. Replace each collar as necessary.
3. Inspect the rocker arm for cracks or damage. Replace as necessary.
4. Inspect the tie rods (**Figure 25**) for bending, cracks or damage. Replace as necessary.

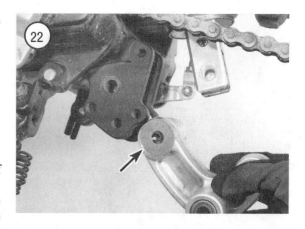

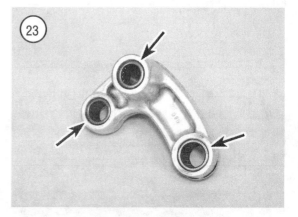

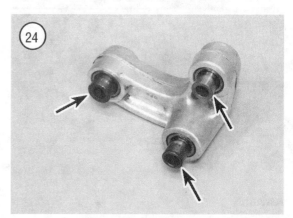

5. Clean the pivot bolts and nuts in solvent. Check the bolts for straightness. If a bolt is bent, it will restrict the movement of the rocker arm.
6. Before installing the spacers, coat the inner surface of the bearings with molybdenum disulfide grease.

BEARING REPLACEMENT

Swing Arm Needle Bearing Replacement

Do not remove the swing arm needle bearings unless they must be replaced. The needle bearings are pressed onto the swing arm. A set of blind bearing

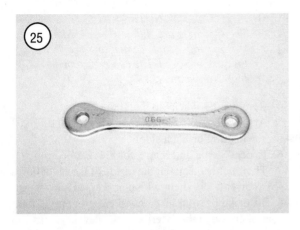

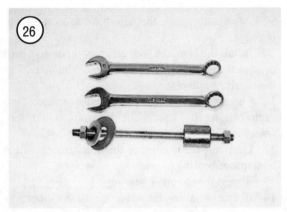

pullers is required to remove the needle bearings. The needle bearings can be installed with a homemade tool.

NOTE
If the needle bearings are replaced, replace the pivot bushings at the same time. These parts should always be replaced as a set.

1. If still installed, remove the pivot bushings (**Figure 14**) from the needle bearings as described in this chapter.

NOTE
In the following steps, the bearing puller grabs the inner surface of the bearing and then withdraws it from the pivot boss in the swing arm.

2. Insert the Suzuki bearing puller (part No. 09921-20240) or an equivalent blind bearing puller through the needle bearing and expand it behind the bearing.
3. Using sharp strokes of the slide hammer, withdraw the needle bearing from the pivot boss.
4. Remove the bearing puller and the bearing.
5. Withdraw the spacer located between the bearings.
6. Repeat for the bearing on the other side.
7. Remove the special tool.
8. Repeat Steps 2-7 for the shock lever pivot bearings on the bottom of the swing arm.
9. Thoroughly clean the inside of the pivot bore with solvent, then dry it with compressed air.
10. To make bearing installation easier, apply a light coat of grease to the exterior of the new bearings and to the inner circumference of the pivot bore.

NOTE
Install one needle bearing at a time. Make sure the bearing is entering the pivot boss squarely, otherwise the bearing and the pivot boss may be damaged.

11. Position the bearing with the manufacturer's marks facing out.

NOTE
The bearing can be easily installed using a homemade tool consisting of a piece of threaded rod, two thick washers, two nuts, a socket that matches the outer race diameter, and two wrenches as shown in Figure 26.

12. Locate and square the new bearing in the pivot bore. Assemble the homemade tool through the pivot bore so the socket presses against the bearing. See **Figure 27**.
13. Hold the nut adjacent to the socket (A, **Figure 27**).
14. Tighten the nut on the opposite side (B, **Figure 27**) and pull the bearing into the pivot bore. Pull the bearing until it is flush with the outer surface of the pivot boss.
15. Disassemble the tool and reinstall it on the opposite side, then repeat for the other bearing.
16. Remove the tool.
17. Make sure the bearings are properly seated. Turn each bearing with by hand, it should turn smoothly.
18. Lubricate the new bearings with grease.

13

19. Repeat for the other set of bearings in the swing arm.

Shock Lever Needle Bearing Replacement

Do not remove the shock lever needle bearings unless they must be replaced. The needle bearings are pressed onto the shock lever. A set of blind bearing pullers is required to remove the needle bearings. The needle bearings can be installed with a homemade tool, or socket and hammer.

NOTE
If the needle bearings are replaced, replace the spacers at the same time. These parts should always be replaced as a set.

1. If still installed, remove the spacers.

NOTE
In the following steps, the bearing puller grabs the inner surface of the bearing and then withdraws it from the pivot areas of the swing arm.

2. Insert the bearing puller through the needle bearing and expand it behind the front bearing.
3. Using sharp strokes of the slide hammer, withdraw the needle bearing from the front pivot hole.

NOTE
The bearings are different sizes. Mark the bearings front, center and rear as they are removed. The center two bearings are identical.

4. Remove the special tool and the bearing.
5. At the center pivot area, repeat Step 2 and Step 3 for the bearing on each side.
6. Repeat Step 2 and Step 3 for the rear bearing.
7. Thoroughly clean out the inside of the pivot bores with solvent. Dry them with compressed air.
8. To make bearing installation easier, apply a light coat of grease to the exterior of the new bearings and to the inner circumference of the pivot bores.
9. Locate and square the new bearing in the pivot bore.
10. Install the bearings with an appropriate size drift or socket that matches the outer race diameter. Tap the bearings into place.
11. Check that the bearing is properly seated. Turn each bearing by hand. The bearing should turn smoothly.
12. Lubricate the needles of the new bearing with a waterproof bearing grease.
13. Repeat for the other bearings.
14. Before installing the spacers, coat the inner surface of the bearings with grease. Install the spacers as described in this chapter.

Table 1 REAR SUSPENSION SPECIFICATIONS

Item	New	Service limit
Swing arm pivot shaft runout (max.)	–	0.3 mm (0.012 in.)

Table 2 REAR SUSPENSION TORQUE SPECIFICATIONS

Item	N•m	in. lb.	ft.-lb.
Shock absorber mounting bolt			
Upper and lower	50	–	37
Shock lever mounting bolt	78	–	57
Swing arm			
Pivot locknut	90	–	66
Pivot nut	100	–	73.5
Pivot shaft	15	133	–
Tie rod nut (both ends)	78	–	57

CHAPTER FOURTEEN

BRAKES

This chapter covers service, repair and replacement procedures for the front and rear brake systems. Brake specifications are located in **Table 1** and **Table 2** at the end of this chapter.

The brake system consists of a hydraulically actuated single disc type system at the front and rear.

DL650A models are equipped with an anti-lock brake system (ABS) that prevents wheel lockup during hard braking or when braking on slippery surfaces.

BRAKE FLUID SELECTION

WARNING
Do not intermix silicone based (DOT 5) brake fluid with glycol-based (DOT 4) brake fluid as it can cause brake system failure.

When adding brake fluid, use DOT 4 brake fluid from a sealed container. DOT 4 brake fluid is glycol-based and draws moisture, which greatly reduces its ability to perform correctly. Purchase brake fluid in small containers and discard any small leftover quantities. Do not store a container of brake fluid with less than 1/4 of the fluid remaining.

BRAKE SERVICE

WARNING
Do not ride the motorcycle unless the brakes work correctly.

WARNING
The proper operation of this system depends on a supply of clean brake fluid (DOT 4) and a clean work environment when any service is being performed. Any debris that enters the system can damage the components and cause poor brake performance.

WARNING
When working on the brake system, do not inhale brake dust. It may contain asbestos, which is a known carcinogen. Do not use compressed air to blow off brake dust. Use an aerosol brake cleaner. Wear a face mask that meets OSHA requirements. Wash hands and forearms thoroughly after completing the work. Wet down the brake dust on brake components before working on the brake system with an aerosol brake cleaner. Secure and dispose of all brake dust and cleaning materials properly.

14

Consider the following when servicing the brake system:

1. The hydraulic components rarely require disassembly. Make sure it is necessary.

2. Keep the reservoir covers in place to prevent the entry of moisture and debris.

3. Clean parts with an aerosol brake parts cleaner or isopropyl alcohol. Never use petroleum-based solvents on internal brake system components. They will cause seals to swell and distort.

4. Do not allow brake fluid to contact plastic, painted or plated parts. It will damage the surface.

5. Before performing any procedure in which there is the possibility of brake fluid contacting the motorcycle, cover the work area with a large piece of plastic.

6. Before handling brake fluid or working on the brake system, fill a small container with soap and water and keep it close to the motorcycle while working. If brake fluid contacts the motorcycle, clean the area and rinse it thoroughly.

7. To help control the flow of brake fluid when filling the reservoirs, punch a small hole into the seal of a new container next to the edge of the pour spout.

8. Do not reuse brake fluid. Dispose of it properly.

9. If the hydraulic system, not including the reservoir cover, has been opened, bleed the system to remove air from the system. Refer to *Brake Bleeding* in this chapter.

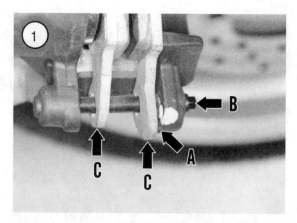

FRONT BRAKE PADS

Inspection

Inspect the front brake pads as described in Chapter Three.

Brake Pad Replacement

1. Place a spacer between the brake lever and the throttle grip and secure it in place. That way if the brake lever is inadvertently squeezed, the pistons will not be forced out of the cylinders.

2. Remove the caliper as described in this chapter.

3. Remove the clip (A, **Figure 1**) and pin (B).

4. Remove both brake pads (C, **Figure 1**) from the caliper assembly.

5. Clean the pad recess and the end of both sets of pistons with a soft brush. Do not use solvent, a wire brush or any hard tool that would damage the cylinders or pistons.

6. Carefully remove any rust or corrosion from the disc.

7. Thoroughly clean the pad pin and clip of any corrosion or road dirt.

8. Check the friction surface of the new pads for any foreign matter or manufacturing residue. If necessary, clean the pads with an aerosol brake cleaner. Make sure the friction compound of the new pads is compatible with the disc material.

9. When new pads are installed in the calipers, the master cylinder brake fluid level will rise as the caliper pistons are repositioned. Perform the following:

   a. Clean all dirt and foreign matter from the top of the master cylinder.

   b. Cover the area beneath the master cylinder to protect parts from brake fluid spills.

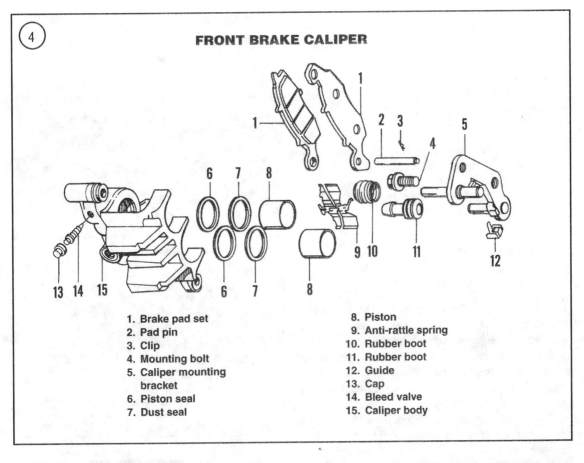

FRONT BRAKE CALIPER

1. Brake pad set
2. Pad pin
3. Clip
4. Mounting bolt
5. Caliper mounting bracket
6. Piston seal
7. Dust seal
8. Piston
9. Anti-rattle spring
10. Rubber boot
11. Rubber boot
12. Guide
13. Cap
14. Bleed valve
15. Caliper body

c. Remove the screws securing the cover (**Figure 2**). Remove the cover and the diaphragm from the master cylinder.

d. Temporarily install both old brake pads into the caliper and seat them against the pistons.

e. Protect the caliper with a shop cloth to prevent scuffing it, then grasp the caliper and brake pad with a large pair of slip-joint pliers. Squeeze the piston back into the caliper. Repeat for each side until the pistons are completely into the caliper.

f. Constantly check the reservoir and make sure the fluid does not overflow. Draw out excess fluid if necessary.

g. The pistons should move freely. If they do not, remove and service the caliper as described in this chapter.

h. Remove the old brake pads.

10. Install the brake pad spring (**Figure 3**).

11. Install the brake pads (C, **Figure 1**) into the caliper, then install the pad mounting pin (B) and clip (A).

12. Carefully install the caliper assembly onto the brake disc. Be careful not to damage the leading edges of the pads during installation.

13. Remove the spacer from the front brake lever.

14. Pump the front brake lever to reposition the brake pads against the brake disc. Roll the motorcycle back and forth and continue to pump the brake lever as many times as it takes to refill the cylinders in the calipers and correctly position the brake pads against the disc.

15. Refill the master cylinder reservoir, if necessary, to maintain the correct fluid level as indicated on the side of the reservoir. Install the diaphragm and cover. Tighten the cover retaining screws securely.

NOTE
For proper brake operation, follow break-in procedure specified by brake pad manufacturer.

FRONT CALIPER

Removal/Installation

Refer to **Figure 4**.

CAUTION
Do not spill brake fluid on the motorcycle. Brake fluid will destroy the finish on plastic, painted or plated surfaces. Use soapy water to wash off spilled brake fluid immediately.

14

1. If the caliper assembly is going to be disassembled for service, perform the following:

a. Remove the brake pads as described in this chapter.

b. Reinstall the caliper assembly onto the brake disc and fork assembly. Tighten the caliper mounting bolts only fingertight.

CAUTION
During the following procedure, do not allow the pistons to come in contact with the brake disc. If this happens the pistons may damage the disc during caliper removal.

NOTE
When performing Step 1c, compressed air may not be necessary for piston removal during caliper disassembly.

c. Slowly apply the brake lever to push the pistons part way out of the caliper assembly for ease of removal during caliper service.

2. Remove the union bolt (A, **Figure 5**) and sealing washers attaching the brake hose to the caliper assembly. There should be two sealing washers—one on each side of the union bolt.

3. Place the loose end of the brake hose in a closable plastic bag to prevent brake fluid from dribbling onto the wheel or fork.

4. Remove the two caliper mounting bolts (B, **Figure 5**) and lift the brake caliper off the disc.

5. Drain any brake fluid remaining in the caliper.

6. If necessary, disassemble and service the caliper assembly as described in this chapter.

7. Install by reversing the preceding removal steps while noting the following:

a. Carefully install the caliper assembly onto the disc being careful not to damage the leading edge of the brake pads.

b. Install the two caliper mounting bolts (B, **Figure 5**) and secure the brake caliper to the front fork. Tighten the caliper mounting bolts to 39 N•m (29 ft.-lb.).

c. If disconnected, connect the brake hose to the caliper. Install a new sealing washer on each side of the union bolt (A, **Figure 5**). Tighten the union bolt to 23 N•m (17 ft.-lb.).

d. If the brake hose was disconnected from the caliper, fill and bleed the brake system as described in this chapter.

Disassembly

Refer to **Figure 4**.

1. Remove the caliper and brake pads as described in this chapter.

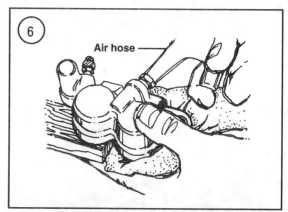

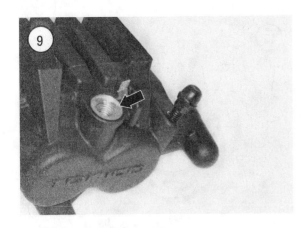

2. Before removing the pistons, identify the pistons by marking their inner bore with a black marker so they can be reinstalled in their original cylinders.

WARNING
Be careful when using compressed air. The piston, dirt or some other material can fly from the caliper at great speed and cause injury. Keep fingers out of the way. Wear safety eyewear and shop gloves and apply compressed air gradually. Do NOT use high pressure air or place the air hose nozzle directly against the hydraulic fluid passageway

in the caliper. Hold the air nozzle away from the inlet allowing some of the air to escape during the procedure.

NOTE
If the pistons were partially forced out of the caliper body during removal, Steps 3-4 may not be necessary. If the pistons or caliper bores are corroded or very dirty, a small amount of compressed air may be necessary to completely remove the pistons from the bores.

3. Place a rag or piece of wood in the path of the pistons (**Figure 6**) and place the caliper on the workbench so that the pistons face down.
4. Blow the piston out with compressed air directed into the hydraulic fluid hole (**Figure 6**).
5. Remove the piston seals and dust seals.
6. Inspect the caliper body as described in this section.

Inspection

1. Carefully slide the caliper mounting bracket (A, **Figure 7**) from the caliper assembly.
2. Clean the caliper and pistons with an aerosol brake cleaner or isopropyl alcohol. Thoroughly dry the parts with compressed air.
3. Make sure the fluid passageways (B, **Figure 7**) in the base of the piston bores are clear. Apply compressed air to the openings to make sure they are clear. Clean the passages if necessary.
4. Inspect the piston and dust seal grooves (**Figure 8**) in the caliper body for damage. If any groove is damaged or corroded, replace the caliper assembly.
5. Inspect the union bolt threaded hole (**Figure 9**) in the caliper body. If worn or damaged, clean out with a metric thread tap or replace the caliper assembly.
6. Remove the bleed valve and dust cap. Inspect the bleed valve. Apply compressed air to the opening and make sure it is clear. If necessary, clean it out. Install the bleed valve, and tighten it to 7.5 N•m (66 in.-lb.).
7. Inspect the bleed valve threaded hole in the caliper body. If worn or damaged, clean the threads with a metric tap or replace the caliper assembly.
8. Remove the pad anti-rattle spring (**Figure 10**) from the caliper.
9. Inspect the caliper body (**Figure 11**) for damage and replace the caliper body if necessary.
10. Inspect the caliper cylinder bores for scratches, scoring or other damage.
11. Measure the cylinder bores with a telescoping gauge (**Figure 12**) or other suitable measuring tool. If using a telescoping gauge, measure it with a

14

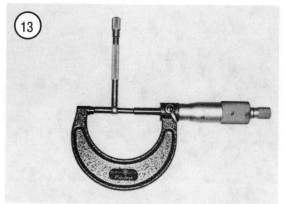

micrometer (**Figure 13**). Refer to the specification listed in **Table 1**.

12. Inspect the pistons (**Figure 14**) for scratches, scoring or other damage.

13. Measure the outside diameter of the pistons with a micrometer (**Figure 15**) or vernier caliper. Refer to the specification listed in **Table 1**.

14. The piston seal helps maintain correct brake pad-to-disc clearance. If the seal is worn or damaged, the brake pads will drag and cause excessive wear and increase brake fluid temperature. It is a good practice to replace the seals whenever disassembling the caliper.

15. Inspect the mounting bracket and pins for wear or damage (**Figure 16**). Replace if necessary.

16. Inspect the brake pads for uneven wear, damage or grease contamination.

NOTE
When the brake system is operating correctly, the inboard and outboard brake pads will show approximately the same amount of wear. If there is a large difference in pad wear, the caliper is not sliding properly along the support bracket shafts causing one pad to drag against the disc. Worn caliper piston seals will also cause uneven pad wear.

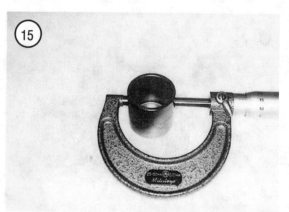

Assembly

1. Install the brake pad anti-rattle spring (**Figure 10**) and make sure it is properly seated.

2. Coat the new dust seals and piston seals and piston bores with clean DOT 4 brake fluid.

3. Carefully install the new piston seals (A, **Figure 17**) into the inner grooves. Make sure the seals are properly seated in their respective grooves.

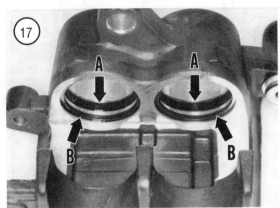

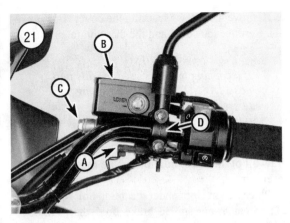

4. Carefully install the new dust seals (B, **Figure 17**) into the outer grooves. Make sure the seals are properly seated in their respective grooves.

5. Coat the pistons with clean DOT 4 brake fluid.

6. Position the pistons with the closed end facing in and install the pistons into the caliper cylinders. Push the pistons in until they bottom (**Figure 18**).

NOTE
*Prior to installing the caliper mounting bracket, apply silicone grease to the bracket pins and to the inside surfaces of the rubber boots (**Figure 19**) on the caliper assembly. This will make installation easier and will ensure that the caliper will move easily after installation on the fork slider.*

7. Carefully slide the caliper mounting bracket (**Figure 20**) onto the caliper assembly. Push the bracket on until it bottoms.

8. Install the caliper and brake pads as described in this chapter.

14

FRONT BRAKE MASTER CYLINDER

Removal/Installation

CAUTION
Do not spill brake fluid on the motorcycle. Brake fluid will destroy the finish on plastic, painted or plated surfaces. Use soapy water to wash off spilled brake fluid immediately.

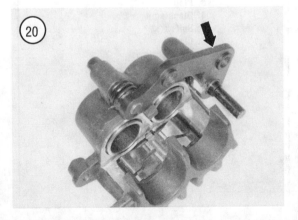

1. Remove the rear view mirror from the master cylinder clamp.

2. Clean the top of the master cylinder of all dirt and foreign matter.

3. Disconnect the two electrical connectors (A, **Figure 21**) from the front brake light switch.

4. Remove the screws securing the cover (B, **Figure 21**). Remove the cover and the diaphragm.

> *WARNING*
> *If a cooking baster is used for this purpose, DO NOT reuse it for cooking purposes due to brake fluid residue within it.*

5. If a shop syringe or a cooking baster is available, draw all of the brake fluid out of the master cylinder reservoir.

6. Place a shop cloth under the union bolt (C, **Figure 21**) to catch any spilled brake fluid that will leak out.

7. Unscrew the union bolt (C, **Figure 21**) securing the brake hose to the master cylinder. Tie the loose end of the hose up to the handlebar and cover the end to prevent the entry of moisture and foreign matter. Cover the loose end with a recloseable plastic bag.

8. Remove the bolts and clamp (D, **Figure 21**) securing the front master cylinder to the handlebar and remove the master cylinder.

9. Install by reversing the preceding removal steps while noting the following:

   a. Position the front master cylinder onto the right handlebar and align the mating surface with the handlebar punch mark.

   b. Position the clamp with the UP mark facing up and install the master cylinder clamp bolts (D, **Figure 21**). Tighten the upper mounting bolt first, then the lower bolt leaving a gap at the bottom. Tighten the bolts to 10 N•m (88 in.-lb.).

   c. Place a new sealing washer on each side of the brake hose fitting (C, **Figure 21**) and install the union bolt. Tighten the union bolt to 23 N•m (17 ft.-lb.).

   d. Bleed the front brakes as described under Bleeding the System in this chapter.

Disassembly

Refer to **Figure 22** when performing this procedure.

1. Remove the master cylinder as described in this chapter.

2. Remove the brake light switch mounting screw, then remove the switch (**Figure 23**).

3. If not already removed, remove the screws securing the cover and remove the cover and diaphragm; pour out any residual brake fluid.

4. Remove the bolt (A, **Figure 24**) and nut securing the brake lever (B) and remove the brake lever.

5. Remove the boot (**Figure 25**) from the piston. The boot is a friction fit. To avoid damaging the boot

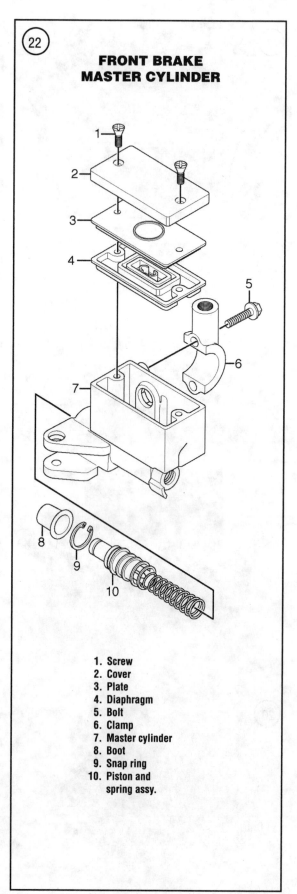

FRONT BRAKE MASTER CYLINDER

1. Screw
2. Cover
3. Plate
4. Diaphragm
5. Bolt
6. Clamp
7. Master cylinder
8. Boot
9. Snap ring
10. Piston and spring assy.

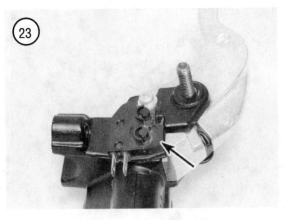

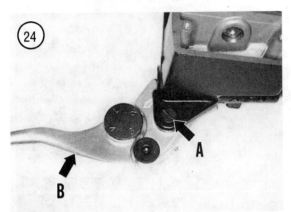

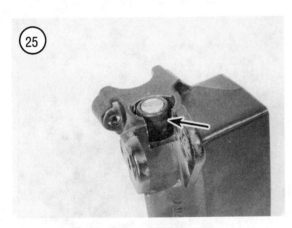

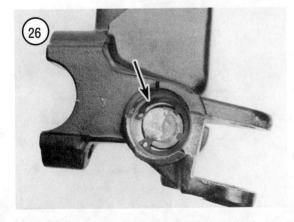

on removal, apply penetrating lubricant around the perimeter of the boot. Carefully pull the bottom edge back so the lubricant can loosen the boot.

6. Remove the snap ring from the master cylinder (**Figure 26**) as follows:

   a. Press down on the piston to relieve pressure on the snap ring, then remove the snap ring.

   b. Slowly relieve the pressure on the piston.

7. Remove the piston/secondary cup assembly (**Figure 27**).

8. Remove the spring and primary cup (**Figure 28**).

Inspection

1. Clean all parts in denatured alcohol or brake cleaning fluid. Inspect the cylinder bore and piston contact surfaces for signs of wear and damage. If either part is less than perfect, replace it.

2. Inspect the piston cups (**Figure 29**) for any signs of wear or damage. Cups are not available separately and must be replaced along with the new piston and spring as an assembly.

3. Inspect the piston contact surface (A, **Figure 30**) for wear and damage. If less than perfect, replace the piston assembly.

14

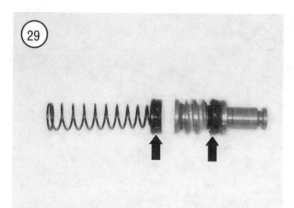

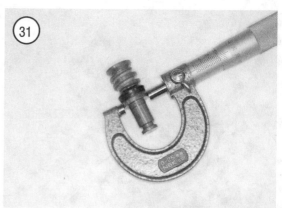

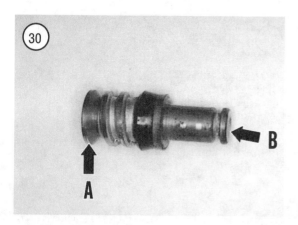

4. Check the end of the piston (B, **Figure 30**) for wear caused by the hand lever. If worn, replace the piston assembly.

5. Measure the outside diameter of the piston with a micrometer (**Figure 31**). Refer to the specification listed in **Table 1**.

6. Make sure the passage (**Figure 32**) in the bottom of the body reservoir is clear. Clean with brake fluid, then apply compressed air to make sure the passage is clear.

7. Check the reservoir cover and diaphragm for damage and deterioration and replace as necessary.

8. Inspect the threads (**Figure 33**) for the union bolt in the body. If worn or damaged, clean out with a suitable size metric thread tap or replace the master cylinder assembly.

9. Inspect the fluid viewing port for signs of hydraulic fluid leakage. If leakage has occurred, replace the master cylinder assembly.

10. Check the hand lever pivot lugs (**Figure 34**) on the master cylinder body for cracks or elongation. If damaged, replace the master cylinder assembly.

11. Inspect the hand lever pivot hole (**Figure 35**). If worn or elongated, replace the lever.

12. Inspect the body cylinder bore surface (**Figure 36**) for signs of wear and damage. If less than per-

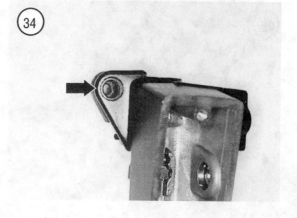

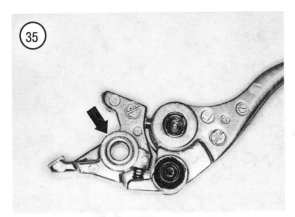

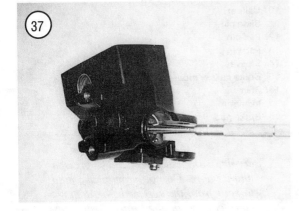

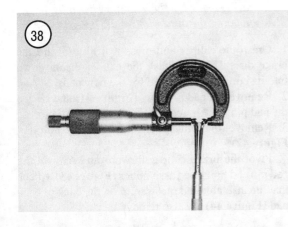

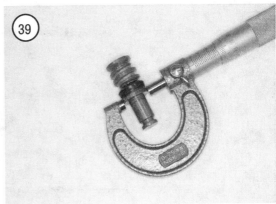

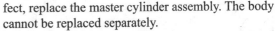

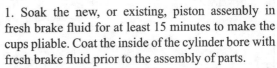

fect, replace the master cylinder assembly. The body cannot be replaced separately.

13. Measure the cylinder bore with a small bore gauge (**Figure 37**). Measure the small bore gauge with a micrometer (**Figure 38**). Refer to the specification listed in **Table 1**.

14. Measure the outside diameter of the piston assembly (**Figure 39**) with a micrometer. Refer to the specification listed in **Table 1**.

Assembly

1. Soak the new, or existing, piston assembly in fresh brake fluid for at least 15 minutes to make the cups pliable. Coat the inside of the cylinder bore with fresh brake fluid prior to the assembly of parts.

> *CAUTION*
> *When installing the piston assembly, do not allow the cups to turn inside out as they will be damaged and allow brake fluid leakage within the cylinder bore.*

2. Position the spring as shown in **Figure 28** so the tapered spring end contacts the primary cup. Install the spring and primary cup into the cylinder bore.

3. Push the piston assembly (**Figure 27**) into the bore and hold it in place. Install the snap ring (**Figure 26**) and make sure it seats correctly in the master cylinder body groove.

4. Install the rubber boot (**Figure 25**) and push it all the way down until seated.

5. Install the brake lever onto the master cylinder body, then install the bolt and nut. Tighten the bolt and nut securely.

6. Reinstall the brake light switch (**Figure 23**) and tighten the screw securely.

7. Install the diaphragm and cover and screws. Do not tighten the cover screws at this time as fluid will have to be added later.

8. Install the master cylinder as described in this chapter.

14

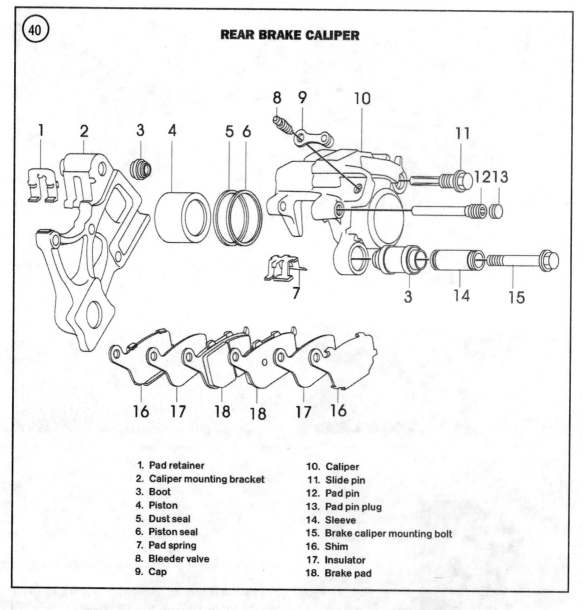

REAR BRAKE CALIPER

1. Pad retainer
2. Caliper mounting bracket
3. Boot
4. Piston
5. Dust seal
6. Piston seal
7. Pad spring
8. Bleeder valve
9. Cap
10. Caliper
11. Slide pin
12. Pad pin
13. Pad pin plug
14. Sleeve
15. Brake caliper mounting bolt
16. Shim
17. Insulator
18. Brake pad

REAR BRAKE PADS

Inspection

Inspect the rear brake pads as described in Chapter Three.

Replacement

Refer to **Figure 40**.

Inspect the rear brake pads (Chapter Three). The brake pads can be replaced with the caliper mounted on the motorcycle.

CAUTION
In the following step, monitor the level of fluid in the master cylinder reservoir. Brake fluid will back flow to the res-
ervoir as the caliper piston is pressed into its bore. Do not allow brake fluid to spill from the reservoir, or damage can occur to painted and plastic surfaces. Immediately clean up any spills, flooding the area with water.

1. Grasp the caliper and press it firmly toward the brake disc. This will push the caliper piston down into its bore, creating room for the new pads.
2. Remove the pad pin plug (**Figure 41**).and loosen the pad pin (A, **Figure 42**).
3. Remove the brake caliper mounting bolt (B, **Figure 42**).
4. Pivot the brake caliper forward and remove the pad pin and brake pad assemblies (**Figure 43**). Check that the insulator and metal shim on the back of each pad (**Figure 44**) are also removed.

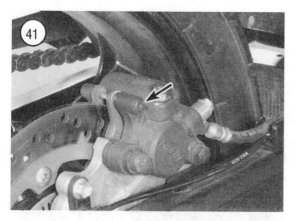

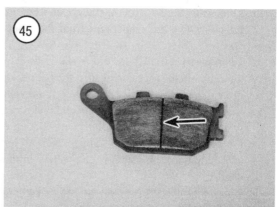

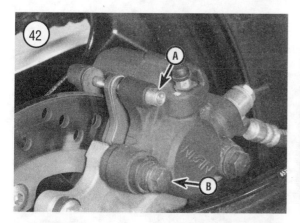

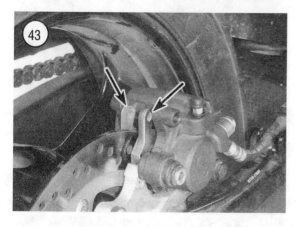

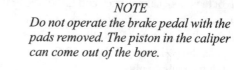

NOTE
Do not operate the brake pedal with the
pads removed. The piston in the caliper
can come out of the bore.

5. Clean the interior of the caliper and inspect for leakage or damage.

6. Inspect the pad pin and plug. Replace the parts if worn, corroded or damaged.

7. Inspect the pads for contamination, scoring and wear.

14

    a. Replace the pads if worn to the wear indicator groove (**Figure 45**).

    b. If the pads are worn unevenly, the caliper is probably not sliding correctly on the slide pin and sleeve. The caliper must be free to float on the pin and sleeve. Buildup or corrosion on the parts can hold the caliper in one position, causing brake drag and excessive pad wear.

8. When new pads are installed in the calipers, the master cylinder brake fluid level will rise as the caliper pistons are repositioned. Perform the following:

    a. Remove the right frame cover as described in Chapter Fifteen.

    b. Clean all dirt and foreign matter from the top of the brake fluid reservoir (**Figure 46**).

    c. Cover the area beneath the reservoir to protect parts from brake fluid spills.

d. Remove the screws securing the cover. Remove the cover and the diaphragm from the reservoir.

e. Temporarily install both old brake pads into the caliper and seat them against the piston.

f. Protect the caliper with a shop cloth to prevent scuffing it, then grasp the caliper and brake pad with a large pair of slip-joint pliers. Squeeze the piston back into the caliper. Repeat for each side until the piston is completely in the caliper.

g. Constantly check the reservoir and make sure the fluid does not overflow. Draw out excess fluid if necessary.

h. The piston should move freely. If they do not, remove and service the caliper as described in this chapter.

i. Remove the old brake pads.

9. Assemble the pads. On the back side of the pad, install the insulator and metal shim. The tabs on the shim should fit over the pad.

10. Install the pad assemblies on each side of the disc, seating the pads against the pad retainer (**Figure 47**) and pad spring.

11. Install the pad pin, guiding it through the holes in the pads. Lightly tighten the pad pin. The pin will be tightened in a later step.

12. Pivot the brake caliper back and install the brake caliper mounting bolt. Tighten the brake caliper mounting bolt to 23 N•m (17 ft.-lb.).

13. Tighten the pad pin to 18 N•m (13 ft.-lb.).

14. Install the pad pin plug.

15. Operate the brake pedal several times to seat the pads.

16. Check the brake fluid reservoir and replenish or remove fluid, as necessary.

17. With the rear wheel raised, check that the wheel spins freely and the brake operates properly.

NOTE
For proper brake operation, follow break-in procedure specified by brake pad manufacturer.

REAR BRAKE CALIPER

Removal/Installation

Refer to **Figure 40**.

NOTE
If removing the pistons hydraulically during disassembly, do not disconnect the brake hose from the caliper.

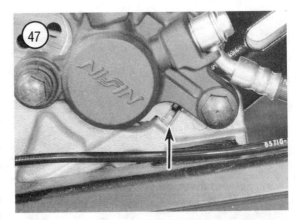

1. If the caliper will be disconnected from the brake hose, drain the system as described in this chapter. After draining, loosen the brake hose union bolt (**Figure 48**) and then lightly tighten the bolt. It is removed in a later step.

2. Remove the brake pads as described in this chapter.

3. Remove the union bolt and seal washers from the brake hose. There should be two sealing washers–one on each side of the union bolt.

4. Place the loose end of the brake hose in a closable plastic bag to prevent brake fluid from dribbling onto the motorcycle.

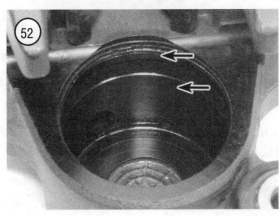

9. Install by reversing the preceding removal steps while noting the following:
    a. If disconnected, connect the brake hose to the caliper.
    b. Install a new sealing washer on each side of the union bolt.
    c. Position the brake hose fitting so it is seated in the notch on the caliper.
    d. Tighten the union bolt to 23 N•m (17 ft.-lb.).
    e. If the brake hose was disconnected from the caliper, fill and bleed the brake system as described in this chapter.
    f. Install the brake pads as described in this chapter.

Disassembly

Refer to **Figure 40**.
1. Remove the brake caliper as described in this chapter.
2. Remove the pads and pad spring (**Figure 50**) from the caliper.
3. Make sure the bleeder valve (A, **Figure 51**) is closed so air cannot escape.

> *WARNING*
> *Wear eye protection when using compressed air to remove the pistons, and keep your fingers away from the piston.*

4. Cushion the caliper pistons with a shop rag and position the caliper with the piston bore facing down. Apply compressed air through the brake hose port (B, **Figure 51**) to pop out the piston.

> *CAUTION*
> *Do not try to pry out the piston. This will damage the piston and caliper bore.*

5. Remove the bleeder valve and cap from the caliper.
6. Remove the dust seal and piston seal (**Figure 52**) from the bore.

Inspection

1. Inspect the caliper body for damage; replace the caliper body if necessary.
2. Inspect the union bolt hole threads. If the threads are slightly damaged; clean them up with a proper size thread tap. If the threads are worn or damaged, replace the caliper assembly.
3. Make sure the hole in the bleed screw is clean and open. Apply compressed air to the opening and

5. Pivot the caliper forward away from the mounting bracket and lift the brake caliper off the disc and mounting bracket.
6. Drain any brake fluid remaining in the caliper.
7. If necessary, disassemble and service the caliper assembly as described in this chapter.
8. To remove the caliper mounting bracket, perform the following:
    a. Remove the rear wheel as described in Chapter Eleven.
    b. Slide the mounting bracket (**Figure 49**) off the locating boss on the swing arm and remove the bracket.

14

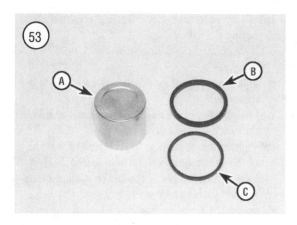

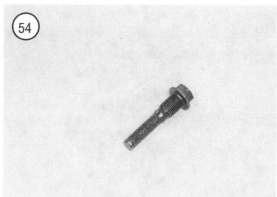

make sure it is clear. Clean out if necessary with fresh brake fluid.

4. Inspect the fluid passage in the base of the cylinder bore. Make sure it is clean and open. Apply compressed air to the opening and make sure it is clear. Clean out if necessary with fresh brake fluid.

5. Inspect the dust seal and piston seal grooves in the caliper body for scoring or other damage. If the grooves are rusty or corroded, replace the caliper assembly.

6. Measure the piston outside diameter and compare to the dimension listed in **Table 1**. Inspect the piston (A, **Figure 53**) for scratches, scoring or other damage. Replace the piston if worn or damaged.

7. Measure the cylinder bore. Replace the caliper assembly if the bore exceeds the specification given in **Table 1**.

8. If serviceable, clean the caliper body with rubbing alcohol and rinse with clean DOT 4 brake fluid.

9. Inspect the caliper mounting bracket for damage. Replace if necessary.

10. Inspect the rubber boots for wear or deterioration. Replace if necessary.

11. Inspect the slide pin (**Figure 54**) on the caliper for scoring, wear or damage. If damaged, replace the stud. Tighten the slide pin to 27 N•m (19.5 ft.-lb.).

12. Inspect the pad retainer (**Figure 55**) on the caliper bracket for wear or damage, replace if necessary.

Assembly

> *NOTE*
> *Never reuse a piston or dust seal that has been removed. Very minor damage or age deterioration can make the seal useless.*

1. Coat the new dust seal and piston seal with fresh DOT 4 brake fluid.

> *WARNING*
> *Check that the seals fit squarely in the cylinder bore grooves. If the seals are not installed properly, the caliper assembly will leak and braking performance will be reduced.*

2. Install the new piston seal and new dust seal (**Figure 52**) into the groove in the caliper assembly. Make sure both seals are properly seated in their grooves.

3. Coat the piston and the caliper cylinder with fresh DOT 4 brake fluid.

4. Position the piston with the sealed end facing out and install the piston into the caliper cylinder. Carefully push in the piston until it bottoms.

5. Install the bleed screw and tighten to 6 N•m (53 in.-lb.).

6. Install the pad spring (**Figure 50**) into the caliper body.

7. Apply a light coat of a Lithium base grease to both front and rear studs and to both rubber boots.

8. Install the brake caliper assembly as described in this section.

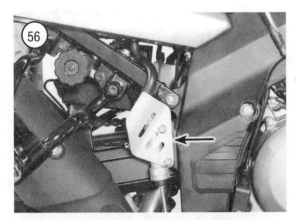

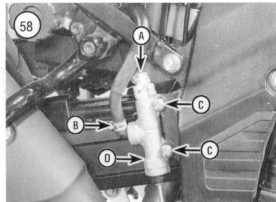

REAR MASTER CYLINDER

Removal/Installation

1. Drain the brake system as described in this chapter.

2. Remove the master cylinder cover (**Figure 56**).

3. Remove the cotter pin and clevis pin (**Figure 57**) that secure the master cylinder clevis to the brake pedal.

4. Remove the union bolt and seal washers from the brake hose fitting (A, **Figure 58**). Have a shop cloth ready to absorb excess brake fluid that drips from the hose. Enclose the hose end to prevent brake fluid from damaging surrounding surfaces.

5. Be prepared to catch brake fluid, then detach the reservoir hose (B, **Figure 58**) from the master cylinder.

6. Unscrew the master cylinder mounting bolts (C, **Figure 58**) and remove the master cylinder (D).

7. Repair the master cylinder as described in this section.

8. Reverse the preceding procedure to install the master cylinder. Note the following:

   a. Tighten the master cylinder mounting bolts to 10 N•m (88 in.-lb.).

   b. Install new seal washers on the union bolt. Tighten the bolt to 23 N•m (17 ft.-lb.).

   c. Install a new cotter pin on the clevis pin.

   d. Fill the brake fluid reservoir and bleed the brake system as described in this chapter.

   e. Adjust rear brake pedal height as described in Chapter Three.

Disassembly/Inspection/Assembly

Refer to **Figure 59**.

1. Remove the master cylinder as described in this section.

2. Remove the snap ring that retains the hose and fitting against the master cylinder (**Figure 60**). Remove the hose assembly and O-ring.

3. Remove the snap ring from the master cylinder as follows:

   a. Unseat the boot from the cylinder bore and fold it toward the clevis. If reusing the boot, apply penetrating lubricant around the perimeter of the boot to prevent damage. Carefully pull the bottom edge back so the lubricant can loosen the boot.

   b. If desired, lock the cylinder in a vise with soft jaws. Grip the cylinder at the mounts. Do not overtighten the vise or cylinder damage could occur.

   c. Press and tilt the pushrod to relieve pressure on the snap ring, and then remove the snap ring (**Figure 61**).

   d. Slowly relieve the pressure on the piston.

4. Remove the pushrod and piston assemblies from the bore (**Figure 62**).

5. Inspect the master cylinder assembly.

   a. Clean all parts being reused with fresh brake fluid.

   b. Inspect the cylinder bore for wear, pitting or corrosion.

   c. Measure the inside diameter of the cylinder bore (**Figure 63**). Refer to **Table 1** for specifications.

14

59 **REAR MASTER CYLINDER AND NON-ABS REAR BRAKE HOSE**

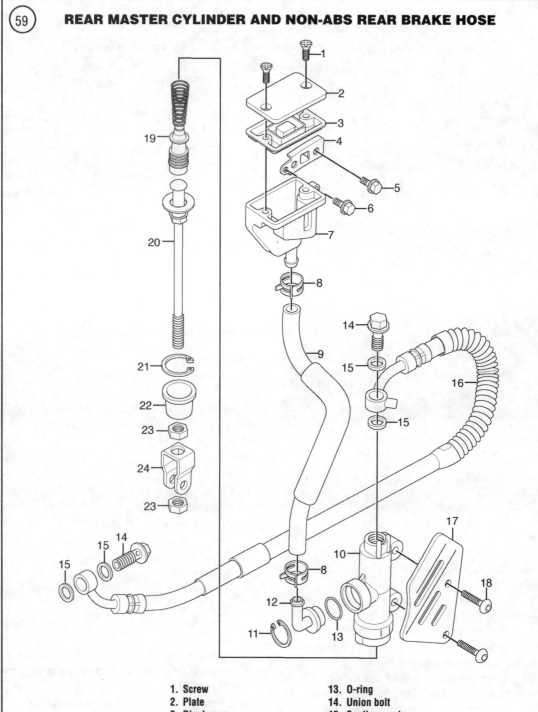

1. Screw	13. O-ring
2. Plate	14. Union bolt
3. Diaphragm	15. Sealing washer
4. Bracket	16. Brake hose
5. Bolt	17. Cover
6. Bolt	18. Bolt
7. Reservoir	19. Spring and piston
8. Hose clamp	20. Push rod
9. Brake hose	21. Snap ring
10. Master cylinder	22. Boot
11. Snap ring	23. Nut
12. Fitting	24. Yoke

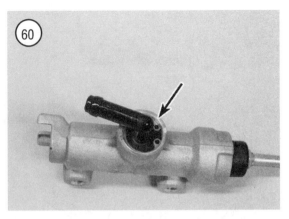

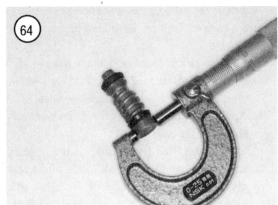

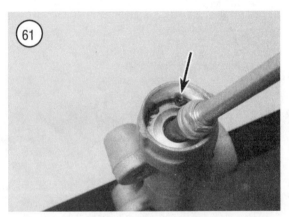

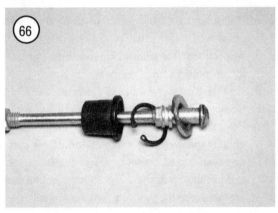

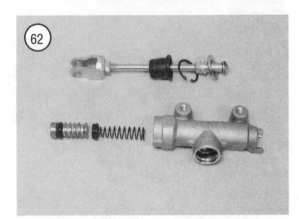

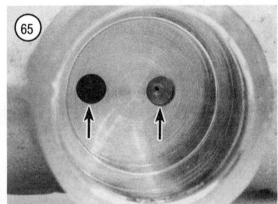

14

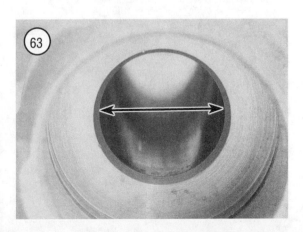

d. Measure the outside diameter of the piston (**Figure 64**). Refer to **Table 1** for specifications.

e. Inspect and clean the threads and orifices (**Figure 65**) in the master cylinder. Clean with compressed air.

f. Inspect the pushrod assembly (**Figure 66**). Check the parts for corrosion and wear. Install a new snap ring on the pushrod, with the sharp edge of the snap ring facing toward the clevis.

g. Inspect the mounting hardware for wear or damage.

6. Assemble the piston, seals and spring as follows. **Figure 67** shows both an assembled and unassembled piston.

    a. Soak the primary seal (A, **Figure 67**) and secondary seal (B) in fresh brake fluid for 15 minutes. This softens and lubricates the seals.

    b. Apply brake fluid to the piston so the seals can slide over the ends.

    c. Identify the wide (open) side of the primary seal. When installed, the wide side of the seal must face in the direction of the arrow (C, **Figure 67**). Install the primary seal onto the piston.

    d. Identify the wide (open) side of the secondary seal. When installed, the wide side of the seal must face in the direction of the arrow (C, **Figure 67**). Install the secondary seal on the piston.

    e. Install the small end of the spring onto the piston.

    f. The assembled piston should appear as in **Figure 68**.

7. Install the piston and pushrod assembly into the master cylinder as follows:

    a. Lubricate the cylinder bore and piston assembly with brake fluid.

    b. If desired, lock the cylinder in a vise with soft jaws.

    c. Apply a small amount of silicone brake grease to the contact area of the pushrod.

    d. Rest the piston assembly in the cylinder.

    e. Compress the snap ring with snap ring pliers.

    f. Press and tilt the pushrod in the cylinder while guiding the snap ring into position. If the snap ring does not easily seat, release the snap ring and use the tip of the pliers to press it into the groove. Keep the pushrod compressed until the snap ring is seated to prevent the piston from coming out of the cylinder.

8. Apply silicone brake grease to the inside of the boot. Seat the boot into the cylinder.

9. Install the locknuts and clevis onto the pushrod. Do not tighten the locknuts until the brake pedal height has been checked.

10. Install a new, lubricated O-ring into the master cylinder (**Figure 69**), and then lock the hose fitting into the O-ring. Install a new snap ring with the flat side facing out.

11. Install the master cylinder as described in this section.

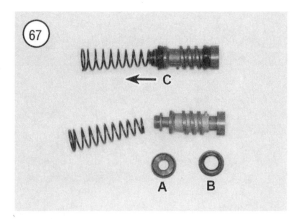

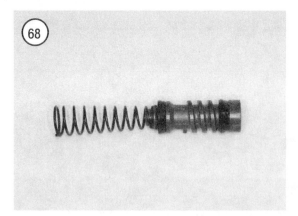

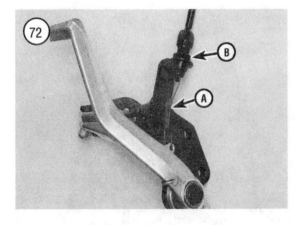

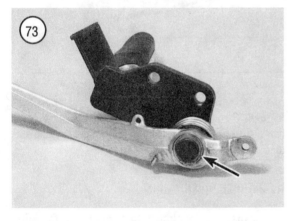

REAR BRAKE PEDAL

Removal/Installation

1. Remove the cotter pin and clevis pin (**Figure 70**) that secure the master cylinder clevis to the brake pedal.

CAUTION
Do not allow the footpeg and brake pedal assembly to hang from the rear brake switch electrical wire.

2. While supporting the footpeg and brake pedal assembly, remove the right footpeg bracket mounting bolts (**Figure 71**). Hold the assembly and remove it.

3. Detach the brake light switch spring (A, **Figure 72**).

4. Remove the rear brake light switch (B, **Figure 72**) from the footpeg bracket.

5. Remove the snap ring (**Figure 73**).

6. Separate the brake pedal and return spring from the pivot post on the footpeg bracket.

7. Install by reversing the preceding removal steps while noting the following:

    a. Apply multipurpose grease to the brake pedal pivot post and the pivot post receptacle on the frame.

    b. Adjust the rear brake light switch as described in Chapter Three.

**BRAKE HOSE REPLACEMENT
(NON-ABS MODELS)**

CAUTION
Make sure to protect the surrounding area from accidental brake fluid spills. Be prepared to catch any spilled brake fluid that might leak from the union bolts or brake fittings.

Note the following:

1. Note the location of clamps and guides during removal.

2. Drain the brake system as described in this chapter.

3. Wash off any spilled brake fluid that may have leaked out of the hoses during removal.

4. On the front brake hoses, the junction fitting is secured to the right fork leg using the fender mounting bolt.

5. Install new sealing washers on each side of the hose fittings.

6. Tighten the union bolts to 23 N•m (17 ft.-lb.).

7. Refill the brake system and bleed the brakes as described in this chapter.

BRAKE DISC

WARNING
Do not true a deeply scored or warped disc. Removing disc material causes the disc to overheat rapidly and warp. Maintain the discs by keeping them clean and corrosion-free. Use a solvent, that is not oil-based, to wipe grit that accumulates on the discs and at the edge of the pads.

14

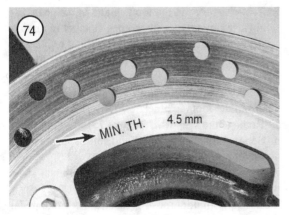

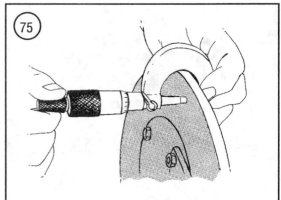

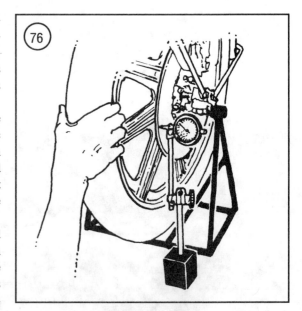

The condition of the brake discs and pads are often a reflection of one another. If disc scoring is evident, inspect the pads and disc as soon as possible. Visually inspect the discs and pads with the wheels mounted on the motorcycle. Perform the inspections described in this section.

It is not necessary to remove the disc from the wheel to inspect it. Small nicks and marks on the disc are not important, but radial scratches deep enough to snag a fingernail reduce braking effectiveness and increase brake pad wear. If these grooves are evident and the brake pads are wearing rapidly, replace the disc.

The Suzuki factory specifications for the standard and wear limits are listed in **Table 1**. The minimum (MIN) thickness is stamped on the disc face (**Figure 74**). If the specification stamped on the disc differs from the wear limit listed in **Table 1**, use the specification on the disc when inspecting it.

Thickness and Runout Inspection

1. Measure the thickness of each disc at several locations around its perimeter (**Figure 75**). Refer to **Table 1** for the service limit. Replace the disc if it is out of specification.
2. Measure disc runout as follows:
   a. Mount a dial indicator on a stable surface and in contact with the disc (**Figure 76**).
   b. Zero the dial indicator gauge.
   c. Turn the wheel and watch the amount of runout measured on the gauge.
   d. Refer to **Table 1** for the service-limit. Replace the disc if it is out of specification.

NOTE
If the disc runout is out of specification, check the condition of the wheel bearings before replacing the disc. Damaged bearings will affect disc runout.

3. On front brake discs, inspect all fasteners (A, **Figure 77**) between the outer and the inner rings of the disc. If any are loose or damaged, replace the disc.

Removal and Installation

The discs are mounted to the hubs with bolts. Remove and install either disc as follows:
1. Remove the wheel from the motorcycle as described in Chapter Eleven.
2. Remove the bolts (B, **Figure 77**) that secure the disc to the hub.
3. Clean the bolts and mounting holes.
4. Reverse this procedure to install the discs. Note the following:
   a. Install the disc with the thickness marking (**Figure 74**) facing out.
   b. Apply ThreeBond 1360 to the bolt threads.
   c. Tighten the bolts in several passes and in a crossing pattern.

d. Tighten the bolts to 23 N•m (17 ft.-lb.).
e. Check the disc for runout as described in this section.

ANTI-LOCK BRAKE SYSTEM (ABS)

DL650A models are equipped with an anti-lock brake system (ABS) that prevents wheel lockup during hard braking or when braking on slippery surfaces. During operation, the ABS rapidly pumps the brake(s), which interrupts the flow of hydraulic fluid to the brake calipers(s) of the wheel approaching lockup.

The ABS system includes a hydraulic unit (HU), front and rear wheel speed sensors, front and rear wheel sensor rotors, ABS indicator and the ABS electronic control unit (ECU). Fuses protect the system.

The ABS ECU monitors the rotational speed of the front and rear wheels using the sensor rotor and speed sensor at each wheel. When the ECU determines that the wheel is approaching lockup, the ECU modulates brake hydraulic pressure using a pump motor and solenoids in the HU. Hydraulic pressure from the master cylinder to the caliper is momentarily interrupted and the reapplied. The ECU repeats this cycle and rapidly pumps the brake(s) until secure braking is restored.

An ABS indicator light is located on the combination meter (**Figure 78**). The light illuminates when the ignition switch is turned on, then extinguishes when the motorcycle exceeds approximately 3 mph (5 km/h).

ABS SERVICE PRECAUTIONS

Before troubleshooting or servicing the ABS, note the following:
1. Handle the ABS components carefully. The HU/ECU can be damaged if dropped.
2. Do not allow dust or water to contact the HU/ECU.
3. The HU/ECU is only available as a unit assembly. Do not attempt disassembly or modification.
4. Turn the ignition switch off before disconnecting or reconnecting ABS electrical connectors. If current is flowing when a connector is disconnected, a voltage spike can damage the ECU.
5. While the ECU is constantly monitoring the ABS, it does not recognize problems in other parts of the brake system unless they affect the ABS. For example, worn brake pads and low brake fluid level. Inspect non-ABS components at the intervals specified in Chapter Three, or more often when operating under severe riding conditions.
6. Be careful not to damage the ABS wiring harness or connectors during service procedures. Note the routing of the wire harness and the type, number and position of fasteners and clamps used to secure the wiring to the frame and other components.
7. The metal brake lines can be creased and permanently damaged from improper handling. Remove, position and secure these lines carefully.
8. Use OEM fasteners (or equivalents) when replacement is required during service.

TROUBLESHOOTING

Refer to Chapter Two for ABS troubleshooting procedures.

HU/ECU

The hydraulic unit (HU) and electron control unit (ECU) are housed in a single unit. The HU/ECU must be serviced as a unit assembly: separate components are not available.

14

Removal/Installation

1. Drain the brake system as described in this chapter.

2. Remove the battery as described in Chapter Nine.

3. Remove the ECM (A, **Figure 79**) from the battery case.

4. Remove the tipover sensor (B, **Figure 79**) from the battery case.

5. Remove the ABS motor relay fuse (C, **Figure 79**) from the battery case.

6. Remove the ABS valve relay fuse (D, **Figure 79**) from the battery case.

7. Remove the fuel pump relay (E, **Figure 79**) from the battery case.

8. Remove the starter relay (F, **Figure 79**) from the battery case.

9. Remove the fuse box and turn signal relay (G, **Figure 79**) from the battery case.

10. Remove the HU/ECU bottom cover as follows:

    a. Remove the bolt (A, **Figure 80**).

    b. Remove both trim clips (B, **Figure 80**) as described in Chapter Fifteen, then remove the cover (C).

11. Remove the battery case mounting screws (A, **Figure 81**) and bolts (B).

12. Remove the battery case (C, **Figure 81**).

13. Loosen the flair nuts securing the following brake lines to the HU/ECU: (A, **Figure 82**) rear brake caliper, (B) front brake calipers, (C) front master cylinder, (D) rear master cylinder.

14. Disconnect the electrical connector (E, **Figure 82**).

15. Remove the front mounting bolt securing the HU/ECU mounting bracket (**Figure 83**).

16. Remove the mounting bolt on each side (**Figure 84**).

17. Remove the HU/ECU assembly (F, **Figure 82**). If necessary, separate the HU/ECU from the mounting bracket.

18. Reverse the removal procedure for installation while noting the following:

    a. Tighten the brake line flair nuts to 16 N•m (142 in.-lb.).

    b. Bleed the front and rear brake systems as described in this chapter.

ABS FRONT WHEEL SPEED SENSOR

ABS Front Wheel Speed Sensor Clearance

For proper operation of the ABS system, the ABS front wheel speed sensor must be positioned a specific distance from the sensor rotor on the front wheel.

1. Raise the front wheel.

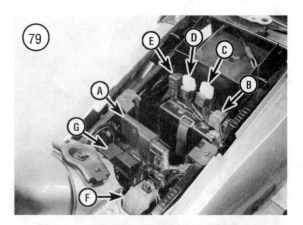

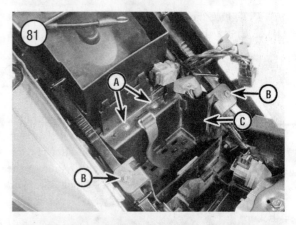

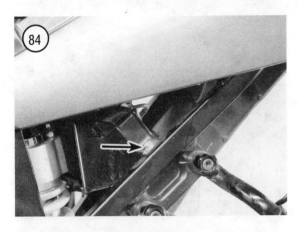

2. Using a feeler gauge measure the clearance between the tip of the sensor and the sensor rotor on the front wheel (**Figure 85**). Note the specified clearance in **Table 1**.

3. Rotate the front wheel and check the clearance at several locations.

4. If the clearance is incorrect, check the following:

   a. Incorrect mounting of the sensor or sensor rotor.

   b. Damaged sensor rotor.

   c. Foreign material on sensor or sensor rotor.

Removal/Installation

1. Remove the air box as described in Chapter Eight.

2. Disconnect the ABS front wheel speed sensor connector (**Figure 86**).

3. Remove the sensor mounting bolt (A, **Figure 87**).

4. Note routing of sensor wire and location of retaining clamps.

5. Remove the ABS front wheel speed sensor (B, **Figure 87**).

6. Clean the sensor and check for damage.

7. Reverse the removal procedure for installation while noting the following:

   a. Tighten the sensor mounting bolt securely.

   b. Check the sensor clearance as described in this section.

ABS REAR WHEEL SPEED SENSOR

ABS Rear Wheel Speed Sensor Clearance

For proper operation of the ABS system, the ABS rear wheel speed sensor must be positioned a specific distance from the sensor rotor on the rear wheel.

1. Raise the rear wheel.

2. Using a feeler gauge measure the clearance between the tip of the sensor and the sensor rotor on the

14

rear wheel (**Figure 88**). Note the specified clearance in **Table 1**.

3. Rotate the rear wheel and check the clearance at several locations.

4. If the clearance is incorrect, check the following:
   a. Incorrect mounting of the sensor or sensor rotor.
   b. Damaged sensor rotor.
   c. Foreign material on sensor or sensor rotor.

Removal/Installation

1. Remove the seat as described in Chapter Eight.

2. Disconnect the ABS rear wheel speed sensor connector (**Figure 89**).

3. Remove the sensor mounting bolt (A, **Figure 90**).

4. Note routing of sensor wire and location of retaining clamps.

5. Remove the ABS rear wheel speed sensor (B, **Figure 90**).

6. Clean the sensor and check for damage.

7. Reverse the removal procedure for installation while noting the following:
   a. Tighten the sensor mounting bolt securely.
   b. Check the sensor clearance as described in this section.

ABS FRONT WHEEL SPEED SENSOR ROTOR

Removal/Installation

1. Remove the front wheel as described in Chapter Eleven.

2. Remove the speed sensor rotor retaining bolts (A, **Figure 91**).

3. Remove the speed sensor rotor (B, **Figure 91**).

4. Inspect the rotor for damage and distortion. Remove foreign debris from the rotor.

5. Reverse the removal steps for installation while noting the following:
   a. Install the rotor so the side stamped 50T is facing out.
   b. Check front wheel speed sensor clearance as described in this section.

ABS REAR WHEEL SPEED SENSOR ROTOR

Removal/Installation

1. Remove the rear wheel as described in Chapter Eleven.

2. Remove the speed sensor rotor retaining bolts (A, **Figure 92**).

3. Remove the speed sensor rotor (B, **Figure 92**).

4. Inspect the rotor for damage and distortion. Remove foreign debris from the rotor.

5. Reverse the removal steps for installation while noting the following:
   a. Install the rotor so the side stamped 50T is facing out.
   b. Check rear wheel speed sensor clearance as described in this section.

ABS BRAKE LINES

The brake lines for the ABS include metal tubing and flexible hoses. The metal brake lines do not require routine replacement unless they are damaged or the end fitting are leaking. While replacing the flexible brake hoses, inspect the metal brake lines for damage. If they have been hit or otherwise deformed, the lines may be restricted, thus decreasing braking effectiveness.

> *WARNING*
> *On ABS-equipped models, the brake system uses flexible brake hoses along with metal brake lines. Because brake pressure is critical in an ABS system, the Suzuki flexible brake hoses are designed to have the same minimal flexing characteristics as the steel lines. When replacing the flexible brake hoses, make sure to install authorized Suzuki replacement hoses specifically designed for use with the ABS system. Using a flexible brake hose of an alternate design will drastically change the characteristics of the brake system.*

Replacement

Refer to **Figure 93** and **Figure 94**.

> *CAUTION*
> *Make sure to protect the surrounding area from accidental brake fluid spills. Be prepared to catch any spilled brake fluid that might leak from the union bolts or brake fittings.*

Note the following:
1. Note the location of clamps and guides during removal.
2. Drain the brake system as described in this chapter.
3. Wash off any spilled brake fluid that may have leaked out of the hoses during removal.
4. The metal lines are equipped with flare nuts to secure the ends. Use a flare nut wrench when loosening or tightening the nut to avoid damage to the nut.

> *CAUTION*
> *Make sure the flare nut threads are properly engaged before tightening the nut.*

5. Tighten the flare nuts to 16 N•m (142 in.-lb.).
6. On the front brake hoses, the junction fitting is secured to the left fork leg using the fender mounting bolt.
7. Install new sealing washers on each side of the hose fittings.
8. Tighten the union bolts to 23 N•m (17 ft.-lb.).
9. Refill the brake system and bleed the brakes as described in this chapter.

BRAKE SYSTEM DRAINING

To drain the brake fluid from the system, have an 8 mm wrench, tip-resistant container and a length of clear tubing that fits snugly on the bleeder valve. Use the following procedure to drain either the front or rear brakes.

> *CAUTION*
> *Brake fluid can damage painted and finished surfaces. Use water to immediately wash any surface that becomes contaminated with brake fluid.*

1. Attach one end of the tubing to the bleeder valve and place the other end into the container (**Figure 95**).
2. Open the bleeder valve so fluid can pass into the tubing.
3. Pump the brake lever/pedal to force the fluid from the system.

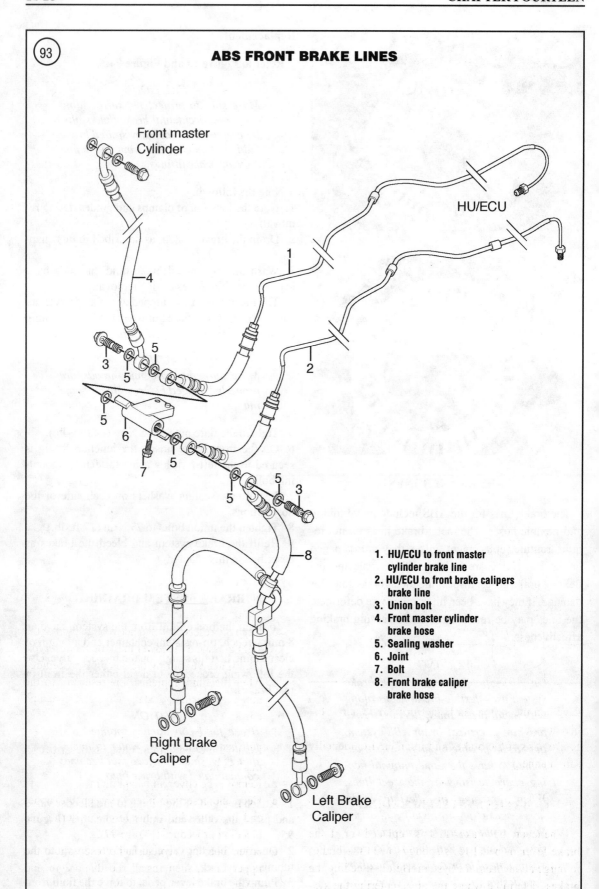

ABS FRONT BRAKE LINES

⑨③

Front master
Cylinder

HU/ECU

1. HU/ECU to front master
   cylinder brake line
2. HU/ECU to front brake calipers
   brake line
3. Union bolt
4. Front master cylinder
   brake hose
5. Sealing washer
6. Joint
7. Bolt
8. Front brake caliper
   brake hose

Right Brake
Caliper

Left Brake
Caliper

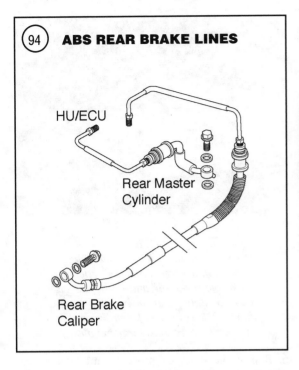

94 **ABS REAR BRAKE LINES**

HU/ECU

Rear Master Cylinder

Rear Brake Caliper

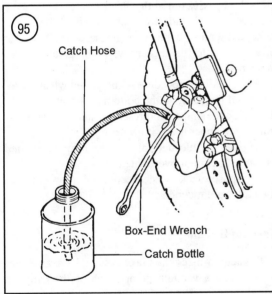

95

Catch Hose

Box-End Wrench

Catch Bottle

4. When the system no longer drips fluid, close the bleeder valve.

5. Dispose of the brake fluid in an environmentally safe manner.

BRAKE SYSTEM BLEEDING

Whenever the brake fluid is replaced, or if the brake lever or pedal feels spongy, bleed the brakes to purge all air from the system. Before bleeding the brakes, determine where the air is entering the system. Check all brake components for leakage, and

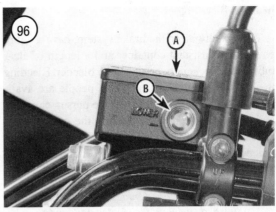

96

fittings and hoses for deterioration, damage or looseness. The brake system can be bled manually or by using a vacuum pump. Both methods are described in this section.

> *CAUTION*
> *Before bleeding brakes, always secure the bike so it is stable and locked in place, particularly the fork. This minimizes the chance of spilled fluid from an open reservoir.*

Brake Fluid Reservoirs

Regardless of the bleeding method used, the reservoir cap of the master cylinder being bled must be removed so the reservoir can be filled with brake fluid. The reservoirs must not be over or under filled. Note the following when working with each reservoir.

1. Front brake reservoir.
   a. After removing the cover (A, **Figure 96**) remove the diaphragm from the reservoir before filling with fluid.
   b. Keep the reservoir filled between the top of the sight glass and the lower mark on the reservoir (B, **Figure 96**) during the bleeding procedure.
   c. After bleeding, replenish the reservoir to the upper mark, then install the diaphragm and cover.
2. Rear brake reservoir.
   a. Remove the right frame cover as described in this chapter.
   b. Remove the cover and diaphragm.
   c. Keep the reservoir filled between the upper and lower marks on the reservoir during the bleeding procedure (**Figure 97**).
   d. After bleeding, replenish the reservoir to the upper mark, then install the diaphragm and cover.
   e. Install the right frame cover.

14

Manual Bleeding

To manually bleed the brake system, have a 8 mm wrench, tip-resistant container and a length of clear tubing that fits snugly on the brake bleeder. Bleeding the system is much easier if two people are available to perform the procedure. One person can open and close the bleeder valve while the other person operates the brake lever or pedal. Use the following procedure to bleed either the front or rear brake.

CAUTION
Brake fluid can damage painted and finished surfaces. Use water and immediately wash any surface that contacts brake fluid.

1. Slip the box-end wrench over the bleeder valve.
2. Attach one end of the tubing to the bleeder valve and place the other end into the container (**Figure 95**).

CAUTION
Do not use brake fluid from an unsealed container. It may be contaminated by moisture absorbed from the air. Use DOT 4 brake fluid from a sealed container.

NOTE
During the bleeding process, the reservoir must contain fluid during the entire procedure. If the reservoir is allowed to empty, air will enter the system and the bleeding process must be repeated.

3. Fill the reservoir to the upper level with DOT 4 brake fluid.
4. Apply pressure (do not pump) to the brake lever or pedal, then open the bleeder valve. As the fluid is forced from the system, the lever/pedal travels its full length of operation. When the lever/pedal can move no farther, hold the lever/pedal in the down position and close the bleeder valve. Do not allow the lever or pedal to return to its up position before the bleeder valve is closed as air will be drawn into the system.

NOTE
Releasing the lever/pedal slowly minimizes the chance of fluid splashing out of the reservoir as excess fluid in the brake line is returned to the reservoir.

5. When the bleeder valve is closed, release the lever/pedal so it returns to its up position. Check the fluid level in the reservoir and replenish, if necessary.

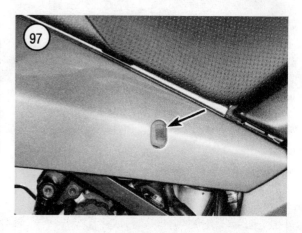

NOTE
If small bubbles (foam) remain in the system after several bleeding attempts, close the reservoir and allow the system to stand undisturbed for a few hours. The system will stabilize and the air can be purged as large bubbles.

6. Repeat the bleeding process until bubble-free, clear fluid passes out of the bleeder valve. Unless the bleeder valve threads are wrapped with Teflon tape, or coated with silicone brake grease, a small amount of air will enter the system when the bleeder valve is opened.
7. The bleeding procedure is completed when the lever/pedal feels firm at the bottom of the stroke.
8. Check the brake fluid reservoir and fill the reservoir to the upper level, if necessary.
9. Tighten the bleeder valve to the torque specified in **Table 2**. Do not overtighten.
10. Dispose of the waste brake fluid in an environmentally safe manner.

Vacuum Bleeding

To vacuum-bleed the brake system, have an 8 mm wrench and a vacuum pump, such as the Mityvac pump shown in **Figure 98**. Use the following procedure to bleed either the front or rear brake.

CAUTION
Do not use brake fluid from an unsealed container. It may be contaminated by moisture absorbed from the air. Use DOT 4 brake fluid from a sealed container.

NOTE
During the bleeding process, the reservoir must contain fluid during the entire procedure. If the reservoir is allowed to empty, air will enter the system and the bleeding process must be repeated.

1. Slip the box-end wrench over the bleeder valve.
2. Check that the union bolts are tight at the master cylinder and caliper.
3. Attach the brake bleeder to the bleeder valve (**Figure 98**). Suspend the tool with wire. This allows the tool to be released when the fluid reservoir needs to be refilled.
4. Fill the reservoir to the upper level with DOT 4 brake fluid.

5. Pump the handle on the brake bleeder to create a vacuum.
6. Open the bleeder valve and draw the air and fluid from the system. Close the valve before the fluid stops moving. If the vacuum pump is equipped with a gauge, close the bleeder before the gauge reads 0 in. Hg. Replenish the fluid level in the reservoir.
7. Repeat the bleeding process until clear fluid (minimal air bubbles) is passing out of the bleeder. Unless the bleeder valve threads are wrapped with Teflon tape, or coated with silicone brake grease, a small amount of air will enter the system when the bleeder valve is opened.
8. The bleeding procedure is completed when the feel of the lever/pedal is firm.
9. Check the brake fluid reservoir and fill the reservoir to the upper level, if necessary.
10. Tighten the bleeder valve to the torque specified in **Table 2**. Do not overtighten.
11. Dispose of the waste brake fluid in an environmentally safe manner.

Table 1 BRAKE SPECIFICATIONS

Item	New	Service limit
ABS brake sensor to rotor clearance (front and rear)	0.3-1.5 mm (0.012-0.059 in.)	–
Brake disc thickness	5.0 mm (0.20 in.)	4.5 mm (0.18 in.)
Brake disc runout (max.)	–	0.3 mm (0.012 in.)
Front brake caliper		
2004-2006 models		
Cylinder bore I.D.	30.230 30.306 mm (1.1902 1.1931 in.)	–
Piston O.D.	30.150 30.200 mm (1.1870 1.1890 in.)	–
2007-2011 models		
Cylinder bore I.D.	27.000 27.076 mm (1.0630 1.0660 in.)	–
Piston O.D.	26.920 26.970 mm (1.0598 1.0618 in.)	–
Front brake master cylinder		
2004-2006 models		
Cylinder bore I.D.	15.870 15.913 mm (0.6248 0.6265 in.)	–
Piston O.D.	15.827 15.854 mm (0.6231 0.6242 in.)	–
2007-2011 models		
Cylinder bore I.D.	14.000 14.043 mm (0.5512 0.5529 in.)	–
Piston O.D.	13.957 13.984 mm (0.5495 0.5506 in.)	–
(continued)		

14

Table 1 BRAKE SPECIFICATIONS (continued)

Item	New	Service limit
Rear brake caliper		
2004-2006 models		
Cylinder bore I.D.	38.180 38.256 mm (1.5031 1.5061 in.)	–
Piston O.D.	38.098 38.148 mm (1.4999 1.5019 in.)	–
2007-2011 models		
Cylinder bore I.D.	38.180 38.230 mm (1.5031 1.5051 in.)	–
Piston O.D.	38.080 38.130 mm (1.4992 1.5012 in.)	–
Rear brake master cylinder		
Cylinder bore I.D.	14.000 14.043 mm (0.5512 0.5529 in.)	–
Piston O.D.	13.957 13.984 mm (0.5495 0.5506 in.)	–

Table 2 BRAKE TORQUE SPECIFICATIONS

Item	N•m	in.-lb.	ft.-lb.
ABS HU/ECU brake pipe flare nut	16	142	–
Front brake caliper bleed valve	7.5	66	–
Front brake caliper mounting bolt	39	–	28
Front brake caliper union bolt	23	–	17
Front brake disc mounting bolt	23	–	17
Front brake master cylinder			
clamp bolts	10	88	–
Front brake master cylinder			
union bolt	23	–	17
Rear brake caliper bleed valve	6	53	–
Rear brake caliper			
Caliper mounting bolt	23	–	17
Slide pin	27	–	19.5
Pad pin	18	–	13
Rear brake caliper union bolt	23	–	17
Rear brake disc mounting bolt	23	–	17
Rear brake master cylinder			
mounting bolts	10	88	–
Rear brake master cylinder union bolt	23	–	17
Rear brake pad pin	18	159	–

CHAPTER FIFTEEN

BODY AND FRAME

This chapter contains removal and installation procedures for the body panels.

Whenever a body or frame member is removed, reinstall all mounting hardware onto the removed part so they will not be misplaced. After each part is removed from the motorcycle, wrap it in a blanket or towel, and place it in a cardboard box. Store it in an area where it will not be damaged.

BODY PANEL FASTENERS

Several types of fasteners are used to attach the various body panels to each other and to the frame. Note the type of fastener used before removing a panel. An improperly released fastener can damage a body panel.

Trim Clip

Quick release trim clips secure various body panels. The plastic trim clips deteriorate with heat, age and use. If necessary, replace trim clips.

To release a trim clip, push the center pin into the head with a Phillips screwdriver (A, **Figure 1**) to release the inner lock so the trim clip can be withdrawn from the body panel (B).

To install a trim clip, push the center pin outward so it protrudes from the head (C, **Figure 1**), and insert the clip through the panels. Lock the trim clip by pushing the pin until it sits flush with the top of the head (D).

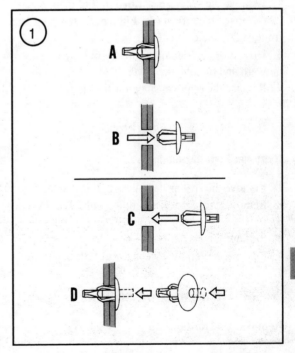

SEAT

Removal/Installation

1. Insert the ignition key into the seat lock (**Figure 2**).
2. Turn the ignition key to release the lock.
3. Lift the rear of the seat while moving the seat rearward.

15

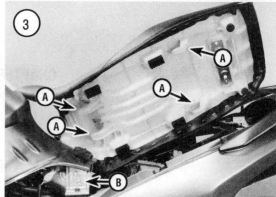

4. Remove the seat.

5. Reverse the removal steps to install the seat. Make sure the seat lugs (A, **Figure 3**) engage the frame and fuel tank brackets (B) and the seat is secure.

FUEL TANK SIDE COVERS

Removal/Installation

1. Remove the seat as described in this chapter.

2. Remove the screw (A, **Figure 4**) securing the front of the side cover (B).

3. Disengage the retaining pins by pulling the cover outward and remove the cover.

4. Reverse the removal steps for installation.

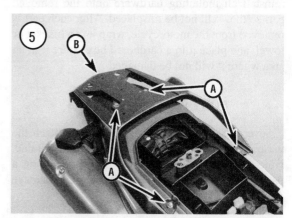

CARRIER

Removal/Installation

1. Remove the seat as described in this chapter.

2. Remove the carrier mounting bolts (A, **Figure 5**).

3. Remove the carrier (B, **Figure 5**).

4. Reverse the removal steps for installation.

FRAME SIDE COVERS

Removal/Installation

1. Remove the carrier as described in this chapter.

2. Remove the fuel tank side cover as described in this chapter.

3. Remove the trim clip on the underside of the cover.

4. Remove the retaining screw (A, **Figure 6**).

5. Disengage the retaining pins by pulling the cover (B, **Figure 6**) outward and remove the cover.

6. Reverse the removal steps for installation.

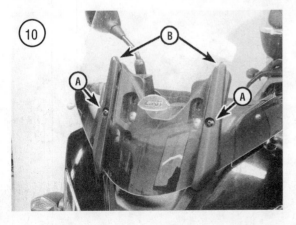

FUEL TANK FRONT COVER

Removal/Installation

1. Remove the trim clips (A, **Figure 7**).
2. Disengage and remove the fuel tank front cover (B, **Figure 7**).
3. Reverse the removal steps for installation.

LOWER COWLING

Removal/Installation

1. Remove the trim clips securing the lower cowling (**Figure 8**).
2. Remove two screws securing the lower cowling and remove the lower cowling.
3. Reverse the removal steps for installation. Insert the two locating pins on the lower cowling into the holes in the center cowling.

SIDE COWLING

Removal/Installation

1. Remove the fuel tank side cover as described in this chapter.
2. Remove the lower cowling as described in this chapter.
3. Remove the fuel tank front cover as described in this chapter.
4. Remove the screw (C, **Figure 7**) securing the instrument panel and side cowling to the fuel tank.
5. Remove the screws securing the side cowling (**Figure 9**).
6. Remove the side cowling.
7. Reverse the removal steps for installation.

WINDSHIELD

Removal/Installation

1. Remove the cover screws (A, **Figure 10**), then remove the covers (B).
2. Remove the windshield retaining screws (**Figure 11**), then remove the windshield.
3. If necessary, remove the retaining screws (A, **Figure 12**) and windshield mounting bracket (B).
4. Reverse the removal steps for installation.

INSTRUMENT PANEL

Removal/Installation

1. Remove the windshield as described in this chapter.

15

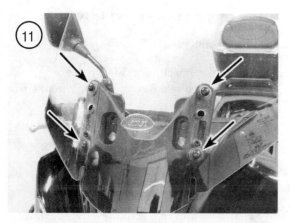

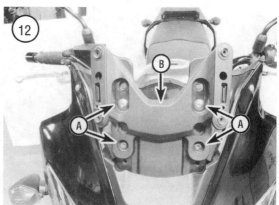

2. Remove the fuel tank front cover as described in this chapter.

3. Remove the screws (C, **Figure 7**) securing the instrument panel and side cowling to the fuel tank.

4. Remove the trim clips (A, **Figure 13**).

5. Remove the screw on each side (**Figure 14**).

6. Disengage the retaining pins by pulling the panel (B, **Figure 13**) outward.

7. Disconnect the combination connector and remove the panel.

8. Reverse the removal steps for installation.

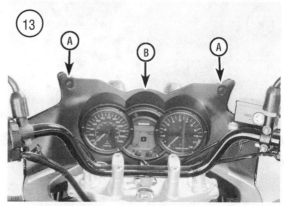

CENTER COWLING AND HEADLIGHT HOUSING

Removal/Installation

1. Remove the windshield and mounting bracket as described in this chapter.

2. Remove the instrument panel as described in this chapter.

3. Remove both side cowlings as described in this chapter.

4. Disconnect the wiring harness connector (**Figure 15**).

5. Unscrew the four nuts securing the cowling to the mounting bracket (**Figure 16**).

6. Remove the center cowling and headlight housing (**Figure 17**).

7. To separate the headlight housing from the center cowling, proceed as follows:

    a. Disconnect the turn signal wires.

    b. Remove the retaining screws.

    c. Disengage the locating pins during separation.

8. Reverse the removal steps for installation.

RIDER FOOTPEG BRACKET

The rider footpegs are attached to removable brackets. The right side bracket also supports the

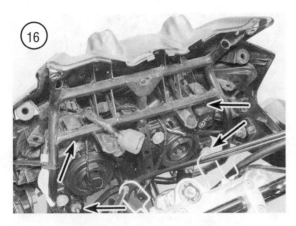

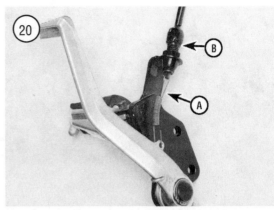

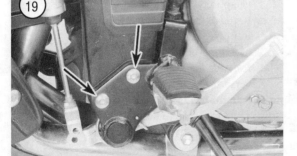

brake pedal and brake light switch. The left side bracket also supports the gearshift lever.

Right Footpeg Bracket
Removal/Installation

1. Remove the cotter pin and clevis pin (**Figure 18**) that secure the master cylinder clevis to the brake pedal.

> *CAUTION*
> *Do not allow the footpeg and brake pedal assembly to hang from the rear brake switch electrical wire.*

2. While supporting the footpeg and brake pedal assembly, remove the right footpeg bracket mounting bolts (**Figure 19**). Hold the assembly and remove it.
3. Detach the brake light switch spring (A, **Figure 20**).
4. Remove the rear brake light switch (B, **Figure 20**) from the footpeg bracket.
5. If necessary, remove the brake pedal as described in Chapter Fourteen.
6. Reverse the removal steps for installation while noting the following:
    a. Tighten the bracket mounting bolts to 26 N•m (19 ft.-lb.).
    b. Adjust the rear brake light switch as described in Chapter Three.

Left Footpeg Bracket
Removal/Installation

1. Remove the clamp bolt (A, **Figure 21**) and slide the shift arm (B) off the shift shaft.
2. Remove the left footpeg bracket mounting bolts (C, **Figure 21**). Hold the assembly and remove it.
3. If necessary, remove the snap ring and separate the gearshift lever from the bracket spindle.
4. Reverse the removal steps for installation while noting the following:

15

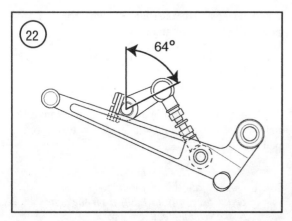

a. Tighten the bracket mounting bolts to 26 N•m (19 ft.-lb.).

b. Install the shift arm onto the shift shaft. The shift arm position should be approximately 64° from vertical (**Figure 22**).

PASSENGER FOOTPEG BRACKET

Removal/Installation

1. Remove the bolts securing the bracket, then remove the bracket.

2. Reverse the removal steps for installation. Tighten the bolts to 23 N•m (17 ft.-lb.).

SIDESTAND

Removal/Installation

1. Place the motorcycle on a suitable jack or wooden blocks on level ground.

2. To replace only the springs, perform the following:

a. Place the sidestand in the raised position. This places the return springs in their relaxed position.

b. Use locking pliers and disconnect the springs from the mounting bracket post. Remove both springs.

c. Reinstall the springs onto the posts.

3. To remove the sidestand leg, perform the following:

a. Remove the sidestand switch as described in Chapter Nine.

b. Remove the springs as previously described.

c. Remove the pivot bolt locknut.

d. Remove the pivot bolt, then remove the sidestand leg.

4. To remove the sidestand assembly, perform the following:

a. Remove the sidestand switch as described in Chapter Nine.

b. Remove the springs as previously described.

c. Remove the bolts securing the sidestand mounting bracket to the frame.

d. Remove the sidestand.

5. Reverse the removal steps for installation while noting the following:

a. Tighten the pivot bolt to 50 N•m (36 ft.-lb.).

b. Tighten the pivot bolt locknut to 40 N•m (29 ft.-lb.).

c. Tighten the sidestand bracket bolts to 100 N•m (74 ft.-lb.).

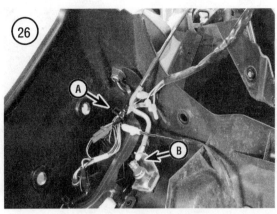

FRONT FENDER

Removal/Installation

1. Remove the rear retaining bolt (A, **Figure 23**) on each side. The bolt also secures the brake hose or fitting.

2. Remove the front retaining bolt (B, **Figure 23**) on each side.

3. Carefully remove the front fender.

4. Reverse the removal steps for installation. Note the nut plates which must be secured in the fender (**Figure 24**).

REAR FENDER

Removal/Installation

1. Remove the seat as described in this chapter.

2. Remove the carrier as described in this chapter.

3. Remove the bolt on each side of the rear fender (**Figure 25**).

4. Lift off and invert the rear fender so the underside is accessible.

5. Disconnect the electrical connectors (A, **Figure 26**).

6. Disconnect the seat lock cable (B, **Figure 26**).

7. Remove the rear fender.

8. Reverse the removal steps for installation.

Table 1 BODY AND FRAME TORQUE SPECIFICATIONS

Item	N•m	in. lb.	ft.-lb.
Passenger footpeg bracket mounting bolts	23	–	17
Rider footpeg bracket mounting bolts	26	–	19
Sidestand bracket bolts	100	–	74
Sidestand pivot bolt locknut	40	–	29
Sidestand pivot bolt	50	–	36

15

Notes

INDEX

16

16

16

WIRING
DIAGRAMS

DL650 US CANADA AUSTRALIA (2004-2006 MODELS)

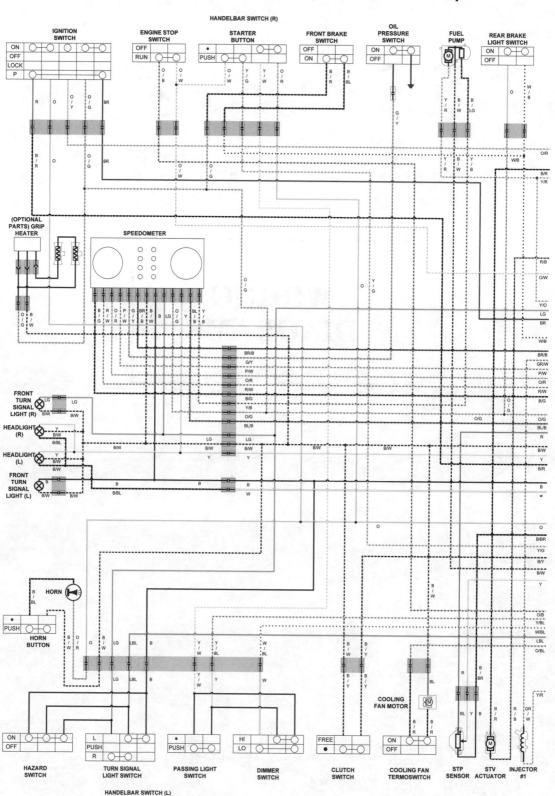

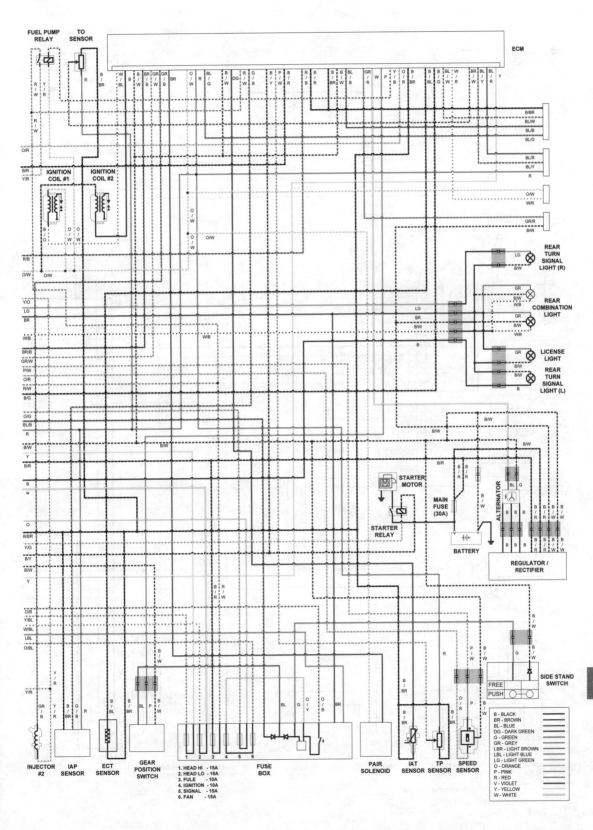

DL650 US AND CANADA (2007-2011 MODELS)

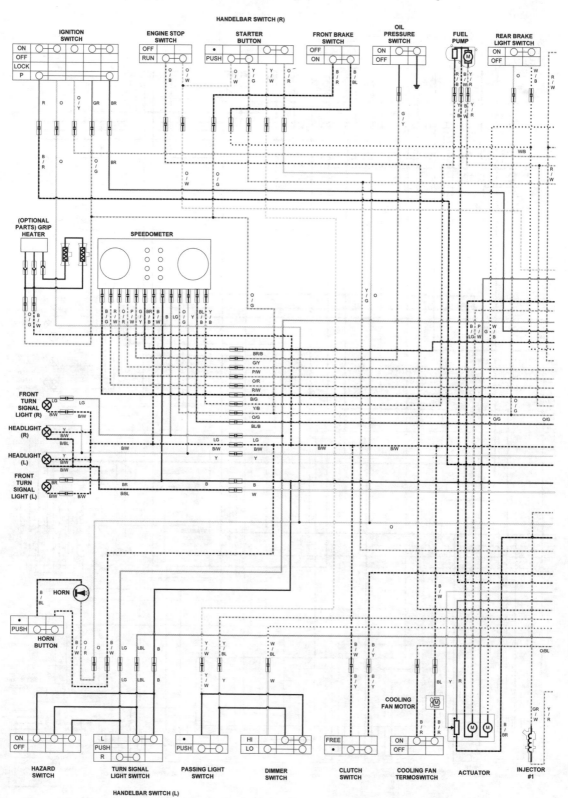

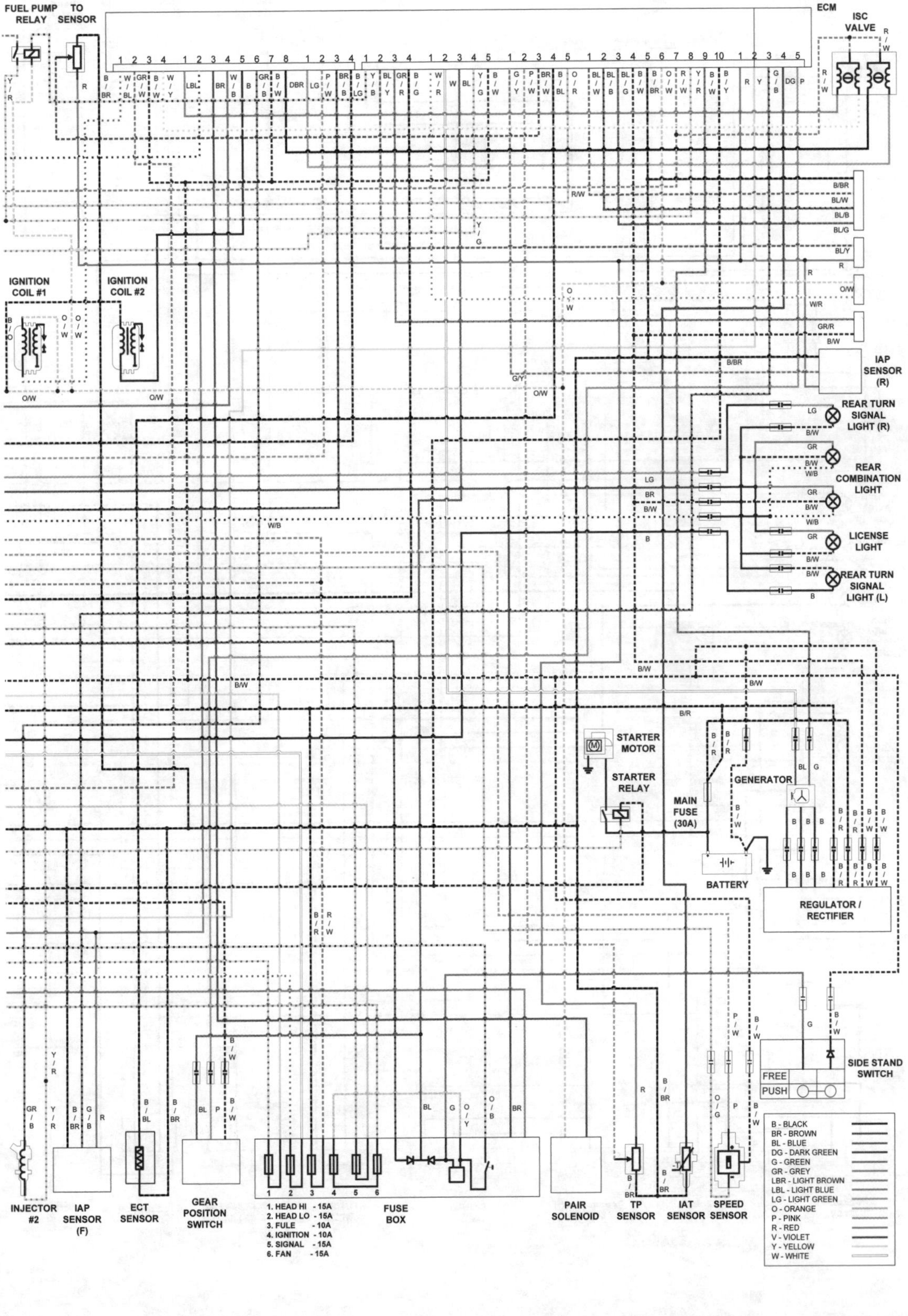
FUEL PUMP RELAY
TO SENSOR
ECM
ISC VALVE
IGNITION COIL #1
IGNITION COIL #2
IAP SENSOR (R)
REAR TURN SIGNAL LIGHT (R)
REAR COMBINATION LIGHT
LICENSE LIGHT
REAR TURN SIGNAL LIGHT (L)
STARTER MOTOR
STARTER RELAY
MAIN FUSE (30A)
GENERATOR
BATTERY
REGULATOR / RECTIFIER
SIDE STAND SWITCH
FREE
PUSH
INJECTOR #2
IAP SENSOR (F)
ECT SENSOR
GEAR POSITION SWITCH
1. HEAD HI - 15A
2. HEAD LO - 15A
3. FULE - 10A
4. IGNITION - 10A
5. SIGNAL - 15A
6. FAN - 15A
FUSE BOX
PAIR SOLENOID
TP SENSOR
IAT SENSOR
SPEED SENSOR
B - BLACK
BR - BROWN
BL - BLUE
DG - DARK GREEN
G - GREEN
GR - GREY
LBR - LIGHT BROWN
LBL - LIGHT BLUE
LG - LIGHT GREEN
O - ORANGE
P - PINK
R - RED
V - VIOLET
Y - YELLOW
W - WHITE

17

DL650A US AND CANADA (2007-2011 ABS MODELS)

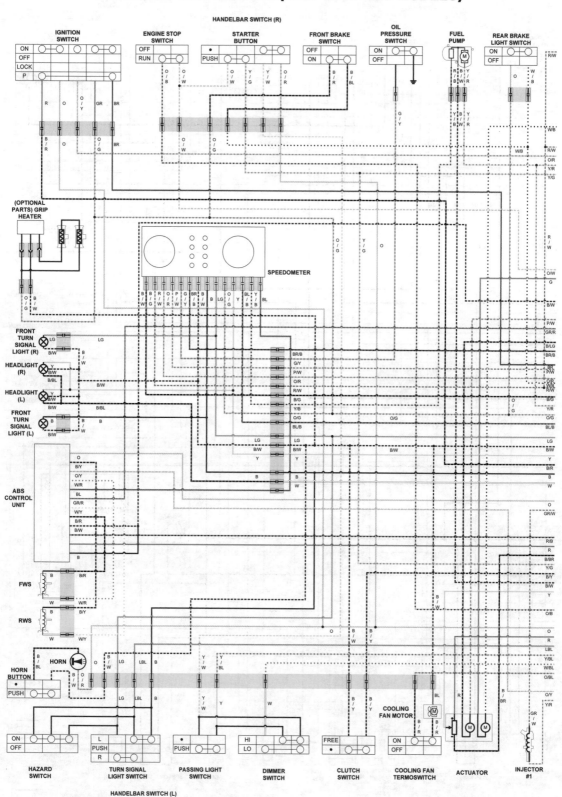